Learning and Attention Disorders in Adolescence and Adulthood

SECOND EDITION

D0708574

Learning and Attention Disorders in Adolescence and Adulthood

Assessment and Treatment

SECOND EDITION

Edited by

Sam Goldstein

Jack A. Naglieri

Melissa DeVries

WILEY

John Wiley & Sons, Inc.

Library of Congress Cataloging-in-Publication Data:

Learning and attention disorders in adolescence and adulthood : assessment and treatment / edited by Sam Goldstein, Jack A. Naglieri, Melissa DeVries.—Second Edition.

p. ; cm.

Includes bibliographical references and index.

ISBN 978-0-470-50518-2 (cloth : alkaline paper); ISBN 978-1-118-06189-3 (ebk);

ISBN 978-1-118-06192-3 (ebk); ISBN 978-1-118-06190-9 (ebk)

1. Attention-deficit disorder in adults. 2. Attention-deficit disorder in adolescence. 3. Learning disabilities. I. Goldstein, Sam, 1952- editor. II. Naglieri, Jack A., editor. III. DeVries, Melissa, editor.

[DNLM: 1. Learning Disorders—therapy. 2. Adolescent. 3. Adult. 4. Attention Deficit Disorder with Hyperactivity—diagnosis. 5. Attention Deficit Disorder with Hyperactivity—therapy. 6. Child. 7. Learning Disorders—diagnosis. 8. Psychotherapy—methods. WS 110]

RC394.A85G65   2011

616.85'89—dc22

Printed in the United States of America

10 9 8 7 6 5 4 3 2 1

For Ryan and Allyson
S.G.

*For Andrea, Scott, Antonia, and
Jack Jr., a source of inspiration*
J.N.

For Derek and Sevilla
M.D.

Contents

Acknowledgments

We would like to thank our editor at Wiley, Patricia Rossi, for her interest and support in pursuing a second edition of this volume. We would also like to thank our colleagues and contributors for their time, expertise, and wisdom. As always, we would like to thank Kathleen Gardner for her editorial assistance in managing and preparing this manuscript.

S.G.

J.N.

M.D.

Contributors

R. Julius Anastasio
Northeastern University
Boston, MA

Kevin M. Antshel, Ph.D.
Associate Professor of Psychiatry
SUNY–Upstate Medical University
Syracuse, NY

Russell Barkley, Ph.D.
Medical University of South Carolina,
    Charleston
Mount Pleasant, SC

Anastasia L. Betts
Regent University
Virginia Beach, VA

Robert B. Brooks, Ph.D.
Harvard Medical School
Boston, MA

Ian Campbell
Central Washington University
Ellensburg, WA

Rob Crawford, M.Ed.
Life Development Institute
Peoria, AZ

Melissa DeVries, Ph.D.
Neurology, Learning and Behavior Center
Salt Lake City, UT

George J. DuPaul, Ph.D.
Lehigh University
Bethlehem, PA

Judith M. Glasser, Ph.D.
Chesapeake ADHD Center of Maryland
Silver Spring, MD

Sam Goldstein, Ph.D.
University of Utah School of Medicine
Salt Lake City, UT

Noel Gregg, Ph.D.
University of Georgia
Athens, GA

Lofton H. Harris, M.S.
University of Pennsylvania School of
    Medicine
Philadelphia, PA

Kevin Hills
Eastern Washington University
Cheney, WA

Patricia H. Latham, J.D.
Partner, Latham and Latham
Washington, DC

Peter S. Latham, J.D.
Partner, Latham and Latham
Washington, DC

Nancy Mather, Ph.D.
University of Arizona
Tucson, AZ

Jack A. Naglieri, Ph.D.
George Mason University
Fairfax, VA

J. Russell Ramsay, Ph.D.
University of Pennsylvania School of
   Medicine
Philadelphia, PA

Nancy Ratey, Ed.M., MCC, SCAC
Strategic Life Coaching
Wellesley, MA

Arthur L. Robin, Ph.D.
Children's Hospital of Michigan
Birmingham, MI

Carol Ann Robbins, Ph.D.
Chesapeake ADHD Center of Maryland
Silver Spring, MD

Bradley M. Rosenfield, Psy.D.
Philadelphia College of Osteopathic
   Medicine
Philadelphia, PA

Anthony L. Rostain, M.D., M.A.
University of Pennsylvania Health
   System
Philadelphia, PA

Jodi Sleeper -Triplett, MCC
JST Coaching, LLC
Herndon, VA

Annmarie Urso, Ph.D.
State University of New York at Geneseo
Geneseo, NY

Robert J. Volpe, Ph.D.
Northeastern University
Boston, MA

We learn more by looking for the answer to a question and not finding it than we do from learning the answer itself.

Lloyd Alexander

Education is learning what you didn't even know you didn't know.

Daniel J. Boorstin

If you hold a cat by the tail you learn things you cannot learn any other way.

Mark Twain

Preface

In 1997, when the first edition of this text was published, the concept of Learning Disabilities (LD) and Attention-Deficit/Hyperactivity Disorder (ADHD) were firmly entrenched within the developmental conditions of childhood. Yet today a search of Google for "adult Learning Disabilities" identified 3 million sites with 2.5 million sites found when the word "treatment" was added. These numbers can be contrasted with over 126 million sites identified for "adulthood." Thus, despite advances the number of sites addressing adult LD are far less than the percentage of adults with likely histories of LD. The same is true for ADHD.

In the last 14 years, ADHD and LD have been recognized as a phenomena that impact individuals throughout their life span. In the last 14 years as well, the rapid pace of technological development has dramatically altered the landscape of high school and postsecondary education. In the 1920s, 20% of parents completed 4 years of high school or more, with 60% having completed at least 8 years of schooling. By the 1980s, the corresponding numbers were 80% and 100%. The shift from farm to urban work over this period meant that greater educational attainment and vocational skill were necessary in order to survive. This is even more true today, when much of what many students learn as part of their postsecondary educational and vocational preparation is obsolete before they begin their first job. It is even more true today than it was 14 years ago that people with specific weaknesses, such as LD and ADHD, find themselves at a significant disadvantage in their efforts to obtain postsecondary education, vocational preparation, and successfully enter the competitive workforce.

A long history of citations suggest that eminent and extremely influential members of society may have experienced LD or ADHD. Albert Einstein, Thomas Edison, Woodrow Wilson, Sir Arthur Conan Doyle, Harvey Cushing, Paul Erlich, and Nobel Prize winner Niels Bohr are mentioned time and time again as examples of people who overcame their childhood disabilities. However, the possibility that they did not actually overcome their disabilities but instead adapted to them and dealt with them successfully on a daily basis was not given serious consideration. As Weiss and Hechtman (1993) suggest, there are five other outcome possibilities besides growing out of problems such as LD and ADHD. Some of these are not mutually exclusive. They are:

1. The condition is still present but resiliency and protective factors allow the adult to compensate and function successfully.

2. The condition in part remits but some aspects or symptoms remain, and are disabling, causing impairment in adulthood.

3. The full syndrome similar to childhood continues to be manifested but in a somewhat altered form compatible with adult status.

4. The childhood disorder predisposes the adult to one or more related mental disorders, increasing the risk of developing these during the adult years.

5. The childhood disorder predisposes the adult to display psychiatric symptoms in general but are not indicative of any specific disorder.

In many ways, the evolution of the concepts, ideas, and understanding of LD and ADHD in adulthood has developed in parallel through overlapping courses. The fields of ADHD and LD in adulthood have been of at least modest interest to a number of researchers since the early 1970s. It was in the 1980s, however, that they began to receive much greater attention. In 1982, the United Nations proclaimed 1983 to1992 the decade of disabled persons and made a commitment to more than 500 million people in the world estimated to have a disability as the result of mental, physical, or sensory impairments. In October 1987, in response to the United Nations Proclamation, the First National Congress for Adults with Special Learning Needs was held. The congress became the foundation upon which the National Association for Adults with Special Learning Needs was founded in 1989, following the first annual National Conference for Adults with Special Learning Needs. In addition, the National Association for Children with Learning Disabilities rededicated itself and the name of its organization to include adults as well.

Along a parallel course, the concept of attention deficit disorder in adults was originally studied by Paul Wender and his colleagues at the University of Utah and by other researchers (Bellak, 1979). In contrast to the adult LD field, however, the adult ADHD field and the concept of the disorder as one of adulthood has now been "warmly" embraced by the public. As Racine and Campbell (1995) have noted, there has been an almost evangelical movement to popularize the idea of adult ADHD, at times leaving limited room for scientific study or debate. Researchers in both fields are concerned that the single-minded pursuit of an ADHD or LD diagnosis will find only these diagnoses—to the person with a hammer, the entire world is a nail.

The National Institute for Literacy (2009) recently has published a review of the research literature on adults with LD and related conditions. The findings in this review note that a significant number of adults in the United States demonstrate inadequate basic academic and related skills. Thirty percent are reported to lack the literacy skills needed to meet reading and computation demands associated with daily life and work (Lasater & Elliott, 2005). Despite societal trends requiring increased literacy skills, census data indicate that more than 40 million Americans have not attained a high school diploma or its equivalent. Although approximately 3 million adults attend a variety of federally funded adult education and training programs targeting their needs (National Commission on Adult Literacy, 2008), many still do not receive services. There are also a variety of programs directly addressing the employment-related needs of this population, particularly in the young adult years. However, many youth with LD and ADHD transition into adult life without support. It is also the case that since there is no single common profile for a late adolescent or adult with LD or ADHD, formal diagnosis and high school completion are documented sources of variability (Mellard & Patterson, 2008).

The authors of the National Institute for Literacy Review provided six consensus statements based on their review of the literature. It is worth reproducing those statements in the opening of this volume:

Consensus Statement 1: The concept of specific learning disabilities is valid and is supported by strong converging evidence. Although there is a lack of consensus over how to define and measure LD and ADHD in the adult years, the reality that challenges are caused by these problems and play a role in school as well as in adult life is well documented (Bradley, Danielson, & Hallahan, 2002).

Consensus Statement 2: Learning disabilities are neurologically based and intrinsic to the individual. Despite the general acceptance of neurological causality for LD and ADHD, issues of measurement and diagnosis continue. At this time there are no clear neurological tests that distinguish individuals with LD and ADHD from other types of low achieving learners or those with related psychiatric problems. However, there is an emerging body of neuroimaging research providing growing evidence for differences in brain structure and function that may ultimately lead to diagnostic instruments (Fletcher, Lyon, Fuchs, & Barnes, 2007).

Consensus Statement 3: Individuals with learning disability show intra-individual differences in skills and abilities. A simple discrepancy model, however, fails to identify the majority in need of help.

Consensus Statement 4: Learning disabilities persist across the life span, though manifestations and intensity may vary as a function of developmental stage and environmental demands. The persistence of LD and ADHD in childhood is indisputable (Barkley, Murphy, & Fischer, 2007; Fletcher, 2003).

Consensus Statement 5: Learning disabilities may occur in combination with other disabling conditions, but they are not due to other conditions, such as mental retardation, behavioral disturbance, lack of opportunities to learn, primary sensory deficits, and multilingualism.

Consensus Statement 6: Learning disabilities are evident across ethnic, cultural, language, and economic groups. For example, from ages 6 through 21, American Indian/Alaskan Native students are 1.5 times more likely than other students and African American students are 1.31 times more likely than other students to receive services for learning disabilities, while white (not Hispanic) students are .88 times as likely to receive services for learning disabilities (U.S. Department of Education, 2005). Cross-cultural research suggests that students exhibit characteristics associated with learning disabilities across countries worldwide (Paulesu et al., 2001; Sideridis, 2007).

The second edition of this text has been greatly expanded. Chapters have been rewritten, and new chapters have been included. The number of contributors has increased as well. We thank our distinguished pool of authors for the knowledge, insight, and scholarly contribution to this volume. This text, as with the first edition, is intended to provide scientist-practitioners in education, medicine, and mental health with a thorough overview of LD and ADHD and a set of practical guidelines to assist the assessment, diagnosis, consultation, and treatment of late adolescents and adults struggling with LD and ADHD. The authors in this volume have made a conscientious effort to distinguish science from nonscience and distinguish nonsense from either of these. Well-controlled research, although difficult, is necessary if we are to make diagnostic decisions and offer treatment ethically. Such research, however, particularly in the fields of adult ADHD and LD continues to require a long-term effort. In the meantime, we must be capable of making diagnostic decisions and offering practical though untested suggestions without unethically recommending nonsense under the rubric "If it can't hurt let's try it." As Jacobson, Mulick, and Schwartz (1995) urge, scientists, practitioners, and others "have an obligation to balance exploratory use of experimental or unproven but seemingly promising techniques with the skilled application of treatment methods that conform to accepted community standards and responsible interpretation of evaluation findings" (p. 762). Practitioners, they continue, "must offer both appropriate treatment and protection from inappropriate care" (p. 762). With an increasing number of children diagnosed with LD and ADHD making the transition to adulthood, it is our hope that the second edition of this volume will serve as a guidepost for those dedicated to helping these individuals throughout their life span.

SAM GOLDSTEIN, PH.D.
Neurology, Learning and Behavior Center
Salt Lake City, Utah

JACK A. NAGLIERI, PH.D.
George Mason University
Washington, D.C.

MELISSA DEVRIES, PH.D.
Neurology, Learning And Behavior Center
Salt Lake City, Utah

REFERENCES

Barkley, R. A., Murphy, K. R., & Fischer, M. (2007). *ADHD in adults: What the science says*. New York, NY: Guilford Press.

Bellak, L. (Ed.). (1979). *Psychiatric aspects of minimal brain dysfunction in adults*. New York, NY: Grune & Stratton.

Bradley, R., Danielson, I., & Hallahan, D. P. (Eds.). (2002). *Identification of learning disabilities: Research to practice*. Mahwah, NJ: Erlbaum.

Fletcher, J. M. (2003, September). *Learning disabilities in adults: Definition and measurement*. Paper presented at the Adult Learning Disabilities Workshop/Symposium on Definition Measurement and Reporting. Washington, DC, National Institute of Literacy.

Fletcher, J. M., Lyon, G. R., Fuchs, L. S., & Barnes, M. A. (2007). *Learning disabilities: From identification to intervention*. New York, NY: Guilford Press.

Jacobson, J. W., Mulick, J. A., & Schwartz, A. A. (1995). A history of facilitated communication: Science, pseudo science and anti-science. *American Psychologist, 50*, 750–765.

Lasater, B., & Elliott, B. (2005). *Profiles of the adult education and training target population: Information from the 2000 census*. Raleigh, NC: RTI International. Retrieved from: www.clasp.org/publications/tanf_ed_2pgr.pdf.

Mellard, D. F., & Patterson, M. B. (2008). Contrasting adult literacy learners with and without specific learning disabilities. *Remedial and Special Education, 29*(3), 133–144.

National Institute for Literacy. (n.d.). *LD Science Q&A*. Washington, DC: Author.

National Commission on Adult Literacy. (2008, June). *Reach higher, America: Overcoming the crisis in the U.S. workforce*. Retrieved from: www.nationalcommissiononadultliteracy .org/report.html.

Paulesu, E., Demonet, J. F., Fazion, F., McCrory, E., Chanoine, V., & Brunswick, N. (2001). Dyslexia: Cultural diversity and biological unity. *Science, 291*, 2165–2167.

Racine, J. D., & Campbell, D. (1995). Adult attention deficit disorder: What's in a name? *Bulletin of the National Academy of Neuropsychology, 12*, 7–8.

Sideridis, G. D. (2007). International approaches to learning disabilities: More alike or more different? *Learning Disabilities Research & Practice, 22*(3), 210–215.

U.S. Department of Education, Office of Special Education and Rehabilitative Services Administration. (2005, January). *Guidelines for assessing the functional capacities of an individual with specific learning disabilities to determine significance of disability for orders of selection purposes technical assistance circular* (RSA-TAC-05–01). Washington, DC: Author. Retrieved from: www.ed.gov/policy/speced/guid/rsa/tac-05-01.doc.

Weiss, G., & Hechtman, L. T. (1993). *Hyperactive children grown up* (2nd ed.). New York, NY: Guilford Press.

PART

I

Background

1

The Changing Face of LD and ADHD in Late Adolescence and Adulthood

SAM GOLDSTEIN
MELISSA DEVRIES

INTRODUCTION

Although in the Bible, God did not completely abandon Job, the proverbial Job's law has been extrapolated to conclude that if someone experiences a single problem, he or she is likely to develop second, third, or fourth problems. There appear to be a large group of adolescents burdened with histories of multiple developmental, behavioral, emotional, and temperamental problems as they begin their transition into adulthood. These numbers appear to be increasing each generation. For this reason, the second edition of this volume is even more important and critical than when initially published nearly 12 years ago.

This second edition begins by providing background information about the childhood and adolescence of people with histories of Learning Disabilities (LD) and Attention-Deficit/Hyperactivity Disorder (ADHD). As child is the father to man, an understanding of the current research regarding childhood and adolescent problems is essential to appreciate the effects of these problems in adulthood. At the time the first edition of this volume was printed, many readers working with the adult population were not too aware of the extensive childhood literature available on LD and ADHD, especially in contrast at the time to the minimal adult literature on these subjects. In the first edition of this volume, it was noted that between 1971 and 1994, nearly 3,000 peer-reviewed studies were published about ADHD. Of these, only 80, or approximately 3%, dealt with adult issues (Resnick & McEvoy, 1995). This percentage appears to be increasing over time, however. For example, between 2005 and 2009,

3

29% of the peer-reviewed articles published in the *Journal of Attention Disorders* were focused on ADHD-related issues in adults. For this reason, Chapters 2 and 3 provide a revised overview of the available literature on the history, presentation, definition, comorbidity, evaluation, and treatment of ADHD and LD in childhood. Chapters 4 and 5 review current knowledge about adult outcome for individuals with histories of these two problems.

This second edition then deviates significantly from the original volume. Chapters 6 through 10 provide a framework for assessment. Chapter 6 provides a neuropsychological framework for evaluating the cognitive and related problems experienced by individuals with ADHD and LD. Chapters 7 and 8 provide overviews of academic and psychiatric assessment in these populations. Chapter 9 provides a model for data integration, through sample reports and case studies. The assessment model is based on a neuropsychological, functional framework. Readers are guided through a process that focuses on evaluating the individual and using the resulting assessment data to help guide important life, vocational, and educational decisions. Finally, Chapter 10 provides an update and overview of the legal rights and qualifications for individuals with these conditions in our society today.

The closing 10 chapters of the book are focused on treatment, beginning with an overview of current research on the medical, nonmedical, and educational interventions directed at adults with histories of LD and ADHD. Treatment chapters then continue and include a resiliency model, a framework for cognitive therapy, classroom and instructional strategies, medications, vocational problems, and lifestyle issues. Also included is a chapter focusing on the increasing application of life coaches to guide individuals with LD and ADHD, particularly through challenging educational and vocational experiences.

It has been 12 years since the publication of the first edition of this volume. During this period of time, there has been an increased emphasis on assessing the effectiveness of schools to prepare all students, not just those with LD and ADHD, to transition successfully into independent living and competitive vocation. This push has led not only to increasing emphasis on high-stakes testing and high school exit examinations but also to an awareness that social/emotional dimension of a child's life must equally be attended to (Cohen, 1999). Strengthening a student's sense of self-esteem and emotional well-being, particularly for students with LD or ADHD, is now recognized as an essential part of the curriculum. The self-confidence and resilience of students with LD and ADHD provides a supporting foundation for enhanced learning, motivation, and self-discipline. Schools must now provide social and emotional interventions for students with LD and ADHD hand in hand with academic education (Merrell, 2002; Weist, Evans, & Level, 2003). In fact, a sustainable school environment must be capable of meeting the social, emotional, and academic needs of all students (Elias, Zins, Graczyk, & Weissberg, 2003). The second edition of this text reflects our renewed interest and commitment to maintaining this focus into the adolescent and adult years for individuals with LD and ADHD. This charge is increasingly important as children's medical, mental health, and general adjustment continues to be eroded by the pressures of our society, making it increasingly more difficult for children to negotiate everyday life successfully and thereby lay a firm foundation for transition into adulthood. As Seligman (1998a, b) has pointed out, attending to those issues that are preventive and create a resilient mindset and wellness will require a significant paradigm shift in mental health professionals and in the educational community. It is the intent of this second edition to introduce and advocate for the implementation of a life span model of effective prevention and positive social and educational science throughout the life span for individuals with ADHD and LD.

LD AND ADHD IN LATE ADOLESCENCE AND ADULTHOOD

Thirty years ago, LD and ADHD were defined as problems of childhood. Yet approaches to remediating these conditions in childhood typically led to minimal if any positive impact in the adult years. (For review, see Goldstein & Teeter Ellison, 2002; Gregg, 2009.) Therefore, it is not surprising that these two conditions have come to be recognized as lifetime phenomena. LD and ADHD affect people across the life span as well as of all socioeconomic classes, ethnicities, cultures, and levels of intelligence (e.g., Faraone, Sergeant, Gillberg, & Biederman, 2003; Morris, Schraufnagel, Chudnow, & Weinberg, 2009). In 1989, Levine referred to the growth and adult LD research as "the early adulthood of a maturing concept" (p. 1). The number of peer-reviewed research studies dealing with LD and ADHD issues in adulthood is growing at an exponential rate. The lifelong nature of these conditions is increasingly well recognized although not always observed as these individuals are no longer in school. Life in many areas, including the workplace, continues to be a struggle for many. Nonetheless, it is still the case that a thorough understanding of the implications these conditions have in the adult years is not well understood. Some researchers suggest that individuals with LD and ADHD have difficulty in adulthood in a broad range of areas beyond just the workplace, including making appropriate choices and decisions, using efficient strategies on a daily basis to assess their functioning, transferring learning from one activity to another, breaking tasks into smaller parts, and overall making good life decisions (Hill, 1984).

The symptom constellation referred to as Attention Deficit Disorder or Attention-Deficit/Hyperactivity Disorder (APA, 2000) has become one of the most widely researched areas in childhood and adolescence with increasing interest throughout the adult life span. In clinic-referred settings, males outnumber females 6 to 1; in epidemiologic studies of community-based settings, the ratio is 3 to 1 (Barkley, Murphy,

& Fischer, 2008). The incidence of diagnosis continues to increase with a 70% increase in the diagnosis of children and nearly a 100% increase in the diagnosis of adults with ADHD between the years 2000 and 2003 (Centers for Disease Control [CDC], 2005). It is now estimated that between 4% to 8% of the general population has received a diagnosis of ADHD (CDC, 2005; Cuffe, Moore, & McKeown, 2005). Females are the fastest-growing group (Medco, 2005). Broad-based definitions of ADHD find epidemiology of nearly 16% in adults; narrower definitions report an incidence of 3% to 4% (Faraone & Biederman, 2005).

In addition to examining the adult impact of these conditions, researchers have begun to question the validity of using childhood constructs to diagnose, evaluate, and treat adults suffering from LD and ADHD (Patton & Polloway, 1992). Some of the theories, ideas, beliefs, and strategies used with children are suggested as inappropriate for adults (Lieberman, 1987). Further, although the literature suggests that some people with histories of these conditions may learn to compensate and succeed in adulthood (Adelman & Vogel, 1990; Polloway, Schewel, & Patton, 1992; Weiss & Hechtman, 1993), it is likely that the majority of individuals with these conditions do not fare as well as the normal population (Gerber et al., 1990; Gregg, 2007; Mannuzza et al., 1993; Newman, Wagner, Cameto, & Knokey, 2009; Wagner, Newman, Cameto, Garza, & Levine, 2005).

Individuals with LD and ADHD do not have an intellectual disability. They fall on a normal curve for intellectual abilities but are typically weak in one or more specific abilities necessary for academic and vocational achievement. Given their deficits, however, it is not surprising that a common misconception among the public, and still to some extent among mental health and educational professions, has been that LD, ADHD, and intellectual disability are variations of the same phenomenon. They are not. Even more perplexing has been the relationship between LD and ADHD (e.g., Bonafina, Newcorn, McKay, Koda, & Halperin, 2000; Preston, Heaton, McCann, Watson, & Selke, 2009). Attention problems were long considered part and parcel of LD. In fact, some researchers suggested that the majority of children with ADHD experienced LD (Safer & Allen, 1976). It is now known, however, that while groups of individuals with diagnoses of LD and ADHD respectively may overlap by as much as 40%, the majority of each group does not experience the other problem (Barkley, 1990, 2005). In fact, weaknesses in the underlying intellectual and neuropsychological abilities that may be responsible for each condition likely do not overlap (Naglieri, Salter, & Edwards, 2004). The majority of individuals with LD typically experience problems with sequential or simultaneous processing while those with ADHD typically experience problems with planning or attention processing. However, failure to practice for proficiency, a problem typically associated with ADHD in academic settings, leads to the commonsense conclusion that inattentive individuals may not perform well and thus fall behind in school, possibly leading to an LD classification (Schnoes,

Reid, Wagner, & Marder, 2006). In this volume, LD is considered primarily as a pro-blem of faulty input. That is, a number of specific weak abilities hinder the acquisition of the knowledge necessary to become competent in reading, writing, spelling, arith-metic, and other basic academic skills. ADHD is considered a performance or output problem. Thus, individuals with ADHD typically know what to do but, because of their poor planning, limited attention to detail, and/or impulsive responding, typically do not do what they know efficiently. It quickly becomes apparent that individuals with both conditions are significantly compromised in nearly all walks of life.

According to the preponderance of available data, outcomes for young adults with histories of LD or ADHD are not good (Spencer, Biederman, & Mick, 2007). Members of this group typically are under- or unemployed, struggle to achieve vocational skills at a rate commensurate with others or, for that matter, with their basic intelligence, and do not achieve at a rate commensurate with their personal or academic poten-tial (Gregg, 2007; Newman et al., 2009; Smith, 1992). In 1982, for example, it was reported that 36% of all juvenile delinquents, a group made up disproportionately of persons from low-income families, suffered from LD (Dunivant, 1982). It is still the case that young adults with LD and ADHD are overrepresented in the penal system (Rutherford, Bullis, Anderson, & Griller-Clark, 2002; Shelton, 2006). The educa-tional, employment, personal, and emotional lives of these individuals appear to dem-onstrate the nearly irreversible effects of their childhood experiences and struggles.

Individuals with LD appear to constitute the largest disability group (Interagency Committee on Learning Disabilities, 1987; SRI International, 1990; U.S. Department of Education, 2002). It is likely that more than half of individuals with disabil-ity experience LD, ADHD, or both of these conditions. Traditionally, the focus in dealing with these conditions in late adolescence and adulthood has been primar-ily on transition—that is, helping these individuals successfully make the move to independent living and competitive vocation. This has led to the development of support services in 2- and 4-year colleges, vocational training programs, job train-ing and employment programs. There has also been increased attention to mental health issues. Individuals with ADHD and to some extent those with LD are sig-nificantly more vulnerable to emotional problems (Biederman, 2005; Biederman, 1993) and addictive disorders (Rowland, Lesesne, & Abramowitz, 2002; Wilens, Biederman, Spencer, & Francis1994). In 1984, the Office of Special Education and Rehabilitation Services (Will, 1984) initiated the development of programs to pre-pare students with LD and other disabilities for successful transition into adulthood. This program paralleled the shift in the community during which support groups for children with disabilities began to broaden their scope and even change their names. For example, the National Association for Children with Learning Disabilities changed its name to the Learning Disabilities Association and sought to represent all ages. This is also true for the Children with ADHD group, as it added the term "adult" to its title. Through the 1970s, the concept of lifelong interventions for people with learning and other disabilities eventually came to the forefront (Wiederholt, 1982). At the federal level, however, as late as 1978, the Rehabilitation Services Administration refused to acknowledge LD or ADHD as a mental or physical disorder that might limit employment eligibility. This appeared to be the last bastion of discrimination against individuals with these conditions. In 1983, the federal government organized a conference of professionals to define the needs of adults with LD (including ADHD in this focus). Seven basic issues were discussed (Gerber, 1983; Gerber & Mellard, 1985):

1. Understanding, defining, and identifying adults with LD and related disorders.
2. Improving the social skills of this population.
3. Understanding the vocational needs of this population.
4. Developing a system for education and information exchange among professionals studying and treating adult LD.
5. Identifying the issues critical to this population's successful adjustment to the community.
6. Focusing on family issues.
7. Identifying and further investigating programs and their fit with this population at a postsecondary educational level.

It was clear by the late 1980s that LD and ADHD were coming to be viewed less as educational issues of childhood and more as conditions with broad impact across the life span. In the United States, researchers and clinicians began studying countries such as Denmark, where adults with LD were reported as experiencing less unemployment and better adjustment compared to those in the United States and even compared to the Danish national average (Gerber, 1984).

In 1987, the National Joint Commission on Learning Disabilities, an organization made up of eight professional advocacy groups, issued a paper titled "A Call to Action" in which these conclusions were drawn and recommendations were made:

1. LD is both persistent and pervasive in an individual's life. The manifestation of LD and other conditions can be expected to change during the life span of the individual.
2. At present there is a paucity of appropriate diagnostic procedures for assessing and determining the status and needs of adults with LD and related conditions. This situation has resulted in the misuse and misinterpretation of tests that have been designed for and standardized on younger people.
3. Older adolescents and adults with LD and related conditions are frequently denied access to appropriate academic instruction, pre-vocational preparation and career counseling necessary for the development of adult abilities and skills.

4. Few professionals have been prepared adequately to work with adults with LD and related conditions.

5. Employers frequently do not possess awareness, knowledge, or sensitivity to the needs of adults with LD and related conditions. In general, corporate as well as public and private agencies have been ignorant of this population and therefore have failed to accept their responsibility to develop and implement programs.

6. Adults with LD and related conditions may experience personal, social and emotional difficulties that affect their adaptation to life tasks. These difficulties may be an integral aspect of these conditions or may have resulted secondarily from past failures.

7. Advocacy efforts on behalf of adults with LD and related conditions are currently inadequate.

8. Federal, state and private funding agencies concerned with LD and related conditions have not supported program development initiatives for adults. (p. 172)

In the vocational arena, the Americans with Disabilities Act of 1990 outlawed discrimination in the workplace against people with any type of disability. The President's Committee for the Employment of People with Disabilities recommended an eight-pronged plan for dealing with transition and employment for adults with histories of learning problems. The plan addressed work preparation, vocational entry, job site accommodations, job advancement, attitudes, policy and legislation, social relations, definition, and diagnosis (Gerber & Brown, 1990). With the 2009 implementation of the Americans with Disabilities Amendments Act (ADAA, 2008) came changes to the definition of what constitutes a disability, for example, by including two nonexhaustive lists of "major life activities" that may be limited by a condition being considered a disability. The ADAA also expands its focus to what constitutes discrimination in the workplace. Overall its aim is to continue the "broad" definition of disability and reduce the burden of proof placed on the applicant or employee in order to speed entry into the workforce.

The need to legislate guidelines and programs in the workplace for individuals with LD and ADHD becomes obvious when the outcome for this population is considered. The National Longitudinal and Transition Study (Wagner, 1989) found that 61% of youth with LD and related conditions graduated from high school in comparison to 56% of youth with other disabilities but 75% of the general population. It has been reported that 35% of youth with LD drop out of school with minimal educational training and poor vocational preparation. Few of these dropouts are aware of the extent to which their disabilities will affect them in adulthood; nor do they understand the dismal vocational and life future potentially ahead of them. Of greater concern, however, is the fact that they also do not appreciate their legal rights (Aune, 1991; Gerber & Rieff, 1991; Madaus, Gerber, & Price, 2008). Most dropouts with these conditions assume that their lives will improve once they leave school.

Unemployment rates for dropouts, whether they have LD or not, have been approximately twice as high over the last 20 years as for high school graduates (U.S. Department of Labor, Bureau of Labor Statistics, 1987, 2010). Studies of high school students with LD have suggested that although dropout rates appear to be declining, a surprisingly large number still drop out. Planty et al. (2008) reported that 25% of students with learning disabilities dropped out of high school in the 2005–06 school year. Valdez, Williamson, and Wagner in 1990 reported that of the total student population, 32% dropped out while Malcolm et al. (1990) reported 56%. Zigmond and Thorton (1985) provided a dropout rate of 53% for high school students with LD. Wagner (1989) reported that just under 17% of individuals with histories of LD or related conditions were taking any kind of course work in a postsecondary institution. Nine percent were at vocational or trade schools; 7% were at 2-year colleges, and only 1% were at 4-year colleges. These figures should be contrasted with the 56% of the general population that goes on to postsecondary education. Sitlington and Frank (1990) found that few students with LD and ADHD were employed in areas that required technical or vocational training. Thus, even when they graduated from high school, such youth appear to be ill-prepared for the work they are given. Past studies have consistently found that these individuals are employed in entry-level positions, change jobs frequently, and are often passed over for promotion (Forquean, Meisgeier, Swank, & Williams, 1991; Sitlington & Frank, 1990). Although Price, Gerber, and Mulligan (2003) noted that the majority of their sample with LD had been promoted at least once at their workplace, most of the participants had not revealed their disability to their employer.

The available data also suggest that despite their average intelligence, those with LD may derive little long-term benefit from the academic remediation provided in childhood (Frauenheim & Heckerl, 1983). However, remedial education in childhood has been found to improve lifetime reading ability (Naylor, Felton, & Wood, 1990). Fairweather and Shaver (1991) reported a successful outcome for students with disabilities participating in postsecondary vocational training. In their review, however, an emphasis on occupational training and links with vocational and high school programs was found to be the best predictors of a better outcome.

At an increasing rate, individuals with LD and ADHD are enrolling in college after high school. The Higher Education and Adult Training for People with Handicaps (HEATH) Resource Center of the American Council on Education reported that the proportion of first-time full-time freshmen with disabilities attending college increased twofold between 1978 and 1985 from 2.6% to 7.4% and has continued to increase (National Center for Education Statistics [NCES], 2006). Among the 2.6% in 1978, almost 5% reported having LD compared with over 14% in 1985 and 29% in 1999 (NCES, 1999).

The U.S. Department of Education National Center for Educational Statistics began collecting and analyzing data on handicapped full- and part-time college students in

1986. At that time, over 10%, or nearly 1.3 million, of 12.5 million students in post-secondary programs reported having one or more disability. Of that number, just over 12% (approximately 160,000) reported having a learning disability, 39% a visual handicap, 20% a hearing disability, and just over 17% an orthopedic handicap. Interestingly, at that time ADHD was not among the handicaps evaluated. The accuracy of these data has been questioned by those who argue that at least in the 1980s persons with sensory and motor impairments were more likely to report their disabilities than those with learning or attention problems (U.S. Department of Education, 1987). Nevertheless, the dramatic increase in the number of inquiries about college programs for students with LD and ADHD suggested that the growth in the number of such students would be likely to continue (Bogart, Eidelman, & Kujawa, 1988; Gregg, 2007; Hartman, 1991). The increase in postsecondary college enrollment for individuals with LD and ADHD must also be contrasted with data suggesting that these students have difficulty staying in college and completing these programs (NCES, 1999; Sitlington & Frank, 1990). Whether this finding reflects lack of fit between the students' capabilities and the program or lack of appropriate support services remains unknown.

The transition to adulthood appears to contain an interim period when all youth adjust to the increasing demands of maturity (Arnett, 2000; Halperin, 1992). Not surprisingly, the more difficult the childhood and adolescent years, the greater problems experienced during these interim years. Preparation, however, can greatly ease the challenges experienced during this period, especially for vulnerable individuals. Some theorists have hypothesized that this is especially true for those with LD and ADHD. It may be that adults with these conditions perceive their world very differently than others as a result of both impairment and experience (Shessel & Reiff, 1999). Problems that compromise a child's ability to function effectively in the classroom likely also compromise an adult's ability to function effectively in life. Schools were originally designed to prepare individuals to become functioning, productive, and successful members of society (Goldstein, 1995). It is therefore not surprising that the daily frustrations and failures some children experience at school carry over, influencing their attitudes, beliefs, and behavior as adults. The combination of their disabilities and experiences may lead to patterns of pessimism, difficulty handling change, and personality differences (Brooks, 2002; Lerner, 1985). It has been suggested that the residual effects of these conditions combined with frustration at school and lack of satisfaction in finding a comfortable niche in adulthood reverberate in the emotional sphere as well. Individuals in the adult years with ADHD demonstrate significantly higher rates of psychiatric conditions, particularly depression and anxiety (Barkley et al., 2008). For some adults with LD a seeming inability to understand why life continues to be a struggle creates a tragic and self-perpetuating cycle of loneliness and despair (Reiff & Gerber, 1994). Thus, helping these individuals during their adolescent years to recognize, understand, and accept their disabilities as a means of preparing them for the many demands of adulthood has become a mainstay of transitions programs (Meaux, Green, & Broussard, 2009).

It still remains true that far more information is available about the adult lives of individuals with ADHD than with LD. Difficulty with social skills, memory, organization, auditory processing, linguistic abilities, attention, and impulsivity are all thought to contribute to poor work performance (Clement-Heist, Siegel, & Gaylord-Ross, 1992; Corley & Taymans, 2002; Latham & Latham, 1993; Mpofu, Watson, & Chan, 1999). The lack of scientific data, however, has led some researchers to report wide-ranging problems for individuals with LD (Blalock, 1981; Hoffman et al., 1987) while others report minimal problems (Felton, 1986; Gerber, 1988). With ADHD, the data are clear. These individuals hold lower-paying jobs, have more job changes, and are not promoted. They typically experience a wide range of health and lifestyle problems as well (Gittleman, Mannuzza, Shenker, & Bonagura, 1985). Despite increased awareness and treatment opportunities for ADHD, this pattern has not been altered significantly. (For review, see Barkley et al., 2008.) It is also of interest to note that in 1990 Hughes and Smith reported that there was not a single scientific, peer-reviewed study published that directly evaluated the efficacy of developmental education programs for college students with LD. Most published articles consisted of program descriptions, opinions, surveys, and commentary (Fairweather & Shaver, 1991; Nelson, Dodd, & Smith, 1990). As technology advances, skills required in the workplace are becoming increasingly complex. Higher and higher levels of educational attainment and intellect are needed to compete successfully for jobs with workers without disabilities (Brown, 1984). Thus, in addition to their primary work with LD and ADHD, vocational and transitional programs have worked to change employer attitudes toward hiring workers with these conditions. Despite advocacy and legislation over the last 20 years, employers continue to be hesitant about hiring workers with disabilities. In 1987, Minskoff, Sautter, Hoffman, and Hawks reported that in a population of 326 surveyed employers, only half indicated they would hire someone with LD for a job they supervised. This was a surprising finding because the question was phrased in a way that made clear that the individual possessed all of the qualifications for the job (Price & Gerber, 2001). Finally, Shapiro and Lentz (1991) reported that many students with LD and related conditions did not end up in jobs for which they were trained. These authors implied that general work skills, rather than a specific job skill, should be emphasized in vocational training programs. These authors also reported that employers were more willing to make allowances for disabilities they could see than they were for disabilities that are difficult to understand and quantify, such as LD and ADHD.

Werner (1994) and Brooks (2002) proposed the concept of "balances" in explaining adult outcome for children with disabilities. Specific risk factors such as LD or ADHD do not in and of themselves guarantee adverse outcome. A variety of other influences can insulate and protect a child with LD or ADHD, leading to the observation that a variety of forces can contribute to resilience in the face of adversity. Since these conditions represent a lifetime phenomenon, it is not surprising that even early researchers failed to propose a clear relationship between intervention and positive adult outcome (Rogan & Hartman, 1976, 1990). In fact, some individuals with histories of LD and ADHD who receive minimal support during their childhood and experience other lifetime traumas are often able to make satisfactory progress into adulthood (Gerber & Reiff, 1991; Gerber, Ginsberg, & Reiff, 1992; Werner, 2005). In their exceptionally interesting text, *Speaking for Themselves: Ethnographic Interviews with Adults with Learning Disabilities*, Gerber and Reiff (1991) described a discovery that researchers in the field of resilience have demonstrated with other populations: A variety of factors within the individual, in the immediate environment, and in the larger community interact in a complex way to shape life outcome. In fact, these authors suggest that a certain amount of risk in childhood actually may stimulate resilience and stress hardiness.

The concept of resilience—that is, the effect of factors that increase the likelihood that children facing adversities such as LD or ADHD will grow up to be functional and successful—has grown in importance as clinicians and researchers have come to recognize that specific interventions for specific populations may yield symptom relief but by themselves may be insufficient to insulate an individual for later success. (For review, see Goldstein & Brooks, 2005.) The longitudinal work of Werner (1989), Werner and Smith (1992, 2001), and Fonagy, Steele, Steele, Higgitt, and Target (1994) exemplifies this field of study. Their findings reveal a number of consistent trends:

1. The impact of reproductive (birth-related) problems diminishes with time.
2. The developmental outcome for almost every biological risk condition depended on family variables—that is, it was less the characteristics of the child (e.g., having LD or ADHD) and more the characteristics of the family that determined the outcome and fate of each child. This phenomenon was even more evident for children with mild biological risks, such as LD and ADHD. Thus, child rearing conditions were found to be powerful determinants of the outcome of the children studied.

Werner (2005) summarized worldwide longitudinal studies defining 13 child and environmental factors associated with resilience:

1. An affectionate and engaging temperament
2. A sociable personality
3. The capacity for autonomous behavior
4. Above-average intelligence
5. Good reading skills
6. High achievement motivation in school

7. A positive self-concept
8. Good impulse control
9. An internal locus of control
10. Good planning skills
11. Faith
12. The capacity for humor
13. A willingness to help others

Werner (2005) reported these 11 environmental phenomena associated with a positive outcome and thereby associated with resilience:

1. Smaller family size
2. Maternal competence at child rearing
3. Maternal mental health
4. An adult available to develop a close bond with the child
5. Supportive siblings
6. Extended family involvement in the child's life
7. Living above the poverty level
8. The capacity to make and maintain friendships
9. Supportive teachers and a safe educational experience
10. Success in school
11. Involvement in prosocial organizations

Werner and Smith (1992) reported that 2 out of 3 vulnerable children exemplified by those born into poverty experiencing a moderate to severe degree of perinatal stress, living in a family environment troubled by chronic discord, parental alcoholism, or mental illness who encountered 4 or more risk factors by age 2 developed serious learning or behavior problems by age 10 as well as mental health problems, delinquency, or teenage pregnancy by age 18. However, 1 out of 3 of these high-risk individuals was able to transition into a functional young adult. For these children, it appeared that their internal locus of control, good temperament, good response to parenting, capacity to succeed at school, relationships with others, and ability to develop a good self-concept best predicted their outcome. In 1992, Gerber et al. suggested that certain factors appear to increase resilient outcome for adults with histories of LD. These included stamina and persistence, goodness of fit between the person's abilities and the environment, a pattern of support by family members, the person's ability to take control of his or her own life, and creativity. Exactly how much each of these factors contributes to any individual's outcome is not well understood. It is also important to note that by far the majority of adults with histories of LD continue to experience a variety of life problems, including a higher-than-average risk of unemployment

(Malcolm, Polatajko, & Simons, 1990). Thus, adults with LD "should not be viewed simply as children with disabilities who have grown up" (Bassett, Polloway, & Patton, 1994, p. 11). If appropriate vocational and educational programs are not provided to these individuals as they leave high school, it is likely that they will struggle vocationally and experience even greater life adjustment problems than when they were younger. The idea that adults continued to develop through the life span has inspired a number of researchers, including state theorists such as Erickson (1950), theorists focusing on age experience (Baltes, Reese, & Lipsitt, 1980), and theorists studying ego and moral development (Gilligan, 1982).

Understanding functional and dysfunctional personality traits that persons with LD and ADHD are prone to develop is of value but does not directly address the practical issues involved in helping this population successfully transition into adulthood. Baltes et al. (1980) proposed what has been called an integrative model of life span development for adults. At any given moment, an individual's thoughts, feelings, and behavior are influenced by normative age-graded events, such as those related to biological and environmental influences correlated with age (e.g., marriage); history-graded events (e.g., economic depression, political change); and events idiosyncratic to a particular individual but not tied to age or immediate cultural experience (e.g., an accident, religious conversion, etc.). This pluralistic model takes into account the effect of previous life experience on current and future functioning. It encompasses the many forces that shape the adult outcome of children, a profile that is consistent with a resilience model.

It is also the case that beyond academics and vocational endeavors, individuals with ADHD and LD struggle in a broad range of life arenas. Over 30 years ago, it was suggested that children with LD were not as popular as other children (Bryan, 1976). Peer popularity for those with LD and in particular ADHD has repeatedly supported this conclusion (Nixon, 2001; Pelham & Milich, 1984). Children with ADHD and LD are more likely to be rejected and neglected than their nonimpaired peers (Rosenberg & Gaier, 1977; Schumacher & Hazel, 1984; for review, see Barkley, 2005). The daily social frustrations that these children face likely makes a significant contribution to adult outcomes of poor self-concept and interpersonal challenges. Many adults with histories of LD and ADHD are thought to be bitter about their early lives and schooling, experiencing a diminished sense of self-worth and reduced life competence (Gerber et al., 1992; Hallowell & Ratey, 1994).

The developmental impact of these conditions also hinders this population in making a successful social transition socially, emotionally, and interpersonally (Rieff & Gerber, 1989). Adults with LD and ADHD may have difficulty reading social situations (Gerber, 1978; Pelham & Bender, 1982), resulting in poor judgment, impaired social reasoning, and generally inappropriate social skills (Lerner, 1993). A number of studies have suggested that these individuals are less sensitive to the thoughts and feelings of others (Dickstein & Warren, 1980). They may also have difficulty discerning and understanding humor (Pickering, Pickering, & Buchanan, 1987). Over 30 years ago, Wiig and Semel (1976) posited that individuals with LD may suffer from social perception deficits that lead to frustration characterized by emotional problems, hostility, insecurity, and even aggression. This certainly occurs for late adolescents and adults with the social learning problems characteristic of Autism Spectrum Disorders.

The negative feedback individuals with LD and ADHD receive about themselves, their competencies, and their potential may very well become a self-fulfilling prophecy that creates a vicious circle of low self-esteem, impaired motivation, and repeated failure (Rieff, 1987). Although the relationship between LD and lifetime psychiatric problems is still not well established, this population is evaluated more negatively by peers and is at increased risk for juvenile delinquency, school dropout, and possibly psychiatric hospitalization (Gregg, 2007; Roff, Sells, & Golden, 1972). There is also no doubt that adults with histories of ADHD are at significantly greater risk for the development of a wide range of psychiatric and lifestyle problems, including antisocial personality, substance abuse, depression, and anxiety. (For review, see Barkley et al., 2008)

While it is now accepted that children with LD and ADHD are likely to experience greater emotional challenges than their peers without LD and ADHD, it is still not clear how much they struggle or how specific these struggles are in predicting future problems. A vast number of variables coalesce to explain the life outcome of any individual. Thus, it would be unfair to state that a child with LD or ADHD is more seriously disturbed than a child without these conditions or that an adult with these conditions will always struggle emotionally and interpersonally. However, it is not surprising that adults with histories of these conditions report higher rates of anxiety (Johnson, 1991; McGough et al., 2005), social problems (Meyers & Messer, 1981; Schütte & Petermann, 2006) and limited social and family relations (Eakin et al., 2004; White, 1985). It is also possible that the daily struggles of these children lead to vulnerability as adults in the same way that the struggles of any child with a medical, developmental, or emotional problem may lead to future challenges. Gerber et al. (1992) suggested on the basis of interviews with successful adults with histories of LD that even these resilient individuals experience anger about their lifetime of academic and related struggles.

Problems in daily life are clearly different from problems in school. However, the skills required for success in adult life—for example, work, personal relationships, activities of everyday living—are strikingly similar to the skills required to be successful in school. The demands of the workplace vary far more than those of the school setting. However, a comparison between school and the "typical desk job" finds that both require:

1. Arriving on time
2. Being and remaining organized

3. Possessing the knowledge necessary for a more competent performance
4. Planning, strategizing, and working with information in sequence
5. Often attending to repetitive, uninteresting tasks
6. Completing tasks in a timely fashion
7. Remaining in a sedentary position for a long period of time
8. Making good choices
9. Working independently
10. Keeping track of possessions
11. Listening to and following directions
12. Controlling emotions and dealing with frustration

Nearly 30 years ago, it was suggested that the most common difficulties encountered by adults with LD were related to language-based deficits that impaired reading and spelling (Blalock, 1982). Overall, however, adults with LD may confront fewer challenges due to poor reading, writing, spelling, and arithmetic skills than they did as children as the daily demands of their lives do not call for competence in these skills multiple times during the day. Rather, those with LD and ADHD likely struggle with tasks requiring efficient daily functioning, especially in the areas of vocation, organization, planning, language comprehension, impulse control, and social relations. The major sources of referral for adults with LD are not programs promoting adult literacy or vocational training but those focused on rehabilitation. It is now recognized that the traditional discrepancy model that was employed for so many years in school settings to identify children with LD or ADHD not only does not work efficiently in the childhood years but is equally ineffective in the adult world. The focus of assessment for adults must be on strengths rather than weaknesses and compensation rather than remediation. Further, assessment of LD and ADHD in adulthood needs to take into account a person's entire life rather than concentrating on performance in a single setting. Thus, laboratory-based measures are less important, and measures of daily functional impairment are paramount. This approach is well supported by current research literature demonstrating that adults with histories of these conditions often function in everyday life above or below levels suggested by laboratory testing with much greater variation than found among children (Adler, Barkley, & Newcorn, 2008; Naugle & Chelune, 1990). Vocational rehabilitation services through state and federal funding have been available to individuals with LD and ADHD since 1981. Funding constraints, however, are leading some states to cut back on these services. This trend has continued over nearly a 20-year period. Data from the Rehabilitation Services Administration (1990, 2003) indicated in 2003 that 7.8% of all clients in rehabilitation had histories of LD compared to only 5% in 1988 and 1.3% in 1983. However, the process of assessment traditionally used to qualify clients and plan treatment is less effective for LD and ADHD populations than for the general population with other types of rehabilitation needs. Differences have been reported not only in tests and cutoff scores used to indicate significance but, alarmingly, in the fact that although almost a third of individuals with histories of LD or ADHD applying for benefits are recommended for assessment, only 6% received a neuropsychological evaluation in 1991 (Sheldon & Prout, 1991).

Thirty million adult Americans are estimated to be illiterate. Anderson (1994) distinguishes 9 groups that constitute the adult illiterate population:

1. Those who have learning disabilities
2. Those with intellectual handicaps
3. Those with limited educational opportunities
4. Dropouts
5. Slow learners
6. Those who "fall through the cracks"
7. Those from poor-quality schools
8. Those for whom English is a second language
9. Unwed mothers

Some researchers have suggested that the majority of illiterate adults have histories of LD or ADHD. This has yet to be clearly demonstrated, however. Most public schools in the United States serve between 2% to 4% of their population as learning disabled, well below the estimated 10% to 20% that likely experience some type of learning or attention problem (Altarac & Saroha, 2007; Baumgaertel, Wolraich, & Dietrich, 1995; Bird et al., 1988; Burd, Klug, Coumbe, & Kerbeshian, 2003; Nichols & Chen, 1981). Thus, it may be that the individuals with undetected LD and ADHD in high school become functionally illiterate adults. However, it is more likely that the majority of those described as illiterate comprise not only people with histories of LD or ADHD but also those with histories of intellectual handicap, those with limited educational opportunities, slow learners, dropouts, even those for whom English is a second language.

The group with limited educational opportunities is of interest as their struggles may result less from lack of ability than from inadequate opportunity. Dunivant (1982) reports that among incarcerated individuals, the level of reading achievement was nearly 3 years below the grade at which the prisoner dropped out of school. Hogenson (1974) reported that 63% of juvenile delinquents had histories of reading disability. Despite recent efforts to address this problem, academic challenges continue to represent a significant problem for the incarcerated population (Rogers-Adkinson, Melloy, Stuart, Fletcher, & Rinaldi, 2008). It has also been demonstrated that a significant minority—up to 40% of individuals with histories of ADHD—are at risk for delinquency. An equal number of these individuals likely experience learning problems as well. (For review, see Barkley, 2005.)

Educational risk factors are powerful predictors of psychiatric and adjustment problems. Over 20 years ago, Costello (1989) reviewed a number of large studies identifying factors associated with increased risk of psychiatric problems. In many of these studies, academic or cognitive problems at school were associated with the development of emotional and learning disabilities. These data are still relevant today.

Table 1.1 summarizes these factors and their general risks.

Table 1.1 Other Factors Associated with Increased Risk for Psychiatric Disorder

Reference	Factor	Risk Increased For
J. Anderson, Williams, McGee, & Silva (age 11) (1989)	Lower cognitive abilities	ADD, multiple
	Lower academic or self-esteem	Emotional, ADD, multiple
	Lower general self-esteem	Emotional, ADD, multiple
	Poor health	Any
	Poor peer socialization	Multiple
	Family disadvantage	Emotional, ADD
Bird et al. (ages 4–16) (1988)	Lower academic achievement	Behavioral, depressed
	Poor family functioning	Depressed
	High life stress	Behavioral, depressed
Velez, Johnson, & Cohen (ages 9–19) (1989)	Family problems	Behavioral
	Repeated school grade	Any
	High life stress	Behavioral, overanxious
Costello (ages 7–11) (1989)	Urban (versus suburban)	Behavioral
	Repeated school grade	Behavioral
	High life stress	Any
	No father in home	Oppositional
Offord, Boyle, & Racine (ages 4–16) (1989)	Family dysfunction	Any
	Repeated school grade	Behavioral
	Parental psychiatric problems	Somatization (boys only)
	Parent arrested	Conduct and oppositional
	Chronic mental illness	Any (4–11 only for hyperactivity)

Note: "Development in Child Psychiatric Epidemiology [Special section]," by E. J. Costello, 1989, *Journal of the American Academy of Child and Adolescent Psychiatry, 28,* p. 838. Used with permission.

REFERENCES

Adelman, P. B., & Vogel, S. A. (1990). College graduates with learning disabilities: Employment attainment and career patterns. *Learning Disability Quarterly, 13,* 154–166.

Adler, L. A., Barkley, R. A., & Newcorn, J. H. (2008). ADHD and comorbid disorders in adults. *Journal of Clinical Psychiatry, 69,* 1328–1335.

Altarac, M., & Saroha, E. (2007). Lifetime prevalence of learning disability among US children. *Pediatrics, 119* (Supplement), S77–S83.

American Psychiatric Association. (2000). *Diagnostic and Statistical Manual of Mental Disorders, Fourth Edition Text Revision.* Washington, DC: American Psychiatric Association.

Americans with Disabilities Amendments Act. Public Law No. 110–325 (2008).

Anderson, C. W. (1994). Adult literacy in learning disabilities. In P. J. Gerber & H. B Reiff (Eds.), *Learning disabilities in adulthood,* 121–129. Stoneham, MA: Butterworth-Heinemann.

Anderson, J., Williams, S., McGee, R., & Silva, P. (1989). Cognitive and social correlates of DSM-III disorders in preadolescent children. *Journal of Child Psychology and Psychiatry, 28,* 842–846.

Arnett, J. J. (2000). Emerging adulthood: A theory of development from late teens through the twenties. *American Psychologist, 55,* 469–480.

Astin, A., Green, K., Korn, W., Schalit, M., & Bertz, E. (1988). *The American freshman: National norms for 1988.* Los Angeles, CA: University of California Press.

Aune, E. (1991). A transition model for postsecondary-bound students with learning disabilities. *Learning Disabilities Research and Practice, 6,* 177–187.

Baltes, P. B., Reese, H. W., & Lipsitt, L. D. (1980). Lifespan development psychology. *Annual Review of Psychology, 31,* 65–110.

Barkley, R. A. (1990). *Attention deficit hyperactivity disorder: A handbook for diagnosis and treatment.* New York, NY: Guilford Press.

Barkley, R. A. (2005). *Attention deficit hyperactivity disorder: A handbook for diagnosis and treatment.* New York, NY: Guilford Press.

Barkley, R. A., Anastopoulos, A. A., Guevremont, D. C., & Fletcher, K. E. (1991). Adolescents with ADHD: Patterns of behavioral adjustment, academic functioning and treatment utilization. *Journal of the American Academy of Child and Adolescent Psychiatry, 30,* 752–761.

Barkley, R. A., Murphy, K. R., & Fischer, M. (2008). *ADHD in adults: What the science says.* New York, NY: Guilford Press.

Bassett, D. S., Polloway, E. A., & Patton, J. R. (1994). Learning disabilities: Perspectives on adult development. In P. J. Gerber & H. B. Reiff (Eds.), *Learning disabilities in adulthood,* 10–19. Stoneham, MA: Butterworth-Heinemann.

Baumgaertel, A., Wolraich, M. L., & Dietrich, M. (1995). Comparison of diagnostic criteria for attention deficit disorders in a German elementary school sample. *Journal of the American Academy of Child and Adolescent Psychiatry, 34,* 629–638.

Biederman, J. (2005). Attention-deficit/hyperactivity disorder: A selective overview. *Biological Psychiatry, 57,* 1215–1220.

Biederman, J., Faraone, S. V., Spencer, T., Wilens, T., Norman, D., Lapey, K. A., Mick, E., Lehman, B. K., & Doyle, A. (1993). Patterns of psychiatric comorbidity, cognition and psychosocial functioning in adults with attention deficit hyperactivity disorder. *American Journal of Psychiatry, 150,* 1792–1798.

Bird, H. R., Canino, G., Rubio-Stipec, M., Gould, M. S., Ribera, J., Sesman, M., Woodbury, M., . . . Moscoso, M. (1988). Estimates of the prevalence of childhood maladjustment in a community survey in Puerto Rico. *Archives of General Psychiatry, 45,* 1120–1126.

Blalock, J. (1981). Persistent problems and concerns of young adults with learning disabilities. In W. Cruickshank & A. Silver (Eds.), *Bridges to tomorrow* (Vol. 2; pp. 3–56). Syracuse, NY: Syracuse University Press.

Blalock, J. (1982). Residual learning disabilities in young adults: Implications for rehabilitation. *Journal of Applied Rehabilitation Counseling, 13,* 9–13.

Brown, D. (1984). Employment considerations for learning disabled adults. *Journal of Rehabilitation, 2,* 74–77, 88.

Bogart, S. K., Eidelman, L. J., & Kujawa, C. L. (1988). Helping learning disabled students in college. *Education Digest, 53,* 48–51.

Bonafina, M. A., Newcorn, J. H., McKay, K. E., Koda, V. H., & Halperin, J. M. (2000). ADHD and reading disabilities: A cluster analytic approach for distinguishing subgroups. *Journal of Learning Disabilities, 33,* 297–307.

Brooks, R. (2002). Changing the mindset of adults with ADHD: Strategies for fostering hope, optimism and resilience. In S. Goldstein & A. Teeter Ellison (Eds.), *Clinician's guide to adult ADHD: Assessment and intervention,* 127–146. New York, NY: Academic Press.

Bryan, T. H. (1976). Peer popularity of learning disabled children. *Journal of Learning Disabilities, 9,* 307–311.

Burd, L., Klug, M. G., Coumbe, M. J., & Kerbeshian, J. (2003). Children and adolescents with attention deficit hyperactivity disorder: Prevalence and cost of care. *Journal of Child Neurology, 18,* 555–561.

Bursuck, W. D., Rose, E., Cowen, S., & Yahaya, M. A. (1989). Nationwide survey of postsecondary education services for students with learning disabilities. *Exceptional Children, 56,* 236–245.

Centers for Disease Control. (2005). Mental health in the United States: Prevalence of diagnosis and medication treatment for Attention Deficit Hyperactivity Disorder—United States, 2003. *Morbidity and Mortality Weekly Report, 54,* 842–847.

Clement-Heist, K., Siegel, S., & Gaylord-Ross, R. (1992). Simulated and *in situ* vocational social skills training for youths with learning disabilities. *Exceptional Children, 58,* 336–345.

Cohen, J. (Ed.). (1999). Educating minds and hearts: Social emotional learning and the passage into adolescence. New York, NY: Teachers College Press.

Corley, M. A., & Taymans, J. M. (2002). Adults with learning disabilities: A review of the literature. In the National Center for Adult Learning and Literacy (Ed.), *The Annual Review of Adult Learning and Literacy* (Vol. 3). Retrieved from http://www.ncsall.net/?id=575

Costello, E. J. (1989). Developments in child psychiatric epidemiology [Special section]. *Journal of the American Academy of Child and Adolescent Psychiatry, 28,* 836–841.

Covey, S. (1989). *The seven habits of highly effective people.* New York: Simon & Schuster.

Cuffe, S. P., Moore, C. G., & Mckeown, R. E. (2005). Prevalence and correlates of ADHD symptoms in the National Health Interview Survey. *Journal of Attention Disorders, 9,* 392–401.

Dickstein, E., & Warren, D. (1980). Role-taking deficits in learning disabled children. *Journal of Learning Disabilities, 13,* 378–382.

Dunivant, N. (1982). *The relationship between learning disabilities and juvenile delinquency.* Washington, DC: U.S. Department of Justice, National Institute for Juvenile Justice and Delinquency Prevention.

Eakin, L., Minde, K., Hechtman, L., Ochs, E., Krane, E., Bouffard, R., et al. (2004). The marital and family functioning of adults with ADHD and their spouses. *Journal of Attention Disorders, 8,* 1–10.

Elias, M. J., Zins, J. E., Graczyk, P. A., & Weissberg, R. P. (2003). Implementation, sustainability and scaling up of social-emotional and academic innovations in public schools. *School Psychology Review, 32,* 303–319.

Erikson, E. (1950). *Childhood and society.* New York: Norton.

Fairweather, J. S., & Shaver, D. M. (1991). Making the transition to postsecondary education and training. *Exceptional Children, 57,* 264–270.

Faraone, S. V., & Biederman, J. (2005). What is the prevalence of adult ADHD? Results of a population screen of 966 adults. *Journal of Attention Disorders, 9,* 384–391.

Faraone, S. V., Sergeant, J., Gillberg, C., & Biederman, J. (2003). The worldwide prevalence of ADHD: Is it an American condition? *World Psychiatry, 2,* 104–113.

Felton, R. (1986, November). *Bowman-Gray follow-up study.* Paper presented at the Orton Dyslexia National Conference, Philadelphia, PA.

Fonagy, P., Steele, M., Steele, H., Higgitt, A., & Target, M. (1994). The Emanuel Miller Memorial Lecture 1992: The theory and practice of resilience. *Journal of Child Psychology and Psychiatry, 35,* 231–257.

Fourquean, J. M., Meisgeier, C., Swank, P. R., & Williams, R. E. (1991). Correlates of postsecondary employment outcomes for young adults with learning disabilities. *Journal of Learning Disabilities, 24,* 400–405.

Frauenheim, J. G., & Heckerl, J. R. (1983). A longitudinal study of psychological and achievement test performance in severe dyslexic adults. *Journal of Learning Disabilities, 16,* 339–347.

Gerber, P. J. (1978). *A comparative study of social perceptual ability of learning disabled and nonhandicapped children* (Unpublished doctoral dissertation). University of Michigan, Ann Arbor.

Gerber, P. J. (1983). Conference summary and generation of final research priorities. In *Special rehabilitation needs of learning disabilities adults* (pp. 50–61). Washington, DC: National Institute for Handicapped Research.

Gerber, P. J. (1984). *A study of the school to work transition for learning disabled students and the learning disabled adult in society in the Netherlands and Denmark.* New York, NY: World Rehabilitation Fund.

Gerber, P. J. (1988). *Highly successful learning disabled adults: Insights from case interviews.* Paper presented at the annual conference of the Association for Handicapped Student Services Programs in Postsecondary Education, New Orleans, LA.

Gerber, P. J., & Brown, D. (1990). Report of the pathways to employment consensus conference on employability of persons with learning disabilities. *Learning Disabilities Research and Practice, 6,* 475–487.

Gerber, P. J., Ginsberg, R. J., & Reiff, H. B. (1992). Identifying alterable patterns in employment success for highly successful adults with learning disabilities. *Journal of Learning Disabilities, 25,* 475–487.

Gerber, P. J., & Mellard, D. (1985). Rehabilitation of learning disabled adults: Recommended research priorities. *Journal of Rehabilitation, 51,* 62–64.

Gerber, P. J., & Reiff, H. B. (1991). *Speaking for themselves: Ethnographic interviews with adults with learning disabilities.* Ann Arbor, MI: University of Michigan Press.

Gerber, P. J., Schneiders, C. A., Paradise, L. V., Reiff, H. B., Ginsberg, R., & Popp, P. A. (1990). Persisting problems of adults with learning disabilities: Self-reported comparisons from their school age years. *Journal of Learning Disabilities, 23,* 570–573.

Gilligan, C. (1982). *In a different voice: Psychological theory and women's development.* Cambridge, MA: Harvard University Press.

Gittleman, R., Mannuzza, S., Shenker, R., & Bonagura, N. (1985). Hyperactive boys almost grown up. *Archives of General Psychiatry, 42,* 937–947.

Goldstein, S. (1989). *Observation checklist.* Salt Lake City, UT: Neurology, Learning and Behavior Center.

Goldstein, S. (1995). *Understanding and managing children's classroom behavior.* New York, NY: Wiley.

Goldstein, S., & Brooks, R. (Eds.) (2005). *Handbook of resilience in children.* New York, NY: Kluwer/Academic Press.

Goldstein, S., & Goldstein, M. (1990). *Managing attention disorders in children: A guide for practitioners.* New York: Wiley.

Goldstein, S., & Teeter Ellison, A. (2002). *Clinician's guide to adult ADHD: Assessment and intervention (practical resources for the mental health professional).* San Diego, CA: Academic Press.

Gregg, N. (2007). Underserved and unprepared: Postsecondary learning disabilities. *Learning Disabilities Research & Practice, 22,* 219–228.

Gregg, N. (2009). *Adolescents and adults with learning disabilities and ADHD: Assessment and accommodation.* New York, NY: Guilford Press.

Hallowell, E. M., & Ratey, J. J. (1994). *Driven to distraction.* New York: Pantheon.

Halperin, A. (1992). Transition: Old wine in new bottles. *Exceptional Children, 58,* 202–213.

Hartman, R. (1991). LD among high achieving students. *Information from HEATH, 10,* 2–12.

Herzog, J. E., & Falk, B. (1991). A follow-up study of vocational outcomes of young adults with learning disabilities. *Journal of Postsecondary Education and Disability, 9*, 219–226.

Hill, J. W. (1984, May). *Unrecognized learning disabilities in adulthood: Implications for adult education*. Paper presented at the annual meeting of the American Association of Mental Deficiency, Minneapolis, MN.

Hoffman, F. J., Sheldon, K. L., Minskoff, E. H., Sautter, S. W., Steidle, E. F., Baker, D. P., Bailey, M. B., & Echols, L. D. (1987). Needs of learning disabled adults. *Journal of Learning Disabilities, 20*, 43–52.

Hogenson, D. L. (1974). *Reading and juvenile delinquency*. Towson, MD: Orton Dyslexia Society.

Hughes, C. A., & Smith, J. O. (1990). Cognitive and academic performance of college students with learning disabilities: A synthesis of the literature. *Learning Disability Quarterly, 13*, 66–79.

Interagency Committee on Learning Disabilities. (1987). *Learning disabilities: A report to the U.S. Congress*. Washington, DC: U.S. Department of Health and Human Services.

Johnson, C. (1981). LD adults: The inside story. *Academic Therapy, 16*, 435–442.

Latham, P. S., & Latham P. H. (1993). *ADD and the law*. Washington, DC: JKL Communications.

Lerner, J. (1985). *Learning disabilities: Theories, diagnosis, and teaching strategies* (4th ed.). Boston, MA: Houghton-Mifflin.

Lerner, J. (1993). *Learning disabilities: Theories, diagnoses, and teaching strategies* (6th ed.). Boston, MA: Houghton-Mifflin.

Levine, M. D. (1989). Learning disabilities at 25: The early adulthood of a maturing concept. *Learning Disabilities, 1*, 1–11.

Lieberman, L. M. (1987). Is the learning disabled adult really necessary? *Journal of Learning Disabilities, 20*, 64.

Madaus, J. W., Gerber, P. J., & Price, L. A. (2008). Adults with learning disabilities in the workforce: Lessons for secondary transition programs. *Learning Disabilities Research & Practice, 23*, 148–153.

Malcolm, C. B., Polatajko, H. J., & Simons, J. (1990). A descriptive study of adults with suspected learning disabilities. *Journal of Learning Disabilities, 23*, 518–520.

Mannuzza, S., Gittleman-Klein, R. G., Bessler, A. A., Malloy, P., & LaPudula, M. (1993). Adult outcome of hyperactive boys: Education achievement, occupational rank, and psychiatric status. *Archives of General Psychiatry, 50*, 565–576.

Matthews, R. M., Whang, R. L., & Fawcett, S. B. (1982). Behavioral assessment of occupational skills of learning disabled adolescents. *Journal of Learning Disabilities, 15*, 38–41.

McGough, J. J., Smalley, S. L., McCracken, J. T., Yang, M., Del'Homme, M., Lynn, D. E., et al. (2005). Psychiatric comorbidity in adult attention deficit hyperactivity disorder: Findings from multiplex families. *American Journal of Psychiatry, 162,* 1621–1627.

Meaux, J. B., Green, A., & Broussard, L. (2009). ADHD in the college student: A block in the road. *Journal of Psychiatric and Mental Health Nursing, 16,* 248–256.

Medco Health Solutions (2005). New research: ADHD medication use growing faster among adults than children. Retrieved from http://phx.corporate-ir.net/phoenix .zhtml?c=131268&p=irol-newsArticle&ID=756843&highlight=

Merrell, K. W. (2002). Social-emotional intervention in schools: Current status, progress, and promise. *School Psychology Review, 31,* 143–147.

Meyers, G. S., & Messer, J. (1981). The social and vocational adjustment of learning disabled/behavior disordered adolescents after h. s.: A pilot survey. In *Proceedings from the International Conference on the Career Development of Handicapped Individuals* (pp. 70–83). Washington, DC: National Institute of Education.

Minskoff, E. H., Sautter, S. W., Hoffman, F. J., & Hawks, R. (1987). Employer attitudes toward hiring the learning disabled. *Journal of Learning Disabilities, 20,* 53–57.

Minskoff, E. H., Sautter, S., Sheldon, K. L., Steidle, E. F., & Baker, D. P. (1988). A comparison of learning disabled adults and high school students. *Learning Disabilities Research, 3,* 115–123.

Morris, M. A., Schraufnagel, C. D., Chudnow, R. S., & Weinberg, W. A. (2009). Learning disabilities do not go away: 20- to 25-year study of cognition, academic achievement, and affective illness. *Journal of Child Neurology, 24,* 323–332.

Mpofu, E., Watson, E., & Chan, S.-Y. (1999). Learning disabilities in adults: Implications for rehabilitation intervention in work settings. *Journal of Rehabilitation, 65,* 33–41.

Naglieri, J. A., Salter, C. J., & Edwards, G. H. (2004). Assessment of children with attention and reading difficulties using the PASS theory and Cognitive Assessment System. *Journal of Psychoeducational Assessment, 22,* 93–105.

National Center for Education Statistics. (1999). *Students with disabilities in postsecondary education: A profile of preparation, participation, and outcomes.* Washington, DC: U.S. Department of Education.

National Center for Education Statistics. (2005). *Stats in brief.* Washington, DC: U.S. Department of Education.

National Joint Commission on Learning Disabilities. (1987). Adults with learning disabilities: A call to action. *Journal of Learning Disabilities, 20,* 172–175.

Naugle, R. I., & Chelune, G. J. (1990). Integrating neuropsychological and "real life" data: A neuropsychological model for assessing every day functioning. In D. E. Tupper & D. D. Cicerone (Eds.), *The neuropsychology of everyday life: Assessment and basic competencies* (pp. 57–74). Boston, MA: Kluwer.

Naylor, C. E., Felton, R. H., & Wood, F. B. (1990). Adult outcome in developmental dyslexia. In G. T. Pavlidis (Ed.), *Perspectives in dyslexia* (Vol. 2; pp. 213–227). Chichester, United Kingdom: Wiley.

Nelson, J. R., Dodd, J. M., & Smith, D. J. (1990). Faculty willingness to accommodate students with learning disabilities: A comparison among academic divisions. *Journal of Learning Disabilities, 23*, 185–189.

Newman, L., Wagner, M., Cameto, R., & Knokey, A.-M.(2009). *The post-high school outcomes of youth with disabilities up to 4 years after high school. A Report of Findings from the National Longitudinal Transition Study-2 (NLTS2) (NCSER 2009–3017).* Menlo Park, CA: SRI International.

Nichols, P. L., & Chen, T. C. (1981). *Minimal brain dysfunction: A prospective study.* Hillsdale, NJ: Erlbaum.

Nixon, E. (2001). The social competence of children with attention deficit hyperactivity disorder: A review of the literature. *Child and Adolescent Mental Health, 6*, 172–180.

Offord, D. R., Boyle, M. H., & Racine, Y. (1989). Ontario child health study: Correlates of disorder. *Journal of American Academy of Child and Adolescent Psychiatry, 28*, 856–860.

Patton, J. R., & Polloway, E. A. (1992). Learning disabilities: The challenges of adulthood. *Journal of Learning Disabilities, 25*, 410–416.

Pelham, W. E., & Bender, M. E. (1982). Peer relationships and hyperactive children: Description and treatment. In K. Gadow & I. Bailer (Eds.), *Advances in learning and behavioral disabilities* (Vol. 1; pp. 365–436). Greenwich, CT: JAI.

Pelham, W. E., & Milich, R. (1984). Peer relations of children with hyperactivity/attention deficit disorder. *Journal of Learning Disabilities, 17*, 560–568.

Pickering, E., Pickering, A., & Buchanan, M. (1987). LD and nonhandicapped boys' comprehension of cartoon humor. *Learning Disability Quarterly, 10*, 45–51.

Planty, M., Hussar, W., Snyder, T., Provasnik, S., Kena, G., Dinkes, R., et al. (2008). *The conditions of education 2008.* Washington, DC: National Center for Education Statistics.

Polloway, E. A., Schewel, R., & Patton, J. R. (1992). Learning disabilities in adulthood: Personal perspectives. *Journal of Learning Disabilities, 25*, 520–522.

Poplin, M. (1988). The reductionist fallacy in learning disabilities: Replicating the past by reducing the present. *Learning Disability Quarterly, 7*, 389–400.

Preston, A. S., Heaton, S. C., McCann, S. J., Watson, W. D., & Selke, G. (2009). The role of multidimensional attentional abilities in academic skills of children with ADHD. *Journal of Learning Disabilities, 42*, 240–249.

Price, L. A., & Gerber, P. J. (2001). At second glance: Employers and employees with learning disabilities in the Americans with Disabilities Act era. *Journal of Learning Disabilities, 34*, 202–210.

Price, L. A., Gerber, P. J., & Mulligan, R. (2003). The Americans with Disabilities Act and adults with learning disabilities as employees: The realities of the workplace. *Remedial and Special Education, 24*, 350–358.

Rehabilitation Services Administration (1990). Program assistance circular. Washington DC: U.S. Department of Education, Office of Special Education and Rehabilitation Services.

Reiff, H. B. (1987). *Cognitive correlates of social perception in students with learning disabilities* (Unpublished doctoral dissertation). University of New Orleans, New Orleans, LA.

Reiff, H. B., & Gerber, P. J. (1989). Social cognition and cognitive processing in students with learning disabilities. *Learning Disabilities: A Multidisciplinary Journal, 1*, 56–62.

Reiff, H. B., & Gerber, P. J. (1994). Social/emotional and daily living issues for adults with learning disabilities. In P. J. Gerber & H. B. Reiff (Eds.), *Learning disabilities in adulthood* (pp. 72–81). Boston, MA: Andover.

Resnick, R. J., & McEvoy, K. (Eds.). (1995). *Bibliographies in psychology: Vol. 14. Attention deficit hyperactivity disorder. Abstracts of the psychological and behavioral literature, 1971–1994*. Washington DC: American Psychological Association.

Roff, M., Sells, S., & Golden, M. (1972). *Social adjustment and personality development in children*. Minneapolis, MN: University of Minnesota Press.

Rogan, L. L., & Hartman, L. D. (1976). *A follow-up study of learning disabled children as adults*. Washington, DC: Department of Health, Education, and Welfare, Office of Education, Bureau for the Education of the Handicapped.

Rogan, L. L., & Hartman, L. D. (1990). Adult outcomes of learning disabled students ten years after initial follow-up. *Learning Disabilities Focus, 5*, 91–102.

Rogers-Adkinson, D., Melloy, K., Stuart, S., Fletcher, L., & Rinaldi, C. (2008). Reading and written language competency of incarcerated youth. *Reading and Writing Quarterly: Overcoming Learning Difficulties, 24*, 197–218.

Rosenberg, B., & Gaier, E. (1977). The self-concept of the adolescent with learning disabilities. *Adolescence, 12*, 489–498.

Rowland, A. S., Lesesne, C. A., & Abramowitz, A. J. (2002). The epidemiology of attention-deficit/hyperactivity disorder (ADHD): A public health view. *Mental Retardation and Developmental Disabilities Research Reviews, 8*, 162–170.

Rutherford, R. B., Bullis, M., Anderson, C. W., & Griller-Clark, H. M. (2002). *Youth with disabilities in the correctional system: Prevalence rates and identification issues*. Washington, DC: Center for Effective Collaboration and Practice.

Safer, D. J., & Allen, R. P. (1976). *Hyperactive children: Diagnosis and management*. Baltimore, MD: University Park Press.

Schnoes, C., Reid, R., Wagner, M., & Marder, C. (2006). ADHD among students receiving special education services: A national survey. *Exceptional Children, 72*, 483–496.

Schumacher, J., & Hazel, S. (1984). Social skills assessment and training for the learning disabled: Who's on first and what's on second? *Journal of Learning Disabilities, 17*, 422–431.

Schütte, V., & Petermann, F. (2006). Social relations and pair relationship in adults with ADHD: A description of phenomenon on the basis of a questionnaire study. *Verhaltenstherapie & Verhaltensmedizin, 27,* 157–172.

Seligman, M. E. P. (1998). Building human strength: Psychology's forgotten mission. *APA Monitor, 29,* 2.

Shapiro, E. S., & Lentz, F. E. (1991). Vocational-technical programs: Follow-up of students with learning disabilities. *Exceptional Children, 58,* 47–59.

Sheldon, K. L., & Prout, H. T. (1991). Vocational rehabilitation and learning disabilities: An analysis of state policies. *Journal of Rehabilitation, 51,* 59–61.

Shelton, D. (2006). A study of young offenders with learning disabilities. *Journal of Correctional Health Care, 12,* 36–44.

Shessel, I., & Reiff, H. B. (1999). Experiences of adults with learning disabilities: Positive and negative impacts and outcomes. *Learning Disability Quarterly, 22,* 305–316.

Sitlington, P., & Frank A. R. (1990). Are adolescents with learning disabilities successfully crossing the bridge in adult life? *Learning Disability Quarterly, 13,* 97–111.

Smith, J. O. (1992). Falling through the cracks: Rehabilitation services for adults with learning disabilities. *Exceptional Children, 58,* 451–460.

Spencer, T., Biederman, J., & Mick, E. (2007). Attention-deficit/hyperactivity disorder: Diagnosis, lifespan, comorbidities, and neurobiology. *Ambulatory Pediatrics, 7,* 73–81.

SRI International. (1990). *The National Longitudinal Transition Study of Special Education Students. Vol. 2. Youth categorized as learning disabled.* Washington, DC: U.S. Department of Education, Office of Special Education Programs.

Swanson, H., & Trahan, M. (1986). Characteristics of frequently cited articles in learning disabilities. *Journal of Special Education, 20,* 167–182.

U.S. Department of Education. (1987). *Profile of handicapped students in postsecondary education* (National Center for Education Statistics, 1987 National Postsecondary Student Aid Study, Report No. 0065–000–00375–9). Washington DC: U.S. Government Printing Office.

U.S. Department of Education. (2002). *Twenty-fourth annual report to Congress on the implementation of the Individuals with Disabilities Education Act.* Washington DC: U.S. Government Printing Office.

U.S. Department of Education. (2003). *Longitudinal study of the vocational rehabilitation services program: VR services and outcomes.* Washington DC: U.S. Government Printing Office.

U.S. Department of Labor, Bureau of Labor Statistics. (1987). *Occupational outlook handbook.* Washington, DC: U.S. Government Printing Office.

U.S. Department of Labor, Bureau of Labor Statistics (2010). *Labor force statistics from the current population survey: Employment status and disability status, December 2009.* Retrieved from http://www.bls.gov/cps/cpsdisability.htm

Valdez, K. A., Williamson, C. L., & Wagner, M. M. (1990). *The National Longitudinal Transition Study of Special Education Students, Statistical Almanac: Vol. 2. Youth categorized as learning disabled.* Palo Alto, CA: SRI International.

Velez, C. N., Johnson, J., & Cohen, P. (1989). A longitudinal analysis of selected risk factors for childhood psychopathology. *Journal of the American Academy of Child and Adolescent Psychiatry, 28,* 861–864.

Wagner, M. (1989). *Youth with disabilities during transition: An overview of descriptive findings from the National Longitudinal Transition Study.* Menlo Park, CA: SRI International.

Wagner, M., Newman, L., Cameto, R., Garza, N., & Levine, P. (2005). *After high school: A first look at the postschool experiences of youth with disabilities. A report from the National Longitudinal Transition Study-2 (NLTS2).* Menlo Park, CA: SRI International.

Weiss, G., & Hechtman, L. T. (1993). *Hyperactive children grown up* (2nd ed.). New York, NY: Guilford Press.

Weist, M. D., Evans, S. W., & Lever, N. A. (Eds.). (2003). *Handbook of school mental health: Advancing practice and research.* New York: Kluwer Academic/Plenum.

Werner, E. E. (1989). High-risk children in young adulthood. A longitudinal study from birth to 32 years. *American Journal of Orthopsychiatry, 59,* 72–81.

Werner, E. E. (1994). Overcoming the odds. *Developmental and Behavioral Pediatrics, 15,* 131–136.

Werner, E. E. (2005). What can we learn about resilience from large-scale longitudinal studies? In S. Goldstein & R. Brooks (Eds.), *Handbook of resilience in children* (pp. 91–105). New York, NY: Kluwer/Academic Press.

Werner, E. E., & Smith, R. S. (1992). *Overcoming the odds: High risk children from birth to adulthood.* Ithaca, NY: Cornell University Press.

Werner, E. E., & Smith, R. S. (2001). *Journeys from childhood to midlife: Risk, resilience, and recovery.* Ithaca, NY: Cornell University Press.

White, W. J. (1985). Perspectives on education and training of learning disabled adults. *Learning Disability Quarterly, 8,* 231–236.

Wiederholt, J. L. (1982). Lifespan instruction for the learning disabled. *Topics in Learning and Learning Disabilities, 2,* 1–89.

Wiig, E. H., & Semel, E. M. (1976). *Language disabilities in children and adolescents.* Columbus, OH: Merrill.

Wilens, T. E., Biederman, J., Spencer, T. J., & Frances, R. J. (1994). Comorbidity of attention deficit hyperactivity disorder and the psychoactive substance use disorders. *Hospital and Community Psychiatry, 45,* 421–435.

Will, M. (1984). *OSERS programming for the transition of youth with disabilities: Bridges from school to working life.* Washington, DC: Office of Special Education and Rehabilitative Services.

Zigmond, N., & Thornton, H. (1985). Follow-up of postsecondary age learning disabled graduates and dropouts. *Learning Disabilities Research, 1,* 50–55.

2

Learning Disabilities in Childhood

SAM GOLDSTEIN

Learning Disabilities (LD), including Reading Disabilities (RD), are the most prevalent group of neurobehavioral disorders affecting children and adults. There is a strong genetic component to these disabilities. Unlike most other psychological or developmental disorders, LD are not a single, relatively well-defined entity or syndrome. Rather, LD encompass an extremely heterogeneous group of problems with diverse characteristics that can result from a variety of biological influences, including genetic factors, environmental insults to the brain, and possibly, as recent research on brain development suggests, extreme lack of early environmental stimulation. As a result, the multifaceted field of LD is complex and often contentious with many competing theories, definitions, diagnostic procedures, and suggested avenues of intervention.

Within the framework of this chapter, it is not possible to adequately describe or attempt to integrate the many competing viewpoints and claims surrounding the construct of LD. This task has been undertaken by other writers in the field who have approached LD from a broad, historical perspective as well as from the viewpoint of best current practices (Burkhardt, Obiakor, & Rotatori, 2004; Lerner, 1993; Mercer, 1991; Swanson, Harris, & Graham, 2003; Torgesen, 1991). This chapter approaches LD from biomedical, neuropsychological, and information-processing perspectives.

CONCEPT OF LD

LD as a category of human exceptionality evolved from observations of physicians and educators as they studied and attempted to assist children with brain injuries. Alfred Strauss and Laura Lehtinen published their classic work, *Psychopathology and Education of the Brain-Injured Child*, in 1947. In 1966, Clements, as head of a task force sponsored by the U.S. Department of Heath, Education, and Welfare, strongly supported use of the term "minimal brain dysfunction," which became popularized as MBD (Mercer, 1991).

The terms "minimal brain injury" or "minimal brain dysfunction" were used to describe children of normal intelligence who appeared similar to some individuals with known brain injury in that they exhibited a combination of hard or soft signs of neurological deficiency concomitantly with educational and sometimes behavioral disorders. Minimal brain dysfunction was believed to be responsible for observed deficits in processes such as auditory and visual perception, symbol learning, short- and long-term memory, concept formation and reasoning, fine and gross motor functions, and integrative functions, resulting in disorders of receptive and expressive language, reading, writing, mathematics, physical skill development, and interpersonal adjustment. In addition, behavioral traits such as distractibility, impulsivity, perseveration, and disinhibition were often found in children with MBD syndrome (Cruickshank, Bentzen, Ratzeburg, & Tannhauser, 1961; Fletcher, Shaywitz, & Shaywitz, 1999; Gardner, 1973; Johnson & Myklebust, 1967). Thus, from the first, the field of LD centered around a medical model with the term "minimal brain dysfunction" being applied to an extremely heterogeneous group of individuals.

Johnson and Myklebust (1967) discussed the limitations of extant terminologies. They suggested that "minimal" was inappropriate to describe individuals whose resulting disabilities had much greater than minimal impact on their learning functions and that the words "brain injury" or "brain dysfunction" were viewed as too stigmatizing by many individuals with LD and their parents.

In 1963, at a national organizing conference of concerned parents and professionals held in Chicago, Samuel Kirk proposed use of the term "Learning Disabilities" (Lerner, 1993). This term was quickly accepted by parents and gained ascendance when federal and state governments adopted it at the time special education services were expanded to include students of average or better intelligence with otherwise unexplained academic LD (Mercer, 1991; U.S. Office of Education, 1977). Kirk viewed LD from a psycholinguistic perspective, which proposed that underlying specific deficiencies in central nervous system functioning result in deficits in psychoneurological learning processes, which, in turn, explain observed LD. Based on the psycholinguistic-process model of Charles Osgood, Kirk described LD according to learning channels (auditory/verbal or visual/motor), learning levels (rote or conceptual), and specific processes (perception, reception, memory, integration, expression, etc.; Kirk & Kirk, 1971). Naglieri and Das (2002), based on A. R. Luria's model of intellectual processes, described four critical processes essential for effective learning. Luria's PASS model involves planning, simultaneous processing, attention, and successive processing. Weaknesses in various combinations of these processes have been associated with specific LD.

Although the view of LD as neurologically based process deficits remained widespread, during the 1970s, a behavioral approach to the topic was promulgated. Process deficits were roundly criticized as hypothetical constructs that could not validly or reliably be diagnosed and that had little or no demonstrable relationship to effective interventions (Hammill & Larsen, 1974, 1996; Larsen, Parker, & Hammill, 1982). Proponents of this view advocated criterion-referenced or curriculum-based assessment of a multitude of specific skills and interventions based on a detailed analysis of the component parts of each skill to be taught/learned along with ecological analysis and modification of the learning environment. Well-designed and group-validated approaches to curriculum instruction were held to be appropriate and effective for all students, including slow learners, without reference to supposed internal processing deficits or disabilities. This approach, now referred to as response to intervention, has become increasingly popular and advocated for within special education programs in public schools.

While debate raged, a third approach to understanding and assisting those with LD added a new dimension. Based on research centered at the University of Virginia (Hallahan, 1980) and the University of Kansas (Schumaker, Deshler, Alley, & Warner, 1983), cognitive learning models were applied to the understanding and treatment of LD. From a cognitive framework, learners are viewed as directing their own learning by focusing on topics and skills that are personally meaningful and by developing active strategies for information acquisition. One outgrowth of cognitive theory has been the holistic or constructivist approach to teaching and learning, including whole-language methods of reading instruction. Although the tenets of cognitive theory have been applied to the population with LD in a number of ways, a major emphasis has been helping students to develop more reflective, accurate, and efficient approaches to learning tasks (i.e., learning how to learn). Students are taught to consciously employ self-monitoring strategies and effective learning/study strategies. This model, which emphasizes focusing on how students learn versus what students learn, may have influenced the scientific discipline away from more deficit-based conceptualizations when explaining LD (Wong, 1987).

PREVALENCE OF LD

Determining prevalence rates, or the frequency of occurrence, of LD in the population might appear at first glance to be a relatively straightforward process. However, since prevalence rates for any disease or disability are dependent on having a clear-cut definition of the disorder under consideration and since there is no consensually accepted or experimentally validated definition of LD, the process of determining the prevalence of LD is a quagmire. At the present time, incidence figures for this nondefinitive disorder or group of disorders cannot be determined precisely and are essentially broad estimates.

Important considerations regarding the determination of LD prevalence were presented by MacMillan (1993) and Lyon (1996). In a discussion of operationalizing disability definitions, MacMillan described *prevalence rate* as referring to the total percentage of the population that is affected by a disorder while *detection rate* refers to the number of known or identified cases. For LD, prevalence and detection rates may, indeed likely do, differ. Depending on the stringency of identification criteria, prevalence estimates for LD have varied from as low as 1% to as high as 30% of the school-age population (Lerner, 1993). In the 2006–07 academic year, 5.4% of all 3- to 21-year-olds were served under the Individuals with Disabilities Education Act as students with a specific learning disability (U.S. Department of Education, 2008). Mercer (1991) suggested that those with severe specific LD might comprise approximately 1.5% of students, while the inclusion of students with mild LD could raise that figure to about 4% or 5% (National Health Interview Survey, 2003). Other studies focusing on a specific classification of LD indicate that from 5% to 8% of school-age children exhibit arithmetical disabilities (Geary, 2003) and 5% to 17.5% with dyslexia (Shaywitz, 1998). It is still estimated that 52% of all students being served in special education have a classification of LD with an actual count exceeding 2.5 million (Kavale & Forness, 2003).

ETIOLOGY AND GENETICS OF LD

From the time of the earliest medical reports that described cases of dyslexia, LD have been viewed as stemming from central nervous system dysfunction, more precisely, from dysfunction of specific portions of the cerebral cortex (Doris, 1986; Huston, 1992). This long-standing presumption is being reinforced and validated by modern cognitive neuroscience. Language-specific processing of the brain in areas surrounded by the sylvian fissure have been associated with a variety of language functions. The temporoparietal cortex receives projections containing but not limited to visual and auditory information. The posterior superior temporal gyrus or Wernicke's area is associated with a variety of language functions, particularly involving comprehension. However, it is likely oversimplistic to describe temporoparietal areas as those responsible for the reception of language whereas frontal regions responsible for expressive language. It is more likely that a distributed network is responsible for full coherence of the language system (Joseph, Nobel, & Eden, 2001).

Positron emission tomography (PET) and functional magnetic resonance imaging (fMRI) have been used extensively to extend an understanding of how specific components of learning map onto the brain (Richards, 2001; Rumsey et al., 1997; B. A. Shaywitz, Lyon, & Shaywitz, 2006). As these techniques have become more refined and technologically advanced, an understanding of structural differences implicated in LD has progressed. Despite their limitations, these techniques have revealed much about structures of the brain associated with visual word form (Fritch, Friston, Liddle, & Frackowiak, 1991), orthography (Cao, Bitan, Chou, Burman, & Booth, 2006; Flowers, Wood, & Nailer, 1991), phonology (Rumsey et al., 1997), semantics (Baillieux et al., 2009; Pugh et al., 1996), and calculation (Davis et al., 2009; Kucian et al., 2006). However, a great deal of variability has been found within and between studies such that multiple sites within similar regions of the brain have been implicated in these processes (Poeppel, 1996).

Very few functional neuroimaging studies have been conducted with children, in part due to the fact that PET requires the application of radioactive material. At least one study using fMRI has mapped language dominance in children with partial epilepsy, finding results similar to those observed in adults (Hertz-Pannier et al., 1997). Readers interested in an extended discussion of learning and brain imaging are referred to Berninger (2004).

LD traditionally have been viewed as neurological deficits intrinsic to genetic and other biological factors within the individual and not of environmental origin. However, current research is documenting the intimate connection between environment and neuroanatomical development (Dawson & Fischer, 1994; Hutenlocher, 1991; Mustard, 2006). The pervasive effects of early environmental programming on the formation and pruning of neural networks and the theoretical relationship of this process to the occurrence of neurologically based specific LD is an area that is only beginning to be considered.

The prenatal, perinatal, and postnatal environmental factors associated with brain development and brain injury are best viewed as potential causes of LD due to uncertainties and inconsistences in the relationships among age at onset, the severity of circumstance or condition, the degree of transient or permanent brain dysfunction, and the broad range of possible effects on learning. For example, clinical studies have documented cases in which major structural deficits, even loss of an entire brain hemisphere, result in few observable signs of LD while many individuals with severe LD have no obvious structural deficits (Bigler, 1992; Bigler, Lajiness-O'Neill, & Howes, 1998; Satz, 1990). In addition, confounding variables, such as socioeconomic status, parenting style, and early interventions, mediate the degree to which a neurological abnormality will result in impaired learning. In many or most cases of LD, etiology is presumably not a factor. In some cases an environmental cause is directly known or fairly certain while in other cases the environmental contribution to etiology is cloudy, involving a subtle interplay of potential factors that may be undocumented or unknown.

In the last 40 years, experimental research has provided strong support for a genetic factor in some forms of LD. The familial occurrence of reading, spelling, and writing disabilities has been investigated using a variety of methodologies, such as study of family history and pedigree analysis, determination of concordance rates among identical and fraternal twins, comparison of linear regression in reading scores between identical and fraternal twins, and chromosomal analysis of family members.

The earliest widely cited family pedigree study of RD, conducted by Hallgren in 1950 (cited in Pennington, 1991), consisted of a statistical analysis of dyslexia in 112 families. Among first-degree relatives (parents and siblings of an identified child), the risk for co-occurrence of this disorder was 41%, which is much higher than the usual prevalence estimates for the general population of 5% to 10%. Huston (1992), reporting on Hallgren's study, indicated that of the 112 families, in 90 families, one parent was dyslexic; in 3 families both parents were dyslexic; and in 19 families neither parent had dyslexia. Although Hallgren's study has been criticized for methodological flaws, later studies carried out with greater technical precision, such as that of Finucci, Guthrie, Childs, Abbey, and Childs (1976, cited in DeFries, 1991), have found similar familial rates in the range of 35% to 45%. Finucci (1978) also published a critical review of the early investigations of dyslexia and genetics. Even more recent studies continue to demonstrate considerable evidence supporting that dyslexia and even dysgraphia have a developmental, genetic influence (Raskind, 2001).

The Colorado Family Reading Study, begun in 1973, compared reading abilities of 125 children with reading disability (probands) and their family members to 125 matched control children who did not have a reading disability and their family members. The total number of subjects in this study was 1,044, making it an extensive family study. Results clearly demonstrated that RD are familial in nature. Scores for siblings of proband subjects were significantly lower than scores for siblings of control subjects on measures of both reading and symbol processing speed. A similar pattern of significant results was observed for the parents of probands and controls. An interesting finding was that, on average, brothers of probands had significantly more reading impairment than sisters of probands. Similarly, fathers of probands were, on average, less skilled readers than mothers of probands; however, the score difference between fathers and mothers was less than the score difference between male and female siblings (DeFries, 1991). Although RD have now conclusively been shown to be familial in nature, familial occurrence suggests but does not demonstrate genetic heritability. Empirical investigations to ascertain the genetic inheritance of LD, specifically reading disability, have included concordance studies of twins, multiple regression studies of twins, segregation analysis studies, and chromosomal linkage studies.

Comparison of pairs of identical and fraternal twins has been used to investigate the genetic component of reading disability in the same way that other twin studies have researched the heritability of intelligence and a variety of other personal characteristics. Many twin studies have employed a comparison of concordance rates to test for genetic etiology. A pair of twins is concordant for reading disability if both twins have a reading disability; if just one twin has a reading disability, the pair is discordant. Identical twins share an identical genetic makeup while fraternal twins share about 50% of heritable variation (LaBuda & DeFries, 1990). To the extent that reading disability is genetically determined, the concordance rate for pairs of identical twins should be considerably higher than for pairs of fraternal twins when at least one member of each identical and fraternal pair has been identified as having a reading disability.

Two of the earlier reports of concordance rates for reading disability in twins were those of Hermann (1959) and Zerbin-Rudin (1967). Both of these researchers pooled the findings of smaller previous studies, possibly with some overlap in their reporting of cases. The concordance rates reported by both authors were nearly identical. Based on their combined data, as reported by Huston (1992), there was, on average, 100% concordance for 29 identical twin pairs and about 34% concordance for 67 fraternal twin pairs.

Due to technical differences in the method for determining concordance rates, different authors sometimes report different concordance figures for the same study (i.e., some authors report pairwise concordance rates and others report proband-wise concordance rates). The first method counts each concordant twin pair one time. The latter method considers each member of a concordant pair as a separate research subject and, therefore, counts each concordant pair twice. Using proband-wise concordance increases the percentage of concordance for both identical and fraternal twin pairs (LaBuda & DeFries, 1990). For example, in the Zerbin-Rudin study, a pairwise concordance rate for fraternal twin pairs was 34% (12 of 34 cases) as reported by Huston (1992); however, the proband-wise concordance rate for those same twin pairs was 52% (24 [12 + 12] of 46 [34 + 12] cases) as reported by DeFries (1991).

Bakwin (1973, cited by LaBuda & DeFries, 1990) studied 31 pairs of identical and 31 pairs of fraternal twins, finding 84% pairwise concordance for identical twin males and 83% for identical twin females. Interestingly, the pairwise concordance rate for male fraternal twins was 42% while the rate for female fraternal twins was just 8%. Bakwin also investigated the environmental factors of birthweight and birth order as predictors of reading disability but found no significant differences between twins who read normally and twins with a reading disability on these variables.

Stevenson, Graham, Fredman, and McLoughlin (1987, cited by Thomson, 1990) conducted a large-scale study of the reading and spelling abilities of 285 13-year-old twins divided into several subgroups according to type and severity of skill deficiencies. In contrast to other concordance studies of twins, these authors reported, overall, relatively similar pairwise concordance rates for identical and fraternal twin pairs, 32% and 21%, respectively. Their findings suggest a fairly low level of heritability for RD. However, with IQ controlled, Stevenson et al. found a strong genetic influence on spelling ability.

The most technologically sound large-scale twin study, the Colorado Twin Study, was begun in 1982 as part of the Colorado Reading Project. With IQ controlled

(Verbal or Performance IQ = 90 or above) and other types of selection criteria in place, the Colorado Study examined reading disability in 101 pairs of identical twins and 114 pairs of fraternal twins. The pairwise concordance rate of 52% for identical twins was lower than for most earlier studies while the rate for fraternal twins was fairly typical at 33% (LaBuda & DeFries, 1990). Although there is some variation in the concordance figures generated by different studies, taken as a whole, they do provide strong evidence for a genetic factor in the etiology of reading disability.

In summary, family studies, concordance studies of twins, and multiple regression studies of twins have shown that RD run in families, that they are heritable, and that the heritable component is approximately 50%. Currently, segregation analyses point to genetic transmission via a partially dominant or dominant major gene effect. Genetic linkage studies have provided strong evidence that in some families and subject populations studied, reading disability is linked to chromosome 6p or chromosome 15p. Both segregation analyses and linkage analyses have led to the conclusion that phenotypic reading disability is genotypically heterogeneous (i.e., increased susceptibility to reading disability can be produced by multiple genetic profiles). Furthermore, preliminary evidence suggests that within a single individual, the component processes of reading may be influenced by separate genes at different loci.

SUBTYPING LD

Although public agencies have chosen to define learning disability primarily based on a discrepancy between achievement and IQ-based estimates of potential achievement, this statistical definition does little to facilitate an understanding of the underlying processes that contribute to successful and, in this case, unsuccessful achievement. Although it has been suggested that LD is a broad, nonspecific syndrome for which cause must be identified, it has yet to be demonstrated that different causes lead to different types of LD or for that matter require different treatments.

The work of Boder (1973) and Bakker (1979), though some 30 years old, exemplify efforts to classify and identify LD on the basis of educational criteria. Boder described three subtypes of children with LD: (1) a dysphonetic group lacking word analysis skills and having difficulty with phonetics; (2) a dyseidetic group experiencing impairment in visual memory and discrimination; and (3) a mixed dysphonetic, dyseidetic group. The dysphonetic group included two-thirds of those identified as having LD with the dyseidetic group constituting approximately 10%. Bakker's work described L- and P-type dyslexias. Children with L-type dyslexia read quickly but made errors of omission, additions, and word mutilation. The P-type group tended to work slowly and make time-consuming errors involving fragmentations and repetitions.

Among the interesting and promising attempts to define LD are those studies involving multivariate analysis. Efforts to subgroup LD using such analyses find that differences between good and poor readers may reflect impairment in minor skills such as oral word rhyming, vocabulary, discrimination of reversed figures, speed of perception for visual forms, and sequential processing (Doehring, 1968). In 1979, Petrauskas and Rourke utilized a factor analytic method to describe the difficulties of a group of deficient readers. They found these readers falling statistically into four subtypes: (1) primarily verbal problems; (2) primarily visual problems; (3) difficulty with conceptual flexibility and linguistic skills; and (4) no identified specific weakness. The first of these two groups corresponds with Boder's analysis. The third may reflect children with weaker intellectual skills while the fourth may in fact reflect the long-standing clinical perception that there are a group of children who experience achievement problems possibly secondary to nonneurologic factors (e.g., emotional disorder).

Mattis, French, and Rapin (1975) identified three distinct syndromes of LD based on a factor analysis. These included: (1) children struggling to read as the result of language problems; (2) children with articulation and graphomotor problems affecting academic achievement; and (3) children with visuospatial perceptual disorder. The third group displayed better verbal than nonverbal intellectual abilities. Almost 80% of the children with an impairment fell in the first two groups. Denckla (1972, 1977) reported similar statistics, noting that approximately 16% of children with LD experienced some type of visuospatial or perceptual motor problem.

Thus, there is a consensus among factor analytic studies attributing a large group of children with problems related to verbal weaknesses and a smaller but significant group related to perceptual weaknesses. Joschko and Rourke (1985), based on an analysis of the Wechsler Intelligence Scale for Children, found a clear distinction between children with learning problems stemming from verbal weaknesses and those whose problems stem from non-verbal weaknesses.

Satz and Morris (1981) found five distinct groups of children with RD, again along this verbal–nonverbal continuum. These included:

1. Those with language impairment.
2. Those with specific language problems related to naming.
3. Those with mixed global language and perceptual problems.
4. Those with perceptual-motor impairment only.
5. An expected group similar to that reported by Petraskas and Rourke (1979) in which no significant impairments were identified.

Some researchers have hypothesized that this latter group of children simply has not experienced adequate education to develop essential achievement skills while others, as noted, suggest an emotional basis for this group of children's problems. Using cluster analysis of a neuropsychological battery, Phillips (1983) identified a fairly similar profile of five subtypes of LD, including individuals with normal test scores, auditory processing problems, difficulty with receptive and expressive language, spatial weaknesses, and a global pattern of low test scores.

Rourke (1989) concluded that cluster-analytic studies have identified some association between learning delay and a wide variety of perceptual, linguistic, sequential, and cognitive skills. This finding is reinforced by the work of others over nearly a 40-year period (Benton, 1975). According to Swartz (1974), a pattern consisting of depressed scores on four Wechsler subtests, the ACID pattern (an acronym for Arithmetic, Coding, Information, and Digit Span subtest) characterizes the weaknesses of most children with LD. Although this view is held by many others and has been advanced most recently by Kaufman (1997), not all children with LD display this pattern. Children who do, however, are thought to have a particularly poor prognosis for academic performance in reading, spelling, and arithmetic (Ackerman, Dykman, & Peters, 1977). Some researchers have suggested that in a population of children with LD demonstrating this pattern, one subgroup experiences particularly poor auditory-verbal memory and sequencing while a second group experiences poor visuospatial abilities. This distinction is similar to that described by Joschko and Rourke in 1985. However, these authors reported a further distinction in the ACID pattern by age between a younger group 5 to 8 years old and an older group 9 to 15 years old. On the basis of an extensive neuropsychological battery, these authors found a distinct pattern of differences resulting in four subtypes. Joschko and Rourke noted that "although the ACID subtypes generated in this research do not differ significantly in terms of level of academic performance, the plots of the factor score profiles for each of the reliable subtests indicate that they have qualitatively different ability profiles which may have practical applications" (p. 77). However, even these authors noted that effective remediation has not been tied clearly to this manner of ability profiling.

The inclusion of LD among the disorders evaluated and diagnosed by the medical and mental health community has been considered an adjunct to formal psychiatric, psychological, or neuropsychological evaluation. However, as it has been recognized that children with LD appear more likely than others to develop psychiatric problems, efforts have been made to refine the clinical diagnosis of learning impairments. The *Diagnostic and Statistical Manual of Mental Disorders* (4th ed., text revision; *DSM-IV-TR*; American Psychiatric Association, 2000) lists four academic skill disorders:

1. RD
2. Mathematics Disorder (MD)
3. Disorder of Written Expression
4. LD, Not Otherwise Specified

All four are qualified as reflecting the collection of standardized test data, indicating performance substantially below what would be expected, based on the individual's age, intelligence, and educational experience. According to these definitive criteria, the problem must interfere with the child's academic performance or activities of daily living. The "Not Otherwise Specified" category reflects LD as an isolated weakness— for example, difficulty with spelling independent of other written language problems. The *DSM-IV-TR* also contains a Developmental Coordination Disorder diagnosis reflecting weak large or fine motor skills that may interfere with academic achievement or daily living but are not due to a specific medical condition. Readers interested in an extensive discussion of subtypes of LD in childhood are referred to Silver and Hagin (1990) or Swanson et al. (2003).

NEUROPSYCHOLOGICAL MODEL TO ASSESS LEARNING DISABILITY

The consensus in current factor analytic research is that there are two broad groups of skills necessary for efficient learning:

1. *Auditory-verbal processes.* Weaknesses in these areas result in RD and other language-based learning problems.
2. *Visual, perceptual, and motor processes.* Weaknesses in these areas may result in reading problems but more likely affect handwriting, mathematics, and certain social skills.

Tables 2.1 and 2.2 present a model for conceptualizing these skills and examples of them in a 2-by-2 grid. The model conceptualizes learning skills on rote/automatic and conceptual levels, linguistically and visually.

As it has also been demonstrated that there is a significant but small group of children experiencing achievement problems in the absence of either of these sets of skill weaknesses, neuropsychologists are urged to consider the impact of foundational skills

Table 2.1 Categories of Academic Skills

	Auditory-Verbal	Visual-Motor
Conceptual	Verbal-conceptual	Visual nonverbal conceptual
Rote/Automatic	Auditory-motor Auditory perceptual	Letter perception Spatial organization and nonverbal integration
	Rote auditory-sequential memory	Rote visual-sequential memory and retrieval
	Rote and association memory and retrieval	Motor sequencing and fine motor control

Source: Adapted from table prepared by Sally I. Ingalls. Copyright 1991 by Neurology, Learning and Behavior Center, Salt Lake City, UT. Adapted with permission.

Table 2.2 Levels of Processing Related to LD and Disability Characteristics

	Auditory-Verbal	Visual-Motor
Conceptual	Language semantics; word meaning, definition, vocabulary	Social insight and reasoning; understand strategies of games, jokes, motives of others, social conventions, tact
	Listening comprehension; understanding and memory of overall ideas	Mathematical concepts; use of 0 in $+$, $-$, $\times$; place value; money equivalencies; missing elements, etc.
	Specificity and variety of verbal concepts for oral or written expression	Inferential reading comprehension; draw conclusions
	Verbal reasoning and logic	Understand relationship of historical events across time; understand scientific concepts
		Structure ideas hierarchically; outlining skills
		Generalization abilities
		Integrate material into a well-organized report
Rote/ Automatic	Early speech; naming objects	Assemble puzzles and build with construction toys
	Auditory processing; clear enunciation of speech; pronouncing sounds or syllables in correct order	Social perception and awareness of environment
	Name colors	Time sense; doesn't ask "Is this the last recess?"
	Recall birth date, phone number, address, etc.	Remember and execute correct sequence for tying shoes
	Say alphabet and other lists (days, months) in order	Easily negotiate stairs; climb on play equipment; learn athletic skills; ride bike
	Easily select and sequence words with proper grammatical structure for oral or written expression	Execute daily living skills such as pouring without spilling, spreading a sandwich, dressing self correctly
	Auditory "dyslexia": discriminate sounds, esp. vowels, auditorily; blend sounds to words; distinguish words that sound alike (e.g., mine/mind)	Use the correct sequence of strokes to form manuscript or cursive letters
	Labeling and retrieval RD: auditory and visual perception okay but continually mislabels letters, sounds, common syllables, sight words (b/d, her/here)	Eye-hand coordination for drawing, assembling art projects, and handwriting

Poor phonic spelling	Directional stability for top/bottom and left/right tracking
Poor listening and reading comprehension due to poor short-term memory, especially for rote facts	Copy from board accurately
Labeling and retrieval Math Disorder: trouble counting sequentially; mislabels numbers (e.g., 16/60); poor memory for facts about numbers and sequences of steps for computation (e.g., long division)	Visual "dyslexia" confused when viewing visual symbols; poor visual discrimination; reversals/inversions/transpositions due to poor directionality; may not recognize the shape or form of a word that has been seen many times before (i.e., "word-blind")
Recall names, dates, and historical facts	Spelling: poor visual memory for the nonphonetic elements of words
Learn and retain new scientific terminology	

Source: Adapted from table prepared by Sally I. Ingalls. Copyright 1991 by Neurology, Learning and Behavior Center, Salt Lake City, UT. Adapted with permission.

such as an environment conducive to learning, problems with attention and impulse control, self-esteem as a learner, and other emotional (e.g., depression/anxiety) and behavioral (oppositional defiance, Conduct Disorder) problems as contributing to delayed achievement (Goldstein & Mather, 1998).

As can be seen in this model, language-based LD are directly related to impaired language skills, especially those related to phonological processes (Bishop & Adams, 1990; Pennington, 1991; Scarborough, 1990, 1998; Tunick & Pennington, 2002). Further, for many children, poor comprehension results from poor rote language skills, such as inability to distinguish similar sounds, that then leads to poor auditory discrimination and weak phonetics. Problems with verbal short-term memory are also common among individuals with reading impairment. Memory requires phonological skill. Poor readers may experience problems recalling letters, digits, words, or phrases in exact sequence. Although the majority of children with language-based LD struggle to master basic foundational academic skills, others are capable of learning to read but struggle when the curriculum begins to accelerate in third or fourth grade and they must read to learn due to weak conceptual, linguistic skills. It is also not surprising that related language-based skills such as spelling and writing are impaired in children with reading disability. For many, spelling is even more impaired than reading (Berninger, Nielsen, Abbott, Wijsman, & Raskind, 2008; Snowling & Hulme, 1991; Wanzek et al., 2006).

Weaknesses in visuomotor skills tend to cause problems with arithmetic and handwriting, often independent of associated reading disability. Included in problems for this group of children are difficulties involving social awareness and judgment. These problems do not appear to be primarily language based and have been referred to collectively in the neuropsychology literature as nonverbal LD (Pennington, 1991; Rourke, 1989). Children with this pattern have been reported to experience problems with spatial organization, attention to visual detail, procedural skills, and mathematics; problems shifting psychological set from one operation to another, graphomotor weaknesses, poor factual memory, and poor judgment and reasoning (Rourke, 1985). Neuropsychologists can reliably conclude that children with nonverbal LD experience greatest deficits in visual, perceptional, and organizational skills; psychomotor coordination; and complex tactile perceptual abilities (Harnadek & Rourke, 1994). Finally, it is also suspected that individuals with nonverbal LD experience greater internalizing problems related to depression and anxiety than those with language-based LD. It is unclear whether this pattern contributes to or is a consequence of the disability.

In the PASS model, Naglieri and Das (2002) note characteristic weaknesses in planning and attention processes for youth receiving diagnoses of Attention-Deficit/Hyperactivity Disorder, isolated weaknesses in planning for youth with mathematics LD and isolated weaknesses in successive processes for youth with phonics-based reading disability.

EVALUATING LEARNING DISABILITY IN THE CONTEXT OF A COMPREHENSIVE EVALUATION

A number of volumes provide thorough, in-depth models for assessment utilizing a myriad of tests and batteries. Interested readers are referred to Reynolds and Fletcher-Janzen (2007) and Pennington (2009). Due to space limitations, this section briefly reviews assessment measures. The basic tasks facing the evaluator are to define achievement levels as well as answer questions concerning underlying intellectual and neuropsychological skills essential to learning. Assets and liabilities must be identified.

Intellectual and Neuropsychological Abilities

Traditionally, measures of intellectual ability have emphasized a verbal/quantitative/nonverbal test structure. Although these approaches still are utilized in many popular measures of intelligence, alternative approaches have also been widely received, such as those aimed at assessing more basic underlying psychological processes rather than measuring success on tasks that are largely knowledge based (Naglieri & Goldstein, 2009). The three most popular approaches to the assessment of intellectual and neuropsychological ability include:

1. *Global ability.* The Wechsler Intelligence Scale for Children-IV (Wechsler, 2003) is theoretically based on Spearman's general ability factor, or *g*, and

focuses on a global ability score while also providing composite scores for verbal and perceptual reasoning, working memory, and processing speed. In younger age groups, the Wechsler Preschool and Primary Scale of Intelligence-III (Wechsler, 2002) provides similar data.

2. *Broad and narrow cognitive abilities.* The Woodcock-Johnson III Tests of Cognitive Abilities (Woodcock, McGrew, & Mather, 2001b) is based on the Cattell-Horn-Carroll theory. This measure, while also providing an estimate of global ability, emphasizes a number of broad and narrow cognitive ability scores that can assist in defining an individual's strengths and weaknesses (Wendling, Mather, & Schrank, 2009).

3. *Underlying psychological processes.* The Cognitive Assessment System (CAS; Naglieri & Das, 1997) is theoretically rooted in the works of Luria (e.g., Luria, 1982) and the PASS theory (Naglieri & Das, 2005). It focuses on measuring cognitive and neuropsychological constructs such as executive function, selective attention, nonverbal processing, and sequencing. Although still providing a global ability score, the structure and content of the CAS is less knowledge based and thus allows for the examination of underlying cognitive processes and abilities and their role in the acquisition of academic knowledge.

Achievement

The most widely used of these instruments, the Woodcock-Johnson III Tests of Achievement (Woodcock, McGrew, & Mather, 2001a), is the most comprehensive. It offers by far the most thorough, well-developed assessment of academic skills. The factor analytic model fits well with the concepts presented in this chapter concerning the underlying neuropsychological deficits contributing to learning disability. Subtest analysis often reveals patterns consistent with verbal, visual, rote, or conceptual weaknesses. Although achievement/intelligence discrepancies are most widely used to identify LD, the issue of high IQ individuals with average achievement identified as having a learning disability continues to be controversial. An age/achievement discrepancy nonetheless is a good target for the neuropsychologist, with a standard deviation and a half below the age mean used as a cutoff.

In the absence of a comprehensive battery such as the Woodcock, it is recommended that evaluators address a collection of basic achievement data in four areas:

1. *Reading.* A measure should be used to obtain single-word reading reflecting phonetics skill and sight word achievement. An estimate of the ability to read within context and comprehend what is read should also be obtained. Achievement tests such as the Woodcock-Johnson III Tests of Achievement (Woodcock et al., 2001a), the Gilmore (Gilmore & Gilmore, 1968), the Gray Oral Reading Test–4th Edition (Wiederholt & Bryant, 2001), or the Test of

Reading Comprehension–4th Edition (Brown, Wiederholt, & Hammill, 2009) can provide clinicians with these data.

2. *Spelling.* Estimates of sight word memory for spelling and phonetic ability can be analyzed qualitatively utilizing the Wide Range Achievement Test-4 (Wilkinson & Robertson, 2005).

3. *Mathematics.* The Wide Range Achievement Test-4 (Wilkinson & Robertson, 2005) or the Key Math Diagnostic Assessment-3 (Connolly, 2007) can be utilized to generate observations of conceptual versus rote sequential mathematics skills.

4. *Written Language.* Written language skills of thematic maturity, vocabulary, capacity to organize ideas, grammar, punctuation, and general execution can be observed utilizing the Story Writing subtest from the Test of Written Language-4 (Hammill & Larsen, 2009).

INTERVENTIONS FOR LD

Views differ regarding the nature and etiology of LD; views also differ about what constitutes appropriate and effective interventions for individuals with LD. Lyon and Moats (1988) discussed critical issues in the instruction of students with LD. Numerous authors, representing different theoretical orientations and instructional paradigms, have presented intervention methodologies developed or adapted for learners with disabilities. These include:

- Psycholinguistic process or specific abilities approach (Johnson & Myklebust, 1967; Kirk & Kirk, 1971).
- Behavioral approaches, including direct instruction and data-based instruction (Lindsley, 1971; Lovitt, 1984; Marston & Tindal, 1995; White, 1986).
- Cognitive approaches, including constructivism and instruction in learning strategies (Deshler & Lenz, 1989; Fuchs & Fuchs, 1994 ; Swanson, 1993; Wong, 1991).
- Neuropsychological approaches (Hooper, Willis, & Stone, 1996; Rourke, Fisk, & Strang, 1986).

Mercer (1991) and Lerner (1993) have provided a lucid discussion of these instructional approaches and their application to individuals with LD. Mercer and Mercer (1993), Mather (1991), Mather and Jaffe (1992), and Lerner (1993) outline a broad array of specific teaching strategies and techniques that have been utilized successfully with atypical learners, including those with LD.

Recent research is leading to better development of causal theories of learning disability and to promising avenues of intervention for the LD subtypes or specific information-processing weaknesses explicated by those theories. As Torgesen (1993) reports: "The two most completely developed current causal theories of LD are the nonverbal learning disabilities syndrome ... and the theory of reading disabilities involving limitations in phonological processing" (p. 158).

A great deal of attention and research has been directed toward understanding phonological processing skills and their relation to the development of reading skills (Lyon, 1996; Pennington, 1991; Shaywitz, 1996; Stanovich, 1993; Stanovich & Siegel, 1994; Torgesen, Wagner, & Rashotte, 1997; Wagner & Torgesen, 1987). A number of well-designed, longitudinal studies have documented the efficacy of instruction in phonological awareness and/or phonemic analysis and synthesis for the initial development of reading skills and for improving reading in children with reading deficiencies (Ball & Blachman, 1988; Blachman, Ball, Black, & Tangel, 1994, cited in Lyon, 1996; Hatcher, Hulme, & Ellis, 1994; Lundberg, Frost, & Petersen, 1988).

At the conclusion of their research report, Hatcher et al. (1994) suggest that children differ in their ability to acquire phonological competence and pose the question of how to best facilitate acquisition of underlying phonological skills. In this critical area of instruction, research-based practices are emerging. In an important contribution, Torgesen, Wagner, and Rashotte (1997) discussed approaches to the prevention and remediation of phonologically based RD. Research with the Auditory Discrimination in Depth Program (Lindemood & Lindemood, 1969) has shown that intensive instruction led to significant gains in reading and spelling skills for 281 subjects, ages 5 to 55 years old (Truch, 1994). Employing a new and promising approach, Merzenich et al. (1996) acoustically modified speech to train sound discrimination abilities in children with language-based learning impairments. Subjects engaged in highly motivating discrimination tasks with speech stimuli altered by a computer algorithm that stretched the duration or increased the volume of sound elements critical to the discrimination process. After a few weeks' instruction, children in the study markedly improved their ability to discriminate phonemes and recognize both brief and fast sequences of speech stimuli. They also showed significant improvement in language comprehension abilities. Although acoustically modified speech is a logically conceived and an exciting intervention concept, experts in the field of dyslexia and LD, as reported by Travis (1996), suggested caution in regard to its potential benefits. Recent research has raised further doubts about the efficacy of this intervention (Watson et al., 2003).

Just as well-designed research can validate intervention practices and techniques for LD, it can also identify methods that are contraindicated for many students with LD. In education as a whole, and in special education, there continues a great debate about the relative merits of code-oriented versus whole-language approaches to reading instruction (Ediger, 2000; Foorman, 1995). Based on available research, most professionals in the field of LD have concluded that when used as the primary mode of instruction, the whole-language method is less effective than structured, explicit instruction in phonics for children with RD (Hatcher, Hulme, & Snowling, 2004; Iverson & Tunmer, 1993; Liberman & Liberman, 1992; Pressley & Rankin, 1994; Shapiro, 1992; Stanovich, 1994; Torgesen et al., 1994).

SUMMARY

A neuropsychological perspective of LD provides an understanding of the underlying forces that impact rate and level of achievement across academic domains. A neuropsychological perspective provides an understanding of the reasons why some children struggle academically. Adult evaluators must be well versed in academic assessment and school issues. This chapter provided an overview of the current literature concerning the history, etiology, definition, evaluation, treatment, and efforts to accelerate achievement for adolescents and adults with LD. There is an increasing appreciation within educational systems for the role underlying neuropsychological processes play in rates of achievement. An increasing body of research is demonstrating that not only do brain structures and function impact learning, but also that, over time, achievement changes the brain in a bidirectional manner.

REFERENCES

Ackerman, P. T., Dykman, R. A., & Peters, J. E. (1977). Teenage status of hyperactive and non-hyperactive learning disabled boys. *American Journal of Orthopsychiatry*, 47, 577–596.

American Psychiatric Association. (2000). *Diagnostic and statistical manual of mental disorders* (4th ed., text revision). Washington, DC: Author.

Baillieux, H., Vandervliet, E. J. M., Manto, M., Parizel, P. M., De Deyn, P. P., & Mariën, P. (2009). Developmental dyslexia and widespread activation across the cerebellar hemispheres. *Brain and Language*, 108, 122–132.

Bakker, D. J. (1979). Hemisphere differences and reading strategies: Two dyslexias? *Bulletin of the Orton Society*, 29, 84–100.

Bakwin, H. (1973). Reading disability in twins. *Developmental Medicine and Child Neurology*, 15, 184–187.

Ball, E. W., & Blachman, B. A. (1988). Phoneme segmentation training: Effect on reading readiness. *Annals of Dyslexia*, 38, 208–225.

Benton, A. L. (1975). Developmental dyslexia: Neurological aspects. In W. J. Friedlander (Ed.), *Advances in neurology* (Vol. 17, pp. 1–47). New York, NY: Raven.

Berkow, R., & Fletcher, A. J. (Eds.). (1992). *The Merck manual of diagnosis and therapy* (16th ed.). Rahway, NJ: Merck Research Laboratories.

Berninger, V. W. (2004). The reading brain in children and youth: A systems approach. In B. Y. L. Wong (Ed.), *Learning about learning disabilities* (pp. 197–248). San Diego, CA: Elsevier Academic Press.

Berninger, V. W., Nielsen, K. H., Abbott, R. D., Wijsman, E., & Raskind, W. (2008). Writing problems in developmental dyslexia: Under-recognized and under-treated. *Journal of School Psychology, 46*, 1–21.

Bigler, E. D. (1992). The neurobiology and neuropsychology of adult learning disorders. *Journal of Learning Disabilities, 25*, 488–506.

Bigler, E. D., Lajiness-O'Neill, R., & Howes, N.-L. (1998). Technology in the assessment of learning disability. *Journal of Learning Disabilities, 31*, 67–82.

Bishop, D. V., & Adams, C. (1990). A prospective study of the relationship between specific language impairment, phonological disorders and reading disabilities. *Journal of Child Psychology and Psychiatry, 31*(7), 1027–1050.

Blachman, B. A., Ball, E., Black, R., & Tangel, D. (1994). Kindergarten teachers develop phoneme awareness in low-income inner-city classrooms: Does it make a difference? *Reading and Writing: An Interdisciplinary Journal, 6*, 1–17.

Boder, E. (1973). Developmental dyslexia: A diagnostic approach based on three atypical reading patterns. *Developmental Medicine and Child Neurology, 15*, 663–687.

Brown, V. L., Weiderholt, J. L., & Hammill, D. D. (2009). *Test of Reading Comprehension* (4th ed.). Austin, TX: PRO-ED.

Burkhardt, S., Obiakor, F. E., & Rotatori, A. F. (Eds). (2004). *Current perspectives on learning disabilities* (Vol. 16). Oxford, United Kingdom: Elsevier.

Cao, F., Bitan, T., Chou, T.-L., Burman, D. D., & Booth, J. R. (2006). Deficient orthographic and phonological representations in children with dyslexia revealed by brain activation patterns. *Journal of Child Psychology and Psychiatry, 47*, 1041–1050.

Cardon, L. R., Smith, S. D., Fulker, D. W., Kimberling, W. J., Pennington, B. F., & DeFries, J. C. (1994). Quantitative trait locus for reading disability in chromosome 6. *Science, 266*, 276–279.

Connolly, A. J. (2007). *Key Math Diagnostic Assessment* (3rd ed.). San Antonio, TX: Pearson.

Cruickshank, W. M., Bentzen, F. A., Ratzeburg, R. H., and Tannhauser, M. T. (1961). *A teaching method for brain-injured and hyperactive children*. Syracuse, NY: Syracuse University Press.

Davis, N., Cannistraci, C. J., Rogers, B. P., Gatenby, J. C., Fuchs, L. S., Anderson, A. W., & Gore, J. C. (2009). Aberrant functional activation in school age children at-risk for mathematical disability: A functional imaging study of simple arithmetic skill. *Neuropsychologia, 47*, 2470–2479.

Dawson, G., & Fischer, K. W. (Eds.). *Human behavior and the developing brain*. New York, NY: Guilford Press.

DeFries, J. C. (1991). Genetics and dyslexia: An overview. In M. Snowling & M. Thomson (Eds.), *Dyslexia: Integrating theory and practice* (pp. 3–20). London, United Kingdom: Whurr.

DeFries, J. C., & Gillis, J. J. (1993). Genetics of reading disability. In R. Plomin & G. E. McClearn (Eds.), *Nature, nurture and psychology* (pp. 163–194). Washington, DC: American Psychological Association.

Denckla, M. B. (1972). Clinical syndromes in learning disabilities: The case for split-ting versus lumping. *Journal of Learning Disabilities, 5,* 401–406.

Denckla, M. B. (1977). The neurological basis of reading disability. In F. G. Roswell & G. Natchez (Eds.), *Reading disability: A human approach to learning* (pp. 56–72). New York, NY: Basic Books.

Deshler, D. D., and Lenz, B. K. (1989). The strategies instructional approach. *International Journal of Disability, Development and Education, 36,* 203–224.

Doehring, D. G. (1968). *Patterns of impairment in specific reading disability.* Bloomington, IN: Indiana University Press.

Doris, J. (1986). Learning disabilities. In S. J. Ceci (Ed.), *Handbook of cognitive, social, and neuropsychological aspects of learning disabilities* (Vol. 1, pp. 3–53). Hillsdale, NJ: Erlbaum.

Ediger, M. (2000). Issues in reading instruction. Retrieved from Education Resources Information Center (ERIC) database (ED445320): http://www.eric.ed.gov/

Finucci, J. M. (1978). Genetic considerations in dyslexia. In H. R. Myklebust (Ed.), *Progress in learning disabilities* (Vol. 4, pp. 41–63). New York: Grune & Stratton.

Finucci, J. M., Guthrie, J. T., Childs, A. L., Abbey, H., & Childs, B. (1976). The genetics of specific reading disability. *Annals of Human Genetics, 40,* 1–23.

Fletcher, M., Shaywitz, S. E., & Shaywitz, B. A. (1999). Comorbidity of learning and attention disorders: Separate but equal. *Pediatric Clinics of North America, 46,* 885–897.

Flowers, D. L., Wood, F. B., & Nailer, C. E. (1991). A regional cerebral blood flow cor-relates of language processes in reading disability. *Archives of Neurology, 48,* 637–643.

Foorman, B. R. (1995). Research on the great debate: Code-oriented versus whole-language approaches to reading instruction. *School Psychology Review, 24,* 376–392.

Fritch, D., Friston, K. J., Liddle, P. F., & Frackowiak, R. S. J. (1991). A PET study of word finding. *Neuropsychologia, 29,* 1137–1148.

Fuchs, D., & Fuchs, L. S. (Eds.). (1994). Implications of constructivism for stu-dents with disabilities and students at risk: Issues and directions. *Journal of Special Education, 28.*

Gardner, R. A. (1973). *MBD: The family book about minimal brain dysfunction.* New York, NY: Jason Aronson.

Geary, D. C. (2003). Learning disabilities and arithmetic: Problem solving differ-ences and cognitive deficits. In H. L. Swanson, K. R. Harris, & S. Graham (Eds.), *Handbook of learning disabilities* (pp. 199–212). New York, NY: Guilford Press.

Geschwind, N., & Behan, P. (1982). Left handedness: Association with immune dis-ease migraine and developmental learning disorder. *Proceedings of the National Academy of Sciences, United States of America, 79,* 5097–5100.

Gilger, J. W., Vorecki, I. B., DeFries, J. C., & Pennington, B. F. (1994). Comingling and segregation analysis of reading performance in families of normal reading prob-lems. *Behavior Genetics, 24,* 345–355.

Gilmore, J. V., & Gilmore, E. C. (1968). *Gilmore Oral Reading Test.* New York, NY: Harcourt, Brace.

Goldstein, S. (1997). *Managing attention and learning disorders in late adolescence and adulthood*. New York, NY: Wiley.

Goldstein, S., & Mather, N. (1998). *Overcoming underachieving: An action guide to helping your child succeed in school*. New York, NY: Wiley.

Hallahan, D. P. (Ed.). (1980). Teaching exceptional children to use cognitive strategies. *Exceptional Education Quarterly, 1*, 1–102.

Hammill, D. D., & Larsen, S. C. (1974). The effectiveness of psycholinguistic training. *Exceptional Children, 41*, 5–14.

Hammill, D. D., & Larsen, S. C. (1996). *Test of Written Language* (3rd ed.). Austin, TX: PRO-ED.

Hammill, D. D., & Larsen, S. C. (2009). *Test of Written Language* (4th ed.). Austin, TX: PRO-ED.

Harnadek, M. C. S., & Rourke, B. P. (1994). Principal identifying features of the syndrome of non-verbal learning disabilities in children. *Journal of Learning Disabilities, 27*, 144–154.

Hatcher, P. J., Hulme, C., and Ellis, A. W. (1994). Ameliorating early reading failure by integrating the teaching of reading and phonological skills: The phonological linkage hypothesis. *Child Development, 65*, 41–57.

Hatcher, P. J., Hulme, C., & Snowling, M. J. (2004). Explicit phoneme training combined with phonic reading instruction helps young children at risk of reading failure. *Journal of Child Psychology and Psychiatry, 45*, 338–358.

Hermann, K. (1959). *Reading disability: A medical study of word-blindness and related handicaps*. Springfield, IL: Charles C. Thomas.

Hertz-Pannier, L., Gaillard, W. D., Mott, S. H., Cuenod, C. A., Bookheimer, S. Y., Weinstein, S., . . . & Theodore, W. H. (1997). Non-invasive assessment of language dominance in children and adolescents with functional MRI: A preliminary study. *Neurology, 48*, 1003–1012.

Hooper, S. R., Willis, W. G., & Stone, B. H. (1996). Issues and approaches in the neuropsychological treatment of children with learning disabilities. In E. S. Batchelor & R. S. Dean, *Pediatric neuropsychology: Interfacing assessment and treatment for rehabilitation* (pp. 211–247). Boston, MA: Allyn and Bacon.

Huston, A. M. (1992). *Understanding dyslexia: A practical approach for parents and teachers*. Lanham, MD: Madison Books.

Hutenlocher, P. (1991, September 26). *Neural plasticity*. Paper presented at the Brain Research Foundation Women's Council, University of Chicago.

Iverson, S., & Tunmer, W. E. (1993). Phonological processing skills and the Reading Recovery Program. *Journal of Educational Psychology, 85*, 112–126.

Johnson, D., & Myklebust, H. (1967). *Learning disabilities: Educational principles and practices*. New York, NY: Grune & Stratton.

Joschko, M., & Rourke, B. P. (1985). Neuropsychological subtypes of learning-disabled children who exhibit the ACID pattern on the WISC. In B. P. Rourke (Ed.),

Neuropsychology of learning disabilities: Essentials of subtype analysis (pp. 65–88). New York, NY: Guilford Press.

Joseph, J., Noble, K., & Eden, G. (2001). The neurobiological basis of reading. *Journal of Learning Disabilities, 34*, 566–579.

Kaufman, A. S. (1997). *Intelligence testing with the WISC-III* (4th ed.). New York, NY: Wiley.

Kavale, K. A., & Forness, S. R. (2003). Learning disability as a discipline. In H. L. Swanson, K. R. Harris, & S. Graham (Eds.), *Handbook of learning disabilities* (pp. 76–93). New York, NY: Guilford Press.

Kirk, S. A., & Kirk, W. D. (1971). *Psycholinguistic learning disabilities: Diagnosis and remediation*. Urbana, IL: University of Illinois Press.

Kucian, K., Loenneker, T., Dietrich, T., Dosch, M., Martin, E., & von Aster, M. (2006). Impaired neural networks for approximate calculation in dyscalculic children: A functional MRI study. *Behavioral and Brain Functions, 2*. Retrieved from http://www.behavioralandbrainfunctions.com/content/2/1/31

LaBuda, M. C., & DeFries, J. C. (1990). Genetic etiology of reading disability: Evidence from a twin study. In *Perspectives on dyslexia* (Vol. 1), *Neurology, neuropsychology and genetics* (pp. 47–76). New York, NY: Wiley.

Larsen, S. C., Parker, R. M., & Hammill, D. D. (1982). Effectiveness of psycholinguistic training: A response to Kavale. *Exceptional Children, 49*, 60–66.

Learning Disabilities Association. (1995, July/August). Thyroid function and learning disabilities: Is there a connection? *Learning Disabilities Association Newsbriefs, 30*(4), 17.

Lerner, J. W. (1993). *Learning disabilities: Theories diagnosis and teaching strategies* (6th ed.). Boston, MA: Houghton Mifflin.

Liberman, I. Y., & Liberman, A. M. (1992). Whole language versus code emphasis: Underlying assumptions and their implications for reading instruction. In P. B. Gough, L. C. Ehri, & R. Treiman (Eds.), *Reading acquisition* (pp. 343–366). Hillsdale, NJ: Erlbaum.

Lindemood, C., & Lindemood, P. (1969). *Auditory Discrimination in Depth*. Boston, MA: Teaching Resources.

Lindsley, O. R. (1971). Precision teaching in perspective: An interview with Ogden R. Lindsley (A. Duncan, Interviewer). *Teaching exceptional children, 3*, 114–119.

Lovitt, T. C. (1984). *Tactics for teaching*. Columbus, OH: Merrill.

Lundberg, I., Frost, J., & Petersen, O. (1988). Effects of an extensive program for stimulating phonological awareness in preschool children. *Reading Research Quarterly, 23*(3), 263–283.

Luria, A. R. (1982). *Language and cognition*. New York, NY: Wiley.

Lyon, G. R. (1996). Learning disabilities. *Future of Children, 6*(1), 54–76.

Lyon, G. R., & Moats, L. (1988). Critical issues in the instruction of the learning disabled. *Journal of Consulting and Clinical Psychology, 56*, 830–835.

MacMillan, D. L. (1993). Development of operational definitions in mental retardation: Similarities and differences with the field of learning disabilities. In G. R. Lyon,

D. B. Gray, J. F. Kavanaugh, & N. A. Krasnegor (Eds.), *Better understanding learning disabilities: New views from research and their implications for education and public policies* (pp. 117–152). Baltimore, MD: Paul H. Brookes.

Marston, D., & Tindal, G. (1995). Performance monitoring. In A. Thomas & J. Grimes (Eds.), *Best practices in school psychology* (Vol. 3, pp. 597–608). Washington, DC: National Association of School Psychologists.

Mather, N. (1991). *An instructional guide to the Woodcock-Johnson Psycho-Educational Battery* (rev. ed.). Brandon, VT: Clinical Psychology Publishing.

Mather, N., & Jaffe, L. E. (1992). *Woodcock-Johnson Psycho-Educational Battery: Recommendations and reports* (rev. ed.). New York, NY: Wiley.

Mattis, S., French, J., & Rapin, I. (1975). Dyslexia in children and young adults: Three independent neuropsychological syndromes. *Developmental Medicine and Child Neurology, 17,* 150–163.

Mercer, C. D. (1991). *Students with learning disabilities* (4th ed.). New York, NY: Macmillan.

Mercer, C. D., & Mercer, A. R. (1993). *Teaching students with learning problems* (4th ed.). New York, NY: Maxwell Macmillan.

Merzenich, M. M., Jenkins, W. M., Johnston, P., Schreiner, C., Miller, S. L., & Tellal, P. (1996). Temporal processing deficits of language learning-impaired children ameliorated by training. *Science, 271,* 77–81.

Mustard, J. F. (2006). Experience-based brain development: Scientific underpinnings of the importance of early child development in a global world. *Paediatric Child Health, 11,* 571–572.

Naglieri, J. A., & Conway, C. (2009). The Cognitive Assessment System. In J. A. Naglieri & S. Goldstein (Eds.), *Practitioner's guide to assessing intelligence and achievement* (pp. 27–59). Hoboken, NJ: Wiley.

Naglieri, J. A., & Das, J. P. (1997). *Cognitive Assessment System.* Itasca, NY: Riverside.

Naglieri, J. A., & Das, J. P. (2002). Practical implications of general intelligence and PASS cognitive processes. In R. J. Sternberg & E. L. Grigorenko (Eds.), *The general factor of intelligence: How general is it?* (pp. 855–884). New York, NY: Erlbaum.

Naglieri, J. A., & Das, J. P. (2005). Planning, Attention, Simultaneous, Successive (PASS) theory: A revision of the concept of intelligence. In D. P. Flanagan & P. L. Harrison (Eds.), *Contemporary intellectual assessment* (2nd ed., pp. 136–182). New York, NY: Guilford Press.

Naglieri, J., & Goldstein, S. (2009). Understanding the strengths and weaknesses of intelligence and achievement tests. In J. A. Naglieri & S. Goldstein (Eds.), *Practitioner's guide to assessing intelligence and achievement* (pp. 3–10). Hoboken, NJ: Wiley.

National Health Interview Survey. (2003). QuickStats: Percentage of children aged 5–17 years ever having diagnoses of Attention Deficit/Hyperactivity Disorder (ADHD) or Learning Disability (LD), by sex and diagnosis—United States. Retrieved from http://www.cdc.gov/mmwr/preview/mmwrhtml/mm5443a8.htm

Olson, R. K., Wise, B., Conners, F., Rack, J., & Fulker, D. (1989). Specific deficits in component reading and language skills: Genetic and environmental influences. *Journal of Learning Disabilities, 22,* 339–348.

Pauls, D. L. (1996, March). Genetic linkage studies. In G. R. Lyon (Chair), *Critical Discoveries in Learning Disabilities: A summary of findings by NIH Research Programs in Learning Disabilities.* Workshop conducted at the Learning Disability Association International Conference, Dallas, TX.

Pennington, B. F. (1991). *Diagnosing learning disorders: A neuropsychological framework.* New York, NY: Guilford Press.

Pennington, B. F. (2009). *Diagnosing learning disorders: A neuropsychological framework* (2nd ed.). New York, NY: Guilford Press.

Pennington, B. F., Bender, B., Puck, M., Salbenblatt, J., & Robinson, A. (1982). Learning disabilities in children with sex chromosome anomalies. *Child Development, 53,* 1182–1192.

Pennington, B. F., Gilger, J. W., Pauls, D., Smith, S. A., Smith, S., & DeFries, J. C. (1991). Evidence for major gene transmission of developmental dyslexia. *Journal of the American Medical Association, 266,* 1527–1534.

Pennington, B. F., Smith, S. D., Kimberling, W. J., Greene, P. A., & Haith, M. M. (1987). Left handedness and immune disorders in familial dyslexics. *Archives of Neurology, 44,* 634–639.

Petrauskas, R., & Rourke, B. P. (1979). Identification of subgroups of retarded readers: A neuropsychological multivariate approach. *Journal of Clinical Neuropsychology, 1,* 17–37.

Phillips, G. W. (1983). Learning the conversation concept: A meta-analysis (Doctoral dissertation, University of Kentucky). *Dissertation Abstracts International, 44,* 1990B.

Poeppel, D. (1996). A critical review of PET studies of phonological processing. *Brain and Language, 55,* 317–351.

Pressley, M., & Rankin, J. (1994). More about whole language methods of reading instruction for students at risk for early reading failure. *Learning Disabilities Research & Practice, 9*(3), 157–168.

Pugh, K. R., Shaywitz, B. A., Shaywitz, S. E., Constable, R. T., Skudlarski, P., Fulbright, R. K., . . . Gore, J. C. (1996). Cerebral organization of component processes in reading. *Brain: A Journal of Neurology, 119,* 1221–1238.

Raskind, W. H. (2001). Current understanding of the genetic basis of reading and spelling disability. *Learning Disability Quarterly, 24,* 141–157.

Reynolds, C. R., & Fletcher-Janzen, E. (2007). *Encyclopedia of special education* (3rd ed.). Hoboken, NJ: Wiley.

Richards, T. L. (2001). Functional magnetic resonance imaging and spectroscopic imaging of the brain: Application of fMRI and fMRS to reading disabilities and education. *Learning Disability Quarterly, 24,* 189–203.

Rourke, B. P. (1985). *Neuropsychology of learning disabilities: Essentials of subtype analysis*. New York, NY: Guilford Press.

Rourke, B. P. (1989). *Nonverbal learning disabilities: The syndrome and the model*. New York, NY: Guilford Press.

Rourke, B. P., Fisk, T. L., & Strang, J. D. (1986). *The neuropsychological assessment of children: A treatment oriented approach*. New York, NY: Guilford Press.

Rumsey, J. M., Horowitz, B., Donahue, B. C., Nace, K., Maisog, J. M., & Andreason, P. (1997). Phonologic and orthographic components of word recognition: A PET-rCBF study. *Brain, 120*, 739–759.

Satz, P. (1990). Developmental dyslexia: An etiological reformulation. In G. Th. Pavlidis (Ed.), *Perspectives on dyslexia* (Vol. 1, pp. 3–26). Chichester, United Kingdom: Wiley.

Satz, P., & Morris, R. (1981). Learning disability subtypes: A review. In F. J. Priozzolo & M. C. Wittrock (Eds.), *Neuropsychological and cognitive processing in reading* (pp. 109–141). New York, NY: Academic Press.

Scarborough, H. S. (1990). Very early language deficits in dyslexic children. *Child Development, 61*, 1728–1743.

Scarborough, H. S. (1998). Early identification of children at risk for reading disabilities. In B. K. Shapiro, P. J. Accardo, & A. J. Capute (Eds.), *Specific reading disability: A view of the spectrum* (pp. 75–119). Timonium, MD: York Press.

Schumaker, J. B., Deshler, D. D., Alley, G. R., & Warner, M. M. (1983). Toward the development of an intervention model for learning disabled adolescents: The University of Kansas Institute. *Exceptional Child Quarterly, 4*, 45–74.

Shapiro, H. R. (1992). Debatable issues underlying whole language philosophy: A speech pathologist's perspective. *Language, Speech, and Hearing Services in Schools, 23*, 308–311.

Shaywitz, B. A., Lyon, G. R., & Shaywitz, S. E. (2006). The role of functional magnetic reasonance imaging in understanding reading and dyslexia. *Developmental Neuropsychology, 30*, 613–632.

Shaywitz, S. E. (1996). Dyslexia. *Scientific American, 275*(5), 98–104.

Shaywitz, S. E. (1998). Current concepts: Dyslexia. *New England Journal of Medicine, 338*(5), 307–312.

Silver, A. A., & Hagin, R. A. (1990). *Disorders of learning in childhood*. New York, NY: Wiley.

Smith, S. D., Kimberling, W. J., & Pennington, B. F. (1991). Screening for multiple genes: Influencing dyslexia. *Reading and Writing, 3*, 285–298.

Smith, S. D., Kimberling, W. J., Pennington, B. F., & Lubs, H. A. (1983). Specific reading disability: Identification of an inherited form through linkage analysis. *Science, 219*, 1345–1347.

Smith, S. D., Pennington, B. F., Kimberling, W. J., & Ing, P. S. (1990). Genetic linkage analysis with specific dyslexia: Use of multiple markers to include and exclude possible loci. In G. Th. Pavlidis (Ed.), *Perspectives on dyslexia* (Vol. 1), *Neurology, neuropsychology and genetics*. New York, NY: Wiley.

Snowling, M., & Hulme, C. (1991). Speech processing and learning to spell. In W. Ellis (Ed.), *All language and the creation of literacy* (pp. 33–39). Baltimore, MD: Orton Dyslexia Society.

Stanovich, K. E. (1993). The construct validity of discrepancy definitions of reading disability. In G. R. Lyson, D. B. Gray, J. F. Kavanaugh, & N. A. Krasnegor (Eds.), *Better understanding learning disabilities: New views from research and their implications for education and public policies* (pp. 273–307). Baltimore, MD: Paul H. Brookes.

Stanovich, K. E. (1994). Constructivism in reading education. Implications of constructivism for students with disabilities and students at risk: Issues and directions [Special issue]. *Journal of Special Education, 28*, 259–274.

Stanovich, K. E., & Siegel, L. S. (1994). Phenotypic performance profile of children with reading disabilities: A regression-based test of the phonological-core variable-difference model. *Journal of Educational Psychology, 86*, 24–53.

Stevenson, J., Graham, P., Fredman, G., & McLoughlin, V. (1987). A twin study of genetic influence on reading and spelling ability and disability. *Journal of Child Psychology and Psychiatry, 28*, 229–247.

Strauss, A., & Lehtinen, L. (1947). *Psychopathology and education of the brain-injured child*. New York, NY: Grune & Stratton.

Swanson, H. L. (1993). Principles and procedures in strategy use. In L. J. Meltzer (Ed.), *Strategy assessment and instruction for students with learning disabilities: From theory to practice* (pp. 61–92). Austin, TX: PRO-ED.

Swanson, H. L., Harris, K. R., & Graham, S. (Eds.). (2003). *Handbook of learning disabilities*. New York, NY: Guilford Press.

Swartz, G. A. (1974). *The language-learning system*. New York, NY: Simon & Schuster.

Tesman, J. R., & Hills, A. (1994). Developmental effects of lead exposure in children. *Social Policy Report: Society for Research in Child Development, 8*(3), 1–16.

Thomson, M. (1990). *Developmental dyslexia* (3rd ed.). London, United Kingdom: Whurr.

Torgesen, J. K. (1991). Learning disabilities: Historical and conceptual issues. In B. Y. L. Wong (Ed.), *Learning about learning disabilities* (pp. 3–37). San Diego, CA: Academic Press.

Torgesen, J. K. (1993). Variations on theory in learning disabilities. In G. R. Lyon, D. B. Gray, J. F. Kavanaugh, & N. A. Krasnegor (Eds.), *Better understanding learning disabilities: New views from research and their implications for education and public policies* (pp. 153–170). Baltimore, MD: Paul H. Brookes.

Torgesen, J. K., Wagner, R. K., & Rashotte, C. A. (1994). Longitudinal studies of phonological processing and reading. *Journal of Learning Disabilities, 27*, 276–286.

Torgesen, J. K., Wagner, R. K., & Rashotte, C. A. (1997). Approaches to prevention and remediation of phonologically based reading disabilities. In B. A. Blachman (Ed.),

Foundation as of reading acquisition and dyslexia: Implications for early intervention (pp. 287–304). Mahway, NJ: Erlbaum.

Travis, J. (1996). Let the games begin. *Science News, 149,* 104–106.

Truch, S. (1994). Stimulating basic reading processes using Auditory Discrimination in Depth. *Annals of Dyslexia, 44,* 60–80.

Tunick, R. A., & Pennington, B. F. (2002). The etiological relationship between reading disability and phonological disorder. *Annals of Dyslexia, 52,* 75–95.

U.S. Department of Education, Institute of Education Sciences. (2008). Children 3 to 21 years old served in federally supported programs for the disabled, by type of disability: Selected years, 1976–77 through 2006–07. Retrieved from http://nces.ed.gov/programs/digest/d08/tables/dt08_050.asp

U.S. Office of Education. (1977). Assistance to states for education of handicapped children: Procedures for evaluating specific learning disabilities. *Federal Register, 42,* G1082–G1085.

Wagner, R. K., & Torgeson, J. K. (1987). The nature of phonological processing and its causal role in the acquisition of reading skills. *Psychological Bulletin, 101*(2), 192–212.

Wanzek, J., Vaughn, S., Wexler, J., Swanson, E. A., Edmonds, M., & Kim, A.-H. (2006). A synthesis of spelling and reading interventions and their effects on the spelling outcomes of students with LD. *Journal of Learning Disabilities, 39,* 528–543.

Watson, C. S., Kidd, G. R., Horner, D. G., Connell, P. E. J., Lowther, A., Eddins, D. A., . . . Watson, B. U. (2003). Sensory, cognitive and linguistic factors in the early academic performance of elementary school children: The Benton-I.U. project. *Journal of Learning Disabilities, 36*(2), 165–197.

Wechsler, D. (2002). *Wechsler Preschool and Primary Scale of Intelligence* (3rd ed.). San Antonio, TX: Psychological Corporation.

Wechsler, D. (2003). *Wechsler Intelligence Scale for Children* (4th ed.), *Administration and scoring manual.* San Antonio, TX: Psychological Corporation.

Wendling, B. J., Mather, N., & Schrank, F. A. (2009). Woodcock-Johnson III Tests of Cognitive Abilities. In J. A. Naglieri & S. Goldstein (Eds.), *Practitioner's guide to assessing intelligence and achievement* (pp. 191–229). Hoboken, NJ: Wiley.

White, O. R. (1986). Precision teaching—Precision learning. *Exceptional Children, 52,* 522–534.

Wiederholt, J. L., & Bryant, B. R. (1992). *Gray Oral Reading Tests* (3rd ed.). Austin, TX: PRO-ED.

Wilkinson, G. S., & Robertson, G. J. (2005). *The Wide Range Achievement Test* (4th ed.). Lutz, FL: Psychological Assessment Resources.

Wong, B. Y. L. (1987). How did the results of medicognitive research impact on the learning disabled individual? *Learning Disability Quarterly, 10,* 189–195.

Wong, B. Y. L. (1991). Assessment of meta-cognitive research in learning disabilities: Theory, research, and practice. In H. L. Swanson (Ed.), *Handbook on the assessment of learning disabilities: Theory, research and practice* (pp. 265–284). Austin, TX: PRO-ED.

Woodcock, R. W., McGrew, K. S., & Mather, N. (2001a). *Woodcock-Johnson III Tests of Achievement*. Itasca, IL: Riverside.

Woodcock, R. W., McGrew, K. S., & Mather, N. (2001b). *Woodcock-Johnson Tests of Cognitive Abilities and Tests of Achievement* (3rd ed.). Rolling Meadows, IL: Riverside.

Zerbin-Rudin, E. (1967). Congenital word-blindness. *Bulletin of the Orton Society, 17,* 47–55.

3

Attention-Deficit/Hyperactivity Disorder in Childhood

SAM GOLDSTEIN
MELISSA DEVRIES

The childhood cognitive and behavioral problems categorized as disorders of attention, impulsivity, and hyperactivity have over the past 50 years presented a clinical challenge for educators and psychologists. The symptom constellation referred to as Attention Deficit Disorder or Attention-Deficit/Hyperactivity Disorder (ADHD) (American Psychiatric Association [APA], 2000) has become one of the most widely researched areas in childhood and adolescence with an increasing interest throughout the adult life span. Problems arising from this constellation of symptoms have constituted the most chronic childhood behavior disorder over the past 40 years (Rowland, Lesesne, & Abramowitz, 2002; Wender, 1975) and the largest single source of referrals to mental health centers (Barkley, 1990; Gadow, Sprafkin, & Nolan, 2001). In clinic-referred settings, males outnumber females 6 to 1. In epidemiological studies of community-based settings, the ratio is 3 to 1 (Barkley, 1990; Derks, Hudziak, & Boomsma, 2009). The incidence of diagnosis continues to increase, with a 70% increase in the diagnosis of children and nearly a 100% increase in the diagnosis of adults between 2000 and 2003 (Centers for Disease Control [CDC], 2005). It is now estimated that between 4% to 8% of the population has received a diagnosis of ADHD (CDC, 2005; Cuffe, Moore, & McKeown, 2005). Females are the fastest-growing group (Medco Health Solutions, 2005). Broad-based definitions of ADHD find epidemiology of nearly 16% in adults; narrower definitions report an incidence of 3% to 4% (Faraone & Biederman, 2005). Additionally, incidence has been reported to be higher in populations of individuals with other impairments (Altfas, 2002).

Even as psychologists utilize the current diagnostic criteria involving symptoms of inattention, hyperactivity, and impulsivity, increasing data have been generated to suggest that, for the majority of affected children, impulsivity and impaired executive functions represent core deficits. (For review, see Barkley, 2006; Goldstein & Schwebach, 2005). Children with ADHD typically experience difficulty in all aspects and situations of their lives. Their behavior is often uneven, unpredictable, and inconsistent. Psychologists evaluating ADHD today must be concerned not only with the core symptoms of this disorder and their impact on childhood but with the significant secondary impact these problems have on children's current and future lives as well as the lives of their family members. An increasing body of research is demonstrating increased vulnerability. Adults with ADHD face psychiatric, emotional, cognitive, academic, vocational, substance, and antisocial problems (Barkley, Fisher, Smallish, & Fletcher, 2004; Barkley & Gordon, 2002; Barkley, Murphy, & Fischer, 2008; Murphy, Barkley, & Bush, 2002).

In part, the controversy and at times confusion concerning various aspects of ADHD may in part be the result of a tradition to view this disorder as a unitary phenomenon with a single cause. Voeller (1991) suggests that rather than viewing ADHD as a single behavioral abnormality with associated comorbidities, it may be better to conceptualize ADHD as a "cluster of different behavioral deficits, each with a specific neuro-substrate of varying severity occurring in variable constellations and sharing a common response to psychostimulants" (S4). There is no doubt, however, that the cluster of symptomatic problems that comprise the diagnosis of ADHD represents a distinct disorder from others of childhood and adulthood (Accardo, Blondis, & Whitman, 1990; Barkley & Murphy, 2006; Biederman et al., 1996). A significant percentage of affected youth continue to demonstrate the condition into adulthood, often underreporting their symptoms and impairment relative to observers (Barkley, Fisher, Smallish, & Fletcher, 2002; Barkley et al., 2008). The consensus among researchers and clinicians is that the core symptoms of ADHD affect a significant minority of our population. For affected individuals, however, ADHD represents a poor fit between societal expectations and these individuals' abilities to meet those expectations. This phenomenon is distinct from other disorders of child- and adulthood and can be reliably evaluated and effectively treated.

TOWARD A WORKING DEFINITION OF ADHD

From a neuropsychological perspective, the concept of attention as an executive function has gained increasing popularity. Sustained mental effort, self-regulation, planning, execution, and maintenance are considered measures of executive functioning (Daigneault, Braun, & Whitaker, 1992). Mirskey, Anthony, Duncan, Ahearn, and Kellam (1991) developed a neuropsychological model of attention defining four basic concepts involving the ability to focus, execute, sustain, or code and shift. Eight traditional assessment measures of attention were used in a factor analytic study to arrive at this model.

Increasingly, there is a consensus that ADHD represents a problem of faulty performance rather than faulty input. It is not so much that this population of individuals does not know what to do; rather, they do not do what they know consistently. It is a problem of inconsistency rather than inability (Goldstein & Goldstein, 1998). Even in their adaptive skills, this pattern of difference between possessing a skill and using it efficiently has been well defined for individuals with ADHD (Stein, 1997).

As the fifth edition of the *Diagnostic and Statistical Manual of Mental Disorders* (*DSM-5*) is not expected to be published until 2012, it is important for psychologists to possess a working understanding of the *Diagnostic and Statistical Manual of Mental Disorders* (4th ed., text revision; *DSM-IV-TR*; APA, 2000) diagnostic criteria for ADHD, a practical understanding of the manner in which the symptoms impact the individual's functioning, and a diagnostic strategy. The traditional disease model is not relevant to the definition of ADHD (Ellis, 1985; Levy, Hay, McStephen, Wood, & Waldman, 1997). ADHD is more like obesity or intelligence. Individuals differ not in having or not having the traits but in the degree of manifestation. ADHD symptoms are multidimensional rather than unitary (Guevremont, DuPaul, & Barkley, 1993; Woo & Rey, 2005). However, there continues to be discussion as to which dimensions represent the most distinguishing deficits of the disorder. The frequency and severity of symptoms fluctuate across settings, activities, and caregivers (Purper-Ouakil, Wohl, Michel, Mouren, & Gorwood, 2004; Tarver-Behring, Barkley, & Karlsson, 1985; Zentall, 1984). Neuropsychological profiles have also been demonstrated to differ between subtypes (Chabildas, Pennington, & Willicutt, 2001). However, these differences have not lent themselves to a differential diagnosis. There is a general consensus, however, that symptoms of ADHD load into two broad factors defined by those related to the behavioral manifestation of faulty attention and those related to hyperactivity and impulsivity (Crystal, Ostrander, Chen, & August, 2001; Faraone, Biederman, & Friedman, 2000). Symptoms of hyperactivity and impulsivity appear to co-occur at such a high frequency that it is difficult on a factor analytic basis to separate them. However, research has demonstrated subtype differences in neuropsychological profiles and patterns of comborbidity (Eiraldi, Power, & Nezu, 1997; Elia, Ambrosini, & Berrettini, 2008; Schmitz et al., 2002; Wåhlstedt, Thorell, & Bohlin, 2009). It is also important for psychologists to recognize that at times the lines blur between the symptoms and consequences or impairments of ADHD. Thus, a diagnostic strategy for ADHD should include identifying symptoms as well as a list of skills and life impairments hypothesized to be directly impacted by symptoms (Gordon et al., 2006). Having the symptoms but not having a negative impact would, in fact, preclude the diagnosis of ADHD, according to current *DSM-IV-TR* criteria.

The *DSM-IV* diagnostic criteria published in 1994 made an effort to move forward and correct the mistaken course that ADHD represents a unipolar disorder. The field studies for the ADHD diagnosis were more comprehensive and better structured than previous efforts. The *DSM-IV-TR* (APA, 2000) criteria are identical to the *DSM-IV* criteria. Since *DSM-III* (APA, 1980) each succeeding diagnostic protocol has focused increasingly on the issue of impairment. Impairment has and will continue to be a critical lynchpin in making the diagnosis of ADHD but is not well explained by symptom severity (Gordon et al., 2006). Further, the measurement of neuropsychological processes may also be considered as part of the *DSM-5* criteria for ADHD (Naglieri & Das, 2005).

Of the 276 children diagnosed with ADHD in the *DSM-IV* field studies, 55% had the Combined Type, 27% the Inattentive Type, and 18% the Hyperactive-Inattentive Type (Lahey et al., 1994). Less than half of the ADHD Hyperactive Type (44%) received that diagnosis when *DSM-III* criteria for ADD with Hyperactivity were used. These two diagnoses, therefore, overlapped only partially. The Hyperactive-impulsive group had fewer symptoms of inattention in comparison to children with the Combined Type. They also had fewer symptoms of hyperactive-impulsive problems, suggesting that this represents a less severe variant of the disorder. The Hyperactive-impulsive group contained 20% females; the Combined group, 12% females; and the Inattentive group, 27% females. This latter number represents clinical perceptions that females more often demonstrate the Inattentive Type of ADHD (Biederman et al., 2002). This overrepresentation has not been well explained by any theoretical model (Silverthorn, Frick, Kuper, & Ott, 1996) nor has it been understood why preliminary research suggests that females with ADHD may be less likely to demonstrate executive function deficits than males (Seidman et al., 1997). The Hyperactive-impulsive population was also younger in the field studies. Additionally, they had fewer disruptive symptoms of oppositional defiance or Conduct Disorder than the Combined Type of ADHD.

A number of researchers have demonstrated the validity of the current *DSM-IV* diagnostic conceptualization for ADHD utilizing a variety of clinical and laboratory measures. Such research has included a full battery of neuropsychological tests (Brand, Das-Smaal, & De Jonge, 1996; Halperin et al., 1993; Harrier & DeOrnellas, 2005); reversal and memory tasks (O'Neill & Douglas, 1996); executive function tasks (Clark, Prior, & Kinsella, 2000; Geurts, Verte, Oosterlaan, Roeyers, & Sergeant, 2005; Hart & Harter, 2001); and neurological evaluation (Luk, Leung, & Yuen, 1991; Mahone & Wodka, 2008). The general consistency of symptom, comorbid and related findings among large, well-controlled clinic and epidemiologic studies suggest that the conceptualization of ADHD in *DSM-IV* has become increasingly more refined. Nonetheless, these criteria continue to focus excessively on inattention as the primary problem for the disorder, limiting the scope and focus on the impact of impulsivity as the core deficit. This perpetuates a number of major misconceptions, including that the Inattentive Type of ADHD represents a subtype of the Combined Disorder (Anastopoulos, Barkley, & Shelton, 1994). Increasing research suggests that it does not (Barkley, 2001; Milich, Balentine, & Lynam, 2001; but also see Stawicki, Nigg, & van Eye, 2006). More likely, the Inattentive Type represents a distinct disorder, primarily reflecting difficulty attending to repetitive, effortful tasks and problems with organization. Carlson and Mann (2002) described children with the Inattentive Type ADHD as distinct from the Combined Type as possessing hypoactivity, lethargy, and a lack of ability to stay focused. The problems this group experiences may very well be the result of faulty skills as opposed to inconsistent or inadequate use of skills. There are also emerging data raising questions about the lack of stability of *DSM-IV* ADHD subtypes over time as children mature (Lahey, Pelham, Loney, Lee, & Wilcutt, 2005).

GENETICS AND ETIOLOGY OF ADHD

ADHD is among the most common disorders of childhood. It is estimated that it affects between 5% and 8% of the population throughout life. Estimates vary, with the American Psychiatric Association suggesting an incidence of 4% to 6% (APA, 2000). Statistics vary depending on populations studied, thresholds, and definitional criteria (Sherman, Iacono, & McGue, 1997). The genetic contribution has been postulated by a number of authors (Hechtman, 1993; Rutter et al., 1990; Stevenson, 1992; Swanson et al., 2000). The underlying mechanism genetically has recently been suggested to be associated with a single dopamine transporter gene (Cook et al., 1995) as well as with a variation in the DRD4 (LaHoste et al., 1996) and DRD5 (Lowe et al., 2004) receptor genes and in the DAT1 transporter (Winsberg & Comings, 1999). Further, it has been suggested that the trait locus for reading disability on chromosome 6 identified by Cardon et al. (1994) may also be a locus for ADHD (Warren et al., 1995).

Eaves et al. (1993) note two complementary approaches to the genetic analysis of ADHD. The first, a dimensional approach, involves the study of a normal range of activity and assumes that ADHD is at one end of the continuum or trait. The second, a categorical approach, is based on studying children of families who meet diagnostic criteria and assumes that ADHD is a discrete disorder (Faraone et al., 1992). It is important for psychologists to recognize that dimensional approaches have been found to better predict life outcome (Fergusson & Horwood, 1992).

Among trait approaches, Willerman (1973) found the heritability of scores on an activity questionnaire to be 0.77 for a sample of 54 monozygotic and 39 dizygotic twin pairs. However, Goodman and Stevenson (1989) reported a heritability estimate of greater than 1 in a sample of 285 twin pairs. This finding appeared to be due to an extremely low dizygotic correlation. Corresponding dizygotic correlations for father and teacher reports were much higher, resulting in heritability estimates from 0.48 to 0.68. A subsequent twin study by Thapar, Hervas, and McGuffin (1995), using the same three activity items, confirmed the low dizygotic correlation in maternal ratings and suggested the role of reciprocal sibling interactions in which twins interact with each other to be different or mothers' ratings exaggerate differences between their dizygotic twins. The low dizygotic correlation may, however, be unique to these specific questions about activity level. Edelbrock, Rende, Plomin, and Thompson (1995) reported correlations predominantly from mothers' ratings of 0.86 for monozygotic twins and 0.29 for dizygotic twins, giving a heritability estimate of 0.66. Zahn-Waxler, Schmitz, Fulker, Robinson, and Emde (1996) obtained a very similar estimate (0.72). However, somewhat lower heritability values were obtained from fathers' and teachers' ratings, and the correlations between raters was low.

From a categorical or diagnostic approach, Goodman and Stevenson (1989) demonstrated a proband-wise concordance rate of 51% in 39 monozygotic twin pairs and 30% in 54 dizygotic twin pairs, yielding a heritability estimate of 0.64. Similarly, Coolidge, Thede, and Young (2000) demonstrated a proband-wise concordance rate of 81% for 67 monozygotic twin pairs and 18% for 42 dyzygotic twin pairs, yielding a heritability estimate of 0.82. DeFries and Fulker (1985, 1988), utilizing a statistical method developed by Gillis, Gilger, Pennington, and DeFries (1992), estimated the heritability of ADHD as 0.91 plus or minus 0.36 for twins participating in a research project.

The issue of phenotypic definition as indicated by the variation in estimates of siblings' risk is 53%, 25%, or 17%, depending on whether the behavior is defined as hyperactivity, Attention Deficit Disorder, or ADHD, speaks to the complexity of relating phenotype to genotype (Biederman, Faraone, Keenan, & Benjamin, 1992; Biederman, Faraone, Keenan, Knee, & Tsuang, 1990; Elia et al., 2009; Faraone et al., 1992; Safer, 1973). Levy et al. (1997), based on a cohort of 1938 families with twins and siblings ages 4 to 12 years recruited from the Australian National Health and Medical Research Council Twin Registry, reported that ADHD is best viewed as the extreme of behavior that varies genetically throughout the entire population rather than as disorder with discrete determinants. In this study, as with others, heritability estimates for monozygotic versus dizygotic twins was significantly higher. As Levy et al. note, ADHD has an exceptionally high heritability compared with other behavioral disorders. These authors reported that 82% of monozygotic twins and 38% of dizygotic twins met an eight-symptom ADHD cutoff for proband concordances.

Studies linking polymorphisms in the dopaminergic system to ADHD (Comings, Wu, & Chiu, 1996) and the DRD4 receptor polymorphisms to dimensional aspects of impulsivity (Benjamin et al., 1996; Ebstein et al., 1996) suggest that polymorphisms identified to date do not account for all of the relevant, heritable variation. The findings of Sherman et al. (1997) suggest that future molecular-genetic studies of ADHD may yield more information defining ADHD as a disorder composed of two quantitatively, continuously distributed dimensions—inattention and hyperactivity/impulsivity—rather than a homogeneous categorical disorder.

Etiology of ADHD must also be considered from a related disorders or teratogen basis. Fragile X, Turner syndrome, Tourette's, neurofibromatosis, sickle cell anemia, phenylketonuria, Noonan syndrome, and Williams syndrome are all chromosomal and genetic abnormalities in which attentional problems and ADHD have been reported

(Hagerman, 1991; Mautner, Kluwe, Thakker, & Laerk, 2002). Bastain et al. (2002) suggest that expensive laboratory tests for genetic disorders are not indicated unless a genetic disorder is suspect due to family history, clinical signs, or low IQ. Toxins result-ing in disorders such as fetal alcohol syndrome, cocaine exposure in utero, lead and vapor abuse, perinatal complications; medical problems such as hypothyroidism and encephalitis; even radiation therapy secondary to leukemia have all been reported as responsible for creating inattentive and impulsive problems. (For review, see Barkley, 2006; Goldstein & Goldstein, 1998.) ADHD and depressive symptoms are commonly identified after pediatric traumatic brain injury but may predate the trauma (Bloom et al., 2001).

The neurobiology of ADHD implicates impairment in brain structure, particu-larly differences in size of certain structures, interacting with metabolic differences (Zametkin & Rapoport, 1987). Efficient brain metabolism in prefrontal and cingulate regions as well as the right thalamus caudate, hippocampus, and cerebellum have been reported in adults with ADHD (Zametkin, Nordahl, & Gross, 1990; Zimmer, 2009). Regional abnormalities of glucose metabolism demonstrated by positron emission tomography studies generally demonstrate a fundamental biologic difference between ADHD and normal subjects. Castellanos et al. (1996) suggest that connections between the right prefrontal cortex, caudate, and cerebellum reflect the brain's "brak-ing system," a system that operates inefficiently in individuals with ADHD. Semrud-Clikeman et al. (2000) found reversed caudate asymmetry on MRI scans of 10 males diagnosed with ADHD. They noted the right prefrontal cortex, cerebellum, and basal ganglia appear to be associated with behavioral measures of inattention and inhibi-tion. Children with ADHD have been found unable to activate the caudate nucleus, suggesting core abnormality in this function for ADHD (Vaiyda et al., 2005). These authors conclude that children with ADHD experience reduced engagement of a frontal-striatal-temporal-parietal network when engaging in inhibitory tasks.

DEVELOPMENTAL COURSE AND COMORBIDITY

Although the core problems children with ADHD experience are homogeneous, reflecting difficulty with impulse control, attention, and hyperactivity, each child's presentation is unique in terms of the manifestation of these problems and associated comorbid factors (Goldstein & Goldstein, 1998). As an increasing body of scientific data is generated concerning the developmental course and adult outcome of children with ADHD, it appears that the comorbid problems they develop rather than the diag-nosis of ADHD best predicts their life outcome. ADHD in isolation appears to best predict school struggles, difficulty meeting expectations within the home setting, and possible mild substance abuse as an adult. However, it does not predict the significant negative emotional, behavioral, and personality outcomes that have been reported.

Infants who have been noted to demonstrate difficult temperament do not handle changes in routines well. They exhibit a low frustration threshold and a high intensity of response (Carey, 1970; Chess & Thomas, 1986; Thomas & Chess, 1977; West, Schenkel, & Pavuluri, 2008). In follow-up studies of such infants, as many as 70% develop school problems (Teglasi, Cohn, & Meshbesher, 2004; Terestman, 1980). These infants appear at greater risk than others of receiving a diagnosis of ADHD. It is also important to note that these difficult infants exert a significant negative impact on the developing relationship with caregivers—a relationship that is critical in predicting a child's life outcome (Katz, 1997).

Although early symptoms of ADHD may be viewed as transient problems of young children, research data suggest that ignoring these signs results in the loss of valuable treatment time. At least 60% to 70% of children later diagnosed with ADHD could have been identified by their symptoms during the preschool years (Cohen, Sullivan, Minde, Novack, & Helwig, 1981). Behavioral difficulties present during preschool have been shown to be predictive of continued behavioral problems in approximately 45% of preschool children (Lahey et al., 2004). Young children manifesting symptoms of ADHD are more likely to present with speech and language problems than are children not suffering from those symptoms (Baker & Cantwell, 1987; Geurts & Embrechts, 2008) and to develop a wide range of behavioral problems (Cantwell, Baker, & Mattison, 1981; Cohen, Davine, & Meloche-Kelly, 1989; DuPaul, McGoey, Eckert, & Van Brakle, 2001). Current research cogently suggests that the comorbidity of speech and language disorders with ADHD merits routine screening of children suspected of ADHD and language disorders, especially during their younger years. Children with concurrent ADHD and language disorders appear to have a much poorer prognosis than those with ADHD alone (Baker & Cantwell, 1992; G. P. Hill, 2000).

Within school settings, children with ADHD appear to be victims of their temperament and of their learning history, which often involves beginning but not completing tasks. The negatively reinforcing model utilized by most educators in this circumstance tends to focus on misbehavior rather than on termination of the behavior. This may further disrupt the classroom by having a disinhibitory effect on other students. Although 25 years ago it was suggested that children with ADHD were intellectually less competent than their peers, it appears more likely that weak performance on intellectual tasks results from the impact of impulsivity and inattention on test-taking behavior rather than an innate lack of intelligence (Barkley, 1995). Kaplan, Crawford, Dewey, and Fisher (2000) identified a normal IQ distribution in children diagnosed with ADHD. Children with ADHD often underperform but may not underachieve during the elementary years. However, by high school, it has been reported that at least 80% of these children fall behind in a basic academic subject requiring repetition and attention for competence, such as basic math knowledge, spelling, or written language. (For review, see Barkley, 2006; Goldstein & Goldstein, 1998.) Depending on diagnostic criteria, approximately 20% to 30% of children with ADHD also suffer from a concomitant, often language-based, learning disability. (For review, see Willcutt & Pennington, 2000.) Although it has been hypothesized that ADHD may prevent a child from achieving his or her academic potential (Frazier, Youngstrom, Glutting, & Watkins, 2007; Stott, 1981), the presence of a learning disability may make a child appear more inattentive than others (Aaron, Joshi, Palmer, Smith, & Kirby, 2002; McGee & Share, 1988).

Sociometric and play study suggests that children with ADHD are not chosen as often by their peers to be best friends or partners in activities (Bagwell, Molina, Pelham, & Hoza, 2001; Pelham & Milich, 1984). They appear to be cognizant of their difficulties, an awareness that likely precipitates lower self-esteem for children with ADHD (Gentschel & McLaughlin, 2000; Glow & Glow, 1980). Moreover, they appear to experience either high-incidence–low-impact problems that result in poor social acceptance or low-incidence–high-impact problems that result in social rejection (Pelham & Milich, 1984). In addition, these children have difficulty adapting their behavior to different situational demands (McQuade & Hoza, 2008; Whalen, Henker, Collins, McAuliffe, & Vaux, 1979). It has been suggested that the impulsive behavioral patterns of children with ADHD are most responsible for their social difficulty, making those with comorbid hyperactive-impulsive problems of greater severity at even greater risk of developing social difficulties (Hodgens, Cole, & Boldizar, 2000; Pelham & Bender, 1982). ADHD has been found to be a risk factor heading to a wide variety of ineffective social coping strategies as youth transition into adolescence (Young, Chadwick, Heptinstall, Taylor, & Songua-Barke, 2005). It should also be noted that children who are good responders demonstrating symptom and impairment reduction with medication appear to exhibit fewer chronic social impairments (Gallagher et al., 2004).

Some primary symptoms of ADHD may diminish in intensity by adolescence (Perkins, 2008; Weiss & Hechtman, 1979). However, most adolescents with ADHD continue to experience significant problems (Milich & Loney, 1979; for review see Barkley, 2006; Goldstein & Ellison, 2002). At least 80% of adolescents with ADHD continue to manifest symptoms consistent with ADHD. Sixty percent develop at least one additional disruptive disorder (Barkley, Fischer, Edelbrock, & Smallish, 1990). Between 20% and 60% of adolescents with ADHD are involved in antisocial behavior, with a normal occurrence of 3% to 4% (Barkley et al., 2006; Satterfield, Hoppe, & Schell, 1982). At least 50% to 70% of these adolescents develop Oppositional Defiant Disorder, often during younger years, with a significant number progressing to Conduct Disorder (Barkley, Fischer, Edelbrock, & Smallish, 1989; van Lier, van der Ende, Koot, & Verhulst, 2007). However, the high prevalence of antisocial problems in adolescents with ADHD likely reflects the comorbidity of ADHD with other disruptive disorders, principally Conduct Disorder (Barkley, McMurray, Edelbrock, & Robbins, 1989;

Marshal & Molina, 2006). As Barkley (1997) succinctly points out, the preponderance of the available data suggests that while ADHD is clearly a risk factor for the development of adolescent antisocial problems, life experience, principally factors within families, most powerfully contribute to the onset and maintenance of delinquency, Conduct Disorder, and subsequent young adult antisocial problems (Dalsgaard, Mortenson, Frydenberg, & Thomsen, 2002).

NEUROPSYCHOLOGICAL IMPAIRMENTS IN ADHD

The ecological validity of laboratory tests to identify, define, and determine the presence and severity of symptoms of ADHD has been increasingly questioned (Barkley, 1991b; Barkley & Grodzinsky, 1994). As ADHD is a disorder defined by behavior in the real world, it is not surprising that laboratory measures frequently fall short in defining and identifying symptoms of the disorder in comparison to naturalistic observation, history, and organized report in the form of questionnaires. Nonetheless, it has been increasingly recognized that clinicians take comfort supplementing their clinical impressions with laboratory-generated, objective scores (DuPaul, Guevremont, & Barkley, 1991). It is increasingly accepted, however, that these scores do not make the diagnosis of ADHD but may be helpful in the process of differential diagnosis (e.g., when is impulsivity a function of ADHD versus other disorders?) as well as facilitating the process of differentiating severity or related prognosis in a group of individuals with ADHD (Gordon, 1995; Hall, Halperin, Schwartz, & Newcorn, 1997).

The development of a norm-referenced, psychometric assessment battery specifically designed for ADHD has been an elusive goal for researchers and clinicians. Thus, it is not surprising when one reviews the extensive literature attempting to hypothetically and objectively define specific neuropsychological impairments occurring consistently in children with ADHD that no tried and true battery or pattern of impairment comes to light. As Levine (1992) has noted, ADHD symptoms appear to reflect "elusive entities and . . . mistaken identities" (p. 10). The comorbidity issue and the lack of specificity that many tests hold in discriminating ADHD from other disorders further complicates this endeavor. Compromised scores may be due to a variety of causes, leading some researchers to suggest that a profile of test scores be utilized in defining and explaining neuropsychological impairments in children with ADHD (Aylward, Verhulst, & Bell, 1993; Naglieri, 2000). Clinicians should be aware that clinic or laboratory tests alone or in combination have been found to result in classification decisions that frequently disagree with the diagnosis of ADHD when it is based on parent interview, history, and behavior rating scales (Doyle, Biederman, & Seidman, 2000; DuPaul, Anastopoulos, Shelton, Guevremont, & Metevia, 1992). Further, Szatmari et al. (1990) report that neuropsychological tests appear to distinguish children with ADHD from those with pure anxiety or affective disorders. However, they may not as efficiently distinguish ADHD from other disruptive disorders. These authors concluded that neuropsychological tests were more strongly associated with externalizing than internalizing diagnoses. They appear to correlate with psychiatric symptoms at school but not at home. Further, traditional neuropsychological instruments used to infer attention and impulse problems often do not correlate with each other (Naglieri et al., 2005). Thus, it is not surprising that the literature suggests that when results of the standardized behavior ratings, observations, and history conflict with laboratory measures, the latter should be disregarded in favor of the former as these are considered more ecologically valid sources of data (Barkley, 1991a; Pelham, Fabiano, & Massetti, 2005; Rapport, Timko, & Wolfe, 2006).

Cherkes-Julkowski, Stolzenberg, and Siegal (1991) suggest that perhaps the dropoff in performance for children with ADHD is a function of an inability to control focus of attention. These authors suggest that when prompts are provided during testing, children with ADHD perform significantly better. In a study evaluating children with ADHD with and without medication compared to children with Learning Disabilities (LD) and a group of normal controls, the greatest gains for prompts were observed in the unmedicated group with ADHD. However, clinicians should be cautioned that prompts, especially on measures designed to evaluate response inhibition, may actually test the ability of the child to follow directions rather than to inhibit. Clinicians should also keep in mind that there are data to suggest that level of reinforcement during test performance may also have an impact on scores. Devers, Bradley-Johnson, and Johnson (1994) found improvement in Verbal IQ scores of 12 points accrued when token reinforcers followed immediately for correct responses. The impact of praise on test performance has not been systematically evaluated. Finally, Draeger, Prior, and Sanson (1986) reported a deterioration in the performance of children with ADHD on a Continuous Performance Test, more so than controls, when the examiner left the room. These authors suggest that even examiner presence acts to mitigate test performance. It may well be that some children who perform poorly on test measures under these circumstances have an application rather than an ability deficit.

EVALUATION

Due to the pervasive, multisetting nature of problems related to ADHD and the high comorbidity with other childhood disorders, assessment for ADHD in childhood must be accompanied by a thorough emotional, developmental, and behavioral evaluation. It should be noted, however, that the diagnosis of ADHD should be firmly based on the accepted standard, in this case the *DSM-IV-TR* diagnostic criteria. Clinicians should be aware that efforts to include additional data to prove/disprove the diagnosis run the risk of introducing increasing variance (Naglieri, Goldstein, & Schwebach, 2004). The comprehensive evaluation should collect data concerning the child's behavior at home, with friends, and at school; academic and intellectual functioning; medical status; and emotional development. It is suggested that clinicians consider the next five-step process to accompany the evaluation of ADHD. Clinicians should:

1. *Obtain a complete history.* This is not a cursory process. Sufficient time (approximately 1.5 to 2 hours) should be set aside to obtain a narrative of the child's development, behavior, extended family history, family relations, and current functioning. Within the context of the interview, efforts should be made to trace a developmental course that appears to fit ADHD as well as to identify core symptoms and those related to other childhood disorders. Obtaining thorough knowledge of the diagnostic criteria for common and uncommon (e.g., high-functioning autism) childhood internalizing and externalizing disorders should be a paramount concern for clinicians to facilitate the identification of high- as well as low-incidence disorders.

2. *Review school records, including report cards and results of group achievement testing.* If weak performance or LD are suspected or if the child is already receiving special education services, the clinician should review all assessment data as well as the child's Individualized Education Plan. Then it is proper to decide which tests and what amount of time should be used to arrive at the most accurate evaluation of the child. Clinicians should be cautioned, as just reviewed in step 5, that no specific laboratory tests to evaluate ADHD have demonstrated sufficient positive and negative predictive power to be relied on. The primary purpose of face-to-face assessment with a child should involve addressing issues related to the child's emotional status, self-esteem, cognitive development, and LD. Observation of the child's behavior during assessment may also yield clues regarding his or her interpersonal style and temperament.

3. *Supplement data obtained from the history with a number of standardized, factor-analyzed questionnaires concerning children's problems.* At least two adults who interact with the child on a regular basis, ideally a parent and a teacher, should be requested to complete questionnaires. For general child assessment, the most valuable questionnaire is the Child Behavior Checklist (Achenbach & Edelbrock, 1991). This well-developed questionnaire organizes childhood behavior on a disruptive/nondisruptive continuum. Recent research supports that the Attention Problems Scale correlates well with the current two-factor DSM-IV ADHD diagnosis (Achenbach, 1996). Also helpful are the Conners' Teacher Rating Scales—Revised (Conners, 1997), the Comprehensive Teacher's Rating Scale (Ullman, Sleator, & Sprague, 1988), the Childhood Attention Problems Scale (Edelbrock, 1990), and the Academic Performance and ADHD Rating Scales (DuPaul, 1990). However, these questionnaires alone do not provide sufficient information for diagnosis. They simply provide

an organized report of behavior. They describe what the observer sees but not why it is being seen.

4. *Generate a consistent set of data and a series of hypotheses to explain the child's behavior across a variety of settings, based on the history and questionnaires.*

5. *Administer tests.* Although a number of paper-and-pencil tasks have been used over the years in research settings to identify symptoms of ADHD, most do not lend themselves easily to clinical use. In research studies, some tests, such as the Matching Familiar Figures Test (Kagan, 1964), appear to have strong positive and negative predictive power for identifying impulsive children. However, in clinical practice, such instruments have not proven reliable for confirming the diagnosis of ADHD. Computerized instruments designed to measure sustained attention and the ability to inhibit impulsive responding (Conners, 1995; Gordon, 1993; Greenberg, 1991) have become increasingly popular among clinicians. However, it is important to remember that although these instruments may demonstrate strong positive predictive power (e.g., if the child fails the task, it strongly confirms the presence of symptoms related to ADHD), they possess poor negative predictive power (e.g., if the child passes the task, conclusions cannot be drawn one way or the other concerning the diagnosis) (McGee, Clark, & Symons, 2000). Nonetheless, many clinicians rely on such instruments to provide additional data as part of the diagnostic process rather than a specific data point to confirm or disconfirm the diagnosis of ADHD (Riccio, Reynolds, & Lowe, 2001). The interested reader is referred to Conners (1994) or Homack and Reynolds (2005) for a thorough review of the literature concerning computerized assessment of ADHD. A number of studies have suggested that measurement of specific intellectual processes may differentiate youth with various subtypes of ADHD (Naglieri, 1999; Paolito, 1999). However, data generated by instruments such as the Cognitive Assessment System (Naglieri & Das, 1997) are not necessary in making the diagnosis of ADHD but can provide useful information concerning differences in cognitive processes among diagnosed youth.

TREATMENT

Treatment of ADHD across the life span must be multidisciplinary, multimodal, and maintained over a long period. (For review, see Goldstein & Ellison, 2002; Goldstein & Goldstein, 1998; Teeter, 1998). By far, the most effective short-term interventions for ADHD are the combined use of medical, behavioral, and environmental techniques. Medication has been shown to reduce the manipulative power of the child's behavior in eliciting certain responses from teachers, peers, and family members.

An extensive literature attests to the benefits of medicine, specifically stimulants, in reducing key symptoms of ADHD and thus improving daily functioning (Klein, 1987;

for review, see Barkley, 2006; Goldstein & Goldstein, 1998). Stimulants and other drugs principally impacting dopamine and norepinephrine (Volkow et al., 2001) have consistently have been reported to improve academic achievement and productivity as well as accuracy of class work (Douglas, Barr, O'Neill, & Britton, 1986; Evans et al., 2001), attention span, reading comprehension, and complex problem solving, and to enhance inhibitory processes (Balthazor, Wagner, & Pelham, 1991; Pelham, 1987; Rubinstein, Malone, Roberts, & Logan, 2006). Related problems, including peer interactions, peer status, and even relationships with family members, have been reported improved with these drugs as well (Phelps, Brown, & Power, 2002; Whalen & Henker, 1991).

Behavior management increases the salience of behaving in a way consistent with environmental expectations. The manipulation of the environment (e.g., making tasks more interesting and payoffs more valuable) reduces the risk of problems within the natural setting. Zentall (1995) suggests that students with ADHD possess an active learning style with a demonstrated need to move, talk, respond, question, choose, debate, and even provoke. Thus, in classroom settings, children with ADHD do not fare well in sedentary situations. Managing interventions have included positive and negative contingent teacher attention, token economies, peer-mediated and group contingencies, time out, home school contingencies, and reductive techniques based on reinforcement and cognitive behavioral strategies (Abramowitz & O'Leary, 1991; DuPaul, Rutherford, & Hosterman, 2008). Environmental and task modifications are also critical for classroom success for the child with ADHD. However, additional research is needed, especially in the area of school-based intervention for adolescents with ADHD.

Though popular, the use of cognitive strategies (e.g., teaching a child to stop, look, and listen) as well as other nontraditional treatments (e.g., dietary manipulation, electroencephalogram biofeedback, etc.) to reduce symptoms of ADHD have not stood the test of scientific research and thus should not be advocated as first-line treatments of choice for children with ADHD. Shure (1994), however, suggests that the patient application of cognitive training over a long period of time, applied in the real-world setting, can improve the self-regulatory skills of children with ADHD. The interested reader is referred to Braswell (1998) for a review of these issues.

Regardless of the treatment modality employed, the basic underlying premise in managing problems of ADHD involves increasing the child's capacity to inhibit before acting. This is consistent with the theoretical construct that the core problem for ADHD reflects an inability to permit sufficient time to think or respond consistently to consequences.

SUMMARY

Psychologists in clinical settings, given their theoretical background, training, and assessment skills, are in a unique position to evaluate and treat children with ADHD. At this time, clinicians must be prepared to rely extensively on history, report, and observation and less so on structured laboratory testing when attempting to understand the behavior and problems of children with ADHD. This chapter provided an overview of the current literature concerning the definition, evaluation, and treatment of ADHD in children.

REFERENCES

Aaron, P. G., Joshi, R. M., Palmer, H., Smith, M., & Kirby, E. (2002). Separating genuine cases of reading disability from reading deficits caused by predominantly inattentive ADHD behavior. *Journal of Learning Disabilities, 35,* 425–435.

Abramowitz, A. J., & O'Leary, S. G. (1991). Behavior interventions for the classroom: Implications for students with ADHD. *School Psychology Review, 20,* 220–234.

Accardo, P. J., Blondis, T. J., & Whitman, B. Y. (1990). Disorders of attention and activity level in a referral population. *Pediatrics, 85,* 426–431.

Achenbach, T. M. (1996). Subtyping ADHD: The request for suggestions about relating empirically based assessment to *DSM-IV. ADHD Report, 4,* 5–9.

Achenbach, T. M., & Edelbrock, C. (1991). *Normative data for the Child Behavior Checklist* (rev. ed.). Burlington, VT: University of Vermont Department of Psychiatry.

Altfas, J. R. (2002). Prevalence of ADHD among adults in obesity treatment. *Biomedical Psychology, 2,* 1–14.

American Psychiatric Association (APA). (1980). *Diagnostic and statistical manual of mental disorders* (3rd ed.). Washington, DC: Author.

American Psychiatric Association. (1994). *Diagnostic and statistical manual of mental disorders* (4th ed., rev.). Washington, DC: Author.

American Psychiatric Association. (2000). *Diagnostic and statistical manual of mental disorders* (4th ed., text rev.). Washington, DC: Author.

Anastopoulos, A. D., Barkley, R., & Shelton, T. (1994). The history and diagnosis of attention deficit/hyperactivity disorder. *Therapeutic care and education, 3,* 96–110.

Aylward, G. P., Verhulst, S. J., & Bell, S. (1993, September). *Inter-relationships between measures of attention deficit disorders: Same scores, different reasons.* Paper presented at the Society for Behavioral Pediatrics Meeting, Providence, RI.

Bagwell, C. L., Molina, D. S., Pelham, W. E., & Hoza, B. (2001). ADHD and problems in peer relations: Predictions from childhood to adolescence. *Journal of the American Academy of Child and Adolescent Psychiatry, 40,* 1285–1299.

Baker, L., & Cantwell, D. P. (1987). A prospective psychiatric follow-up of children with speech/language disorders. *Journal of the American Academy of Child Psychiatry, 26,* 546–553.

Baker, L., & Cantwell, D. P. (1992). Attention Deficit Disorder and speech/language disorders. *Comprehensive Mental Health Care, 2,* 3–16.

Balthazor, M. J., Wagner, R. K., & Pelham, W. E. (1991). The specificity of the effects of stimulant medication on classroom learning-related measures of cognitive processing for Attention Deficit Disorder children. *Journal of Abnormal Child Psychology, 19,* 35–52.

Barkley, R. A. (1990). *Attention-Deficit Hyperactivity Disorder: A handbook for diagnosis and treatment.* New York, NY: Guilford Press.

Barkley, R. A. (1991a). Attention-Deficit Hyperactivity Disorder. *Psychiatric Annals, 21,* 725–733.

Barkley, R. A. (1991b). The ecological validity of laboratory and analogue assessment methods of ADHD symptoms. *Journal of Abnormal Child Psychology, 19,* 149–178.

Barkley, R. A. (1995). ADHD and I.Q. *ADHD Report, 3,* 1–3.

Barkley, R. A. (1997). *Defiant children: A clinician's manual for assessment and parent training* (2nd ed.). New York, NY: Guilford Press.

Barkley, R. A. (2001). The inattentive type of ADHD as a distinct disorder: What remains to be done. *Clinical Psychology: Science and Practice, 8,* 489–501.

Barkley, R. A. (2006). *Attention Deficit Hyperactivity Disorder* (3rd ed.). New York, NY: Guilford Press.

Barkley, R. A., Fischer, M., Edelbrock, C. S., & Smallish, L. (1990). The adolescent outcome of hyperactive children diagnosed by research criteria: I, An eight year prospective follow-up study. *Journal of the American Academy of Child and Adolescent Psychiatry, 29,* 546–557.

Barkley, R. A., Fischer, M., Smallish, L., & Fletcher, K. (2004). Young adult follow-up of hyperactive children: Antisocial activities and drug use. *Journal of Child Psychology and Psychiatry, 45,* 195–207.

Barkley, R. A., Fischer, M., Smallish, L., & Fletcher, K. (2006). Young adult outcome of hyperactive children: Adaptive functioning in major life activities. *Journal of the American Academy of Child and Adolescent Psychiatry, 45,* 192–202.

Barkley, R. A., & Gordon, M. (2002). Research on comorbidity, adaptive functioning and cognitive impairments in adults with ADHD: Implications for a clinical practice. In S. Goldstein & A. T. Ellison (Eds.), *Clinician's guide to adult ADHD: Assessment and intervention* (pp. 43-69). New York, NY: Academic Press.

Barkley, R. A., & Grodzinsky, G. M. (1994). Are tests of frontal lobe functions useful in a diagnosis of attention deficit disorders? *Clinical Neuropsychologists, 8,* 121–139.

Barkley, R. A., McMurray, M. B., Edelbrock, C. S., & Robbins, K. (1989). The response of aggressive and non-aggressive ADHD children to two doses of methylphenidate. *Journal of the American Academy of Child and Adolescent Psychiatry, 28,* 873–881.

Barkley, R. A., & Murphy, K. R. (2006). *Attention-Deficit/Hyperactivity Disorder* (3rd ed.) *A handbook for diagnosis and treatment.* New York, NY: Guilford Press.

Barkley, R. A., Murphy, K. R., & Fischer, M. (2008). *ADHD in adults: What the science says.* New York, NY: Guilford Press.

Bastain, T. M., Lewczyk, C. M., Sharp, W. S., James, R. S., Long, R. T., Eagen, P. B., . . . Castellanos, F. X. (2002). Cytogenetic abnormalities in ADHD. *Journal of the American Academy of Child and Adolescent Psychiatry, 41,* 806–810.

Benjamin, J., Li, L., Patterson, C., Greenberg, B. D., Murphy, D. L., & Hamer, D. H. (1996). Population and familial association between the D4 dopamine receptor gene and measures of novelty seeking. *National Genetics, 12,* 81.

Biederman, J., Faraone, S. V., Keenan, K., Benjamin, J., Krifcher, B., Moore, C., . . . Tsuang, M. T. (1992). Further evidence for family-genetic risk factors in attention deficit hyperactivity disorder: Patterns of comorbidity in probands and relatives in psychiatrically and paediatrically referred samples. *Archives of General Psychiatry, 49,* 728–738.

Biederman, J., Faraone, S. V., Keenan, K., Knee, D., & Tsuang, M. T. (1990). Family-genetic and psychosocial risk factors in *DSM-III* attention deficit disorders. *Journal of the American Academy of Child and Adolescent Psychiatry, 29,* 526–533.

Biederman, J., Faraone, S. V., Mick, E., Wozniak, J., Chen, L., Ouelette, C., Marrs, A., . . . Lelon, E. (1996). Attention deficit hyperactivity disorder in juvenile mania: An overlooked comorbidity? *Journal of the American Academy of Child and Adolescent Psychiatry, 35,* 997–1008.

Biederman, J., Faraone, S. V., Milberger, S., Curtis, S., Chen, L., Marrs, A., . . . Spencer, T. (1995). Predictors of persistence and remission of ADHD: Results from a four-year prospective follow-up study of ADHD children. *Journal of the American Academy of Child and Adolescent Psychiatry, 35,* 343–351.

Biederman, J., Mick, E., Faraone, S. V., Braaten, E., Doyle, A., Spencer, T., . . . Johnson, M. A. (2002). Influence of gender on Attention Deficit Hyperactivity Disorder in children referred to a psychiatric clinic. *American Journal of Psychiatry, 159,* 36–42.

Bloom, D. R., Levin, H. S., Ewing-Cobbs, L., Saunders, A. E., Song, J., Fletcher, J. M., & Kowatch, R. A. (2001). Lifetime and novel psychiatric disorders after pediatric traumatic brain injury. *Journal of the American Academy of Child and Adolescent Psychiatry, 40,* 572–579.

Brand, E. F., Das-Smaal, E. A., & De Jonge, B. F. (1996). Subtypes of children with attention disabilities. *Child Neuropsychology, 2,* 109–122.

Braswell, L. (1998). Cognitive behavioral approaches as adjunctive treatments for ADHD children and their families. In S. Goldstein & M. Goldstein (Eds.), *Managing attention deficit hyperactivity disorder in children: A guide for practitioners* (2nd ed., pp. 533–544). New York, NY: Wiley.

Cantwell, D. P., Baker, L., & Mattison, R. (1981). Prevalence, type and correlates of psychiatric disorder in 200 children with communication disorder. *Journal of Developmental and Behavioral Pediatrics, 2,* 131–136.

Cardon, L. R., Smith, S. D., Fulker, D. W., Kimberling, W. J., Pennington, B. F., & DeFries, J. C. (1994). Quantitative trait locus for reading disability in chromosome 6. *Science, 266,* 276–279.

Carey, W. B. (1970). A simplified method for measuring infant temperament. *Journal of Pediatrics, 77,* 188–194.

Carlson, C. L., & Mann, M. (2002). Sluggish cognitive tempo predicts a different pattern of impairment in the Attention Deficit Hyperactivity Disorder—Predominantly

Inattentive Type. *Journal of Clinical Child and Adolescent Psychology*, *31*, 123–129.

Castellanos, F. X., Giedd, J. N., Marsh, W. L., Hamburger, S. D., Vaituzis, A. C., Dickstein, D. P., . . . Rapoport, J. L. (1996). Quantitative brain magnetic resonance imaging in Attention-Deficit Hyperactivity Disorder. *Archives of General Psychiatry*, *53*, 607–616.

Centers for Disease Control (CDC). (2005). *Morbidity and Mortality Weekly Report*, *54*(34). Retrieved from www.cdc.gov/mmwr

Chabildas, N., Pennington, B. F., & Willicutt, E. G. (2001). A comparison of the neuropsychological profiles of the *DSM-IV* subtypes of ADHD. *Journal of Abnormal Child Psychology*, *29*, 529–540.

Cherkes-Julkowski, M., Stolzenberg, J., & Siegal, L. (1991). Prompted cognitive testing as a diagnostic compensation for attentional deficits: The Raven Standard Progressive Matrices and Attention Deficit Disorder. *Learning Disabilities*, *2*, 1–7.

Chess, S., & Thomas, A. (1986). *Temperament in clinical practice*. New York, NY: Guilford Press.

Clark, C., Prior, M., & Kinsella, G. J. (2000). Do executive function deficits differentiate between adolescents with ADHD and oppositional defiant/conduct disorder: A neuropsychological study using the Six Elements Test and the Hayling Sentence Completion Test. *Journal of Abnormal Child Psychology*, *28*, 403–414.

Cohen, N. J., Davine, M., & Meloche-Kelly, M. (1989). Prevalence of unsuspected language disorders in a child psychiatric population. *Journal of the American Academy of Child and Adolescent Psychiatry*, *28*, 107–111.

Cohen, N. J., Sullivan, S., Minde, K. K., Novak, C., & Helwig, C. (1981). Evaluation of the relative effectiveness of methylphenidate and cognitive behavior modification in the treatment of kindergarten-aged hyperactive children. *Journal of Abnormal Child Psychology*, *9*, 43–54.

Comings, D. E., Wu, S., & Chiu, C. (1996). Polygenic inheritance of Tourette syndrome, stuttering, Attention Deficit Hyperactivity, Conduct and Oppositional Defiant Disorder. *American Journal of Medical Genetics*, *67*, 264–288.

Conners, C. K. (1994). *Conners' Continuous Performance Test (Version 3.0)* [User's Manual]. Toronto, ON: Multi-Health Systems.

Conners, C. K. (1995). *Continuous Performance Test*. North Tonawanda, NY: Multi-Health Systems.

Conners, C. K. (1997). *Conners' Rating Scales* (rev. ed.). North Tonawanda, NY: Multi-Health Systems.

Cook, E. H., Jr., Stein, M. A., Krasowski, M. D., Cox, N. J., Olkon, D. M., Kieffer, J. E., & Leventhal, B. L. (1995). Association of attention deficit disorder and the dopamine transporter gene. *American Journal of Human Genetics*, *56*, 993–998.

Coolidge, F. L., Thede, L. L., & Young, S. E. (2000). Heritability and the comorbidity of attention deficit hyperactivity disorder with behavioral disorders and executive function deficits: A preliminary investigation. *Developmental Neuropsychology*, *17*, 273–287.

Crystal, D. S., Ostrander, R., Chen, R., & August, G. J. (2001). Multi-method assessment of psychopathology among *DSM-IV* subtypes of children with ADHD: Self, parent and teacher reports. *Journal of Abnormal Child Psychology, 29*, 189–205.

Cuffe, S. P., Moore, C. G., & Mckeown, R. E. (2005). Prevalence and correlates of ADHD symptoms in the National Health Interview Survey. *Journal of Attention Disorders, 9*(2), 392–401.

Daigneault, S., Braun, C. M. J., & Whitaker, H. A. (1992). An empirical test of two opposing theoretical models of prefrontal function. *Brain and Cognition, 19*, 48–71.

Dalsgaard, S., Mortenson, P., Frydenberg, M., & Thomsen, P. H. (2002). Conduct problems: Gender and adult psychiatric outcome of children with ADHD. *British Journal of Psychiatry, 181*, 416–421.

Douglas, V. I., Barr, R. G., O'Neil, M. E., & Britton, B. G. (1986). Short-term effects of methylphenidate on the cognitive, learning, and academic performance of children with attention deficit disorder in the laboratory and classroom. *Journal of Child Psychology and Psychiatry, 27*, 191–211.

DeFries, J. C., & Fulker, D. W. (1985). Multiple regression analysis of twin data. *Behavioral Genetics, 15*, 467–473.

DeFries, J. C., & Fulker, D. W. (1988). Multiple regression analysis of twin data: Etiology of deviant scores versus individual differences. *Acta Geneticae Medicae et Gemellologiae (Roma), 37*, 205–216.

Derks, E. M., Hudziak, J. J., & Boomsma, D. I. (2009). Genetics of ADHD, hyperactivity, and attention problems. In K. Yong-Kyu (Ed.), *Handbook of behavior genetics* (pp. 361–378). New York, NY: Springer Science + Business Media.

Devers, R., Bradley-Johnson, S., & Johnson, C. M. (1994). The effect of token reinforcement on WISC-R performance for fifth through ninth grade American Indians. *Psychological Record, 44*, 441–449.

Doyle, A. E., Biederman, J., & Seidman, L. J. (2000). Diagnostic efficacy of neuropsychological test scores for discriminating boys with and without ADHD. *Journal of Consulting and Clinical Psychology, 68*, 477–488.

Draeger, S., Prior, M., & Sanson, A. (1986). Visual and auditory attention performance in hyperactive children: Competence or compliance. *Journal of Abnormal Child Psychology, 14*, 411–424.

DuPaul, G. J. (1990). *Academic-performance Rating Scale and ADHD Rating Scale.* Worcester, MA: Department of Psychiatry, University of Massachusetts.

DuPaul, G. J., Anastopoulos, A. D., Shelton, T. L., Guevremont, D. C., & Metevia, L. (1992). Multimethod assessment of Attention-Deficit Hyperactivity Disorder: The diagnostic utility of clinic-based tests. *Journal of Clinical Child Psychology, 21*, 394–402.

DuPaul, G. J., Guevremont, D. C., & Barkley, R. A. (1991). Attention Deficit Hyperactivity Disorder in adolescence: Critical assessment parameters. *Clinical Psychological Review, 11*, 231–245.

DuPaul, G. J., McGoey, K. E., Eckert, T. L., & Van Brakle, J. V. (2001). Preschool children with ADHD: Impairments in behavioral, social and school functioning. *Journal of the American Academy of Child and Adolescent Psychiatry, 40*, 508–515.

DuPaul, G. J., Rutherford, L. E., & Hosterman, S. J. (2008). Attention-Deficit/ Hyperactivity Disorder. In R. J. Morris & N. Mather (Eds.), *Evidence-based interventions for students with learning and behavioral challenges* (pp. 33–58). New York, NY: Routledge/Taylor & Francis Group.

Eaves, L. J., Silberg, J. L., Hewitt, J. K., Meyer, J., Rutter, M., Simonoff, E., . . . Pickles, A. (1993). Genes, personality and psychopathology: A latent class analysis of liability to symptoms of Attention Deficit Hyperactivity Disorder in twins. In R. Plomin & G. McClean (Eds.), *Nature, nurture and psychology* (pp. 285–303). Washington, DC: American Psychological Association.

Ebstein, R. P., Novick, O., Umansky, R., Priel, B., Osher, Y., Blaine, D., . . . Belmaker, R. H. (1996). Dopamine D4 receptor (D4 DR) exon III polymorphism associated with the human personality trait of novelty seeking. *National Genetics, 12*, 78–80.

Edelbrock, C. (1990). *Childhood attention problems (CAP) scale.* In R. A. Barkley (Ed.), *Attention-Deficit Hyperactivity Disorder: A handbook for diagnosis and treatment* (pp. 320–321). New York, NY: Guilford Press.

Edelbrock, C., Rende, R., Plomin, R., & Thompson, L. A. (1995). A twin study of competence and problem behavior in childhood and early adolescence. *Journal of Psychology and Psychiatry, 36*, 775–785.

Eiraldi, R. B., Power, T. J., & Nezu, C. M. (1997). Patterns of comorbidity associated with subtypes of Attention Deficit/Hyperactivity Disorder among six-to-twelve year-old children. *Journal of the American Academy of Child and Adolescent Psychiatry, 36*, 503–514.

Elia, J., Ambrosini, P., & Berrettini, W. (2008). ADHD characteristics: I, Concurrent co-morbidity patterns in children & adolescents. *Child and Adolescent Psychiatry and Mental Health, 2.* doi:10.1186/1753-2000-2-15.

Elia, J., Arcos-Burgos, M., Bolton, K. L., Ambrosini, P. J., Berrettini, W., & Muenke, M. (2009). ADHD latent class clusters: *DSM-IV* subtypes and comorbidity. *Psychiatry Research, 170*, 192–198.

Ellis, A. W. (1985). The cognitive neuropsychology of development (and acquired) dyslexia: A critical survey. *Cognitive Neuropsychology, 2*, 169–205.

Evans, S. W., Pelham, W. E., Smith, B. H., Bukstein, O., Gnagy, E. M., Greiner, A. R., . . . Baron-Myak, C. (2001). Dose-response effects of methylphenidate on ecologically valid measures of academic performance and classroom behavior in adolescents with ADHD. *Experimental and Clinical Psychopharmacology, 9*, 163–175.

Faraone, S. V., & Biederman, J. (2005). What is the prevalence of adult ADHD? Results of a population screen of 966 adults. *Journal of Attention Disorders, 9*(2), 384–391.

Faraone, S. V., Biederman, J., Chen, W. J., Krifcher, B., Keenan, K., Moore, C., . . . Tsuang, M. (1992). Segregation analyses of Attention Deficit Hyperactivity Disorder. *Psychiatric Genetics, 2*, 257–275.

Faraone, S. V., Biederman, J., & Friedman, D. (2000). Validity of *DSM-IV* subtypes of Attention-Deficit/Hyperactivity Disorder: A family study perspective. *Journal of the American Academy of Child and Adolescent Psychiatry, 59*, 300–307.

Fergusson, D. M., & Horwood, L. J. (1992). Attention deficit and reading achievement. *Journal of Child Psychology and Psychiatry, 33*, 375–385.

Frazier, T. W., Youngstrom, E. A., Glutting, J. J., & Watkins, M. W. (2007). ADHD and achievement: Meta-analysis of the child, adolescent, and adult literatures and a concomitant study with college students. *Journal of Learning Disabilities, 40*, 49–65.

Gadow, K. D., Sprafkin, J., & Nolan, E. (2001). *DSM-IV* symptoms in community and clinic preschool children. *Journal of the American Academy of Child and Adolescent Psychiatry, 40*, 1383–1392.

Gallagher, R., Fleiss, K., Etkovich, J., Cousins, L., Greenfield, B., Martin, D., & Pollack, S. (2004). Social functioning in children with ADHD treated with long-term methylphenidate and multi-modal psychosocial treatment. *Journal of the American Academy of Child and Adolescent Psychiatry, 43*, 820–829.

Gentschel, D. A., & McLaughlin, T. F. (2000). Attention Deficit Hyperactivity Disorder as a social disability: Characteristics and suggested methods of treatment. *Journal of Developmental and Physical Disabilities, 12*, 333–347.

Geurts, H. M., & Embrechts, M. (2008). Language profiles in ASD, SLI, and ADHD. *Journal of Autism and Developmental Disorders, 38*, 1931–1943.

Geurts, H. M., Verte, S., Oosterlaan, J., Roeyers, H., & Sergeant, J. A. (2005). ADHD subtypes: Do they differ in their executive functioning profile? *Archives of Clinical Neuropsychology, 20*, 457–477.

Gillis, J. J., Gilger, J. W., Pennington, B. F., & DeFries, J. C. (1992). Attention Deficit Disorders in reading disabled twins: Evidence for a genetic etiology. *Journal of Abnormal Child Psychology, 20*, 303–315.

Glow, R. A., & Glow, P. H. (1980). Peer and self-rating: Children's perception of behavior relevant to hyperkinetic impulse disorder. *Journal of Abnormal Psychology, 8*, 471–490.

Goldstein, S. (1997). *Managing attention disorders in late adolescence and adulthood: A guide for practitioners*. New York, NY: Wiley.

Goldstein, S. (2002). Continuity of ADHD in adulthood: Hypothesis and theory meets reality. In S. Goldstein & A. T. Ellison (Eds.), *Clinician's guide to adult ADHD: Assessment and intervention*. New York, NY: Academic Press.

Goldstein, S., & Ellison, A. T. (2002). *Clinician's guide to adult ADHD: Assessment and intervention*. New York, NY: Academic Press.

Goldstein, S., & Goldstein, M. (1998). *Understanding and managing Attention Deficit Hyperactivity Disorder in children: A guide for practitioners* (2nd ed.). New York, NY: Wiley.

Goldstein, S., & Schwebach, A. (2005). Attention Deficit Disorder in adults. In S. Goldstein & C. Reynolds (Eds.), *Handbook of neurodevelopmental and genetic disorders in adults*. New York, NY: Guilford Press.

Goodman, R., & Stevenson, J. (1989). A twin study of hyperactivity: II, The aetiological role of genes, family relationships and perinatal activity. *Journal of Child Psychology and Psychiatry, 30,* 691–709.

Gordon, M. (1993). Do computerized measures of attention have a legitimate role in ADHD evaluations? *ADHD Report, 1,* 5–6.

Gordon, M. (1995). *How to own and operate an ADHD clinic.* DeWitt, NY: Gordon Systems.

Gordon, M., Antshel, K., Faraone, S., Barkley, R., Lewandowski, L., Hudziak, J., . . . Cunningham, C. (2006). Symptoms versus impairment: The case for respecting DSM-IV's Criterion D. *Journal of Attention Disorders, 9*(3), 465–475.

Greenberg, L. (1991). *Test of Variables of Attention (TOVA).* St. Paul, MN: Attention Technology.

Guevremont, D. C., DuPaul, G. J., & Barkley, R. A. (1993). Behavioral assessment of attention deficit hyperactivity disorder. In J. L. Matson (Ed.), *Handbook of hyperactivity in children.* Needham Heights, MA: Allyn & Bacon.

Hagerman, R. (1991). Organic causes of ADHD. *ADD-VANCE, 3,* 4–6.

Hall, S. J., Halperin, J. M., Schwartz, S. T., & Newcorn, J. H. (1997). Behavioral and executive functions in children with Attention Deficit Hyperactivity Disorder and reading disability. *Journal of Attention Disorders, 1,* 235–247.

Halperin, J. M., Newcorn, J. H., Matier, K., Sharma, V., McKay, K. E., & Schwartz, S. (1993). Discriminant validity of Attention-Deficit Hyperactivity Disorder. *Journal of the American Academy of Child and Adolescent Psychiatry, 32,* 1038–1043.

Harrier, L. K., & DeOrnellas, K. (2005). Performance of children diagnosed with ADHD on selected planning and reconstitution tests. *Applied Neuropsychology, 12,* 106–119.

Hart, C. C., & Harter, S. L. (2001, October 31–November 3). *Measurement of right frontal lobe functioning and ADHD.* Paper presented at the 21st Annual Meeting of the National Academy of Neuropsychology, San Francisco, CA.

Hechtman, L. (1993). Genetic and neurobiological aspects of Attention Deficit Hyperactivity Disorder: A review. *Journal of Psychiatric Neuroscience, 9,* 193–201.

Hill, G. P. (2000). A role for the speech-language pathologist in multidisciplinary assessment and treatment of Attention-Deficit/Hyperactivity Disorder. *Journal of Attention Disorders, 4,* 69–79.

Hill, J. C., & Schoener, E. P. (1996) Age-dependent decline of Attention Deficit Hyperactivity Disorder. *American Journal of Psychiatry, 153,* 1143–1146.

Hodgens, J., Cole, J., & Boldizar, J. (2000). Peer-based differences among boys with ADHD. *Journal of Clinical Child Psychology, 29,* 443–452.

Homack, S. R., & Reynolds, C. R. (2005). Continuous Performance Testing in differential diagnosis of ADHD. *ADHD Report, 13*(5), 5–9.

Ingersoll, B., & Goldstein, S. (1993). *Attention Deficit Disorder and Learning Disabilities: Myths, realities and controversial treatments.* New York, NY: Doubleday.

Kagan, J. (1964). The Matching Familiar Figures Test. Unpublished. Harvard University, Cambridge, MA.

Kaplan, B. J., Crawford, S. G., Dewey, D. M., & Fisher, G. C. (2000). The I.Q.'s of children with ADHD are normally distributed. *Journal of Learning Disabilities, 33*, 425–432.

Katz, M. (1997). *Playing a poor hand well*. New York, NY: Norton.

Klein, R. G. (1987). Pharmacotherapy of childhood hyperactivity: An update. In H. Y. Meltzer (Ed.), *Psychopharmacology: The third generation of progress* (pp. 1215–1224). New York, NY: Raven Press.

Lahey, B. B., Applegate, B., McBurnett, K., Biederman, J., Greenhill, L., Hyund, G., . . . Shaffer, D. (1994). *DSM-IV* field trial for attention deficit hyperactivity disorder in children and adolescents. *American Journal of Psychiatry, 151*, 1673–1685.

Lahey, B. B., Pelham, W. E., Loney, J., Kipp, H., Ehrhardt, A., Lee, S. S., . . . Massetti, G. (2004). Three-year predictive validity of *DSM-IV* attention deficit hyperactivity disorder in children diagnosed at 4–6 years of age. *American Journal of Psychiatry, 161*, 2014–2020.

Lahey, B. B., Pelham, W. E., Loney, J., Lee, S., & Willcutt, E. (2005). Instability of the *DSM-IV* subtypes of ADHD from preschool through elementary school. *Archives of General Psychiatry, 62*, 896–902.

LaHoste, G. J., Swanson, J. M., Wigal, S. B., Glabe, C., Wigal, T., King, N., & Kennedy, J. L. (1996). Dopamine D4 receptor gene polymorphism is associated with Attention Deficit Hyperactivity Disorder. *Molecular Psychiatry, 1*, 121–124.

Levine, M. D. (1992). Commentary: Attentional disorders: Elusive entities and their mistaken identities. *Journal of Child Neurology, 7*, 449–453.

Levy, F., Hay, D. A., McStephen, M., Wood, C., & Waldman, I. (1997). Attention-Deficit Hyperactivity Disorder: A category or a continuum? Genetic analysis of a large-scale twin study. *Journal of the American Academy of Child and Adolescent Psychiatry, 36*, 737–744.

Lowe, N., Kirley, A., Hawi, Z., Sham, P., Wickham, H., Kratochvil, C. J., . . . Gill, M. (2004). Joint analysis of the DRD5 marker concludes association with ADHD confined to the predominantly inattentive and combined subtypes. *American Journal of Human Genetics, 74*, 348–356.

Luk, S. L., Leung, P. W., & Yuen, J. (1991). Clinic observations in the assessment of pervasiveness of childhood hyperactivity. *Journal of Child Psychology and Psychiatry and Allied Disciplines, 32*, 833–850.

Mahone, E. M., & Wodka, E. L. (2008). The neurobiological profile of girls with ADHD. *Developmental Disabilities Research Reviews, 14*, 276–284.

Marshal, M. P., & Molina, B. S. G. (2006). Antisocial behaviors moderate the deviant peer pathway to substance use in children with ADHD. *Journal of Clinical Child and Adolescent Psychology, 35*, 216–226.

Mautner, V. F., Kluwe, L., Thakker, S. D., & Laerk, R. A. (2002). Treatment of ADHD in neurofibromatosis Type 1. *Developmental Medicine and Child Neurology, 44*, 164–170.

McGee, R. A., Clark, S. E., & Symons, D. K. (2000). Does the Conners' Continuous Performance Test aid in ADHD diagnosis? *Journal of Abnormal Child Psychology, 28*, 415–424.

McGee, R. A., & Share, D. L. (1988). Attention Deficit Disorder Hyperactivity and academic failure: Which comes first and what should be treated? *Journal of the American Academy of Child and Adolescent Psychiatry, 27,* 318–325.

McQuade, J. D., & Hoza, B. (2008). Peer problems in Attention Deficit Hyperactivity Disorder: Current status and future directions. *Developmental Disabilities Research Reviews, 14,* 320–324.

Medco Health Solutions. (2005). New research: ADHD medication use growing faster among adults than children (news release). Retrieved from http://phx.corporate-ir .net/phoenix.zhtml?c=131268&p=irol-newsArticle&ID=756843&highlight=

Milich, R. S., Balentine, A. C., & Lynam, D. R. (2001). ADHD Combined Type and ADHD predominantly Inattentive Type are distinct and unrelated disorders. *Clinical Psychology: Science and Practice, 8,* 463–488.

Milich, R. S., & Loney, J. (1979). The role of hyperactive and aggressive symptomatology in predicting adolescent outcome among hyperactive children. *Journal of Pediatric Psychology, 4,* 93–112.

Mirskey, A. F., Anthony, B. J., Duncan, C. C., Ahearn, M. B., & Kellam, S. G. (1991). Analysis of the elements of attention: A neuropsychological approach. *Neuropsychology Review, 2,* 109–145.

Murphy, K., Barkley, R., & Bush, T. (2002). Young adults with ADHD: Subtype differences in comorbidity, educational and clinical history. *Journal of Nervous and Mental Disease, 190,* 1–11.

Naglieri, J. A. (1999). *Essentials for CAS assessment.* New York, NY: Wiley.

Naglieri, J. A. (2000). Can profile analysis of ability test scores work? An illustration using the PASS theory and CAS with an unselected cohort. *School Psychology Quarterly, 15,* 419–433.

Naglieri, J. A., & Das, J. P. (1997). *Cognitive Assessment System.* Itasca, IL: Riverside.

Naglieri, J. A., & Das, J. P. (2006). Are intellectual processes important in the diagnosis and treatment of ADHD? *ADHD Report,14,* 1-6.

Naglieri, J. A., Goldstein, S., Delauder, B., & Schwebach, A. (2005). Relationships between the WISC-III and the Cognitive Assessment System with Conners' Rating Scales and Continuous Performance Tests. *Archives of Clinical Neuropsychology, 20,* 385–401.

Naglieri, J. A., Goldstein, S., & Schwebach, A. (2004). Can there be reliable identification of ADHD with divergent conceptualization and inconsistent test results? *ADHD Report, 12,* 6–9.

O'Neill, M. E., & Douglas, V. I. (1996). Rehearsal strategies and recall performance with boys with and without Attention Deficit Hyperactivity Disorder. *Journal of Pediatric Psychology, 21,* 73–88.

Paolito, A. W. (1999). Clinical validation of the Cognitive Assessment System for children with ADHD. *ADHD Report, 1,* 1–5.

Pelham, W. E. (1987). What do we know about the use and effects of CNS stimulants in ADD? In J. Loney (Ed.), *The young hyperactive child: Answers to questions about diagnosis, prognosis and treatment* (pp. 99–110). New York, NY: Haworth Press.

Pelham, W. E., & Bender, M. E. (1982). Peer relationships in hyperactive children. In K. D. Gadow & I. Bialer (Eds.), *Advances in learning and behavioral disabilities* (Vol. 1, pp. 365–436). Greenwich, CT: JAI.

Pelham, W. E., & Milich, R. (1984). Peer relations of children with hyperactivity/attention deficit disorder. *Journal of Learning Disabilities, 17,* 560–568.

Pelham, W. E., Jr., Fabiano, G. A., & Massetti, G. M. (2005). Evidence-based assessment of attention deficit hyperactivity disorder in children and adolescents. *Journal of Clinical Child and Adolescent Psychology, 34,* 449–476.

Perkins, C., Jr. (2008). Symptoms changes in ADHD found as children grow into adolescence. *Primary Psychiatry, 15,* 26.

Phelps, L., Brown, R. T., & Power, T. J. (2002). Externalizing disorders. In L. Phelps, R. T. Brown, & T. J. Power (Eds.), *Pediatric psychopharmacology: Combining medical and psychosocial interventions* (pp. 101–131). Washington, DC: American Psychological Association.

Purper-Ouakil, D., Wohl, M., Michel, G., Mouren, M. C., & Gorwood, P. (2004). Variations dans l'expression clinique du trouble déficit attentionnel/hyperactivité (TDAH): Rôle du contexte, du développement et de la comorbidité thymique. *L'Encéphale: Revue de psychiatrie clinique biologique et thérapeutique, 30,* 533–539.

Rapport, M. D., Timko, T. M., Jr., & Wolfe, R. (2006). Attention-Deficit/Hyperactivity Disorder. In M. Hersen (Ed.), *Clinician's handbook of child behavioral assessment* (pp. 401–435). San Diego, CA: Elsevier Academic Press.

Riccio, C. A., Reynolds, C. R., & Lowe, P. A. (2001). *Clinical applications of continuous performance tests: Measuring attention and impulsive responding in children and adults.* New York, NY: Wiley.

Rowland, A. S., Lesesne, C. A., & Abramowitz, A. J. (2002). The epidemiology of Attention-Deficit/Hyperactivity Disorder (ADHD): A public health view. *Mental Retardation and Developmental Disabilities Research Reviews, 8,* 162–170.

Rubinstein, S., Malone, M. A., Roberts, W., & Logan, W. J. (2006). Placebo-controlled study examining the effects of Selegiline in children with Attention-Deficit/Hyperactivity Disorder. *Journal of Child and Adolescent Psychopharmacology, 16,* 404–415.

Rutter, M., MacDonald, H., Lecoutier, A., Harrington, R., Bolton, P., & Bailey, A. (1990). Genetic factors in child psychiatric disorders: II, Empirical findings. *Journal of Child Psychology Psychiatry, 31,* 39–83.

Safer, D. J. (1973). A familia factor in minimal brain dysfunction. *Behavioral Genetica, 3,* 175–186.

Satterfield, J. H., Hoppe, C. M., & Schell, A. M. (1982). A perspective study of delinquency in 110 adolescent boys with Attention Deficit Disorder and 88 normal adolescent boys. *American Journal of Psychiatry, 139,* 795–798.

Schmitz, M., Cadore, L., Paczko, M., Kipper, L., Chaves, M., Rohde, L. A., . . . Knijnik, M. (2002). Neuropsychological performance in *DSM–IV* ADHD subtypes: An exploratory study with untreated adolescents. *Canadian Journal of Psychiatry, 47,* 863–869.

Seidman, L. J., Biederman, J., Faraone, S. V., Weber, W., Mennin, D., & Jones, J. (1997). A pilot study of neuropsychological functioning in girls with ADHD. *Journal of the American Academy of Child and Adolescent Psychiatry, 36,* 366–373.

Semrud-Clikeman, M., Steingard, R. J., Filipek, P., Biederman, J., Bekken, K., & Renshaw, P. F. (2000). Using MRI to examine brain-behavior relationships in males with attention deficit disorder with hyperactivity. *Journal of the American Academy of Child and Adolescent Psychiatry, 39,* 477–484.

Sherman, D. K., Iacono, W. G., & McGue, M. K. (1997). Attention-Deficit Hyperactivity Disorder dimensions: A twin study of inattention and impulsivity-hyperactivity. *Journal of the American Academy of Child and Adolescent Psychiatry, 36,* 745–753.

Shure, M. (1994). *Raising a Thinking Child.* New York, NY: Henry Holt.

Silverthorn, P., Frick, P. J., Kuper, K., & Ott, J. (1996). Attention Deficit Hyperactivity Disorder and sex: A test of two etiological models to explain the male predominance. *Journal of Clinical Child Psychology, 25,* 52–59.

Stawicki, J. A., Nigg, J. T., & van Eye, A. (2006). Family psychiatric history evidence on the nosological relations of *DSM-IV* ADHD combined and inattentive subtypes: New data and meta-analysis. *Journal of Child Psychology and Psychiatry, 47,* 935–945.

Stein, M. (1997). We have tried everything and nothing works: Family-centered pediatrics and clinical problem solving. *Journal of Developmental and Behavioral Pediatrics, 18,* 114–119.

Stevenson, J. (1992). Evidence for genetic etiology in hyperactivity in children. *Behavior Genetics, 22,* 337–344.

Stott, D. H. (1981). Behavior disturbance and failure to learn: A study of cause and effect. *Educational Research, 23,* 163–172.

Swanson, J. M., Flodman, P., Kennedy, J., Spence, M. A., Moyzis, R., Schuck, S., . . . Posner, M. (2000). Dopamine genes and ADHD. *Neuroscience and Biobehavioral Reviews, 24,* 21–25.

Szatmari, P., Offord, D. R., Siegel, L. S., Finlayson, M. A., & L. Tuff. (1990). The clinical significance of neurocognitive impairments among children with psychiatric disorders: Diagnosis and situational specificity. *Journal of Child Psychology and Psychiatry, 31,* 287–299.

Tarver-Behring, S., Barkley, R. A., & Karlsson, J. (1985). The mother-child interactions of hyperactive boys and their normal siblings. *American Journal of Orthopsychiatry, 355,* 202–209.

Teeter, P. A. (1998). *Interventions for ADHD: Treatment in developmental context*. New York, NY: Guilford Press.

Teglasi, H., Cohn, A., & Meshbesher, N. (2004). Temperament and learning disability. *Learning Disability Quarterly, 27*, 9–20.

Terestman, N. (1980). Mood quality and intensity in nursery school children as predictors of behavior disorder. *American Journal of Orthopsychiatry, 50*, 125–138.

Thapar, A., Hervas, A., & McGuffin, P. (1995). Childhood hyperactivity scores are highly heritable and show siblings competition effects: Twin study evidence. *Behavioral Genetica, 35*, 537–544.

Thomas, A., & Chess, S. (1977). *Temperament and development*. New York, NY: Brunner/Mazel.

Ullmann, R. K., Sleator, E. K., & Sprague, R. K. (1988). *ADD-H: Comprehensive Teacher's Rating Scale* (2nd ed.). Champaign, IL: MetriTech.

Vaidya, C. J., Bunge, S. A., Dudukovic, N. M., Zalecki, C. A., Elliott, G. R., & Gabrieli, J. D. (2005). Altered neurosubstraits of cognitive control and childhood ADHD: Evidence from functional magnetic resonance imaging. *American Journal of Psychiatry, 162*, 1605–1613.

van Lier, P. A., van der Ende, J., Koot, H. M., & Verhulst, F. C. (2007). Which better predicts conduct problems? The relationship of trajectories of conduct problems with ODD and ADHD symptoms from childhood into adolescence. *Journal of Child Psychology and Psychiatry, 48*, 601–608.

Voeller, K. S. (1991). Towards a neurobiologic nosology of attention deficit hyperactivity disorder. *Journal of Child Neurology, 6*, S2–S8.

Volkow, N. D., Wang, G., Fowler, J. S., Logan, J., Gerasimov, M., Maynard, L., . . . Franceschi, D. (2001). Therapeutic doses of oral methylphenidate significantly increase extra cellular dopamine in the human brain. *Journal of Neuroscience, 21*, 1–5.

Wåhlstedt, C., Thorell, L. B., & Bohlin, G. (2009). Heterogeneity in ADHD: Neuropsychological pathways, comorbidity and symptoms domains. *Journal of Abnormal Child Psychology, 37*, 551–564.

Warren, R. P., Odell, J. D., Warren, L. W., Burger, R. A., Maciulis, A., Daniels, W. W., & Torres, A. R. (1995). Reading disability, Attention-Deficit Hyperactivity Disorder and the immune system. *Science, 268*, 786–787.

Weiss, G., & Hechtman, L. (1979). The hyperactive child syndrome. *Science, 205*, 1348–1354.

Wender, P. H. (1975). The minimal brain dysfunction syndrome. *Annual Review of Medicine, 26*, 45–62.

West, A. E., Schenkel, L. S., & Pavuluri, M. N. (2008). Early childhood temperament in pediatric Bipolar Disorder and Attention Deficit Hyperactivity Disorder. *Journal of Clinical Psychology, 64*, 402–421.

Whalen, C. K., & Henker, B. (1991). Therapies for hyperactive children: Comparisons, combinations and compromises. *Journal of Consulting and Clinical Psychology, 59*, 126–137.

Whalen, C. K., Henker, B., Collins, B., McAuliffe, S., & Vaux, A. (1979). Peer interaction in a structured communication task: Comparisons of normal and hyperactive boys and of methylphenidate (Ritalin) and placebo effects. *Child Development, 50*, 388–401.

Willcutt, E. G., & Pennington, B. F. (2000). Comorbidity of reading disability and attention-deficit/hyperactivity disorder: Differences by gender and subtype. *Journal of Learning Disabilities, 33*, 179–191.

Willerman, L. (1973). Activity level and hyperactivity in twins. *Child Development, 44*, 288–293.

Winsberg, B. G., & Comings, D. E. (1999). Association of the dopamine transported gene (DAT1) with poor methylphenidate response. *Journal of the American Academy of Child and Adolescent Psychiatry, 38*, 1474–1477.

Woo, B. S. C., & Rey, J. M. (2005). The validity of the *DSM-IV* subtypes of Attention-Deficit/Hyperactivity Disorder. *Australian and New Zealand Journal of Psychiatry, 39*, 344–353.

Young, S., Chadwick, O., Heptinstall, E., Taylor, E., & Sonuga-Barke, E. J. S. (2005). The adolescent outcome of hyperactive girls. *European Child and Adolescent Psychiatry, 14*, 245–254.

Zahn-Waxler, C., Schmitz, S., Fulker, D., Robinson, J. & Emde, R. (1996). Behavior problems in five-year-old monozygotic and dizygotic twins: Genetic and environmental influences, patterns of regulation, and internationalization of control. *Developmental Psychopathology, 8*, 103–122.

Zametkin, A. J., Nordahl, T. E., & Gross, M. (1990). Cerebral glucose metabolism adults with hyperactivity in childhood onset. *Archives of General Psychiatry, 50*, 333–340.

Zametkin, A. J., & Rapoport, J. L. (1987). Neurobiology of attention deficit disorder with hyperactivity: Where have we come in 50 years? *Journal of American Academy of Child and Adolescent Psychiatry, 26*, 676–686.

Zentall, S. S. (1984). Context effects in the behavioral ratings of hyperactivity. *Journal of Abnormal Child Psychology 12*, 345–352.

Zimmer, L. (2009). Positron emission tomography neuroimaging for a better understanding of the biology of ADHD. *Neuropharmacology, 57*, 601–607.

CHAPTER

4

Adults with Learning Disabilities: Barriers and Progress

Noel Gregg

ADULTS WITH LEARNING DISABILITIES: BARRIERS AND PROGRESS

The adult population with Learning Disabilities (LD) represents the largest categories of individuals with disabilities at secondary and postsecondary institutions (Gregg, 2009). Approximately two-thirds of those receiving special education services in secondary schools are identified as demonstrating LD (Newman, 2006). Historically, professionals have given far less attention to the adult population with LD than to younger children. Most funding initiatives, for example, were directed toward elementary school-age students with the faulty assumption that early identification would minimize the need for services as such individuals entered adulthood. However, recently federal agencies signaled a change related to the importance placed on funding research specific to the adult population, particularly agencies such as the National Institute for Child Health and Development, the National Institute for Literacy, and the Office of Vocational and Adult Education. For example, in 2001, these three agencies published a research solicitation committing a total of $18.5 million over the 5-year period from 2002 to 2006 ($3.7 million per year) to support adult literacy research (Miller, McCardle, & Hernandez, 2010). Substantial funding opportunities continue, as noted by the Adult Basic and Literacy Education State Grants currently receiving substantial resources directed toward increasing adult literacy (www2.ed.gov/about/offices/list/ovae/index.html). Thus, attention is being redirected from primarily focusing on the prevention of illiteracy to ways in which literacy proficiency can be enhanced once individuals experiencing low literacy are outside the K–12 education system.

This chapter provides a panoramic view of the outcome data specific to the adult population with LD at postsecondary institutions (i.e., school and work) as a means to inform future research and policy. Information was synthesized in this chapter by using outcome data from large-scale surveys, research literature, and learning from program evaluations or technical reports. The chapter does not include the perceptions elicited by professionals directly working with adults and/or individuals with LD. Such an omission does represent a limitation to the findings in this chapter. Outcome data specific to adult learning proficiencies and practices are the focus of the chapter. Evidence pertaining to specific perceptions, attitudes, or cognitive processing research will not be addressed. These questions provide the framework for interpreting the evidence presented throughout this chapter:

- What demographics define the adult population with LD?
- What does the risk and resilience research inform us about adults with LD?
- What do we know about the career and workforce outcomes of the adults with LD?
- What do we know about literacy proficiency and the adult population with LD?
- What do we know about accommodating environments for adults with LD?
- How does technology accommodate learning and work outcomes for the adult population with LD?

DEFINING AND DESCRIBING THE ADULT POPULATION WITH LD

LD is a condition that by definition defines an adult as having a developmental disorder in learning as compared to age-expected behaviors and requires evidence that an individual is substantially limited in major life activities (Gregg, 2009). However, as Barkley (2006) suggests when discussing the developmental disorder of Attention-Deficit/Hyperactivity Disorder (ADHD), (a) the symptoms are not "static pathological states or absolute deficits in formerly typical functioning" (p. 265), and (b) the symptoms must be determined by "age-relative thresholds" (p. 265). Social/emotional, cognitive, language, and achievement abilities influence individual learning differently across the life span, and the recognition of age-specific markers is critical to reliable and valid diagnostic decision making appropriate for the adult population (Gregg, 2009).

The diagnostic criteria professionals set in determining the severity thresholds for symptoms, history, and behaviors (emotional, cognitive, and achievement) for the adult population are not mandated by law; therefore, policies vary significantly across institutions and/or agencies (Gregg, 2009). The two most common practices applied by professionals in identifying severity levels are discrepancies across performance and cutoff standards. These eligibility criteria are central to the policies and practices that provide access to services and/or accommodations. Therefore, the prevalence rate for the adult population with LD varies as a function of different eligibility criteria set by the policies and practices of agencies. For instance, the U.S. Employment and Training

Administration (1991) estimated the incidence of adults with LD among Job Training Partnership Act recipients to be 15% to 23% percent (Corley & Taymens, 2002). According to Corley and Taymens (2002), 10% to 50% of individuals participating in adult education programs experience LD. The prevalence figures for the college-bound population with LD are reported to be approximately 3% to 5% of student enrollment (U.S. Department of Education, National Center for Educational Statistics [NCES], 2006). Due to variability in eligibility criteria, the adult population with LD represents a very heterogeneous group of individuals in relation to severity, ability, and background. This fact is important to keep in mind when drawing inferences pertaining to adult outcomes.

Results from the National Longitudinal Transitional Survey-2 (NLTS-2; Wagner, Newman, Cameto, Garza, & Levine, 2005) capture the profile of secondary students with LD transitioning to postsecondary settings. The NLTS-2 outcome data provide evidence that students with LD enrolled in secondary schools demonstrate significantly lower literacy skills as compared to peers with LD. Wagner and colleagues found that over 50% of secondary students with LD performed below the 16th percentile on reading comprehension measures. Ineffective secondary curricula, poverty, and lack of student-adult connections have been identified as significant contributors to such dismal outcomes (Morocco, Aguilar, Clay, Brigham, & Zigmond, 2006).

Not surprisingly, the high school dropout rate for adolescents with LD is 2 to 3 times more than their peers (U.S. General Accounting Office, 2003; Young & Browning, 2005). Transition-to-college figures are equally dismal for the adult population with LD. Only one-tenth the rate of the general population without disabilities enrolls in postsecondary education or training (Stodden, Jones, & Chang, 2002; Wagner et al., 2005; Young & Browning, 2005). In addition, the adult population with LD is 20% to 60% more likely to access welfare programs (Burgstahler, 2003; Young & Browning, 2005) and serves time in correctional institutions at significantly elevated rates (Burrell & Warboys, 2000; Christle, Jolivette, & Nelson, 2000; National Council on Disability, 2003; Stenhjem, 2005).

Socioeconomic status (SES) presents a major barrier to successful postsecondary transition for individuals with LD (Gregg, 2007, 2009). We know that SES remains the most significant predictor of occupational aspirations and postsecondary transitional status (Rojewski & Kim, 2003). Postsecondary career attainment is highly correlated with "systematic patterns of educational placement and social expectations" that remains indirectly a function of SES (Rojewski & Kim, 2003, p. 106). Evidence is clear that youth with LD from low-income households perform less well academically than their peers with or without disabilities, separate from race/ethnicity (Rojewski & Kim, 2003). Outcome data from the NLTS-2 illustrate that students with LD from households with low incomes ($25,000 or less per year) score significantly lower on achievement measures than youth from moderate-income households (those earning $25,000 to $75,000 per year). For instance, Wagner et al. (2005) note that a "low-income Hispanic youth with disabilities is likely to score 15 points lower on reading comprehension measures than a White peer from a moderate-income household, holding other factors in the analysis constant" (p. 48).

The relationship of race or ethnic differences to academic performance continues to receive little attention by research or policy makers interested in the adolescent or adult population (Gregg, 2007; C. Murray & Naranjo, 2008). Yet there is strong evidence that African American and Hispanic students with LD are less likely to have access to postsecondary learning environments (Wagner et al., 2005). In addition, White youth with LD score significantly higher on academic performance measures than their peers with LD who are African American or Hispanic (Wagner et al., 2005). Investigation of the direct and indirect relationship among SES, race, and ethnic differences is a critical research agenda that policy makers and researchers need to address in greater breadth and depth than currently is available in the literature.

Researchers continue to provide empirical-based evidence for the disparity across genders in LD identification practices among the adult population, with females more often underrepresented (Gregg, 2009; Vogel, 1990). Therefore, the potential is greater for females to have access to accommodations and/or services necessary for success at postsecondary learning or work environments less often. However, the NLTS-2 outcome data did provide some interesting findings related to employment trends among young women. Evidence from their follow-up studies indicate that more females with LD in 2003 (a 16-percentage-point increase) were engaging in school, work, or preparation for work after graduating from high school as compared to their cohorts in 1987 (Wagner et al., 2005). Despite such a positive finding, an increasing number of males (87%) as compared to females (79%) earned above-minimum wages.

RISK AND RESILIENCE OUTCOMES

Researchers investigating the internal and external risk factors that predict individual outcomes provide important evidence to better understanding educational and employment outcomes. Masten (2001) defines resilience as "a class of phenomena characterized by good outcomes in spite of serious threat to adaptation or development" (p. 228). As noted by Gregg (2007), however, risk factors can be arbitrarily labeled, contributing to inverse relationships. As an example, a milder type of LD (causal factor) might produce less academic stress (risk), provide greater access to higher education (risk), and allow for more professional advancements (access). Again, any conclusions drawn about adults with LD must factor into the decision making heterogeneity of the population.

Follow-up and follow-along research studies of adults with LD provide a window of opportunity by which to observe the influence of living with a disability. However, as noted by Gregg (2009), the definitions and eligibility criteria used in the childhood identification of the participants across this body of research often are not consistent with today's policies and practices. The majority of follow-up studies focused on the adult population with LD include participants who are primarily Caucasian and male, from middle- to upper-middle-class families that were referred to clinics for learning problems (Bruck, 1992; Fink, 1998; Gerber, Ginsberg, & Reiff, 1992; Rogan & Hartman, 1990; Sitlington & Frank, 1990; Spekman, Goldberg, & Herman, 1992; Vogel & Adelman, 1992; Vogel, Hruby, & Adelman, 1993). Therefore, it is again important to recognize the limitations of this literature due to the heterogeneity of the population of adults with LD.

Researchers focusing on the resilience of adults with LD have depended primarily on qualitative and descriptive methodologies in measuring success. For instance, Spekman et al. (1992) and Goldberg, Higgins, Raskind, and Herman (2003) identified three factors that differentiated successful adults with LD from unsuccessful adults with LD using the Frostig Center data:

1. Successful adults adapted to life events through self-awareness and acceptance of their LD, were proactive and persevering, and were able to demonstrate emotional stability and the ability to tolerate stress.
2. Successful adults were able to set appropriate goals and become goal directed.
3. Successful adults were able to establish and use effective support systems.

Gerber et al. (1992) studied 71 adults with LD identified as "successful." They grouped factors of resilience into two categories: *internal decisions* and *external manifestations* (p. 99). *Internal decisions* were comprised of desire, goal orientation, and reframing. *External manifestations* were seen as persistence, goodness of fit, learned creativity, and social ecologies (p. 99). Gerber et al. suggested that success was the result of an interactive process rooted in the individual's ability to take control through the interplay of internal and external factors.

Based on an extensive review of empirical evidence, Masten (2001) identifies the specific global factors that are significantly related to resilience in the general population. She includes these factors: positive relationship with caring adults, cognitive and self-regulation skills, positive self-concept, and motivation. Using Masten's empirically based risk and resilience factors, Gregg (2009) reviewed the literature in an attempt to provide a more comprehensive understanding of resilience for the adolescent and adult population with LD. As noted in Table 4.1, positive relationships with caring adults (e.g., mentors, parents) appears to be one of the primary protective factors while self-regulation (i.e., temperament, self-efficacy, self-concept, motivation) is more of an indirect risk for success. Despite qualitative and descriptive evidence that risk and resilience factors are critical to learning, very little empirically based research is available specific to the relationship of these indicators to the performance of the adult population with LD.

Table 4.1 Risk and Resilience Research

Factors	Research	Summary
Positive Relationships with Caring Adults		
Mentors	Gerber et al., 1992	Protective factor
	Reiff, Gerber, & Ginsberg, 1997	
	Spekman et al., 1992	
	Werner, 1993	
Parents	Cosden, Brown, & Eliott, 2002	Protective factor
	Reynolds, 1999	
	Rothman & Cosden, 1995	
	Wong, 2003	
Self-Regulation		
Temperament	McNamara, Willoughby,	Indirect risk
	Chalmers, & Cura, 2005	
Self-efficacy	Klassen, 2007	
social	Hampton & Mason, 2003	
academic	Hoza, Gerdes, et al., 2004	
Self-concept	Hoza, Pelham, Dobbs, Owens,	
	& Pillow, 2004	
Motivation	Bear, Minke, Griffin, & Deemer, 1998	
	Butler, 1998	
	Hoza, Pelham, Waschbusch, Kipp, & Owens, 2001	
	Hoza, Waschbusch, Pelham, Molina, & Milich, 2000	
	McNamara et al., 2005	
	McPhail & Stone, 1995	
	Rubin, McCoach, McGuire, & Reis, 2003	
	C. A. Stone & May, 2002	

Comorbidity

The diagnosis of LD places an adult at a greater risk for other coexisting psychiatric and/or developmental disorders (Gregg, 2009). In a meta-analysis of research on the prevalence and cause and effects of diagnostic psychiatric disorders among children and adolescents, Angold, Costello, and Erkanli (1999) suggest: "There is little evidence that any one disorder directly causes any other disorder, but it is likely that some homotypic comorbid patterns (depression with dysthymia and Obsessive Compulsive Disorder with Conduct Disorder [OCD]) represent developmental sequences of unitary underlying developmental psycho-pathologic process (at least in some individuals)" (p. 78). The three most common comorbid disorders reported in the adult population with LD include ADHD, anxiety, and depression (Gregg, 2009). However, with each of these disorders, identification of comorbidity is dependent on the eligibility criteria used by the researcher. There is no evidence that ADHD, anxiety, or depression leads to an LD diagnosis or that LD leads to other comorbid conditions (Angold et al., 1999; Gregg, 2009; Nelson & Gregg, in press).

The majority of researchers investigating the relationship of anxiety and depression to the adult population with LD have utilized college populations (Gregg, 2009; Nelson & Gregg, in press). As mentioned earlier, to make inferences for all adults with LD across the very different subgroups (e.g., severity, type, educational experience) is troubling and leads to inaccurate conclusions. College students with LD are but one subset of the larger population of adults. We know that only two-thirds of high school graduates in the general population even attend college (U.S. Department of Education, 2006). Relative to their peers with or without LD, far fewer high school students with LD attend college (Gregg, 2009). For example, results from the NLTS-2 indicated that only 1 in 10 high school students with LD attend 4-year colleges (Wagner et al., 2005). Therefore, we can conclude that college students with LD are small subpopulations of the much larger general population of adults with these disorders. What is lacking in the literature is empirical evidence to determine whether college students with LD are more likely to possess better coping skills, higher cognitive abilities, and greater academic success as compared to non-college adults with LD. Although we have empirical evidence that college populations with ADHD utilize different types of coping skills than their peers without LD, research specific to individuals with LD is not as available in the literature (Glutting, Youngstrom, & Watkins, 2005; Rabiner, Anastopoulos, Costello, Hoyle, & Swartzweldr, 2008). Therefore, college students with LD may possess specific characteristics that differ from the general population of adults with LD, particularly in relation to disorders such as anxiety, depression, and/or ADHD.

There is an extreme paucity of research specific to the relationship between anxiety and depression specific to the adult population with LD. Hoy et al. (1997) and Carroll and Iles (2006) found that college students with LD reported more symptoms of anxiety than college students without LD; however, Riddick, Sterling, Farmer, and Morgan (1999) failed to find such differences. Nelson and Gregg (in press) located only two studies in which adults with LD were compared to a non-LD control group. Both Hoy et al. (1997) and Mattek and Wierzbicki (1998) found that the two groups did not significantly differ on measures of self-reported depressive symptoms. The lack of research evidence specific to the incidence of depression or anxiety and the adult population with LD is troubling.

Career and Workforce Outcomes

Adult literacy proficiency exerts a significant influence on economic indicators. As much as 55% of long-term differences in the growth rate of gross domestic product per capita and productivity growth at the national and international level are influenced by a country's adult literacy rates (T. S. Murray et al., 2009). Researchers have provided evidence that adults with higher literacy skills work more, experience less unemployment, earn more, spend less time unemployed, and rely less on government support (Green & Riddell, 2007; Osberg, 2000). Higher literacy levels of workers positively influence the success of firms as they integrate communication tools and technologies at a greater rate in the workplace (Educational Testing Service, 2003; T. S. Murray & McCracken, 2008). In addition, a strong relationship exists between literacy and adult health, including the probability of illness, length of recovery, and age at death (Kutner, Greenberg, Jin, & Paulsen, 2006; T. S. Murray et al., 2009; Rudd, Kirsch, & Yamamoto, 2004). Literacy proficiency correlates very highly to the social and economic growth of a country. Providing adequate literacy interventions and accommodations for this population is likely to become more important as the global knowledge economy grows (Gregg, 2009).

Employment statistics suggest that adults with LD appear to function equal to their peers in obtaining jobs upon graduation from high school (Wagner et al., 2005). However, since no comprehensive study of employment outcomes for adults with LD has been conducted, the outcome data we have are based primarily on personal and professional experience (Gregg, 2009; Young & Browning, 2005). Adults with LD primarily take semiskilled and usually part-time jobs (Wagner et al., 2005). According to Wagner's research, although 86% of young adults with LD earn more than minimum wage, only about 36% of them work full time. In addition, she noted that there was no real change in earnings for youth with LD from the original National Longitudinal Transitional Study (NLTS, 1987) and the second study (NLTS-2; Wagner et al., 2005), even when wages were adjusted for inflation. The most disturbing fact is that the majority of these individuals earn less than the federal poverty threshold (U.S. Census Bureau, 2004). The low literacy level demonstrated by a significant number of adults suggests a negative influence for their postsecondary success in learning or employment (Day & Newburger, 2002; Wagner et al., 2005).

The nature of an adolescent's susceptibility to career-related risks varies as to the type and severity of LD. Little attention has been directed toward the career development needs of transitioning adolescents with LD, particularly the workbound population (Rojewski & Kim, 2003). Several career-related barriers that have been associated with LD include social stigma (Stone, Stone, & Dipboye, 1992), employment discrimination (Unger, 2001), inadequate academic and vocational training (Ochs & Roessler, 2001), and poor self-efficacy and lower career aspirations (Fabian & Liesener, 2005; Rojewski & Yang, 1997). Several researchers have argued strongly that educators have as much responsibility for students who are at risk of dropping out of school or go to work directly after high school graduation as those bound for a 4-year college or university (Gray & Herr, 2006; Rojewski & Gregg, in press).

Literacy Outcomes

As noted earlier, a significant number of adults with LD demonstrate literacy proficiencies that seriously interfere with their success in today's learning and work environment (Bruck, 1992; Gregg, 2009; Shaywitz et al., 2003). As part of the NLTS-2, students with LD were administered assessments in reading, mathematics, science, and social studies using six subtests from the Woodcock-Johnson III (Woodcock, McGrew, & Mather, 2001). Across the academic areas, between 30% and 60% of students with LD performed below a standard score of 85. The largest noted area of underachievement for this population was in the area of reading.

Additional documentation of the low literacy proficiencies for the adult population with LD can be found in the large-scale adult literacy assessments. For instance, the National Assessment for Adult Literacy (NAAL; Kutner, Greenberg, & Baer, 2005) found that approximately 30 million Americans are estimated to perform at below basic prose literacy levels. Approximately 22% of the NAAL population performing below the basic prose levels demonstrated multiple disabilities (e.g., psychological and LD), and of that group, 2% to 4% demonstrated only LD. High school data from the National Assessment of Education Progress provide similar findings: Over a quarter of 12th grade students perform at below basic levels in reading and/or writing near the end of high school (NCES, 2007). Quantitative literacy is also systematically evaluated every few years through several large-scale adult self-report literacy assessments (NAAL; Kutner et al., 2007) and the International Adult Literacy and Lifeskills Survey. An outcome from many of these large-scale, self-report surveys is the recognition of the importance of literacy competencies for success in the workplace. Researchers provide evidence for the strong correlation between literacy and a successful employment history (Kutner et al., 2005; Liming & Wolf, 2009).

Instructional and Testing Accommodation Outcomes

Sociocultural theory continues to contribute to our understanding of the literacy proficiency of adults with LD, particularly in the area of accommodating learning and testing situations. According to Vygotsky (1993, 1998), a dialectic relationship exists between an individual's primary and secondary disabilities (Kozulin & Gindis, 2007). An individual's *primary learning disability* refers to the cognitive processing deficits interfering with literacy tasks while the *secondary disability* refers to the cognitive and social consequences of the disorder. When discussing disabilities, Vygotsky emphasized the role of social mediation and the acquisition of symbolic tools to accommodate learning (1993, 1998). He encouraged professionals to acquire alternative but essentially equivalent roads for acquiring meaning. Although Vygotsky used the term "compensatory strategies," today we refer to them as "accommodations."

Accommodations adjust the manner in which learning or testing situations are presented and/or evaluated so that individuals can either access or demonstrate knowledge in a fair and equitable fashion. Several published literature reviews specific to the adolescent and adult population provide empirical evidence as to the effectiveness of specific accommodations for accessing literacy (Cahalan-Laitusis, 2003; Chi & Pearson, 1999; Gregg, 2009; Gregg, & Nelson, in press; Johnstone, Altman, Thurlow, & Thompson, 2006; McArthur, 2006; Sireci, Li, & Scarpati, 2003; Thompson, Blount, & Thurlow, 2002; Tindal & Fuchs, 1999; Tindal, Heath, Hollenbeck, Almond, & Harniss, 1998; Tindal & Ketterlin-Geller, 2004).

In addition, Vygotsky (1993, 1999) encouraged the construction of more supportive learning contexts and actually advocated for the inclusion of all individuals with disabilities in school and work environments. The concept of universal design (UD) is the most recent movement to provide all individuals equal access to learning. The UD concept was created to reflect the approach of proactively including accessible design features while minimizing the need for individually retrofitted accommodations in learning and work environments (Gregg, 2009). Through the evolution of UD, additional design concepts including universal design for learning, universal design for instruction, and universal design for testing are receiving more attention by researchers. At this time, research surrounding universal design for testing has the most empirically based evidence for the principles of UD (Cohen, Gregg, & Deng, 2005; Johnstone, Thompson, Bottsford-Miller, & Thurlow, 2008).

Accommodating adults with LD is common practice across instructional, testing, and work settings. However, very little empirically based literature is available to support or reject the effectiveness of many of the accommodations for this population. Empirically based research specific to the accommodation of instruction and employment settings is significantly underrepresented in the literature. In an extensive review of the literature, Gregg (2009) found no empirically based studies in which work accommodations were even investigated specific to the adolescent or adult population with LD. She found that the effectiveness of instructional accommodations was represented by only 7 reading studies, 10 writing studies, and 1 mathematics study. Although testing accommodation research predominates in the literature, Gregg found only 31 studies specific to the adolescent or adult population with LD. Of these 31 studies, 57% were specific to the postsecondary entrance exams. The homogeneity of the participants across these studies does not accurately represent the heterogeneity of the adolescent and adult population with LD. Therefore, generalizing the results of the test accommodation literature to specific subgroups of the adolescent and adult population with LD (e.g., gender, race, ability level, educational level) must be done with great caution (Gregg, 2009).

As mentioned previously, the accommodation studied most often among the adolescent and adult population with LD is extended time. Gregg and Nelson recently completed a meta-analysis of studies comparing scores of adolescents and adults with and without LD on accommodated tests (Gregg & Nelson, in press). The literature is lacking in quantity of studies, restricted in types of design methodologies, and underrepresentative of the diversity of individuals demonstrating the disorder. After a thorough review of the literature, they found only 9 studies in which adequate empirical data were available to be included in their meta-analysis. A most interesting finding of the Gregg and Nelson study was the lack of detailed descriptive information about the participants in these studies. Only 1 of the 9 studies they identified reported any substantive (i.e., ability and achievement current functioning) or topical marker variables (i.e., cognitive processing current functioning) for the populations investigated. Only 3 studies reported the type of eligibility criteria used to operationalize LD. Therefore, the generalizability to the adult population with LD findings is questionable.

Technology Outcomes

For many adults with LD, low literacy proficiency presents a negative impact on postsecondary work and educational outcomes. Therefore, UD solutions that provide these individuals digital media options for alternative means of accessing print become critical in both the educational and the work environment. However, very little empirically based research is available to measure the effectiveness of technology accommodations and/or UD solutions for the adult population with LD (Gregg, 2009, in press).

Traditionally, assistive technologies (AT) have been seen as central to the solution for helping individuals with LD access learning, but there is a growing awareness that AT may not be enough in the world of work and education (Gregg, 2009). According to Silver-Pacuila and Reder (2008), "it is the interaction among the learner's skills, the opportunities they encounter, and the supports available that determines threshold levels of literacy and language proficiency" (p. 4). On the NAAL, adult technology users with LD were more likely to have higher literacy scores (Pacuila & Reder, 2008).

However, many adults with LD report that using technology in learning or work environments can pose a challenge. These individuals are often unfamiliar with the skills and strategies needed for reading in open learning environments (e.g., Internet). Professionals working with adult learners with LD must become better at empowering these individuals with knowledge—for example, providing on-site and virtual training modules; offering hands-on direct instruction; providing access to today's tools for success, such as digital audio players (iPods), audio digital recorders, and AT software; ensuring availability of resources and materials (including print materials in digital format); and developing technical and learning supports via online portals necessary to access information in real time (Gregg, in press). Too often, adults with LD have to be satisfied with parallel reading experiences (i.e., read-only when the material is in an accessible medium, which may be available at a much later time), precluding equal competitive opportunities in postsecondary learning or work environments (Gregg & Banerjee, 2009). In other words, although accessibility might exist in some settings, it is often neither efficient nor effective.

Electronic text (e-text) is fast becoming the medium by which a large percentage of our society with or without print disabilities reads. One can buy an e-text of a book, newspaper, or magazine and have it delivered wirelessly to a laptop or handheld device in less than 1 minute at little to no cost (Gregg, 2009). However, e-text is not accessible for many adults with LD unless it is used in conjunction with a product like text-to-speech (TTS) software. A technology software accommodation that holds great promise for adults with LD is embedded e-text supports. Such supports are embedded in e-text used along with additional software: online notebook (notational resource), TTS and links to definitions, highlighting, and text summaries. A growing body of research is providing strong validation for the effectiveness of embedded supports in enhancing reading for adolescents and adults with LD (Anderson-Inman, 2004; Anderson-Inman & Horney, 2007; Anderson-Inman, Horney, Chen, & Lewin, 1994; Horney & Anderson-Inman, 1994, 1999). The utilization of embedded e-text solutions at the postsecondary level—for learning or work—has received less attention.

Another important feature of e-text for adults with LD is its portability. Digital files can be downloaded via e-mail or Internet portals and used in a variety of learning environments. Current advancements in TTS technology allow books and PDF files to be easily downloaded to computers or MP3 players, to then be read through specialized TTS software. In addition, speech-to-text (STT) technology, using such devices as digital recorders (e.g., Belkin audio recorders), provides a tool for adolescents or adults to instantly record their ideas or messages, which can then be downloaded into handheld devices that read information back to them.

Mobile phones are becoming the most dominant communication medium (Gregg, 2009). More than half the population owns cell phones (more than 3.3 billion wireless users worldwide), as compared to 1.6 billion who own televisions (Gregg, 2009). For adults with LD, the phone is fast providing the most comprehensive accommodation tool for managing the literature tasks facing them in the world of learning or work. The implications for the learning and work environments are just beginning to receive attention by researchers.

FUTURE DIRECTIONS

In the past, research specific to the adult population with LD has drawn very heavily from the K–12 frameworks guiding learning and assessment. The lack of cognitive and achievement models that account for adult learning is a contributing factor to the rather dismal outcome research reported throughout this chapter (Miller et al., 2010). Adults with LD engage in literacy across multiple domains, with a range of environments, and for multiple purposes (Alvermann & Xu, 2003; Blackburn, 2005; Cowan, 2004; Fisher, 2007; Hicks, 2004; Hull & Schultz, 2001; Jocson, 2008; Knobel, 1999; Lewis & Fabos, 2005; Mahiri & Sablo, 1996; Moje, 2000, 2008; Moll, 1994; Morrell & Duncan-Andrade, 2003; Noll, 1998). Researchers involved in better understanding the population with LD have not given a great deal of attention to out-of-school learning practices. This is a critical omission since adults with LD remind us that successful literacy practice in a school context may be considered ineffective in other environments (e.g., employment). It is not clear what the relationship between postsecondary literacy proficiencies/skills are and social and/or economic success. Moje and Luke (2009) noted that individuals with reading difficulties often diminish the value of the various kinds of reading they do on a regular basis, assuming it not to count as reading or failing to see themselves as readers.

The research surrounding community-based and after-school programs for media-intensive and arts-based instruction also has implications for the adolescent and adult population with LD (e.g., Buckingham, 2003; Eccles & Gootman, 2002; Soep & Chavez, 2005). Often drawing on popular cultural forms, including music, film, and digital media, such programs include literacy-related skills and practices by immersing participants in language-rich and multimodal activities. They often are conceptualized as providing alternative educational spaces where adolescents and/or adults with LD who are alienated from school can find reentry points to reenage with learning. Research that has compared individuals who participate in these programs with their nonaffiliated peers has suggested superior academic and social performance (Hull, Kenney, Marple, & Forsman-Schneider, 2006).

Considerable attention has also highlighted the critical need to increase the number of U.S. citizens pursuing science, technology, engineering, and mathematics (STEM) careers in order for adults to remain competitive in our global economy. As noted by Friedman (2005) in his best-selling book *The World Is Flat: A Brief History of the Twenty-First Century*, "We are not producing, in this country, in America, enough young people going into science, technology, and engineering—the fields that are going to be essential for entrepreneurship and innovation in the 21st century" (p. 23). The National Science Board (2004) has also stressed the need "to improve success in science and engineering study by American undergraduates from all demographic groups" (p. 23). In addition, the National Science Foundation reports (NSF; 1996, 2000, 2004) encourage critical attention toward strengthening efforts for recruiting and retaining chronically underrepresented populations into STEM fields. We know that adolescents and adults with LD are among the most marginalized of these groups (Gregg, 2009; Wolanin & Steele, 2004) and face significant obstacles and barriers to accessing higher education STEM programs (Burgstahler, 2003; NSF, 2000). However, very little attention has been directed by researchers and policy makers toward understanding the barriers faced by adult learners accessing STEM courses and job situations (Gregg, 2009).

Enhancing greater collaboration and pathways between secondary and postsecondary institutions is one means toward providing greater options for increasing the STEM learning and employment opportunities for the adult population with LD (Gregg, 2007). Models need to be developed and validated that will strengthen the capacities for individuals with LD to access and succeed in STEM programs across critical junctures: high school to work; high school to 2-year college; 4-year college to graduate school; postsecondary graduation to careers. To increase participation and retention in STEM fields, service models at the secondary and postsecondary will need to be innovative and integrate a variety of options, such as virtual mentoring and training, in-person mentoring, social networking, video analysis of student and faculty performance, and learning communities (student and professional). In addition, professionals teaching at secondary and postsecondary institutions will be required to increase evidence-based STEM learning competencies specific to learning motivation, use of prior knowledge, intellectual engagement, use of evidence, and sense making (Heck, Banilower, & Rosenberg, 2008).

Virtual worlds provide a platform by which an increasing number of adults with LD can have the opportunity to access knowledge, supports, and interventions both in their school or employment settings. Virtual worlds have shown significant promise for mentoring and teaching (Bruckman, 1998; Turkay, 2008). Research on virtual reality has demonstrated that people identify with their avatars and transfer positive experiences to them (Bailenson & Fox, 2009), which in turn increases motivation, engagement, self-efficacy, and social skills (Holden, Bearison, Rode, Rosenberg, & Fishman, 1999; Kizelshteyn, 2008). Electronic mentoring that can be located in virtual environments also has great potential for the adult population situated across multiple literacy domains and environments (e.g., learning or employment). A mentoring island could be developed by an institution or agency that would serve individuals with disabilities. It could provide a realistic way for busy adults with LD to receive guidance on accommodations, cope with their disability issues, navigate transition points, locate and use school or work resources, build meaningful relationships, and engage in communication with key stakeholders. The design of the virtual world should follow best practices in UD and AT for virtual environments. Unfortunately, Gregg (2007) notes that in response to negative postsecondary outcomes for the adolescent and adult population, many "professionals continue to overrely on past directives that divert thinking and resources away from unique solutions for change" (p. 219). Equity to access learning and employment opportunities for the adult population with LD is going to require greater use of novel and innovative solutions.

Another factor contributing to the dismal learning and employment outcomes discussed throughout this chapter for the adult population with LD might rest with the research methodologies frequently used for interpreting findings. The empirical evidence provided by a great deal of research related to adults with LD should be called into question by professionals concerned that traditional research designs do not always address the complex, multivariate, and multilevel complexity of learning and instruction, particularly out-of-school learning. To better address the efficacy of learning, some professionals have encouraged greater use of design research. Design research methodologies require intensive and long-term collaboration involving both researchers and practitioners integrating both qualitative and quantitative data. Such research designs are iterative, interventionist, and theory oriented (Cobb, Confrey, diSessa, Lehrer, & Schauble, 2003). Examples of design research endeavors are well represented across the fields of literacy, mathematics, science, and technology (Hoadley, 2005; Hull et al., 2006; Moje et al., 2004; Steffe & Thompson, 2000). However, design research methodologies have been utilized very infrequently by researchers investigating the learning, social, and employment settings adults with LD participate in on a daily basis.

Adults with LD represent a diverse population in ability and experience and in the context in which they learn and work on a daily basis. Solutions to improve school and employment outcomes will require collaborative and unique systems developed by business and government resources. Social contexts change over time, requiring practices and policies to be adjusted accordingly (Gregg, 2007). The information throughout this chapter has highlighted the dismal school- and work-related demographics for adults with LD. Economic and political forces are modifying and often limiting available resources as well as requiring different accountability structures for providing services. The solutions for enhancing more positive school and employment outcomes for the population with LD will require innovative thinking across constituencies within the current and future world contexts.

REFERENCES

Alvermann, D. E., & Xu, S. H. (2003). Children's everyday literacies: Intersections of popular culture and language arts instruction. *Language Arts, 81*(2), 145–155.

Anderson-Inman, L. (2004). Reading on the Web: Making the most of digital text. *Wisconsin State Reading Association Journal, 4,* 8–14.

Anderson-Inman, L., & Horney, M. A. (2007). Supported eText: Assistive technology through text transformations. *Reading Research & Practice, 14,* 153–160.

Anderson- Inman, L., Horney, M. A., Chen, D., & Lewin, L. (1994, April). Hypertext literacy: Observations from the ElectroText Project. *Language Arts, 71,* 37–45.

Angold, A., Costello, E. J., & Erkanli, A. (1999). Comorbidity. *Journal of Child Psychiatry, 40*(1), 57–87.

Bailenson, J. N., & Fox, J. (2009). Virtual self-modeling: The effects of vicarious reinforcement and identification on exercise behaviors. *Media Psychology, 12,* 1–25.

Barkley, R. A. (2006). *Attention-deficit hyperactivity disorder: A handbook for diagnosis and treatment* (3rd ed.). New York, NY: Guilford Press.

Bear, G. G., Minke, K. M., Griffin, S. M., & Deemer, S. A. (1998). Achievement related developmental differences. *Journal of Learning Disabilities, 31,* 91–104.

Blackburn, M. V. (2005). Agency in borderland discourses: Examining language use in a community center with Black queer youth. *Teachers College Record, 107*(1), 89–113.

Bruck, M. (1992). Persistence of dyslexics' phonological awareness deficits. *Developmental Psychology, 28,* 874–886.

Bruckman, A. (1998). Community support for constructionist learning. *Computer Supported Cooperative Work (CSCW): The Journal of Collaborative Computing, 7,* 47–86. Retrieved from http://www.cc.gatech.edu/~asb/papers/cscw.html.

Buckingham, D. (2003). *Media education: Literacy, learning, and culture.* Cambridge, MA: Polity.

Burgstahler, S. (2003). *DO-IT: Helping students with disabilities transition to college and careers.* Minneapolis, MN: University of Minnesota, National Center on Secondary Education and Transition. Retrieved from http://www.ncset.org/publications/viewdesc.asp?id=1168

Burrell, S., & Warboys, L. (2000, July). *Special education and the juvenile justice system.* Washington, DC: Office of Juvenile Justice and Delinquency Prevention. Retrieved from http://www.ncjrs.org/html/ojjdp/2000_6_5/contents.html

Butler, D. (1998). Metacognition and learning disabilities. In B. Y. L. Wong (Ed.), *Learning about learning disabilities* (2nd ed., pp. 277–307). San Diego, CA: Academic Press.

Cahalan-Laitusis, C. (2003). *Accommodations on high-stakes writing tests for students with disabilities.* Retrieved from http://www.ets.org/Media/Research/pdf/RR-04-13.pdf

Carroll, J. M., & Iles, J. E. (2006). An assessment of anxiety levels in dyslexic students in higher education. *British Journal of Educational Psychiatry, 76,* 651–662.

Chi, C. W. T., & Pearson, P. D. (1999, June). *Synthesizing the effects of test accommodations for special education and limited English proficient students.* Paper presented at the National Conference on Large Scale Assessment, Snowbird, UT.

Christle, C. A., Jolivette, K., & Nelson, C. M. (2000). *Youth aggression and violence: Risk, resilience, and prevention.* Arlington, VA: Education Resources Information Center (ERIC) Clearinghouse on Disabilities and Gifted Education. Retrieved from http://www.ericdigests.org/2001-4/youth.html

Cobb, P., Confrey, J., diSessa, A., Lehrer, R., & Schauble, L. (2003). Design experiments in educational research. *Educational Researcher, 32*(1), 9–13.

Cohen, A., Gregg, N., Deng, M. (2005). The role of extended time and item content on a high-stakes mathematics test. *Journal of Learning Disabilities Research & Practice, 20*, 225–233.

Corley, M. A., & Taymans, J. (2002). Adults with learning disabilities: A review of the literature. In the National Center for the Study of Adult Learning and Literacy (Ed.), *The annual review of adult learning and literacy* (Vol. 3, pp. 44–83). Hoboken, NJ: Wiley. Retrieved from http://www.ncsall.net/?id=568

Cosden, M., Brown, C., & Eliott, K. (2002). Development of self-understanding and self-esteem in children and adults with learning disabilities. In B. Y. L. Wong & M. Donahue (Eds.), *Social dimensions of learning disabilities* (pp. 33–51). Mahwah, NJ: Erlbaum.

Cowan, P. (2004). Devils or angels: Literacy and discourse in lowrider culture. In J. Mahiri (Ed.), *What they don't learn in school: Literacy in the lives of urban youth* (pp. 47–74). Oxford, United Kingdom: Peter Lang.

Day, J., & Newburger, E. (2002). *The big payoff: Educational attainment and synthetic estimate of work-life earnings. Current Population Reports No.* P23–210. Washington, DC: U.S. Census Bureau.

Eccles, J., & Gootman, J. (Eds.). (2002). *Community programs to promote youth development.* Washington, DC: National Academic Press.

Educational Testing Service (ETS). (2003). *Digital transformation: A framework for ICT literacy.* Princeton, NJ: Author.

Fabian, E. S., & Liesener, J. J. (2005). Promoting the career potential of youth with disabilities. In S. D. Brown & R. W. Lent (Eds.), *Career development and counseling: Putting theory and research to work* (pp. 551–572). Hoboken, NJ: Wiley.

Fink, R. (1998). Literacy development in successful men and women with dyslexia. *Annals of Dyslexia, 48*, 311–347.

Fisher, M. T. (2007). *Writing in rhythm: Spoken word poetry in urban classrooms.* New York, NY: Teachers College Press.

Friedman, M. (2005). *The world is flat: A brief history of the twenty-first century.* New York, NY: Farrar, Straus, & Giroux.

Gerber, P. J., Ginsberg, R., & Reiff, H. B. (1992). Identifying alterable patterns in employment success for highly successful adults with learning disabilities. *Journal of Learning Disabilities, 25*, 475–487.

Glutting, J. J., Youngstrom, E. A., & Watkins, M. W. (2005). ADHD and college students: Exploratory and confirmatory factor structures with student and parent data. *Psychological Assessment, 17*, 44–55.

Goldberg, R. J., Higgins, E. L., Raskind, M. H., & Herman, K. L. (2003). Predictors of success in individuals with learning disabilities: A qualitative analysis of a 20-year longitudinal study. *Learning Disabilities Research & Practice, 18*(4), 222–236.

Gray, K. C., & Herr, E. L. (2006). *Other ways to win: Creating alternatives for high school graduates* (3rd ed.). New York, NY: Corwin.

Green, D. A., & Riddell, C., (2007). *Literacy and the labor market: The generation of literacy and its impact on earning and statistics*. Ottawa, Canada: Human Resources and Skills Development Canada (HRSDC).

Gregg, N. (2007). Underserved and unprepared: Postsecondary learning disabilities. *Learning Disabilities Research & Practice, 22*, 219–228. doi: 10.1111/j.1540-5826.2007.00250.

Gregg, N. (2009). *Adolescents and adults with learning disabilities and ADHD: Assessment and accommodation*. New York, NY: Guilford Press.

Gregg, N. (in press). Increasing access to learning for the adult basic education learner with learning disabilities: Evidence-based accommodation research. *Journal of Learning Disabilities*.

Gregg, N., & Banerjee, M. (2009). Reading comprehension solutions for college students with dyslexia in an era of technology. In G. Reid (Ed.), *Dyslexia: A handbook for research and practice* (pp. 32–60). New York, NY: Routledge.

Gregg, N., & Nelson, J. (in press). A meta-analysis of the test accommodation research specific to adolescents and adults with LD. *Journal of Learning Disabilities*.

Hampton, N. Z., & Mason, E. (2003). Learning disabilities, gender, sources of efficacy, self-efficacy beliefs, and academic achievement in high school students. *Journal of School Psychology, 41*, 101–112.

Heck, D., Banilower, E. R., & Rosenberg, S. (2008). Studying the effects of professional development: The case of the NSF's local systemic change through teacher enhancement initiative. *Journal for Research in Mathematics Education, 39*, 113–152.

Hicks, D. (2004). Growing up girl in working-poor America: Textures of language, poverty, and place. *ETHOS, 32*(2), 214–232.

Hoadley, C. M. (2005). Design-based research methods and theory building: A case study of research with *SpeakEasy*. *Educational Technology, 45*(10), 42–47.

Holden, G., Bearison, D. J., Rode, D. C., Rosenberg, G., & Fishman, M. (1999). Evaluating the effects of a virtual environment (STARBRIGHT World) with hospitalized children. *Research on Social Work Practice, 9*, 365.

Horney, M. A., & Anderson-Inman, L. (1994). The ElectroText Project: Hypertext reading patterns of middle school students. *Journal of Educational Multimedia and Hypermedia, 3*, 71–91.

Horney, M. A., & Anderson-Inman, L. (1999). Supported text in electronic reading environments. *Reading and Writing Quarterly, 15*, 127–168.

Hoy, C., Gregg, N., Wisenbaker, J., Bonham, S., King, M., & Moreland, C. (1996). Clinical model versus discrepancy model in determining eligibility for learning disabilities services at a rehabilitation setting. In N. Gregg, C. Hoy, & A. Gay (Eds.), *Adults with learning disabilities: Theoretical and practical perspectives* (pp. 55–67). New York, NY: Guilford Press.

Hoza, B., Gerdes, A. C., Hinshaw, S. P., Arnold, L. E., Pelham, W. E., Molina, B. S., . . . Wigal, T. (2004). Self-perceptions of competence in children with ADHD and comparison children. *Journal of Consulting and Clinical Psychology, 72*, 382–391.

Hoza, B., Pelham, W. E., Dobbs, J., Owens, J. S., & Pillow, D. R. (2002). Do boys with Attention-Deficit/Hyperactivity Disorder have positive illusory self concepts? *Journal of Abnormal Psychology, 111*, 268–278.

Hoza, B., Pelham, W. E., Waschbusch, D. A., Kipp, H., & Owens, J. S. (2001). Academic task persistence of normally achieving ADHD and control boys: Performance, self-evaluations and attributions. *Journal of Consulting and Clinical Psychology, 69*, 281–283.

Hoza, B., Waschbusch, D. A., Pelham, W. E., Molina, B. S. G., & Milich, R. (2000). Attention-Deficit/Hyperactivity Disordered and control boys' responses to social success and failure. *Child Development, 71*, 432–446.

Hull, G., Kenney, N., Marple, S., & Forsman-Schneider, A. (2006). *Many versions of masculine: Explorations of boys' identity formation through multimodal composing in an after-school program.* Robert F. Bowne Foundation's Occasional Papers Series. New York, NY: Robert F. Bowne Foundation.

Hull, G., & Schultz, K. (2001). Literacy and learning out of school: A review of theory and research. *Review of Educational Research, 71*(4), 575–611.

Jocson, K. M. (2008). *Youth poets: Empowering literacies in and out of schools.* New York, NY: Peter Lang.

Johnstone, C. J., Altman, J., Thurlow, M. L., & Thompson, S. J. (2006). *A summary of research on the effects of test accommodations: 2002 through 2004* (Technical Report 45). Minneapolis, MN: University of Minnesota, National Center on Educational Outcomes. Retrieved from http://education.umn.edu/NCEO/OnlinePubs/Tech45/

Johnstone, C. J., Thompson, S. J., Bottsford-Miller, N. S., & Thurlow, M. L. (2008). Universal design and multimethod approaches to item review. *Educational Measurement: Issues and Practice, 27*, 25–36.

Kizelshteyn, M. (2008). Therapy and the metaverse. *Washington University Undergraduate Research Digest, 4*, 17–26. Retrieved from http://www.turtlethink.com/WUURD%202008_Kizelshteyn.pdf

Klassen, R. M. (2007). Using predictions to learn about the self-efficacy of early adolescents with and without learning disabilities. *Contemporary Educational Psychology, 32*, 173–187.

Knobel, M. (1999). *Everyday literacies.* New York, NY: Peter Lang.

Kozulin, A., & Gindis, B. (2007). Sociocultural theory and education of children with special needs. In H. Daniels, M. Cole, and J. Wertsch (Eds.), *The Cambridge companion to Vygotsky* (pp. 332–362). New York, NY: Cambridge University Press.

Kutner, M., Greenberg, E., & Baer, J. (2005). *National Assessment of Adult Literacy (NAAL): A first look at the literacy of America's adults in the 21st century* (NCES 2006–470). Washington, DC: U.S. Department of Education, National Center for Education Statistics. Retrieved from http://nces.ed.gov/NAAL/PDF/2006470.PDF

Kutner, M., Greenberg, E., Jin, Y., Boyle, B., Hsu, Y., Dunleavy, E., & White, S. (2007). *Literacy in everyday life: Results from the 2003 National Assessment of Adult*

Literacy (NCES 2007–480). Washington, DC: U.S. Department of Education, National Center for Education Statistics.

Kutner, M., Greenberg, E., Jin, Y., & Paulsen, C. (2006). *The health literacy of American adults: Results from the 2003 National Assessment of Adult Literacy* (NCES 2006–483). Washington, DC: U.S. Department of Education, National Center for Education Statistics. Retrieved from http://nces.ed.gov/Pubs2007/2007480.pdf

Lackaye, T., Margalit, Z., & Zinman, T. (2006). Comparisons of self-efficacy, mood, effort, and hope between students with learning disabilities and their non-LD-matched peers. *Learning Disabilities Research & Practice, 21*(2), 111–121.

Lewis, C., & Fabos, B. (2005). Instant messaging, literacies, and social identities. *Reading Research Quarterly, 40*(4), 470–501.

Liming, D., & Wolf, M. (2008, Fall). Job outlook by education, 2006-16. *Occupational Outlook Quarterly, 52*(3), 2–29.

MacArthur, C. A. (2006). The effects of new technologies on writing and writing processes. In C. A. MacArthur, S. Graham, & J. Fitzgerald (Eds.), *Handbook of writing research* (pp. 248–262). New York, NY: Guilford Press.

Mahiri, J., & Sablo, S. (1996). Writing for their lives: The non-school literacy of California. *Journal of Negro Education, 65*(2), 164–180.

Masten, A. S. (2001). Ordinary magic: Resilience processes in development. *American Psychologist, 56*(3), 227–238.

Mattek, P. W., & Wierzbicki, M. (1998). Cognitive and behavioral correlates of depression in learning disabled and non-learning disabled adult students. *Journal of Clinical Psychology, 54*, 831–837.

McNamara, J. K., Willoughby, T., Chalmers, H., & Cura, Y. L. C. (2005). Psychosocial status of adolescents with learning disabilities with and without comorbid attention deficit hyperactivity disorders. *Learning Disabilities Research & Practice, 20*(4), 234–244.

McPhail, J. C., & Stone, C. A. (1995). The self-concept of adolescents with learning disabilities: A review of the literature and a call for theoretical elaboration. In T. E. Scruggs & M. A. Mastropieri (Eds.), *Advances in learning and behavioral disabilities* (Vol. 9, pp. 193–226). Greenwich, CT: JAI Press.

Miller, B., McCardle, P., & Hernandez, R. (2010). Advances and remaining challenges in adult literacy research. *Journal of Learning Disabilities, 43*(2), 101–107.

Moje, E. B. (2000).Youth cultures, literacies, and identities in and out of school. In J. Flood, S. B. Heath, & D. Lapp (Eds.), *Handbook of research in teaching the communicative and visual arts* (pp. 207–219). Mahwah, NJ: Erlbaum.

Moje, E. B. (2008). Foregrounding the disciplines in secondary literacy teaching and learning: A call for change. *Journal of Adolescent and Adult Literacy, 52*(2), 96–107.

Moje, E. B., Ciechanowski, K. M., Kramer, K. E., Ellis, L. M., Carrillo, R., & Collazo, T. (2004). Working toward third space in content area literacy: An examination of everyday funds of knowledge and discourse. *Reading Research Quarterly, 39*(1), 38–71.

Moje, E. B., & Luke, A. (2009). Literacy and identity: Examining the metaphors in history and contemporary research. *Reading Research Quarterly, 44*(4), 415–437.

Moje, E. B., Peek-Brown, D., Sutherland, L. M., Marx, R. W., Blumenfeld, P., & Krajcik, J. (2004). Explaining explanations: Developing scientific literacy in middle-school project-based science reforms. In D. Strickland & D. E. Alvermann (Eds.), *Bridging the gap: Improving literacy learning for preadolescent and adolescent learners in grades 4–12* (pp. 227–251). New York, NY: Carnegie Corporation.

Moll, L. C. (1994). Literacy research in community and classrooms: A sociocultural approach. In R. B. Ruddell, M. R. Ruddell, & H. Singer (Eds.), *Theoretical models and processes of reading* (4th ed., pp. 179–207). Newark, DE: International Reading Association.

Morocco, C. C., Aguilar, C. M., Clay, K., Brigham, N., & Zigmond, N. (2006). Good high schools for students with disabilities: Introduction to the special issue. *Learning Disabilities Research & Practice, 21*(3), 135–145.

Morrell, E., & Duncan-Andrade, J. (2003). What they do learn in school: Hip-hop as a bridge to canonical poetry. In J. Mahiri (Ed.), *What they don't learn in school: Literacy in the lives of urban youth* (pp. 247–268). New York, NY: Peter Lang.

Murray, C., & Naranjo, J. (2008). Poor, Black, learning disabled, and graduating: An investigation of factors and processes associated with school completion among high-risk urban youth. *Remedial and Special Education, 29*(3), 145–160.

Murray, T. S., & McCracken, M. (2008). *The economic benefits of literacy: Theory, evidence, and implications for public policy.* Ottawa, Canada: Canadian Council and the Canadian Language and Literacy Network.

Murray, T. S., McCracken, M., Willms, D., Jones, S., Shillington, R., & Stucken, J. (2009). *Addressing Canada's literacy challenge: A cost-benefit analysis.* Ottawa, Canada: DataAngel.

National Center for Education Statistics (NCES). (2007, May). The condition of education 2007 in brief. Retrieved from www.nces.ed.gov/programs/coe

National Council on Disability. (2003, May). *Addressing the needs of youth with disabilities in the juvenile justice system: The current status of evidence-based research.* Washington, DC: Author. Retrieved from http://www.ncd.gov/newsroom/publications/2003/juvenile.htm

National Science Foundation (NSF). (1996). *Shaping the future: New expectations for Undergraduate education in science, mathematics, engineering, and technology* (NSF 96–139). Washington, DC: Government Printing Office.

National Science Foundation. (2000). *Land of plenty: Diversity as America's competitive edge in science, engineering and technology.* Arlington, VA: Author.

National Science Foundation. (2006). *Women, minorities, and persons with disabilities in science and engineering* (NSF 04–317). Arlington, VA: Author. Retrieved from http://www.nsf.gov/statistics/wmpd/

Nelson, J. M., & Gregg, N. (in press). Depression and Anxiety Among Transitioning Adolescents and College Students with ADHD, Dyslexia, or Comorbid ADHD/Dyslexia. *Journal of Learning Disabilities.*

Newman, L. (2006, July). *Facts from NLTS2: General education participation and academic performance of students with learning disabilities*. Menlo Park, CA: SRI International. Retrieved from http://ies.ed.gov/ncser/pubs/20063001/index.asp

Noll, E. (1998). Experiencing literacy in and out of school: Case studies of two American Indian youths [Sioux Indians]. *Journal of Literacy Research, 30*(2), 205–232.

Ochs, L., & Roessler, R. T. (2001). Students with disabilities: How ready are they for the 21st century? *Rehabilitation Counseling Bulletin, 49*, 775–781.

Osberg, L. (2000). *Schooling, literacy and individual earnings*. Ottawa, Canada: Statistics Canada and Human Resources Development Canada.

Rabiner, D. L., Anastopoulos, A. D., Costello, J., Hoyle, R. H., & Swartzweldr, H. S. (2008). Adjustment to college in students with ADHD. *Journal of Attention Disorders, 11*, 680–699.

Reiff, H. B., Gerber, P. J., & Ginsberg, R. (1997). *Exceeding expectations: Highly successful adults with learning disabilities*. Austin: TX: PRO-ED.

Reynolds, A. W. (1999). *High risk college students with emotional disorders as well as learning disabilities*. Unpublished doctoral dissertation, University of Georgia, Athens, GA.

Riddick, B., Sterling, C., Farmer, M., & Morgan, S. (1999). Self-esteem and anxiety in the educational histories of adult dyslexic students. *Dyslexia, 5*, 222–248.

Rogan, L. L., & Hartman, L. D. (1990). Adult outcome of learning disabled students ten years after initial follow-up. *Learning Disabilities Focus, 5*, 91–102.

Rojewski, J. W., & Gregg, N. (in press). Career choice patterns and behavior of work-bound youth with disabilities. In J. Kauffman & D. Hallahan (Eds.), *Handbook of special education*. New York, NY: Routledge.

Rojewski, J. W., & Kim, H. (2003). Career choice patterns and behavior of work-bound youth during early adolescence. *Journal of Career Development, 30*, 89–108.

Rojewski, J. W., & Yang, B. (1997). Longitudinal analysis of select influences on adolescents' occupational aspirations. *Journal of Vocational Behavior, 51*, 375–410. doi: 10.1006/jvbe.1996.1561.

Rothman, H., & Cosden, M. (1995). The relationship between self-perception of a learning disability and achievement, self-concept, and social support. *Learning Disability Quarterly, 18*, 203–221.

Rubin, L. M., McCoach, B., McGuire, J. M., & Reis, S. M. (2003). The differential impact of academic self-regulatory methods on academic achievement among university students with and without learning disabilities. *Journal of Learning Disabilities, 36*, 270–286.

Rudd, R., Kirsch, I., & Yamoto, K. (2004). *Literacy and health in America*. Princeton, NJ: ETS.

Shaywitz, S. E., Shaywitz, B. A., Fulbright, R. K., Skudlarksi, P., Mencl, W. E., Constable, R. T., . . . Gore, J. C. (2003). Neural systems for compensation and persistence: Young adult outcome of childhood reading disability. *Society of Biological Psychiatry, 54,* 25–33.

Silver-Pacuila, H., & Reder, S. (2008). *Investigating the language and literacy skills required for independent on-line learning.* Washington, DC: National Institute for Literacy.

Sireci, S. G., Li, S., & Scarpati, S. (2003). *The effects of test accommodations on test performance: A review of the literature* (Center for Education Assessment Research Report No. 485). Amherst, MA: School of Education, University of Massachusetts, Amherst.

Sitlington, P. L., & Frank, A. R. (1990). Are adolescents with learning disabilities successfully crossing the bridge into adult life? *Learning Disability Quarterly, 13,* 17–111.

Soep, E., & Chavez, V. (2005). Youth radio and the pedagogy of collegiality. *Harvard Educational Review, 75*(4), 409–434.

Spekman, N. J. , Goldberg, R. J., & Herman, K. L. (1992). Learning disabled children grow up: A search for factors related to success in the young adult years. *Learning Disabilities Research & Practice, 7,* 161–170.

Stenhjem, P. (2005, February). *Youth with disabilities in the juvenile justice system: Prevention and intervention strategies.* Minneapolis, MN: University of Minnesota, National Center on Secondary Education and Transition. Retrieved from http://www.ncset.org/publications/viewdesc.asp?id=1929

Steffe, L. P., & Thompson, P. W. (2000). Teaching experiment methodology: Underlying principles and essential elements. In R. Lesh & A. E. Kelly (Eds.), *Research design in mathematics and science education* (pp. 267–307). Hillsdale, NJ: Erlbaum.

Stodden, R., Jones, M., & Chang, K. (2002). *Services, supports and accommodations for individuals with disabilities: An analysis across secondary education, postsecondary education, and employment* (White Paper). Manoa, HI: University of Hawaii, Postoutcomes Network of the National Center on Secondary Education and Transition. Retrieved from http://www.ncset.hawaii.edu/publications/pdf/services_supports.pdf

Stone, C. A., & May, A. L. (2002). The accuracy of academic self-evaluations in adolescents with learning disabilities. *Journal of Learning Disabilities, 35*(4), 370–383.

Stone, E. F., Stone, D. L., & Dipboye, R. L. (1992). Stigmas in organizations: Race, handicaps, and physical unattractiveness. In K. Kelly (Ed.), *Issues, theory, and research in industrial and organizational psychology* (pp. 385–457). New York, NY: Elsevier Science.

Thompson, S., Blount, A., & Thurlow, M. (2002). *A summary of research on the effects of test accommodations: 1999 through 2001* (Technical Report 34). Minneapolis, MN: University of Minnesota, National Center on Educational Outcomes. Retrieved from www.education.umn.edu/NCEO/OnlinePubs/Technical34.htm

Tindal, G., & Fuchs, L. (1999). *A summary of research on test changes: An empirical basis for defining accommodations.* Lexington, KY: University of Kentucky, Mid-South Regional Resource Center.

Tindal, G., Heath, B., Hollenbeck, K., Almond, P., & Harniss, M. (1998). Accommodating students with disabilities on large-scale tests: An empirical study of student response and test administration demands. *Exceptional Children, 64*, 439–450.

Tindal, G., & Ketterlin-Geller, L. R. (2004). *Research on mathematics test accommodations relevant to NAEP testing.* Paper prepared for the National Assessment Governing Board (NAGB) Conference on increasing the participation of Students with Disabilities (SD) and Limited English Proficiency (LEP) Students in the National Assessment of Educational Progress (NAEP), New York, NY. Retrieved from http://www.nagb.org/publications/conferences/tindal.pdf

Turkay, S. (2008). *Global Kids, Inc's science through Second Life curriculum evaluation.* New York, NY: Global Kids, Inc. Retrieved from http://www.holymeatballs.org/StSLEvaluation.pdf

Unger, D. D. (2001). *Employer's attitudes toward people with disabilities in the workforce: Myths or realities.* Richmond, VA: Virginia Commonwealth University. Retrieved from http://www.worksupport.com

U.S. Census Bureau. (2004). *Population estimates.* Washington, DC: Author. Retrieved from http://onlinelibrary.wiley.com/doi/10.1111/j.1540-5826.2007.00250.x/pdf

U.S. Department of Education. (2006, April). *26th annual (2004) report to Congress on the implementation of the Individuals with Disabilities Education Act* (Vol. 1). Washington, DC: Office of Special Education and Rehabilitative Services, Office of Special Education Programs. Retrieved from http://www2.ed.gov/about/reports/annual/osep/2004/index.html

U.S. Employment and Training Administration. (1991). *The learning disabled in employment and training programs* (Research and Evaluation Report No. 91-E). Washington, DC: U.S. Department of Labor.

U.S. Government Accountability Office (GAO). (2003, July 31). *Special education: Federal actions can assist states in improving postsecondary outcomes for youth* (GAO 03–773). Washington, DC: Author. Retrieved from http://www.gao.gov/products/GAO-03-773

Vogel, S. A. (1990). Gender differences in intelligence, language, visual-motor abilities, and academic achievement in students with learning disabilities: A review of the literature. *Journal of Learning Disabilities, 23*, 44–52.

Vogel, S. A., & Adleman, P. B. (1992). The success of college students with learning disabilities: Factors related to educational attainment. *Journal of Learning Disabilities, 25*(7), 430–441.

Vogel, S. A., Hruby, P. J., & Adelman, P. B. (1993). Educational and psychological factors in successful and unsuccessful college students with learning disabilities. *Learning Disabilities Research & Practice, 8*(1), 35–43.

Vygotsky, L. S. (1993). *The collected works of L. S. Vygotsky* (Vol. 2), *The fundamentals of defectology (abnormal psychology and learning disabilities).* (J. E. Know & C. B. Stevens, Trans.; R. W. Rieber & A. S. Carton, Eds.). New York, NY: Plenum Press.

Vygotsky, L. S. (1998). *The collected works of L. S. Vygotsky, Volume 5: Child psychology.* (J. E. Know & C. B. Stevens, Trans.; R. W. Rieber, Ed.). New York, NY: Plenum Press.

Wagner, M., Newman, L., Cameto, R., Garza, N., & Levine, P. (2005). *After high school: A first look at the postschool experiences of youth with disabilities. A report from the National Longitudinal Transition Study-2 (NLTS2).* Menlo Park, CA: SRI International. Retrieved from ERIC database (ED494935).

Werner, E. F. (1993). Risk and resilience in individuals with learning disabilities: Lessons learned from the Kauai longitudinal study. *Learning Disabilities Research & Practice, 8,* 28–35.

Wolanin, T. R., & Steele, P. E. (2004). *Higher education opportunities for students with disabilities.* Washington, DC: Institute for Higher Education Policy.

Wong, B. Y. L. (2003). General and specific issues for researchers' consideration in applying the risk and resilience framework to the social domain of learning disabilities. *Learning Disabilities Research & Practice, 18*(2), 68–76.

Woodock, D., McGrew, K., & Mather, N. (2001). *Woodcock-Johnson III (Cognitive and Achievement Batteries).* Itasca, IL: Riverside.

Young, G., & Browning, J. (2005). Learning disabilities/dyslexia and employment: A mythical view. In G. Reid & A. Fawcett (Eds.), *Dyslexia in context: Research, policy and practice* (pp. 25–59). London, United Kingdom: Whurr.

5

---❯◆❮---

Children with ADHD Grown Up

Kevin M. Antshel

Russell Barkley

lthough Attention-Deficit/Hyperactivity Disorder (ADHD) was long considered to be relevant only to children (Hill & Schoener, 1996), within the past
25 years, longitudinal evidence has accumulated suggesting that ADHD often persists into adulthood (Barkley, Murphy, & Fischer, 2008; Faraone, Biederman, & Mick,
2006; Mannuzza, Klein, Bessler, Malloy, & LaPadula, 1993). It is certainly possible that
someone may be first diagnosed as having ADHD in adulthood (Faraone et al., 2006),
but 98% of such cases have an onset in childhood prior to 16 years of age (Barkley
et al., 2008); those who do clinical work undoubtedly have had the experience of an
adult with no history of ADHD presenting for an ADHD evaluation. The primary
focus of this chapter, however, is to describe what we know about the longitudinal
course of *children* with ADHD as they age into *adulthood*.

SYNDROMAL PERSISTENCE AND DIAGNOSIS IN ADULTS

While this may change with the 5th edition of the *DSM*, currently, the gold standard
and most commonly applied method for diagnosing ADHD across the life span is the
Diagnostic and Statistical Manual of Mental Disorders (4th ed., text revision) *DSM-IV-TR*.
It is the most empirically based criteria for diagnosing ADHD yet developed. A common method of identifying adults who have continued to maintain their ADHD diagnosis is to supplement structured diagnostic interviews for adult psychopathology with
the child module for ADHD. Criterion A of the *DSM-IV-TR* lists 9 inattentive and
9 hyperactive/impulsive symptoms. A 6-symptom threshold is required in both children and adults.

The validity of these symptoms and/or thresholds for identifying syndromal persistence of ADHD, however, may not be appropriate for adults. For example, in two longitudinal samples followed into adulthood, Barkley (Barkley et al., 2008) studied DSM symptom thresholds. As adults, nearly all of the control participants endorsed 3 or fewer symptoms of inattention and 3 or fewer of hyperactive impulsive behavior. Conversely, all of the ADHD group endorsed 3 or more inattention symptoms, and 72% endorsed 3 or more hyperactive symptoms (Barkley et al., 2008). Four symptoms on the inattention or hyperactive-impulsive DSM lists effectively exclude *all* typically developing adults, which suggests that high sensitivity can occur with fewer than 6 symptoms currently required by the DSM-IV-TR. The fifth edition of the DSM (DSM-5) is currently field-testing criteria for adults with ADHD and may eventually follow suit in recommending a reduced symptom threshold and even new symptoms to be used for adult diagnosis of ADHD.

Although it is possible to differentiate adults with ADHD from typical controls with 4 symptoms, differentiating ADHD from other clinical disorders (e.g., anxiety disorders, etc.) may be more difficult. Barkley (Barkley et al., 2008) found that three DSM-IV inattentive symptoms were the most specific to ADHD, classifying 87% of the ADHD group correctly and 44% of the clinical control group: (1) fails to give close attention to details; (2) difficulty sustaining attention to tasks; and (3) fails to follow through on instructions. Three hyperactive/impulsive symptoms accurately classified 76% of ADHD cases and 49% of clinical control cases: (1) fidgets with hands/feet or squirms in seat; (2) difficulty engaging in leisure quietly; and (3) interrupts or intrudes on others (Barkley et al., 2008).

In addition to the DSM-based algorithm for identifying syndromal persistence of ADHD, the Utah criteria proposed by Wender (1995) are used to diagnose ADHD in adults. The Utah criteria and the Wender Utah Rating Scale (Ward, Wender, & Reimherr, 1993) use 7 symptoms to diagnose adult ADHD:

1. Inattentiveness
2. Hyperactivity
3. Mood lability
4. Irritability and hot temper
5. Impaired stress tolerance
6. Disorganization
7. Impulsivity

The Utah criteria have been criticized by others in that (a) by requiring both hyperactivity and inattention, the Inattentive subtype is excluded (McGough & Barkley, 2004); (b) irritability and hot temper are semi-independent of ADHD symptoms

(Loeber, Burke, Lahey, Winters, & Zera, 2000); and (c) the diagnosis of ADHD cannot be made with coexisting Major Depressive Disorder (MDD), a relatively common finding in adult ADHD (Kessler et al., 2006).

Diagnosing ADHD in children requires consultation with school personnel (e.g., teachers) about the child's school functioning and behavior (Pliszka, 2007). Many adults who were diagnosed with ADHD as children are no longer in school. Thus, it is not often possible to acquire information on current functioning from independent sources such as teachers. Similarly, in child ADHD, parent and teacher reports are often considered more reliable than the child's report (Achenbach, McConaughy, & Howell, 1987). Nonetheless, the persistence of ADHD in adults is often assessed with considerable or sole emphasis on self-report. Data suggest that, much like children with ADHD (Gerdes, Hoza, & Pelham, 2003; Hoza, Pelham, Dobbs, Owens, & Pillow, 2002), adults with ADHD may present with an optimistic bias and report functioning as better than it truly may be (Knouse, Bagwell, Barkley, & Murphy, 2005). Thus, clinicians who assess for syndromal persistence of ADHD would be wise to obtain collateral reports, such as from parents, siblings, or others who know the adult well. For example, in a longitudinal project following children with ADHD until age 21, only 5% of young adults reported enough symptoms to meet diagnostic criteria; when parent-reported information was considered, 46% of the sample met diagnostic criteria (Barkley et al., 2008).

Epidemiological data suggest that *DSM-IV*–defined ADHD occurs in approximately 8% of the pediatric population (Canino et al., 2004; Froehlich et al., 2007; Kessler et al., 2005). Epidemiological research suggests that ADHD prevalence in adults is 4.4% (Kessler et al., 2006). Using recent census data, this prevalence rate suggests that approximately 11 million adults in the United States have ADHD.

These epidemiological studies on both children and adults are consistent with longitudinal research following children with ADHD into adulthood. Most of these longitudinal data report that 50% to 70% of children with ADHD continue to show impairing symptoms into adulthood (Faraone et al., 2006). The decline in ADHD prevalence as a function of time may be due to the finding that ADHD symptoms decline in typically developing populations as a function of age (DuPaul, Power, & Anastopoulos, 1998; Hart, Lahey, Loeber, Applegate, & Frick, 1995). This is especially so for the symptoms of hyperactivity more than those of inattention and impulsivity. The loss of syndromal persistence in these populations may also be a function of *DSM* symptoms and symptom thresholds that are developmentally inappropriate and too restrictive, respectively, to be applied to adults (Barkley et al., 2008)

Barkley et al.'s longitudinal data suggests that ADHD remission in young adulthood is unrelated to severity of disorder, age of onset, childhood IQ, or childhood conduct problems at study entry, or severity of ADHD, Oppositional Defiant Disorder (ODD), or Conduct Disorder (CD), or duration of stimulant treatment by adolescence (Barkley et al., 2008). In other words, their data suggest that it is difficult to predict who will remit in their symptoms in adulthood based on routinely used psychological measures.

Instead, genetics may offer a better alternative for predicting persistence of ADHD. Genes appear to be a strong predictor of who continues to demonstrate clinically significant ADHD in adulthood versus those whose symptoms are in remission. For example, prevalence rates of ADHD are significantly higher among the relatives of children with persistent ADHD compared to relatives of children with remitted ADHD (Biederman, Faraone, Monuteaux, Bober, & Cadogen, 2004; Faraone, Biederman, & Monuteaux, 2000). Similarly, parents of children with persistent ADHD were 20 times more likely to have ADHD themselves than parents of controls whereas parents of children with nonpersistent ADHD showed only a fivefold increased risk (Faraone, Biederman, Feighner, & Monuteaux, 2000).

NEUROPSYCHOLOGY OF ADULT ADHD

A meta-analysis suggested that children with ADHD have an IQ about 9 points lower than typically developing peers (Frazier, Demaree, & Youngstrom, 2004). Similar data have been reported in adults with ADHD (Barkley et al., 2000; Biederman et al., 1993; Bridgett & Walker, 2006; Bush et al., 1999; DuPaul et al., 2001; Murphy, Barkley, & Bush, 2001). Lower performance on the Wechsler Adult Intelligence Scale–3rd Edition (WAIS-III) Arithmetic and Coding–Digit Symbol may account for a substantial portion of the IQ differences noted between ADHD and community controls (Hervey, Epstein, & Curry, 2004).

Controlled processing deficits are commonly observed in pediatric ADHD. Children with ADHD perform less well on laboratory tasks that assess vigilance, motoric inhibition, organization, planning, complex problem solving, and verbal learning and memory (Seidman, Biederman, Faraone, Weber, & Ouellette, 1997). Although the literature about the neuropsychology of adult ADHD is not as voluminous as the child literature, adults with ADHD appear impaired on these same cognitive domains (Hervey et al., 2004).

Since the DSM-III (American Psychiatric Association [APA], 1980), ADHD has been conceptualized as a disorder of attention. Although the hyperactive and impulsive symptoms of childhood may diminish with age, there is significant evidence demonstrating that attention deficits do not diminish with age (Biederman, Mick, & Faraone, 2000). For example, much like children with ADHD, adults with ADHD also perform less well on tasks that require vigilance, or the ability to sustain attention (Downey, Stelson, Pomerleau, & Giordani, 1997; Gansler et al., 1998; Seidman, Biederman, Weber, Hatch, & Faraone, 1998). There is also some evidence that "rare target" paradigms (few targets, many nontargets) such as the Gordon Diagnostic System or Test of Variables of Attention appear to be more difficult for adults with

ADHD than those paradigms with higher signal probabilities (DuPaul et al., 2001; Johnson et al., 2001; Klee, Garfinkel, & Beauchesne, 1986; Seidman et al., 1998).

Response inhibition has been hypothesized to play a central role in pediatric ADHD (Barkley, 1997). Continuous Performance Test (CPT) commission errors are a common laboratory measure of this construct. Unlike attention deficits (which seem to emerge more reliably in rare target CPTs as reflected in more variable reaction times and higher omission errors), response inhibition deficits emerge more reliably in higher signal probabilities such as the Conners, CPT, Go/No-Go, or Stop Signal paradigms. Several studies have reported that adults with ADHD make more errors of commission on high signal CPTs relative to both clinical and community control participants (Epstein, Conners, Sitarenios, & Erhardt, 1998; Epstein, Johnson, Varia, & Conners, 2001; Walker, Shores, Trollor, Lee, & Sachdev, 2000).

The term "executive functioning" refers to the set of neuropsychological capacities required to organize and direct behavior across time to anticipate future events or achieve future goals (Fuster, 1997; Welsh & Pennington, 1988). It includes such constructs as inhibition, nonverbal working memory, verbal working memory, emotion/ motivation self-regulation, and planning and problem solving (generativity or reconstitution) (Barkley, 1997). Substantial evidence exists to show that children and adults with ADHD are, as a group, impaired on measures of these constructs (Barkley, 1997; Frazier et al., 2004; Hervey et al., 2004). Some evidence exists to suggest that deficits are greater in those executive functions lateralized more to the right hemisphere than left, such as nonverbal working memory, nonverbal fluency, and sustaining response inhibition (Barkley & Fischer, in press; Barkley & Murphy, 2010; Barkley & Murphy, in press).

Although executive function deficits are considered to be present in both pediatric and adult ADHD, the evidence for such deficits is highly dependent on the methods used to assess executive function. If executive function is evaluated using neuropsychological tests, then only a minority of ADHD cases (<35%) are found to be impaired; if rating scales are used, the vast majority (95%) are classified as clinically impaired (Barkley & Fischer, in press; Barkley & Murphy, 2010, in press; Gioia, Isquith, Guy, & Kenworthy, 2000). Thus, it is not surprising that performance on one of the most well-established tests of executive functioning, the Wisconsin Card Sorting Test (WCST) (Heaton, Chelune, Talley, Kay, & Curtiss, 1993), is not impaired in adults with ADHD. Multiple studies have failed to report a significant difference between adults with ADHD and community controls on WCST categories completed (Barkley et al., 2000; Johnson et al., 2001; Seidman et al., 1998) and number of errors, both perseverative (Gansler et al., 1998; Seidman et al., 1998) and nonperseverative (Seidman et al., 1998). In fact, poor performance on this test may be more related to concept formation rather than executive function and may be more a function of low IQ rather than severity of ADHD (Barkley et al., 2008).

Given the importance of attention and working memory to memory encoding and storage, it is not surprising that adults with ADHD have been demonstrated to have memory deficits. Adults with ADHD also appear to have more difficulty managing auditory/verbal information relative to visual information (Hervey et al., 2004). Although differences emerge between adults with ADHD and community controls on the WAIS-III Digit Span (Bush et al., 1999; Seidman et al., 1998), the effect size of the differences are much larger on the California Verbal Learning Test (Delis, Kramer, Kaplan, & Ober, 2000). For example, adults with ADHD perform less well on overall rates of learning (Barkley et al., 2000; Holdnack, Moberg, Arnold, Gur, & Gur, 1995), recall (Holdnack et al., 1995; Lovejoy, Graczyk, O'Hare, & Neuman, 2000), recognition (Holdnack et al., 1995; Riordan et al., 1999), and semantic clustering (Holdnack et al., 1995; Seidman et al., 1998). The weaker performance on the semantic clustering index may indicate failure to adopt a strategy (Delis et al., 2000). Children and adults with ADHD also have difficulties with nonverbal working memory, as often measured by delayed spatial memory tasks, self-ordered pointing (such as the Simon Game), and design fluency tasks (Barkley et al., 2008). In fact, the deficits on such tasks are often more severe than those found on verbal working memory tasks (Rapport et al., 2008).

Although executive function tests are often organized into the executive function constructs just noted, ratings of executive function deficits as they occur in daily life activities in natural settings reveal a different set of constructs. These can be organized into five categories:

1. Self-stopping (inhibition) that incorporates problems with behavioral, cognitive, verbal, and emotional impulsiveness.
2. Self-management relative to time, which includes planning.
3. Self-organization and problem solving.
4. Self-motivation.
5. Self-activation and sustained concentration (Barkley & Murphy, in press).

Such constructs are often found to be unrelated to executive function tests or to share less than 10% of their variance for any single test and less than 20% for the best combination of executive function tests (Barkley & Fischer, in press; Barkley & Murphy, in press; Burgess, Alderman, Evans, Emslie, & Wilson, 1998; Chaytor, Schmitter-Edgecombe, & Burr, 2006; Wood & Liossi, 2006). Thus, conclusions by some investigators (Jonsdottir, Bouma, Sergeant, & Scherder, 2006; Marchetta, Hurks, Krabbendam, & Jolles, 2008) that ADHD does not appear to be a disorder of executive function based on executive function test results are contradicted by the results of research using more ecologically valid rating scales of executive function in everyday life activities.

NEUROBIOLOGY OF ADULT ADHD

Pediatric ADHD studies most consistently document smaller whole-brain volume and a smaller cerebellum (especially the right vermis), right dorsolateral prefrontal cortex, anterior cingulate cortex, caudate nucleus, and corpus callosum, especially the genu and splenium (Bush, Valera, & Seidman, 2005; Hutchinson, Mathias, & Banich, 2008; Mackie et al., 2007; Paloyelis, Mehta, Kuntsi, & Asherson, 2007; Valera, Faraone, Murray, & Seidman, 2007). Many of these same regions are also smaller in adults with ADHD. Nonetheless, compared to the vast pediatric ADHD literature, the adult ADHD neuroimaging literature, especially structural, is rather sparse (Zang et al., 2005).

Functional neuroimaging studies have documented anomalous patterns of activation relative to community controls on a working memory task (Bush et al., 2005). Despite equivalent performance, adults with ADHD had less cerebellar and occipital activation as well as mild (yet not statistically significant) reductions in dorsolateral prefrontal cortex activation. Schweitzer et al. (2000) also reported occipital activation in adults with ADHD during a working memory task. Another functional neuroimaging study of adult ADHD reported more significant hypoactivation of the premotor and superior prefrontal cortices (Zametkin et al., 1990). Anterior cingulate cortex hypoactivation has also been reported in the adult ADHD functional neuroimaging literature (Bush et al., 1999; Zametkin et al., 1990). Ernst, Zametkin, Phillips, and Cohen (1998) have speculated that as a function of developmental maturation, the dopaminergic anomalies in ADHD observed in adult ADHD have shifted from the basal ganglia and midbrain to the prefrontal cortex.

Using magnetic resonance spectroscopy, an imaging method that evaluates the spectra of N-acetylaspartate (NAA), choline, creatine, and myo-inositol, adult ADHD research found lowered NAA concentration in the left dorsolateral prefrontal cortex (Hesslinger, Thiel, Tebartz van Elst, Hennig, & Ebert, 2001). Reduced levels of NAA are thought to reflect neuronal loss or dysfunction. In a single photon emission computed tomography (SPECT) study, Dougherty et al. (1999) found striatal dopamine transporter to be elevated by about 70% in adults with ADHD. K. Krause, Dresel, Krause, Kung, and Tatsch (2000) also reported increased dopamine transporter in the striatum of adults with ADHD. In addition, their data demonstrated that after methylphenidate treatment, ligand binding to the dopamine transporter was reduced to normal levels (K. Krause et al., 2000). Others (van Dyck et al., 2002) have not reported altered dopamine transporter levels in a SPECT study of striatal binding in adults with ADHD. The higher availability of dopamine transporter has been speculated to be etiologically relevant to the increased rate of cigarette smoking in adults with ADHD (J. Krause, Krause, Dresel, la Fougere, & Ackenheil, 2006).

PSYCHIATRIC COMORBIDITIES IN ADULT ADHD

Adults with syndromal persistence of ADHD very often meet diagnostic criteria for a comorbid psychiatric disorder. Although approximately 25% of adults with ADHD do not have a comorbid disorder (Biederman et al., 1993), anxiety, mood, and Substance Use Disorders (SUDs) are commonly reported in adult ADHD (Barkley, Murphy, & Fischer, 2007; Biederman et al., 1993a; Borland & Heckman, 1976; Heiligenstein, Conyers, Berns, & Miller, 1998; Murphy & Barkley, 1996a; Shekim, Asarnow, Hess, Zaucha, & Wheeler, 1990; Thomson et al., 2005) and do not differ in prevalence rates as a function of gender (Lahey et al., 1994).

Prevalence rates of anxiety disorders in adults are often similar to if not higher than those found in children with ADHD; approximately 25% to 30% of children with ADHD (MTA Collaborative Group, 1999a, 1999b) and adults with ADHD (Barkley, Murphy, & Kwasnik, 1996; Biederman et al., 1993; Kessler et al., 2006; Mannuzza et al., 1993; MTA Collaborative Group, 1999b; Shekim et al., 1990) suffer from anxiety disorders, most often Generalized Anxiety Disorder. Panic disorder, Obsessive Compulsive Disorder (OCD), and Social Phobia are less common yet can be comorbid conditions (Kessler et al., 2006; Shekim et al., 1990; Torgersen, Gjervan, & Rasmussen, 2006).

MDD occurs in children with ADHD, particularly those with CD (Angold, Costello, & Erkanli, 1999). Similarly, approximately 20% to 30% of adults with ADHD have comorbid MDD (Barkley et al., 2007; Barkley et al., 1996; Biederman et al., 1993b; Kessler et al., 2006; Mannuzza et al., 1993). In one longitudinal study, rates of MDD rose to age 21 and then declined on follow-up to age 27 in hyperactive children followed to adulthood (Barkley et al., 2008). In contrast, rates of suicidal ideation and attempts reached their peak during the high school years and declined thereafter, although both remained higher than that of the control group to the age 27 follow-up (Barkley et al., 2008).

Relative to child ADHD, SUDs are more common in adult ADHD (Barkley et al., 2008). For example, lifetime SUD prevalence rates range from 21% to 53% (Barkley et al., 1996; Biederman et al., 1993b; Faraone et al., 2007; Mannuzza et al., 1993) with alcohol SUDs being the most common. Cannabis and cocaine use disorders are both also relatively common in adults with ADHD (Biederman et al., 1995; Wilens, 2004). Although comorbid Conduct or Bipolar Disorder increases the risk for SUDs (Mannuzza et al., 1993; G. Weiss, Hechtman, Milroy, & Perlman, 1985), ADHD alone is an independent risk factor for later SUDs (Biederman et al., 1995; Molina & Pelham, 2003). Adults with ADHD and SUDs have both a greater severity of SUD (Chalfant, Rapee, & Carroll, 2007; Schubiner et al., 2000) and an earlier onset of SUD relative to adults with SUD yet without ADHD (Biederman et al., 1997).

FUNCTIONAL OUTCOMES IN ADULT ADHD

To meet *DSM-IV-TR* diagnosis for ADHD, one must be functionally impaired in two or more domains of major life activities (APA, 2000). In children, academic, social, and family functioning are the most frequently impaired (MTA Collaborative Group, 1999a, 1999b, 2004). Academic impairments continue to persist in adolescents and young adults (Barkley et al., 2008); nonetheless, impairments in diverse domains such as dating/marital relations, financial management, occupational, driving, child rearing and behavior management, maintaining health, and managing a household are consistently reported in adults with ADHD (Barkley, Fischer, Smallish, & Fletcher, 2006; Barkley et al., 2008; G. Weiss & Hechtman, 1993; M. D. Weiss & Weiss, 2004; Wender, Wolf, & Wasserstein, 2001). Some data suggest that adult ADHD is *more* functionally impairing in these domains than most other outpatient psychiatric disorders, such as anxiety disorders or depression (Barkley et al., 2008).

Educational impairments, home responsibilities, and occupational domains are the three most functionally impaired domains in adults with ADHD (Barkley et al., 2008). Financial management and managing daily chores/responsibilities are also impaired more in adults with ADHD relative to adults with other psychiatric disorders but not ADHD (Barkley et al., 2008). In children, the association between the number of ADHD symptoms and functional impairment is modest ($r = 0.3$), especially if indexed by highly specific measures, such as grade point average (Gordon et al., 2006). However, if ratings of impairment employ more global indicators of academic, social, or other domains, the relationship is often higher. This is especially so in adults with ADHD, where these relationships may be more robust ($r = 0.7$) (Barkley et al., 2008).

In children with ADHD, *DSM-IV-TR* inattentive symptoms that best predict impairment are not listening, losing things, being forgetful, and avoiding tasks requiring sustained mental effort (inattentive symptoms) (Mota & Schachar, 2000). The best *DSM-IV-TR* inattentive symptoms for predicting impairments in adults with ADHD were being easily distracted and being unable to sustain attention to tasks (Barkley et al., 2008). Interrupts, blurts out, cannot wait turn, does not play quietly, and leaves seat were the best hyperactive symptoms (Mota & Schachar, 2000). Feeling restless and having difficulties waiting their turn were the two best *DSM-IV-TR* hyperactive symptoms) (Barkley et al., 2008). Thus, impairing symptoms for children may not be necessarily most impairing for adults with ADHD.

Academic underachievement (Busch et al., 2002; Faraone et al., 1993) and Learning Disabilities (LD) (Faraone et al., 1993; Semrud-Clikeman et al., 1992; Willcutt & Pennington, 2000) are well documented in the pediatric ADHD literature. Academic retention (~30%), requiring academic tutoring (~50%), special education classroom placement (~30%), and/or dropping out of school (10%–35%) all occur in children with ADHD (Barkley, Anastopoulos, Guevremont, & Fletcher, 1991;

Barkley, DuPaul, & McMurray, 1990; Faraone et al., 1993; Szatmari, Offord, & Boyle, 1989; Wilson & Marcotte, 1996). Comorbid CD diagnosis exacerbates the risk for dropping out of school (Fischer, Barkley, Edelbrock, & Smallish, 1990), yet ADHD appears independently associated with the other educational risks (Mannuzza et al., 1993; Wilson & Marcotte, 1996).

Young adults with ADHD complete fewer years of education, with nearly one-third failing to complete high school (Barkley et al., 2008). Relatively few young adults with ADHD attempt college (20%), and fewer graduate from college (5%) (G. Weiss & Hechtman, 1993). Compared to children with ADHD who are followed into adulthood, clinically diagnosed adults with ADHD have higher intellectual levels, have graduated from high school, and have at least attempted college (Barkley et al., 2008).

Possibly as a function of academic struggles and not having a college degree, children with ADHD often become adults with ADHD who have significantly lower occupational status (Mannuzza et al., 1993; G. Weiss & Hechtman, 1993). Adults with ADHD have lower socioeconomic status than siblings without ADHD, have more part-time employment outside of full-time employment, and change jobs more often (Barkley et al., 2006; Barkley et al., 2008; De Quiros & Kinsbourne, 2001; G. Weiss & Hechtman, 1993). Over half of adults with ADHD have been fired from employment (Murphy & Barkley, 1996b), and supervisor ratings of employee performance are lower for adults with ADHD compared to their non-ADHD counterparts (Barkley et al., 2006; G. Weiss & Hechtman, 1993). The severity of self-reported ADHD symptoms and supervisor ratings of ADHD severity together are strong predictors of occupational functioning in adults with ADHD (Barkley et al., 2008). Similarly, years of education and the number of self-rated current oppositional/defiant symptoms are strong predictors of the number of times an adult with ADHD has been fired from a job (Barkley et al., 2008).

Although educational and occupational domains are the best-researched functional domains, adults with ADHD may also have problems related to maintaining health-conscious behavior (e.g., exercise, proper diet, etc.) (Barkley, 2002; Milberger, Biederman, Faraone, Chen, & Jones, 1997). Fewer than 50% of adults with ADHD exercise frequently (compared to 65% of community controls) (Barkley et al., 2008). Financial impairments, such as having trouble sticking to a budget, exceeding credit card limits, failing to pay for utilities resulting in their termination, being in debt, and going on shopping "sprees," are reported in adult ADHD (Barkley et al., 2008; De Quiros & Kinsbourne, 2001). Severity of ADHD symptoms and the number of childhood CD symptoms are both associated with financial management difficulties (Barkley et al., 2008).

Teens and adults with ADHD are more likely to have numerous problems in the domain of motor vehicle operation. Extensive research on driving documents a greater frequency of speeding citations, greater likelihood of having had an at-fault accident, and greater likelihood of having their license suspended or revoked (Barkley & Cox, 2007; Barkley et al., 2008; Barkley et al., 1996; Fried et al., 2006). Similarly suggesting an optimistic bias, adults with ADHD often judge themselves to be average or slightly better-than-average drivers when their actual driving history is worse than normal (Knouse et al., 2005).

Adults with ADHD self-report a lower quality of their marital relationships, if married, and are more likely to have extramarital affairs (Barkley et al., 2008). Parenting stress is also reported to be significantly higher in adults with ADHD (Barkley et al., 2008; Johnston & Mash, 2001), possibly due in part to their own higher rate of depression but also to the higher incidence of pediatric ADHD and ODD in offspring of adults with ADHD (Biederman et al., 1995); over half of the offspring of adults with ADHD meet criteria for ADHD themselves (Biederman et al., 1995). Mothers with ADHD are less effective at monitoring child behavior and less consistent with discipline (Murray & Johnston, 2006).

TREATING ADHD IN ADULTS

Adult ADHD is a significantly impairing psychiatric disorder and requires treatment. In pediatric ADHD, stimulant medications are a front line management strategy (Pliszka, 2007); approximately 70% of children with ADHD will show an efficacious response to stimulant medications such as methylphenidate or mixed-salt amphetamines. (For reviews, see Biederman et al., 1996; Faraone, Sergeant, Gillberg, & Biederman, 2003.) Similar response rates have been reported in the adult ADHD literature (Biederman et al., 2004). Atomoxetine is a nonstimulant that is approved by the Food and Drug Administration for managing adult ADHD and may be particularly effective for adults with ADHD and comorbid depression (Spencer et al., 2006) or for those with a comorbid SUD addictive potential (Wee & Woolverton, 2004).

Most adults with ADHD have significant psychiatric comorbidity that requires clinical attention and management. One aspect in which the psychiatric comorbidity is evident in treatment strategies is pharmacotherapy. Although the evidence for the efficacy of polypharmacy is limited at this time, multiple researchers have asserted that polypharmacy may be more likely in adult ADHD than pediatric ADHD (Adler, Reingold, Morrill, & Wilens, 2006; Barkley et al., 2007; M. Weiss & Hechtman, 2006; Wender et al., 2001).

Psychosocial treatments are also typically recommended in adult ADHD (Dodson, 2005). What constitutes the psychosocial component, however, appears to be somewhat different in adult ADHD relative to pediatric ADHD. For example, neither cognitive behavioral therapy (CBT) nor cognitive therapy has much research support in pediatric ADHD (Abikoff & Gittelman, 1985; Baer, 1991; Bloomquist, 1991; DuPaul & Eckert, 1997; Dush, Hirt, & Schroeder, 1989). Nonetheless, there are some data to suggest that CBT may be more efficacious in adults with ADHD (Rostain & Ramsay, 2006; Safren et al., 2005).

SUD interventions may also be necessary. ADHD aggravates the SUD, resulting in a more severe disorder (Spencer et al., 1998) and poorer outcomes (Ercan, Coskunol, Varan, & Toksoz, 2003). Thus, ADHD interventions should be initiated first to determine the extent to which ADHD is contributing to SUDs (Barkley et al., 2008; Johnston & Mash, 2001).

Facilitating the transition to adulthood has been an increasing focus in the ADHD literature (Davis & Sondheimer, 2005; Verity & Coates, 2007). For example, the transition to adulthood is defined by young adults themselves as accepting responsibility for oneself, gaining autonomy and independence, and becoming financially independent (Arnett & Taber, 1994; Shanahan, 2000). In many ways, these attributes and qualities are often very difficult for individuals with ADHD. Many psychosocial treatment approaches focus explicitly on these domains.

SUMMARY

There is now considerable evidence that ADHD often persists into adulthood. ADHD in adults is less common than ADHD in children. Nonetheless, in cases that persist into adulthood, the functional impairments, psychiatric comorbidities, neuropsychological and neurobiological anomalies, and treatments are highly comparable to those seen in children. And although the response of adults with ADHD to the ADHD medications appears high and comparable to that seen in child ADHD, new psychosocial treatments may be required to address the more varied forms of impairments in major life activities in adults than is the case for children with ADHD.

REFERENCES

Abikoff, H., & Gittelman, R. (1985). Hyperactive children treated with stimulants. Is cognitive training a useful adjunct? *Archives of General Psychiatry, 42*(10), 953–961.

Achenbach, T. M., McConaughy, S. H., & Howell, C. T. (1987). Child/adolescent behavioral and emotional problems: implications of cross-informant correlations for situational specificity. *Psychological Bulletin, 101*(2), 213–232.

Adler, L. A., Reingold, L. S., Morrill, M. S., & Wilens, T. E. (2006). Combination pharmacotherapy for adult ADHD. *Current Psychiatry Reports, 8*(5), 409–415.

American Psychiatric Association. (1980). *Diagnostic and statistical manual of mental disorders (3rd ed.)*. Washington, DC: Author.

American Psychiatric Association. (2000). *Diagnostic and statistical manual of mental disorders (4th ed., text rev.)*. Washington, DC: Author.

Angold, A., Costello, E. J., & Erkanli, A. (1999). Comorbidity. *Journal of Child Psychology and Psychiatry, 40*(1), 57–87.

Arnett, J. J., & Taber, S. (1994). Adolescence Terminable and Interminable: When Does Adolescence End? *Journal of Youth and Adolescence, 23*, 517–537.

Baer, R. A., & Nietzel, M. T. (1991). Cognitive and behavioral treatment of impulsivity in children: A meta-analytic review of the outcome literature. *Journal of Clinical Child Psychology, 20*, 400–412.

Barkley, R., Murphy, K., & Fischer, M. (2007). *ADHD in Adults: What the Science Says.* New York: Guilford Press.

Barkley, R. A., Murphy, K. R., & Fischer, M. (2008). *ADHD in adults: What the science says.* New York, NY: Guilford Press.

Barkley, R. A. (1997). Behavioral inhibition, sustained attention, and executive functions: Constructing a unifying theory of ADHD. *Psychological Bulletin, 121*(1), 65–94.

Barkley, R. A. (2002). Major life activity and health outcomes associated with attention-deficit/hyperactivity disorder. *Journal of Clinical Psychiatry, 63*(Suppl. 12), 10–15.

Barkley, R. A., Anastopoulos, A. D., Guevremont, D. C., & Fletcher, K. E. (1991). Adolescents with ADHD: Patterns of behavioral adjustment, academic functioning, and treatment utilization. *Journal of the American Academy of Child and Adolescent Psychiatry, 30*(5), 752–761.

Barkley, R. A., & Cox, D. (2007). A review of driving risks and impairments associated with attention-deficit/hyperactivity disorder and the effects of stimulant medication on driving performance. *Journal of Safety Research, 38*(1), 113–128.

Barkley, R. A., DuPaul, G. J., & McMurray, M. B. (1990). Comprehensive evaluation of attention deficit disorder with and without hyperactivity as defined by research criteria. *Journal of Consulting and Clinical Psychology, 58*(6), 775–789.

Barkley, R. A., & Fischer, M. (in press). Predicting impairment in major life activities and occupational functioning in hyperactive children as adults: Self-reported executive function (EF) deficits versus EF tests. *Developmental Neuropsychology.*

Barkley, R. A., Fischer, M., Smallish, L., & Fletcher, K. (2006). Young adult outcome of hyperactive children: Adaptive functioning in major life activities. *Journal of the American Academy of Child and Adolescent Psychiatry, 45*(2), 192–202.

Barkley, R. A., & Murphy, K. R. (2010). Impairment in occupational functioning and adult ADHD: The predictive utility of executive function (EF) ratings versus EF tests. *Archives of Clinical Neuropsychology, 25*(3), 157–173.

Barkley, R. A., & Murphy, K. R. (in press). Evaluating executive function (EF) deficits in daily life activities: Scale development and relationships with EF tests and severity of ADHD. *Psychopathology and Behavioral Assessment.*

Barkley, R. A., & Murphy, K. R. (in press). Impairment in major life activities and adult ADHD: The predictive utility of executive function (EF) ratings versus EF tests. *Neuropsychology.*

Barkley, R. A., Murphy, K. R., & Kwasnik, D. (1996). Motor vehicle driving competencies and risks in teens and young adults with attention deficit hyperactivity disorder. *Pediatrics, 98*(6, Pt 1), 1089–1095.

Barkley, R. A., Shelton, T. L., Crosswait, C., Moorehouse, M., Fletcher, K., Barrett, S., . . . Metevia, L. (2000). Multi-method psycho-educational intervention for preschool children with disruptive behavior: Preliminary results at post-treatment. *Journal of Child Psychology and Psychiatry, 41*(3), 319–332.

Biederman, J., Faraone, S. V., Mick, E., Spencer, T., Wilens, T., Kiely, K., . . . Warburton, R. (1995). High risk for attention deficit hyperactivity disorder among children of parents with childhood onset of the disorder: a pilot study. *American Journal of Psychiatry, 152*(3), 431–435.

Biederman, J., Faraone, S. V., Milberger, S., Guite, J., Mick, E., Chen, L., . . . Perrin, J. (1996). A prospective 4-year follow-up study of attention-deficit hyperactivity and related disorders. *Archives of General Psychiatry, 53*(5), 437–446.

Biederman, J., Faraone, S. V., Monuteaux, M. C., Bober, M., & Cadogen, E. (2004). Gender effects on attention-deficit/hyperactivity disorder in adults, revisited. *Biological Psychiatry, 55*(7), 692–700.

Biederman, J., Faraone, S. V., Spencer, T., Wilens, T., Norman, D., Lapey, K. A., . . . Doyle, A. (1993a). Patterns of psychiatric comorbidity, cognition, and psychosocial functioning in adults with attention deficit hyperactivity disorder. *American Journal of Psychiatry, 150*(12), 1792–1798.

Biederman, J., Faraone, S. V., Spencer, T., Wilens, T., Norman, D., Lapey, K. A., et al. (1993b). Patterns of psychiatric comorbidity, cognition, and psychosocial functioning in adults with attention deficit hyperactivity disorder. *American Journal of Psychiatry, 150*(12), 1792–1798.

Biederman, J., Faraone, S. V., Spencer, T., Wilens, T., Norman, D., Lapey, K. A., et al. (1993c). Patterns of psychiatric comorbidity, cognition, and psychosocial functioning in adults with attention deficit hyperactivity disorder. *American Journal of Psychiatry, 150*(12), 1792–1798.

Biederman, J., Mick, E., & Faraone, S. V. (2000). Age-dependent decline of symptoms of attention deficit hyperactivity disorder: Impact of remission definition and symptom type. *American Journal of Psychiatry, 157*(5), 816–818.

Biederman, J., Wilens, T., Mick, E., Faraone, S. V., Weber, W., Curtis, S., . . . Soriano, J. (1997). Is ADHD a risk factor for psychoactive substance use disorders? Findings from a four-year prospective follow-up study. *Journal of the American Academy of Child and Adolescent Psychiatry, 36*(1), 21–29.

Bloomquist, M. L., August, G. J., & Ostrander, R. (1991). Effects of a school-based cognitive-behavioral intervention for ADHD children. *Journal of Abnormal Child Psychology, 19*, 591–605.

Borland, B. L., & Heckman, H. K. (1976). Hyperactive boys and their brothers: A 25-year follow-up study. *Archives of General Psychiatry, 33*, 669–675.

Bridgett, D. J., & Walker, M. E. (2006). Intellectual functioning in adults with ADHD: a meta-analytic examination of full scale IQ differences between adults with and without ADHD. *Psychological Assessment, 18*(1), 1–14.

Burgess, P. W., Alderman, N., Evans, J., Emslie, H., & Wilson, B. A. (1998). The ecological validity of tests of executive function. *Journal of the International Neuropsychological Society, 4*(6), 547–558.

Busch, B., Biederman, J., Cohen, L. G., Sayer, J. M., Monuteaux, M. C., Mick, E., . . . Faraone, S. V. (2002). Correlates of ADHD among children in pediatric and psychiatric clinics. *Psychiatric Services, 53*(9), 1103–1111.

Bush, G., Frazier, J. A., Rauch, S. L., Seidman, L. J., Whalen, P. J., Jenike, M. A., . . . Biederman, J. (1999). Anterior cingulate cortex dysfunction in attention-deficit/hyperactivity disorder revealed by fMRI and the counting stroop. *Biological Psychiatry, 45*(12), 1542–1552.

Bush, G., Valera, E. M., & Seidman, L. J. (2005). Functional neuroimaging of attention-deficit/hyperactivity disorder: a review and suggested future directions. *Biological Psychiatry, 57*(11), 1273–1284.

Canino, G., Shrout, P. E., Rubio-Stipec, M., Bird, H. R., Bravo, M., Ramírez, R., . . . Martínez-Taboas, A. (2004). The *DSM-IV* rates of child and adolescent disorders in Puerto Rico: prevalence, correlates, service use, and the effects of impairment. *Archives of General Psychiatry, 61*(1), 85–93.

Chalfant, A. M., Rapee, R., & Carroll, L. (2007). Treating anxiety disorders in children with high functioning autism spectrum disorders: a controlled trial. *Journal of Autism and Developmental Disorders, 37*(10), 1842–1857.

Chaytor, N., Schmitter-Edgecombe, M., & Burr, R. (2006). Improving the ecological validity of executive functioning assessment. *Archives of Clinical Neuropsychology, 21*(3), 217–227.

Davis, M., & Sondheimer, D. (2005). Child mental health systems' efforts to support youth in transition to adulthood. *Journal of Behavioral Health Services and Research, 32*, 27–42.

Delis, D. C., Kramer, J. H., Kaplan, E., & Ober, B. A. (2000). *California Verbal Learning Test (2nd ed.)*. San Antonio, TX: The Psychological Corp.

De Quiros, G. B., & Kinsbourne, M. (2001). Adult ADHD: Analysis of self-ratings on a behavior questionnaire. *Annals of the New York Academy of Sciences, 931*, 140–147.

Dodson, W. W. (2005). Pharmacotherapy of adult ADHD. *Journal of Clinical Psychology, 61*(5), 589–606.

Dougherty, D. D., Bonab, A. A., Spencer, T. J., Rauch, S. L., Madras, B. K., & Fischman, A. J. (1999). Dopamine transporter density in patients with attention deficit hyperactivity disorder. *Lancet, 354*(9196), 2132–2133.

Downey, K. K., Stelson, F. W., Pomerleau, O. F., & Giordani, B. (1997). Adult attention deficit hyperactivity disorder: psychological test profiles in a clinical population. *Journal of Nervous and Mental Disease, 185*(1), 32–38.

DuPaul, G. J., & Eckert, T. L. (1997). The effects of school-based interventions for attention deficit hyperactivity disorder: A meta-analysis. *School Psychology Digest, 26,* 5–27.

DuPaul, G. J., Power, T., & Anastopoulos, A. (1998). *ADHD Rating Scale-IV: Checklists, norms, and clinical interpretation.* New York, NY: Guilford Press.

DuPaul, G. J., Schaughency, E. A., Weyandt, L. L., Tripp, G., Kiesner, J., Ota, K., & Stanish, H. (2001). Self-report of ADHD symptoms in university students: cross-gender and cross-national prevalence. *Journal of Learning Disabilities, 34*(4), 370–379.

Dush, D. M., Hirt, M. L., & Schroeder, H. E. (1989). Self-statement modification in the treatment of child behavior disorders: a meta-analysis. *Psychological Bulletin, 106*(1), 97–106.

Epstein, J. N., Conners, C. K., Sitarenios, G., & Erhardt, D. (1998). Continuous performance test results of adults with attention deficit hyperactivity disorder. *The Clinical Neuropsychologist, 12*(2), 155–168.

Epstein, J. N., Johnson, D. E., Varia, I. M., & Conners, C. K. (2001). Neuropsychological assessment of response inhibition in adults with ADHD. *Journal of Clinical and Experimental Neuropsychology, 23*(3), 362–371.

Ercan, E. S., Coşkunol, H., Varan, A., & Toksöz, K. (2003). Childhood attention deficit/hyperactivity disorder and alcohol dependence: a 1-year follow-up. *Alcohol and Alcoholism, 38*(4), 352–356.

Ernst, M., Zametkin, A., Phillips, R., & Cohen, R. (1998). Age-related changes in brain glucose metabolism in adults with attention-deficit/hyperactivity disorder and control subjects. *The Journal of Neuropsychiatry and Clinical Neurosciences, 10,* 168–177.

Faraone, S. V., Biederman, J., Feighner, J. A., & Monuteaux, M. C. (2000). Assessing symptoms of attention deficit hyperactivity disorder in children and adults: which is more valid? *Journal of Consulting and Clinical Psychology, 68*(5), 830–842.

Faraone, S. V., Biederman, J., Lehman, B. K., Spencer, T., Norman, D., Seidman, L. J., . . . Tsuang, M. T. (1993). Intellectual performance and school failure in children with attention deficit hyperactivity disorder and in their siblings. *Journal of Abnormal Psychology, 102*(4), 616–623.

Faraone, S. V., Biederman, J., & Mick, E. (2006). The age-dependent decline of attention deficit hyperactivity disorder: a meta-analysis of follow-up studies. *Psychological Medicine, 36*(2), 159–165.

Faraone, S. V., Biederman, J., & Monuteaux, M. C. (2000). Toward guidelines for pedigree selection in genetic studies of attention deficit hyperactivity disorder. *Genetic Epidemiology, 18*(1), 1–16.

Faraone, S. V., Biederman, J., Spencer, T., Mick, E., Murray, K., Petty, C., . . . Monuteaux, M. C. (2006). Diagnosing adult attention deficit hyperactivity disorder: are late onset and subthreshold diagnoses valid? *American Journal of Psychiatry, 163*(10), 1720–1729; quiz 1859.

Faraone, S. V., Sergeant, J., Gillberg, C., & Biederman, J. (2003). The worldwide prevalence of ADHD: is it an American condition? *World Psychiatry, 2*(2), 104–113.

Faraone, S. V., Wilens, T. E., Petty, C., Antshel, K., Spencer, T., & Biederman, J. (2007). Substance use among ADHD adults: implications of late onset and subthreshold diagnoses. *American Journal on Addictions, 16*(Suppl. 1), 24–32; quiz 33–24.

Fischer, M., Barkley, R. A., Edelbrock, C. S., & Smallish, L. (1990). The adolescent outcome of hyperactive children diagnosed by research criteria: II, Academic, attentional, and neuropsychological status. *Journal of Consulting and Clinical Psychology, 58*(5), 580–588.

Frazier, T. W., Demaree, H. A., & Youngstrom, E. A. (2004). Meta-analysis of intellectual and neuropsychological test performance in attention-deficit/hyperactivity disorder. *Neuropsychology, 18*(3), 543–555.

Fried, R., Petty, C. R., Surman, C. B., Reimer, B., Aleardi, M., Martin, J. M., . . . Biederman, J. (2006). Characterizing impaired driving in adults with attention-deficit/hyperactivity disorder: A controlled study. *Journal of Clinical Psychiatry, 67*(4), 567–574.

Froehlich, T. E., Lanphear, B. P., Epstein, J. N., Barbaresi, W. J., Katusic, S. K., & Kahn, R. S. (2007). Prevalence, recognition, and treatment of attention-deficit/hyperactivity disorder in a national sample of US children. *Archives of Pediatrics and Adolescent Medicine, 161*(9), 857–864.

Fuster, J. M. (1997). *The prefrontal cortex.* New York, NY: Raven.

Gansler, D. A., Fucetola, R., Krengel, M., Stetson, S., Zimering, R., & Makary, C. (1998). Are there cognitive subtypes in adult attention deficit/hyperactivity disorder? *Journal of Nervous and Mental Disease, 186*(12), 776–781.

Gerdes, A. C., Hoza, B., & Pelham, W. E. (2003). Attention-deficit/hyperactivity disordered boys' relationships with their mothers and fathers: child, mother, and father perceptions. *Development and Psychopathology, 15*(2), 363–382.

Gioia, G. A., Isquith, P. K., Guy, S. C., & Kenworthy, L. (2000). Behavior rating inventory of executive function. *Child Neuropsychology, 6*(3), 235–238.

Gordon, M., Antshel, K., Faraone, S., Barkley, R., Lewandowski, L., Hudziak, J. J., . . . Cunningham, C. (2006). Symptoms versus impairment: the case for respecting *DSM-IV's* Criterion D. *Journal of Attention Disorders, 9*(3), 465–475.

Hart, E. L., Lahey, B. B., Loeber, R., Applegate, B., & Frick, P. J. (1995). Developmental change in attention-deficit hyperactivity disorder in boys: a four-year longitudinal study. *Journal of Abnormal Child Psychology, 23*(6), 729–749.

Heaton, R. K., Chelune, G. J., Talley, J. L., Kay, G. G., & Curtiss, G. (1993). *Wisconsin Card Sorting Test manual: Revised and expanded.* Odessa, FL: Psychological Assessment Resources.

Heiligenstein, E., Conyers, L. M., Berns, A. R., & Miller, M. A. (1998). Preliminary normative data on *DSM-IV* attention deficit hyperactivity disorder in college students. *Journal of American College Health, 46*(4), 185–188.

Hervey, A. S., Epstein, J. N., & Curry, J. F. (2004). Neuropsychology of adults with attention-deficit/hyperactivity disorder: a meta-analytic review. *Neuropsychology, 18*(3), 485–503.

Hesslinger, B., Thiel, T., Tebartz van Elst, L., Hennig, J., & Ebert, D. (2001). Attention-deficit disorder in adults with or without hyperactivity: where is the difference? A study in humans using short echo (1)H-magnetic resonance spectroscopy. *Neuroscience Letters, 304*(1–2), 117–119.

Hill, J. C., & Schoener, E. P. (1996). Age-dependent decline of attention deficit hyperactivity disorder. *American Journal of Psychiatry, 153*(9), 1143–1146.

Holdnack, J. A., Moberg, P. J., Arnold, S. E., Gur, R. C., & Gur, R. E. (1995). Speed of processing and verbal learning deficits in adults diagnosed with attention deficit disorder. *Neuropsychiatry, Neuropsychology, and Behavioral Neurology, 8*(4), 282–292.

Hoza, B., Pelham, W. E., Jr., Dobbs, J., Owens, J. S., & Pillow, D. R. (2002). Do boys with attention-deficit/hyperactivity disorder have positive illusory self-concepts? *Journal of Abnormal Psychology, 111*(2), 268–278.

Hutchinson, A. D., Mathias, J. L., & Banich, M. T. (2008). Corpus callosum morphology in children and adolescents with attention deficit hyperactivity disorder: a meta-analytic review. *Neuropsychology, 22*(3), 341–349.

Johnson, D., Epstein, J., Waid, R., Latham, P., Voronin, K., & Anton, R. (2001). Neuropsychological performance deficits in adults with attention deficit/hyperactivity disorder. *Archives of Clinical Neuropsychology, 16*, 587–604.

Johnston, C., & Mash, E. J. (2001). Families of children with attention-deficit/hyperactivity disorder: review and recommendations for future research. *Clinical Child and Family Psychology Review, 4*(3), 183–207.

Jonsdottir, S., Bouma, A., Sergeant, J. A., & Scherder, E. J. (2006). Relationships between neuropsychological measures of executive function and behavioral measures of ADHD symptoms and comorbid behavior. *Archives of Clinical Neuropsychology, 21*(5), 383–394.

Kessler, R. C., Adler, L., Barkley, R., Biederman, J., Conners, C. K., Demler, O., . . . Zaslavsky, A. M. (2006). The prevalence and correlates of adult ADHD in the United States: results from the National Comorbidity Survey Replication. *American Journal of Psychiatry, 163*(4), 716–723.

Kessler, R. C., Berglund, P., Demler, O., Jin, R., Merikangas, K. R., & Walters, E. E. (2005). Lifetime prevalence and age-of-onset distributions of DSM-IV disorders in the National Comorbidity Survey Replication. *Archives of General Psychiatry, 62*(6), 593–602.

Klee, S., Garfinkel, B., & Beauchesne, H. (1986). Attention deficits in adults. *Psychiatric Annals, 16*(1), 52–56.

Knouse, L. E., Bagwell, C. L., Barkley, R. A., & Murphy, K. R. (2005). Accuracy of self-evaluation in adults with ADHD: evidence from a driving study. *Journal of Attention Disorders, 8*(4), 221–234.

Krause, J., Krause, K. H., Dresel, S. H., la Fougere, C., & Ackenheil, M. (2006). ADHD in adolescence and adulthood, with a special focus on the dopamine transporter and nicotine. *Dialogues in Clinical Neuroscience, 8*(1), 29–36.

Krause, K., Dresel, S. H., Krause, J., Kung, H. F., & Tatsch, K. (2000). Increased striatal dopamine transporter in adult patients with attention deficit hyperactivity disorder: Effects of methylphenidate as measured by single photon emission computed tomography. *Neuroscience Letters, 285*(2), 107–110.

Lahey, B. B., Applegate, B., McBurnett, K., Biederman, J., Greenhill, L., Hynd, G. W., . . . Richters, J. (1994). DSM-IV field trials for attention deficit hyperactivity disorder in children and adolescents. *American Journal of Psychiatry, 151*(11), 1673–1685.

Loeber, R., Burke, J. D., Lahey, B. B., Winters, A., & Zera, M. (2000). Oppositional defiant and conduct disorder: a review of the past 10 years (pt. 1). *Journal of the American Academy of Child and Adolescent Psychiatry, 39*(12), 1468–1484.

Lovejoy, M. C., Graczyk, P. A., O'Hare, E., & Neuman, G. (2000). Maternal depression and parenting behavior: a meta-analytic review. *Clinical Psychology Review, 20*(5), 561–592.

Mackie, S., Shaw, P., Lenroot, R., Pierson, R., Greenstein, D. K., Nugent, T. F., III, . . . Rapoport, J. L. (2007). Cerebellar development and clinical outcome in attention deficit hyperactivity disorder. *American Journal of Psychiatry, 164*(4), 647–655.

Mannuzza, S., Klein, R. G., Bessler, A., Malloy, P., & LaPadula, M. (1993). Adult outcome of hyperactive boys: Educational achievement, occupational rank, and psychiatric status. *Archives of General Psychiatry, 50*(7), 565–576.

Marchetta, N. D., Hurks, P. P., Krabbendam, L., & Jolles, J. (2008). Interference control, working memory, concept shifting, and verbal fluency in adults with attention-deficit/hyperactivity disorder (ADHD). *Neuropsychology, 22*(1), 74–84.

McGough, J. J., & Barkley, R. A. (2004). Diagnostic controversies in adult attention deficit hyperactivity disorder. *American Journal of Psychiatry, 161*(11), 1948–1956.

Milberger, S., Biederman, J., Faraone, S. V., Chen, L., & Jones, J. (1997). ADHD is associated with early initiation of cigarette smoking in children and adolescents. *Journal of the American Academy of Child and Adolescent Psychiatry, 36*(1), 37–44.

Molina, B. S., & Pelham, W. E., Jr. (2003). Childhood predictors of adolescent substance use in a longitudinal study of children with ADHD. *Journal of Abnormal Psychology 112*(3), 497–507.

Mota, V. L., & Schachar, R. J. (2000). Reformulating attention-deficit/hyperactivity disorder according to signal detection theory. *Journal of the American Academy of Child and Adolescent Psychiatry, 39*(9), 1144–1151.

MTA Collaborative Group. (1999a). A 14-month randomized clinical trial of treatment strategies for attention-deficit/hyperactivity disorder. *Archives of General Psychiatry, 56*(12), 1073–1086.

MTA Collaborative Group. (1999b). Moderators and mediators of treatment response for children with attention-deficit/hyperactivity disorder: the Multimodal Treatment Study of Children with Attention-deficit/hyperactivity disorder. *Archives of General Psychiatry, 56*(12), 1088–1096.

MTA Collaborative Group. (2004). National Institute of Mental Health Multimodal Treatment Study of ADHD follow-up: changes in effectiveness and growth after the end of treatment. *Pediatrics, 113*(4), 762–769.

Murphy, K., & Barkley, R. A. (1996a). Attention deficit hyperactivity disorder adults: Comorbidities and adaptive impairments. *Comprehensive Psychiatry, 37*(6), 393–401.

Murphy, K., & Barkley, R. A. (1996b). Attention deficit hyperactivity disorder adults: Comorbidities and adaptive impairments. *Comprehensive Psychiatry 37*(6), 393–401.

Murphy, K., Barkley, R. A., & Bush, T. (2001). Executive functioning and olfactory identification in young adults with attention deficit-hyperactivity disorder. *Neuropsychology, 15*, 211–220.

Murray, C., & Johnston, C. (2006). Parenting in mothers with and without attention-deficit/hyperactivity disorder. *Journal of Abnormal Psychology, 115*(1), 52–61.

Paloyelis, Y., Mehta, M. A., Kuntsi, J., & Asherson, P. (2007). Functional MRI in ADHD: a systematic literature review. *Expert Review of Neurotherapeutics, 7*(10), 1337–1356.

Pliszka, S. (2007). Practice parameter for the assessment and treatment of children and adolescents with attention-deficit/hyperactivity disorder. *Journal of the American Academy of Child and Adolescent Psychiatry, 46*(7), 894–921.

Rapport, M. D., Alderson, R. M., Kofler, M. J., Sarver, D. E., Bolden, J., & Sims, V. (2008). Working memory deficits in boys with attention-deficit/hyperactivity disorder (ADHD): the contribution of central executive and subsystem processes. *Journal of Abnormal Child Psychology, 36*(6), 825–837.

Riordan, H. J., Flashman, L. A., Saykin, A. J., Frutiger, S. A., Carroll, K. E., & Huey, L. (1999). Neuropsychological correlates of methylphenidate treatment in adult ADHD with and without depression. *Archives of Clinical Neuropsychology, 14*(2), 217–233.

Rostain, A. L., & Ramsay, J. R. (2006). A combined treatment approach for adults with ADHD: Results of an open study of 43 patients. *Journal of Attention Disorders, 10*(2), 150–159.

Safren, S. A., Otto, M. W., Sprich, S., Winett, C. L., Wilens, T. E., & Biederman, J. (2005). Cognitive-behavioral therapy for ADHD in medication-treated adults with continued symptoms. *Behavior Research and Therapy, 43*(7), 831–842.

Schubiner, H., Tzelepis, A., Milberger, S., Lockhart, N., Kruger, M., Kelley, B. J., & Schoener, E. P. (2000). Prevalence of attention-deficit/hyperactivity disorder and conduct disorder among substance abusers. *Journal of Clinical Psychiatry, 61*(4), 244–251.

Schweitzer, J. B., Faber, T. L., Grafton, S. T., Tune, L. E., Hoffman, J. M., & Kilts, C. D. (2000). Alterations in the functional anatomy of working memory in adult attention deficit hyperactivity disorder. *American Journal of Psychiatry, 157*(2), 278–280.

Seidman, L. J., Biederman, J., Faraone, S. V., Weber, W., & Ouellette, C. (1997). Toward defining a neuropsychology of attention deficit-hyperactivity disorder: performance of children and adolescents from a large clinically referred sample. *Journal of Consulting and Clinical Psychology, 65*(1), 150–160.

Seidman, L. J., Biederman, J., Weber, W., Hatch, M., & Faraone, S. V. (1998). Neuropsychological function in adults with attention-deficit hyperactivity disorder. *Biological Psychiatry, 44*(4), 260–268.

Semrud-Clikeman, M., Biederman, J., Sprich-Buckminster, S., Lehman, B. K., Faraone, S. V., & Norman, D. (1992). Comorbidity between ADDH and learning disability: a review and report in a clinically referred sample. *Journal of the American Academy of Child and Adolescent Psychiatry, 31*(3), 439–448.

Shanahan, M. J. (2000). Pathways to Adulthood in Changing Societies: Variability and Mechanisms in Life Course Perspective. *Annual Review of Sociology, 26,* 667–692.

Shekim, W. O., Asarnow, R. F., Hess, E., Zaucha, K., & Wheeler, N. (1990). A clinical and demographic profile of a sample of adults with attention deficit hyperactivity disorder, residual state. *Comprehensive Psychiatry, 31*(5), 416–425.

Spencer, T. J., Biederman, J., Wilens, T., Prince, J., Hatch, M., Jones, J., . . . Seidman, L. (1998). Effectiveness and tolerability of tomoxetine in adults with attention deficit hyperactivity disorder. *American Journal of Psychiatry, 155*(5), 693–695.

Spencer, T. J., Faraone, S. V., Michelson, D., Adler, L. A., Reimherr, F. W., Glatt, S. J., & Biederman, J. (2006). Atomoxetine and adult attention-deficit/hyperactivity disorder: the effects of comorbidity. *Journal of Clinical Psychiatry, 67*(3), 415–420.

Szatmari, P., Offord, D. R., & Boyle, M. H. (1989). Correlates, associated impairments and patterns of service utilization of children with attention deficit disorder: findings from the Ontario Child Health Study. *Journal of Child Psychology and Psychiatry, 30*(2), 205–217.

Thomson, J. A., Tolmie, A. K., Foot, H. C., Whelan, K. M., Sarvary, P., & Morrison, S. (2005). Influence of virtual reality training on the roadside crossing judgments of child pedestrians. *Journal of Experimental Psychology: Applied, 11*(3), 175–186.

Torgersen, T., Gjervan, B., & Rasmussen, K. (2006). ADHD in adults: a study of clinical characteristics, impairment and comorbidity. *Nordic Journal of Psychiatry, 60*(1), 38–43.

Valera, E. M., Faraone, S. V., Murray, K. E., & Seidman, L. J. (2007). Meta-analysis of structural imaging findings in attention-deficit/hyperactivity disorder. *Biological Psychiatry, 61*(12), 1361–1369.

Van Dyck, C. H., Quinlan, D. M., Cretella, L. M., Staley, J. K., Malison, R. T., Baldwin, R. M., . . . Innis, R. B. (2002). Unaltered dopamine transporter availability in adult attention deficit hyperactivity disorder. *American Journal of Psychiatry, 159*(2), 309–312.

Verity, R., & Coates, J. (2007). Service innovation: transitional attention-deficit hyperactivity disorder clinic. *Psychiatric Bulletin, 31,* 99–100.

Walker, A. J., Shores, E. A., Trollor, J. N., Lee, T., & Sachdev, P. S. (2000). Neuropsychological functioning of adults with attention deficit hyperactivity disorder. *Journal of Clinical and Experimental Neuropsychology, 22*(1), 115–124.

Ward, M. F., Wender, P. H., & Reimherr, F. W. (1993). The Wender Utah Rating Scale: An aid in the retrospective diagnosis of childhood attention deficit hyperactivity disorder. *American Journal of Psychiatry, 150,* 885–890.

Wee, S., & Woolverton, W. L. (2004). Evaluation of the reinforcing effects of ato-moxetine in monkeys: comparison to methylphenidate and desipramine. *Drug and Alcohol Dependence, 75*(3), 271–276.

Weiss, G., & Hechtman, L. (1993). *Hyperactive children grown up* (2nd ed.). New York, NY: Guilford Press.

Weiss, G., Hechtman, L., Milroy, T., & Perlman, T. (1985). Psychiatric status of hyper-actives as adults: a controlled prospective 15-year follow-up of 63 hyperactive chil-dren. *Journal of the American Academy of Child and Adolescent Psychiatry, 24*(2), 211–220.

Weiss, M. D., & Hechtman, L. (2006). A randomized double-blind trial of paroxetine and/or dextroamphetamine and problem-focused therapy for attention-deficit/hyperactivity disorder in adults. *Journal of Clinical Psychiatry, 67*(4), 611–619.

Weiss, M. D., & Weiss, J. R. (2004). A guide to the treatment of adults with ADHD. *Journal of Clinical Psychiatry, 65*(Suppl. 3), 27–37.

Welsh, M. C., & Pennington, B. F. (1988). Assessing frontal lobe functioning in chil-dren: views from developmental psychology. *Developmental Neuropsychology, 4*, 199–230.

Wender, P. H. (1995). *Attention-Deficit Hyperactivity Disorder in Adults*. New York, NY: Oxford University Press.

Wender, P. H., Wolf, L. E., & Wasserstein, J. (2001). Adults with ADHD. An over-view. *Annals of the New York Academy of Sciences, 931*, 1–16.

Wilens, T. (2004). Attention-deficit/hyperactivity disorder and the substance use disorders: The nature of the relationship, subtypes at risk and treatment issues. *Psychiatric Clinics of North America, 27*(2), 283–301.

Willcutt, E. G., & Pennington, B. F. (2000). Comorbidity of reading disability and attention-deficit/hyperactivity disorder: differences by gender and subtype. *Journal of Learning Disabilities, 33*(2), 179–191.

Wilson, J. M., & Marcotte, A. C. (1996). Psychosocial adjustment and educational outcome in adolescents with a childhood diagnosis of attention deficit disorder. *Journal of the American Academy of Child and Adolescent Psychiatry, 35*(5), 579–587.

Wood, R. L., & Liossi, C. (2006). The ecological validity of executive tests in a severely brain injured sample. *Archives of Clinical Neuropsychology, 21*(5), 429–437.

Zametkin, A. J., Nordahl, T. E., Gross, M., King, A. C., Semple, W. E., Rumsey, J., . . . Cohen, R. M. (1990). Cerebral glucose metabolism in adults with hyperactivity of childhood onset. *New England Journal of Medicine, 323*(20), 1361–1366.

Zang, Y. F., Jin, Z., Weng, X. C., Zhang, L., Zeng, Y. W., Yang, L., . . . Faraone, S. V. (2005). Functional MRI in attention-deficit hyperactivity disorder: evidence for hypofrontality. *Brain and Development, 27*(8), 544–550.

PART

II

Assessment

6

Assessment of Cognitive and Neuropsychological Processes

JACK A. NAGLIERI

SAM GOLDSTEIN

INTRODUCTION

Assessment of intelligence plays an important role in the process of determining if an adolescent or adult has a disability. For those suspected of having a Specific Learning Disability (SLD), the intelligence test provides an important reference point to compare to levels of achievement. For those who may have Attention-Deficit/Hyperactivity Disorder (ADHD), the measure of intelligence is used to rule out other disabilities that may better explain the person's behavior. Intelligence tests have and will continue to provide a critical component of any comprehensive assessment needed to determine the presence of disabilities, such as SLD and ADHD. Their importance, however, demands a thorough understanding of the strengths and limitations of these tests of ability, an appreciation of the research on their effectiveness, and an examination of modern views of assessing intelligence. The goal of this chapter is to address these issues.

This chapter reexamines intelligence as measured by traditional IQ tests with special attention to the utility such tests have for diagnosis. In order to achieve this goal, the chapter includes a brief overview of the history and definitions of intelligence and examines examples of measures of intelligence more closely. Emphasis will be placed on the importance of understanding how intelligence is conceptualized and measured by different tests and the implications this has for assessment. The chapter also provides a conceptual model of assessment of basic psychological processes and how that information can aid in the diagnostic process and treatment of adolescents and adults.

DEFINITIONS OF LEARNING AND ATTENTION DISORDERS

Learning Disabilities and IQ

Learning Disabilities (LD) are defined in the *Diagnostic and Statistical Manual of Mental Disorders* (4th ed., text revision; *DSM-IV-TR*) (American Psychiatric Association [APA], 2000) on the basis of an inconsistency between ability and achievement (reading, math, or written expression, or a nonspecified area) when that difference is not better accounted for by inadequate education, cultural or ethnic differences, impaired vision or hearing, or mental retardation. The definition of LD included in the *DSM-IV* is based on finding achievement scores on individually administered, standardized tests in reading, mathematics, or written expression that are substantially below that expected for age, schooling, and level of intelligence. The size of the discrepancy should be more than 2 standard deviations, but a difference of at least 1 standard deviation is acceptable if the IQ test score may have been influenced by an associated disorder in cognitive processing, a mental disorder, or the ethnic or cultural background of the individual. Importantly, LD should significantly interfere with achievement or daily living that involves reading, math, or writing. The *DSM-IV* also recognizes that problems with cognitive processing (e.g., deficits in visual perception, linguistic processes, attention, or memory) may have preceded or are associated with LD.

The term "Specific Learning Disability" is defined in the Individuals with Disabilities Education Act (IDEA) and is used for students up to age 21 as specified by the U.S. federal government. This definition has similarities and differences from that used in the *DSM-IV*. The similarities include an academic failure despite evidence that the student's scores are not better explained by inadequate education, cultural or ethnic differences, or impaired vision or hearing, mental retardation, or other disability. The differences between IDEA and *DSM-IV* include: (a) the age range for which the definition applies; (b) the disability is described as a "specific" learning disability; and (c) the definition of the disability is a disorder in basic psychological processes. The definition is:

Specific learning disability means a disorder in one or more of the basic psychological processes involved in understanding or in using language, spoken or written, which may manifest itself in an imperfect ability to listen, think, speak, read, write, spell, or to do mathematical calculations. The term includes such conditions as perceptual handicaps, brain injury, minimal brain dysfunction, dyslexia, and developmental aphasia. The term does not include children who have problems that are primarily the result of visual, hearing, or motor disabilities, or mental retardation, emotional disturbance, or of environmental, cultural, or economic disadvantage. (IDEA, 2004)

The two different approaches to defining SLD reflect differences in the field regarding the best way to conceptualize and operationalize identification of the disorder. Insofar as assessment of adolescents and adults is concerned, both the *DSM-IV* and IDEA definitions involve some kind of academic skills deficit despite adequate instruction, making the evaluation of achievement a critical component of the comprehensive assessment. These two definitions also involve assessment of ability, defined either as traditional IQ or as some measure of basic psychological process to establish an ability achievement difference. Such a difference provides evidence of unexpected poor performance relative to ability. Importantly, both approaches to diagnosis stress the importance of ensuring that cultural or linguistic issues do not influence the scores obtained on these tests and thereby bias the process.

ADHD and IQ

The essential feature of ADHD described in the *DSM-IV* (APA, 2000) is a "persistent pattern of inattention and/or hyperactivity-impulsivity that is more frequently displayed and more severe than is typically observed in individuals at a comparable level of development" (p. 78). The diagnostic criteria for the three subtypes of ADHD are:

A. Persistent pattern of inattention and/or hyperactivity-impulsivity that is more frequently displayed and is more severe than is typically observed in individuals at comparable level of development. Individual must meet criteria for either (1) or (2):

  (1) Six (or more) of the following symptoms of inattention have persisted for at least six months to a degree that is maladaptive and inconsistent with developmental level:

  Inattention

   (a) often fails to give close attention to details or makes careless mistakes in schoolwork, work or other activities
   (b) often has difficulty sustaining attention in tasks or play activity
   (c) often does not seem to listen when spoken to directly
   (d) often does not follow through on instructions and fails to finish schoolwork, chores or duties in the workplace (not due to oppositional behavior or failure to understand instructions)
   (e) often has difficulty organizing tasks and activities
   (f) often avoids, dislikes, or is reluctant to engage in tasks that require sustained mental effort (such as schoolwork or homework)
   (g) often looses things necessary for tasks or activities (e.g., toys, school assignments, pencils, books or tools)
   (h) is often easily distracted by extraneous stimuli
   (i) is often forgetful in daily activities

  (2) Six (or more) of the following symptoms of hyperactivity-impulsivity have persisted for at least six months to a degree that is maladaptive and inconsistent with developmental level:

Hyperactivity

(a) often fidgets with hands or feet or squirms in seat
(b) often leaves seat in classroom or in other situations in which remaining seated is expected
(c) often runs about or climbs excessively in situations in which it is inappropriate (in adolescents or adults, may be limited to subjective feelings of restlessness)
(d) often has difficulty playing or engaging in leisure activities quietly
(e) is often "on the go" or often acts as if "driven by a motor"
(f) often talks excessively

Impulsivity

(g) often blurts out answers before questions have been completed
(h) often has difficulty awaiting turn
(i) often interrupts or intrudes on others (e.g., butts into conversations or games)

B. Some hyperactive-impulsive or inattentive symptoms must have been present before age 7 years.

C. Some impairment from the symptoms is present in at least two settings (e.g., at school [or work] and at home).

D. There must be clear evidence of interference with developmentally appropriate social, academic or occupational functioning.

E. The disturbance does not occur exclusively during the course of a Pervasive Developmental Disorder, Schizophrenia, or other Psychotic Disorders and is not better accounted for by another mental disorder (e.g., Mood Disorder, Anxiety Disorder, Dissociative Disorder, or a Personality Disorder) (APA, 2000, pp. 92–93).

The three subtypes of ADHD are:

ADHD, *Predominantly Inattentive Type:* This subtype is used if 6 (or more) symptoms of inattention (but fewer than 6 symptoms of hyperactivity-impulsivity) have persisted for at least 6 months.

ADHD *Predominantly Hyperactive-Impulsive Type:* This subtype should be used if 6 (or more) symptoms of hyperactivity-impulsivity (but fewer than 6 of inattention) have persisted for at least 6 months.

ADHD *Combined Type:* This subtype should be used if 6 (or more) symptoms of inattention and 6 (or more) symptoms of hyperactivity-impulsivity have persisted for at least 6 months.

Adolescents with ADHD are identified within the schools using the *Other health impairment designation* in IDEA, which is described without specific reference to IQ in this way:

Other health impairment means having limited strength, vitality, or alertness, including a heightened alertness to environmental stimuli, that results in limited alertness with respect to the educational environment, that
(i) Is due to chronic or acute health problems such as asthma, attention deficit disorder or attention deficit hyperactivity disorder, diabetes, epilepsy, a heart condition, hemophilia, lead poisoning, leukemia, nephritis, rheumatic fever, sickle cell anemia, and Tourette syndrome; and
(ii) Adversely affects a child's educational performance. (*U.S. Department of Education*, 2006, p. 46757)

The role IQ tests have in diagnosis of these two disorders differs in that ability is necessary for meeting the requirements of the *DSM-IV* when assessing children with SLD but not for ADHD. For SLD, IQ plays a key role in differentiating those whose low achievement is related to low ability (e.g., no discrepancy between IQ and achievement) and those for whom achievement is unexpected given their overall ability (Kavale, 2002). For ADHD, IQ is used to determine if the symptoms related to this disorder are related to a disorder other than attention deficit. In both these instances, however, the way in which intelligence is measured has a direct impact on the information that is received. This fact can lead to obstacles for individuals with disabilities as well as those from culturally and linguistically diverse populations. It is important to reexamine the scores obtained using these various measures of ability.

HOW IS IQ MEASURED?

IQ has been measured for more than 100 years using verbal, quantitative, and nonverbal test questions. The tests of today were initially formulated in 1905 (Binet & Simon, 1905) and in 1939 with the publication of the Wechsler-Bellevue Scales (Wechsler, 1939). These tests measure *general ability* through questions that can be described as verbal (e.g., vocabulary or word analogies), performance (arranging blocks to match a simple design or assembling puzzles to make a common object), or quantitative (e.g., math word problems or math calculation). The performance tests have been described as nonverbal because it is an easier concept to understand, not because of any intention to measure nonverbal ability. Similarly, the verbal tests have come to be described as measures of verbal ability. In fact, these tests were developed without a theoretical basis, as noted by Pintner (1923) when he wrote, "we did not start with a clear definition of general intelligence . . . [but] borrowed from every-day life a vague term implying all-round ability and . . . we [are] still attempting to define it more sharply and endow it with a stricter scientific connotation" (p. 53). Despite the theoretical limitations, these tests represent one of the most influential contributions made by psychology to society in general (Anastasi & Urbina, 1997). They also have become ingrained in our culture as *the* way to measure ability.

There is considerable empirical support for the concept of general intelligence (see Jensen, 1998, for a review), especially when measured by tests such as the Wechsler and the Stanford-Binet. Among the most important sources of validity evidence for IQ tests is the fact that the tests predict school achievement, even though they do not correlate more highly with achievement than more modern measures of intelligence (Naglieri & Bornstein, 2003; Ramsey & Reynolds, 2004). Researchers have recognized that the content of the verbal and quantitative tests on these measures of ability are often similar to those included on tests of achievement. This is problematic for individuals who have a history of academic failure due to a disability or have had limited opportunity to learn and therefore have not had the chance to acquire verbal and quantitative skills. Suzuki and Valencia (1997) argued that verbal and quantitative questions found on most traditional IQ tests interfere with accurate assessment, especially for minority children.

Test questions that require knowledge of English are found on both traditional IQ tests and measures of achievement. For example, IQ tests require knowledge of English, and sometimes very similar words are used on both types of tests. For example, examinees are required to define a word like "bat" on subtests included in the Stanford-Binet-5 or Wechsler Intelligence Scale for Children–4th Edition intelligence tests and the Woodcock-Johnson Tests of Achievement (WJ-III Achievement; Woodcock, McGrew, & Mather, 2001a). The WJ-III Tests of Cognitive Abilities (WJ-III Cognitive; Woodcock, McGrew, & Mather, 2001b) battery contains a Verbal Comprehension subtest that has an item similar to "Tell me another word for small." The WJ-III Achievement contains a Reading Vocabulary question like, "Tell me another word for little." In addition, an item on the WJ-III Achievement Reading Vocabulary test is something like, "Tell me another word for (examiner points to the word big)," and in the WJ-III Cognitive, the examiner asks something like, "Tell me another word for tiny." Additionally, the WJ-III Cognitive Verbal Comprehension test contains Picture Vocabulary items, and the WJ-III Achievement includes Picture Vocabulary items, some of which are very similar. The lack of distinction between these items exaggerates the relationship between IQ and achievement (Naglieri & Bornstein, 2003).

The Stanford-Binet-5 (SB-5 Roid, 2003) includes Quantitative Reasoning questions that, for example, require the student to calculate the total number of circles on a page (e.g., 3 circles in one box plus 4 in a second box plus 1 in a third box). The same type of question appears on the Wechsler Adult Intelligence Scale–4th Edition (WAIS-IV; Wechsler, 2008) Arithmetic subtest, which requires the examinee to answer word problems read by the examiner (e.g., Bob has 20 toys and 5 children; if each child gets the same number of toys, how many toys will each child have?). Tests of achievement require these same skills. For example, on the WJ-III Achievement Applied Problems subtest, items are also math word problems (e.g., A boy saved 50 cents each week for 2 years; how much did he have?). Similarly, an SB-5 Quantitative Reasoning item requires the child to complete a simple math problem (e.g., $4 + 2 = ?$) just as the WJ-III Achievement test on Math Fluency (e.g., $7 + 2 = ?$) and the Wechsler Individual Achievement Test–2nd Edition (WIAT-II; Wechsler, 1992) on Numerical Operations (e.g., $3 + 2 = ?$) do.

The similarity of questions on tests of ability and achievement increases their apparent validity when the IQ and achievement tests are correlated. And although it is reasonable that verbal and math skills should be part of a test of achievement, the inclusion of these test questions on measures of ability is problematic for two reasons. First, there are many adolescents and adults who have had a low-quality education. For example, Hispanics age 25 and older are less likely to have a high school diploma (57%) than non-Hispanic Whites (88.7%). Importantly, 27.0% of Hispanics have less than a ninth-grade education compared with only 4.0% of non-Hispanic Whites, and only 14.2% of Hispanics are in managerial or professional occupations compared with 35.1% of non-Hispanic Whites (Ramirez & de la Cruz, 2002). In order to equitably evaluate the level of ability for a population such as this, or any others with limited opportunity to learn due to some SLD, tests that do not assess intelligence using verbal and quantitative skills are necessary. Second, because when SLD is defined as an ability/achievement discrepancy, the similarity in the content of the two tests decreases the probability that the scores will differ. What is known about the performance of individuals with SLD and ADHD and those with limited academic skills on these measures of ability?

GROUP PROFILES BY ABILITY TEST

Because ability tests play such an important role in the diagnostic process, it is crucial to understand the sensitivity each test may have to any unique characteristics of those with an SLD or attention deficit. Clinicians need to know if an adolescent or adult has a specific deficit in ability that is related to a specific academic learning problem. There has been considerable research on, for example, Wechsler subtest profile analysis, and most researchers conclude that no profile has diagnostic utility for individuals with SLD or ADHD (Kavale & Forness, 1995). The failure of subtest profiles has led some to argue (e.g., Naglieri, 1999) that scale, rather than subtest, variability should be examined, especially if the separate scales have ample theoretical and empirical support. In the sections that follow, research on the scale profiles is presented first for those ability tests that are used for adolescents and adults, and then for those that can be used only with adolescents. The goal is not to describe these instruments; interested readers should examine their respective test manuals. Instead, the goal is to examine the mean scores of the scales from each test. This examination helps us understand if the ability test shows a particular pattern for a specific clinical group. Such information could have important implications for understanding the cognitive characteristics of that clinical group and allow for possible diagnostic and intervention considerations. These findings, however, must be taken with recognition that the samples are not matched across the various studies, the accuracy of the diagnosis may not have been verified, and some of the sample sizes may be small. Notwithstanding these limitations, the findings do provide important insights into the extent to which these various tests can be used for assessment of adolescents and adults suspected of having an SLD or attention deficit.

WAIS-IV

The WAIS-IV manual (Wechsler, 2008) is a valuable resource for information about the performance of several diagnostic groups on the test. The research evidence was drawn from a variety of clinical settings using well articulated criteria for inclusion. The manual states that limitations regarding these samples included: lack of random selection, diagnostic procedures may have varied from clinician to clinician, sample sizes were limited, and the groups were not necessarily representative of the diagnostic or national sample. Despite these limitations, the data do provide some useful information. Figure 6.1 provides a summary of the WAIS-IV research for groups of individuals with Reading Disabilities (RD), Math Disorder (MD), and attention deficits. These three groups were mostly diagnosed according to the *DSM-IV-TR* or, for the SLD students, a discrepancy between ability and achievement as specified by school district guidelines. The WAIS-IV manual also provides comparisons to matched control groups. The results suggested that individuals with RD had low scores on all the scales with the highest score on the Processing Speed Index (PSI). Similarly, the group with MD was low on all scales except PSI. Interestingly, this group was lowest on the Working Memory Index (WMI). The mean Verbal Comprehension Index (VCI) and Perceptual Reasoning Index (PRI) scores of the group with ADHD were about average, and the WMI and PSI scales were only slightly lower. In summary, these findings suggest that the WAIS-IV Index profiles for individuals with RD and MD were similar in shape. The group with MD typically earned lower means with the exception of the VCI and PSI, on which the groups differed minimally. The sample of individuals with ADHD was generally average with somewhat lower scores on the WMI and PSI scales.

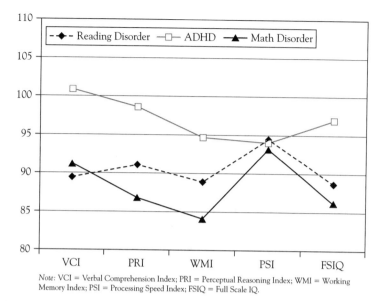

Note: VCI = Verbal Comprehension Index; PRI = Perceptual Reasoning Index; WMI = Working Memory Index; PSI = Processing Speed Index; FSIQ = Full Scale IQ.

Figure 6.1   Graphic Representation of Mean Scores for Various Groups on the WAIS-IV

All three groups earned essentially the same PSI mean score. These findings do not suggest that there are distinctive profiles for these groups of individuals, although analysis of the frequency of individual WAIS-IV profiles could yield useful information.

SB-5

The SB-5 (Roid, 2003) manual provides helpful information about scale profiles for students with LD in math (N = 49), reading (N = 212), and writing (N = 44), and those with ADHD (N = 94). The groups were identified by school district personnel and enrolled in public school programs. The method used for diagnosis of the children and adolescents with ADHD was not specified. The results illustrated in Figure 6.2 suggest that these various groups had some similarities and differences. For example, the group with ADHD had a low score on Working Memory, as did the group with a Writing Learning Disability. These two groups showed considerable similarity in profiles across the SB-5 scales. The groups with Reading and Math disabilities were similar on all scales, except the group with Math disability had a low score on the Quantitative scale. Interestingly, the highest SB-5 scores were obtained by the sample of students with a learning disability in writing. These comparisons need to be considered in light of the fact that there was no matching of samples on the basis of demographic variables, which could have influenced the findings.

WJ-III

Wendling, Mather, and Shrank (2009) provide a summary of the performance of individuals greater than 18 years of age on the WJ-III. The samples utilized in their

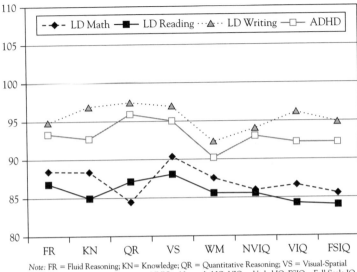

Note: FR = Fluid Reasoning; KN = Knowledge; QR = Quantitative Reasoning; VS = Visual-Spatial Processing; WM = Working Memory; NVIQ = Nonverbal IQ; VIQ = Verbal IQ; FSIQ = Full Scale IQ.

Figure 6.2   Graphic Representation of Mean Scores for Various Groups on the SB-5

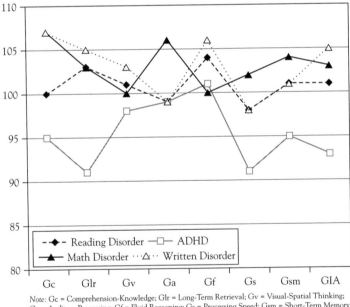

Note: Gc = Comprehension-Knowledge; Glr = Long-Term Retrieval; Gv = Visual-Spatial Thinking; Ga = Auditory Processing; Gf = Fluid Reasoning; Gs = Processing Speed; Gsm = Short-Term Memory; GIA = General Intellectual Ability.

Figure 6.3   Graphic Representation of Mean Scores for Various Groups on the WJ-III

study differed for each variable. For example, the sample sizes for the group with ADHD ranged from 39 to 117 for the Gc (Verbal Comprehension) and Gf (Concept Formation) variables, respectively. The results provided in Figure 6.3 are also limited by the lack of matching of groups on demographic variables, yet the findings are still important. The individuals with WD and RD had similar profiles except for the Gc. Those with MD were similar to the group with WD except for Gf and Gc. Interestingly, all of the scores for these three groups of individuals with a disorder were very close to or above 100. The sample with ADHD differed the most from the other three groups on the Glr (Visual Auditory Learning) and Gs (Visual Matching speed test).

RESULTS FOR OTHER ABILITY TESTS

Two important measures of ability can be used for adolescents but for which adult norms have not been developed. These are the Kaufman Assessment Battery for Children–2nd Edition (KABC-II; Kaufman & Kaufman, 2004) and the Cognitive Assessment System (CAS; Naglieri & Das, 1997). The KABC-II uses two different conceptual frameworks, one based on the work of A. R. Luria and another that uses the Cattell-Horn-Carroll (CHC) theory of cognitive abilities. (For more detail, see Kaufman & Kaufman, 2004, and Lichtenberger, Sotelo-Dynega, & Kaufman, 2009.) The CAS is a multidimensional measure of cognitive processing based on the Planning, Attention, Simultaneous, and Successive (PASS) theory of intelligence (see Naglieri, 1999, 2005; Naglieri & Das, 1997). These two instruments were designed to measure intelligence from a cognitive processing perspective and therefore utilize tests developed to measure abilities apart from verbal and quantitative skills. There are several sources of information about the profiles these tests yield for children and adolescents with various LD.

KABC-II

The KABC-II manual provides information about scale profiles for a variety of special populations. The clinical validity studies were conducted during standardization of the test, and only those cases that met specific classification criteria of the diagnostic category were used. Figure 6.4 provides a summary of the KABC-II findings for groups of individuals with RD, MD, Writing Disorder (WD), and ADHD. The test manual also provides comparisons to groups applying statistical controls for differences in demographic variables. The results suggest that groups with RD and WD were very similar; both had their lowest scores on Learning and Sequential scales. The group with WD was generally similar across all KABC-II scales. All three of these groups earned mean scores that were less than 90. In contrast, the group with ADHD earned higher scores that were similar and ranged from 93 to 96. The sample with autism was generally low on all variables and differed from the other groups on that basis. These findings suggest that there are no distinctive profiles for these groups of individuals, although analysis of each child's individual profiles could yield useful information in clinical settings.

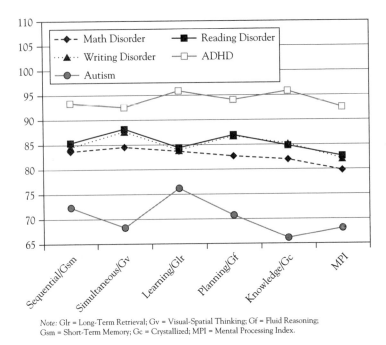

Note: Glr = Long-Term Retrieval; Gv = Visual-Spatial Thinking; Gf = Fluid Reasoning;
Gsm = Short-Term Memory; Gc = Crystallized; MPI = Mental Processing Index.

Figure 6.4   Graphic Representation of Mean Scores for Various Groups on the KABC-II

CAS

The CAS manual provides research on PASS scale profiles for a variety of special groups. The samples were conducted during standardization of the test using specific classification criteria for each diagnostic category, but like the data provided earlier, the samples were not matched on basic demographic characteristics. Findings for the CAS are provided in the manual (Naglieri & Das, 1997) for individuals with RD ($N = 22$) and ADHD ($N = 66$). These samples were combined with more recent studies of children with ADHD (Naglieri, Goldstein, Iseman, & Schweback, 2003; Van Luit, Kroesbergen, & Naglieri, 2005), RD (Naglieri, Otero, DeLauder, & Matto, 2007), and Autism Spectrum Disorder (Goldstein & Naglieri, 2009). The results presented in Figure 6.5 suggest that groups with RD and attention disorders were similar on Simultaneous and Attention scales but not on Planning and Successive scales. The group of students with ADHD had a specific weakness in Planning, and those in the RD group had a specific weakness in Successive processing ability. The group with autism showed a different profile: specifically, low on the Attention scale. These findings suggest that these three groups showed different PASS profiles that are related to their respective cognitive descriptions seen in the literature. That is, the low score in Planning supports Barkley's (1997) view that ADHD involves problems with behavioral inhibition and self-control, which is associated with poor executive control (Planning, as described by Goldberg, 2002, and Naglieri & Das, 2005).

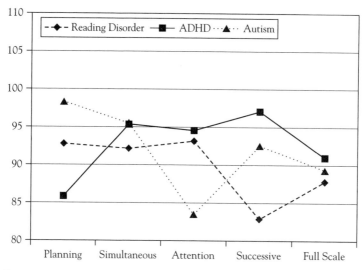

Figure 6.5   Graphic Representation of Mean Scores for Various Groups on the CAS

Low scores in Successive processing for the sample with reading decoding problems is consistent with the phonological skills deficit these individuals, experience (Das, Naglieri, & Kirby, 1994). Children with autism have been described as having difficulties in shifting attention (Klinger, O'Kelly, & Mussey, 2009), which was supported by these CAS data.

PROFILES ACROSS ABILITY TESTS
Groups with RD

The comparison of scale profiles for individuals with RD across the various ability tests is shown in Figure 6.6. Examination of the mean scores by scale for the several ability tests suggests that some are more sensitive to the cognitive characteristics of individuals with RD than others. The WAIS-IV, WJ-III, SB-5, and KABC-II showed relatively little variability within each test with a range of means of 5.6, 6.0, 3.8, and 3.8 standard scores, respectively. That is, the pattern of scores on the separate scales of which these tests are comprised did not suggest that a specific cognitive disorder was uncovered. The sample of individuals with RD earned their lowest score on the WJ-III Processing Speed (98), which was a few points higher than their PSI on the WAIS-IV (standard score of about 95). The WJ-III PSI scores were the lowest score on that test but the WAIS-IV PSI score was the highest of the four scores on that test. Interestingly, the individuals with RD earned scores that clustered around 90 on the WAIS-IV and 100 on the WJ-III. In fact, none of the WJ-III scores was less than 98.

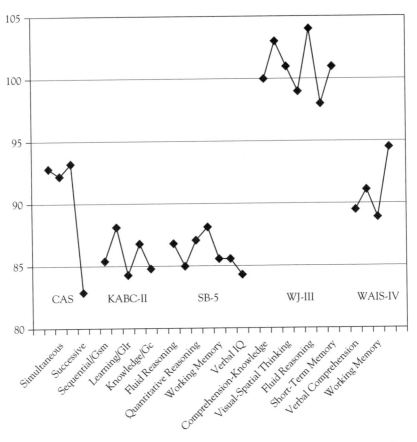

Figure 6.6 Graphic Representation of Mean Scores for Individuals with RD across Several Tests of Ability

These findings suggest that the WJ-III yielded the highest scores among the five ability tests and none of that test's scale mean scores indicated that as a group, these individuals with RD were below normal. Both the SB-5 and the KABC-II scores were around 86, but also with a relatively small range. That is, these two tests did not show evidence of a specific cognitive weakness but rather overall depressed performance.

The group with RD earned scores that ranged from 83 on the CAS Successive processing scale to a high score of 93 in Planning ability (range of scores is 10 points). The CAS showed the most variability; there were scores in the average range (Planning, Simultaneous, and Attention) and one score that was at about the 12th percentile. The CAS profile for the sample with RD suggested that this group has a specific academic (Reading) *and* a specific cognitive (Successive) weakness. This means that as a group, these individuals have difficulty working with stimuli that are arranged in a specific serial order, as in the sequence of sounds that make words, sequence of letters to spell words, and the sequences of groups of sounds and letters needed to make words. Whereas some of the other tests do include scales that are sensitive to Successive processing ability, such as the KABC-II Sequential/Gsm scale, the remaining scales on that test were low, reducing the range of scores. The findings for the samples of individuals with ADHD are similar to those for RD.

Groups with ADHD

The mean scores by scale for the several ability tests for individuals with ADHD found in Figure 6.7 suggest that scores for most of the tests were within the 90 to 100 range. The WAIS-IV, SB-5, and KABC-II showed relatively little variability within each test (range means was 6.9, 5.7, and 3.4 standard scores, respectively). The WJ-III showed more variability (range of 10) with the lowest score (91) in Long-Term Retrieval and the highest in Fluid Reasoning. The Long-Term Retrieval (Glr) score measures "a person's facility in storing and recalling associations" (Wendling et al., 2009, p. 192)

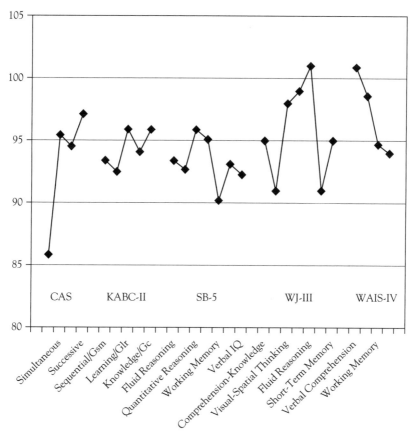

Figure 6.7   Graphic Representation of Mean Scores for Individuals with ADHD across Several Tests of Ability

using a test that requires the child to associate simple shapes and drawings with words and then to use those shapes to make a statement. The CAS showed the most variability (range of 11.3) of the five tests with the lowest score in Planning (85) and highest in Successive (97) processing abilities. This finding suggests that the sample with ADHD had considerable difficulty with use of strategies for solving problems, self-monitoring, and regulation of activity. The CAS is the only test that provides a measure of this neuopsychologically derived ability that is critical to all activities where the person has to determine how to solve a problem; the activities include self-monitoring and impulse control and generation, evaluation, and execution of strategies. This finding is consistent with Barkley's (1997) conceptualization of individuals with ADHD. That is, they have difficulty with planning and anticipation, organization, development and use of organizational strategies, and self-regulation, which, according to Goldberg (2002), is associated with the prefrontal areas of the brain and can be assessed using the Planning scale of the CAS (Goldstein & Naglieri, 2006). These findings suggest that these several tests of ability yield different information about the cognitive ability characteristics of individuals with ADHD. Like the findings for individuals with RD, these results provide some evidence that individuals with reading and attention disorders have a specific cognitive disorder detected by the CAS that helps explain their disability and has implications for intervention. In order to more explicitly explain how a disorder in one or more of the basic psychological processes could be determined, we first discuss how a cognitive process can be defined and then how this view can be applied. These questions were amply discussed by Naglieri (2008) and are summarized here.

HOW TO USE A PROCESSING APPROACH TO SLD DIAGNOSIS

In the current system based on *DSM* and IDEA, ability tests can be used in two ways:

1. A 2 standard deviation discrepancy between ability (e.g., WAIS-IV, SB-5, WJ-III) and achievement may be used.
2. Following from the definition of an SLD in IDEA, a "disorder in one or more of the basic psychological processes" may be identified using the KABC-II or CAS when there is academic failure.

When choosing a test of basic psychological processes, we suggest that the practitioner carefully examine the various options and select those tests that best meet appropriate reliability, validity, and related psychometric qualities. Choosing the best measure of basic psychological processes requires particular attention to the theory used by the test author.

DEFINING A COGNITIVE PROCESS

We suggest that the term "cognitive process" should be used to describe foundational abilities that provide the means by which individuals meet the demands of their environment. These abilities could be defined using statistical methods, such as factor analysis, or they could be defined following neuropsychologically identified abilities. We prefer the latter method. We also suggest that intelligence is best conceptualized as multiple abilities and that, although these abilities act in unison at the same time, each provides a unique contribution to the whole. A group of cognitive processes is needed to meet the multidimensional demands of our complex environment. Multiple cognitive processing abilities provide the ability to complete the same task using different types or various combinations of processes. Because the same task can be achieved using different abilities, interventions can be devised that teach a person to select the cognitive process that works best for him or her. For example, reading requires blending of the separate sounds that make the word (which involves Successive processing), but seeing the word as a whole uses Simultaneous processing.

Cognitive processes are the basis of all mental and physical activity. The application of cognitive processes leads to the acquisition of knowledge and skills. What we know and can do are the result of, not in and of themselves, a cognitive process. For example, a skill, such as reading decoding or math reasoning, is not an example of a cognitive process. A skill like reading is the application of knowledge to achieve some goal. Moreover, a specific skill, such as sound blending to make a word, is not a special type of cognitive processing but instead a basic psychological process that is specifically used for working with serial information (e.g., Successive processing from PASS theory) is used to perform this act. It is the interaction of basic cognitive processes with instruction (and related factors, such as motivation, emotional status, quality of instruction, etc.) that leads to learning and social competence.

The distinction between cognitive processes and knowledge is critical for effective assessment of ability when ability is defined from a processing perspective. Assessment of achievement must be accomplished using tests that adequately evaluate the area of interest (e.g., reading, math, etc.). Assessment of cognitive processes must be conducted using tests that are as free of academic content as possible. Separating measures of achievement and cognitive processes is essential to accurately assess these two constructs. Moreover, it is critical to recognize that while the scope of questions needed to measure knowledge in an achievement test can be aligned with recognized curriculum, cognitive processing tests should be defined by the theory they represent and constructed accordingly.

Using a carefully prescribed approach to defining a basic psychological process is essential for understanding the cognitive weaknesses that underlie both SLD and ADHD. Users should carefully select tests for this purpose and consult the test manuals for information about the theoretical basis of the instrument as well as its psychometric characteristics and especially its validity (Naglieri & Goldstein, 2009).

DISABILITY DETERMINATION: A PRACTICAL SOLUTION

The definition of a learning disability and the method used to identify individuals with the disorder should be consistent (Hale, Kaufman, Naglieri, & Kavale, 2006; Kavale, Kaufman, Naglieri, & Hale, 2005). When using the *DSM* definition of a learning disability, it is important to look at the separate scales the test yields as well as the total IQ score in contrast to achievement test scores to compute the discrepancy. Because the *DSM* does not specify that the total test IQ score must be used, a discrepancy between separate scales from the ability and achievement tests should be examined. According to Naglieri (1999), the goal should be to find a discrepancy between ability and achievement along with a consistency between low achievement and low ability scores. This approach, called the discrepancy/consistency model, can be used with all of the IQ and processing tests described in this chapter. The model is illustrated in Figure 6.8.

When using the IDEA (2004) definition for individuals up to age 21 years, practitioners should aim to determine if the individual has a disorder in "one or more of the basic psychological processes," which is the underlying cause of an SLD. A comprehensive evaluation of the basic psychological processes unites the statutory and regulatory

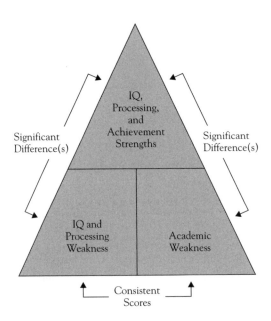

Figure 6.8   Illustration of the Discrepancy/Consistency Model for Disability Determination

components of IDEA. This unites the methods used for identification more closely with the definition, leading to a more defensible approach to diagnosis. The tools used for this assessment, however, must meet the technical criteria included in IDEA. This means valid and reliable tests that are nondiscriminatory. We suggest either the KABC-II (Kaufman & Kaufman, 2008) or the CAS (Naglieri & Das, 1997) or the forthcoming CAS-2 (Naglieri, Das, & Goldstein, in press). There is ample evidence that the CAS in particular, and the theory it was based on, meets the requirements specified in IDEA (see Naglieri, 2005, 2008; Naglieri & Conway, 2009).

Naglieri's (1999) discrepancy/consistency model includes an important component that operationalizes the notion of an exceptional (e.g., unusual) finding. That is, the low ability score should be low relative to the individual's *average* ability score. This is accomplished using the so-called ipsative method originally proposed by Davis (1959), popularized by Kaufman (1979), and modified by Silverstein (1993), which determines when an individual score is reliably different from the individual's average score. This technique has been applied to a number of tests, including, for example, the WISC-IV (Naglieri & Paolitto, 2005), the CAS (Naglieri & Das, 1997), and the SB-5 (Roid, 2003). Naglieri (1999) proposed, however, that in order to be considered evidence of a disability, the low scores should also be well below the national norm. This means that determining if a person's scores within a multiability test vary from one another is important, but the lowest score must be below some reasonable normative value (e.g., 16th percentile). For example, if an adolescent has standard scores of 104 (Planning), 96 (Simultaneous), 95 (Attention), and 84 (Successive), the Successive score is significantly different from the person's average because it is 10.75 standard score points below the mean of 94.75. (See Naglieri, 1999 for details and the values needed for significance for this test.) Because the 84 in Successive is below the person's mean *and* is well below the norm of 100, there is evidence of a disorder in one or more of the basic psychological processes. Combine low processing ability with similar variability in achievement test scores (as shown in Figure 6.8), and evidence for LD is obtained.

SUMMARY AND CONCLUSIONS

The purpose of this chapter was to examine the role various IQ tests and tests of cognitive processing play in determining if an adolescent or adult meets criteria for LD and/or ADD. We reexamined the content of IQ tests prior to looking at the validity of these instruments. In order to determine if these tests yield profiles for groups of individuals previously diagnosed, we summarized research provided by the respective test authors. Overall, we found that no distinctive IQ test profiles were found for the groups of individuals with LD. The test of basic psychological processes that did show a specific cognitive weakness (e.g., a score that was low relative to the other scales provided on the test that were also in the average range *and* low in relation to the norm) for those with a specific reading decoding disorder was the CAS. Similarly, the only test to show evidence of a specific cognitive weakness for individuals with ADHD was also the CAS. This information is useful when the discrepancy/ consistency approach is used.

The findings presented in this chapter suggest that traditional IQ tests that use subtests built on the verbal, quantitative, and nonverbal formats do not appear to be sensitive to the cognitive disorders underlying a learning or attention disorder. In contrast, the cognitive processing tests described here have more carefully defined abilities that, in the case of the CAS, do appear to identify the cognitive processing weakness for those with specific RD and ADHD. Importantly, the cognitive processing weakness found for these two groups are consistent with an understanding of each disorder. For example, those with reading decoding difficulty have problems working with information that is arranged or has to be recalled in a specific sequence (Das et al., 1994). Those with ADHD have a specific problem related to self-regulation of thoughts and actions (Goldstein & Naglieri, 2006). Knowing the cognitive processing failure related to the academic failure not only provides important information for diagnosis/eligibility, but it also provides the opportunity for successful intervention design and/or selection (see Naglieri, 2008; Naglieri & Pickering, 2010).

Since their introduction in the early 1900s, IQ tests have provided a valuable way to measure general ability. As the findings summarized in this chapter suggest, however, the tests have limited utility for diagnosis for persons with LD and ADHD. With the more recent development of new tests that measure basic psychological processes comes the hope of increased utility for diagnosis and treatment. Tests of basic psychological processes offer potential advantages by providing measures of theoretically defined constructs that appear to identify specific areas of cognitive deficits related to the academic failure. More research into the utility of these tests for diagnostic and intervention purposes is clearly warranted.

REFERENCES

American Psychiatric Association (2000). *Diagnostic and Statistical Manual of Mental Disorders* (4th ed., text rev.), Washington, DC: Author.

Anastasi, A., & Urbina, S. (1997). *Psychological testing.* Upper Saddle River, NJ: Prentice-Hall.

Barkley, R. A. (1997). *ADHD and the nature of self-control.* New York, NY: Guilford Press.

Binet, A., & Simon, T. (1905). New methods for the diagnosis of the intellectual level of subnormals. *L'Année Psychologique, 11*, 191–244.

Das, J. P., Naglieri, J. A., & Kirby, J. R. (1994). *Assessment of cognitive processes.* Boston, MA: Allyn & Bacon.

Davis, F. B. (1959). Interpretation of differences among averages and individual test scores. *Journal of Educational Psychology*, 50, 162–170.

Federal Register (2006). Department of Education, 71, 46540–46845.

Goldberg, E. (2002). *The executive brain: Frontal lobes and the civilized mind*. New York, NY: Oxford University Press.

Goldstein, S., & Naglieri, J. A. (2006). The role of intellectual processes in the DSM-V diagnosis of ADHD. *Journal of Attention Disorders*, 10, 3–8.

Goldstein, S., & Naglieri, J. A. (2009). *Autism Spectrum Rating Scale*. Toronto, Canada: Multi Health Systems.

Hale, J. B., Kaufman, A. S., Naglieri, J. A., & Kavale, K. A. (2006). Implementation of IDEA: Using RTI and Cognitive Assessment Methods. *Psychology in the Schools*, 43(7), 753–770.

Individuals with Disabilities Education Improvement Act of 2004 (IDEA), Pub. L. No. 108–446, 118 Stat. 2647 [Amending 20 U.S.C. § § 1400 et seq.].

Jensen, A. R. (1998).

Kaufman, A. S., & Kaufman, N. L. (2004). *Kaufman Assessment Battery for Children* (2nd ed.). Circle Pines, MN: American Guidance Service.

Kaufman, A. S. (1979). *Intelligent testing with the WISC-R*. New York, NY: Wiley.

Kaufman, A. S., Lichtenberger, E. O., Fletcher-Janzen, E., & Kaufman, N. L. (2005). *Essentials of KABC-II assessment*. Hoboken, NJ: Wiley.

Kavale, K. A. (2002). Discrepancy models in identification of learning disability. In R. Bradley, L. Danielson, & D. P. Hallahan (Eds.), *Identification of learning disabilities: Research to practice* (pp. 369–426). Mahwah, NJ: Erlbaum.

Kavale, K. A., & Forness, S. R. (1995). *The nature of learning disabilities: Critical elements of diagnosis and classification*. Mahwah, NJ: Earlbaum.

Kavale, K. A., Kaufman, A. S., Naglieri, J. A., & Hale, J. B. (2005). Changing procedures for identifying learning disabilities: The danger of poorly supported ideas. *School Psychologist*, 59, 16–25.

Klinger, L. G., O'Kelly, S. E., & Mussey, J. L. (2009). Assessment of intellectual functioning in Autism Spectrum Disorders. In J. A. Naglieri & S. Goldstein (Eds.), *Assessment of Autism Spectrum Disorders* (pp. 209–252). Hoboken, NJ: Wiley.

Lichtenberger, E. O., Sotelo-Dynega, M., & Kaufman, A. S. (2009). The Kaufman Assessment Battery for Children (2nd ed.). In J. A. Naglieri & S. Goldstein (Eds.), *A practitioner's guide to assessment of intelligence and achievement* (pp. 61–95). Hoboken, NJ: Wiley.

Naglieri, J. A. (1999). *Essentials of CAS assessment*. New York, NY: Wiley.

Naglieri, J. A. (2005). The Cognitive Assessment System. In D. P. Flanagan & P. L. Harrison (Eds.), *Contemporary intellectual assessment* (2nd ed., pp. 441–460). New York, NY: Guilford Press.

Naglieri, J. A. (2008). Best practices in linking cognitive assessment of students with learning disabilities to interventions. In A. Thomas & J. Grimes (Eds.),

Best practices in school psychology (5th ed., pp. 679–696). Bethesda, MD: National Association of School Psychologists (NASP).

Naglieri, J. A., & Bornstein, B. T. (2003). Intelligence and achievement: Just how correlated are they? *Journal of Psychoeducational Assessment, 21,* 244–260.

Naglieri, J. A., & Conway, C. (2009). The Cognitive Assessment System. In J. A. Naglieri & S. Goldstein (Eds.), *A practitioner's guide to assessment of intelligence and achievement* (pp. 27–60). Hoboken, NJ: Wiley.

Naglieri, J. A., & Das, J. P. (1997). *Cognitive Assessment System.* Itasca, IL: Riverside.

Naglieri, J. A., & Das, J. P. (2005). Planning, Attention, Simultaneous, Successive (PASS) theory: A revision of the concept of intelligence. In D. P. Flanagan & P. L. Harrison (Eds.), *Contemporary intellectual assessment* (2nd ed., pp. 136–182). New York, NY: Guilford Press.

Naglieri, J. A., Das, J. P., & Goldstein, S. (in press). *Cognitive Assessment System* (2nd ed.). Austin, TX: PRO-ED.

Naglieri, J. A., & Goldstein, S. (2009). Understanding the strengths and weaknesses of intelligence and achievement tests. In J. A. Naglieri & S. Goldstein (Eds.), *A practitioner's guide to assessment of intelligence and achievement* (pp. 3–10). Hoboken, NJ: Wiley.

Naglieri, J. A., Goldstein, S., Iseman, J. S., & Schwebach, A. (2003). Performance of children with Attention Deficit Hyperactivity Disorder and anxiety/depression on the WISC-III and Cognitive Assessment System (CAS). *Journal of Psychoeducational Assessment, 21,* 32–42.

Naglieri, J. A., Otero, T., DeLauder, B., & Matto, H. (2007). Bilingual Hispanic children's performance on the English and Spanish versions of the Cognitive Assessment System. *School Psychology Quarterly, 22,* 432–448.

Naglieri, J. A., & Pickering, E. (2010). *Helping children learn* (2nd ed.). Baltimore, MD: Brookes.

Pintner, R. (1923). *Intelligence testing.* New York, NY: Henry Holt.

Ramirez, R. R., & de la Cruz, G. (2002). The Hispanic population in the United States: March 2002. *Current Population Reports,* 20–545. Washington, DC: U.S. Census Bureau.

Ramsey, M. C., & Reynolds, C. R. (2004). Relations between intelligence and achievement tests. In G. Goldstein & S. Beers (Eds.), *Comprehensive handbook of psychological assessment* (pp. 25–50). Hoboken, NJ: Wiley.

Roid, G. (2003). *Stanford-Binet Intelligence Scale* (5th ed.). Itasca, IL: Riverside.

Silverstein, A. B. (1993). Type I, Type II, and other types of errors in pattern analysis. *Psychological Assessment, 5,* 72–74.

Suzuki, L. A., & Valencia, R. R. (1997). Race-ethnicity and measured intelligence. *American Psychologist, 52,* 1103–1114.

U.S. Department of Education. (2006, August 14). Assistance to States for the Education of Children with Disabilities and Preschool Grants for Children with Disabilities. *Federal Register, 71,* 46540–46845.

Van Luit, J. E. H., Kroesbergen, E. H., & Naglieri, J. A. (2005). Utility of the PASS theory and Cognitive Assessment System for Dutch children with and without ADHD. *Journal of Learning Disabilities*, 38, 434–439.

Wechsler, D. (1939). *Wechsler-Bellevue Intelligence Scale*. New York, NY: Psychological Corporation.

Wechsler, D. (2005). *Wechsler Individual Achievement Test* (2nd. ed.). San Antonio, TX: Pearson.

Wechsler, D. (2008). *Wechsler Adult Intelligence Scale* (4th ed.). San Antonio, TX: Pearson.

Wendling, B. J., Mather, N., & Shrank, F. A. (2009). Woodcock-Johnson III Tests of Cognitive Abilities. In J. A. Naglieri & S. Goldstein (Eds.), *A practitioner's guide to assessment of intelligence and achievement* (pp. 191–232). Hoboken, NJ: Wiley.

Woodcock, R. W., McGrew, K. S., & Mather, N. (2001a). *Woodcock-Johnson III Tests of Cognitive Abilities*. Ithasca, IL: Riverside.

Woodcock, R. W., McGrew, K. S., & Mather, N. (2001b). *Woodcock-Johnson III Test of Achievement*. Ithasca, IL: Riverside.

7

Assessment of Academic Achievement

Nancy Mather
Annmarie Urso

This chapter focuses on the assessment of academic performance, including reading, written language, and mathematics, for adolescents and adults with Learning Disabilites (LD) (often referred to as Specific Learning Disabilities [SLD]), and/or Attention-Deficit/Hyperactivity Disorder (ADHD). Both groups of individuals represent the most common referrals for evaluations and exhibit depressed academic functioning as compared to their peers without disabilities (Demaray, Schaefer, & Delong, 2003; Gregg, 2007; Kaufman & Kaufman, 2004). In addition, high comorbidity exists between these two disorders.

The assessment of academic performance is just one important component of a comprehensive evaluation. A comprehensive, individualized assessment is designed to reveal the profile of an individual's unique learning abilities. Such an assessment includes an evaluation of cognitive processes, academic performance, social-emotional functioning, and the environmental factors affecting performance (Kavale, Kaufman, Naglieri, & Hale, 2005). The assessment results are directly linked to individualized recommendations and then, based on the diagnostic conclusions, the evaluator chooses specific interventions and accommodations that will address the person's identified needs. Evaluators are also charged with the responsibility of documenting these disabilities so that these individuals can access accommodations and services in both school and work environments. For students with LD and/or ADHD, differential instruction that addresses the source of the problem is far more effective than global, generalized approaches that do not (Aaron, 1997; Kavale et al., 2005). Thus, as one part of this diagnostic process, the purposes of academic evaluations are to (a) establish present performance levels in areas of achievement, (b) determine what the individual can and cannot currently do, and (c) identify ways to measure and monitor future academic progress. Although individuals with SLD and/or ADHD are often administered standardized assessments, the purposes of the evaluation may differ.

An important distinction in the assessment of school-age students with LD and/ or ADHD as compared to the adult population, including postsecondary students, is who bears responsibility for the cost of the evaluation. Students age 3 to 21 who are enrolled in preK–12 programs are entitled to a free appropriate public education (FAPE) as determined by a multidisciplinary team based on a comprehensive evaluation paid for by the local education authority (LEA). FAPE is mandated by both Section 504 of the Rehabilitation Act of 1973 (U.S. Department of Education, Office for Civil Rights, 2007a), and the Individuals with Disabilities Education Act of 2004 (IDEA, 2004). The LEA is responsible for assessment costs that are part of the comprehensive evaluation to identify a student's academic needs, including those done by medical professionals who are not reimbursed by a student's health insurance coverage. Once a student leaves secondary school, the onus of evaluation costs and intervention services are on the individual. A student must self-identify and provide appropriate documentation to the institution in order to receive services (U.S. Department of Education, Office for Civil Rights, 2007b). In addition, there is no guarantee that if an individual received accommodations in the secondary setting, he or she will be eligible for them in a postsecondary learning or work environment (Gregg, 2009).

SPECIAL CONSIDERATIONS IN EVALUATING INDIVIDUALS WITH LD

The category of LD encompasses a heterogeneous group of disorders that adversely impacts the development of some aspects of academic functioning and proficiency. Because of these problems, both adolescents and adults with LD are underprepared to meet the demands of the learning and work environment (Gregg, 2007). The difficulty acquiring academic skills involves a dysfunction in one or more cognitive processes that mediate achievement; thus, these individuals are often described as displaying "unexpected underachievement" (Boada, Riddle, & Pennington, 2008). Essentially, a learning deficit exists in the presence of basic integrities (Johnson & Myklebust, 1967).

Intra-Individual Variations

One key characteristic of individuals with SLD is that a pattern of strengths and weaknesses exists among varying areas of cognition and achievement. This concept of specificity is not new. For example, Travis (1935) observed that in some students, a striking disparity exists between achievement in one area and achievement in another, such as a student who cannot read but can comprehend material that is read aloud, or a student who excels in reading and writing, but struggles with mathematical concepts and applications. These children, who do not achieve as well as would be expected in one or more areas of performance, may be regarded as having a "special defect or disability" (Travis, 1935, p. 43).

In describing children who struggled to learn to read, Monroe (1932) observed: "It seems that we are measuring a discrepancy between reading and other accomplishments which may occur in either direction at any intellectual level" (p. 17). A multiplicity of factors and cognitive processes can contribute to poor academic performance; the causes and correlates of "unexpected" underachievement are, however, beyond the scope of this chapter. What is of relevance, however, is an examination of a person's intra-individual variations among his or her achievement scores, as a piece of confirmatory evidence for the diagnosis of LD. For determination of LD, these phases are often involved:

1. Ruling out emotional, cultural, social, or physical factors related to the learning difficulty.
2. Identifying cognitive processing and academic strengths and weaknesses of the individual.
3. Prescribing evidence-based interventions directly related to an individual's strengths and weaknesses (Kaufman, Lichtenberger, Fletcher-Janzen, & Kaufman, 2005).

Response to Intervention

Since the implementation in 1976 of Public Law No. 94–142, the Education for All Handicapped Children Act, the number of students with LD has increased dramatically (U.S. Department of Education, 2009). As a result, alternatives to standard diagnostic models of achievement/ability discrepancy were explored by the President's Commission on Excellence in Special Education (2001). The resulting recommendations (as well as other factors) led to the inclusion of a progress monitoring requirement in the identification of LD As specified in the IDEA 2004 reauthorization, states may now permit a process that examines whether a student responds to scientific, research-based intervention as *part* of the learning disability evaluation procedure. This process of data collection is often referred to as response to intervention (RTI). Although RTI may be used as part of the process, it is not clear how significant that part should be, or how and when that part is integrated into the diagnostic assessment process.

Many states have been implementing, or are planning to implement, some form of RTI with the hopes of (a) reducing the number of students referred for evaluations, (b) providing research-based early intervention to children in a more timely fashion, (c) ensuring targeted assistance to all children who need help, and (d) increasing the validity of actual placement decisions. Clearly, efficient progress monitoring and early intervention can provide benefits and help improve the quality of instruction to all children. It seems, however, that RTI can be viewed most accurately as a model of prevention and intervention rather than as a method for diagnosing LD (Kavale, Kauffman, Bachmeier, & LeFever, 2008).

Numerous reasons exist for why a student would not fully respond to a certain intervention or treatment, only one of which is a learning disability. Some of the reasons for low achievement are extrinsic (e.g., limited or inadequate instruction), whereas others would be considered intrinsic (e.g., LD or ADHD). Unfortunately, the IDEA 2004 reauthorization does not realign the identification procedures with the definition (a disorder in psychological processing) and contributes further to a disconnection between the LD definition and the selected assessment methodology. In fact, the biggest discrepancy that exists is between the LD definition and how we operationalize it (Hale, Naglieri, Kaufman, & Kavale, 2004; Kavale et al., 2005).

Furthermore, some professionals suggest that LD can be identified solely through achievement deficits and that cognitive assessments do not need to be part of an evaluation. Within any RTI model, a place should be kept for comprehensive evaluations that address the specific referral question that has been posed and help an evaluator determine the specific reasons why a person is struggling with learning. Models that rely solely on RTI for LD identification will: (a) produce numerous sources of measurement error, (b) threaten the validity of the LD concept, (c) result in inaccuracy in identification, and (d) result in potential legal challenges (McKenzie, 2009). RTI is another type of discrepancy model that is based on a discrepancy from grade level, making it a special case of severe discrepancy analysis that assumes everyone is of equal ability or possesses similar academic aptitude (Reynolds, 2005). Sole reliance on an RTI model will not result in valid LD identification; it will result only in a category of underachievement for any student who otherwise might be left behind (Kavale et al., 2008). Regardless of what type of model or combination of models of LD identification are adopted within a school district or by an evaluator (e.g., ability/achievement discrepancy, RTI, pattern of strengths and weaknesses), some type of achievement testing will play a central role.

One further issue regarding the assessment of adults with SLD is arriving at a consensus regarding what constitutes low achievement; this is particularly perplexing with college students, a select group who often score above the mean of the general population in most areas of performance. Part of the confusion stems from the guidelines in the Americans with Disabilities Act of 1990, which indicate that in order to have a disability, a person must have a mental or physical impairment that substantially limits a major activity as compared to the "average person" in the general population. Some have indicated that "substantially limits" equates to functioning below the statistical average, based on achievement scores derived from a bell-curve metric (e.g., at or below the 16th percentile) (e.g., Flanagan, Keiser, Bernier, & Ortiz, 2003). Others have suggested that the concept of substantial limitation refers to the *condition*, *manner*, and *duration* in which one performs an activity, not the actual resulting achievement itself (Mather, Gregg, & Simon, 2005).

LD is not synonymous with underachievement. College students with LD often show average scores in achievement but impairments relative to their classmates having above-average skills (Sparks & Lovett, 2009). Through years of special education, intensive tutoring, and persistence, individuals with LD can improve enough academically to appear to have "compensated" for their disability. This does not mean the disability is no longer present, but only that the person has managed to achieve a certain level of academic success (Mather & Gregg, 2006). The concept of LD encompasses individuals who are functioning well below their own capabilities, regardless of their functioning levels as compared to average peers.

SPECIAL CONSIDERATIONS IN EVALUATING INDIVIDUALS WITH ADHD

As with LD, an assessment for ADHD must be accompanied by a thorough developmental, behavioral, and emotional evaluation (Goldstein & Cunningham, 2009). For students with ADHD who are taking medication(s), testing should occur while they are on their medication so that the results will more accurately reflect their actual competence, as opposed to distractibility or impulsivity (Lichtenberger, Sotelo-Dynega, & Kaufman, 2009). Although poor academic performance is associated with ADHD, not all individuals with ADHD experience academic difficulties (Frazier, Youngstrom, Glutting, & Watkins, 2007). Students with the most severe ADHD and the most impaired achievement, however, are the least likely to complete high school and pursue postsecondary education (Frazier et al., 2007). Similar to the results from previous studies, Barkley (2006) found that teens with hyperactivity were 3 times more likely to have failed a grade and 8 times more likely to have been expelled or dropped out of school. ADHD symptoms continue to affect the academic performance of college students (Frazier et al., 2007). Few students with ADHD actually attend college; if they do, they rarely complete a college degree (Weiss & Hechtman, 1993). Unfortunately, the population of students with ADHD has a long-standing history of lacking academic persistence (Goldstein, 1997).

Barkley (2006) reported that the main complaints among adults with ADHD who refer themselves to clinics involve impairments in attention, inhibition, and self-regulation. Unlike LD, the impaired functioning and academic achievement problems of adolescents and adults with ADHD can be partially explained by poor self-regulation as well as disruptive, impulsive, and/or inattentive behaviors. These behaviors can then result in more generalized school difficulties, such as problems with homework completion, poor study habits, and low test performance. Robin (2006) observed that virtually every adolescent with ADHD has trouble completing homework, taking tests, organizing materials, studying, and listening in class; furthermore, many adolescents and adults also have LD in reading, writing, and/or mathematics that further complicate their school difficulties.

INTERVIEWS

Prior to initiating an academic assessment, an informal, conversational interview can provide the clinician with insights into a person's perceptions of his or her academic difficulties and how they affect school or job performance. For many individuals with LD and/or ADHD, oral language skills are often an area of relative integrity (Kaufman & Kaufman, 2004); therefore, they will be able to address and describe their strengths as well as weaknesses. Tables 7.1 and 7.2 provide examples of the types of questions for individuals with LD and/or ADHD that may clarify an individual's perspectives on why school or work is difficult, and how he or she has attempted to improve performance. For individuals with both disorders, questions from both sets may be appropriate.

For the remainder of this chapter, we discuss the use of both standardized measures of academic achievement and informal measures of academic competence, including curriculum-based measures (CBMs). Both types of assessments are useful as a part of a comprehensive evaluation.

Table 7.1 Academic Performance Interview Questions for Individuals with LD

What school subjects have you most enjoyed? Least enjoyed?

What school subjects have been easy for you? Hard for you?

Do you spend time reading for pleasure?

Does it take you longer to complete assignments than other students/co-workers? If so, what types of assignments?

When work has been too difficult, what have you done?

How have learning difficulties affected your school/job performance?

What have teachers, tutors, or others done to help you improve your school/job performance?

Did/do you receive any accommodations in school? If so, what were/are they and were/are they helpful? How frequently did/do you use them?

Did/do you use assistive technology in any of your classes or at work? If so, what type(s)? Is/was it helpful?

Table 7.2 Academic Performance Interview Questions for Individuals with ADHD

Do you find you are easily distracted in academic settings, the workplace, or in meetings? If so, what do you do to improve concentration?

Have problems with attention affected your academic learning? If so, how?

Have your academic work or work tasks been affected by careless mistakes and errors? If so, how?

Have you had difficulty completing assignments or projects at school or at the workplace? If so, what strategies have you attempted to finish them?

What strategies have you used to improve academic performance?

What strategies have you used to improve your abilities to organize and complete your work?

STANDARDIZED ACADEMIC ASSESSMENTS

Broad-based individualized tests of academic achievement are often used to get overall estimates of how a person is generally performing in reading, writing, and mathematics as well as how he or she is doing on narrower subsets of skills, such as word identification, spelling, or math problem solving. Commonly used diagnostic individual achievement tests include subtests that assess specific skills and concepts. Many standardized tests include similar measures. For example, tests of nonword reading, spelling, and math calculation are included on the Woodcock-Johnson III Normative Update Tests of Achievement (WJ-III-ACH-NU), the Kaufman Test of Educational Achievement II (KTEA-II), and the Wechsler Individual Achievement Test-III (WIAT-III). Different batteries provide greater emphasis on certain aspects of achievement as well as different formats that are designed to pinpoint specific strengths and weaknesses. The WJ-III-ACH-NU has one measure of math fluency whereas the WIAT-III has three measures; the WIAT-III includes both sentence and essay writing whereas the WJ-III-ACH-NU measures various aspects of sentence construction. Thus, results may differ depending on the choice of the test battery as well as the format of the specific subtests. Table 7.3 lists examples of several widely used diagnostic measures of academic performance.

In addition, a review of performance on group administered achievement tests, such as the Iowa or Scholastic Aptitude Tests, can provide an overview and estimate of general academic achievement (Goldstein, 1997). More in-depth testing often is done when a person exhibits markedly poor performance in a specific area, such as low reading performance. One facet of comprehensive clinical evaluations is that all diagnostic conclusions from the test profiles are supported with data from multiple sources (Kaufman, 1994). The evaluator relates observations of behaviors to the test profile and integrates information from a variety of instruments and observations to support or clarify the diagnostic hypotheses (Kaufman, Lichtenberger, & Naglieri, 1999; Lichtenberger, Mather, Kaufman, & Kaufman, 2004). Because the obtained scores may

Table 7.3 Commonly Used Individual Achievement Tests

Test name	Author (Date)	Age range	Abilities	Publisher
Kaufman Test of Educational Achievement, 2nd ed.	Kaufman & Kaufman (2004)	4.6–25 years (4.6–90+ years for brief form)	Reading, math, written language, and oral language	Pearson
Peabody Individual Achievement Test–Revised/Normative Update	Markwardt (1998)	5.0–22.11 years	Reading, mathematics, written language, and general information	Psychological Corporation
Wechsler Individual Achievement Test-III	Wechsler (2009)	4.0–19.11 years	Oral language, reading, written expression, and mathematics	Psychological Corporation
Wide Range Achievement Test–4th Ed.	Wilkinson & Robertson (2007)	5.0–94 years	Reading, spelling, and mathematics	Psychological Assessment Resources (PAR)
Woodcock-Johnson III Normative Update Tests of Achievement	Woodcock, Schrank, McGrew, & Mather (2007)	2.0–90+ years	Oral expression, listening comprehension, written expression, basic reading skills, reading comprehension, math calculation skills, and math reasoning	Riverside

not have a unitary explanation and individuals can obtain low scores for a variety of reasons, an evaluator must corroborate information with other tests. In explaining the findings, the evaluator integrates the referral information, clinical observations of test-taking behaviors, detailed analysis of errors, and an analysis of the profile fluctuations (Kaufman, 1994). For example, when considering different standardized academic measures and making a differential diagnosis between LD and ADHD, it is important to consider the degree of attention that each type of assessment requires for successful performance (Aaron, Joshi, Palmer, Smith, & Kirby, 2002). For example, timed tests may require more sustained attention than tests that measure accuracy of performance alone, whereas math problem-solving tests would have more of a demand on oral language and reasoning abilities.

Reading

The reading process is complex, incorporating at least two facets of performance: word recognition and comprehension (Aaron, Joshi, & Williams, 1999). Each of these areas can develop, or fail to develop, independently of each other. Thus, reading difficulties can be a result of weaknesses in decoding or word recognition skills or weaknesses in listening and language comprehension that underlie the development of reading comprehension (Torgesen & Miller, 2009). A recent meta-analysis of reading research indicates that problems in several distinct areas contribute to the difference in reading abilities in adults with and without Reading Disabilities (RD) (Swanson & Hsieh, 2009). Swanson and Hsieh (2009) found that the cognitive processes related to phonological skills, verbal memory, naming speed, and vocabulary all made significant contributions to adult RD. An evaluator should also consider other extrinsic factors that may be influencing performance.

To help account for the fact that reading difficulties can result from a variety of factors, Aaron, Joshi, Boulware-Gooden, and Bentum (2008) described the component model of reading (CMR) designed to determine the cause of poor reading. This model seems particularly appropriate for gaining an understanding of the factors that are affecting reading performance in both adolescents and adults with LD and/or ADHD. The CMR model includes these domains: (a) cognitive, which includes word recognition and listening and reading comprehension; (b) psychological, which includes factors such as motivation, interest, teacher expectations, and learned helplessness; and (c) ecological, which includes the home and school environment as well as dialect and peer influence. Thus, an evaluator can determine if an individual's poor reading stems from decoding weaknesses, limited vocabulary, poor reading comprehension, or an inadequate home environment. By identifying the source of the reading difficulties, instruction can be carefully planned to address an individual's specific needs.

The cognitive domain of reading performance includes an evaluation of both word recognition (decoding and instant word recognition) and comprehension (listening and reading comprehension). Diagnostic reading tests are used to assess the skills of basic reading, fluency, vocabulary, and comprehension, all important measures of reading for older students. Many standardized measures of reading, such as the Gray Oral Reading Test–4th Edition (GORT-4), include measures of oral reading fluency and rate, whereas others include measures of comprehension based on vocabulary, sentence completion, paragraph construction or contextual fluency (e.g., Test of Reading Comprehension-4 [TORC-4]; Woodcock Reading Mastery

Test–Revised/Normative Update [WRMT-R/NU]) or measures of basic reading skills such as phonemic awareness, phonics knowledge, or irregular and regular word reading (e.g., Woodcock-Johnson III Diagnostic Reading Battery [WJ-III-DRB]; Test of Irregular Word Reading [TIWRE]; Test of Word Reading Efficiency [TOWRE]). Some of the measures are timed (e.g., TOWRE and TIWRE), whereas others measure accuracy of word reading (e.g., WRMT-R/NU). A skilled evaluator will have several assessments in their clinical repertoire to match the presenting symptoms with the appropriate assessment. Table 7.4 indicates commonly used measures of reading performance.

Table 7.4 Commonly Used Standardized Measures of Reading

Test name	Author (Date)	Age range	Abilities	Publisher
Gray Oral Reading Tests (GORT-4)	Wiederholt & Bryant (2001)	6.0–18.11 years	Oral reading skills	PRO-ED
Gray Silent Reading Tests	Wiederholt & Blalock (2000)	7.0–25.0 years	Silent reading comprehension ability	PRO-ED
Test of Irregular Word Reading Efficiency	Reynolds & Kamphaus (2007)	3.0–94 years	Irregular word reading	PAR
Test of Reading Comprehension–4	Brown, Wiederholt, & Hammill (2009)	7.0–17.11 years	Reading comprehension, vocabulary, and contextual fluency	PRO-ED
Test of Silent Word Reading Fluency	Mather, Hammill, Allen, & Roberts (2004)	6.6–17.11 years	Word recognition fluency	PRO-ED
Test of Word Reading Efficiency	Torgesen, Wagner, & Rashotte (1999)	6.0–24.11 years	Regular and irregular word reading accuracy and fluency	PRO-ED
WJ–III Diagnostic Reading Battery	Woodcock, Mather, & Schrank (2004)	2.0–80+ years	Reading achievement and ability	Riverside
Woodcock Reading Mastery Tests–Revised/ Normative Update	Woodcock (1987/1998)	5.0–75+ years	Visual-auditory learning, letter and word identification, word attack, word and passage comprehension	Pearson Assessments

Basic Reading Skills

Standardized assessments of reading include measures of word recognition accuracy that involve reading a list of unrelated real words as well as measures of nonword reading that involve reading nonsense words that conform to English spelling patterns. Performance in nonword reading helps the evaluator document poor phonic skills. When an individual has poor phonic skills and word identification abilities, it is often difficult to differentiate between poor reading performance caused by ADHD and poor reading performance caused by RD. Students with ADHD appear to obtain their lowest scores on standardized tests of reading achievement (Frazier et al., 2007), as do individuals with dyslexia, the most common neurobiological disorder affecting children (Shaywitz & Shaywitz, 2003).

Often what distinguishes individuals with dyslexia from other poor readers is that their listening comprehension ability is significantly higher than their ability to decode words as well as their ability to comprehend what they read (Aaron et al., 2002; Rack, Snowling, & Olson, 1992). Many poor readers, however, whether having RD or ADHD, have weaknesses in phonology or a generalized deficit in phonological processing (Swanson, Mink, & Bocian, 1999). In addition to phonological processing, researchers have attempted to identify other correlates of reading failure, including slow naming speed (e.g., Bell, McCallum, & Cox, 2003; Bowers & Wolf, 1993; Plaza & Cohen, 2003; Wolf & Bowers, 2000), slow processing speed (e.g., Kail, 1991; Kail & Ferrar, 2007; Urso, 2008), and poor auditory memory (e.g., Brady, 1991; Siegel & Ryan, 1989).

Individuals with RD, or dyslexia, exhibit a primary deficit in decoding and spelling skills (Aaron et al., 2002). Thus, they tend to perform poorly on tasks requiring the reading and spelling of nonsense words that conform to the rules of English spelling (e.g., flib), which involves the application of phonics. The individuals' poor word identification skills then affect both their speed of reading and comprehension. In a sample of students with RD, phonological awareness, basic reading skills, and reading fluency were most impaired (Kaufman & Kaufman, 2004). Others have indicated that adults with dyslexia have more generalized problems showing weaknesses in phonological processing, reading, spelling, and arithmetic, whereas adults with ADHD may not have these weaknesses, but often display less accurate performance (Laasonen, Lehtinen, Leppamaki, Tani, & Hokkanen, 2010).

Reading Comprehension

A variety of different procedures exist for measuring reading comprehension tests, and it is likely that scores will differ for individuals depending on the way that comprehension is assessed. Thus, these different formats involve different task demands that measure different skills (Keenan, Betjemann, & Olson, 2008). Some tests use a cloze format where the person must fill in a missing word in a sentence (e.g., WJ III ACH) whereas others use a paragraph followed by specific questions (e.g., KTEA-II). Some tests measure silent reading, whereas others measure oral reading.

The length of the passages is another important consideration. Short passages are more influenced by decoding skills; in longer passages, the decoding problems can often be rectified by use of background knowledge and context (Keenan et al., 2008). Thus, the shorter the passage, the greater the emphasis on accurate decoding, and the longer the passage, the more difficult it is to sustain attention. For individuals with RD, poor comprehension often results from poor word recognition; for individuals with ADHD, comprehension may be more affected by inattention. Adult males with ADHD may perform more poorly on tests of reading comprehension than on measures of phonological processing and word decoding, with poor word-decoding performance more commonly found among children (Samuelsson, Lundberg, & Herkner, 2004). Samuelsson et al. (2004) suggest that this may be because reading comprehension involves many of the higher cognitive control and executive functions that are assumed to be impaired in individuals with ADHD. Unlike individuals with RD, individuals with ADHD appear to have more difficulty on tests of listening comprehension than they do on measures of reading comprehension.

WRITTEN LANGUAGE

Disorders of Written Expression are complex and multifaceted, as writing requires the linking of language, thought, and motor skills. The writer must write legibly, spell words correctly, and translate thoughts into writing. Difficulty in any one aspect of writing can contribute to difficulty in another. For example, motor difficulties may directly impact handwriting and spelling performance, and then poor handwriting and spelling will impact the quality and quantity of written output. Thus, writing is a highly complex, integrated task that has been described as "an immense juggling act" (Berninger & Richards, 2002, p. 173). Table 7.5 includes several widely used measures of written expression and spelling that are appropriate for adolescents and adults.

Handwriting

Three types of graphomotor disorders are prevalent in the adolescent and adult population with LD and/or ADHD: symbolic deficits, motor speed deficits, and dyspraxia (Deul, 1992; Gregg, 2009). With symbolic deficits, the writer has specific phonemic, orthographic, and morphemic weaknesses that affect only writing, not drawing. With motor speed deficits, the writer is capable of good handwriting, but letters and words are produced slowly. With dyspraxia, the writer has limited ability to learn and perform voluntary motor activities, which affects both writing and drawing (Gregg, 2009). In analyzing handwriting, an evaluator would consider overall legibility, letter formation

Table 7.5 Commonly Used Standardized Measures of Written Expression and Spelling

Test name	Author (Date)	Age range	Abilities	Publisher
Oral and Written Language Scales	Carrow-Woolfolk (1995)	3.0–21.0 years	Listening comprehension, oral expression, written expression	PRO-ED
Test of Adolescent and Adult Language, 4th ed.	Hammill, Brown, Larsen, & Wiederholt (2007).	12.0–24.11 years	Includes subtests on written language abilities	PRO-ED
Test of Language Development: Intermediate, 4th ed.	Hammill & Newcomer (2008)	8.0–17.11 years	Sentence combining, picture vocabulary, word ordering, relational vocabulary, morphological comprehension, multiple meanings	PRO-ED
Test of Written Language, 4th ed.	Hammill & Larsen (2008)	9.0–17.0 years	Written language skills	PRO-ED
Tests of Written Spelling, 4th ed.	Larsen, Hammill, & Moats (1999)	6.0–8.11 years	Spelling	PRO-ED
Word Identification and Spelling Test	Wilson & Felton (2004)	7.0–18.11 years	Word identification, spelling, and sound-symbol knowledge	PRO-ED

errors, and writing rate. Legibility is often best determined by attempting to read a student's papers. Letter formation errors are identified by examining words and letters more closely to determine any problematic letters, or problems with the joining of letters in cursive writing. Writing speed is often measured by asking a student to copy a short passage for 1 minute and then comparing the student's performance to that of classmates. Few standardized assessments exist for handwriting evaluation.

Basic Writing Skills

Most standardized tests include a separate measure of spelling. Poor spelling is one of the core characteristics of individuals who have RD or dyslexia; in fact, even successful adults with LD continue to experience significant spelling difficulties (Gregg, 2009). Spelling ability is primarily related to phonemic segmentation, the ability to segment or break apart the sounds in words, an aspect of phonological awareness. Spelling problems in high school students and young adults still reflect specific deficits in the phonological aspects of language (Bruck, 1993; Moats, 1995). In addition, orthography, the knowledge of letter strings and the ability to recall these letter strings, and knowledge of morphology, the meaning units of language, are also necessary for sequencing letters and adding word parts and word endings. Weaknesses in phonological, orthographic, and morphological awareness are common characteristics of older students with dyslexia, and these learners often require more time to recall the motor and orthographic patterns necessary for spelling (Gregg, 2009; Gregg, Coleman, Davis, & Chalk, 2007).

Written Expression

Standardized tests of written expression typically require the individual to write a story to a picture or a prompt within a specified time limit (e.g., 15 minutes). When assessing written expression, it is important to analyze several longer pieces of text (e.g., essays), rather than relying solely on the results obtained from standardized tests, which often include only one writing sample, or several short samples completed within one time frame.

Because reciprocal influences exist between oral and written language, oral language abilities will affect an individual's abilities to compose written text (Berninger & Wolf, 2009). Thus, when evaluating a person's ability to express ideas, an assessment should also include measures of both receptive and expressive oral language. Gregg, Coleman, Stennett, and Davis (2002) found that young adults with LD and/or ADHD had less variety, complexity, and sophistication in their use of sentence structures in written text. In addition, these young adults made many common errors associated in producing grammatical structures, such as omitting words or phrases, reversing word order, substituting related words, overusing simple sentence structures, and using incorrect verb tenses. Berninger (1996) suggested that when assessing written expression, an evaluator should also consider the various "constraints" impacting writing. Understanding the multidimensional impact of constraints, such as limited instruction, specific cognitive or linguistic weaknesses, limited cultural experiences, and poor motivation, can help inform the type and extent of accommodations and instruction needed.

MATHEMATICS

Not as much is known about the relationships among LD, ADHD, and low math performance (Monuteaux, Faraone, Herzig, Navsaria, & Biederman, 2005), but adolescents and adults with LD or ADHD can experience problems in mathematics for a variety of reasons (Gregg, 2009). Two significant problems affecting the analysis of poor math performance have been the use of only one math achievement measure, so the results often represent only one or two aspects of mathematical learning, and the fact that researchers have not reached a consensus definition regarding exactly what constitutes a Mathematics Disorder (Murphy, Mazzocco, Hanich, & Early, 2007). In addition, studies of individuals with ADHD and mathematics are not as prolific as studies involving students with LD, despite the incidence of children with both disorders reported to have a comorbidity rate of 9% to 25% (e.g., Barkley, 2003; Kaufmann & Nuerk, 2008). As with reading and writing, math can be separated into basic skills and applications, but there are fewer standardized measures of math performance. The most widely used math test is the Key Math-3, which is appropriate for use with adolescents and adults up to the age of 21. Table 7.6 illustrates two commonly used individualized achievement measures of mathematics.

Table 7.6 Commonly Used Standardized Measures of Mathematics

Test name	Author (Date)	Age range	Abilities	Publisher
Key Math-3 Diagnostic Assessment	Connolly (2007)	4.6–21.0 years	Conceptual knowledge, computational skills, and problem solving	Pearson
Comprehensive Mathematical Abilities Test	Hresko, Schlieve, Herron, Swain, & Sherbenou (2003)	7.0–18.11 years	Global mathematical ability	PRO-ED

Basic Math Skills

Most standardized tests include a separate assessment of computational or calculation skills, ranging from problems in simple addition to higher-level algebraic equations. Some students with RD also have problems in math calculation (Swanson, Hoskyn, & Lee, 1999) whereas for others, calculation skills are higher than both reading and spelling scores (Bonafina, Newcorn, McKay, Koda, & Halperin, 2000). Calculation skills depend on attentional resources and working memory capabilities—both vital skills for mental mathematics. Geary (1993) discussed the importance of the speed of reasoning, which may underlie the development of accurate representations of math facts, as necessary for automatic fact recall. Individuals with Mathematics Disorder frequently have difficulty with the representation and the retrieval of math facts (Geary, 1993, 2007), implicating weaknesses within both the storage and retrieval processes.

Math Problem Solving

Unless administered to a group, the problems on standardized tests of math problem solving are read to individuals. Although reading ability is eliminated as a confounding variable, listening comprehension is required. Many students with LD and/or ADHD who are poor mathematical problem solvers do not effectively or efficiently process word problems; they either lack the prerequisite skills or do not apply the resources needed to solve such complex cognitive problems. Research on students with ADHD with and without comorbid Mathematics Disorder has yielded these conclusions:

1. Math achievement test scores for students with ADHD Predominantly Inattentive Type were significantly lower than those for students with ADHD Predominantly Hyperactive-Impulsive Type (Marshall, Hynd, Handwerk, & Hall, 1997).

2. Performance is significantly lower on simple mental calculation, complex mental calculation, and written calculations for students with ADHD Combined Type than for students without ADHD (Kaufmann & Nuerk, 2008).

3. Students with ADHD Combined Type but without comorbid LD perform equally well on simple and complex calculation tasks as their non-ADHD peers while struggling with math skills that involve nonverbal number representations (i.e., a mental number line, number value comparisons) (Kaufmann & Neurk, 2008).

As with reading, specific cognitive processes are often linked to mathematical abilities. For example, growth in working memory has been shown to be an important predictor of children's growth in abilities to solve mathematical problems (Swanson, Jerman, & Zheng, 2008).

To assess mathematical problem solving, Montague (1996) described the use of the Mathematical Problem Solving Assessment–Short Form (MPSA-SF), an evaluation tool designed to assess various affective factors, cognitive and metacognitive factors, and strategies associated with mathematical problem solving in middle school students. The MPSA-SF informal assessment examines both problem representation and problem execution. Montague and colleagues have demonstrated the MPSA-SF tool to be an effective measure of problem-solving competence (Montague, 1996, 1997, 2006; Montague, Warger, & Morgan, 2000).

The MPSA-SF is based on the task analysis of math problem-solving skills. To solve math problems effectively, students need to be able follow a sequence of steps:

1. Read the problem for understanding.
2. Paraphrase the problem by putting into their own words.
3. Draw a picture or diagram that demonstrates the relationships among the problem parts.
4. Hypothesize or make a plan to solve the problem.

5. Estimate or predict the answer.

6. Compute the solution.

7. Check that the plan was appropriate and the answer is correct (Montague, 1996).

Thus, appropriate problem representation is the foundation for understanding a problem and devising a plan to solve the problem. Students who have not acquired problem representation strategies will struggle with problem solving. Montague revised the MPSA-SF and has recently conducted a 3-year efficacy study sponsored by the Institute of Education Sciences on nearly 800 students using the new instrument. Information on this instrument is available from www.education.miami.edu/solveit (personal communication, December 6, 2009).

CURRICULUM-BASED ASSESSMENT

Assessment is an essential part of effective teaching, and some researchers have criticized the use of standardized norm-referenced testing as a basis for making instructional decisions (Marston, 1989; Salvia, Ysseldyke, & Bolt, 2010). The curriculum-based paradigm is recognized as an alternative for identifying students with LD in the RTI model (Burns, Dean, & Klar, 2004). The paradigm includes two different forms of education measurement that are being proposed as alternatives to the standardized, norm-referenced model: curriculum-based measurement (CBM) and curriculum-based assessment (CBA). Both CBM and CBA have been used by teachers and school psychologists for over 25 years. (For review, see Deno, 1985; Deno, Fuchs, Marston, & Shin, 2001.) Deno and colleagues originally designed CBM measures for teachers to be able to reliably measure student growth in order to enhance achievement. CBM and CBA assessment have evolved to be used for a variety of purposes that are applicable to older students with LD and ADHD. Within academic settings, CBM and CBA can be useful for: (a) establishing norms for screening and identifying students in the need of special education services; (b) identifying students for special education evaluation who demonstrate a low level of performance and inadequate rate of improvement; and (c) monitoring student progress and planning effective instruction in the general education classroom for included students with disabilities or for those who are reintegrating into general education (Stecker, Fuchs, & Fuchs, 2005).

CBMs

CBMs are widely used informal assessments tied directly to the classroom curriculum. Developed by teachers or designed as standardized benchmark and progress monitoring measures (e.g., AIMSweb®, 2008), CBMs are employed for the purposes of progress monitoring and establishing baseline performance. In these capacities, CBMs are valuable in linking assessment to intervention. Because these measures are brief and curriculum based, they are good tools for directly measuring the effectiveness of instruction and intervention (Deno, 1985). CBM procedures are standardized and conducted regularly to monitor progress, adjust interventions, and measure academic gains. Instructional decisions are made using the data collected from administered CBM probes with criteria for goals and progress rates determined by comparison to a normative group (Deno et al., 2001).

The use of CBMs allows teachers to make informed decisions on planning future instruction. To be effective for students with disabilities, progress monitoring must be paired with instructional modifications, and data-based decision rules must be used for interpreting graphed CBM data to determine the effectiveness of the instructional interventions (Stecker et al., 2005). Computer applications can facilitate the use of decision rules and can reduce teacher time and increase teacher satisfaction (Stecker et al., 2005).

For both students with LD and/or ADHD, motivation is a key to academic success (Sternberg & Williams, 2002). For older students with reading challenges as well as students who are culturally and linguistically diverse, well-established links exist between reading achievement and motivation, and progress monitoring can enhance both (Gardner et al., 2001; Guthrie & Davis, 2003; Wang & Guthrie, 2004).

CBAs

Similar to CBMs, CBAs use brief measures of academic skills administered on a frequent basis. However, unlike CBMs, CBAs have the potential to distinguish ineffective instruction from unacceptable learning, providing data that can be used to identify appropriate instructional-level material and specify methods for intervention (Burns et al., 2004). Gickling and Rosenfield (1995) cited four basic tenets of CBAs:

1. Aligns assessment practices with curriculum instruction
2. Permits contiguous assessment of student progress
3. Aims for high success rates
4. Responds to task variability, task demand, and pace of instruction to establish student success

Salvia et al. (2010) propose that the merits of instruction are assessed by evaluating the instructional environment as well as the challenges this environment presents to learners. To determine if an individual with LD and/or ADHD is receiving instruction that is appropriately challenging, effective, and delivered with fidelity, both the instructional material and the instructional environment should be reviewed. CBAs are designed to evaluate both the environment and the learner.

An appropriate level of instruction is one of the necessary components of an effective learning environment (Ysseldyke & Christenson, 2002). CBAs were specifically designed to determine the instructional challenge of the curriculum by examining instructional levels. Additionally, CBAs use well-established criteria to evaluate student performance; unlike CBMs, CBAs will provide data on both individual student performance and the difficulty level of the material, which can then help identify gaps in intervention (Burns et al., 2004).

CONCLUSIONS

Results from standardized assessments, CBMs, and CBAs are all useful academic assessment tools for planning interventions for students with LD and ADHD. Standardized assessments help us to understand the nature and severity of a specific problem or disorder. The first step in solving a problem is to define it and understand its nature (Boada et al., 2008). With an individual with LD, academic performance is often affected in some specific areas but not others. With an individual with ADHD, a pattern of strengths and weaknesses may also be present, but often the academic tasks that require the most sustained attention are affected. What comprehensive test batteries offer most to clinicians is the chance to observe how different children approach different tasks, particularly when they have to cope with learning and/ or attentional challenges (Lichtenberger et al., 2009). In fact, the way in which a person achieves a score is often more significant than the score itself (Wiznitzer & Scheffel, 2009).

Formative assessments, such as CBMs and CBAs, also provide useful information on the rate at which a student is achieving and the effectiveness of the interventions employed. Various RTI models, however, have placed traditional assessment procedures under scrutiny by questioning the need for comprehensive assessments to accurately and effectively diagnose LD and ADHD. For a more in-depth understanding of why a student is struggling, RTI procedures should be combined with psychometric testing that provides both diagnostic and instructional data and includes cognitive ability testing (Kavale et al., 2008). If a student fails to respond to intervention and the results of a comprehensive evaluation indicate that the student has a processing deficit that impacts academic performance, both the definitional criteria for LD and the limited response to evidence-based instruction as part of the LD eligibility criteria have been addressed, resulting in a balanced model that promotes diagnostic accuracy (Hale, Kaufman, Naglieri, & Kavale, 2006).

In addition, for adults with LD and ADHD in postsecondary and vocational settings, the results of the RTI process will have little meaning for eligibility decisions as well as for the development of rationales for an individual's need for accommodations. Although standardized tests of academic achievement are only a part of the required information for accurate diagnosis, the results can assist with the selection of interventions and accommodation planning. A thorough evaluation that includes both academic and cognitive testing will lead to the development of the most appropriate accommodations and interventions. Evaluators need to be equipped with both an observational lens and a well-equipped tool kit that contains a variety of standardized assessments and informal measures designed to provide information about an individual's current performance levels and his or her particular pattern of strengths and weaknesses. As noted by Keenan et al. (2008): "Progress in science and validity of diagnoses depend on measurement instruments" (p. 298). A valid diagnosis also depends on the knowledge and skill of the evaluator. Individuals with LD and/ or ADHD present a particular challenge both diagnostically and educationally, and it is incumbent upon the involved specialists to meet this challenge (Johnson & Myklebust, 1967).

REFERENCES

Aaron, P. G. (1997). The impending demise of the discrepancy formula. *Review of Educational Research, 67*, 461–502.

Aaron, P. G., Joshi, R. M., Boulware-Gooden, R., & Bentum, K. (2008). Diagnosis and treatment of reading disabilities based on the component model of reading: An alternative to the discrepancy model of reading disabilities. *Journal of Learning Disabilities, 41*, 67–84.

Aaron, P. G., Joshi, R. M., Palmer, H., Smith, N., & Kirby, E. (2002). Separating genuine cases of reading disability from reading deficits caused by predominantly inattentive ADHD behavior. *Journal of Learning Disabilities, 35*, 425–435, 447.

Aaron, P. G., Joshi, M., & Williams, K. A. (1999). Not all reading disabilities are alike. *Journal of Learning Disabilities, 32*, 120–137.

AIMSweb® [Computer software]. San Antonio, TX: PsychCorp.

Americans with Disabilities Act of 1990. Public Law No. 101–336, 104 Stat. 327.

Barkley, R. A. (2003). Issues in the diagnosis of attention deficit/hyperactivity disorder in children. *Brain and Development, 25*, 77–83.

Barkley, R. A. (2006). ADHD in adults: Developmental course and outcome of children with ADHD, and ADHD in clinic-referred adults. In R. A. Barkley (Ed.), *Attention-deficit hyperactivity disorder: A handbook for diagnosis and treatment* (3rd ed., pp. 248–296). New York, NY: Guilford.

Bell, S. M., McCallum, R. S., & Cox, E. A. (2003). Toward a research-based assessment of dyslexia: Using cognitive measures to identify reading disabilities. *Journal of Learning Disabilities, 36*, 505–516.

Berninger, V. W. (1996). *Reading and writing acquisition: A developmental neuropsychological perspective*. Oxford, United Kingdom: Westview Press.

Berninger, V. W., & Richards, T. (2002). *Brain literacy for educators and psychologists.* San Diego, CA: Academic Press.

Berninger, V. W., & Wolf, B. J. (2009). *Teaching students with dyslexia and dysgraphia: Lessons from teaching and science.* Baltimore, MD: Brookes.

Boada, R., Riddle, M., & Pennington, B. F. (2008). Integrating science and practice in education. In E. Fletcher-Janzen & C. R. Reynolds (Eds.), *Neuropsychological perspectives on learning disabilities in the era of RTI: Recommendations for diagnosis and intervention* (pp. 179–191). Hoboken, NJ: Wiley.

Bonafina, M. A., Newcorn, J. H., McKay, K. E., Koda, V. H., & Halperin, J. M. (2000). A cluster analytic approach for distinguishing subgroups. *Journal of Learning Disabilities, 33,* 297–307.

Bowers, P. G., & Wolf, M. (1993). Theoretical links between naming speed, precise timing mechanisms and orthographic skill in dyslexia. *Reading and Writing: An Interdisciplinary Journal, 5,* 69–85.

Brady, S. A. (1991). The role of working memory in reading disability. In S. A. Brady & D. P. Shankweiler (Eds.), *Phonological processes in literacy: A tribute to Isabelle Y. Liberman* (pp. 129–151). Hillsdale, NJ: Erlbaum.

Brown, V., Wiederholt, J. L., & Hammill, D. D. (2009). *Test of reading comprehension* (4th ed.). Austin, TX: PRO-ED.

Bruck, M. (1993). Component spelling skills of college students with childhood diagnoses of dyslexia. *Learning Disability Quarterly, 16,* 171–184.

Burns, M. K., Dean, V. J., & Klar, S. (2004). Using curriculum-based assessment in the responsiveness to intervention diagnostic model for learning disabilities. *Assessment for Effective Intervention, 29*(3), 47–56.

Carrow-Woolfolk, E. (1995). *Oral and Written Language Scales.* Circle Pines, MN: American Guidance Service.

Connolly, J. (2007). *KeyMath 3 Diagnostic Assessment (KeyMath 3 DA).* Minneapolis, MN: Pearson.

Demaray, M. K., Schaefer, K., & Delong, K. (2003). Attention-Deficit/Hyperactivity Disorder (ADHD): A national survey of training and current assessment practices in school. *Psychology in the Schools, 40,* 583–597.

Deno, S. L. (1985). Curriculum-based measurement: The emerging alternative. *Exceptional Children, 52,* 219–232.

Deno, S. L., Fuchs, L. S., Marston, D., & Shin, J. (2001). Using curriculum-based measurement to establish growth standards for students with learning disabilities. *School Psychology Review, 30,* 507–524.

Deul, R. K. (1992). Motor skill disorder. In S. R. Hooper, G. W. Hynd, & R. E. Mattison (Eds.), *Developmental disorders: Diagnostic criteria and clinical assessment* (pp. 239–282). Hillsdale, NJ: Erlbaum.

Flanagan, D. P., Keiser, S., Bernier, J., & Ortiz, S. O. (2003). *Assessment of learning disabilities in adulthood.* Boston, MA: Allyn & Bacon.

Frazier, T. W., Youngstrom, E. A., Glutting, J., & Watkins, M. W. (2007). ADHD and achievement: Meta-analysis of the child, adolescent, and adult literatures and a concomitant study with college students. *Journal of Learning Disabilities, 40,* 49–65.

Gardner, R., Cartledge, G., Seidl, B., Woolsey, M. L., Schley, G. S., & Utley, C. A. (2001). Mt. Olivet after-school program: Peer-mediated interventions for at-risk students. *Remedial and Special Education, 22*(1), 22–33.

Geary, D. C. (1993). Mathematical disabilities: Cognitive, neuropsychological, and genetic components. *Psychological Bulletin, 114,* 345–362.

Geary, D. C. (2007). An evolutionary perspective on learning disabilities in mathematics. *Developmental Neuropsychology, 32,* 471–519.

Gickling, E., & Rosenfield, S. (1995). Best practices in curriculum-based assessment. In A. Thomas & J. Grimes (Eds.), *Best practices in school psychology* (3rd ed., pp. 587–595). Washington, DC: National Association of School Psychologists.

Goldstein, S. (1997). *Managing attention and learning disorders in late adolescence & adulthood: A guide for practitioners.* New York, NY: Wiley.

Goldstein, S., & Cunningham, S. (2009). Current issues in the assessment of intelligence, specific learning disability, and attention deficit hyperactivity disorder. In J. A. Naglieri & S. Goldstein (Eds.), *Practitioner's guide to intelligence and achievement* (pp. 11–23). Hoboken, NJ: Wiley.

Gregg, N. (2007). Underserved and underprepared: Postsecondary learning disabilities. *Learning Disabilities Research & Practice, 22,* 219–228.

Gregg, N. (2009). *Adolescents and adults with learning disabilities and ADHD: Assessment and accommodation.* New York, NY: Guilford Press.

Gregg, N., Coleman, C., Davis, M., & Chalk, J. C. (2007). Timed essay writing: Implications for high-stakes tests. *Journal of Learning Disabilities, 40,* 306–318.

Gregg, N., Coleman, C., Stennett, R. B., & Davis, M. (2002). Discourse complexity of college writers with and without disabilities: A multidimensional analysis. *Journal of Learning Disabilities, 35,* 23–38, 56.

Guthrie, J. T., & Davis, M. H. (2003). Motivating struggling readers in middle school through an engagement model of classroom practice. *Reading and Writing Quarterly, 19,* 59–85.

Hale, J. B., Kaufman, A. S., Naglieri, J. A., & Kavale, K. A. (2006). Implementation of IDEA: Response to intervention and cognitive assessment methods. *Psychology in the Schools, 43,* 753–770.

Hale, J. B., Naglieri, J. A., Kaufman, A. S., & Kavale, K. A. (2004). Specific learning disability classification in the new Individuals with Disabilities Education Act: The danger of good ideas. *School Psychologist, 58*(1), 6–13, 29.

Hammill, D. D., Brown, V. L., Larsen, S. C., & Wiederholt, J. L. (2007). *Test of Adolescent and Adult Language* (4th ed.). Austin, TX: PRO-ED.

Hammill, D. D., & Larsen, S. (2008). *Test of Written Language* (4th ed.). Austin, TX: PRO-ED.

Hammill, D. D., & Newcomer, P. (2008). *Test of Language Development-Intermediate* (4th ed.). Austin, TX: PRO-ED.

Hresko, W. P., Schlieve, P. L., Herron, S. R., Swain, C., & Sherbenou, R. J. (2003). *Comprehensive Mathematical Abilities Test*. Austin, TX: PRO-ED.

Individuals with Disabilities Education Act of 2004 (IDEA). (2004). Pub. L. No. 108-446, 118 Stat. 2647. Retrieved from http://www2.ed.gov/offices/OSERS/Policy/IDEA/the_law.html

Johnson, D. J., & Myklebust, H. R. (1967). *Learning disabilities: Educational principles and practices*. New York, NY: Grune & Stratton.

Kail, R. V. (1991). Developmental change in speed of processing during childhood and adolescence. *Psychological Bulletin, 109*, 490–501.

Kail, R. V., & Ferrer, E. (2007). Processing speed in childhood and adolescence: Longitudinal models for examining developmental change. *Child Development, 78*, 1760–1770.

Kaufman, A. S. (1994). *Intelligent testing with the WISC-III*. New York, NY: Wiley.

Kaufman, A. S., & Kaufman, N. L. (2004). *Kaufman Test of Educational Achievement* (2nd ed.). San Antonio, TX: Pearson.

Kaufman, A. S., Lichtenberger, E. O., Fletcher-Janzen, E., & Kaufman, N. L. (2005). *Essentials of the K-ABC-II Assessment*. Hoboken, NJ: Wiley.

Kaufman, A. S., Lichtenberger, E. O., & Naglieri, J. A. (1999). Intelligence testing in the schools. In C. R. Reynolds & T. Gutkin (Eds.), *The handbook of school psychology* (3rd ed., pp. 307–349). New York, NY: Wiley.

Kaufmann, L., & Nuerk, H. C. (2008). Basic number processing deficits in ADHD: A broad examination of elementary and complex number processing skills in 9- to 12-year-old children with ADHD-C. *Developmental Science, 11*, 692–699.

Kavale, K. A., Kauffman, J. M., Bachmeier, R. J., & LeFever, G. B. (2008). Response-to-intervention: Separating the rhetoric of self-congratulation from the reality of specific learning disability identification. *Learning Disability Quarterly, 31*, 135–150.

Kavale, K. A., Kaufman, A. S., Naglieri, J. A., & Hale, J. (2005). Changing procedures for identifying learning disabilities: The danger of poorly supported ideas. *School Psychologist, 59*, 16–25.

Keenan, J. M., Betjemann, R. S., & Olson, R. K. (2008). Reading comprehension tests vary in the skills that they assess: Differential dependence on decoding and oral comprehension *Scientific Studies of Reading, 12*, 281–300.

Laasonen, M., Lehtinen, M., Leppamaki, S., Tani, P., & Hokkanen, L. (2010). Project DyAdd: Phonological processing, reading, spelling, and arithmetic in adults with dyslexia or ADHD. *Journal of Learning Disabilities, 43*, 3–14.

Larsen, S., Hammill, D. D., & Moats, L. (1999). *Test of Written Spelling* (4th ed.). Austin, TX: PRO-ED.

Lichtenberger, E. O., Mather, N., Kaufman, N. L., & Kaufman, A. S. (2004). *Essentials of assessment report writing*. Hoboken, NJ: Wiley.

Lichtenberger, E. O., Sotelo-Dynega, M., & Kaufman, A. S. (2009). The Kaufman Assessment Battery for Children (2nd ed.). In J. A. Naglieri & S. Goldstein (Eds.), *Practitioner's guide to assessing intelligence and achievement* (pp. 61–93). Hoboken, NJ: Wiley.

Markwardt, F. (1998). *Peabody Individual Achievement Test-Revised-Normative Update*. Circle Pines, MN: American Guidance Service.

Marshall, R. M., Hynd, G. W., Handwerk, M. J., & Hall, J. (1997). Academic underachievement in ADHD subtypes. *Journal of Learning Disabilities, 30*, 635–642.

Marston, D. (1989). Curriculum-based measurement: What is it and why do it? In M. R. Shinn (Ed.), *Curriculum-based measurement: Assessing special children* (pp. 18–78). New York, NY: Guilford.

Mather, N., & Gregg, N. (2006). Specific learning disabilities: Clarifying, not eliminating, a construct. *Professional Psychology, 37*, 99–106.

Mather, N., Gregg, N., & Simon, J. A. (2005). The curse of high stakes tests and high abilities: Reactions to Wong v. Regents of the University of California. *Learning Disabilities: A Multidisciplinary Journal, 13*, 139–144.

Mather, N., Hammill, D., Allen, E., & Roberts, R. (2004). *Test of Silent Word Reading Fluency*. Austin, TX: PRO-ED.

McKenzie, R. G. (2009). Obscuring vital distinctions: The oversimplification of learning disabilities within RTI. *Learning Disability Quarterly, 32*, 203–215.

Moats, L. C. (1995). *Spelling: Development, disability, and instruction*. Timonium, MD: York Press.

Monroe, M. (1932). *Children who cannot read*. Chicago, IL: University of Chicago Press.

Montague, M. (1996). Assessing mathematical problem solving. *Learning Disability Research & Practice, 11*, 228–238.

Montague, M. (1997). Cognitive strategy training in mathematics instruction for students with learning disabilities. *Journal of Learning Disabilities, 30*, 164–177.

Montague, M. (2006). Self-regulation strategies for better math performance. In M. Montague & J. K. Jitendra (Eds.), *Teaching mathematics to middle school students with learning difficulties* (pp. 89–107). New York, NY: Guilford Press.

Montague, M., Warger, C. L., & Morgan, H. (2000). Solve it! Strategy instruction to improve mathematical problem solving. *Learning Disabilities Research & Practice, 15*, 110–116.

Monuteaux, M. C., Faraone, S. V., Herzig, K., Navsaria, N., & Biederman, J. (2005). ADHD and dyscalculia: Evidence for independent familial transmission. *Journal of Learning Disabilities, 38*, 86–93.

Murphy, M. M., Mazzocco, M. M. M., Hanich, L. B., & Early, M. C. (2007). Cognitive characteristics of children with mathematics learning disability (MLD) vary as the function of the cutoff criterion used to define MLD. *Journal of Learning Disabilities, 40*, 458–478.

Plaza, M., & Cohen, H. (2003). The interaction between phonological processing, syntactic awareness, and naming speed in the reading and spelling performance of first-grade children. *Brain and Cognition, 53,* 287–292.

President's Commission on Excellence in Special Education. (2001). *A new era: Revitalizing special education for children and their families.* Washington, DC: U.S. Department of Education.

Rack, J. P., Snowling, M. J., & Olson, R. K. (1992). The nonword reading deficit in developmental dyslexia: A review. *Reading Research Quarterly, 27,* 28–53.

Reynolds, C. R. (2005, August). *Considerations in RTI as a method of diagnosis of learning disabilities.* Paper presented at the Annual Institute for Psychology in the Schools of the American Psychological Association, Washington, DC.

Reynolds, C. R., & Kamphaus, R. W. (2007). *Test of Irregular Word Reading Efficiency.* Lutz, FL: PAR.

Robin, A. L. (2006). Training families with adolescents with ADHD. In R. A. Barkley (Ed.), *Attention-deficit hyperactivity disorder: A handbook for diagnosis and treatment* (3rd ed., pp. 499–546). New York, NY: Guilford.

Salvia, J., Ysseldyke, J. E., & Bolt, S. (2010). *Assessment in special and inclusive education* (11th ed.). Belmont, CA: Wadsworth.

Samuelsson, S., Lundberg, I., & Herkner, B. (2004). ADHD and reading disability in male adults: Is there a connection? *Journal of Learning Disabilities, 37,* 155–168.

Shaywitz, S. E., & Shaywitz, B. A. (2003). Neurobiological indices of dyslexia. In H. L. Swanson, K. R. Harris, & S. Graham (Eds.), *Handbook of learning disabilities* (pp. 514–531). New York, NY: Guilford Press.

Siegel., L. S., & Ryan, E. B. (1989). The development of working memory in normally achieving and subtypes of learning disabled children. *Child Development, 60,* 973–980.

Sparks, R. L., & Lovett, B. J. (2009). College students with learning disabilities diagnoses: Who are they and how do they perform? *Journal of Learning Disabilities, 42,* 494–510.

Stecker, P. M., Fuchs, L. S., & Fuchs, D. (2005). Using curriculum-based measurement to improve student achievement: Review of research. *Psychology in the Schools, 42,* 795–819.

Sternberg, R. J., & Williams, W. M. (2002). *Educational psychology.* Boston, MA: Allyn & Bacon.

Swanson, H. L., Hoskyn, M., & Lee, C. (1999). *Interventions for students with learning disabilities: A meta-analysis of treatment outcomes.* New York, NY: Guilford Press.

Swanson, H. L., & Hsieh, C. J. (2009). Reading disabilities in adults: A selective meta-analysis of the literature. *Review of Educational Research, 79,* 1362–1390.

Swanson, H. L., Jerman, O., & Zheng, X. (2008). Growth in working memory and mathematical problem solving in children at risk and not at risk for serious math difficulties. *Journal of Educational Psychology, 100,* 343–379.

Swanson, H. L., Mink, J., & Bocian, K. M. (1999). Cognitive processing deficits in poor readers with symptoms of reading disabilities and ADHD: More alike than different? *Journal of Educational Psychology, 91*, 321–333.

Torgesen, J. K., & Miller, D. H. (2009). *Assessments to guide adolescent literacy instruction*. Portsmouth, NH: RMC Research Corporation, Center on Instruction.

Torgesen, J. K., Wagner, R., & Rashotte, C. (1999). *Test of Word Reading Efficiency*. Austin, TX: PRO-ED.

Travis, L. E. (1935). Intellectual factors. In G. M. Whipple (Ed.), *The thirty-fourth yearbook of the National Society for the Study of Education: Educational diagnosis* (pp. 37–47). Bloomington, IL: Public School Publishing.

U.S. Department of Education. (2009). *Twenty-eighth annual report to Congress on the implementation of the Individuals with Disabilities Education Act*. Washington, DC: Author.

U.S. Department of Education, Office for Civil Rights. (2007a). *Free and appropriate public education for students with disabilities: Requirements under Section 504 of the Rehabilitation Act of 1973*. Washington, DC: Author.

U.S. Department of Education, Office for Civil Rights (2007b). *Transition of students with disabilities to postsecondary education: A guide for high school educators*. Washington, DC: Author.

Urso, A. (2008). Processing speed as a predictor of poor reading. *Dissertation Abstracts International, Section A: The Humanities and Social Sciences, 69*(3), 923.

Wang, J., & Guthrie, J. T. (2004). Modeling the effects of intrinsic motivation, extrinsic motivation, amount of reading, and past reading achievement on text comprehension between U.S. and Chinese students. *Reading Research Quarterly, 39*, 162–186.

Wechsler, D., (2009). *Wechsler Individual Achievement Test* (3rd ed.). San Antonio, TX: Psychological Corporation.

Weiss, G., & Hechtman, L. (1993). *Hyperactive children grown up* (2nd ed.). New York, NY: Guilford Press.

Wiederholt, J. L., & Blalock, G. (2000). *Gray Silent Reading Tests*. Austin, TX: PRO-ED.

Wiederholt, J. L., & Bryant, B. (2001). *Gray Oral Reading Tests* (4th ed.). Austin, TX: PRO-ED.

Wilkinson, G. S., & Robertson, G. J. (2007). *Wide Range Achievement Test* (4th ed.). Lutz, FL: Psychological Assessment Resources.

Wilson, B. A., & Felton, R. H. (2004). *Word Identification and Spelling Test*. Austin, TX: PRO-ED.

Wiznitzer, M., & Scheffel, D. L. (2009). Learning disabilities. In R. B. David, J. B. Bodensteiner, D. E. Mandelbaum, & B. Olson (Eds.), *Clinical pediatric neurology* (pp. 479–492). New York, NY: Demos Medical.

Wolf, M., & Bowers, P. (2000). The question of naming-speed deficits in developmental reading disabilities: An introduction to the special issue on the double-deficit hypothesis. *Journal of Learning Disabilities, 33*, 322–324.

Woodcock, R. W., Schrank, F. A., McGrew, K. S., & Mather, N. (2007). *Woodcock-Johnson III Normative Update*. Rolling Meadows, IL: Riverside.

Ysseldyke, J. E., & Christenson, S. L. (2002). *Functional assessment of Academic Environment Scale*. Longmont, CO: Sopris West.

8

Assessment of Psychiatric Status and Personality Qualities

J. Russell Ramsay
Bradley M. Rosenfield
Lofton H. Harris

When individuals are referred for an evaluation for Attention-Deficit/ Hyperactivity Disorder (ADHD) or a learning assessment, the request can sound similar to a request for blood work to determine cholesterol levels. To some degree, this metaphor is apt insofar as assessment of learning and attention disorders are not typical components of standard diagnostic interviews conducted in most out-patient mental health clinics. The purpose of such specialized evaluations is to determine if, in fact, there are underlying learning and attention issues that have not been previously identified. What is more, these evaluations must address whether learning and attention problems are present and have made a direct and causal contribution to coping difficulties and impairments, most often but not exclusively in academic settings. However, assessments narrowly limited to evaluating learning and attention disorders run the risk of underestimating the presence of comorbid psychiatric disorders and characterological patterns (not to mention medical conditions). These potential comorbidities may exacerbate or, in some cases, be a primary source of problems related to learning and attention. Hence, adequate assessment of psychiatric and personality factors is an important component of a thorough evaluation for attention and other learning problems.

The purpose of this chapter is to review strategies and inventories for the multidimensional assessment of psychiatric status and personality variables as a component of a comprehensive evaluation of learning and attention disorders in adolescents and adults, with a particular focus on ADHD. We first review evaluation strategies for psychiatric diagnoses followed by a discussion of personality measures. The manner in which these variables may affect diagnosis and treatment planning will be discussed throughout the chapter.

EVALUATION OF PSYCHIATRIC STATUS

Clinical Interview

Comprehensive assessments of learning and attention disorders start off with a review of presenting problems as they manifest across multiple life domains (e.g., school, work, relationships, etc.) and identifying the specific reasons why the individual has sought the evaluation. For example, we typically ask: "Why did you come in for this evaluation, and how are you hoping it can help you?" This sort of open-ended question allows the individual and any family members or significant others participating in the interview to outline the various circumstances that led to the assessment and the desired outcomes. The clinician listens for clues about psychiatric status throughout the assessment process, which will inform later inquiry.

In many cases, it is the cumulative emotional effects and frustrations in response to the impairments associated with undiagnosed learning and attention problems that eventually compel individuals to seek an assessment. In other cases, stressful and unremitting life events, such as academic setbacks, employment problems, or legal entanglements, can bring about anxiety or mood disturbances that, in turn, magnify attention and/or learning problems. For example, some patients describe increased feelings of "frustration," "stress," or being "overwhelmed" when facing seemingly reasonable demands at school, work, or home, which may suggest the presence of anxiety. Descriptions of feeling "down," "unmotivated," "disappointed in myself," or other self-criticisms may indicate depressive symptoms. Inasmuch as these symptoms are present in learning and attention disorders as well as in mood disorders, the challenge for the assessor is to disentangle whether these psychiatric symptoms are causes or effects of learning and attention problems, or some interactive combination thereof.

To further complicate matters, the functional and educational impairments associated with attention and Learning Disabilities (LD) may fluctuate across time and settings. When these difficulties occur, individuals with these sorts of disorders may develop compensatory strategies in an attempt to reduce the impact of the disorder on their ability to function effectively. However, such strategies often prove inadequate when an affected individual is confronted with a particularly difficult life situation, such as an academic or occupational role that reveals long-standing learning or attention issues in the form of emergent functional impairments.

Consequently, in addition to listening for descriptions of emotional reactions to the presenting problems, inquiry about an individual's coping responses to current difficulties may provide clues to guide further questioning. Questions along the lines of "How have you tried to deal with some of the problems you have been facing?" shed light on attempts to implement coping strategies, including both adaptive and maladaptive practices. These attempts at coping may be cognitive, behavioral, and emotional. For example, individuals may report responding with avoidance and procrastination (e.g., "I put things off too long and then have to rush to finish them"), stoically spending inordinate time on tasks (e.g., "I sacrifice sleep and my social life to push through the project, even though I know I'll end up exhausted the next few days"), or other unproductive patterns (e.g., cheating on academic assignments or tests). Conversely, patients may describe the use of some adaptive strategies, such as the use of organizational tools, seeking additional help from a teacher or employer, or insight about one's personal learning style that helps them take steps to manage their attention problems, such as studying in the morning when attention, for some, is highest.

Whenever feasible, it is useful to include family members or significant others in the evaluation in order to get their impressions regarding a patient's attention and learning problems as well as emotional and behavioral functioning. In cases in which a family member or significant other cannot be present for the clinical interview, these individuals may be amenable to a scheduled phone contact or to provide a written narrative of their observations. Parents of adolescents and young adults, particularly college students, often provide important observations of behavioral problems that patients may be legitimately unaware of or minimize. For example, parents of a high school student may observe significant moodiness or agitation that may suggest the presence of a possible mood disorder that is minimized by the student. With young adult and adult patients, significant others may also be able to provide other corroborative assessment data, such as past report cards from school, recent work evaluations or college grades, and their observations of the individual. Collateral reports can be enormously helpful in guiding the assessment.

The open-ended, "conversational" nature of the clinical interview helps build a working alliance to facilitate the rest of the evaluation and treatment phases. Additionally, the information gathered during the clinical interview helps the evaluator to prioritize areas of inquiry to be emphasized during a structured diagnostic interview, which is discussed next.

Structured Diagnostic Interview

A number of structured diagnostic interview formats and protocols are available that are used in the context of assessments for ADHD and learning problems (Barkley & Murphy, 2006; Brown, 1996; Kaufman, Birmaher, Brent, Rao, & Ryan, 1996; Murphy & Gordon, 2006), including the Structured Clinical Interview for DSM-IV (SCID-I; First, Spitzer, Gibbon, & Williams, 1997). Although differing somewhat in particular details, they share an emphasis on the assessment of past and current symptoms based on the DSM-IV (DSM-IV; American Psychiatric Association [APA], 1994) diagnostic criteria. Most structured diagnostic interview formats for older adolescents and adults used in standard mental health settings do not include modules focused on ADHD or learning issues, hence the assessment of attention and LD is considered a clinical specialty. However, a structured approach to the assessment of psychiatric diagnoses is an essential component of a comprehensive evaluation of learning and attention in order to identify comorbidity and make differential diagnoses.

Although looking at the number of diagnostic categories covered in the DSM-IV-TR (4th ed., text revision; APA, 2000) makes conducting an adequate interview appear daunting, information gathered during the clinical interview, use of background questionnaires, and good interviewing skills make it quite manageable. Moreover, psychometrically sound, standardized measures, such as the SCID or other structured approaches, increase diagnostic validity and reliability while reducing the chance of misdiagnosis. The interviewer will have gathered some clinical information regarding an individual's functioning and symptoms during the open-ended clinical interview or from symptom screening questionnaires (e.g., Symptom Checklist 90–Revised; Derogatis, 1986), history (e.g., past treatment, diagnoses, family history), and any background questionnaires completed prior to the evaluation. For example, background inventories with questions regarding academic and behavioral functioning at different grade levels, occupational history and behavior, and questions about past medical and psychiatric treatment, including a list of medications, can be used to guide interview questions (e.g., Barkley & Murphy, 2006; Brown, 1996).

Moreover, although the SCID is comprised of modules for the major Axis I diagnoses, each module has screening questions for the particular diagnostic category to be assessed. For example, if the interviewee denies ever having had a panic attack, there is no need to assess for all the specific symptoms of Panic Disorder. However, as the interviewer gathers information throughout the assessment process, possible clues of diagnostic issues should be considered and reviewed, such as the case of a young woman presenting for issues of distractibility who describes anxiety and then notes that she has a distressing habit of excessive skin picking and hair pulling, which she performs to relieve her anxiety. This information is clearly relevant to diagnosis and treatment planning where addressing her symptoms of trichotillomania becomes a priority, and this condition is likely the source of her attention and downstream academic problems.

Common Comorbid and Differential Diagnoses

Whether using a standardized diagnostic interview format or assessing psychiatric status using a less formal clinical interview, it is useful to rule out different diagnostic categories in order to identify conditions that may be the root causes of attention problems. For example, inquiring about traumatic experiences such as physical or sexual abuse may reveal evidence of Posttraumatic Stress Disorder (PTSD), which even in subthreshold form is associated with symptoms that can interfere with learning and attention. Early trauma has been associated with subsequent attention problems stemming from affect dysregulation and dissociative states that could be mistaken for ADHD (Weinstein, Staffelback, & Biaggio, 2000), although these conditions can coexist. Likewise, inquiring about substance use may also reveal issues that could be either a cause or an effect of the presenting attention and/or learning problems but must be addressed in terms of the assessment and subsequent treatment planning. The next sections address some common areas of inquiry in the assessment of psychiatric status.

Depression

Along with anxiety and substance use problems, depression is one of the most common comorbidity patterns observed in samples of adolescents and adults with ADHD (Barkley, Murphy, & Fischer, 2008). Although it is obviously important to screen for evidence of a major depressive episode and associated suicidal ideation, individuals with ADHD often exhibit milder, chronic forms of dysphoria when facing the impairments associated with their difficulties that warrant clinical intervention.

Depressive symptoms may reflect the mounting frustration and demoralization associated with unrecognized attention and learning problems as individuals face situations in school, work, and other domains of life that demand efficient learning skills and executive functioning. Depression may also represent a distinct mood disorder that presents as or magnifies a learning or attention disorder. The diagnostic interview helps to identify the presence and severity of symptoms, to determine the course of onset of mood issues relative to learning or attention problems, and to factor these issues in the resulting treatment plan.

The Beck Depression Inventory-II (BDI-II; Beck, Steer, & Brown, 1996) is a well-researched and useful clinical scale with which to assess depressed mood and to monitor change in the course of treatment. The BDI-II also includes an item assessing concentration that has been correlated with ADHD (Steer, Ranieri, Kumar, & Beck, 2003). The Beck Hopelessness Scale (BHS; Beck & Steer, 1989) also provides a measure of pessimistic outlooks about the future. Thus, the BDI-II and BHS can be used as indicators of the magnitude of the effects of presenting problems on an individual's view of the future and his or her ability to change, akin to the Problems with Self-Concept subscale of the Conners' Adult ADHD Rating Scale Self-Report–Long Version (Conners, Erhardt, & Sparrow, 1999) or the Affect subscale of the Brown Attention Deficit Disorders Scales (Brown, 1996).

Bipolar Disorder is another condition to be ruled out in the course of a diagnostic interview as part of the assessment of attention and learning problems. Hypomanic and manic episodes are associated with impulsivity, racing thoughts, and difficulties focusing on tasks at hand. ADHD and learning problems may coexist with a bipolar spectrum disorder, and some studies of reverse comorbidity of ADHD have indicated that the prevalence of ADHD among samples of individuals with lifetime Bipolar Disorder is greater than would be predicted by chance (Nierenberg et al., 2005). Whereas attention and learning problems are generally persistent, the mood variations in bipolar spectrum disorders tend to be episodic (Murphy & Gordon, 2006). Inquiring about discrete periods of hypomania or mania in which behaviors are particularly goal oriented (though usually not focused on priority academic or occupational tasks), there is sleep disruption, the person engages in risky and impulsive behaviors, and concentration problems are characterized by racing thoughts helps identify these episodes. Individuals with ADHD may describe difficulties "turning off thoughts" or report that their thoughts may be distracting, but they generally do not describe thoughts as constantly "racing" or "jumbled." Individuals with ADHD may also describe many examples of impulsivity, but usually these examples fit a predictable profile of impulsive behaviors exhibited across time rather than episodes of uncharacteristic impulsive and risky behaviors. Interviewing corroborative reporters can be helpful to discern the presence of discrete mood and manic/hypomanic episodes and issues related to decreased need for sleep that could indicate a bipolar spectrum disorder.

Anxiety

Anxiety is another very common presenting emotional issue in adolescents and adults seeking assessment for learning and attention problems (Barkley et al., 2008). As individuals face mounting difficulties managing the demands of school, work, or other life domains, they may experience newfound problems and setbacks when performing tasks associated with these domains. Hence, individuals with learning and attention problems may feel increased worry about their performance on upcoming tasks based on past functional difficulties. What is more, these individuals may have encountered impairments from their functional difficulties ranging from diminished performance on certain tasks up to receiving official academic or occupational warnings or dismissal. Other examples of significant coping difficulties include financial problems related to disorganization and procrastination, relationship problems, and poor follow-through on the various affairs of daily life.

In most cases, escalating anxiety reflects the direct effects of learning and attention problems on task performance and sense of efficacy. In fact, as individuals become aware of their coping struggles, they may attempt to increase the emotional salience of difficult tasks by emphasizing the potential negative consequences of procrastination or avoidance (e.g., "If I don't get to work on this, I might fail the class"), thereby generating motivation for follow-through. In circumscribed situations, this approach may be helpful, such as completing a task under a deadline pressure—so-called brinksmanship. However, this strategy is generally neither adaptive nor sustainable over time. Moreover, as tasks become more challenging, particularly in cases of attention and learning problems, the associated anxiety increases. This anxiety, in turn, magnifies distractibility that may lead to a self-defeating cycle of avoidance and underperformance.

In some cases, however, learning and attention problems may be the direct result of an Anxiety Disorder. Individuals with chronic, generalized anxiety frequently experience difficulties with concentration (APA, 2000). Adolescents and adults may experience anxiety that is particularly magnified in performance situations, such as test taking in academic settings or in various work roles. Issues related to perfectionism may also lead to problems with procrastination, inordinate time spent on tasks, and, consequently, missing deadlines, as the demand to be "perfect" proves overwhelming. Likewise, social anxiety may create many of the same difficulties. Cases of pure Social Phobia are usually easy to differentiate from ADHD and learning problems due to the context-specific nature of the associated impairments (e.g., public speaking anxiety); individuals with ADHD and learning difficulties may avoid situations based on the task demands rather than concerns about the judgments of others. That being said, individuals with ADHD and learning difficulties may exhibit features of Avoidant Personality as a secondary effect of their coping difficulties.

The Beck Anxiety Inventory (Beck & Steer, 1990) can be a useful tool for measuring anxiety symptoms, although it includes more somatic symptoms (e.g., heart pounding) than cognitive symptoms of anxiety (e.g., worry, fear of the worst happening). Inquiry during the clinical interview regarding the internal experience of individuals while facing difficult situations may shed light on the role anxiety problems might play in their coping difficulties. In particular, reviewing specific examples of procrastination and avoidance helps gather information not only for the assessment of learning and attention problems but also associated emotional factors, namely anxiety, that might exacerbate these difficulties with follow-through on tasks. To this end, it is useful to ask patients to recount a recent incident of avoidance or procrastination in order to uncover possible elements of anxiety (e.g., "What was your plan for working on the project you anticipated would be difficult for you? What thoughts went through your mind when you tried to work on the project? What emotions or physical sensations did you feel? How did the plan turn out?").

Substance Use

Individuals with ADHD are at increased risk for lifetime substance use problems, particularly alcohol use (Barkley et al., 2008). However, the risk may be greater for individuals with ADHD and Conduct Disorder (CD), which can be associated with wide-ranging behavioral problems that interfere with academic, social, and occupational functioning (Barkley, 2006; Barkley et al., 2008; Schubiner et al., 2000). In cases of adolescents or young adults seeking assessment primarily for attention and learning problems, only rarely is there evidence of a level of substance use that fulfills diagnostic criteria for active substance abuse or dependence that has not already been identified. By contrast, in cases of adults seeking treatment for a Substance Use Disorder, evidence of an attention disorder or LD is quite common (Schubiner et al., 2000). Moreover, there may be cases in which an underfunctioning high school or college student is brought in for an evaluation and it is found that substance use and other issues may explain the presenting difficulties and functional changes more so than ADHD or learning problems. Regardless, treatment and stabilization of an active substance dependence or abuse problem must be placed at the top of the treatment plan. Some adults seeking assessment for ADHD might be in sustained full remission from substance use problems and are seeking subsequent treatment for ADHD that might have put them at risk for their substance use problems in the first place.

More common in the assessment of adolescents and adults with attention and learning problems is the possibility that there are problematic substance use patterns that magnify coping difficulties and that must be addressed in treatment. Explicitly inquiring about the use of alcohol and recreational drugs should be a standard part of the interview. Available screening measures, such as the Michigan Alcohol Screening Test (Selzer, 1971), can help guide this assessment. Individuals may describe use of substances to reduce stress and anxiety or for self-medication for concentration difficulties, such as to "quiet my mind." Adolescents and young adults (i.e., college students) may report persistent problematic use patterns, most often marijuana use, which may not obviate the pursuit of interventions for attention and learning problems but that must be addressed in treatment since cannabis may impair attention and concentration both during acute intoxication and withdrawal and may produce Cannabis Induced Anxiety Disorder (APA, 2000).

Inquiring about current prescribed medications helps to identify conditions that are currently being treated that are relevant to the diagnostic interview. It is also useful to inquire as to whether individuals misuse (here defined as not taking a medication as prescribed) their prescription medications. In many cases, misuse is characterized by an underutilization of medications, such as forgetting to take medications for ADHD. However, other cases of misuse are characterized by overuse of prescription medications, such as an individual taking excessive amounts of a sedative or using a sibling's ADHD medication in order to improve focus while studying.

Explicit inquiry about substance use patterns and follow-up inquiry regarding imprecise descriptions of "social drinking" (e.g., "I drink about the same as any other college student") helps gather important clinical data. Even when substance use patterns do not approach levels of abuse, qualitative information about individuals' use patterns may provide useful information. For example, a graduate student seeking an evaluation for ADHD recognized that it was uncharacteristic for her to have two beers in an evening after classes to deal with her stress. The student recognized that she was increasingly anxious about her underperformance in school related to heightened distractibility and decided to seek an assessment for her attention problems. Asking about legal issues and other consequences related to substance use, such as charges related to driving while intoxicated (or being stopped without an official charge), substance use violations on campus, or teens getting grounded by parents for drinking, are other ways to inquire about these use patterns.

Finally, it is also clinically useful to inquire about patterns of caffeine and nicotine use. Both of these substances have been associated with improved ability to focus, although their use or overuse may also be associated with various negative health outcomes. Again, exploring possibilities of using these substances for self-medication provides useful clinical data.

Other Diagnostic Considerations

Although depression, anxiety, and substance use problems are the most common coexisting psychiatric conditions observed in cases of young adults and adults with ADHD (Barkley et al., 2008), there are other conditions to be considered during the clinical interview. These diagnostic considerations are particularly relevant in the assessment of adolescents and young adults, as this period of development is associated with the emergence of a number of psychiatric conditions that may cause or contribute to attention and learning problems.

Although it may be a rare occurrence to uncover evidence of a severe thought disorder in such evaluations, individuals who perform evaluations for attention and learning problems, particularly for older adolescents and young adults, may want to be alert for the potential emergence of early signs of psychosis as an explanation for a decline in academic performance and overall functioning. Early manifestations of psychotic disorders may present as marked changes from previous functioning characterized by executive function problems, such as disorganization and attention difficulties. Later, individuals may present with particularly disorganized behavior with other features, such as delusions, disorganized speech, inappropriate affect, and the like.

Another important issue for which to screen is the presence of some sort of traumatic experience that might be creating attention problems and resultant academic or occupational functioning difficulties, as mentioned earlier. Studies have shown that traumatic events, particularly those experienced in childhood, alter development of regions of the brain responsible for executive functioning, which may lead to symptoms of inattention and impulsivity (Karl et al., 2006). Simply asking the open-ended question during the interview of whether the individual has experienced any traumatic experiences allows people to judge what may be relevant to disclose. When there is an affirmative response, most often what is reported is an example of an emotionally troubling and personally relevant experience, such as the divorce of parents or having to change schools several times while growing up, that does not meet the clinical definition of a trauma (e.g., experiencing an event that involves actual or threatened death, serious injury, or a threat to the physical integrity of self or others). However, individuals who have encountered traumatic events should be screened for PTSD.

The exploration of possible sleep problems is important in the assessment of attention and learning problems (Rosenfield, Ramsay, Cahn, & Pellegrino, 2009). In addition to being a factor in the differential diagnosis of Bipolar Disorder, sleep disorders, such as insomnia, obstructive sleep apnea, and restless leg syndrome, may create problems with fatigue and inattention, thereby creating the downstream functional difficulties in daily life. Individuals with ADHD also are at heightened risk for experiencing disrupted sleep—difficulties winding down and getting to sleep at the end of a day, problems waking up and getting started at the beginning of a day, or some combination thereof. Adults with ADHD have been found to have an altered circadian rhythm, preferring to stay up late and sleep in later the following day (Gau et al., 2007; Rybak, McNeely, Mackenzie, Jain, & Levitan, 2007). It is unclear whether the self-regulation problems associated with ADHD also are associated with regulation of sleep-wake cycles or whether these maladaptive patterns (insofar as they contribute to impairment) are another behavioral manifestation of the disorder, such as procrastinating on sleep, or a combination of both. The possible presence of a Sleep Disorder requires referral for specialized assessment to rule out and specialized treatment to address.

It is useful to have a current medical evaluation to rule out medical conditions that may contribute to psychiatric symptoms and/or learning and attention problems, such as hyper- or hypothyroidism, obstructive sleep apnea, past head injuries, and others. Inquiring about current physical health and functioning is a useful line of questioning to screen for potential medical complications.

Finally, many older adolescents and adults seeking help for attention and learning problems may also exhibit mild or subthreshold versions of many of the aforementioned psychiatric diagnoses or developmental syndromes. That is, there may be features of mild, mixed depressed mood and anxiety that create added coping difficulties but that do not fulfill diagnostic criteria for a major depressive episode or Generalized Anxiety Disorder. Likewise, individuals may exhibit characteristics of a developmental syndrome, such as Asperger's Disorder, that might not warrant a formal diagnosis but is considered in the evaluation and treatment plan.

In addition to previously mentioned psychiatric issues, ranging from relatively circumscribed adjustment reactions, to shadow features, to full diagnostic criteria, personality factors also are important to consider in the evaluation process. There can be a similar continuum from personality qualities and temperaments to full-blown personality disorders. However, these varying characteristics and temperaments are important to consider insofar as they may contribute to attention and learning problems and affect how individuals cope with them. The next section reviews personality variables in the assessment of attention and learning problems.

EVALUATION OF PERSONALITY

Clinical Interview

Even if formal assessment of personality style using personality measures is not an aspect of the evaluation of attention and learning problems, the clinical interview and history taking provide opportunities to explore these factors. Listening for and inquiring about long-standing trends regarding personal experience, behavior, and interpersonal functioning may provide clues about temperamental tendencies that might play a role in a patient's functional difficulties as well as in treatment.

The clinical interview provides a rich source of information regarding how individuals handle a variety of situations. In addition to assessing the executive functioning and learning styles of individuals, review of academic and workplace functioning provides insight on how individuals face various challenges and interpersonal situations. Thus, two workers with ADHD who have similar symptom and impairment profiles may exhibit different personality styles in their handling of these difficulties, such as one person being avoidant and reticent to ask for help and the other person fabricating excuses and perhaps blaming others for on-the-job difficulties. Review of functioning at home and in social settings may provide clinical data about cross-situational patterns that might reflect personality characteristics above and beyond the effects of ADHD or learning problems.

ADHD and other learning issues themselves can be considered akin to temperament (Ramsay & Rostain, 2003) inasmuch as these concerns reflect long-standing influences on individuals' perceptions and interactions with their environments. Thus, it is important to tease apart the aspects of an individual's functioning that reflect these sorts of attention and learning problems from those that indicate personality styles that might make a unique contribution to the presenting problems.

Personality inventories that might be helpful as components of the larger evaluation of learning and attention problems are discussed in the next section. However, just as the assessment of ADHD and learning problems cannot rely on the administration of a single questionnaire or even numerous questionnaires without adequate clinical interview, assessment of personality must include consideration of other factors that might affect the conclusions made. One consideration, particularly in the assessment of adolescents and young adults, is that attitudes and behaviors exhibited in various situations, such as school, work, or family settings, may reflect reactions to developmental transitions and challenges rather than enduring personality patterns. That being said, there may be evidence of emerging personality trends that are important to note. For example, the combination of ADHD and CD is associated with greater functional impairments than ADHD alone (Barkley, 2006). Moreover, evidence of CD before age 15 is one of the diagnostic criteria for Antisocial Personality Disorder (APA, 2000).

Another consideration is whether various attitudes and behaviors reflect context-specific reactions or enduring personality traits. Just as many individuals with ADHD may report recurring symptoms of depression or anxiety in reaction to various life frustrations, such symptoms may not meet diagnostic criteria for Major Depression or Generalized Anxiety. Likewise, individuals with attention and learning problems may report situation-specific maladaptive reactions that do not reflect characterological patterns. Thus, a college student in danger of failing a class may appear somewhat rigid and compulsive about preparation for an upcoming final exam, or a worker who has received a below-average work performance evaluation may appear dependent insofar as he excessively seeks reassurance and support from others for a new project he has been assigned.

Exploration of the circumstances surrounding these sorts of reactions may shed light on whether they reflect recurring patterns of responding or emergent and circumscribed reactions to newfound stressors. What is more, corroborative reporters familiar with the individual being evaluated may be able to provide observations on long-standing patterns. Several personality measures have been studied in samples of adults with ADHD that might be useful adjuncts in an evaluation of attention and learning problems. These personality measures are reviewed in the next section.

Personality Inventories

Structured Clinical Interview for DSM-IV Axis II Disorders (SCID-II)

The SCID-II (First et al., 1997) is a structured interview designed to identify personality disorders as defined by DSM-IV (APA, 1994). There is a prescreening questionnaire on which respondents are presented with examples of behaviors that may reflect recurring patterns and are asked whether they consider themselves to consistently exhibit these behaviors. If a respondent endorses items within a particular personality disorder category, there is follow-up inquiry regarding the module for that personality disorder to determine if symptoms exceed diagnostic threshold.

In the case of young adults and adults with ADHD, Antisocial Personality Disorder is among the most commonly identified personality disorders (Biederman, 2004). However, this comorbidity pattern may be particularly relevant for individuals diagnosed with ADHD Combined Type who previously fulfilled diagnostic criteria for CD. Hence, subsequent features of Antisocial Personality Disorder in adults with ADHD may reflect a developmental pattern associated with the coexisting disruptive behavior problems.

C. J. Miller, Flory et al. (2008) studied the emergence of personality disorders in teens and young adults who were diagnosed with ADHD in childhood using the SCID-II. Individuals diagnosed with ADHD in childhood were more likely to be diagnosed with a personality disorder in late adolescence/young adulthood. The most common personality disorders were Avoidant, Narcissistic, Borderline, Antisocial, and Paranoid Personalities. Differences between individuals with persistent ADHD and those whose symptoms remitted were also examined. Individuals with persistent ADHD had higher rates of Antisocial and Paranoid Personality when compared with remitters.

Recent research has examined Axis II disorders among samples of adults with ADHD. T. W. Miller, Nigg, and Faraone (2007) administered the SCID-II in a controlled study of 363 adults. As predicted, there was a strong association of adult ADHD and Cluster B personality disorders, which are characterized by poor self-regulation (e.g., Antisocial Personality, Borderline Personality). Conceptually, these findings are consistent with the behavioral disinhibition associated with ADHD (Barkley, 2006). Individuals with ADHD also reported higher rates of Cluster C personality disorders than did control participants. These personality disorders, such as Avoidant Personality and Obsessive-Compulsive Personality, are characterized by anxious, fearful patterns of behavior. Conceptually, these personality patterns may reflect difficulties adults with ADHD have regarding initiation and follow-through on tasks and how these difficulties may affect interactions with others.

The coexistence of ADHD and Borderline Personality Disorder has received increased attention owing to the overlap of symptoms related to self-dysregulation and the importance of making a differential diagnosis. It has been suggested that ADHD and Borderline Personality may reflect different dimensions of a similar disorder, at least in some cases (Philipsen, 2006). A 41.8% prevalence of childhood ADHD among women with Borderline Personality Disorder has been reported (Philipsen et al., 2008). Childhood ADHD also predicted more severe symptoms of Borderline Personality Disorder in adulthood. A study comparing adults with ADHD, Borderline Personality, or both revealed significant symptom overlap across groups (Lampe et al., 2007). However, individuals with ADHD, either alone or coexisting with Borderline Personality, consistently exhibited difficulties on various cognitive tasks measuring inhibition, had longer reaction times, and had higher intra-individual variability on attentions tasks. Individuals with Borderline Personality alone performed at the same level as nonclinical control participants. Thus, it is the persistent difficulties related to underlying executive dysfunction during periods of emotional stability that indicate the presence of comorbid ADHD in individuals diagnosed with Borderline Personality.

Anckarsäter et al. (2006) examined various personality features, including Axis II disorders, among adults reporting lifetime developmental disorders, including ADHD. Adults with ADHD reported Cluster B disorders at a higher rate than patients with other developmental disorders. Cluster C disorders were common among adults with ADHD, though less so than rates reported by adults with autistic spectrum disorders. Individuals with ADHD also reported high rates of novelty seeking and harm avoidance and low levels of "character maturity."

The presence of an Axis II personality disorder is important from a diagnostic standpoint insofar as these factors may explain learning and attention problems experienced by many adults or, more commonly, these personality disorders may coexist with ADHD or learning problems. However, the presence of other important personality characteristics, such as novelty seeking, and other measures of personality and temperament have been studied in samples of adults with ADHD, as reviewed in the next sections.

Big Five Personality Dimensions

Studies of the variations of normal personality have yielded the Big Five dimensions, also known as the Five Factors (McCrae & Costa, 1987). These Five Factors are:

1. Extraversion (e.g., sociability, activity, assertiveness in social life).
2. Conscientiousness (e.g., impulse control, goal-oriented behavior, organization).
3. Agreeableness (e.g., trust, altruism, regard for others in interpersonal life).
4. Neuroticism (e.g., negative emotionality and susceptibility to stress and emotional distress).
5. Openness to new experience (e.g., complexity of one's mental and experiential life).

The primary measure of the Five Factors is the NEO Personality Inventory (NEO-PI; Costa & McCrae, 1992). Obtaining a personality profile based on individuals' responses to this questionnaire helps to identify factors that might contribute to learning and attention problems and that may influence interventions.

Nigg et al. (2002) studied the NEO-PI administered across several different samples comprised of adults with a lifetime history of ADHD that persisted into adulthood. A common finding across samples was the association of adult ADHD with low Conscientiousness, low Agreeableness, and high Neuroticism, which were corroborated by spousal ratings. These results were also obtained when comparing individuals with ADHD and non-ADHD controls. More specifically, individuals with ADHD Predominantly Inattentive Type reported low Conscientiousness and high Neuroticism; individuals with ADHD Predominantly Hyperactive-Impulsive Type reported low Agreeableness.

C. J. Miller, Miller, Newcorn, and Halperin (2008) examined Five Factor characteristics in older adolescents and young adults who had been diagnosed with ADHD in childhood. Regardless of whether ADHD was persistent, childhood ADHD was associated with low Conscientiousness in later adolescence and young adulthood. Individuals with persistent ADHD also reported high Neuroticism and low Agreeableness. Childhood history of Oppositional Defiant Disorder (ODD) also contributes to low Agreeableness among individuals with ADHD.

Parker, Majeski, and Collin (2004) found that a Five Factor measure accounted for significant symptom variability among a sample of nearly 600 adults with ADHD. Similar to previous studies reviewed, Conscientiousness and Agreeableness were strong predictors of ADHD status. Conscientiousness was the strongest predictor of ADHD inattention scores, with individuals with ADHD Predominantly Inattentive Type scoring significantly lower than those with Predominantly Hyperactive-Impulsive Type, who, in turn, scored significantly lower than controls. Agreeableness was the strongest predictor of the Predominantly Hyperactivite-Impulsive Type, who scored lower than the Predominantly Inattentive group, who, in turn, scored lower than controls. Regarding other factors, Extraversion was a predictor of hyperactive-impulsive symptoms; inattention symptoms were unrelated to this factor. Neuroticism was a predictor of both ADHD subtypes, and individuals with ADHD scored higher than controls on this factor. The factors of Conscientiousness and Agreeableness are associated with occupational and academic performance as well as driving behavior, which are domains in which individuals with ADHD are often functionally impaired.

Other Personality Measures

The Millon Clinical Multiaxial Inventory-II (MCMI-II; Millon, 1987) is a self-report questionnaire designed to be used with the DSM classification system for personality disorders. May and Bos (2000) examined the personality characteristics of 104 adults with ADHD using the MCMI-II. Four subgroups of ADHD emerged based on comorbidity profile: ADHD only, ADHD-ODD, ADHD-comorbid (a non-ODD comorbid diagnosis), and ADHD-ODD-comorbid. Consequently, different comorbidity groups were associated with different modal personality features. The ADHD-only group endorsed mild features of Histrionic Personality. The ADHD-ODD group endorsed prominent features of Narcissistic, Aggressive-Sadistic, and Negativistic Personality. The ADHD-comorbid group endorsed mild features of Avoidant and Dependent Personality styles. Finally, the ADHD-ODD-comorbid group was associated with elevated scores on all the aforementioned personality characteristics.

Robin, Tzelepis, and Bedway (2008) used the Millon Index of Personality Styles (MIPS; Millon, 1994) to assess the normative personality styles of adults with ADHD. A cluster analysis of the data indicated that 2 replicable clusters emerged across 2 independent subsamples with 91% of the total sample of 311 participants falling into 1 of these 2 clusters. The first cluster was comprised of individuals whose MIPS responses indicated a tendency toward having a pessimistic outlook on life and adopting a reactive (instead of a proactive) approach to dealing with the demands of life. They tended to be self-focused rather than attending to the needs of others. These individuals could be impulsive, disorganized, emphasized their hunches rather than tangible evidence when making decisions, and tended to look inward for stimulation. They could be viewed by others as passive and withdrawn, feeling misunderstood and dissatisfied by their situation, all the while holding a sense of rebelliousness and lack of respect for authority. Although the MIPS does not classify responses in terms of Axis II diagnostic categories, the extreme scores that characterized the first cluster were consistent with Schizoid, Avoidant, Antisocial, Self-Defeating, and Passive-Aggressive styles.

The second cluster was comprised of individuals who tended to have an optimistic outlook and to be proactive in dealing with life events. These individuals also struck a balance between self-interests and the needs of others. Similar to the first cluster, these individuals tended to act impulsivity, were disorganized, handled problems by relying on hunches, and tended to experience chaos in their lives. However, they seemed to get along well with others and were interpersonally adroit, being able to balance assertiveness with knowing when to hold back.

The results reported by Robin et al. (2008) are important for clinical practice. That is, the individuals in the second cluster, while experiencing impairments associated with ADHD, would seem to fit a profile of individuals likely to follow through with a treatment or educational regimen; to respond to therapeutic support; to be able to maintain a resilient, optimistic outlook throughout treatment; and to make use of available resources. These individuals may be able to see good treatment progress from straightforward interventions designed for adults with ADHD. Patients who fit a profile associated with the first cluster, however, may experience greater frustration in treatment and may require comprehensive psychosocial interventions to address the negative outlooks that likely affect daily functioning as well as compliance with treatment recommendations. Although not controlled for in the Robin et al. (2008) study, it may be that comorbidity patterns, ADHD subtype, severity of symptoms, and/or other life experiences may contribute to the personality style differences exhibited in this sample of adults with ADHD.

The assessment of personality in the context of evaluations of learning and attention problems provides a comprehensive view of individuals' functioning. Unlike some psychiatric diagnoses, it would be unlikely that personality variables would completely explain away the presence of learning or attention problems. However, personality factors may contribute to the complexity of a case that may affect treatment planning and follow-through on coping recommendations.

SUMMARY

Including evaluations for psychiatric and personality functioning as components of comprehensive assessments of attention and learning problems for older adolescents and young adults provides additional clinical information needed to understand the functional problems that necessitated the assessment as well as factors that might influence prognosis. In some cases, it may be determined that there is insufficient evidence of ADHD or LD to explain an individual's coping difficulties and that other psychiatric factors explain these problems and warrant treatment. More often, coexisting psychiatric and personality variables magnify extant learning and attention problems and must also be addressed in treatment in order to help the individuals develop effective coping strategies and improve their overall well-being.

REFERENCES

American Psychiatric Association (APA). (1994). *Diagnostic and statistical manual of mental disorders* (4th ed.). Washington, DC: Author.

American Psychiatric Association. (2000). *Diagnostic and statistical manual of mental disorders* (4th ed., text rev.). Washington, DC: Author.

Anckarsäter, H., Stahlberg, O., Larson, T., Hakansson, C., Jutblad, S. B., Niklasson, L., . . . Rastam, M. (2006). The impact of ADHD and autism spectrum disorders on temperament, character, and personality development. *Archives of General Psychiatry, 163,* 1239–1244.

Barkley, R. A. (Ed.). (2006). *Attention-deficit hyperactivity disorder: A handbook for diagnosis and treatment* (3rd ed.). New York, NY: Guilford Press.

Barkley, R. A., & Murphy, K. R. (2006). *Attention-deficit hyperactivity disorder: A clinical workbook* (3rd ed.). New York, NY: Guilford Press.

Barkley, R. A., Murphy, K. R., & Fischer, M. (2008). *ADHD in adults: What the science says.* New York, NY: Guilford Press.

Beck, A. T., & Steer, R. A. (1989). *Manual for the Beck Hopelessness Scale.* San Antonio, TX: Psychological Corporation.

Beck, A. T., & Steer, R. A. (1990). *Beck Anxiety Inventory manual.* San Antonio, TX: Psychological Corporation.

Beck, A. T., Steer, R. A., & Brown, G. K. (1996). *Beck Depression Inventory—Second edition manual.* San Antonio, TX: Psychological Corporation.

Biederman, J. (2004). Impact of comorbidity in adults with attention-deficit/hyperactivity disorder. *Journal of Clinical Psychiatry, 65*(Suppl. 3), 3–7.

Brown, T. E. (1996). *Brown Attention Deficit Disorder Scales.* San Antonio, TX: Psychological Corporation.

Conners, C. K., Erhardt, D., & Sparrow, E. (1999). *Conners' Adult ADHD Rating Scales.* North Tonawanda, NY: Multi-Health Systems.

Costa, P. T., & McCrae, R. R. (1992). *NEO PI-R professional manual.* Odessa, FL: Psychological Assessment Resources.

Derogatis, L. R. (1986). *Manual for the Symptom Checklist 90—Revised (SCL-90-R).* Baltimore, MD: Author.

First, M. B., Gibbon, M., Spitzer, R. L., Williams, J. B. W., & Benjamin, L. (1997). *User's guide for the Structured Clinical Interview for DSM-IV Axis II Personality Disorders.* Washington, DC: American Psychiatric Press.

First, M. B., Spitzer, R. L., Gibbon, M., & Williams, J. B. W. (1997). *User's guide for the Structured Clinical Interview for DSM-IV Axis I Disorders.* Washington, DC: American Psychiatric Press.

Gau, S. S. F., Kessler, R. C., Tseng, W. L., Wu, Y. Y., Chiu, Y. N., Yeh, C. B., & Hwu, H. G. (2007). Association between sleep problems and symptoms of attention-deficit/hyperactivity disorder in young adults. *Sleep, 30,* 195–201.

Karl, A., Schaefer, M., Malta, L. S., Dorfel, D., Rohleder, N., & Werner, A. (2006). A meta-analysis of structural brain abnormalities in PTSD. *Neuroscience and Biobehavioral Reviews, 30*, 1004–1031.

Kaufman, J., Birmaher, B., Brent, D., Rao, U., & Ryan, N. (1996). *Kiddie-SADS—Present and lifetime versions.* Pittsburgh, PA: University of Pittsburgh School of Medicine.

Lampe, K., Konrad, K., Kroener, S., Fast, K., Kunert, H. J., & Herprertz, S. C. (2007). Neuropsychological and behavioural disinhibition in adult ADHD compared to borderline personality. *Psychological Medicine, 37*, 1717–1729.

May, B., & Bos, J. (2000). Personality characteristics of ADHD adults assessed with the Millon Clinical Multiaxial Inventory-II: Evidence of four distinct subtypes. *Journal of Personality Assessment, 75*, 237–248.

McCrae, R. R., & Costa, P. T. (1987). Validation of the five-factor model of personality across instruments and observers. *Journal of Personality and Social Psychology, 52*, 81–90.

Miller, C. J., Flory, J. D., Miller, S. R., Harty, S. C., Newcorn, J. H., & Halperin, J. M. (2008). Childhood attention-deficit/hyperactivity disorder and the emergence of personality disorders in adolescence: A prospective follow-up study. *Journal of Clinical Psychiatry, 69*, 1477–1484.

Miller, C. J., Miller, S. R., Newcorn, J. H., & Halperin, J. M. (2008). Personality characteristics associated with persistent ADHD in late adolescence. *Journal of Abnormal Child Psychology, 36*, 165–173.

Miller, T. W., Nigg, J. T., & Faraone, S. V. (2007). Axis I and II comorbidity in adults with ADHD. *Journal of Abnormal Psychology, 116*, 519–528.

Millon, T. (1987). *Millon Clinical Multiaxial Inventory* (2nd ed.). Minneapolis, MN: National Computer Systems.

Millon, T. (1994). *Millon Index of Personality Styles manual.* San Antonio, TX: Psychological Corporation.

Murphy, K. R., & Gordon, M. (2006). Assessment of adults with ADHD. In R. A. Barkley (Ed.), *Attention-deficit hyperactivity disorder: A handbook for diagnosis and treatment* (3rd ed., pp. 425–450). New York, NY: Guilford Press.

Nierenberg, A. A., Miyahara, S., Spencer, T., Wisniewski, S. R., Otto, M. W., Simon, N., . . . Sachs, G. S. (2005). Clinical and diagnostic implications of lifetime attention-deficit/hyperactivity disorder comorbidity in adults with bipolar disorder: Data from the first 1000 STEP-BD participants. *Biological Psychiatry, 57*, 1467–1473.

Nigg, J. T., John, O. P., Blaskey, L. G., Huang-Pollock, C. L., Willcutt, E. G., Hinshaw, S. P., & Pennington, B. (2002). Big five dimensions and ADHD symptoms: Links between personality traits and clinical symptoms. *Journal of Personality and Social Psychology, 83*, 451–469.

Parker, J. D. A., Majeski, S. A., & Collin, V. T. (2004). ADHD symptoms and personality: Relationships with the five-factor model. *Personality and Individual Differences, 36*, 977–987.

Philipsen, A. (2006). Differential diagnosis and comorbidity of attention-deficit/hyperactivity disorder (ADHD) and borderline personality disorder (BPD) in adults. *European Archives of Psychiatry and Clinical Neuroscience, 256*(Suppl. 1), 42–46.

Philipsen, A., Limberger, M. F., Lieb, K., Feige, B., Kleindienst, N., Ebner-Priemer, U., ... Bohus, M. (2008). Attention-deficit hyperactivity disorder as a potentially aggravating factor in borderline personality. *British Journal of Psychiatry, 192*, 118–123.

Ramsay, J. R., & Rostain, A. L. (2003). A cognitive therapy approach for adult attention-deficit/hyperactivity disorder. *Journal of Cognitive Psychotherapy, 17*, 319–334.

Robin, A. L., Tzelepis, A., & Bedway, M. (2008). A cluster analysis of personality style in adults with ADHD. *Journal of Attention Disorders, 12*, 254–263.

Rosenfield, B., Ramsay, J. R., Cahn, S., & Pellegrino, P. (2009). Cognitive behavioral therapy for insomnia: Evidence-based treatments and encouraging innovations for primary care. In R. A. DiTomasso, B. A. Golden, & H. Morris (Eds.), *The comprehensive handbook of cognitive behavioral approaches in primary care* (pp. 699–726). New York, NY: Springer.

Rybak, Y. E., McNeely, H. E., Mackenzie, B. E., Jain, U. R., & Levitan, R. D. (2007). Seasonality and circadian preference in adult attention-deficit/hyperactivity disorder: Clinical and neuropsychological correlates. *Comprehensive Psychiatry, 48*, 562–571.

Schubiner, H., Tzelepis, A., Milberger, S., Lockhart, N., Kruger, M., Kelley, B. J., & Schoener, E. P. (2000). Prevalence of attention-deficit/hyperactivity disorder and conduct disorder among substance abusers. *Journal of Clinical Psychiatry, 61*, 244–251.

Selzer, M. L. (1971). The Michigan Alcoholism Screening Test (MAST): The quest for a new diagnostic instrument. *American Journal of Psychiatry, 127*, 1653–1658.

Steer, R. A., Ranieri, W. F., Kumar, G., & Beck, A. T. (2003). Beck Depression Inventory-II items associated with self-reported symptoms of ADHD in adult psychiatric outpatients. *Journal of Personality Assessment, 80*, 58–63.

Weinstein, D., Staffelbach, D., & Biaggio, M. (2000). Attention-deficit hyperactivity disorder and posttraumatic stress disorder: Differential diagnosis in childhood sexual abuse. *Clinical Psychology Review, 20*, 359–378.

9

Integration and Formulation of Data

SAM GOLDSTEIN
MELISSA DEVRIES

INTRODUCTION

The biggest mistake an evaluator can make is to offer a diagnosis of Attention-Deficit/ Hyperactivity Disorder (ADHD) or Learning Disabilities (LD) based on a narrow scope of evaluation; limited historical, behavioral, or assessment data; and the presumption that no other conditions or disorders contribute to symptom presentation and impairment. The risk of false diagnosis can be minimized by using a systematic approach. Such an approach will assist in facing the two greatest problems involved in making diagnoses of ADHD and LD in these populations: Alternative etiologies that are difficult to rule out and objective data that do not provide a consistent profile because symptoms of poor academic achievement, impulsiveness, and inattentiveness are common complaints in adulthood. An evaluator is unlikely to encounter "clean cases" in which symptoms are very easily tied to ADHD and/or LD.

This chapter begins with three case reports using a model developed at the Neurology, Learning and Behavior Center in Salt Lake City, where the first author has served over the last 30 years as clinical director. The chapter continues with 24 brief case studies. Together these reports and cases provide a descriptive overview beginning with individuals presenting with generally uncomplicated ADHD or LD and progressing to those with multiple comorbid problems and finally to those whose apparent symptoms of LD or ADHD are in fact caused by other conditions and disorders. These three reports and case studies provide a framework for a model for integrating and formulating data, making diagnoses, and, most important, using diagnostic data to guide treatment decisions and recommendations.

NAME:	Adam L.
CA:	18 years 6 months
CURRENT GRADE:	12

Reason for Evaluation

Adam suffers from Neurofibromatosis Type I (NF1). He was referred by Children's Hospital for a neuropsychological evaluation in an effort to better understand his current functioning and assist with treatment and transitional planning.

Background Information

Ms. L., Adam's mother, was seen to review his social and developmental history. Adam is his parents' only child. Adam's parents divorced when he was 3 years of age. His father completed high school and is employed as a plumber. Mr. L. sees Adam approximately once per week but does not see him consistently. Ms. L. noted that he has gone up to 6 weeks without seeing Adam. Ms. L. is Adam's legal guardian. Ms. L. is a registered nurse, having completed an associate's degree. She noted a history of depression. Ms. L. has an 11-year-old daughter with whom Adam has some rivalry. He tends to "police her." She does not experience developmental or adjustment problems. Mr. L. has 12-year-old female twins.

Adam was the 7-pound, 6-ounce product of a pregnancy noted by toxemia and unplanned cesarean delivery. As an infant Adam had very poor sleep patterns. As a toddler he was disruptive and constantly into things. He has always been quite outgoing. He was generally happy as a toddler but very inconsistent in fitting routines. He had difficulty with persistence and attention. He demonstrated sensory threshold problems.

NF1 was diagnosed at about 2 years of age. Adam also had rhabdomyosarcoma at 2 years of age for which he received 15 months of chemotherapy and 6 to 9 weeks of radiation. He was diagnosed with T-cell lymphoma at almost 8 years of age and received 2 years of chemotherapy. Adam wears corrective lenses. He has poor sleep onset, wakes frequently, and sleeps in on the weekends. He is often tired in the morning. He has periodic migraines.

Adam currently takes Adderall and Neurontin. The Neurontin has improved behavior as well as reduced complaints of peripheral neuropathy. The Adderall appears to help Adam settle down.

Adam appeared to reach early milestones somewhat late. He was talking by 2 years of age but then made very slow developmental progress from 2 to 3 years of age. Preacademic milestones were very slow in developing. Adam received early developmental services and began receiving special services early in his school career. He missed most of second grade due to repeated illness. He was classified as a student with Other Health Impairment.

Adam's large and fine motor skills have been late in developing. Adam does not appear to understand directions and situations as well as others. Intellectually he appears below average.

Adam appears to be on a first- to second-grade level for arithmetic, second-grade level for spelling, and third- to fourth-grade level for reading. Over the past 3.5 years, he has been in a small private school. He has done well with individualized support and assistance. He will remain in this program until he graduates, and then plans are for him to enter the Developmental Program for additional educational services.

Adam is generally socially isolated. He has some friends at school. He likes to direct people and enjoys conversation.

At home Adam fidgets and has difficulty remaining seated. He is easily distracted and does not wait his turn well. He often responds impulsively. He has difficulty paying attention, mostly to chores and homework. He shifts from one uncompleted activity to another. Adam often talks excessively, interrupts, and changes the subject. His affect at times appears flat. He is respectful toward most individuals but least respectful of his mother. He has a history of frustrating easily, temper outbursts, and tantrums. He is a repeat offender of making the same mistakes over and over, and often misses cues. He cannot be left unsupervised for more than just a short period of time. He does not like doing chores, complaining that he gets headaches and sweats when he has to do chores. He resists doing anything that is not "his idea."

Adam at times will work for short-term rewards but not at all for long-term rewards. He creates more problems at home than his sibling. Discipline when needed consists of time out and restriction of privilege. No particular form of discipline has proven effective. Adam enjoys playing games on the computer. He tends to get stuck in discussing certain subjects. He has a poor concept of time. He likes doing Legos. He has the attention span to watch 2 to 3 hours per day of television. He has always enjoyed learning how things work. He likes to take things apart.

Assessment Procedures

Conners, Parent Rating Scale–Revised (Form L)
Child Behavior Checklist
Home Situations Questionnaire
Social Attributes Checklist
PDD Research Screening Questionnaire
Neuropsychological Impairment Scale
Review of Academic File
Behavior Rating Inventory of Executive Function
Peabody Picture Vocabulary Test–IIIA
Expressive Vocabulary Test
Wechsler Adult Intelligence Scale–III
Wechsler Memory Scale–III
Cognitive Assessment System
Conners' Continuous Performance Test
Gordon Diagnostic System
Purdue Pegboard
Rey Complex Figure Drawing

Woodcock-Johnson III Tests of Achievement
Revised Children's Manifest Anxiety Scale
Clinical Interview

Adaptive Functioning

Ms. L.'s responses to the Conners' Rating Scale placed Adam at the following age-adjusted T-scores (mean = 50; s.d. = 10):

	T-scores
Oppositional Behavior	74
Cognitive Problems/Inattention	77
Hyperactivity	101
Anxious/Shy	71
Perfectionism	50
Social Problems	64
Psychosomatic	101
Conners' ADHD Index	80
Conners' Global Index	
Restless-Impulsive	85
Emotional Lability	80
Total	86
Diagnostic and Statistical Manual of Mental Disorders (4th ed., DSM-IV)	
Inattentive	75
Hyperactive-Impulsive	94
Total	77

Even with the 30 mg per day of Adderall, Ms. L. notes that Adam demonstrates 8 inattentive and 5 hyperactive-impulsive symptoms to a clinical degree.

Parent responses to the Child Behavior Checklist place Adam at the following age-adjusted percentiles (50th percentile is average; high score indicates problem):

	Percentile
Withdrawn	70th
Somatic Complaints	98th
Anxious/Depressed	70th
Social Problems	84th
Thought Problems	95th
Attention Problems	98th

Delinquent Behavior	70th
Aggressive Behavior	84th

Adam at times is argumentative and demands attention. He acts immaturely, has difficulty concentrating, and at times appears fearful and worrisome.

Ms. L.'s responses to the Home Situations Questionnaire noted Adam's significant problems across many situations, including routines such as meals, with hygiene, and when parents are on the telephone; problems with behavior in public places and when visiting others; difficulty doing chores, getting to bed, and behaving with babysitters.

On the Social Attributes Checklist, Ms. L. noted that Adam at times has a positive mood. He is often dependent on adults. He doesn't cope with rebuff adequately. At times he can demonstrate empathy and humor. He can at times approach others positively and express wishes and preferences clearly. He struggles to assert rights and needs appropriately and express frustration and anger effectively. He is easily intimidated. At times he is accepted by his peers. He struggles, however, to consistently enter a conversation, take turns, show interest, negotiate, and compromise. Adam often draws inappropriate attention to himself.

Ms. L. was taken through the PDD Research Screening questions. She responded affirmatively to 14 of 18 items, noting that Adam talks excessively about favorite topics that hold limited interest for others. He interprets conversation literally, frequently asks irrelevant questions, has difficulty with conversation, and avoids eye contact when in trouble. He does not appear to understand basic social behavior and exhibits obsessive behavior, particularly being concerned that "everyone is safe." He has an extreme or obsessive interest in movies and TV shows, taping the same program over and over again. He is disorganized, passively inattentive, and overreacts to noise, light, and cold. He limits himself to certain food and clothing. He often has to know everything that is going on.

Impairment

Ms. L.'s responses to the Neuropsychological Impairment Scale yielded normal validity indices. Her response profile placed Adam at these percentiles (50th percentile is average; high score indicates impairment):

	Percentile
Critical Items	90th
Cognitive	99th
Attention	99th
Memory	98th
Frustration	99th
Learning/Verbal	99th
Academic	99th

Review of Previous Evaluation

A psychological evaluation was completed by N.C., Ph.D., in September 2007. The following scores were generated:

Wechsler Intelligence Scale for Children–III

	Standard Scores (mean = 100; s.d. = 15)
Verbal IQ	48
Performance IQ	61
Full-Scale IQ	53

Wechsler Individual Achievement Test

	Standard Scores (mean = 100; s.d. = 15)
Word Reading	66
Reading Comprehension	40
Pseudo Word Decoding	62
Numerical Operations	55
Math Reasoning	51
Spelling	69
Listening Comprehension	63
Oral Expression	67
READING COMPOSITE	48
MATHEMATICS COMPOSITE	45
WRITTEN LANGUAGE COMPOSITE	below norms
ORAL LANGUAGE COMPOSITE	60

Dr. C. noted that Adam's presentation met the diagnostic criteria for the Combined Type of ADHD even while he was taking medication.

School Functioning

A multidisciplinary evaluation team report from the County School District completed when Adam was a third grader in March 1999 yielded these test results:

Stanford-Binet Intelligence Scale–IV

	Standard Scores (mean = 100; s.d. = 15)
Verbal Reasoning	70
Abstract Visual Reasoning	88
Quantitative Reasoning	86
Short-Term Memory	77
Composite	76

Wechsler Individual Achievement Test

	Standard Scores (mean = 100; s.d. = 15)
Composite Reading	69
Composite Math	60

Adam completed the Stanford Achievement Test as a fifth grader in October 2001 performing at these national percentiles:

	Percentiles
Reading	1st
Mathematics	1st
Language	3rd
Science	7th
Social Science	14th
Listening	1st
Complete Battery	2nd

Adam's fifth-grade Individualized Education Plan noted that he was performing academically at about a second-grade level. He was noted to have articulation problems with 8th-percentile receptive vocabulary and 1st-percentile expressive vocabulary.

Current data concerning Adam's functioning at the private school was not obtained at the time this evaluation was completed.

Behavioral Observation

Adam, an adolescent of short stature appearing younger than his chronological age with slightly atypical craniofacial features, was seen for two assessment sessions with a lunchtime break. His behavior during both sessions was similar. Adam wore corrective lenses. He had taken his 2 prescribed medications in the previous 24 hours prior to the evaluation.

Eye contact was appropriate. Adam demonstrated poor articulation. He maintained and initiated conversation but would often change the subject. Receptive vocabulary appeared weak. Adam had difficulty cohesively explaining his thoughts and responses. His thoughts, though at times logical, were not always focused or relevant.

Adam was neither anxious nor sad. Overall he was emotionally stable.

Adam was alert and attentive but concentrated inconsistently. He required frequent prompting from the examiner to remain on task. He was willing to attempt all tasks presented.

No muscular tension or habitual mannerisms were noted. Adam presented with a normal activity level. He was not fidgety. He often appeared easily distracted by both external and internal stimuli.

Adam appeared moderately confident in his skills. He related well to the examiners. He smiled occasionally. Despite his limited abilities, overall it was not significantly difficult to establish a working relationship with this adolescent.

Assessment Results and Interpretation

Autism

A number of subtests from Modules II and III of the Autism Diagnostic Observation Scale were attempted with limited success. The administration of this instrument was then discontinued. Adam experienced significant trouble consistently communicating his thoughts. However, he was able to share joint attention, demonstrated no overt signs of echolalia or atypical sensory response, and was quite social.

Observation during assessment with the Childhood Autism Rating Scale placed Adam below the autism threshold. Adam related adequately to the examiner. He demonstrated appropriate imitation but somewhat abnormal emotional response. This was due primarily to his limited cognitive abilities. He demonstrated no atypical body or object use. He adapted to change and demonstrated no atypical sensory response. His verbal communication, however, was mildly abnormal.

Language

The Peabody was administered as a simple measure of one-word receptive vocabulary. Adam completed this test with a standard score of 74, equivalent to the 4th percentile. This is generally consistent with his performance on this instrument a number of years ago.

The Expressive Vocabulary Test was administered as a simple synonym measure of expressive language. Adam completed this test with a standard score of 61, below the 1st percentile.

Intellectual

The Wechsler Intelligence Scale was administered as an overall screening of intellectual ability and achievement. Age-adjusted scaled scores follow.

	Scaled Scores (mean = 100; s.d. = 3)
Verbal Subtests	
Vocabulary	4
Similarities	1
Arithmetic	3
Digit Span	4
Information	5
Comprehension	4
Letter-Number Sequencing	4

	Scaled Scores (mean = 100; s.d. = 3)
Performance Subtests	
Picture Completion	5
Digit Symbol—Coding	3
Block Design	5
Matrix Reasoning	5
Picture Arrangement	8
Symbol Search	2

	Standard Scores		
	(mean = 100; s.d. = 15)	Percentiles	90% Confidence Interval
Verbal IQ	61	1st	59–67
Performance IQ	70	2nd	66–77
Full-Scale IQ	63	1st	60–67
Verbal Comprehension Index	63	1st	60–70
Perceptual Organization Index	70	2nd	66–78
Working Memory Index	61	–1st	58–69
Processing Speed Index	63	1st	60–75

These scores are generally consistent with those obtained a number of years ago at Children's Hospital. They are somewhat lower than those obtained on the Stanford-Binet but overall not inconsistent in reflecting Adam's markedly slower pattern of cognitive development. His intellectual abilities at this time fall in the mildly intellectually handicapped range.

Learning and Working Memory

The Wechsler Memory Scale was administered as an overall screening of memory ability. Age-adjusted scaled scores follow.

	Scaled Scores (mean = 100; s.d. = 3)
Logical Memory I	4
Faces I	9
Verbal Paired Associates I	4
Family Pictures I	8
Letter-Number Sequencing	6
Spatial Span	1
Logical Memory II	4
Faces II	9
Verbal Paired Associates II	6
Family Pictures II	9
Auditory Recognition	6

	Standard Scores		
	(mean = 100; s.d. = 15)	Percentiles	90% Confidence Interval
Auditory Immediate	65	1st	60–74
Visual Immediate	91	27th	82–103
Immediate Memory	73	4th	67–83
Auditory Delayed	71	3rd	66–84
Visual Delayed	94	34th	85–105
Auditory Recognition Delay	80	9th	74–96
General Memory	78	7th	72–88
Working Memory Index	66	1st	61–80

Executive/Neuropsychological Skills

Ms. L.'s responses to the Behavior Rating Inventory for Executive Function placed Adam at the following percentiles (50th percentile is average; high score indicates problem):

	Percentile
Inhibit	99th
Shift	97th
Emotional Control	99th
Initiate	99th
Working Memory	99th
Plan/Organize	93rd
Organization of Materials	90th
Monitor	99th
BEHAVIORAL REGULATION INDEX	99th
META-COGNITION INDEX	99th
GLOBAL EXECUTIVE COMPOSITE	99th

The Cognitive Assessment System was administered as a neuropsychological screening. Age-adjusted scaled scores follow.

	Scaled Scores (mean = 100; s.d. = 3)
Matching Numbers	1
Planned Codes	1
Nonverbal Matrices	3
Verbal-Spatial Relations	4
Expressive Attention	10
Number Detection	4
Word Series	6
Sentence Repetition	2

	IQ		
	(mean = 100; s.d. = 15)	Percentiles (mean = 50th)	90% Confidence Interval
Planning	47	−1st	47–63
Simultaneous	61	−1st	57–72
Attention	82	12th	76–93
Successive	66	1st	63–76
Full Scale	50	−1st	49–64

Attention

The Gordon Diagnostic Instrument was administered as a computerized measure of Adam's ability to sustain attention and inhibit impulsive responding. He performed in the abnormal range for Vigilance and in the borderline range for Total Correct scores, reflecting a somewhat impulsive, inattentive approach to this measure.

A second attentional measure, the Conners' Continuous Performance Test, was also administered. Adam struggled on this longer task, performing in a range consistent with an inattentive and impulsive pattern. It should be noted that Adam had taken his prescribed stimulant medication on the morning of the assessment.

Motor/Perceptual

Adam appears right-side dominant. He held a pencil in his right hand with a pincer grip. Casual observation did not indicate significant large motor abnormalities. Fine motor skills for motor speed and coordination, based on the Purdue Pegboard performance, appeared at or below the 1st percentile.

Adam's reproductions of the figures on the Developmental Test of Visual Motor Integration yielded a score below the 1st percentile with an age equivalent of 6 years 3 months.

Adam was unable to reproduce the Rey Figure. Adam's Human Figure Drawing is consistent for his 6- to 7-year-old level of cognitive and perceptual development.

Academic

The Woodcock-Johnson was administered as a screening of Adam's academic abilities and fluency. Age-adjusted standard scores follow.

	Standard Scores (mean = 100; s.d. = 15)
Letter/Word Identification	59
Reading Fluency	75
Story Recall	82
Understanding Directions	53
Calculation	42
Math Fluency	67
Spelling	66
Writing Fluency	72
Passage Comprehension	66
Applied Problems	54
Writing Samples	48
Word Attack	71
Spelling of Sounds	69

ORAL LANGUAGE	54
BRIEF ACHIEVEMENT	49
TOTAL ACHIEVEMENT	49
BROAD READING	60
BROAD MATH	41
BROAD WRITTEN LANGUAGE	54
BRIEF READING	56
BASIC READING SKILLS	58
BRIEF MATH	40
MATH CALCULATION SKILLS	43
BRIEF WRITING	52
WRITTEN EXPRESSION	56
ACADEMIC SKILLS	43
ACADEMIC FLUENCY	67
ACADEMIC APPLICATION	40
PHONEME/GRAPHEME KNOWLEDGE	68

Adam's academic achievement is consistent with his overall cognitive and neuropsychological profile. His basic reading, math, and written language skills appear at a late second- to early third-grade level overall.

Emotional/Personality

Adam's responses to the Manifest Anxiety Scale suggest that he fosters more anxious thinking than most youth of his age. His overall score was at the 93rd percentile. He noted that he has trouble making up his mind, becomes nervous if he makes a mistake, worries a lot of the time, is concerned what people may think or say about him, thinks that other people are happier, has his feelings hurt easily, and worries that something bad might happen to him.

During a brief clinical interview, Adam had difficulty responding to the examiner's open-ended questions. The quality of his responses was consistent with that of a much younger child. Adam noted that if he could change something, he wished that he could be taller. When asked for three wishes, he impulsively responded that he wanted a Lamborghini, a semi, and a snowmobile. Adam explained to the examiner that he would like to be a semi truck driver.

Adam reported a normal range of emotions. He reported becoming angry at his sister when "she hits me." He acknowledged that he had a best friend but that friend moved away. He reported having some friends at school and playing basketball with them.

Adam described recess as his favorite part of school and computers as his least favorite. He felt he was smart and denied that he was experiencing any problems at school. Adam reported the medications he currently takes "calm me down." He reported they work effectively and do not cause any side effects. Adam noted that if allowed to, he would not stop attending school. He agreed, however, that sometimes it was difficult to finish schoolwork.

Adam could not explain any of his medical problems. He acknowledged to the examiner that he had been in the hospital many times but could not remember how many times or when. He noted that he sometimes has back and hip pain. He reported finding it difficult to fall asleep, waking frequently, and having nightmares nightly about aliens.

Adam described his mother as nice and his father as funny. He denied that he disliked anything about either one of them, reporting that his parents treated him in a fair way. He denied he created problems at home. He reported going to stores and movies as enjoyable activities. He reported getting along "fine" with his sister.

On the basis of history, presentation, and current test data, Adam presents as a late adolescent with immature thought processes and reality testing. Adam's level of self-awareness is consistent with his markedly delayed cognitive and intellectual development. It would not be unexpected for someone in Adam's situation to demonstrate a pattern of oppositional behavior. This pattern of behavior combined with Adam's impulsivity, a frequent characteristic of youth with NF1, leads to conflicts with caretakers and teachers.

Diagnostic Impression

Adam was diagnosed with NF1 at 2 years of age. He has since had multiple courses of chemotherapy and radiation. He has demonstrated a long history of developmental delay and inattentive, hyperactive, and impulsive behavior. He has been diagnosed and treated as well for ADHD. Although research has not consistently demonstrated a distinct neurocognitive and neurobehavioral profile for youth with NF1, many experience cognitive impairments, ADHD, and disruptive behavior. NF1 has been associated with a higher risk of autism as well.

Adam's lower functioning appears consistent within the range of mild intellectual handicap. His overall functioning appears generally within a 6- to 8-year-old range and likely will remain at this throughout his lifetime. It is not likely that he will be able to live independently or enter the competitive workforce.

As characteristic of many youth with NF1, Adam's presentation also meets the diagnostic criteria for the Combined Type of ADHD. He also demonstrates symptoms though not a full syndrome characteristic of autism, warranting a diagnosis of Pervasive Developmental Disorder–Not Otherwise Specified.

In light of Adam's developmental impairments, it would not be unexpected for him to experience problems with behavior and emotional regulation.

At this time, however, it does not appear that he experiences Major Depression or Generalized Anxiety. His insight, not unexpectedly, is significantly limited.

Recommendations

It is strongly recommended that Adam's educational team review the current evaluation. Adam should be transitioned into a post–high school sheltered workshop/educational setting through his local school district.

As the opportunity arises, if interested, Adam and his family should explore group home living opportunities.

This examiner is prepared to consult with Ms. L. as needed relative to Adam's general functioning and behavior.

It is recommended that Adam's physicians review the current evaluation and maintain his currently prescribed stimulant medication. Should adjustments be made in the medication, this examiner is prepared to assist in the collection of behavioral data within the home and school setting. It is this examiner's opinion, however, that increased medicine will not likely lead to dramatically improved behavior, as Adam's self-regulation problems likely reflect a combination of temperament and neurological dysfunction.

The evaluation should be used to maintain Adam's status as a disabled individual eligible for Social Security benefits.

NAME:	Marcus D.
CURRENT OCCUPATION:	College Student
CA:	21 years 6 months

Reason for Evaluation

Marcus was originally diagnosed in childhood and treated for ADHD. He is seeking evaluation to determine eligibility as a Student with a Specific Disability under the Americans with Disabilities Act.

Assessment Procedures

Neuropsychological Impairment Scale
Test of Memory Malingering
Peabody Picture Vocabulary Test–IIIA
Wechsler Adult Intelligence Scale–IV
Wechsler Memory Scale–IV
Cognitive Assessment System
Conners' Continuous Performance Test
Woodcock-Johnson III–Tests of Achievement

ADHD Behavior Checklist for Adults
Purdue Pegboard
Rey Complex Figure Drawing
Beck Anxiety Inventory
Beck Depression Inventory
Millon Clinical Multiaxial Inventory–III
Clinical Interview

Background Information

Marcus and his parents were seen to review his history and development. Marcus's parents reported that though he was quite bright in elementary school, he was disorganized and hyperactive. He began having more problems and was eventually diagnosed by a local psychiatrist in fourth or fifth grade with ADHD. Medication was attempted inconsistently due to a difference of opinion between parents concerning the use of medication. Marcus eventually began taking medication again in 10th grade. Medicine at that time was of benefit. However, Marcus changed schools frequently in middle and high school. He eventually entered an outpatient drug rehabilitation program in 10th grade, which was beneficial. He completed high school at a parochial school with a 2.6 grade point average. His college grade point average is approximately 3.0. Copies of his transcripts were not reviewed. Marcus reported that this year he has done reasonably well in school but has received accommodation of increased time for tests from his math instructor. He has also had the opportunity to participate in academic support through tutorials.

Marcus reported that he does not currently take any medications for ADHD or other psychiatric conditions. He worked with psychologist P.D. in high school for 1.5 years. He was tested and evidently experienced "some type" of organizational and sequencing problem. He has worked with a number of health professionals, most recently with social worker, M.C., for approximately 1.5 years to receive neurofeedback, and meditation training. The treatment ended approximately 2 years ago. Marcus reported that he has developed skills to be more organized and functional through trial-and-error experience.

Marcus's parents divorced 9 years ago. His father is an attorney. His mother is a consultant. Marcus has an older brother. His older brother works as a personal trainer and modern dancer in New York. Marcus reported he and his older brother are good friends.

Marcus's parents recalled that prior to age 5 he was rather disorganized, distractible, and restless. He qualified for gifted programming in elementary school. He had poor handwriting. Marcus recalled that he was always a good reader and creative writer. He liked art, science, and English but was often unfocused in school. His grades varied dramatically. He never repeated a grade.

Marcus currently is working part time at a monument as a guide. He has worked for up to 8 months in the past as a dishwasher, in parts assembly, in organic farming, and as a school counselor.

Marcus reported a group of friends whom he enjoys activities with. He denied any history of problems making or keeping friends. He reported that he has been teased in the past. He can be argumentative but is improving in his ability to resolve conflicts with peers.

Marcus has had two speeding or moving violations and three car accidents. He has moved three times since completing high school.

Impairment

Marcus's responses to the Neuropsychological Impairment Scale yielded scores within the average range. Marcus did not report excessive levels of impairment in any major domain of life.

Behavioral Observation

Marcus, a young man of average size and appearance, was well groomed and neatly dressed. He wore an earring in each year. Eye contact was appropriate. Marcus was seen for two assessment sessions over a 2-day period. Receptive and expressive language skills appeared good. Marcus maintained and initiated conversation.

Marcus was neither anxious nor sad. Overall, he was calm and emotionally stable.

Marcus was alert and attentive. His concentration was good. He was cooperative and attempted all tasks presented. Marcus was motivated to perform. Persistence was good. No muscular tension or habitual mannerisms were noted. Marcus presented with a normal activity level. He was not fidgety or distracted. He appeared moderately confident in his abilities.

Marcus related well to the examiners and smiled appropriately. His thoughts appeared logical, focused, and relevant. He asked frequent questions during testing and appeared slow, particularly on tasks requiring motor output or rote memory. Overall, however, it was not significantly difficult to establish a working relationship with this pleasant individual.

Assessment Results and Interpretation

Dissimulation

The Test of Memory Malingering was administered as a screening of effort and dissimulation. Marcus completed Trial I with 46 out of 50 correct responses while completing the next two trials with 100% correct responding. The performance suggests he exerted good effort during the course of the evaluation.

Language

The Peabody was administered as a simple measure of one-word receptive vocabulary. Marcus completed this test with a standard score of 110, equivalent to the 75th percentile.

Intellectual

The Wechsler Adult Intelligence Scale (4th ed.) was administered as an overall screening of intellectual achievement and ability. Age-adjusted scaled scores follow.

	Scaled Scores (mean = 100; s.d. = 3)
Verbal	
Similarities	19
Vocabulary	18
Information	14
Perceptual Reasoning	
Block Design	14
Matrix Reasoning	14
Visual Puzzles	13
Working Memory	
Digit Span	7
Arithmetic	8
Processing Speed	
Symbol Search	5
Coding	5

	Standard Scores		
	(mean = 100; s.d. = 15)	Percentiles	90% Confidence Interval
Verbal Comprehension	143	99.8th	137–146
Perceptual Reasoning	121	92nd	115–125
Working Memory	86	18th	81–93
Processing Speed	74	4th	70–84
Full Scale	110	75th	106–113

Memory

The Wechsler Memory Scale was administered as an overall screening of memory ability. Age-adjusted scaled scores follow.

	Scaled Scores (mean = 100; s.d. = 3)
Logical Memory I	7
Logical Memory II	6
Verbal Paired Associates I	10
Verbal Paired Associates II	13
Designs I	12
Designs II	12

Visual Reproduction I	12
Visual Reproduction II	10
Spatial Addition	9
Symbol Span	10

| | Standard Scores | | |
	(mean = 100; s.d. = 15)	Percentiles	90% Confidence Interval
Auditory Memory	94	34th	89–100
Visual Memory	108	70th	103–112
Visual Working Memory	97	42nd	91–103
Immediate Memory	102	55th	97–107
Delayed Memory	102	55th	96–108

Executive/Neuropsychological

The Cognitive Assessment System was administered as a neuropsychological screening. Adjusted 18-year-old (highest normative sample) scaled scores follow.

	Scaled Scores (mean = 10; s.d. = 3)
Matching Numbers	8
Planned Codes	10
Nonverbal Matrices	14
Verbal-Spatial Relations	13
Expressive Attention	9
Number Detection	6
Word Series	4
Sentence Repetition	10

| | IQ | | |
	(mean = 100; s.d. = 15)	Percentiles (mean = 50)	90% Confidence Interval
Planning	94	34th	87–103
Simultaneous	120	91st	111–125
Attention	85	16th	79–96
Successive	84	14th	78–93
Full Scale	94	34th	87–103

Attention

The Conners' Continuous Performance Test was administered as a computerized measure of Marcus's ability to sustain attention and inhibit impulsive responding. He demonstrated an impulsive approach to this task.

Marcus's responses to the ADHD Behavior Checklist for Adults yielded scores within the average range. Marcus did not endorse significant problems with sustained attention, distractibility, or hyperactivity. He reported, however, that he has developed strategies to compensate for his disorganization and listening problems, indicating that without use of these strategies, his self-report would reflect greater symptomatic problems.

Motor/Perceptual

Marcus appears right-side dominant. Motor speed and coordination, based on Purdue Pegboard performance, appeared within the average range.

Marcus's reproduction of the Rey Complex Figure yielded a score at the 50th percentile. Immediate recall of the figure yielded a score at the 25th percentile.

Academic

The Woodcock-Johnson was administered as an assessment of academic ability, fluency, and application. Age-adjusted standard scores follow.

	Standard Scores (mean = 100; s.d. = 15)
Letter/Word Identification	108
Reading Fluency	101
Story Recall	87
Understanding Directions	97
Calculation	102
Math Fluency	63
Spelling	113
Writing Fluency	106
Passage Comprehension	115
Applied Problems	109
Writing Samples	112
Word Attack	112
Spelling of Sounds	109
ORAL LANGUAGE	93
BRIEF ACHIEVEMENT	112
TOTAL ACHIEVEMENT	108
BROAD READING	109

BROAD MATH	99
BROAD WRITTEN LANGUAGE	113
BRIEF READING	113
BASIC READING SKILLS	111
BRIEF MATH	107
MATH CALCULATION SKILLS	89
BRIEF WRITING	115
WRITTEN EXPRESSION	110
ACADEMIC SKILLS	110
ACADEMIC FLUENCY	94
ACADEMIC APPLICATION	115
PHONEME/GRAPHEME KNOWLEDGE	113

Emotional/Personality

Marcus's responses to the Beck Depression Inventory yielded a score within the normal range. Marcus did not report excessive depressive or helpless thoughts.

Marcus's responses to the Beck Anxiety Inventory also yielded a score within the average range.

On the basis of history, presentation, and current test data, Marcus presents as a young adult with adequate reality testing and generally age-appropriate thought processes. Individuals with his personality style tend to be capable of making good impressions on others but often behave in impulsive and restless ways. They tend to be unreliable, seek excitement, and can act rashly with insufficient deliberation or poor judgment. Such individuals can be seen by others as irresponsible or undependable. This profile is consistent with a significant percentage of individuals with histories of ADHD. The profile does not reflect clinical symptomatology for any type of specific psychiatric condition or personality disorder beyond ADHD.

Diagnostic Impression

Marcus was diagnosed as a young child and treated throughout his childhood inconsistently for ADHD. He changed schools frequently, was treated for substance use, and has had a number of moving violations and automobile accidents. These data are all consistent with a childhood history of ADHD.

Current assessment reflects Marcus's superior verbal comprehension and perceptual reasoning abilities but low-average working memory and very slow processing speed, particularly when output with a pencil is required. Memory skills appear just average with low-average auditory memory. Neuropsychological processes are noted by strong simultaneous ability and average planning but low-average attention and successive processing. Marcus's overall neuropsychological abilities at the 34th percentile are markedly below his 99th- and 92nd-percentile verbal comprehension and perceptual reasoning abilities. Marcus's academic skills appear within the average range except for mathematics. Marcus demonstrates a pattern of poor math fluency consistent with processing speed weaknesses characteristic of individuals with ADHD.

Marcus does not report symptoms of depression or anxiety. His personality style is characteristic of individuals with histories of ADHD, including impulsive behavior and a tendency to act with insufficient deliberation and/or poor judgment.

By his report, Marcus has developed a number of compensatory skills that have allowed him to function effectively and minimize daily impairments. Nonetheless, his history and presentation continues to reflect symptomatology and impairments related to ADHD. For this reason, a diagnosis of ADHD–Not Otherwise Specified appears warranted. Additionally, based on *Diagnostic and Statistical Manual of Mental Disorders* (4th ed., text revision; DSM-IV-TR) *DSM-IV-TR* criteria, the discrepancy between Marcus's verbal comprehension and perceptual reasoning and his math fluency, attention and successive processes warrant diagnoses of Developmental Math Disorder and Cognitive Disorder–Not Otherwise Specified.

Marcus's impairments with processing speed, attention to detail, and successive processing cause limitations in the classroom, particularly as it relates to his ability to keep pace with instruction and complete tests in a timely fashion. Under the Americans for Disabilities Act, it would appear reasonable for Marcus to receive accommodations, particularly in math classes, to include additional time on tests and tutorial support as needed.

NAME: Susan P.
CURRENT EMPLOYMENT: Certified Nursing Assistant (CNA)
CA: 21 years 4 months

Reason for Evaluation

Susan has a childhood and young adult history of problems with academics. She has been served as a student with LD throughout her academic career. She has also had bouts of depression and anxiety. Susan has requested an evaluation in an effort to better understand and define her current issues as well as assist with developing accommodations and possibly remediation to facilitate her success in the workplace.

Assessment Procedures

Review of Medical and Academic Records
Conners' Behavior Rating Scales–Parent Form
NRP Rating Form
Neuropsychological Impairment Scale

Brown Attention Disorders Scale
ADHD Behavior Checklist for Adults
Peabody Picture Vocabulary Test–IIIA
Expressive Vocabulary Test
Wechsler Adult Intelligence Scale–IV
Wechsler Memory Scale–IV
Cognitive Assessment System
Woodcock-Johnson III–Tests of Academic Achievement
Conners' Continuous Performance Test
Purdue Pegboard
Rey Complex Figure Drawing
Beck Anxiety Inventory
Beck Depression Inventory
Millon Clinical Multiaxial Inventory–III
Clinical Interview

Review of Previous Evaluation
May 3, 2004

A psychosocial assessment completed by N.C., LCSW, noted that Susan was in a special education classroom for students with behavior disorders. This record also notes that Susan's mother may require a liver transplant in the future. The following diagnoses were made:

Major Depression
Learning Disorder–Not Otherwise Specified (NOS)
Rule Out ADHD

June 1, 2004

A psychiatric assessment was completed by E.C., APRN. Dr. C. noted that Susan reported feeling depressed since seventh grade. In her journal, Susan listed concerns about obesity as well as suicidal thoughts. At the time, Susan had an irritable mood and was anhedonic. She had significant weight gain. She was experiencing problems with sleep, psychomotor agitation, retardation, fatigue, loss of energy, worthlessness, and poor concentration.

Susan also demonstrated symptoms of anxiety. This record notes Susan's aunt with a history of Obsessive/Compulsive Disorder, Anxiety, and Learning disorders. The following diagnoses were made:

Dysthymia that has progressed to a Major Depressive Disorder
Generalized Anxiety Disorder
Specific Phobia to Natural Environment
Social Phobia
Rule Out ADHD
Learning Disorders by History

August 17, 2004

A Children's Medical Center record notes that Susan was prescribed Prozac.

August 31, 2004

A Children's Medical Center record notes that Susan was prescribed Prozac and Adderall.

December 15, 2004

A Children's Medical Center record notes that Susan was prescribed Adderall and Prozac.

January 2, 2005

A Children's Medical Center record notes that Susan was prescribed Adderall and Effexor.

January 27, 2005

A Children's Medical Center record notes that Susan was prescribed Adderall and Effexor.

March 2, 2005

Susan's medical records also note that in June 2004 she was taking Lexapro and in March 2005 she was prescribed Wellbutrin.

Review of Academic Records

A copy of Susan's high school transcript was reviewed. Susan graduated in June 2006 with a grade point average of 2.1. She was ranked 393 in a class of 652.

Copies of Susan's Individualized Education Programs from 11th and 12th grade were reviewed. Susan was classified as a Learning Disabled Student. The following test scores were included.

Woodcock-Johnson III Tests of Achievement

	Standard Scores (mean = 100; s.d. = 15)
Calculation	74
Math Fluency	73
Applied Problems	86
Broad Math	77
Math Calculation Skills	72

Background Information

Susan and her mother, Sue, were seen to review her history and development. Susan is currently living with her grandmother in Mississippi. She has completed her Certified Nursing Assistant course and passed her license exam there and is currently working on an as-needed basis. She has not decided if she will return to Salt Lake City. Susan is seeking evaluation because she wants to know "why life is harder for me." Susan reported her first depressive episode sometime in fourth grade. She has likely had a number of depressive episodes since then. Susan's mother noted that she had an unremarkable early childhood. Her early development was a bit slower than her siblings. Susan has 3 siblings ranging in age from 13 to 19 years. None have experienced developmental or adjustment problems. Susan has most conflict with her 16-year-old brother, Jim, and gets along reasonably well with her brothers Sean and Randy. Susan's father is a city manager. Her mother is a homemaker. Susan's mother's side of the family has a history of learning disability and obesity. Both sides of the family have histories of depression, addiction, and anxiety.

Once she completed high school, Susan moved out to a friend's home and lived there for almost 2 years. She worked full time at the humanitarian center for her church. She had a period where she did not communicate much with her parents, reporting that she was angry for reasons that were explained during the clinical interview. Susan then became involved with a young man and lived with him. She then became very ill and developed diabetes for which she now is treated with insulin. She spent a week in the hospital last summer due to her lack of care for her health. She moved back home, lived with her parents for nearly a year, and this past summer moved to Mississippi.

Susan saw social worker, N.C., every few weeks for a period of time during her high school years. She reported that counseling was supportive but not necessarily helpful.

Susan does not drive. She reported she has made some but not many friends in Mississippi. She currently lives with her grandmother on a ranch in a small town. Susan described herself as having few friends throughout her life. She noted problems with concentration, restlessness, and being withdrawn. She has had an interest in anime throughout high school and a continued interest in watching and reading anime books after high school. She reads anime materials and watches anime videos.

Susan has not had problems with the legal system or substance use or abuse. She has an interest in possibly returning to school to obtain additional education in the health field.

Susan acknowledged that she has been feeling the best she has over a number of years in the past few months. She is not currently taking any psychiatric medications. She denied suicidal thoughts in the last 6 months but noted that she has had continued problems with headache, appetite, moodiness, depression, feeling misunderstood, and being shy with others. Susan also reported that as a child, she was frequently picked on. She recalled she had a "very hard time at school." Susan spends her free time reading, watching television, or studying.

In a correspondence dated November 5, 2009, to the examiner, Susan's grandmother noted that Susan has been living with her since the summer of 2009.

She reports that Susan seems to have symptoms of hypopituitarism. These symptoms include fatigue, headache, low tolerance for stress, muscle weakness, gastrointestinal problems, weight gain, abdominal discomfort, sensitivity to cold, visual disturbance, thirst, excessive urination, diabetes, and menstrual problems. She noted that Susan has "radical mood swings." She further reported that Susan's hands and feet appear quite small and her gait is poor. She appears to drag her feet when she walks. She also noted that Susan would "sleep 14–16 hours a day if allowed to." She appears to enjoy watching children's cartoons. Her appetite is limited because things don't taste good.

Adaptive Functioning

Susan's mother was asked to complete the Conners' Behavior Rating Scale observing Susan as she has presented over the past few years at home. The following age-adjusted scores were obtained (mean = 50; s.d. = 10; high scores indicate problems).

Content Scales

	T-scores
Emotional Distress	81
Upsetting Thoughts	92
Worrying	83
Social Problems	84
Aggressive Behavior	71
Academic Difficulty	86
Language	79
Math	81
Hyperactivity/Impulsivity	50
Separation Fears	47
Perfectionistic and Compulsive Behaviors	69
Violence Potential	69
Physical Symptoms	71

DSM-IV-TR Scales

	T-scores
ADHD Inattentive Type	91
ADHD Hyperactive-Impulsive Type	50
Conduct Disorder	49
Oppositional Defiant Disorder	67

Major Depressive Episode	82
Manic Episode	64
Generalized Anxiety Disorder	84
Separation Anxiety Disorder	47
Social Phobia	86
Obsessive/Compulsive Disorder	79
Autistic Disorder	90
Asperger's Disorder	74

Impairment

On the NRP Rating Form, Susan reported that she can engage in most activities of daily living but has some difficulty starting a conversation in groups, remembering important things to do, getting help when confused, dealing with unexpected changes, handling arguments with others, accepting criticism, controlling crying, showing affection, participating in group activities, controlling her temper, keeping from being depressed, and keeping her emotions from affecting her everyday activities.

Susan's grandmother also completed the NRP Form, noting that Susan has difficulty preparing her own meals, staying involved in activities when fatigued or bored, remembering the names of people she sees often, getting help when confused, handling unexpected changes, handling arguments, controlling crying, accepting criticism from others, participating in group activities, recognizing when something she says upsets others, understanding new instructions, controlling her temper, and keeping her emotions from affecting everyday activities.

Susan's and her grandmother's responses to the Neuropsychological Impairment Scale yielded very elevated Affective Indices; above the 99th percentile. This suggests that affective symptoms likely contribute to Susan's daily impairments. Subscales follow, providing percentile comparisons (50th percentile is average; high score indicates problem).

	Percentile	
	Susan	Grandmother
Critical Items	94th	76th
Cognitive	98th	98th
Attention	98th	98th
Memory	98th	98th
Frustration	98th	98th
Learning/Verbal	98th	98th
Academic		

Behavioral Observation

Susan, a moderately obese young adult, was well groomed and neatly dressed. She was seen for 2 assessment sessions over a 2-day period. During the first day, self-report measures and the history were obtained with the examiner. On the second day, structured testing was completed with Dr. D. as well as the clinical interview being completed with the examiner. Susan's behavior and presentation during both sessions was similar.

Eye contact was appropriate. Susan maintained and initiated conversation. She demonstrated some dysfluency. Receptive language appeared within normal limits.

Susan was mildly anxious during testing and concerned about her performance. She was emotionally stable although teary during the history and clinical interview.

Susan was alert, attentive, and concentrated adequately. She was cooperative and attempted all tasks presented. She was motivated to perform and persistence was good.

No muscular tension or habitual mannerisms were noted. Susan presented with a normal activity level. She was not fidgety but was occasionally distracted. She appeared inclined to distrust her abilities.

Susan related well to the examiners, but she smiled only occasionally. Her thoughts appeared logical, focused, and relevant. Overall, it was not significantly difficult to establish a working relationship with this pleasant individual.

Assessment Results and Interpretation

Language

The Peabody was administered as a simple measure of 1-word receptive vocabulary. Susan completed this test with a standard score of 91, equivalent to the 27th percentile.

The Expressive Vocabulary Test was administered as a simple measure of expressive language. Susan completed this test with a standard score of 82, equivalent to the 12th percentile.

Intellectual

The Wechsler Adult Intelligence Scale (4th ed.) was administered as an overall screening of intellectual achievement and ability. Age-adjusted scaled scores follow.

	Scaled Scores (mean = 10; s.d. = 3)
Verbal	
Similarities	8
Vocabulary	8
Information	12

Perceptual Reasoning

Block Design	5
Matrix Reasoning	6
Visual Puzzles	6
Working Memory	
Digit Span	6
Arithmetic	7
Processing Speed	
Symbol Search	8
Coding	6

	Standard Scores		
	(mean = 100; s.d. = 15)	Percentiles	90% Confidence Interval
Verbal Comprehension	96	39th	91–101
Perceptual Reasoning	75	5th	71–81
Working Memory	80	9th	76–87
Processing Speed	87	14th	79–93
Full Scale	80	9th	77–84

Despite possessing average verbal comprehension, Susan demonstrates poor perceptual reasoning, working memory, and processing speed.

Memory

The Wechsler Memory Scale was administered as an overall screening of memory ability. Age-adjusted scaled scores follow.

	Scaled Scores (mean = 10; s.d. = 3)
Logical Memory I	11
Logical Memory II	10
Verbal Paired Associates I	12
Verbal Paired Associates II	13
Designs I	6
Designs II	9
Visual Reproduction I	5
Visual Reproduction II	9
Spatial Addition	7
Symbol Span	9

| | Standard Scores | | |
	(mean = 100; s.d. = 15)	Percentiles	90% Confidence Interval
Auditory Memory	109	73rd	103–114
Visual Memory	84	14th	80–89
Visual Working Memory	88	21st	93–95
Immediate Memory	89	23rd	84–95
Delayed Memory	102	55th	96–108

Susan demonstrates average verbal memory but below-average visual memory. This is consistent with differences between verbal comprehension and perceptual reasoning abilities.

Executive/Neuropsychological

The Cognitive Assessment System was administered as a neuropsychological screening. Eighteen-year-old (oldest normative sample) adjusted scaled scores follow.

	Scaled Scores (mean = 10; s.d. = 3)
Matching Numbers	2
Planned Codes	6
Nonverbal Matrices	9
Verbal-Spatial Relations	5
Expressive Attention	7
Number Detection	7
Word Series	4
Sentence Repetition	7

| | IQ | | |
	(mean = 100; s.d. = 15)	Percentiles (mean = 50)	90% Confidence Interval
Planning	61	1st	62–78
Simultaneous	82	12th	76–91
Attention	82	12th	76–93
Successive	75	5th	70–84
Full Scale	66	1st	63–78

Despite possessing average simultaneous and attention processes, Susan possesses borderline successive and very poor planning abilities. Planning requires the ability to strategize, self-monitor, organize, and learn as well as work efficiently. Susan's problems with planning and successive processing offer a broad-based understanding of her significant problems academically and with transitioning into adult life.

Attention

The Conners' Continuous Performance Test was administered as a computerized measure of Susan's ability to sustain attention and inhibit impulsive responding. Susan performed within the normal range on this instrument.

Motor/Perceptual

Susan appeared right-side dominant. Motor speed and coordination, as measured by the Purdue Pegboard, appeared within the low-average range. Of interest was the fact that Susan performed better with her left, or nondominant, hand (20th percentile) than with her right, or dominant, hand (1st percentile).

Susan's reproduction of the Rey Complex Figure was awkwardly drawn. The reproduction yielded a score below the 1st percentile. Susan's immediate recall of the figure yielded a score at the 2nd percentile. Susan's problems on this task clearly reflect her planning deficits.

Academic

The Woodcock-Johnson was administered as an assessment of academic ability, fluency, and application. Age-adjusted standard scores follow.

	Standard Scores (mean = 100; s.d. = 15)
Letter/Word Identification	84
Reading Fluency	80
Story Recall	84
Understanding Directions	80
Calculation	69
Math Fluency	72
Spelling	80
Writing Fluency	77
Passage Comprehension	85
Applied Problems	77
Writing Samples	84
Word Attack	74
Spelling of Sounds	83

(Continued)

(continued)

	Standard Scores (mean = 100; s.d. = 15)
ORAL LANGUAGE	78
BRIEF ACHIEVEMENT	77
TOTAL ACHIEVEMENT	74
BROAD READING	80
BROAD MATH	68
BROAD WRITTEN LANGUAGE	74
BRIEF READING	81
BASIC READING SKILLS	75
BRIEF MATH	71
MATH CALCULATION SKILLS	65
BRIEF WRITING	81
WRITTEN EXPRESSION	78
ACADEMIC SKILLS	73
ACADEMIC FLUENCY	74
ACADEMIC APPLICATION	75
PHONEME/GRAPHEME KNOWLEDGE	75

Basic academic achievement is best predicted by patterns of neuropsychological processes. Susan's neuropsychological processes appear at the 1st percentile. Thus, it is not unexpected that her academic skills generally appear below the 5th percentile. Susan's overall achievement appears at a fifth-grade level.

Emotional/Personality

Susan's responses to the Brown Attention Disorders Scale yielded a score of over 90 points. Scores above 50 are considered indicative of self-reports of attention problems. However, scores at this elevation are usually indicative of attention problems further fueled by significant psychiatric problems.

Susan's responses to the ADHD Behavior Checklist for Adults yielded a self-report within the range of individuals experiencing significant attention problems. Susan notes she has trouble giving close attention to details as well as problems sustaining attention or effort. She is easily distracted and forgetful in daily activities. In contrast, Susan did not report significant symptoms of hyperactivity.

Susan's responses to the Beck Depression Inventory yielded a score of 31, indicative of moderate to severe depressive reports. Susan noted that she is very sad and unhappy, feels discouraged about the future, sees failures in her life, does not derive much satisfaction, feels guilty all of the time, is disappointed with herself, blames herself for her thoughts, has thoughts of killing herself but would not do it, has a great deal of difficulty making decisions, does not sleep well, and fatigues very easily.

Susan's responses to the Beck Anxiety Inventory yielded a score of 53, indicative of severe anxiety reports.

On the basis of history, presentation, and current test data, Susan presents as an adult with adequate reality testing and generally age-appropriate thought processes. Her personality profile is characterized as an individual who is likely subjected to the flux of her enigmatic attitudes and contradictory behavior. Such individuals often have a checkered history of disappointments in personal and family relationships.

Susan's Millon profile is characteristic of individuals who are pervasively apprehensive and intense and variable in their moods and who tend to experience prolonged periods of dejection and self-deprecation. Such individuals often withdraw, isolate, and distance themselves from others. Individuals with this personality style often possess a long-standing expectation that others will be rejecting or disparaging. This expectation precipitates profound gloom, self-defeating and negative behavior, and irrational negativism. Such individuals often vacillate in their moods and typically desire affection but are at risk for self-destructive acts. Despite longing for warmth and acceptance, individuals with this personality style often withdraw to maintain a self-distance from close psychological involvement.

Surface apathy is often characteristic in individuals with this personality style. However, below their front of apathy often lie contrary feelings that can break through in displays of temper toward those they view as being unsupportive, critical, or disapproving.

Individuals with this personality style often experience a low sense of self-worth. They typically and painfully contemplate the pitiful and futile state of their identity. They tend to have a tendency toward extreme introspection, which only further compounds their identity problems. Such individuals often expect ridicule and derision. They can detect the most minute traces of indifference expressed by others. Their inability to communicate ideas and feelings in a relevant manner further alienates them from others.

Susan's Millon profile was strongly indicative of self-demeaning comments and feelings of inferiority, suggesting Major Depression. Irritability, anxiety, and depressed moods suggest Susan likely vacillates between keeping her dysphoric feelings in check and voicing them, thus preventing her from stabilizing her emotions.

On the Millon, Susan responded affirmatively to the following critical items:

I feel weak and tired much of the time.
I have a hard time keeping my balance when walking.
I can't seem to sleep and wake up just as tired as when I went to bed.

I don't have the energy to concentrate on my everyday responsibilities
    anymore.
When I have a choice I prefer to do things alone.
A long time ago I decided it is best to have little to do with people.
I am alone most of the time and I prefer it that way.
In social groups I am almost always very self-conscious and tense.
Lately I have gone all to pieces.
My moods seem to change a great deal from one day to the next.
I began to feel like a failure some years ago.
I feel terribly depressed and sad much of the time now.
I have felt downhearted and sad for much of my life since I was quite young.
I feel deeply depressed for no reason I can figure out.
I frequently feel that there is nothing inside me like I'm empty and hollow.
Looking ahead as each day begins makes me feel terribly depressed.
I have never been able to shake the feeling that I am worthless to others.

In the clinical interview, Susan reported that she is much less sad and depressed currently than 6 months ago. Nonetheless, she is worried about "falling back." She acknowledged to the examiner that she tried overdosing with medication at age 17 but does not currently have any active suicidal thoughts.

Between 18 and 19 years of age, Susan reported after she moved out of her home that "everything was fine." She indicated she was working and living with a friend. At age 19, for reasons that are unclear, she became very depressed. Her father came home from his placement abroad. Susan reported she did not feel like she was part of the family. She had two boyfriends, the second of whom was physically aggressive. In January through March 2008, Susan reported she felt "really ill" and was eventually diagnosed with diabetes and moved in with her parents. During this period of time, her brother attacked her over an anger issue and by her report was very violent with her. Susan noted that she moved to Mississippi in part to get away from this brother. She acknowledged, however, that she has been jealous of her brothers.

Susan reported that she has been bullied as a child and has been mentally and physically abused by her mother, indicating that her mother's moods are inconsistent and that her mother would scream or yell at her. Susan also reported that it is her impression that her mother wanted a boy for her first child and instead Susan was born.

Diagnostic Impression

Susan has a childhood and young adult history of problems with academics. She has been treated for a variety of psychiatric and developmental disabilities. She requested evaluation in an effort to better understand and define her current presentation.

Susan's past diagnoses and treatments have included depression, anxiety, phobia, ADHD, and learning disability. She has been treated with multiple classes of psychiatric medications. Susan received special education services throughout school. Measures of academic achievement from high school suggest that she always functioned within the borderline range of academic abilities.

Susan and her grandmother currently report moderate to significant problems related to impairment throughout the day. Susan's grandmother reports that Susan demonstrates multiple physical symptoms, including fatigue, headache, low tolerance for stress, weight gain, mood swings, and poor gait.

Current assessment reflects Susan's average verbal comprehension and verbal memory abilities with poor perceptual reasoning, working memory, and processing speed. Neuropsychological processes are noted by generally low-average simultaneous and attention with borderline successive but very poor planning processes, falling at or below the 1st percentile. Planning reflects the ability to problem-solve, strategize, and work efficiently. Planning allows you to gain new knowledge, retain that knowledge, and use it effectively in day-to-day activities. It would appear that Susan's very poor planning skills reflect the primary foundational impairment that has caused her significant challenges in school and in transitioning into adult life. Poor planning is also likely responsible for her inability to drive as well. Susan's current academic achievement appears at a fifth-grade level, consistent with her neuropsychological processes but clearly well below her average verbal comprehension and verbal abilities.

The combination of Susan's nonverbal or right-hemisphere deficits as well as her currently reported physical impairments, particularly obesity and poor gait, raise questions about a possible medical or genetic etiology. Her presentation may be consistent for a condition such as Fragile X or hypopituitarism.

Based on *DSM-IV-TR* criteria, Susan's symptoms and impairments meet diagnostic criteria for Major Depression–Recurrent, ADHD Inattentive Type (ADHD-I), and a Cognitive Disorder–NOS.

Recommendations

It is recommended that Susan provide this evaluation to her physician and consider both genetic and endocrinology evaluations.

Susan would benefit from cognitive-behavioral therapy for depression.

Susan may wish to work with a cognitive rehabilitation specialist focusing specifically on strategies to improve her planning and sequencing skills in everyday life. Because of her significant cognitive weaknesses, Susan may also qualify under Section 504 of the Americans with Disabilities Act as a disabled worker or student. This may afford her some additional accommodations at work and school, particularly involving mastering new tasks and acquiring new knowledge.

CASE 1: ADHD

R.B., a 48-year-old male, was self-referred at the insistence of his spouse. R.B. reported a normal childhood. However, his mother died when he was 3 years of age, and he was raised by a grandmother and great-aunt until he was 6, at which time his father remarried. He denied any significant behavioral, cognitive, or emotional problems in childhood but noted that he should have been retained in third grade because of poor reading skills. Nonetheless, R.B. progressed through high school and graduated with a 4-year college degree and a B average.

R.B. was employed in sales full time. He had worked for the same company for 9 years but expressed concern that he had missed promotions because he was disorganized and had difficulty getting along with supervisors.

R.B. and his first wife have been married for 20 years. They have 4 children. Their youngest, an 11-year-old boy, was diagnosed with ADHD, which in part prompted R.B. to consider assessment for himself.

R.B. described chronically feeling tense, unable to relax, and fatigued and having difficulty with concentration and memory. R.B. noted that at times he feels stupid and that his moods will change frequently or unpredictably. He reported numerous citations for speeding violations but only 1 automobile accident.

R.B.'s self-report on the Wender and Brown questionnaires crossed the clinical cut-offs. R.B.'s father reported that, as a child, R.B. was easily distracted and fidgety, had difficulty sustaining attention, and often seemed not to listen. R.B.'s wife's observations on the Brown questionnaire crossed the clinically significant threshold. Fourteen out of 18 *DSM-IV-TR* symptoms of ADHD were also acknowledged by R.B.'s wife.

R.B.'s presentation was unremarkable. On demanding tasks, however, he frequently became frustrated and less efficient. His mannerisms were appropriate. Brief structured assessment detected average verbal and nonverbal intellectual skills. R.B. demonstrated difficulty sustaining attention on a computerized measure of continuous performance.

Data generated from the Beck and Millon did not reflect significant symptoms of depression; however, personality characteristics suggested that R.B.'s veneer of confidence covered strong feelings of inadequacy, impulsive acts resulting from minimal deliberation, poor judgment, and difficulty admitting responsibility. Rationalization and projection were identified as primary psychological defenses.

The preponderance of the data most powerfully reflected R.B.'s lifetime patterns of ADHD symptoms. Given his intelligence and lack of learning problems, R.B. had developed numerous strategies to manage problems and allow him to function adequately on a daily basis.

Recommendations included a trial of medication, video resources relevant to ADHD, and psychosocial interventions as well as further consultation concerning R.B.'s current problems at work.

CASE 2: ADHD

M.B., an almost 16-year-old female, demonstrated a history of disruptive behavior consistent with ADHD from preschool. Family history was positive for ADHD in a number of immediate and extended family members. M.B.'s treatment history included preschool play therapy at 4 years of age and intermittent counseling with a number of mental health professionals throughout childhood and early adolescence. More recently, counselors reported M.B.'s reluctance to discuss her feelings and life problems and her general tendency to deny the need for treatment. M.B.'s medical treatment history included the therapeutic use of a number of stimulants, including Ritalin and Dexedrine; imipramine begun in midadolescence due to concerns about mood fluctuations; and more recently, a trial of Zoloft due to parental complaints of disruptive behavior at home.

M.B.'s parents described the home situation as her primary area of difficulty. M.B.'s mother reported an ongoing and fairly severe pattern of conflict between herself and her daughter. M.B.'s father was often placed in the role of mediator. Approaching late adolescence, M.B. had become more independent, challenging her parents' authority, their post–high school goals for her, and what she perceived as their unequal treatment of her and her older sister. Current referral resulted from a particularly nasty family battle coinciding with a poor report card.

Despite behavioral difficulties, M.B.'s academic records reflected average grades in general. A number of M.B.'s teachers reported that she appeared to be capable of better work. She had become more passive in some classes and was actively missing in other classes.

Questionnaires completed by M.B.'s parents reflected scale elevations on the Child Behavior Checklist, including aggressive and withdrawn behavior, as well as inattentiveness. On a Conners' questionnaire, M.B. presented at above the 98th percentile without stimulant medication. Problems were noted with distractibility, inattention, failing to finish things, wide or drastic mood changes, excitability, and impulsivity. With the present regime of Dexedrine and Zoloft, M.B.'s parents reported a marked decline in these problems. Nonetheless, continued situational problems, primarily with noncompliance, were reported at home.

M.B. was an attractive adolescent. She was pleasant and cooperative during the assessment process. No overt signs of depression or anxiety were noted. M.B. related well to the examiner.

Brief structured assessment reflected M.B.'s average to high-average verbal and nonverbal skills. Her approach to test tasks became increasingly more hesitant as task complexity increased. When prompted by the examiner, it was clear that M.B.'s intellectual skills were likely even better than these average measures reflected.

M.B.'s responses to self-report measures did not yield symptoms related to anxiety or depression. Her personality was typified by a confident social style of seeking attention and a tendency to seek praise and approval from others through immature or histrionic means. M.B.'s personality reflected an adolescent easily excited and then quickly bored. This pattern did not appear to result from hostile or malicious tendencies but rather from M.B.'s somewhat self-centered narcissism. Nonetheless, she presented with a fairly clear self-concept and a general measure of comfort when describing herself and her current life. M.B.'s primary focus of problems was on the unfair means by which her parents had related and continued to relate to her. She reported her family as the primary source of tension and conflict.

By history and presentation, M.B. met symptom criteria for ADHD. Although M.B.'s parents reported improvements in her behavior at home with the introduction of the Zoloft, an anecdotal log over a period of weeks did not clearly support their perceptions. M.B. and her parents, however, reported that the Dexedrine appeared to be beneficial when M.B. chose to participate and complete schoolwork.

Further psychiatric consultation was recommended in an effort to provide clear target symptoms to evaluate the potential need for and benefits from the antidepressant medication. M.B. decided to continue with the Dexedrine and to make an effort to participate more actively in school so as not to jeopardize her upcoming graduation. M.B. was also provided with additional information about ADHD in adolescence and adulthood. Finally, after communicating with a number of other professionals who had failed to improve family relations, the examiner decided to recommend individual counseling for M.B. in an effort to provide her with some additional support and guidance as she began planning her future life. M.B.'s parents were given additional information concerning ADHD and urged to allow M.B. to take a more active and independent role in her life.

CASE 3: ADHD AND GIFTED INTELLECT

D.O., a 17.5-year-old 11th-grade male, was referred because of a history of poor academic motivation, symptoms suggestive of ADHD, and recent reports of increasingly low self-esteem. D.O.'s family history was significant for Obsessive/Compulsive Disorder, ADHD, alcoholism, and depression.

D.O.'s history was positive for a fall at 2 years of age, which resulted in a concussion followed by a convulsion. For several years afterward, when D.O. fell or got hurt, he would either black out or experience a convulsion. No clear etiologies for these problems were identified.

During his fifth-grade year, D.O. was diagnosed with ADHD by a family physician. A trial of Cylert was initially beneficial, but then benefits seemed to wane. In 10th grade, because of continued problems with inattentiveness, a brief trial of Ritalin was attempted, with equivocal results.

D.O.'s parents recalled being concerned about him before he entered kindergarten because of his late-summer birthday and tendency to bore easily. D.O. was placed in a gifted educational program in fourth and fifth grades but did not perform well and was moved back into a regular educational setting.

In 11th grade, D.O. was described as disorganized, not completing assignments, inattentive, and scoring poorly academically. D.O. had a group of friends and was not involved in antisocial or substance abuse problems.

D.O.'s parents reported that he had become more withdrawn, less involved with friends, and more resistant at home. School was described as a major area of conflict between D.O. and his parents. Nonetheless, D.O. was described by his parents as loving and kind.

Psychiatric evaluation completed in 2008 yielded a diagnosis of ADHD. A second evaluation completed in 2002 noted ADHD as well as depressive symptoms, including sadness, decreased appetite, loss of interest in pleasurable activities, fatigue, and poor concentration.

Complicating D.O.'s problems was a 15-year-old brother who was physically bigger and much more accomplished at school than D.O. This brother frequently tormented and intimidated D.O.

Parent responses to the Child Behavior Checklist were consistent with significant problems on the withdrawn, attention problems, and delinquent behavior scales. The Conners' Parent hyperactivity/impulsivity index was above the 98th percentile, reflecting marked problems with failing to finish things, being inattentive, and being easily frustrated in his efforts. Interestingly, D.O. was described as only mildly impulsive and not particularly restless.

Reports from D.O.'s teachers noted mild difficulty with inattentive behavior. However, only one teacher felt that this problem was excessive. Teachers described D.O. as not a behavior problem and frequently overlooked because he did not misbehave or contribute in class.

D.O. was an adolescent of average size and appearance. He drove himself to the evaluation, meeting his parents for the intake session. His affect appeared flat. He did not smile very often. Nonetheless, he was cooperative and completed all tasks presented.

Intellectual assessment placed D.O. in the gifted range, at the 98th percentile. D.O.'s performance on a computerized measure of sustained attention demonstrated a tendency to become more inconsistent as time passed. Numerous indices of impulsive responding were noted. D.O.'s academic skills appeared advanced, although his nonphonetic spelling, rote mathematical knowledge, and written language skills (grammar, punctuation, etc.) appeared in the average range at best. From a personality perspective, D.O. seemed to perceive himself as fairly well functioning. His personality style was consistent with someone who may act impulsively but who is not experiencing any specific emotional problems. Nonetheless, D.O. acknowledged that he was beginning to feel less confident that he could succeed at school and progress successfully to college.

D.O.'s history and current presentation were consistent with a diagnosis of ADHD-I. As he matured, D.O. demonstrated significantly fewer problems with overt hyperactivity and impulsivity. It was clear that, from an early age, D.O. was often able to use his gifted intellect to compensate in many situations. At the time of assessment, D.O. did not demonstrate enough symptoms for a diagnosis of depression or anxiety. Concern existed, however, about D.O.'s lowered academic self-esteem as well as D.O.'s perception of his family, specifically his relationship with his younger brother, as a source and focus of tension.

D.O.'s parents were given additional information about ADHD in adolescents. They were also referred to a number of resources about facilitating parent and adolescent communication. It was recommended that D.O.'s physician once again consider the use of stimulant medication if D.O. expressed an interest in participating in this form of treatment. An effort was made to ensure that D.O. understood his assets as well as his liabilities. The use of a computer, calculator, and possibly an academic coach to assist with complex assignments and school problems was recommended. Finally, it was recommended that D.O. participate in short-term counseling, picking specific goals, such as improving his performance in a specific class or his relationship with sibling. D.O.'s personality style was such that he was unlikely to be interested in or willing to participate in long-term counseling, given his perception that if left alone he was capable of working out his own problems without support.

CASE 4: ADHD, LD, AND LOW SELF-ESTEEM

J.N., a 16-year-old 10th-grade male, was referred because of a history of inattention and poor school performance and increasing concerns about social relations and self-esteem. J.N. was the third of his parents' five children. Sibling history was significant for learning and language problems. Family history was significant for ADHD.

J.N.'s medical and developmental history noted recurrent ear infections and placement of pressure equalization tubes. J.N. had a history of lazy eye and suffered from hay fever. J.N. received surgery in second grade to correct his visual problem. For this reason he repeated the second grade. From an early age, J.N. was described as not taking enough time to complete tasks appropriately, struggling with instructions, and showing poor early academic achievement.

J.N. had never received special education assistance despite his struggles with school, and his parents reported he was at least two grade levels behind in basic academic subjects. J.N. had also never received counseling or any kind of medication for attention or emotional problems.

Within the home setting, J.N. was described as being in frequent and escalating conflict with siblings. Socially, he appeared rather isolated, and he had never had a best friend. He spent the majority of his time at home watching television or playing Nintendo. He worked well for short-term but not for long-term rewards. He passed his driver's license examination after a number of failures.

The one shining light in J.N.'s life was his exceptional soccer playing. He played on a competitive team. His coach noted, however, that at times J.N. was inattentive. J.N. had also earned his Eagle Scout badge in Boy Scouts.

J.N.'s parents noted that he was increasingly hesitant to try new activities that he felt he could not succeed at. He complained of boredom and difficulty finding pleasurable activities. Nonetheless, J.N.'s parents felt they had a positive relationship with him.

Parental questionnaires revealed significant scores on the Child Behavior Checklist for attention, withdrawn, and delinquent problems. On the Conners' questionnaire, the *DSM-IV* index was above the 98th percentile as a result of J.N.'s restlessness, distractibility, inattention, and inability to finish tasks. Moderate problems were described with excitability and impulsivity.

Assessment at school was completed when J.N. was in eighth grade and failing. Intellectual assessment detected borderline verbal skills but average nonverbal abilities. Educational assessment noted well-below-average reading, math, and written language skills. Teacher reports at that time consistently described inattentiveness and difficulty completing schoolwork. Nonetheless, no steps were taken at school to provide remedial or compensatory activities.

J.N.'s 10th-grade report card listed a C– average. J.N. was failing one class and receiving D grades in three others. Teacher reports on standardized questionnaires described moderate problems with academic performance, primarily reflecting difficulty in working independently and persisting on and completing tasks and an increased need for the teacher's attention and time. J.N. was not described as significantly disruptive but was noted to be somewhat isolated socially.

J.N. was an adolescent of average appearance. He was seen for two assessment sessions. As the assessment progressed, J.N. appeared to become more fatigued, stressed, and apathetic about what he perceived to be his failure. He was rather distant with the examiner, rarely initiating conversation. His approach to the test tasks was mildly impulsive.

Structured assessment yielded a Wechsler Verbal IQ of 76, a Performance IQ of 91, and a Full-Scale IQ of 83. J.N.'s pattern of weak verbal and stronger nonverbal skills was consistent with previous assessment. Verbally, J.N. performed best on tasks requiring rote memory and much weaker on tasks requiring reasoning and judgment. Further assessment of J.N.'s memory, however, reflected very poor rote recall. His performance on a computerized measure of attention and the ability to inhibit impulsive responding was consistent for individuals struggling with attentional skills.

Academic screening noted well-below-average spelling abilities and reading skills at an early seventh-grade level at best. J.N.'s written language skills were also quite poor.

A qualitative description of J.N.'s academic performance noted retrieval problems and label difficulty (e.g., a/the). These problems were not serious but did affect his accuracy in reading. They did not appear to affect his comprehension as much.

He was somewhat better at reading in context than at reading words in isolation. J.N. also tended to transpose words as he read, reflecting rote sequential weakness. His visual processing for reading appeared adequate, but J.N. was not an efficient reader. He tended to omit or insert words as well as to miss word endings. He recognized words that he saw but occasionally made errors because of his tendency to predict by context. He did not always fully comprehend what he read, likely due to the effort he needed to expend to decode the material. His visual memory for spelling was weak. His phonic spelling for short words was adequate but for longer words was poor. J.N. struggled to sequence the sounds of multisyllable words. Finally, J.N.'s conceptual knowledge of mathematics was good. Surprisingly, his rote knowledge of number facts was also good.

J.N.'s cognitive and academic test data and history were somewhat difficult to integrate. On measures of intellectual skills, J.N. scored poorest on tasks requiring semantic knowledge and concept formation and performed better on rote tasks, such as general information. On the memory battery, he scored better on ability to recall meaningful information but worse on rote recall. The overall pattern reflected some type of auditory processing, rote memory, or sequential language disability. Further consultation with a speech language pathologist yielded data consistent with this hypothesis. J.N.'s problems appeared to be exacerbated by a history of inattentive, impulsive behavior.

Although J.N. denied excessive feelings of depression or anxiety, he acknowledged perceiving that other students were able to do things more easily than he could and that other people were happier in their lives. J.N. was rather limited in his responses during the clinical interview. His personality style was that of an adolescent who often felt misunderstood and unappreciated. J.N. seemed to expect criticism and feared condemnation by others. In response, he appeared to be acting more and more defensively and precipitating the reaction he feared and anticipated. J.N. seemed increasingly to expect that things would not work out well for him. He appeared to lack confidence in himself and others. Overall, J.N. was having a more painful early adolescence than others.

Despite the lack of early identification, J.N.'s history and functioning was consistent with a diagnosis of ADHD. Retrospectively, J.N.'s presentation at the time appeared consistent with a *DSM-IV* diagnosis of ADHD-I, although a history of impulsive and at times restless behavior had been reported. Structured testing reflected J.N.'s language-based LD, which affected auditory processing, rote memory, and sequential linguistic skills. These weaknesses resulted in a pattern of poor reading, spelling, and written language abilities. In addition, although J.N.'s presentation and history did not meet the symptomatic cutoff for a mood or anxiety disorder, it was clear that he was struggling to adjust emotionally to the demands of adolescence.

Short-term counseling was recommended as a way to help J.N. begin focusing on his strengths and develop a clear sense of his identity and future goals. Concerns were raised that J.N.'s fragile trust might be easily shaken, resulting in a reluctance to invest in counseling. The importance of building a trusting relationship between J.N. and a counselor was strongly emphasized. It was also recommended that J.N. and his family review with their physician the risks and benefits of a trial of stimulant medication as part of J.N.'s treatment plan. Private academic tutoring was recommended to teach J.N. basic school success skills (e.g., note taking, organization, etc.) as well as to improve his reading decoding accuracy, comprehension, and written language skills. J.N. was urged to use a computer to complete assignments as often as possible. Additional information about ADHD was given to J.N. and his parents. It was also strongly recommended that J.N. continue playing soccer, as this activity was a significant builder of self-esteem. Finally, given J.N.'s history and pattern of test data, careful transition planning was recommended to help J.N. to begin examining future vocational opportunities.

CASE 5: ADHD AND LD

A.G., a 15-year-old ninth-grade female, demonstrated a history of immature social behavior, developmental delay, poor academic achievement, and complaints of inattentive behavior. Limited information was available concerning A.G.'s biological father. He had never met A.G., but he was reportedly a good student and subsequently became a physician. A.G.'s mother married just after A.G. was born. The marriage lasted 8 years. Concerns were raised about A.G.'s having been sexually abused by her stepfather. A.G.'s current adoptive father and mother have been married for 7 years. Maternal family history was positive for ADHD, anxiety, and LD.

A.G. was reported to have been cyanotic at birth and requiring incubator care. During her first 2 years of life, she experienced multiple medical complications and was frequently hospitalized. A.G.'s pituitary and thyroid glands were reported to be underdeveloped, for which A.G. was receiving a number of medications.

A.G.'s achievement of developmental milestones was always slow. She was retained in kindergarten and received special education services throughout her academic career. In contrast to her slow development, there were no complaints about disruptive behavior. A.G. was reported to relate well to adults but to be extremely immature and to lack insight in interactions with peers, resulting in increased social isolation.

Within the home setting, A.G. was described as impulsive, inattentive, and restless. She did not work well for long-term rewards. Responses to parental questionnaires yielded elevations on the Child Behavior Checklist for the scales of somatic complaints, anxious/depressed, social, thought, and attention problems. A.G.'s Conners' Parent DSM-IV index was above the 98th percentile. Situational problems were noted within both the home and public settings.

A.G. was an attractive, neatly groomed adolescent. A.G.'s conversational skills were limited. She was calm, attentive, and responsive. She appeared to distrust her abilities. Nonetheless, with prompting, she was willing to attempt all tasks presented.

Standardized assessment detected weaker nonverbal than verbal abilities and an overall level of intellectual skill in the mildly handicapped range. Nonetheless, A.G. performed within the average range on tasks of verbal reasoning and vocabulary, struggling with comprehension. A review of past records revealed intellectual scores in the borderline range. Academic data placed A.G. in the low-average range for rote skills such as work reading but below the 2nd percentile for comprehension and written language. Responses to teachers' questionnaires noted fairly consistent work completion problems in more academically demanding classes as well as inattentive behavior and social isolation.

Measures of memory skills detected borderline abilities, with near-average ability to recall meaningful information but great difficulty in recalling rote, repetitive information. Performance on a computerized measure, even when compared to a lower developmental level, reflected marked problems in sustaining attention and inhibiting impulsive responding.

A.G.'s history and data reflected significant weaknesses in verbal and nonverbal conceptual abilities. A.G. solved problems very inefficiently. She did not appear to learn well across trials or to initiate or develop strategies. She appeared to lack an internal framework to consistently guide her behavior. Conceptual problems revealed her very poor understanding of mathematics. A.G. attempted rote solutions in math when she could recall them but used them without any conceptual insight. Her interpretive comprehension was very poor. She struggled to identify the main point, draw conclusions, and generalize when reading. She did not appear to connect ideas or to put information into hierarchies well.

A.G.'s responses to self-report measures did not suggest marked problems with hopelessness, unhappiness, or helplessness. In contrast, she reported significant feelings of anxiety, including difficulty making up her mind, worrying about herself and others, and believing that she was a nervous person.

A.G.'s personality appeared, not surprisingly, to be marked by strong dependency needs and anxious seeking of attention and reassurance from others as well as intense fear of separation from those providing support. A.G.'s behavior could be unpredictable, irritable, and pessimistic. Her interpersonal insight appeared limited. This problem resulted in A.G.'s being taken advantage of by a number of friends as well as potential boyfriends.

A.G.'s overall profile was consistent with some unknown organic etiology for her problems. Oxygen deprivation at birth appeared to be the most plausible explanation, combined with A.G.'s early complicated medical history. From a developmental perspective, A.G. demonstrated at best borderline intellectual skills with fairly significant verbal and nonverbal conceptual weaknesses. As life had become more complex, A.G. appeared to struggle more. The pattern of conceptual weakness with significant visual perceptual difficulties resulted in significant mathematical problems. In contrast, A.G.'s rote reading skills seemed adequate, though her comprehension was limited.

Finally, A.G.'s history presented symptoms of inattentiveness, impulsivity, and hyper-activity consistent enough to meet the *DSM-IV-TR* diagnostic criteria for ADHD Combined Type (ADHD-C).

A trial of stimulant medication resulted in parent and teacher reports of improved behavior. A.G. also began working with a counselor on a regular basis in an effort to gain support and improve her insight. Continued academic support was recommended in order to help A.G. consider a variety of vocations in planning for post–high school training. Finally, A.G.'s parents were given additional insight into her daily functioning and suggestions for communicating, disciplining, and interacting with A.G. effectively.

CASE 6: LD AND ADHD

S.K., a 27-year-old male, was self-referred because of a reported history of learning and attention problems. S.K. reported having had lifetime difficulty with reading, listening, focusing, following through, and being impulsive. It was his impression that he had developed compensatory strategies and had a stimulating lifestyle. S.K. reported par-ticipating in competitive mogul skiing and motorcycle racing. He described numerous head injuries without loss of consciousness or serious repercussions. He felt, however, that he had problems with memory and financial difficulties that were secondary to his attentional problems. S.K. reported five speeding violations over the past 3 years and two automobile accidents over 8 years.

S.K. was currently employed as a sales representative and skiing coach. He gradu-ated from high school with a C average and reported receiving special education services. S.K. denied a family history of psychiatric problems but reported that his grandfather had had ADHD.

S.K.'s responses to adult self-report ADHD questionnaires yielded scores beyond the clinical cutoff. S.K.'s parents completed a number of retrospective questionnaires and described S.K. as a child and adolescent who was unable to finish tasks, hyperac-tive, fidgety, and inattentive. S.K. was also described as having social problems and LD. S.K.'s mother described his childhood learning problems as related to memory and labeling difficulty. As a young child, S.K. was in "perpetual motion" and struggled with early academic achievement. A speech pathologist and family friend described S.K. as a child as presenting with severe word-finding problems, difficulty following multiple commands, problems with reading comprehension, impulsivity, hyperactivity, and inat-tention. Nonetheless, S.K. had never been treated for ADHD in childhood.

Structured assessment yielded a Wechsler Full-Scale IQ of 91 (Verbal IQ = 83; Performance IQ = 106). When compared to individuals of his age and academic his-tory, S.K.'s nonverbal abilities were rated above average and his verbal abilities nearly 1.5 standard deviations below average. This pattern was amplified on the memory battery on which S.K. performed below the 1st percentile verbally but at the 60th percentile nonverbally. Further, S.K.'s fund of verbal and nonverbal information was poor, which was not surprising, given his academic struggles. Neuropsychological screening also revealed problems with reasoning, judgment, and concept formation. Academic assessment reflected low-average basic academic skills, with spelling at well below 1st-percentile ability.

The pattern of S.K.'s errors when reading and spelling reflected basic weaknesses in perceiving and recognizing phonemic sounds of language. S.K. spelled *enter* as *intire*, *material* as *miteral*, and *recognize* as *recagnise*. When reading, he used a sight-word approach. Analysis of mathematical errors revealed that S.K. did not know basic mathematical facts.

From a personality perspective, S.K. had an easygoing and nonconforming style. He appeared to seek challenges and risks with a tendency toward exhibitionist and contentious behavior. S.K. seemed to be an individual seeking praise and attention and who was easily bored. Underlying S.K.'s basic personality appeared to be a very strong, competitive, and power-oriented attitude, an air of self-assurance, and a sometimes careless indifference to the feelings of others.

S.K.'s history and presentation met the diagnostic profile for ADHD-I. Although somewhat impulsive, S.K.'s presentation did not meet 6 of the 9 criteria necessary for the hyperactive-impulse component of this diagnosis. S.K.'s history also reflected a lifetime pattern of developmental impairments comprising weak verbal abilities and above-average nonverbal skills. The data were consistent with severe verbal memory problems and rote verbal LD.

It was recommended that a psychiatric consultation be considered to evaluate the potential risks and benefits of psychotropic medication as part of S.K.'s treatment plan. S.K. was given additional resources about ADHD in adulthood. Although S.K. might have benefited from short-term counseling, he made it very clear during the assessment that he was interested in diagnosis but not necessarily in treatment.

CASE 7: ADHD AND LD

J.H., a 43-year-old male, was self-referred because of complaints of short-term memory problems and inattention. J.H. denied significant childhood problems but reported that his academic performance at school had been unacceptable. He recalled being left back one year in elementary school. He also described being picked on by others.

J.H. had never married. Immediate family history was positive for ADHD in a sibling and in his father. J.H. had completed a 4-year college degree. He recalled being bored at school. He graduated with a B– grade point average. He was employed in sales for a number of years, then as a bus driver, and at the time of assessment in telephone mutual-fund sales.

J.H. denied a history of substance abuse or previous psychiatric treatment. He reported receiving four or five traffic citations for moving violations over the past 10 years. He also reported five automobile accidents.

J.H.'s responses to the Brown questionnaire yielded a score above the clinical cutoff. J.H. acknowledged problems paying attention, initiating activities, tracking when reading, remembering certain kinds of information easily, procrastinating, and being easily distracted. In contrast, J.H.'s responses to the Wender questionnaire yielded a score below the clinical cutoff because J.H. denied problems with restlessness, irritability, or stress. J.H.'s parents reported that as a child, J.H. was easily distracted, did not follow instructions, and had difficulty sustaining attention. Their responses were very consistent with the *DSM-IV* description of ADHD.

J.H. was an adult of average size and appearance. During the interview he was very pleasant. During structured testing he showed signs of increasing stress and anxiety. His thoughts appeared logical, focused, and relevant.

Assessment yielded average intellectual scores for a college graduate male of J.H.'s age. Nonetheless, a significant degree of subtest scatter was noted; J.H. experienced marked problems on simple rote measures requiring sustained attention but performed well above average on measures of general information, vocabulary, verbal reasoning, and comprehension. Administration of a memory battery detected 7th-percentile verbal memory skills but 77th-percentile nonverbal memory skills. Despite an exceptionally good fund of verbal information and knowledge, J.H. struggled to process, recall, and, over the short term, retain meaningful and nonmeaningful verbal information. These test data appeared to confirm J.H.'s lifetime complaints of short-term memory difficulty. Brief academic screening yielded above-average reading but below-average spelling and arithmetic performance, primarily due to rote rather than conceptual errors.

J.H. had no significant complaints of depression or anxiety. His personality was that of someone concerned with public appearance, wanting to be seen by others as composed, virtuous, and conventional. Such individuals often downplay distressing problems in their lives.

Although requested, J.H.'s school transcripts were never provided. J.H. also declined to participate in further assessment. Based on the data generated, J.H. appeared to have struggled from an early age with a rote LD that continued to plague him through college and in vocational endeavors. Further discussion with J.H. revealed that he had moved from sales to bus driving because of missed promotions resulting from his poor memory. J.H. seemed to have been able to use his good intellectual skills to compensate for his rote memory problems, but he continued to be painfully aware of his difficulties. Further, J.H.'s history and current presentation appeared consistent with the *DSM-IV* categorization of ADHD-I.

J.H. reported that a brief trial of stimulant medication produced improved memory and attention at work. A number of texts about ADHD as well as texts to assist with organization and memory were recommended. Finally, as J.H. was preparing to take a number of examinations to progress in his current vocation, short-term consultation with an educational therapist was recommended in order to provide J.H. with additional study skills and memory strategies.

CASE 8: ADHD AND LD

S.C., an almost 17-year-old male 11th grader, had a history of inattentiveness, poor school performance, and a reported period of depression. S.C. was adopted by his physician father and mother. No information was available about his biological family. S.C.'s older adopted sister had struggled with chronic depression.

From an early age, S.C. was hyperactive and inattentive. He had a childhood history of chronic headaches of unknown etiology. Stimulant medication was initiated in first grade with reported benefits but also side effects, including increased headache. Stimulants had been attempted intermittently throughout S.C.'s childhood and adolescent years.

S.C.'s parents reported that as he reached adolescence, he became markedly less hyperactive and impulsive but was still inattentive. Despite his performance problems at school, he was described as an average student. In junior high school, he struggled socially and was ostracized by a small group of disruptive males. S.C.'s parents felt that he had never recovered socially or emotionally from that experience, and in high school, he continued to be extremely isolated socially. S.C.'s parents noted during the previous 6 months an increase in withdrawn, apathetic, and seemingly unhappy behavior.

A year prior to the assessment, S.C. was diagnosed with depression by a local psychologist. Short-term therapy appeared to yield some immediate benefits, but S.C. was not interested in continuing counseling. During this series of counseling sessions, S.C. raised concerns about possible homosexuality but decided that this was something he feared rather than something he felt.

Questionnaires completed by S.C.'s parents noted significant scale elevations on the Child Behavior Checklist for somatic complaints, social problems, anxious/depressed, and attention problems. On the hyperkinesis index of the Conners' questionnaire, S.C. was above the 98th percentile. He was described as at times argumentative with family members but in general socially isolated. Responses by S.C., as well as by his parents, to the Brown questionnaire yielded scores above the clinical cutoff suggestive of problems with inattention.

Standardized questionnaires completed by S.C.'s teachers noted his social isolation and difficulty completing schoolwork but no other disruptive or withdrawn complaints. Teachers noted that S.C. appeared polite and insightful and that he was not a discipline problem. A review of past group achievement tests noted S.C.'s very weak spelling and math computation scores together with above-average vocabulary, listening comprehension, and language scores.

S.C. was a slightly overweight adolescent wearing loose-fitting clothing. He was pleasant, and he warmed up quickly during the two evaluative sessions. He appeared to distrust his abilities while working and made frequent negative self-statements.

Intellectually, S.C. performed on the Wechsler with a Verbal IQ of 95, a Performance IQ of 125, and a Full-Scale IQ of 106. S.C.'s nonverbal skills were markedly better than his verbal abilities. He struggled on tasks that required sustained and divided attention. A brief memory battery detected very good logical memory skills and weaker rote memory skills. S.C.'s reproduction and spontaneous recall of a complex figure was in the 95th percentile, reflecting his exceptional perceptual abilities. Performance on a computerized battery did not reflect problems in sustaining attention or managing impulses.

S.C.'s self-report did not reflect significant complaints of anxiety or depression. S.C. noted, however, that he felt other people were happier than he was. He was open and introspective during the clinical interview. His personality was that of an adolescent who tended to be too self-critical and self-deprecating. S.C. appeared to have a long history of social awkwardness and hesitation in dealing with others. Further interviews reflected S.C.'s somewhat obsessive worries about his social deficits and academic failures. His personality style was such that he rarely acted out or displayed resentment. He had adopted a strategy of fading into the social background, assuming a passive role. As a consequence, S.C. had become more and more peripheral in social interactions, drifting further into a detached, ineffective life pattern. On a positive note, although S.C. described social interactions as painful, he clearly reported a desire to improve his social life, and he appeared to be a sensitive, empathetic person willing to help others in need.

S.C.'s early history and current symptoms appeared consistent with the *DSM-III-R* diagnosis of ADHD. The constellation of symptoms was consistent with the *DSM-IV* categorization of ADHD-I. From a cognitive perspective, S.C. demonstrated exceptional nonverbal, or right-hemisphere, skills and average verbal abilities. The overall pattern appeared to reflect mild rote LD with academic achievement further impaired by S.C.'s inattentiveness and declining effort and participation in school. S.C.'s emotional history and current data revealed problems on the depression dimension, with a categorical *DSM-IV* diagnosis consistent with mild dysthymia and increasing social avoidance.

A course of psychotherapy was initiated with S.C., initially providing a high level of sympathy and understanding and patiently working to develop a trusting relationship. With support, S.C.'s attitude and affect improved. His willingness to take social risks increased, and he slowly developed a social network. His participation in school improved as well. By his choice, S.C. decided to delay the initiation of any type of psychotropic medication. S.C., with his therapist, began exploring post–high school vocational and academic options.

CASE 9: ADHD AND RIGHT-HEMISPHERE DISORDER

S.F., an almost 19-year-old high school graduate male, had a history of inconsistent school performance and social isolation. S.F.'s fraternal twin had a history of ADHD but was academically competent. S.F.'s family history was positive for LD and depression. S.F.'s medical history was unremarkable, although he had received pressure equalization tubes twice at a young age and had suffered from a number of allergies. He had been nocturnally enuretic through 7 years of age. At 13 and 17 years of age, brief trials of antidepressants were attempted with little reported benefit.

S.F. had a history of awkward fine and large motor skills, delayed motor skill development, and poor handwriting. S.F. was reported to have achieved well in reading and spelling but to have struggled with mathematical skills from a young age. He received special education services periodically throughout his academic career. He required support through high school but was able to graduate. He earned marginal grades during one semester in a community college. S.F. decided to join the workforce full time temporarily and was employed as a checker at a large department store.

S.F.'s parents described him as having poor judgment and not working well for rewards. Nonetheless, he was not described as having behavior or disruptive problems growing up. S.F.'s parents noted that he had always been somewhat isolated socially. Their responses to the Child Behavior Checklist yielded scores in the clinically significant range for social, attention, and anxious/depression scales. On the Conners' questionnaire, S.F. obtained a *DSM-IV* index above the 98th percentile. He was reported as able to initiate social interaction but as rather isolated in general. He had two childhood friends with whom he had maintained a reasonably close relationship. S.F.'s and his parents' responses to the Brown questionnaire yielded scores above the clinical cutoff range suggestive of inattentiveness.

At age 14, an in-depth psychoeducational evaluation had been completed. S.F. obtained a Wechsler Verbal IQ of 114, a Performance IQ of 98, and a Full-Scale IQ of 107. S.F.'s verbal skills, including fund of information, reasoning, and vocabulary, appeared well above average.

On the Woodcock-Johnson Psycho-Educational Battery, cognitive cluster, S.F.'s oral abilities were scored at the 99th percentile with visual perception scores below the 20th percentile. Academically, S.F. at the time scored at the 99th percentile for reading but at the 54th percentile for mathematics. A diagnosis of LD related to organizational and visual-motor skills was made.

A review of S.F.'s academic file noted group achievement test scores consistently above average in reading but below average in mathematics. ACT testing (college entrance), completed 2 years before, measured 73rd-percentile reading skills, 60th-percentile English skills, and 10th-percentile mathematical skills in comparison to college-bound high school students.

S.F. was a soft-spoken young adult of average size and appearance. He related well to the examiner and was cooperative and responsive. Brief neuropsychological screening with S.F. indicated clear and consistent right-hemisphere problems related to rote and conceptual non-verbal skills. S.F.'s performance on a computerized attention battery revealed difficulty with perceptual sensitivity, mild impulsiveness, and difficulty in sustaining attention.

During the interview, S.F. was quite open and responsive with the examiner. He described his limited social life and while discussing dating noted that it was often difficult for him to understand "what girls like." He spoke fairly introspectively and was clearly frustrated by his academic and social problems. He reported enjoying his current job but felt that it was not something he could make into a career.

S.F.'s personality appeared characteristic of individuals with a right-hemisphere weakness. He was self-critical and self-deprecating. S.F. was rather apprehensive, socially oversensitive, awkward, shy, hesitant, and uncomfortable when interacting with others. S.F. appeared to be rather sad and reported recurrent anxieties about school and work. A pervasive disharmony of mood appeared increasingly to characterize his daily functioning. Concerned with social rebuff, S.F. was unlikely to act out or become openly resentful. He appeared to lack initiative and competitiveness and struggled to achieve the level of autonomous behavior required for adolescents entering adulthood. He perceived himself as rather weak, fragile, and ineffective. Not surprisingly, given his excellent verbal intellect, S.F. reported feeling confused and uncertain about his life direction, believing that others had a much clearer sense of their identity and goals. On the positive side, S.F. presented as gentle and compassionate, accepting others regardless of their frailties or vulnerabilities and willing to provide help and support when needed. He viewed his family as a support and a resource.

S.F.'s cognitive, academic, and emotional presentation was consistent with right-hemisphere weakness. Individuals with this condition struggle with social interaction in nondisruptive ways and end up being neglected. They struggle to read and interpret social cues effectively, demonstrate a passive pattern of inattentive and disorganized behavior, and are prone to emotionally distressing rather than disruptive behavioral symptoms. S.F. also demonstrated the visual perceptual and relative mathematical weakness consistent with nonverbal, or right-hemisphere, LD.

From a categorical perspective, S.F.'s history was consistent with the *DSM-IV* diagnosis of ADHD-I. In addition, his emotional functioning was consistent with a diagnosis of dysthymia and increasing adjustment problems reflecting mixed emotional features.

S.F. and his parents were given additional insight into and information about S.F.'s disabilities and how the disabilities had affected his past history and current life functioning. Psychotherapy was initiated in an effort to help S.F. begin to focus on his assets and thus develop a more effective set of coping skills. Because S.F. hesitated to make what might be considered a fuss over his problems, fearing that a therapist might be angry or rejecting if he complained too bitterly, initial progress in therapy was slow though clearly positive. S.F. was also referred for a psychiatric consultation because he had decided to consider the potential benefits of medication as part of a treatment plan. S.F. planned to continue working for the present and considered applying for supportive services for learning-disabled students as he prepared to reenter college.

CASE 10: ADHD, MULTIPLE SCLEROSIS, AND GENERALIZED ANXIETY

R.B., a 46-year-old male college graduate, was self-referred because of reported increasing difficulty with memory, attention, and stress. At age 34, R.B. had been diagnosed with multiple sclerosis. He expressed concern that over the past few years he had been having worsening problems with memory, resulting in a demotion at work from supervisor to computer data entry technician.

R.B. recalled a childhood history suggestive of ADHD. He described engaging in high-risk behavior, being in multiple accidents, and displaying inattentiveness. He recalled obtaining B grades in high school, nonetheless, completing an associate's degree and finally a 4-year degree with a B average. His recent agreed-on demotion at work resulted from his inability to master the skills necessary to supervise others on a new computer system.

R.B. recalled multiple accidents as a child, including being buried in a cave-in at 11 years of age and nearly dying from lack of oxygen. He reported being legally blind in his left eye and having a history of mild hearing loss secondary to the multiple sclerosis. R.B. denied an extended family history of psychiatric problems but noted that an uncle committed suicide for unknown reasons.

R.B. and his first wife were married for 23 years. Their five children had all done fairly well at school. He noted that one child had possibly had a history of ADHD.

Symptomatically, R.B. described having occasional migraines, ringing in his ears, and difficulty with short-term and immediate memory. These symptoms caused him many daily problems at work and at home. Responses to the Brown questionnaire by R.B. and his wife yielded scores above the clinical cutoff, suggestive of problems with inattentiveness in adulthood. R.B. and his wife noted his difficulty in sustaining activities, tendency to leave things unfinished, and increasing difficulty in initiating activities. It must be noted, however, that on this questionnaire, both R.B. and his wife's scores were extremely high, strongly suggesting compounding psychiatric problems contributing to R.B.'s attention difficulties. On retrospective questionnaires, R.B.'s mother recalled that as a child, he was impulsive, inattentive, and rather hyperactive.

R.B. was a moderately obese individual of otherwise normal appearance. He appeared to be mildly dysnomic and had difficulty following instructions during structured testing. During testing he demonstrated a moderate degree of performance anxiety, at one point reporting that he felt overwhelmed. He appeared to distrust his abilities. It was clear that he struggled to sequence, detail, and reason.

Extended neuropsychological assessment yielded intellectual scores in the low-average range for individuals for R.B.'s demographic background. His greatest problems involved more complex abstract tasks, such as the Comprehension and Similarities subtests of the Wechsler. Intratest scatter on all tasks appeared to reflect potentially better or previously better functioning. R.B. performed best on simple rote tasks. His nonverbal memory skills appeared to be stronger that his verbal memory skills overall. R.B. obtained a standard score equivalent to the 87th percentile on the Peabody Picture Vocabulary Test, strongly suggestive of better intellectual functioning in the past. General academic assessment reflected above-average academic skills, with mathematical skills at the 84th percentile and reading skills at the 77th percentile. R.B.'s self-report on the Beck was consistent with mild depression. He appeared to be experiencing a prolonged period of futility and dejection.

R.B.'s personality appeared to be characterized by anxious dependency, the persistent seeking of reassurance from others, and the expectation that things were likely to get worse. R.B. appeared to be an individual using guilt and self-condemnation as means of coping with stress. His sense of helplessness appeared to be strong. Increasingly, however, R.B. appeared to be turning to anger and resentment about his life situation as ways of dealing with his emotional distress.

R.B.'s history and presentation produced enough data to be consistent with the DSM-IV-TR diagnosis of ADHD. However, R.B.'s problems with inattentiveness appeared to be compounded by emotional and cognitive difficulties. R.B. demonstrated difficulty simultaneously processing multiple sources of information, a slow speed of information processing, and intermittent problems with reasoning. These problems appeared to be exacerbated in part by R.B.'s anxious, hesitant response. These types of frontal lobe cognitive weaknesses were uncharacteristic, given R.B.'s history. R.B.'s difficulty tracking the ebb and flow of changing environmental or nonverbal stimuli, his difficulty tracking efficiently through instructions, and his previously mentioned difficulties appeared consistent with a small population of multiple sclerosis patients. In the majority of multiple sclerosis cases, physical symptoms manifest themselves long before cognitive or behavioral symptoms. However, when cognitive symptoms are manifested, they often present as low cognitive efficiency and difficulty with frontal lobe functions, including abstraction, concept formation, judgment, mental speed, and, for some individuals, concentration.

Finally, from an emotional perspective, it was not surprising that R.B. was experiencing increasing unhappiness and stress, given his disease, current life situation, and forced vocational change.

Based on the assessment data, R.B.'s physician initiated a trial of stimulant medication. R.B. reported marked benefits at work. R.B. and his wife noted marked improvements in his daily functioning at home as well. R.B. was referred for short-term counseling so that he could learn stress management skills. Based on what he perceived as a discriminatory change in his vocational status due to his disease, R.B. also initiated arbitration with his employer.

CASE 11: ADHD, ANXIETY, AND DYSTHYMIA

G.H., a 47-year-old male, was self-referred because of concerns about ADHD. G.H. reported childhood symptoms of inattentiveness and difficulty with concentration. He noted that he had difficulty learning, forgot things, and had problems with organization and setting priorities.

G.H. graduated from high school with a C average and received a bachelor's degree in botany with a C+ average. G.H. recalled school as being very difficult. G.H. had worked for a number of years as a civilian employee of the air force.

G.H. denied a family history of psychiatric problems. He noted, however, that as a child, he angered easily and had engaged in antisocial behavior, including shooting out streetlights. G.H. recalled adolescence as particularly painful.

He reported a history of frequent motor accidents, including a spinal injury at age 35 that required two surgeries. G.H. also noted head injuries from previous motorcycle accidents, falls from trees as a child, and parachute jumping in the military. G.H. reported receiving approximately 10 traffic citations for moving violations and having been in three automobile accidents.

G.H.'s psychiatric history revealed a diagnosis of depression a number of years earlier and a trial of Prozac. He reported that the medication had seemed to be beneficial, but for reasons that were unclear, he did not follow through with medication treatment.

G.H. and his first wife had been married for 7 years. They had two children. The eldest, 4 years of age, had been recently diagnosed with ADHD. G.H. noted that interacting daily with the children was extremely stressful.

G.H.'s responses to self-report instruments were much higher than the clinical cutoff suggestive of ADHD. The overall pattern appeared to indicate symptoms of inattentiveness, compounded by problems with stress, anxiety, and depression. G.H.'s wife described her husband as being forgetful in daily activities and as having problems with organization, following instructions, and being inattentive. Nonetheless, she described these problems as being much less severe than her husband did. G.H.'s mother on retrospective questionnaires noted that G.H. had had difficulty concentrating and was impulsive and hyperactive as a child. Although G.H. reported symptoms of unhappiness, his responses to the Beck Depression Inventory did not cross into the clinically significant range.

Brief cognitive screening placed G.H. in the average range intellectually. Basic academic skills also appeared in the average range. There were no indices of specific LD.

By history and symptom presentation, G.H. clearly met the criteria for a *DSM-IV* diagnosis of ADHD. Further interviews with G.H. revealed fairly strong feelings of inadequacy, hypersensitivity to criticism, and a pattern of social inhibition. G.H.'s wife later noted that he had become more isolated from family members, choosing to not participate in family activities. G.H.'s presentation and profile, as well as his responses to personality instruments, revealed symptoms consistent with long-standing dysthymia, anxiety, and possibly the entrance into a major depressive episode.

G.H.'s physician reinitiated a trial dose of Prozac, which G.H. found beneficial. Supportive psychotherapy was strongly recommended and undertaken. G.H. and his wife were given additional information about ADHD.

CASE 12: ADHD, LD, AND ANXIETY

S.T., a 15-year-old tenth grader, was referred because of a history of inattentiveness, impulsive behavior, and poor school performance. S.T. was the youngest of his family's five children. An older sibling had experienced LD. Otherwise, there did not appear to be any extended family history of emotional or disruptive behavioral problems. S.T.'s parents were both college graduates.

S.T. had appeared to be cyanotic at birth. He was jaundiced and a number of congenital heart defects were diagnosed. These were corrected at 25 months of age. S.T.'s developmental history was unremarkable. His medical history revealed unilateral migraine occurring in clusters every few months. S.T. was also reported to be somewhat anxious and overconcerned about his health, especially his heart.

S.T.'s coordination was described as average; however, he was described as poor in athletics. His handwriting was also described as poor. S.T.'s parents recalled a pattern of his beginning each school year adequately but slowly and steadily falling behind. In 10th grade, S.T. was struggling consistently to complete schoolwork.

Socially, S.T. was somewhat isolated, without a best friend or a consistent group of friends. Within the home setting, he was described as fidgety, easily distracted, inattentive, easily frustrated, and experiencing difficulty with self-control. S.T. was described as somewhat oppositional and strong-willed. He boasted, lied, and embellished, which alienated others.

Parental questionnaires noted S.T.'s problems on the Child Behavior Checklist, including those related to anxiety, depression, social difficulty, inattentiveness, and disruptive behavior. S.T. had experimented with tobacco and alcohol. He had run away from home once. He enjoyed making small fires with a lighter. Parent responses to the Conners' questionnaire placed S.T. above the 98th percentile on the *DSM-IV* index. A variety of situational problems were described.

In general, S.T.'s teachers described him as inattentive, impulsive, and hyperactive. He was noted as having difficulty following instructions and persisting on task.

Teacher responses to the Comprehensive Teacher's Rating Scale placed S.T. below the 10th percentile in almost all classes with problems for attention span and hyperactivity. Nonetheless, none of the teachers described S.T. as purposely disruptive. All noted his difficulty completing schoolwork.

A review of S.T.'s group academic testing revealed 80th-percentile overall academic skills in ninth grade, with 88th-percentile reading, 42nd-percentile spelling, and 39th-percentile mathematical skills. S.T.'s social studies score was at the 82nd percentile and his science score at the 92nd percentile.

Individual academic testing completed with S.T. the same year detected above-average reading comprehension, average mathematical skills, and slightly below-average spelling and written language skills. A Wechsler Intelligence Scale for Children was completed when S.T. was 14.5 years of age and yielded a Verbal IQ of 123, a Performance IQ of 106, and a Full-Scale IQ of 116.

In general, S.T. was calm and pleasant during the assessment. His thoughts appeared logical and focused. He related well to the examiner. No odd mannerisms were noted.

A readministration of the Wechsler yielded a Full-Scale IQ of 113. The quality of S.T.'s responses suggested even better intellectual potential. Further, S.T. performed at the 96th percentile on the Peabody Picture Vocabulary Test. Measures of verbal memory detected excellent conceptual and general memory and weaker rote memory skills.

A screening of S.T.'s academic abilities measured average spelling and mathematical skills and above-average word reading and comprehension skills. S.T.'s written story was characterized by good themes and ideas but poor organization.

The preponderance of the data reflected S.T.'s exceptionally good conceptual verbal and nonverbal abilities. His mathematical achievement appeared to be impaired by his weakness in abstract nonverbal reasoning, compounded with his impulsive lack of attention to detail. In combination with spelling and written language weaknesses, the data appeared to reflect a mild rote memory difficulty exacerbated by S.T.'s inattentiveness.

S.T.'s responses to self-report measures placed him at the 87th percentile on the Reynolds Adolescent Depression Scale and the 83rd percentile on the Revised Children's Manifest Anxiety Scale. S.T. reported having more helpless, unhappy, and anxious thoughts than others. His personality appeared to reflect an adolescent who was excessively self-depreciating, vulnerable, and defenseless. During the interview, S.T. reported feeling misunderstood, unappreciated, and demeaned by others. He had learned to be on guard against ridicule. He seemed to find within himself few of the attributes that he admired in others. When compared to the standardization sample, his responses to the Millon Adolescent Personality Inventory reflected his strong feelings of confusion and identity difficulty. He described his family as a source of tension and conflict.

Diagnostically, S.T. demonstrated a history of high-average to likely superior intellectual skills. His history and current functioning were consistent with a diagnosis of

ADHD-C. Further, despite being exceptionally bright, S.T. demonstrated slight conceptual weaknesses with abstract nonverbal reasoning and rote memory that appeared to affect his spelling and mathematical and written language skills. From an emotional perspective, S.T. demonstrated symptoms consistent with anxiety and the possible onset of a Major Depressive Disorder.

S.T. was referred for psychiatric consultation in order to evaluate the potential benefits of psychotropic medication as part of his treatment plan. Short-term counseling was recommended as a way to help S.T. focus on his positive traits and deal in a more effective way with his anxious, helpless thoughts. S.T. and his family were given additional information about ADHD and LD and were taught strategies to improve communication and problem solving at home. Finally, it was recommended that S.T. work with an academic coach to improve his study and organizational skills. S.T.'s school counselor was also apprised of his intellectual strengths and mild learning problems so that the counselor could better help S.T. over the coming years in planning for post–high school education or vocational experiences.

CASE 13: ADHD, LD, AND ADJUSTMENT PROBLEMS

S.J., a nearly 18-year-old male, was referred because of a history of disruptive behavior and poor school performance. S.J. dropped out of school in 10th grade but was currently completing requirements for a general equivalency diploma (GED).

S.J. was the eldest of his parents' two children. His younger 14-year-old brother did not have a history of behavioral or developmental problems. S.J.'s parents were college graduates. There was a family history of alcoholism, ADHD, and the suicide of a grandparent.

S.J.'s developmental milestones were reached without difficulty. His medical history was unremarkable. School problems were first observed in second grade when S.J. appeared to begin struggling. He began receiving special education services. By 10th grade, S.J. was skipping school and flunking classes.

S.J. had a small group of friends and was dating. His parents noted a long history of inattentive, impulsive behavior. S.J. was charged at age 16 as a minor in possession of alcohol and, on turning age 17, with forging his parents' checks. He was later placed in a detention center for 14 days for probation violation. His treatment history also included residential rehabilitation in an alcohol and drug abuse facility. S.J.'s accomplishments included being an all-star baseball player for 4 years and hunting with his father on a regular basis.

Parental responses to standardized questionnaires reflected problems with anxiety, depression, inattention, and delinquent behavior. The Conners' Parent *DSM-IV* index placed S.J. at above the 98th percentile. Although S.J.'s parents described him as sensitive, they also noted that he could be quite manipulative.

Group achievement tests completed when S.J. was in 10th grade measured 21st-percentile reading skills, 32nd-percentile language skills, 19th-percentile mathematical skills, and a total battery at the 23rd percentile.

S.J. was a casually dressed, handsome adolescent. He was passively cooperative but did not appear particularly motivated during structured testing.

S.J. obtained a Full-Scale IQ of 86, a Performance IQ of 87, and a Verbal IQ of 86 on the Wechsler. Within verbal areas, S.J.'s pattern of scores was consistent with complex language processing problems. Weaknesses were noted with conceptual reasoning, verbal comprehension, and factual information. Relative strengths were noted in rote skills. S.J. performed at the 32nd percentile on the Peabody Picture Vocabulary Test and the 27th percentile on the Test of Nonverbal Intelligence. On the memory battery, he performed at the 4th percentile overall, with low-average nonverbal memory skills and below 1st-percentile verbal memory. S.J. struggled to learn and recall both simple and complex verbal information.

Academic screening placed S.J. in the average range, with slightly weaker spelling skills. His reading for accuracy was quite good, but his comprehension was barely at the fifth-grade level. The preponderance of the data indicated that S.J. had problems processing and dealing with conceptual and abstract information. It was not surprising that his academic problems grew as the demands of high school increased.

S.J.'s responses to self-report attention measures yielded a score above the clinically significant cutoff for the Brown questionnaire but below the cutoff for the Wender questionnaire. Although S.J. acknowledged symptoms of inattention and difficulty initiating activities, he denied stress-related problems. S.J.'s responses to the anxiety and depression questionnaires yielded scores above the 90th percentile. S.J. reported becoming anxious easily, worrying, and perceiving that life was unfair.

The data and personality measures reflected a late adolescent with an immediate history of moody, impulsive, and unpredictable behavior. S.J. appeared to feel misunderstood and unappreciated. Thus, he was easily offended by minor trifles and quickly provoked into angry, resentful outbursts. S.J. appeared to lack confidence in others and reported being disappointed in the responses he received. His view of himself suggested a rather aimless, undirected existence. His family was described as a source of tension and conflict. S.J.'s responses to the Millon Adolescent Clinical Inventory were consistent with those of adolescents with repeated problems as the result of impulsive behavior.

Although there was no doubt that S.J. demonstrated symptoms related to ADHD, his overall profile appeared to be compounded by a long-standing pattern of language-based LD that affected his reasoning and concept formation. Although S.J.'s rote academic skills (e.g., word reading) appeared adequate, his reading comprehension was quite limited. His overall behavioral profile at the time of assessment was consistent with a DSM-IV diagnosis of a chronic Adjustment Disorder with Mixed Disturbance of

Emotions and Conduct. There was also no doubt that S.J. demonstrated symptoms of Oppositional Defiant Disorder and at least two symptoms in the past year consistent with Conduct Disorder.

S.J. was directed to the vocational rehabilitation program in his community. Further language assessment was recommended as part of the overall vocational evaluation. S.J. and his parents were given additional information about ADHD and LD in late adolescence and adulthood. S.J. was also urged to consider counseling to help him learn strategies to manage his anger, impulsivity, and frustration. Finally, given S.J.'s endorsement of ADHD, anxious, and depressive symptoms, psychiatric consultation was suggested in order to obtain further diagnostic opinion about the potential benefits of medication treatment.

CASE 14: ADHD, PAST SUBSTANCE ABUSE, AND OBSESSIVE/COMPULSIVE PERSONALITY

R.J., a 43-year-old male with 2 years of college experience, was referred by his neurologist. R.J. was employed as a silver refinery operator. R.J. sought a medical consultation because of what he described as dissociative-like experiences beginning at age 11. R.J. described these as "the unusual sensation that he is watching a movie and that his life is not real."

R.J. reported a childhood history of inattention, overactivity, and LD. R.J.'s father committed suicide after learning he had cancer. His mother died as the result of AIDS contracted from a blood transfusion. R.J.'s four siblings had not experienced similar developmental or emotional problems.

R.J.'s life history was complex. At the time of assessment, he had been divorced for 7.5 years; his wife had declared her lesbianism and gone to live with a girlfriend. R.J.'s two daughters were in their late teens. Both had dropped out of school and were working. Neither had experienced behavioral or developmental problems.

R.J. had to consciously think about every action no matter how trivial. He related this to a machine in which every movement has to be directed and controlled. He noted that he could cover up his problems well and that most people were not aware of how hard he had to think before acting. He reported mild obsessive behaviors involving repeated checking, explaining "I have to be sure." He also reported experiencing no emotions.

R.J. had immigrated to the United States 15 years before the assessment. He worked for a number of companies producing metal products throughout his vocational history. He had never been reprimanded or discharged from work.

R.J. reported that his alcohol problems started because of his attempts to treat his feelings of disassociation. R.J. reported he had not drunk in the past 5 years.

Symptomatically, R.J. described a wide range of difficulties involving numbness in his limbs; problems with memory, dizziness, and ringing in his ears; difficulty with attention and concentration; and, at times, problems completing daily activities. R.J.'s responses to self-report attention questionnaires yielded scores well above the clinical cutoff, reflecting not only problems with inattentiveness but also problems with stress and general inefficiency in daily living. R.J.'s responses to the Beck Depression Inventory yielded a score below the clinical cutoff for mild depression.

R.J. was an average-appearing adult. He was soft spoken and mildly dysnomic. No excessive signs of anxiety were observed. Although English was R.J.'s second language, he reported speaking fluent English since childhood.

R.J. completed the Wechsler with average scores. His fund of information and rote verbal memory tested weakest; on measures of higher-order thinking (Similarities subtest), he scored well above average. R.J.'s performance on the memory battery was also average. Screening of R.J.'s academic skills revealed above-average word reading and comprehension but low-average spelling and arithmetic. His performance on arithmetic problems reflected lack of conceptual knowledge and errors in attention to detail.

R.J.'s responses to personality measures reflected an individual with a well-established need for social approval, self-condemnation, and a general naivete about psychological matters, including deficits in insight. R.J.'s personality style was that of someone inclined to blame himself, to deny strong feelings, and to fear that expressing emotion might lead to a loss of emotional control. The overall profile, however, did not appear consistent with that of an individual struggling with true dissociative problems.

R.J.'s history and current symptomatic complaints met the diagnostic criteria for ADHD. Questions existed, however, about the complication of these symptoms as the result of what appeared to be a long-standing pattern of dysthymia and Generalized Anxiety. Further, R.J.'s behavior appeared consistent with an Obsessive/Compulsive Personality.

During a brief trial of low-dose stimulant medication R.J. reported feeling better, and his complaints of disassociation lessened. R.J. was provided with reading materials about adult ADHD and was taught strategies to manage anxiety. Although counseling was strongly recommended, R.J. chose to not participate further.

CASE 15: LD, BORDERLINE IQ, SOMATIZATION, BORDERLINE PERSONALITY, AND ADHD

C.B., a 26-year-old male, was self-referred because of long-standing complaints of LD, temper outbursts, and attention problems. C.B. was currently unemployed.

By correspondence, C.B.'s mother recalled that C.B. was developmentally delayed from a very early age. It was suspected that C.B. may have experienced brain damage due to birth trauma. C.B. received special education services throughout his school career. He was teased and socially isolated. C.B.'s mother recalled that he was inattentive, impulsive, and hyperactive as a child.

On graduating from high school, C.B. was employed in a number of positions part time and attempted to attend college. He was frequently fired from jobs because of his absence or tardiness. He tried and failed four different courses of study.

C.B.'s physician reported that over the past 10 years, C.B. had made frequent visits as the result of diffuse, undefinable physical complaints. These included difficulty with various aches and pains, dizziness, sexual problems, and rectal bleeding.

C.B. was married to his first wife for approximately 1 year. Their marriage appeared to have been extremely stressful and conflicted. They had separated for a number of weeks and recently reconciled. One reason for their separation was C.B.'s use of phone sex lines several times each day over the past 5 to 6 months, resulting in phone bills of $400 to $500 per month. Further, C.B. had recently met another woman at a multiple marketing conference. They had started speaking by phone every day.

C.B. reported five speeding tickets and several car accidents. He denied any history of substance abuse.

C.B.'s responses to self-report attention measures yielded a score just above the clinical cutoff on the Brown questionnaire due to complaints of procrastination, inattentiveness, and difficulty with memory and organization. On the Wender, C.B.'s scores were low because his complaints of irritability, restlessness, or stress intolerance were minimal.

Questionnaires completed by C.B.'s parents described a childhood characterized by hyperactivity, inattention, and impulsivity. A spousal checklist described C.B.'s problems with tasks requiring sustained mental effort and his distractibility, restlessness, and impulsive behavior.

C.B. was an average, neatly groomed young adult. All of the conversations he initiated during his two assessment sessions focused on illnesses. He appeared overconfident but rather disorganized in his approach to the test tasks.

C.B.'s Wechsler measured a Verbal IQ of 74, a Performance IQ of 81, and a Full-Scale IQ of 76. Compared to a demographically corrected population, C.B.'s overall IQ was nearly 2 standard deviations below expectation. In general, C.B.'s intellectual skills were in the borderline range. He completed the Peabody Picture Vocabulary Test with a performance at the 5th percentile and the Test of Nonverbal Intelligence with a performance at the 14th percentile. A memory battery measured below 1st-percentile memory skills. C.B. demonstrated low-average rote skills but struggled to recall any type of complex information. A brief screening of C.B.'s academic abilities detected low-average word reading skills but very poor comprehension. Spelling and arithmetic skills appeared to be at a late elementary school level.

C.B.'s history and current assessment data reflected a disturbed personality. Although C.B.'s behavior reflected a style of friendliness and sociability, it appeared to hide an abrasive hypersensitivity to criticism and a marked tendency to project blame onto others. C.B.'s behavior was unpredictable, impulsive, resentful, and moody. Relationships were shallow and fleeting. They were often characterized by manipulative deceptions and were frequently disrupted by C.B.'s caustic comments and hostile outbursts. C.B. appeared to be unable to delay gratification, acting on impulses with insufficient deliberation and poor judgment. As a result, others perceived C.B. as irresponsible and undependable. C.B.'s history and Millon profile suggested that he was prone to manic episodes of an expansive and hostile nature. During these periods he was talkative, restless, distractible, hostile, excitable, and interpersonally disruptive. During at least two of these periods, he had frightened his wife enough that she had moved out of the house. Once he nearly strangled her. If provoked during these outbursts, it was clear that C.B. could explode into uncontrollable rage.

Diagnostically, C.B. appeared to be functioning in the borderline range of intellectual skill. Not surprisingly, therefore, his learning abilities were quite poor as a result of what appeared to be complex memory problems and poor conceptual abilities. C.B. demonstrated symptoms of ADHD. However, these appeared to be one part of C.B.'s more global personality, intellectual, and memory problems. C.B.'s symptom presentation was consistent with diagnoses of Somatization and Borderline Personality Disorder. C.B. presented with affective instability, chronic feelings of emptiness, inappropriate intense anger, and self-damaging impulsivity.

C.B. was referred to a day treatment program for further observation and treatment planning.

CASE 16: ACQUIRED ADHD AND RELATED COGNITIVE PROBLEMS SECONDARY TO TRAUMATIC BRAIN INJURY

M.M., a 23-year-old college student, was referred by his neurosurgeon. Two years prior to the evaluation, while at work, M.M. was struck by a falling piece of pipe and seriously injured. Assessment was requested because of ongoing problems related to this injury. M.M. described difficulty with blurred vision, muscle weakness, immediate and short-term memory, concentration, reasoning, and dysnomia.

At the time of the accident, M.M. had been employed as a welder. He had been attending school part time. At the time of the evaluation, he had returned to school full time with worker's compensation support.

M.M. denied a preaccident history of psychiatric problems or substance abuse. He acknowledged, however, that there was a history of alcoholism in his family. M.M. reported a B+ average in high school and a summary ACT score of 24.

A review of M.M.'s medical records revealed multiple physical problems, concussion, and posttraumatic amnesia as the result of the work-related accident. A 12% permanent impairment in cognitive functioning had been assigned. A review of cognitive and related testing completed during M.M.'s recovery indicated that he had recovered to low-average cognitive, memory, and academic skills.

M.M. was a casually dressed, well-groomed, tall adult. Although slightly anxious, his behavior and interaction with the examiner was appropriate.

On the Wechsler, M.M. obtained a Verbal IQ of 111, a Performance IQ of 98, and a Full-Scale IQ of 106. Corrected demographic scores placed M.M. well in the average range. M.M.'s performance on the memory battery, in contrast, placed him at the 4th percentile for verbal skills and the 66th percentile for nonverbal skills. M.M. struggled to recall, immediately and over the short term, both simple and complex verbal information. In contrast, he performed much better when recalling nonverbal information.

M.M. achieved a performance at the 66th percentile on the Peabody Picture Vocabulary Test, a performance at the 77th percentile on the Test of Nonverbal Intelligence, and an average performance on the Halstead Category Test. M.M.'s performance on related neuropsychological measures placed him in the low-average range. He performed at the 15th percentile for completion time on the Tactual Performance Test and struggled somewhat to divide his attention efficiently on Trail B.

Academic screening revealed M.M.'s above-average basic academic skills. His reading comprehension, however, was just average, in contrast to his higher rote skills, such as independent word reading and spelling.

M.M.'s performance on a computerized attention battery reflected his problems in sustaining attention and inhibiting impulsive responding. M.M.'s self-reports placed him at the cutoff on the Brown questionnaire indicative of concentration difficulty.

M.M.'s personality was that of a somewhat egocentric individual, self-reliant and competitive. M.M.'s self-reports did not reveal strong indices of symptoms of depression or anxiety. However, M.M. described a period of depression immediately following his accident. Overall, there did not appear to be any major posttraumatic change in M.M.'s personality.

The preponderance of the data suggested that M.M. functioned fairly well before his accident. Since that time, although he appeared to make a good recovery, residual, and likely permanent, problems were noted in M.M.'s ability to concentrate efficiently, in his speed and efficiency in processing information, and in his short-term and immediate verbal memory.

It was the examiner's impression that M.M.'s solid premorbid skills, combined with his personality, had helped him make a fairly good recovery from a very serious traumatic brain injury.

M.M. was started by his physician on a low-dose trial of stimulant medication. He subjectively reported benefits at school and during daily activities. Further ophthalmologic consultation for visual problems was recommended. M.M. was also asked to consider working with a cognitive rehabilitation specialist as he completed school and reentered the workforce.

CASE 17: MEMORY PROBLEMS, ACQUIRED ADHD, AND DEPRESSION SECONDARY TO BRAIN INJURY

A.L., a 40-year-old female stained-glass artist, collided head-on with another bicyclist while bicycling on a steep hillside. Although she was wearing a helmet, A.L. lost consciousness for a brief period of time. She suffered numerous physical injuries and was reported to have experienced a convulsion at the site of the accident. A.L. reported pretraumatic amnesia of a few moments and posttraumatic amnesia of nearly 12 hours. She was referred for assessment 6 months after the accident because of her continued complaints of cognitive difficulty.

A.L.'s history appeared unremarkable. She completed two years of college and had been self-employed over the previous 10 years as a very successful stained-glass artist. At the time of the accident, she had been separated from her second husband of 9 years and was engaged in a custody battle for their three daughters.

A.L. recalled always being quite active as a child and adolescent but denied any behavioral, emotional, or academic problems. A.L. graduated from high school with a B+ average.

At the time of assessment, A.L. continued to receive physical therapy three times per week. Symptoms included neck, arm, back, and head pain; sleep problems; obsessive worrying; feelings of hopelessness; difficulty with short-term memory; problems with concentration; and feeling of apathy. These core difficulties resulted in a diffuse set of problems affecting A.L. throughout each day.

A.L. was an attractive, well-groomed adult. Her behavior during assessment was appropriate. Her work style, however, was characterized by a tendency to make minor errors of detail and to attempt to work very slowly in an effort to compensate. A.L. was motivated to perform and appeared to make her best effort.

On the Wechsler, A.L. obtained a Verbal IQ of 114, a Performance IQ of 97, and a Full-Scale IQ of 106. Demographically, this placed A.L. in the average range with a significant discrepancy between her verbal and nonverbal skills. Interestingly, A.L.'s weakest performance was on the Block Design and Object Assembly subtests. These two tasks measure skills in which, given A.L.'s vocational history, she would be expected to be quite strong.

A.L. completed the Peabody Picture Vocabulary Test with a score at the 66th percentile and the Test of Nonverbal Intelligence with a score at the 70th percentile. On the neuropsychological battery, A.L. completed the Halstead Category Test with a score at the 99th percentile for individuals of her demographic background. A.L. did not have problems on the Halstead; she could form an idea and track that idea consistently. On the Test of Nonverbal Intelligence, however, A.L. appeared to experience some difficulty switching from idea to idea as she attempted to complete the task.

A.L. completed the memory battery with average scores. However, she appeared to have greatest problems recalling complex verbal information. Her performance on measures of distractibility, divided attention, and impulsiveness yielded scores in the low-average range. Academic screening also placed A.L.'s skills in the average range.

A.L.'s self-reports yielded a score beyond the clinical cutoff on the Brown questionnaire due to current complaints of inattention and difficulty initiating activities. On the Beck she scored 26, indicative of moderate depressive thinking.

A.L.'s personality style suggested someone who had difficulty admitting responsibility for problems or was prone to rationalize or project problems. She appeared to be someone who when upbeat could be high-spirited and animated but could quickly revert to anger to control others. However, the majority of her history suggested that prior to the accident in question, A.L. had not experienced any symptoms related to mood or anxiety. Her profile at the time of assessment strongly suggested a major depressive episode and Generalized Anxiety.

Diagnostically, A.L. demonstrated a diffuse pattern of emotional, cognitive, and behavioral difficulty secondary to a traumatic brain injury. Cognitively, A.L. experienced problems processing information quickly as a result of her difficulty with attention to detail, poor visual perception, and limited concentration. Symptoms consistent with acquired ADHD were reported by A.L. as well as other family members. From an emotional perspective, A.L. appeared to have entered a major depressive episode. Her functioning reflected problems related to anxiety and posttraumatic stress as well. At the time of assessment she appeared to be on a downward spiral in terms of her efficiency at daily living.

A.L.'s physician initiated trials of antidepressant and stimulant medications. A serotonin-based antidepressant improved A.L.'s general mood and reduced her obsessive worrying within a few weeks. The initiation of the stimulant resulted in A.L.'s reporting increased daily efficiency and, for the first time in 6 months, the ability to begin stained-glass work. Cognitive rehabilitation on a weekly outpatient basis was initiated to provide A.L. with additional compensatory strategies to improve her efficiency at everyday activities. Supportive psychotherapy was also initiated to help A.L. understand her experiences in the previous 6 months and to reverse the downward spiral of her emotional problems.

CASE 18: ORGANIC PERSONALITY, LD, AND ADHD SYMPTOMS SECONDARY TO TRAUMATIC BRAIN INJURY

A.R., a 48-year-old female, was referred by her rehabilitation specialist because of increasing disruptive and emotional symptoms. Although A.R. had a long history of developmental impairments as the result of severe anoxia at birth, over the previous

6 years symptoms of depression, anxiety, obsessiveness, and anorexia had escalated steadily and significantly.

A.R. was the only survivor of a set of triplets. Both of her siblings died during their first 3 months of life. Despite being slow in development, A.R., with special education support, was able to graduate from high school. She had been employed in the family jewelry business since that time. She continued to live at home with her parents. Now in their late 70s, A.R.'s parents were having increasing difficulty supporting and managing her. A.R. was described as increasingly rigid, aggressive, and obsessive.

A.R. described her current symptomatic complaints, including crying; having suicidal thoughts; feeling lonely, apathetic, and sad; lacking appetite; and angering easily.

On the retrospective measures, A.R.'s parents recalled that, as a child, she was inattentive, impulsive, and rather restless. She was never diagnosed or treated for hyperactivity or attention deficit.

A.R.'s medical records revealed diagnoses of minimal brain dysfunction and at 30 years of age initiation of treatment with antidepressant and antipsychotic medications. Cognitive testing completed when A.R. was 40 years of age yielded a Verbal IQ of 74, a Performance IQ of 66, and a Full-Scale IQ of 69. Discharge diagnoses from a psychiatric hospitalization at age 40 included Major Depression, an Organic Personality Disorder, an Obsessive/Compulsive Personality Disorder, and mild mental retardation.

Neurology consultation at the time of the present evaluation yielded impressions of symptoms of anxiety and depression, possibly the result of progressive neurological problems.

A.R. was a neatly groomed, middle-age female. She was anxious during both assessment sessions and cried frequently. Her conversation was often self-centered. She was easily redirected, however. With support, A.R.'s concentration was good. She quickly became apologetic as tasks became more difficult. Her thoughts appeared logical though mildly unfocused and irrelevant.

Cognitive assessment on the Wechsler yielded a Verbal IQ of 76, a Performance IQ of 70, and a Full-Scale IQ of 73. A.R.'s skills appeared evenly balanced, with slightly stronger verbal than nonverbal abilities. A memory battery, however, measured below 1st-percentile memory skills, again with slightly better verbal than visual memory. A.R. was unable to complete either the Test of Nonverbal Intelligence or the Halstead Category Test. Computerized measures revealed her difficulty in sustaining attention and her tendency to respond impulsively. A.R. appeared to be extremely slow in processing information on a number of neuropsychological tests. Academically, she performed in the low-average range for reading and spelling. Her handwriting was quite fast, efficient, and well integrated. Her arithmetic skills, in contrast, were at the 2nd percentile for her age.

On self-report measures, A.R. described depressive symptoms in the severe range. From a personality perspective, it appeared that much of A.R.'s behavior was intended to gain the attention and favor of others, not only by appearing in an attractive or positive light but also by exposing her troubled state. A.R. demonstrated a very clear tendency toward self-defeating cycles. Her markedly deflated self-worth and her expectations of failure and humiliation appeared to constrain her efforts to function more efficiently and autonomously. A.R. appeared to feel that others had either depreciated or disapproved of her occasional attempts at autonomy. She seemed to perceive no alternative but to depend on supporting persons and groups. She deeply resented this restriction, however, and was impelled to act in a petulant, unpredictable, and often aggressive manner. It was clear that over the past 20 years, A.R.'s discontent, impulsive outbursts, and chronic moodiness had tended to evoke rejection and humiliating reactions from others. This in turn reinforced her self-protective social withdrawal and retreat into increasing isolation.

Diagnostically, A.R.'s fretful and anxious feelings were interwoven with clear signs of a Major Depressive Disorder overlying a characterologic mix of dysthymic features. A.R.'s thinking at times appeared to be somewhat fragmented. Irritable and fretful at the time of assessment, A.R. appeared to be experiencing a significant level of dysphoria, sufficient to justify a diagnosis of Generalized Anxiety as well. Her symptoms and preoccupations were consistent with a Somatoform Disorder that appeared to be contributing to her gastrointestinal discomfort, pain, hypochondriasis, and anorexia.

A.R.'s cognitive strengths and weaknesses, as well as her concentration difficulty, reflected a long-standing history of organically based problems. Her symptomatic difficulties were not consistent with a typical pattern of developmental or intellectual handicap but appeared to reflect the checkerboard pattern of loss as the result of neurologic insult.

A.R. did not read or follow nonverbal routines or expectations very well. She missed the usual signals about when to start or stop tasks. She did not realize what tasks were required to do well. As a result, this difficulty combined with her anxiety and resulted in very poor problem solving, judgment, and comprehension. It appeared that most of the time A.R. did not have a good grasp of what was going on around her. This pattern of organic problems appeared to be responsible for her anxiety difficulties. Further, A.R. demonstrated very few coping abilities, even for someone of her intellectual capability. She did not appear to see, do, or understand as an adult, so she was unable to act like one. She appeared to have major right-hemisphere problems, a difficulty she had experienced since birth. She struggled with visual-motor and perceptual skills. Her mathematical skills reflected her weakest area of academics. Individuals with this pattern often struggle with emotionally distressing symptoms related to anxiety and depression. Despite her perceptual difficulties, however, A.R.'s handwriting and spelling skills were spared.

The examiner raised the possibility that A.R.'s skills were declining. This finding would not be inconsistent for someone with her history reaching middle age. Additional evidence of a slow decline included increased problems reading, some slurring in her speech, increased motor tremors, and an escalation in psychiatric symptoms.

Very clearly, A.R.'s parents were no longer capable of caring for her or providing the structure she needed on a daily basis. A.R. was referred to a state rehabilitation team in an effort to begin making plans for her transition into a group home setting. Continued psychological and psychiatric support was strongly recommended. A.R. was referred to a day treatment psychiatric program in an effort to obtain additional observations of her behavior and to make decisions concerning the potential benefits of psychotropic medications.

CASE 19: LD, OPPOSITIONAL PROBLEMS, AND POSSIBLE ADHD

J.M., a 15-year-old ninth-grader, was referred because of disruptive behavior, increasing reports of emotional distress, and LD. J.M.'s family history was extremely complex. J.M.'s mother was married to her fourth husband and had a history of depression and previous psychiatric hospitalization. J.M. did not get along with his stepfather. In addition, J.M.'s relationship with his biological father was inconsistent. His father had molested stepdaughters and had been charged with incest, convicted, and imprisoned. J.M.'s half-brother had had a history of criminal behavior and had been murdered in prison.

J.M.'s early developmental milestones were unremarkable, although J.M.'s mother recalled that he had received speech language therapy. J.M. struggled in school, was retained, and then evidently moved a year ahead. He began receiving special education services in the second grade. J.M.'s mother married her fourth husband 5 years before assessment. At that time J.M. developed severe psychiatric symptoms and was placed in a residential psychiatric program. At the time of assessment, J.M. was participating in outpatient group therapy for adolescents with histories of alcohol abuse. J.M.'s criminal history included being charged and convicted of stealing the family car, stealing his stepfather's work products, and possession of marijuana. J.M. was described as socially isolated. He tended to interact with older adolescents, most of whom had been involved with repeated juvenile offenses.

Within the home setting, J.M.'s mother noted that he had a long history of inattentiveness, impulsivity, and disorganization. J.M. was described as having had temper tantrums from a young age. He was aggressive with minimal provocation. J.M.'s mother indicated that at the time of assessment, she had a very poor relationship with him.

Psychiatric records from the previous year revealed diagnoses of Mixed Substance Abuse, dysthymia, LD, and Oppositional Defiant Disorder. Not surprisingly, J.M.'s mother's responses to the Child Behavior Checklist indicated significant complaints of disruptive and nondisruptive problems, well above the 98th percentile. J.M. also scored above the 98th percentile on the *DSM-IV* index of the parent Conners' questionnaire.

A review of J.M.'s school records reflected average academic skills with weak spelling in first grade. This pattern continued through fourth grade. By eighth grade, J.M.'s group achievement tests measured his reading at the 6th percentile, math at the 21st percentile, language at the 3rd percentile, spelling at the 2nd percentile, and an overall battery at the 4th percentile. A review of report cards did not indicate problems with attention, work completion, or behavior in kindergarten through second grade. By third grade, complaints were noted about delayed spelling and handwriting as well as marginal mathematical skills. Problems by fourth grade also included difficulty with reading achievement. Fifth-grade notes reflected the first complaints about J.M.'s disruptive behavior, at a time that coincided with his mother's fourth marriage. In sixth grade, J.M. was out of school 51 days due to illnesses.

Assessment at school 2 years prior to the evaluation yielded an average Wechsler IQ but a Verbal IQ of 90 and a Nonverbal IQ of 111. The evaluator described J.M. as guilty, anxious, and hostile.

J.M. was a tall, mature-appearing adolescent. His face was marred by severe acne. His nails were mildly bitten. He wore a baseball cap and kept his coat on during the assessment. J.M.'s affect was somewhat flat, but he was not particularly resistant. In fact, once he warmed up during the assessment process, he became rather pleasant.

J.M. obtained a Full-Scale Wechsler IQ of 90, a Verbal IQ of 87, and a Performance IQ of 96. Intratest scatter suggested that J.M.'s potential IQ was likely better than this measure reflected. Memory assessment yielded 63rd-percentile visual memory skills but only 10th-percentile verbal memory skills. J.M. demonstrated significant problems with rote sequential memory. He performed at the 11th percentile on the Peabody Picture Vocabulary Test and at the 34th percentile on the Test of Nonverbal Intelligence. No signs of difficulty in sustaining attention or inhibiting impulses were noted on a computerized attention battery. Academically, J.M. appeared to be at the seventh-grade level for arithmetic. The data seemed to indicate that J.M.'s verbal and nonverbal conceptual abilities were average but somewhat underdeveloped as a result of his educational history and poor school motivation. His LD appeared to reflect problems with rote verbal memory, causing difficulty with number facts, spelling, following instructions, vocabulary, and comprehension.

J.M.'s self-reports did not reflect any complaints of anxiety or unhappiness. During the interview, J.M. noted he would like to have more control over his life and the lives of others. When asked who he would like to be for a day, he responded, "God." J.M. also acknowledged frequent and repeated drug use beginning at age 13, including marijuana, alcohol, and hallucinogens.

J.M.'s behavior was typified by unpredictable and pessimistic moods, an edgy irritability, and a tendency to engage in self-defeating behaviors. J.M.'s responses to the Millon Adolescent Personality Inventory reflected his feelings of being misunderstood and unappreciated. J.M. expressed momentary thoughts and feelings impulsively and was easily provoked by outside stimuli into sudden and unpredictable reactions. He appeared to anticipate being disillusioned by others and for this reason would behave obstructively. Parent and family relationships were fraught with wrangles and antagonism, provoked by J.M.'s characteristic carelessness and complaining passive-aggressive attitude. His behavior induced others to react in a negative manner. As a consequence, J.M. felt all the more misunderstood and unappreciated. Further, he appeared to be rather self-critical, oversensitive, and defensive. He lacked empathy and viewed the problems of others rather harshly. Family difficulties were reported to be a central focus of J.M.'s expressed problems.

Diagnostically, J.M. demonstrated a long-standing pattern of language-based LD. As a result of these weaknesses, J.M.'s verbal memory skills appeared quite poor. Further, it appeared that J.M.'s family and life history had slowly and consistently impaired his overall adjustment and behavior. J.M. demonstrated symptoms consistent with diagnoses of oppositional defiance, Conduct Disorder, and Mixed Substance Abuse. Although J.M. denied significant complaints of anxiety or depression, his overall behavior and reports of his comments to his parents suggested dysthymia somewhat. J.M.'s overall pattern and presentation, however, also appeared to demonstrate early risks of an emerging Borderline Personality Disorder. Finally, although symptoms of ADHD were present, the history and current presentation strongly argued that these behaviors were etiologically related to other developmental and emotional problems. Moreover, at the time of assessment, J.M. did not meet the full criteria necessary for a diagnosis of ADHD.

Given the history and increasing conflict between J.M. and his parents, it was strongly recommended that a residential treatment program for disruptive, substance-abusing adolescents be considered. Academic support and consideration of vocational training with an academic mentor, someone whom J.M. was willing to trust, were strongly recommended. Finally, although medications might have been beneficial for J.M., it was suggested that until he was in a consistent environment, medication treatments be withheld, especially in light of his history of substance abuse.

CASE 20: DYSTHYMIA AND POSSIBLE ADHD

J.S., an 18-year-old 12th grader, was referred by her educational team at a private, residential school for adolescents. Concerns were raised about J.S.'s difficulty remaining on task and about possible LD.

J.S.'s mother committed suicide when J.S. was 7 years of age. Her father later remarried. J.S. had not gotten along with her stepmother, and in part this was responsible for her out-of-home school placement.

J.S.'s early developmental history was unremarkable. J.S. participated in gifted educational programming during her first few years of elementary school. By junior high school, there appeared to be increasing complaints of off-task behavior. J.S. became rebellious as a freshman in high school and struggled academically. By her sophomore year, she had run away from home a number of times and was later placed in an adolescent psychiatric treatment center for 9 months.

J.S.'s father described her as from an early age being rather inattentive, shifting from one uncompleted activity to another, acting impulsively, and demonstrating poor self-control. Residential staff at J.S.'s school described symptoms related to social isolation, frequent somatic complaints, inattentiveness, and mild disruptive behavior.

A review of J.S.'s records revealed diagnoses of Major Depression, Cyclothymia, and a Mixed Personality Disorder with avoidant and narcissistic features. Intellectual assessment when J.S. was 15 years of age measured a Wechsler Verbal IQ of 96, a Performance IQ of 114, and a Full-Scale IQ of 104. "Information processing deficiencies" were hypothesized to be responsible for J.S.'s weak fund of information and vocabulary.

J.S.'s teachers noted marked variability in her attentional skills, with some teachers reporting good attention and others poor attention. In addition, some teachers described J.S. as overactive, impulsive, restless, and fidgety while others noted minimal difficulties in these areas.

J.S. was a casually dressed, neatly groomed adolescent. She appeared mildly anxious, although her affect was generally flat. She was inclined to distrust her abilities but willing to persist with support. Her thoughts appeared logical, focused, and relevant.

Intellectual assessment measured a Verbal IQ of 86, a Performance IQ of 110, and a Full-Scale IQ of 96. In agreement with the previous assessment, this pattern reflected a fairly consistent trend of weak verbal and stronger nonverbal abilities. J.S. performed at the 86th percentile on the Peabody Picture Vocabulary Test but at only the 18th percentile on the Test of Nonverbal Intelligence. Her performance on the memory battery revealed above-average verbal and nonverbal memory for meaningful information but poor sequential memory. Performance on a computerized attention measure indicated difficulty in sustaining attention and inhibiting impulsive responding. Academic assessment as well reflected difficulty in sustaining attention and inhibiting impulsive responding. Academic assessment reflected difficulty with comprehension and poor written language skills. J.S.'s rote skills did not appear to be particularly weak. Most of her problems appeared to be the result of an overall conceptual weakness. Her slow and steady decline on academic achievement measures during her career, starting from an initial good performance at school, appeared consistent with an individual suffering from conceptual rather than rote LD. Higher-level language processing problems were subsequently identified following a speech and language assessment. In general, J.S. struggled when tasks became more verbally complex and abstract.

J.S.'s self-report measures did not reflect symptoms of depression or anxiety. However, J.S. scored above the clinical cutoff on the Brown questionnaire, describing symptoms consistent with inattention, disorganization, and mild restlessness.

The clinical interview revealed J.S.'s apparent amnesia for the period of time immediately preceding and following her mother's suicide, despite the fact that J.S. discovered her mother's body. Although J.S. denied that the loss of her mother contributed to the increase in her behavioral problems a number of years ago, she was willing to acknowledge that her problems apparently began at this time. J.S. chose to focus the majority of her complaints on her relationship with her stepmother. J.S. also recalled that her father "was really weird" after her mother's death and that her father and stepmother evidently had had some kind of relationship prior to her mother's death.

J.S.'s behavior was characterized by submissive dependency and fears of abandonment, leading her to be compliant and obliging with anyone willing to pay attention to her. J.S. did not appear to value herself in terms of her own traits but in terms of the traits of those to whom she felt most attached. By allying herself with the attributes and attractiveness of others, J.S. created an illusion of sharing their competence. On the Millon Adolescent Personality Inventory, J.S. reported being unhappy with her body maturation and attractiveness. She described serious problems in her family setting. It appeared that her inability to function on a more complex cognitive level was in part responsible for the development of these personality traits.

The question of ADHD was complex for J.S. The preponderance of the data did not reflect consistent long-standing problems with ADHD symptoms. The more serious onset of these symptoms appeared to follow the loss of J.S.'s mother. Even at the time of assessment, complaints of inattentiveness were inconsistent from one classroom to the next. A diagnosis of ADHD was deferred until J.S. could be worked with more closely.

The data, however, very clearly reflected J.S.'s higher-level language processing difficulty. She struggled to integrate information into concepts and hierarchies. Her reading comprehension problems and the types of writing errors that she made clearly reflected her verbal linguistic conceptual limitations. At a very young age, she functioned exceptionally well because of her rote strengths. Thus, during the first few grades while learning to read, J.S. did well. As school became more complex and her life was complicated by emotional stress and as the need to read to learn increased, J.S.'s struggles increased.

The examiner raised questions about the possible contribution of Post–Traumatic Stress Disorder leading to a general dysthymic adjustment to life following the death of J.S.'s mother.

J.S.'s educational team was directed to begin guiding her toward post–high school vocational options. J.S. was interested in photography, and efforts were undertaken to help her apply to 2-year colleges offering photography course work. Suggestions were also made to assist J.S. with academic tasks. A strong focus was placed on helping J.S. organize information and work at a concrete level, seeing and dealing with what was directly in front of her. The use of carefully sequenced instructions and working slowly from one step to the next, especially in more complex academic classes, were also emphasized.

J.S. was provided with additional information about LD in adolescence and adulthood. J.S. was referred to counseling in an effort to help her identify life goals and possibly make some modifications in her personality style. It was recommended that J.S. participate in consultation in 6 to 12 months to once again address the issue of ADHD and the possible risks and benefits of medication treatment.

CASE 21: APPARENT ADHD SYMPTOMS SECONDARY TO PERSONALITY

R.Z., a 21-year-old female college junior, was referred because of reports of increasing difficulty with academic achievement. After viewing a television program dealing with adult ADHD, R.Z. hypothesized that her growing problems at school might be related to attention deficit.

R.Z.'s childhood and developmental history were unremarkable. She denied that as a child she experienced problems with inattention, impulsivity, or hyperactivity. She reported, however, being somewhat unmotivated, but she graduated from high school with a B+ average. In college, R.Z. received Cs and Ds and failed calculus, linear algebra, chemical principles, and differential equations. R.Z. noted that she could "charm her way through high school but can't anymore." R.Z. acknowledged, however, that she did not spend much time studying in college.

R.Z. had been employed for 3.5 years as a grocery store checker. She lived at home with her parents while attending college. Her brother was diagnosed with ADHD as a child. Other siblings had not experienced attention or developmental problems. There was no extended family history of psychiatric or behavioral difficulties.

R.Z. received two speeding tickets but had not had any other legal problems. She described herself as lacking the willpower to start tasks and to put off enjoyable activities. She reported dating on a casual basis.

R.Z.'s mother noted that, as a child, R.Z. experienced very mild problems with attention but that these did not cause her any difficulty in daily functioning. R.Z. evidently excelled in elementary school but struggled somewhat when placed in a gifted junior high school program. Responses by R.Z. and her mother to the Brown questionnaire yielded scores just below the clinically significant cutoff. R.Z. was described as being easily sidetracked, procrastinating, and inconsistent.

R.Z. was an attractive, well-groomed female. It was not difficult to establish a working relationship with her.

Cognitive screening revealed an individual with average intellectual skills. Consistent with her responses and interaction during the clinical interview, R.Z.'s Millon profile indicated an individual working very hard to present a socially acceptable front but also resistant to admitting personal shortcomings. R.Z.'s behavior was typified by an easygoing and nonconforming social style, the seeking of attention as a means of excitement, and self-dramatizing behavior. R.Z. appeared to be easily excited and quickly bored. A general intolerance of inactivity was reflected in her impulsiveness, her attraction to, at times, dangerous behavior, and a seeming disregard for consequences.

Although R.Z. demonstrated some symptoms consistent with ADHD, she did not present with sufficient symptoms or severity of symptoms to warrant a diagnosis of ADHD. In addition, her school performance and academic history revealed problems in some courses that required substantial effort and thus more study time but not in others. A review of R.Z.'s high school transcript noted honors classes such as chemistry, geography, advanced algebra, physics, and trigonometry. Her struggles in college appeared to be a function of her personality and her lack of investment in preparing assignments and studying for tests.

Just as R.Z. withdrew when she was not the best in her early school years, she found it increasingly difficult to complete tasks requiring effort that might not result in the highest score. Finally, R.Z.'s self-report suggested no symptoms of anxiety, depression, or other psychiatric disturbance.

R.Z. was referred for a series of supportive counseling sessions in an effort to help her better understand the ways in which her personality style affected her daily functioning and to help her make academic and vocational decisions. Given R.Z.'s belief that her problems stemmed from ADHD, it was recommended that the issue of ADHD as a contributing factor be reconsidered after R.Z. had participated in supportive counseling and made some changes in her approach to academic tasks.

CASE 22: LD, MILD ANXIETY, AND APPARENT ADHD

J.J., a 16-year-old 10th-grade female, was referred because of poor schoolwork, questions about anxiety, and inattentive behavior. J.J. was the eldest of three siblings. One of the younger siblings had a history of LD and ADHD. The family history was positive for ADHD and LD.

J.J. had been a normal infant, toddler, and preschooler. Developmental milestones were reached within normal limits. An atypical period of repetitive hand-washing was noted at 10 years of age when one of J.J.'s younger siblings was born. This behavior remitted spontaneously.

The year prior to assessment, J.J. became increasingly noncompliant in completing schoolwork. Her parents noted that her life appeared to be "directed by her emotions." In general, they reported a positive relationship with her.

J.J. had been evaluated at 10 years of age when referred because of learning and possible emotional problems. A Wechsler completed at the time measured a Verbal IQ of 96, a Performance IQ of 86, and a Full-Scale IQ of 90. Academic screening at that time indicated low-average written language and reading skills and average mathematical skills. Questionnaires completed by parents and teachers reflected shy but not inattentive behavior. Diagnoses at the time included Overanxious Disorder and a specific LD.

Parental responses to the Child Behavior Checklist noted problems with attention, anxiety, depression, and social withdrawal. J.J. presented at above the 98th percentile on the hyperkinesis index. She was described as somewhat argumentative with family members. She appeared to have a reasonably good peer network.

Teacher responses to the Conners' questionnaire indicated problems in one class with completing tasks but no significant complaints in other classes. A review of J.J.'s report cards noted a comment of "excellent seat work habits" in first grade. Nonetheless, by second grade, J.J. was described as struggling with reading and spelling. In third grade, she was described as pleasant, cooperative, and a good worker. Her fifth-grade teacher also noted her effort despite academic struggles. Junior high school began with A and B grades, but by eighth grade, J.J. was having much more difficulty.

A review of group achievement tests revealed average to low achievement throughout elementary school. In ninth grade, J.J. achieved at the 81st percentile for reading, 37th percentile for mathematics, 58th percentile for language skills, and 17th percentile for spelling, and obtained a basic total battery at the 45th percentile.

J.J. was an attractive, well-groomed adolescent. She was alert and attentive. Her concentration was good. She appeared inclined to distrust her abilities. Overall, she related well to the examiner.

J.J. obtained a Verbal IQ of 97, a Performance IQ of 87, and a Full-Scale IQ of 92 on the Wechsler. These scores, however, appeared to underestimate J.J.'s abilities. The quality of her verbal responses and insight suggested better potential. Her pattern was often to respond correctly to more difficult task items while failing easier items. She performed at the 78th percentile on the Peabody Picture Vocabulary Test. Memory screening detected average to above-average verbal memory for complex information but low-average rote memory. J.J.'s performance on a computerized battery did not reflect problems in sustaining attention or any difficulty with impulsivity. Nonetheless, J.J. experienced some difficulty initially grasping the nature of the task.

Academic screening placed J.J. in the average range. She presented as a quick, accurate visual processor when reading. She had difficulty summarizing and comprehending, however. Her written story was well done with respect to vocabulary and theme.

J.J.'s test data and history reflected something of an enigma. She appeared to possess excellent capacity for awareness, insight, and depth, but these skills were not often triggered unless J.J. was carefully directed. She appeared to go through the world usually perceiving, organizing, and understanding on a superficial, disorganized, discrete, rather concrete level. Her basic problem appeared to be one of immediate abstraction and insight. J.J. appeared to have difficulty grasping and organizing new tasks as they were presented, but typically, with added experience, she was able to sort out, see what was required to perform well, understand the nature and demands of tasks, and then perform them with accuracy and efficiency. Her basic academic skills appeared good. In problem-solving situations when concept, insight, or generalization processes were not triggered, J.J. appeared weaker. Her mathematical skills indicated mild conceptual weakness. Her spelling weaknesses reflected a lack of rule generation and generalization as opposed to poor phonics or weak visual memory.

Her parents' and J.J.'s responses to the Brown questionnaire placed her above the clinical cutoff for inattentive problems. J.J.'s responses to a depression questionnaire placed her in the nonsignificant range. However, on a questionnaire screening anxiety, J.J. described herself as worrying excessively, having her feelings hurt easily, and experiencing difficulty making up her mind.

J.J.'s history and her responses to the Millon profile suggested that underneath her calm facade, she experienced a high degree of emotional lability and irritable hypersensitivity to criticism. J.J. appeared to struggle to express attitudes that were contrary to her actual feelings and thus would display short-lived dramatic or superficial emotions. J.J. appeared to be easily excited and quickly bored.

J.J. also demonstrated a history of mild anxiety. Although she and her parents reported some degree of inattentive symptoms, the history, combined with an insufficient number of symptoms presenting, precluded a diagnosis of ADHD.

A psychiatric consultation was recommended to determine whether a psychotropic medication might ease J.J.'s anxiety difficulties. J.J. was also directed to work with an academic coach in an effort to help her function more efficiently on an independent basis. Short-term counseling was also recommended to help J.J. better understand her rather complex pattern of difficulties and the manner in which she functioned.

CASE 23: BIPOLAR AND BORDERLINE PERSONALITY DISORDER

M.T., a 45-year-old female with a master's degree in education, was self-referred, having read a book on ADHD. Despite her advanced degree, M.T. had only taught as a substitute teacher.

M.T. reported having been anxious since childhood but having her symptoms become exaggerated "since my kids have been teenagers." She described her current problems as disorganization, anxiety, unstable emotions, worry, impatience, impulsivity, and a negative attitude. M.T. described a history of frequent, abrupt, and unpredictable mood changes. Nonetheless, she denied a significant history of a major depressive episode.

M.T. denied a childhood history of developmental or behavioral problems. M.T. had been married to her first husband for 25 years. She described her marriage positively. M.T. had two adopted children, one in college, the other completing high school. The younger had a history of ADHD and LD. M.T. reported frequent and chronic conflicts with her children, noting that they thought she wanted to run their lives. She denied a close history with her parents, describing her mother as "a witch to live with." Her relationships with five siblings were also described as negative. M.T. had something derogatory to say about each.

M.T.'s responses to self-report attention measures yielded scores well above the clinical cutoff. M.T. described excessive problems with inattention, procrastination, stress intolerance, impulsivity, distractibility, anger control, and fatigue. Her husband described his wife's difficulty with organization and consistency. He noted that she failed to follow through with attention to detail and was easily distracted. These behaviors had been present throughout their marriage.

M.T. was an attractive woman, neatly groomed, and of average appearance. She maintained and initiated conversation. Her conversational style was often animated and rapid. She would start one conversation and then almost tangentially switch to others. She was quite active during the clinical interview, leaning forward and back in her chair and slapping at the table for emphasis.

Given M.T.'s academic history, cognitive and academic assessments were not completed. M.T.'s responses to the Beck Depression Inventory yielded a score well below the clinical cutoff. Her responses to the Millon Clinical Multiaxial Inventory, however, were much more revealing.

M.T.'s behavior appeared to reflect her inflated sense of self-worth, a superficially charming style, and the persistent seeking of attention and stimulation. This pattern was repeatedly evident in her immature exhibitionistic and self-dramatizing behavior. M.T.'s relationships appeared characteristically shallow, self-indulgent, and fleeting. She appeared only minimally aware that her undependability and exploitation were seen by others as inconsistent and presumptuous. Over the years, one by one, she had relegated friends and family members to positions of antagonism with her caustic comments. Her behavior did not appear to reflect hostile or malicious tendencies but was derived from feelings of omnipotence and the arrogant assumption that she did not have to follow everyone else's rules. M.T.'s history revealed her pattern of, at times, manic hyperactivity and excitement. Her history also reflected repetitive periods of euphoria and hostility marked by pressured speech, less need for sleep, hyperdistractibility, and general restlessness. Periods of buoyant cheerfulness appeared to be manifested for brief spans of time only to be suddenly and unpredictably replaced by temper outbursts, belligerence, and explosive anger.

Diagnostically, M.T. presented as an individual with likely above-average intellectual skills and academic achievement. Despite her advanced degree, she had never entered the workforce. Although her self-reports and those of her husband reflected symptoms consistent with ADHD, the overall profile suggested that these symptoms were more likely secondary to Borderline Personality Disorder and possibly Bipolar Disorder. At the time of assessment, M.T.'s endorsed symptomatology was consistent with a manic episode. She demonstrated inflated self-esteem, wide and rapid mood changes, irritability, pressured speech, and distractibility. M.T.'s borderline personality qualities included affective instability, frequently in response to anxiety or provoking situations.

M.T. was carefully counseled that the source of her inattentive problems appeared to be emotional and not developmental. She was referred for further psychiatric consultation. A recommendation was also made for supportive psychotherapy, given the examiner's concern that M.T.'s outbursts over the years were becoming more severe in their presentation.

CASE 24: BIPOLAR DISORDER, BORDERLINE PERSONALITY DISORDER, AND BORDERLINE IQ

W.K., a 24-year-old female high school graduate, was referred after her friend suggested that her problems might be the result of ADHD. W.K. reported a childhood history of learning difficulty, inferior feelings, depression, and possibly inattention. She described peers as particularly abusive and aggressive. She reported a history of LD. She had received special education services throughout her high school career. She attended a 2-year college for one semester but later dropped out. At the time of the assessment, W.K. was recently divorced and unemployed.

W.K. described physical symptoms, including headache and aches and pains, feelings of tension and depression, thoughts of suicide, feelings of inferiority, difficulty with concentration, mood swings, and sexual problems. She also noted that "I don't think I have ever rested for a long time, I never really sleep." W.K. noted that one of the more significant problems in her marriage was her dislike of sexual activities, explaining that she did not like being nude.

The symptomatic problems that W.K. described were ego-dystonic. She noted that they were quite troublesome; she would like to "function like a normal person." W.K. described a long history of getting mad easily, losing her temper, and acting aggressively toward persons or objects; of frequent, abrupt, and unpredictable mood changes; and of impulsive behavior as well. She had received two moving violations and had been in two automobile accidents.

W.K. was an only child. Her family history was positive for ADHD and LD.

On self-report measures related to attention, W.K.'s scores were far beyond the clinical cutoff. W.K. endorsed nearly all items on these questionnaires to the extreme. On the Retrospective Attention Profile, her mother reported that, as a child, W.K. was extremely hyperactive and fidgety, daydreamed, did not follow directions, and acted impulsively. Nonetheless, her mother described W.K. as usually happy as a child.

W.K. was a well-groomed, attractive woman. She worked hard throughout the structured assessment. She was alert and attentive, manifesting good concentration. Her approach to test tasks was methodical.

On the Wechsler, W.K. obtained a Verbal IQ of 74, a Performance IQ of 83, and a Full-Scale IQ of 76. The overall profile reflected generally weak intellectual skills. Her performance on the memory battery indicated a similar relative verbal weakness, with W.K. performing at the 2nd percentile for verbal memory, 17th percentile for nonverbal memory, and 4th percentile for overall memory skills. Not surprisingly, given her intellectual weaknesses, W.K. experienced greatest problems on tasks requiring complex memory.

W.K. completed the Peabody Picture Vocabulary Test with a score at the 4th percentile and the Test of Nonverbal Intelligence with a score at the 7th percentile. Academic screening placed W.K.'s academic skills at or below the 5th percentile. Reading comprehension skills were measured at a sixth-grade level.

W.K.'s responses to the Beck Depression Inventory yielded a score suggesting a moderate level of reported depressive symptoms. Her moods appeared highly labile, with impulsive, angry outbursts alternating with recurrent depressive complaints and sulking.

W.K.'s responses to the Millon Clinical Multiaxial Inventory reflected an irritable hypersensitivity to criticism, low frustration tolerance, shortsighted hedonism, immature behavior, and an erratic search for momentary excitement and stimulation. Impulsive and unmoderated emotions surged readily to the surface for W.K., making her behavior capricious, distractible, and egocentric. Unpredictable, contrary, manipulative, and volatile, W.K. frequently elicited rejection rather than the support she sought from others. Her moods appeared brittle and variable. She appeared to be an individual capable of displaying short-lived, dramatic but superficial emotions. Her moods appeared to be highly reactive to external stimuli. Feeling misunderstood and disappointed with life, W.K. had begun behaving in an irrational, negativistic, critical, and envious manner, begrudging others for their good fortune.

Diagnostically, W.K. demonstrated a long-standing history of borderline intellectual skills of uncertain etiology. Although she was strong at simple, rote types of tasks, her abstract and conceptual reasoning skills presented at well below the 2nd percentile. Her arithmetic skills were at a late elementary school level. Further, W.K.'s memory for complex verbal and nonverbal information was extremely weak.

W.K. endorsed symptoms of rapidly alternating moods accompanied by manic and depressive episodes. Symptoms included agitation, insomnia, and suicidal thoughts. Her pervasive pattern of instability in interpersonal relationships, her instability, and her impulsivity were consistent with a diagnosis of Borderline Personality Disorder.

Although symptoms of ADHD were reported, the overall profile did not warrant a diagnosis of ADHD at the time.

W.K. was referred for psychiatric consultation to evaluate the potential benefits of psychotropic medication as part of her treatment plan. W.K. was also urged to participate in supportive psychotherapy and to consider evaluation with her local vocational rehabilitation office. With her approval, the results of the assessment were explained to W.K.'s parents in an effort to help them advocate for their daughter.

CHAPTER

10

=≫·◆·≪=

Legal Rights and Qualification Under the Americans with Disabilities Act

PETER S. LATHAM
PATRICIA H. LATHAM

INTRODUCTION

The purpose of this chapter is to provide a clear explanation of the primary disability antidiscrimination laws that pertain to individuals with cognitive disabilities, such as Learning Disabilities (LD) and Attention-Deficit/Hyperactivity Disorder (ADHD) in higher education and employment. The approach is analytical and practical. Consistent with the objectives of clarity and brevity, the strictly legal method of case citations has been simplified. We have used basic citations that show the deciding court, the year of decision, and, where available, a reference to a legal reporter by volume and page. Note that the full text of all cases can be located at the Internet home page for the particular court in question.

THE CONSTITUTION: BASIS OF ALL DISABILITY LAW

The government of the United States of America is a limited one. The powers of the federal government may be exercised through legislation that is authorized by, and enacted pursuant to, specific provisions of the Constitution. As a result, the federal legal rights accorded individuals with disabilities are found in or derived from the Constitution of the United States or those statutes enacted by Congress pursuant to constitutional provisions.

There are three relevant constitutional provisions: the Commerce Clause, the Spending Clause, and the Fourteenth Amendment. They are set forth, in pertinent part, next.

The Commerce Clause provides that Congress has the authority "to regulate Commerce . . . among the several States" (Constitution, Art. I, § 8, Cl. 4).

The Spending Clause provides that "the Congress shall have Power To lay and collect Taxes . . . to . . . provide for the . . . general Welfare of the United States" (Constitution, Art. I, § 8, Cl. 4).

The Fourteenth Amendment provides that

Section 1. . . . No state shall make or enforce any law which shall abridge the privileges or immunities of citizens of the United States; nor shall any state deprive any person of life, liberty, or property, without due process of law; nor deny to any person within its jurisdiction the equal protection of the laws.

***

Section 5. The Congress shall have power to enforce, by appropriate legislation, the provisions of this article.

Note that the Fourteenth Amendment applies to states and not to the federal government. The Fifth Amendment applies to the federal government and contains the prohibition against deprivation "of life, liberty, or property, without due process of law." Although the Fifth Amendment does not contain the equal protection guarantees, in practice, it has been interpreted to include them. Note also that the Fourteenth Amendment provides for the enactment of implementing legislation. Disability legislation must be authorized by one or more of these provisions in order to be valid constitutionally. Those statutes that exceed constitutional authority would be invalid. Regulations issued under a statute may not exceed statutory authority in order to be valid.

The Constitution does more than authorize statutes. It also directly protects individuals with disabilities from discrimination.

The Fifth Amendment (which applies to the federal government) and the Fourteenth Amendment (which applies to the states) contain prohibitions against the deprivation "of life, liberty, or property, without due process of law." There are two types of due process: substantive due process and procedural due process.

Substantive Due Process

A statute violates substantive due process when it seeks to deny an individual one or more of his or her fundamental rights. In general, fundamental rights have included the right to privacy, the right to associate, and other rights set forth in the Constitution.

For example, it would be a violation of substantive due process for a state to refuse to educate all children who are members of a particular religious group.

Procedural Due Process

Procedural due process is basically the requirement that the government may not take life, liberty, or property without using fair procedures that are applicable to all. For example, a hearing that did not allow for an adequate presentation of evidence by all parties to it would violate procedural due process.

STATUTES

To protect individuals with disabilities in higher education and employment, Congress has enacted two key federal statutes, the Rehabilitation Act of 1973 (RA) and the Americans with Disabilities Act of 1990 (ADA). Although the focus of this chapter is the ADA, it is helpful to understand the RA, which contains similar language and was enacted many years earlier.

Rehabilitation Act of 1973

The RA made discrimination against individuals with disabilities unlawful in three areas: (1) employment by the executive branch of the federal government, (2) employment by most federal government contractors, and (3) activities that are funded by federal subsidies or grants. This latter category includes all public elementary and secondary schools and most postsecondary institutions. The statutory section that prohibits discrimination in grants was numbered § 504 in the original legislation, and the RA is often referred to simply as Section 504. Other sections, for example, create a limited requirement for affirmative action in the hiring of persons with disabilities by the executive branch of the federal government and most federal government contractors. Under Section 504, individuals with impairments that substantially limit a major life activity, such as learning, are entitled to academic adjustments and auxiliary aids and services so that courses, examinations, and services will be accessible to them.

The RA is authorized by the Spending Clause of the United States Constitution, which provides that "the Congress shall have Power To lay and collect Taxes . . . to . . . provide for the . . . general Welfare of the United States" (Constitution, Art. I, § 8, Cl. 1).

Under this authority, the federal government provides funding for services, such as education, which it could not provide directly itself. The funding is accomplished by the use of grants that are much like contracts. Any contract, by definition, requires the agreement of the parties. Special issues arise regarding the question of what the states have agreed to when they receive grants authorized under the Spending Clause. For example, in *Barnes v. Gorman* (2002), the Supreme Court has held that the states have *not* agreed to accept liability for punitive damages for violations of the RA.

Americans with Disabilities Act of 1990

In 1990, the Congress enacted the ADA. This act extended the concepts of Section 504 to (1) employers with 15 or more employees (Title I); (2) all activities of state and local governments, including but not limited to employment and education (Title II); and (3) virtually all places that offer goods and services to the public, termed "places of public accommodation" (Title III). In addition, ADA standards apply to employment by the Congress.

Two constitutional provisions authorize the ADA:

1. Titles I and III are authorized by the Commerce Clause, which provides that Congress has the authority to "regulate Commerce . . . among the several States" (Constitution, Art. I, § 8, Cl. 4).
2. Title II is authorized by the Fourteenth Amendment, discussed earlier.

The ADA has been amended by the ADA Amendments Act of 2008 (ADAAA). The basic purpose of the amendments is to expand the coverage of the ADA to a broader range of persons with impairments.

Two points should be noted:

1. Congress clearly believed that the ADA, as interpreted by the courts, had been too narrowly interpreted.
2. Congress intended to rectify the situation by mandating that all persons with "physical or mental disabilities" should "fully participate in all aspects of society" and that none shall have diminished rights. To achieve this result, the Congress made changes to the original ADA.

The ADAAA became effective on January 1, 2009. As decided in the case *Rohr v. Salt River Project Agricultural Improvement and Power District* (2009), it does not apply to claims for damages based on actions that took place before the effective date of the ADAAA. Based on a number of cases, it does apply to actions for injunctive relief that were pending on January 1, 2009 (e.g., *EEOC v. Argo Distribution L.L.C.*, 2009; *Kiesewetter v. Caterpillar, Inc.*, 2008; *Jenkins v. National Board of Medical Examiners*, 2009). However, the distinction may not be of great significance. Courts faced with cases that are technically not covered by the ADAAA tend to interpret the "old" ADA to be consistent with the ADAAA.

INDIVIDUAL WITH A DISABILITY
RA

The RA bans discrimination by:

- The U.S. government (29 U.S.C. § 791).
- U.S. government contractors (29 U.S.C. § 793).
- Recipients of federal funds (29 U.S.C. § 794).

This latter provision (popularly known as Section 504) covers all federal grant and aid recipients. Most notably, it applies to most elementary, secondary, and postsecondary educational institutions. It also served as the model for the ADA.

ADA

The ADA was intended to extend the basic disability rights set forth in the RA to most of society. The RA follows federal dollars. It applies to most federal employment, to federal government contractors, and to federal grant and aid recipients. The ADA prohibits discrimination in three major areas:

1. Private employment (Title I)
2. The activities of state and local governments (public schools, employment, licensing, public programs, etc.) (Title II)
3. Access to privately owned places of public accommodation (private schools, hotels, theaters, etc.) (Title III)

A Common Language

The ADA was based on the RA and contains definitions that are identical to that statute. For this reason, court decisions regarding a definition under the ADA would be instructive as to that definition in the RA as well. Together, the ADA and RA were intended to create the same basic rights. Both laws, for example, are intended to protect the civil rights of qualified individuals with disabilities. The relationship between the two laws is best understood in light of the Supreme Court's decision in *Bragdon v. Abbott* (1998). Speaking for the Court, Mr. Justice Kennedy explained the relationship:

> The ADA's definition of disability is drawn almost verbatim from the definition of "handicapped individual" included in the Rehabilitation Act of 1973, 29 U. S. C. §706(8)(B) (1988 ed.), and the definition of "handicap" contained in the Fair Housing Amendments Act of 1988, 42 U. S. C. §3602(h)(1)

(1988 ed.). Congress' repetition of a well-established term carries the implication that Congress intended the term to be construed in accordance with pre-existing regulatory interpretations.

The ADA had once followed the earlier statute, the RA. Now, on the contrary, the interpretation of the RA will be influenced by the ADAAA. The ADAAA provides that, under the RA:

The term "disability" means . . . a physical or mental impairment that constitutes or results in a substantial impediment to employment; or [*a physical or mental impairment that substantially limits one or more major life activities,*] the meaning given it in . . . the Americans with Disabilities Act of 1990 (42 U.S.C. 12102).

In other words, the RA must now be interpreted in accordance with the ADA. See also *EEOC v. Argo Distribution L.L.C.* (2009).

In any event, the two laws utilize a set of common definitions. The central definition is that of an "individual with a disability."

STATUTORY LANGUAGE

The ADA contains the following definition of a disability. The act [42 U.S.C. § 12102(2)] provides in pertinent part:

The term "disability" means, with respect to an individual—

(A) a physical or mental impairment that substantially limits one or more of the major life activities of such individual;

(B) a record of such an impairment; or

(C) being regarded as having such an impairment.

Note that the ADA defines an individual with a disability in precisely the same way as the RA does. [See 29 U.S.C. § 706(8)(B).] Under both laws, "Test A" is the most important one. "Test B" ("record of such impairment") was intended to prevent discrimination on the basis of past impairments. "Test C"—"being regarded as having such an impairment"—was intended to prevent discrimination on the basis of conditions such as disfiguring burns, which, while not disabling in themselves, might lead to discrimination based on an erroneous perception that an individual has a particular disability.

The RA/ADA approach is to define "disability" conceptually. Any impairment that substantially limits a major life activity can qualify. Although the statutes and their implementing regulations have identified some impairments, the list is by no means exhaustive. As new impairments occur, they may qualify as disabilities when they sub-stantially limit a major life activity. However, as we shall see, the ADAAA has created an extensive list.

Definition of Physical or Mental Impairment

The RA/ADA applies to any individual with a disability, which includes one who has a physical or mental impairment that substantially limits one or more of such person's major life activities.

The term "physical or mental impairment" under the RA/ADA is:

(h) Physical or mental impairment means:

Any physiological disorder, or condition, cosmetic disfigurement, or anatomical loss affecting one or more of the following body systems:

(1) Neurological, musculoskeletal, special sense organs, respiratory (including speech organs), cardiovascular, reproductive, digestive, genito-urinary, hemic and lymphatic, skin, and endocrine; or

(2) Any mental or psychological disorder, such as mental retardation, organic brain syndrome, emotional or mental illness, and specific learning disabi-lities. (29 C.F.R. § 1630.2)

Note that the RA and ADA expressly apply to individuals with "Specific Learning Disabilities" (SLD). That term has been held to have the same meaning as that con-tained in the Individuals with Disabilities Education Act of 2004 (IDEA). See *Lyons v. Smith* (1993).

Original Definition of "Substantially Limits"

Not every impairment that affects a major life activity is a disability under the ADA. Only those whose effects substantially limit a major life activity can be considered disabilities. The concept of substantial limitation has been developed by regula-tions and court decisions. It is the intention of the ADAAA to undo many of these decisions.

Four Supreme Court decisions defined the ADA prior to its amendment.

In *Sutton v. United Air Lines* (1999), the Supreme Court ruled that "when judging whether that person is 'substantially limited' in a major life activity and thus 'disabled' under the Act," a court must consider "that if a person is taking measures to correct for, or mitigate, a physical or mental impairment, the effects of those measures—both positive and negative—must be taken into account."

Sutton concerned the question whether the beneficial effects of prosthetic devices should be considered in evaluating the extent of an impairment (the Court held they should). Companion cases ruled that the beneficial effects of medication

(*Murphy v. United Parcel Service*, 1999), and coping or compensatory strategies (*Albertsons, Inc., v. Kirkingburg*, 1999), should also be considered. Had there been negative consequences of the prosthetic devices, medications, or coping strategies, these would also have been required to be considered.

In *Rohr v. Salt River Project Agricultural Improvement and Power District* (2009), the Court described the impact of the ADAAA on *Sutton*. It said that

---

the ADAAA rejects the requirement enunciated in *Sutton* that whether an impairment substantially limits a major life activity is to be determined with reference to mitigating measures. . . . The ADAAA makes explicit that the "substantially limits" inquiry "shall be made without regard to the ameliorative effects of mitigating measures such as . . . medication, medical supplies, equipment, or appliances . . . ; use of assistive technology; reasonable accommodations or auxiliary aids or services; or learned behavioral or adaptive neurological modifications." . . . Impairments are to be evaluated in their *unmitigated* state, so that, for example, diabetes will be assessed in terms of its limitations on major life activities when the diabetic does *not* take insulin injections or medicine and does not require behavioral adaptations such as a strict diet. [Citations omitted.]

In *Toyota Motor Manufacturing, Kentucky, Inc., v. Williams* (2002), the Supreme Court ruled that in order to be substantially limited, an individual must have an impairment that is permanent or long term and that severely restricts the individual from doing activities that are of central importance to most people's daily lives. The ADAAA has repudiated that ruling in *Jenkins v. National Board of Medical Examiners* (2009).

In many other cases, the courts had found that individuals with LD or ADHD have impairments that do not rise to the level of disabilities under the RA and ADA.

In *Ristrom v. Asbestos Workers Local 34* (2004), an employee with ADHD and depression had been discharged from an apprenticeship program. He sued under the ADA. The Court found that he was not a person with a disability under the ADA. The employee failed to prove that his ADHD and depression limited his ability to learn as compared to the average person in the general population. It was not sufficient to show that certain subjects or educational contexts are challenging or frustrating. The man had graduated from high school and had held a full-time job. See also *Wright v. CompUSA* (2003) and *Calef v. Gillette Co.* (2003).

Under the ADAAA

The ADAAA seeks to undo much of this case law.

The act attempts to repudiate the principles set forth in *Sutton, Murphy, Kirkingburg, Toyota, Rohr,* and *Jenkins* by addressing in the amendment the issues that the Supreme Court had not addressed:

> (E) (i) The determination of whether an impairment substantially limits a major life activity shall be made without regard to the ameliorative effects of mitigating measures such as—
>
> (I) medication, medical supplies, equipment, or appliances, low-vision devices (which do not include ordinary eyeglasses or contact lenses), prosthetics including limbs and devices, hearing aids and cochlear implants or other implantable hearing devices, mobility devices, or oxygen therapy equipment and supplies;
>
> (II) use of assistive technology;
>
> (III) reasonable accommodations or auxiliary aids or services; or
>
> (IV) learned behavioral or adaptive neurological modifications.
>
> (ii) The ameliorative effects of the mitigating measures of ordinary eyeglasses or contact lenses shall be considered in determining whether an impairment substantially limits a major life activity.
>
> (iii) As used in this subparagraph—
>
> (I) the term "ordinary eyeglasses or contact lenses" means lenses that are intended to fully correct visual acuity or eliminate refractive error; and
>
> (II) the term "low-vision devices" means devices that magnify, enhance, or otherwise augment a visual image.

Note that, generally, under the amended ADA, mitigating measures will not be considered in determining disability, but Congress expressly allows ordinary glasses and contact lenses to be considered. See *Rohr v. Salt River Project* (2009).

The ADAAA also provides that an "impairment that substantially limits one major life activity need not limit other major life activities in order to be considered a disability."

Congress directs that "the definition of disability in this Act shall be construed in favor of broad coverage of individuals under this Act, to the maximum extent permitted by the terms of this Act," and the "term 'substantially limits' shall be interpreted consistently with the findings and purposes of the ADA Amendments Act of 2008." Those purposes could not be more broadly stated. Those added by the ADAAA, for example, provided that

> physical or mental disabilities in no way diminish a person's right to fully participate in all aspects of society, yet people with physical or mental disabilities have been precluded from doing so because of discrimination; others who have a record of a disability or are regarded as having a disability also have been subjected to discrimination.

Effectively, this example expands the statutory definition of "substantially limits." The courts must interpret the term in a broad and inclusive manner to "in no way diminish a person's right to fully participate in all aspects of society." An example of broader court interpretation is *Jenkins v. National Board of Medical Examiners* (2009). There, a medical student with a "reading disorder" sued under the ADA to obtain accommodations on the United States Medical Licensing Examination. District Court denied the requested injunction, holding that "there is ample evidence that Jenkins processes written words slowly, and that his condition prevents him from succeeding where success is measured by one's ability to read under time pressure." Citing *Toyota*, the court ruled that time pressured reading is not one of the "meaningful tasks central to most people's daily lives." The Sixth Circuit reversed, holding that the meaningful central tasks standard of *Toyota* had been repudiated by the Congress when it enacted the ADAAA. The Supreme Court then ignored the *Toyota* ruling and found that the evidence suggested that "Jenkins reads written language in a slow and labored fashion when compared to the general public." Moreover, the Court concluded, "Reading is a major life activity under the existing precedent of this circuit and the amended ADA." The Sixth Circuit then sent the case back to be heard under the appropriate legal standard.

The ADAAA also sought to overturn a line of cases that held that illnesses such as cancer were not disabilities until the impact was truly substantially limiting. Other cases held that illnesses such as depression were not disabilities if they were episodic. The ADAAA overturns that line of cases and provides that an "impairment that is episodic or in remission is a disability if it would substantially limit a major life activity when active."

MAJOR LIFE ACTIVITIES

The ADAAA expands the list of major life activities originally identified by the original ADA. The amendment says that "major life activities include, but are not limited to, caring for oneself, performing manual tasks, seeing, hearing, eating, sleeping, walking, standing, lifting, bending, speaking, breathing, learning, reading, concentrating, thinking, communicating, and working."

The ADAAA goes further to specify that many body functions are themselves major life activities. The act provides that "a major life activity also includes the operation of major bodily function, including but not limited to, functions of the immune system, normal cell growth, digestive, bowel, bladder, neurological, brain, respiratory, circulatory, endocrine, and reproductive functions.

Under the ADA, Attention-Deficit Disorder (ADD), ADHD, and SLD were considered to be impairments. Some limited major life activities as previously defined and some did not. Under the ADA as amended by the ADAAA, these impairments are more likely to be found to have limited substantially one or more of the major life activities of "learning, reading, concentrating, thinking, communicating, and working."

The major life activity of thinking may be substantially limited by ADD, ADHD, and SLD. In *EEOC v. Chevron Phillips Chemical Co.* (2009) the Court held that an employee's chronic fatigue syndrome (CFS) substantially limited thinking, sleeping, and caring for oneself. The Court described the impact on thinking in terms more frequently associated with ADD, ADHD, and SLD:

With respect to thinking, Netterville [the employee] testified that she suffered from episodes of aphasia, including times when she forgot her own son's name, an inability to concentrate, forgetfulness about how to perform routine tasks, and falling asleep or losing focus while driving. This testimony is sufficient to support a finding that Netterville's CFS created a substantial limitation on Netterville's ability to think relative to the average person.

The major life activity of sleeping may be substantially limited by medications, such as those used to address ADD and ADHD. In *McAlindin v. County of San Diego* (1999), the Court found that the major life activity of sleeping had been substantially limited. The Court found "enough evidence of sleep disturbance" to warrant a trial, where "plaintiff testified that he had 'great difficulty' sleeping, was sometimes unable to sleep, and took medications that disrupted his normal sleep patterns and caused drowsiness at work."

OTHERWISE QUALIFIED

Prior to the enactment of the ADAAA, most litigated cases concerned the question of whether the individual did or did not have a disability. Most of those cases would be resolved in favor of a disability finding under the ADAAA. However, while Congress purported to reverse most disability rulings, it left untouched the requirement that an individual with a disability must be otherwise qualified to participate in an educational program or to perform the essential tasks of a job in the workplace. One can reasonably anticipate that the "otherwise qualified" requirement will prove to be an increased focus of litigation under the ADAAA.

The ADA does not fully protect all individuals with disabilities, only those who are "otherwise qualified" for the educational program, test, license, or job at issue. However, the very facts that establish disability status may also show that the individual is not otherwise qualified.

The ADA, which has language similar to that of the RA, applies only to a "qualified individual with a disability." For example, 42 U.S.C. § 12111 provides in pertinent part:

---

(8) Qualified individual with a disability

> The term "qualified individual with a disability" means an individual with a disability who, with or without reasonable accommodation, can perform the essential functions of the employment position that such individual holds or desires.

Thus, under both the ADA and RA, an "otherwise qualified" individual is one who, although possessed of a disability, would be eligible for the education, job, or program benefit, with or without a reasonable accommodation. See *Wynne v. Tufts University School of Medicine* (1992).

In *Mathews v. Denver Post* (2001), an individual with epilepsy had a job as a mailer. After a seizure, his doctor recommended he not work around mail machinery, and the man requested that he do only the part of his job that did not involve working around the machinery. The *Denver Post* terminated him because working with the machinery was essential to his job and so he could not perform the essential functions of his mailer job. The Court agreed, holding that he was not qualified because he could not perform those essential job functions.

The fact that an individual has been accepted to a program and performed at an acceptable level for a period of time does not ensure that he or she is qualified. In *Powell v. National Board of Medical Examiners* (2004), the Court held that a medical student with LD was not entitled under Title III of the ADA or Section 504 to extra test time on the first of three medical licensing exams administered by the National Board of Medical Examiners. The Court also found that the medical school did not violate Title II of the ADA by applying to the student its requirement that medical students must pass this first licensing exam in order to proceed into the third year of medical school. She had failed the test twice without accommodations. The Court found that she never had been an above-average student and had college grades and entrance test scores well below those of her fellow medical students. Her neuropsychologist had concluded that advanced postsecondary courses would pose difficulties. Thus, the Court reasoned, she was not qualified to be in medical school.

The ultimate lack of qualifications occurs when an individual poses a "direct threat" to those with whom he or she interacts in the academic or workplace setting. In *Robertson v. Neuromedical Ctr.* (1998), for example, the Fifth Circuit upheld the termination of a neurologist with ADHD. Holding that there was no duty to accommodate Robertson in his medical practice, the court said:

Robertson posed a "direct threat" to the health and safety of others in the workplace. Robertson's short-term memory problems had already caused various mistakes to be made in patients' charts and in dispensing medicine. Most significantly, Robertson voiced his own concerns about his ability to take care of patients, stating that it was only a matter of time before he seriously hurt someone. In light of this evidence, we agree with the district court's conclusion that any accommodations in this case would be unjustified from the standpoint of the basic medical safety of Dr. Robertson's patients. See *McRae v. Potter* (N.D. Ill. Apr. 19, 2002), *Shiring v. Runyon* (1996).

We have established that, under the ADAAA, otherwise qualified individuals with impairments such as ADHD and SLD that limit substantially the major life activities of "learning, reading, concentrating, thinking, communicating, and working" are protected by both the RA and the ADA as amended. The term "substantially limit" is to be interpreted in a broad and inclusive manner. How do these protections play out in higher education and the workplace?

HIGHER EDUCATION

The RA applies to higher educational institutions that receive federal funds. The receipt of federal money, not the nature of the institution, determines whether the RA applies. Educational institutions that receive no federal funds are not subject to the RA.

Under the ADA, the nature of the institution, not the receipt of federal funds, is the decisive factor. All public educational institutions are governed by Title II, whether they receive federal funds or not. All private educational institutions, except those that are religiously controlled, are governed by Title III.

Postsecondary institutions are governed by the RA and ADA in three principal areas: (1) testing (for admissions, evaluation of academic performance, and graduation); (2) the delivery of course materials; and (3) nonacademic benefits of campus life, such as sports, dormitory living, and the like. In this chapter, as in prior chapters, we will be using the definition of an individual with a disability we discussed earlier. It is a person who "has a physical or mental impairment that substantially limits one or more of such person's major life activities."

The RA/ADA approach to higher education is fundamentally the same as in other areas. *Discrimination* against individuals with disabilities is prohibited, and *qualified individuals* with disabilities are entitled to *reasonable accommodations* in meeting the *essential requirements* of the educational program.

Court cases involving the issue of who is an individual with a disability under the RA and ADA have been discussed earlier. The focus of this section is on accommodations in higher education.

Reasonable Accommodations in Education

In general, there is no obligation under either the RA or ADA for a postsecondary institution to design an individualized course of study for an individual with a disability. A postsecondary institution must, however, provide equal access to classroom and other educational materials. This duty is described in the regulations as an obligation to provide course and testing modifications as well as auxiliary aids and services.

An educational institution has no obligation to alter the fundamental requirements of its programs as an accommodation under the RA/ADA. A student who cannot comply with the essential course requirements of the program may be expelled, even if he or she has a disability. For example, in *Ellis v. Morehouse Sch. of Med.* (1996), an individual with dyslexia requested and received a decelerated first-year curriculum and double time within which to complete his examinations. The medical school refused to provide a decelerated program for the third and fourth years, which consisted of clinical rather than classroom programs, on the grounds that the accommodations would require modification of the essential nature of the clinical programs. The Court held in favor of the medical school. The student was not qualified to be in medical school if he could not meet its requirements.

Testing and Fundamental Academic Requirements

A postsecondary institution must provide equal access to classroom materials and examinations. Appropriate auxiliary aids are required in testing a qualified individual with a disability, unless the use of auxiliary aids would fundamentally alter the measurement of the skills or knowledge being tested or would result in an undue burden on the institution. The regulations provide that the selection and administration of tests must be nondiscriminatory. Each examination must be

selected and administered so as to best ensure that, when the examination is administered to an individual with a disability that impairs sensory, manual, or speaking skills, the examination results accurately reflect the individual's aptitude or achievement level or whatever other factor the examination purports to measure, rather than reflecting the individual's impaired sensory, manual, or speaking skills (except where those skills are the factors that the examination purports to measure). 28 CFR § 36.309(b)

Test Selection

Standardized testing for admission to educational programs is permissible. Testing that relies on a single criterion is unlawful where that criterion can be shown to be an inaccurate predictor of performance and the use of that criterion has no compelling justification. The issue of testing was considered in *Stutts v. Freeman* (1983).

The Court found discriminatory (under the RA) the use, as a single criterion for employment as a heavy equipment operator apprentice, of a written test that could not be shown to be an accurate predictor of performance.

A review of an institution's educational program should enable it to identify those features of the program that are essential and those that are not. At the postsecondary level, accommodations need be given only for those features of a program that are nonessential. For example, a student with dyslexia would not be entitled to additional test time in a speed-reading test. Time in that case is essential.

When challenged, an educational institution may be required to validate testing constraints and methods that it considers essential. For further information, see *Wynne v. Tufts University School of Medicine* (1992) and *Guckenberger et al. v. Boston University* (1997). Generally, universities and testing entities may select the type of test they deem appropriate for all students, such as multiple-choice tests. See *Stern v. University of Osteopathic Med. and Health Sciences* (2000).

Test Administration

Tests must be administered to students in a manner that does not discriminate against people with disabilities. Therefore, reasonable accommodations in testing must be provided to individuals with disabilities, according to *Morisky v. Broward County* (1996). According to 28 CFR § 36.309(a), examinations and courses must be offered in a "place and manner accessible to persons with disabilities or other alternative accessible arrangements for such individuals" must be offered. Moreover, 28 CFR § 36.309(b) states that examinations must be structured in such a way that their results "accurately reflect the individual's aptitude or achievement level or whatever other factor the examination purports to measure." The examinations may not reflect "the individual's impaired sensory, manual, or speaking skills" unless (1) the purpose of the test is to measure those factors and (2) the measurement of those factors has a valid educational purpose. See generally *Morisky v. Broward County* (1996) and *Wynne v. Tufts University School of Medicine* (1992). In *Letter of Findings Issued to Educational Testing Service* (1993), the Office for Civil Rights (OCR) of the Department of Education concluded that the Educational Testing Service could not arbitrarily limit extended time to double time but rather must give consideration to a documented request for triple time.

Examinations tailored to individuals with disabilities must be administered in facilities that are "accessible" to those individuals. 28 CFR § 36.309(b)(2) states that the examinations are generally required to be modified "in the length of time permitted for completion" and in the "manner in which the examination is given."

Auxiliary aids and services must be provided in testing. Modifications are not required where they would alter the fundamental nature of the course or pose an undue hardship. According to 28 CFR § 36.309(b)(3), auxiliary aids in examinations may include taped examinations, interpreters or other effective methods of making orally delivered materials available to individuals with hearing impairments, Brailled or large-print examinations and answer sheets or qualified readers for individuals with visual impairments or LD, transcribers for individuals with manual impairments, and other similar services and actions. The ADAAA provides:

SEC. 4. ADDITIONAL DEFINITIONS.

As used in this Act:

(1) AUXILIARY AIDS AND SERVICES.—The term "auxiliary aids and services" includes—
   (A) qualified interpreters or other effective methods of making aurally delivered materials available to individuals with hearing impairments;
   (B) qualified readers, taped texts, or other effective methods of making visually delivered materials available to individuals with visual impairments;
   (C) acquisition or modification of equipment or devices; and
   (D) other similar services and actions.

According to 28 CFR § 36.309(b)(4), alternative accessible arrangements, including "provision of an examination at an individual's home with a proctor," may be utilized if accessible facilities are not available. These modifications and auxiliary aids must be provided to those individuals with disabilities who require them. See *Stern v. University of Osteopathic Med. and Health Sciences* (2000); *Bartlett v. New York State Bd of Law Exam'rs* (2001); and *Detroyer v. Oakland Cmty College* (2001).

Required Testing Modifications

Testing modifications are required for a qualified individual with a disability if they will not alter the fundamental nature of the program being offered or create an undue burden. As stated in 28 CFR § 36.309(b)(3) of the regulations:

---

(3) A private entity offering an examination covered by this section shall provide appropriate auxiliary aids for persons with impaired sensory, manual, or speaking skills, unless that private entity can demonstrate that offering a particular auxiliary aid would fundamentally alter the measurement of the skills or knowledge the examination is intended to test or would result in an undue burden.

Delivery of Educational Materials

A postsecondary institution must provide equal access to classroom and other educational materials. This duty is described in the regulations as an obligation to provide course modifications and auxiliary aids and services.

Course modifications are required. The institution offering the course

> must make such modifications to that course as are necessary to ensure that the place and manner in which the course is given are accessible to individuals with disabilities. . . . Required modifications may include changes in the length of time permitted for the completion of the course, substitution of specific requirements, or adaptation of the manner in which the course is conducted or course materials are distributed. 28 CFR §§ 36.309(c)(1),(2)

Auxiliary aids and services in the presentation of the course are required. According to 28 CFR § 36.309(c)(3), the institution offering the course:

> shall provide appropriate auxiliary aids and services for persons with impaired sensory, manual, or speaking skills, unless the private entity can demonstrate that offering a particular auxiliary aid or service would fundamentally alter the course or would result in an undue burden.

The auxiliary aids and services must "recognize individual communications needs" and must provide "contemporaneous communication" of the entire educational experience—including class participation—being offered. Their selection is to be guided by an interactive process involving the student and the institution.

Auxiliary aids in courses

> may include taped texts, interpreters or other effective methods of making orally delivered materials available to individuals with hearing impairments, Brailled or large print texts or qualified readers for individuals with visual impairments and learning disabilities, classroom equipment adapted for use by individuals with manual impairments, and other similar services and actions. 28 CFR § 36.309(c)(3)

Alternative accessible arrangements, including videotaped lectures, cassettes, and prepared notes, may be utilized, according to 28 CFR § 36.309(c)(5). As with aids in examinations, these auxiliary aids in courses must be provided to those individuals with disabilities who require them. Ordinarily, students with disabilities who require aids in examinations and courses would so request and would provide appropriate supporting documentation.

Fundamental Academic Requirements

No postsecondary institution is required to lessen the quality of the education it provides (*Letter of Findings Issued to Golden Gate University*, 1996). Postsecondary institutions are not required to permit course substitutions where the required course is considered essential (*Letter of Findings Issued to Wingate University*, 1996). See also *Guckenberger v. Boston University* (1997).

Selecting the Appropriate Accommodation

The first step in selecting an appropriate accommodation is to request one. In order to obtain an accommodation (called academic adjustments and auxiliary aids and services), the individual must contact the appropriate university office and follow the procedure for documenting the disability and the need for particular accommodations. A failure to comply with reasonable procedures will bar the student's claim (*Letter of Findings Issued to Highline Community College*, 1996). A timely request for accommodation in compliance with institutional procedures is essential. See *Letter of Findings Issued to University of California, Los Angeles* (1996) and *Letter of Findings Issued to Philadelphia College of Optometry* (1996) for further information.

Accommodations Must Be Requested

Accommodations are required only for individuals with disabilities who request them. In *Letter of Findings Issued to St. Louis Community College at Meramec* (1996), the Department of Education held that a student with ADHD who met admissions criteria was a qualified individual with a disability. When the student requested additional time for tests, but not the right to use loose-leaf sheets for laboratory note-taking and the right to transcribe those notes into the lab book, the educational institution was permitted to lower his laboratory grades for failure to comply with the requirement that all notes be entered directly during the laboratory session. An institution is not obligated to provide assistance that has not been requested. See *Letter of Findings Issued to Almont Community Sch. Dist.* (1996). It is lawful for a university to establish reasonable standards and procedures to obtain academic adjustments.

Documentation Requirements

Applicants and students who are seeking to obtain accommodations must present reasonable documentation to support the requested accommodations. In *Dubois v. Alderson-Broaddus College, Inc.* (1997), the Court considered the case of a student who was granted accommodations (oral rather than written exams) but was required to give 48-hour notice of his need for these accommodations. The student objected and sued under the ADA. The Court held that the student had not established that he was an individual with a disability because his only documentation consisted of a psychologist's report that stated that he "might suffer from a specific learning disability." The student had also refused to take a Wechsler Adult Intelligence Scale to confirm the diagnosis (*Letter of Findings Issued to State University of New York*, 1993). See also *Letter of Findings Issued to Frostburg State University* (1995).

Note that the foregoing regulations were adopted prior to the enactment of the ADAAA. New regulations have not been promulgated. It appears likely that the vast increase in the number of individuals receiving the term "individual with a disability" in the ADAAA will lead to an expansion of reasonable accommodations. In *Jenkins v. National Board of Medical Examiners* (2009), the Court remanded the case to be tried under the standards of the ADAAA. It noted that the

---

scope of the ADA's coverage has been broadened. This breadth heightens the importance of the district court's responsibility to fashion appropriate accommodations. If the district court in this case finds that Jenkins is disabled under the more inclusive terms of the amended ADA, the court must still determine specifically what NBME [National Board of Medical Examiners] must do to comply with the requirement that a professional licensing board offer its examination "in a place and manner accessible to persons with disabilities." 42 U.S.C. § 12189 This nuanced determination is not governed by previous, voluntarily provided accommodations that Jenkins has received, nor necessarily by what accommodations were required under the narrower previous definition of disability.

EMPLOYMENT

Earlier in this chapter we considered the application of the RA/ADA to postsecondary education. Now we consider the application of the RA/ADA to employment. Court cases involving the issue of who is an individual with a disability under the RA and ADA have been extensively discussed already. The principal focus of this section is on accommodations in the workplace.

Remember that we defined an individual with a disability as a person who "has a physical or mental impairment that substantially limits one or more of such person's major life activities."

The RA/ADA approach to employment is fundamentally similar to other areas. *Discrimination* against individuals with disabilities is prohibited, and *qualified individuals* with disabilities are entitled to *reasonable accommodations* in meeting the *essential requirements* of the employer.

RA

The RA applies to three classes of employer:

1. The federal government, less the judiciary and armed forces
2. Most government contractors, by virtue of their contracts
3. Recipients of federal funds

Under the ADA, the nature of the institution, not the receipt of federal funds, is the decisive factor. Employers are governed primarily by Title I.

Title I of the ADA

Title I covers employers with 15 or more employees. The basic requirement of Title I, as specified in 42 U.S.C. § 12112(a), is that

> No covered entity shall discriminate against a qualified individual with a disability because of the disability of such individual in regard to job application procedures, the hiring, advancement, or discharge of employees, employee compensation, job training, and other terms, conditions, and privileges of employment.

These provisions are implemented by regulations such as 29 C.F.R. § 1630. Note: These regulations do not reflect the ADAAA. The Department of Justice and the Equal Employment Opportunity Commission (EEOC) recently have issued regulations implementing the ADAAA.

Title I of the ADA—42 U.S.C. § 12112(b)—protects individuals with disabilities from discrimination in employment. The EEOC describes the ADA's requirements in this way:

> Under www.eeoc.gov/policy/ada.html, Americans with Disabilities Act, it is illegal to discriminate in any aspect of employment, including:
> - hiring and firing;
> - compensation, assignment, or classification of employees;
> - transfer, promotion, layoff, or recall;
> - job advertisements;
> - recruitment;
> - testing;
> - use of company facilities;
> - training and apprenticeship programs;
> - fringe benefits;
> - pay, retirement plans, and disability leave; or
> - other terms and conditions of employment.

OTHERWISE QUALIFIED

Basic Rule

The ADA does not protect all individuals with disabilities. It applies only to a "qualified individual with a disability," as previously discussed.

The requirements of the ADA have been summarized by the EEOC:

> QUALIFIED INDIVIDUAL WITH A DISABILITY
> A qualified employee or applicant with a disability is someone who satisfies skill, experience, education, and other job-related requirements of the position held or

desired, and who, with or without reasonable accommodation, can perform the essential functions of that position.

Just what are the essential functions or duties of a job?

Essential Job Requirements

An individual with a disability must prove that he or she is able to meet the essential requirements of a job, with or without a reasonable accommodation. If the record shows that an individual cannot perform without a reasonable accommodation, he or she must prove that a particular accommodation would enable him or her to perform. See *Bombard v. Fort Wayne Newspapers, Inc.* (1996).

Just what are the essential job requirements? The courts have devoted a significant effort to answering that question. Three essential requirements include:

1. Prerequisite qualifications, such as physical, mental, academic, and work experience requirements.
2. Hard-core job skills.
3. Requirements for cooperativeness and good citizenship in the workplace.

The ability to work cooperatively with supervisors and coworkers is essential and may prove challenging for some persons with ADD, ADHD, and/or SLD. Employers are entitled to require such "good citizenship." Examples of the courts' rulings in this regard are:

- **Ability to refrain from bizarre and disruptive office behavior and an ability to get along with a supervisor:** *Dazey v. Department of the Air Force* (1992); *Mancini v. General Elec. Co.* (1993).
- **Ability to refrain from "combative exchanges" with fellow employees:** *Hardy v. Sears, Roebuck & Co.* (1996).
- **Regular attendance:** *Jackson v. Veterans Admin.* (1994); *Jackson v. Department of Veterans Affairs* (1994); *Kennedy v. Applause, Inc.* (1996); *Leatherwood v. Houston Post Co.* (1995); *Tyndall v. National Educ. Ctrs.* (1994); *Wilder v. Southeastern Pub. Serv. Auth.* (1994).
- **Honesty:** *Grinstead v. Pool Co. of Texas* (1994); *Harris v. Polk County* (1996); *Hartman v. City of Petaluma* (1994); *Waites v. MCI* (1998).
- **Safety:** *Allmond v. Akal Security, Inc., et al.* (2009); *Bussey v. West* (1996); *City of Columbus v. Lowe* (1995); *Wilson v. Phillips Petroleum Co.* (1998).
- **Drug-free workplace:** *Shafer v. Preston Memorial Hospital Corporation* (1997).

Adequate Social Skills

Persons with cognitive disorders are often challenged by the requirement that employees possess social skills adequate to their tasks. *Taylor v. Food World, Inc.* (11th Cir. 1998) concerned Gary, a clerk for Food World, who suffers from Asperger's Disorder, a form of autism involving Pervasive Developmental Disorders. As a result of this condition, Gary often spoke more loudly than necessary and engaged in echolalia (constant repetitive speech) that he was unable to control. In addition, Gary's communication and social interaction skills were impaired, as were certain living and survival skills. For example, Gary tended to make inappropriate comments or ask personal questions of strangers. On September 13, 1994, the store manager for Food World terminated Gary's employment. The manager told Gary's mother that the decision to terminate Gary was based on customer complaints that Gary was loud, overly friendly, and overly talkative.

Gary sued under the ADA, but the District Court dismissed his suit. The Eleventh Circuit ordered the suit reinstated, saying:

> We do not think that the record shows, as a matter of law, that Gary could not carry out the tasks of his job without offending customers. . . . Although Gary did ask customers questions, there is an issue of fact as to whether these questions were offensive or inappropriate. Because a genuine issue of material fact exists as to whether Gary was qualified, summary judgment on this ground is precluded.

Duty to Manage Medication

Some persons with ADD/ADHD or LD may be required to take medications in order to ameliorate the effects of their conditions. While the beneficial effects of medications may render them qualified for the job, there may arise a concomitant duty to manage the medications.

TESTING

Employment-related testing under the ADA must comply with the same rules applicable to postsecondary education discussed earlier in the chapter. Specifically, testing must be justified, where essential, and modified to accommodate reasonably an individual with a disability.

According to 42 U.S.C. § 12113(a), justification is required:

> It may be a defense to a charge of discrimination under this chapter that an alleged application of qualification standards, tests, or selection criteria that screen out or tend to screen out or otherwise deny a job or benefit to an individual with a disability has been shown to be job-related and consistent with business necessity, and such performance cannot be accomplished by reasonable accommodation, as required under this subchapter.

Testing for a Disability

The ADA generally prohibits an employer from inquiring whether an individual has a disability or the extent of it. The ADA also prohibits medical examinations and inquiries, absent a showing that such inquiries are job related and consistent with business necessity.

Karracker et al. v. Rent-A-Center (2005) involved personality testing to screen for promotion with the company. The personality test included over 500 questions from the Minnesota Multiphasic Personality Test (MMPI). The court found that the MMPI measures conditions, such as depression, paranoia, and mania, and is used in diagnosing psychiatric disorders. Accordingly, the court held that the MMPI is a medical examination or inquiry not permitted under the ADA to be used for routine pre-employment or pre-promotion screening.

Testing for Qualifications

It is important to note that, in general, prospective employers are permitted to test potential employees to determine whether they possess the ability to meet the essential requirements of a job.

In *Thompson v. Borg-Warner Protective Servs Corp.* (1996), the Court considered the case of an applicant for a security guard position with a security service company. The applicant was interviewed and requested to complete a multiple-choice survey, which was intended to assess the applicant's alienation, trustworthiness, and drug attitudes. The interviewer advised the applicant that his answers would make security guard employment unlikely. The applicant became angry and protested the use of the survey, at which point the company refused to hire him because he lacked the temperament and self-control necessary to be a security guard. Thompson then sued under the ADA, contending that the survey was an unlawful inquiry to determine whether applicants had disabilities. The Court held the survey to be lawful and, in doing so, pointed out that alienation, untrustworthiness, and current drug use were indicators of an inability to perform the essential functions of a security guard. Since none of these was protected by the ADA, the prospective employer is entitled to inquire concerning them.

Drug Testing

Drug testing is permitted if justified by business necessity. In *Roe v. Cheyenne Mt. Conf. Resort* (1997), the Court struck down a company policy that required each employee to report every drug ingested, including all lawful prescription medications. A suit was brought by an employee who took prescription medication for asthma to prohibit the company from requiring disclosure of her medications. The company did not contend that the policy was justified by business necessity or specific job-related requirements, and, in fact, as the Court pointed out, the company was free at all times to test employees for illegal drug use.

REASONABLE ACCOMMODATIONS

Reasonable accommodations are of three general types:

1. Those required to ensure equal opportunity in the job application process
2. Those that enable the individual with a disability to perform the essential features of a job
3. Those that enable individuals with disabilities to enjoy the same benefits and privileges as those available to individuals without disabilities

The most common accommodations are those that enable the individual with a disability to perform the essential features of a job. Cases decided by the courts are detailed next.

Supervisor Feedback to Guide Performance

In *Commeree v. Hantman* (1999), the Court found requested accommodations for a senior-level employee to be unreasonable. The Court considered a request by the assistant head for the Architect of the Capitol. This individual had ADD and sought, as a reasonable accommodation, a nondistracting workplace, multistaged tasks, written instructions (by text or e-mail), intermediate deadlines, a single supervisor, and assistance in setting up a time management system. The Architect of the Capitol denied the requested accommodations and offered as alternatives (1) permission for the assistant head to remain in his job without accommodations, (2) retirement with disability, or (3) acceptance of a lesser-paying position with accommodations. Commeree refused and brought suit alleging disability discrimination. The Court held for the Architect of the Capitol because the accommodations requested were not reasonable. They put Commeree in the position of an employee who needed supervision rather than a supervisor who must exercise independent judgment, interface with subordinates, and juggle tasks when necessary. The Court further held that the Architect of the Capitol is not required to reallocate supervisory functions as an accommodation.

Flex Time

Flex time means a specific and agreed-on earlier or later starting time coupled with a correspondingly earlier or later leaving time. Flex time may be a reasonable accommodation in some circumstances.

Reassignment

Sometimes a nonessential function that poses a problem for an individual with a disability can be transferred to another employee. However, some requests are unreasonable. Reassignment to a vacant permanent position may be a reasonable accommodation, but there are limits on the duty to accommodate. In *Howell v. Michelin Tire Corp.* (1994), the Court held that an employer has no obligation to create a permanent "light duty" position for an individual with a disability.

Working at Home

Working at home is an accommodation that, in some workplace situations, may be reasonable. In *Misek-Falkoff v. IBM Corp.* (1994), the Court held that work at home must be considered but is usually denied unless available to others. The nature of the job, nature of the disability, length of time on job, and need for supervision are to be considered.

Additional Time

Additional time for an individual with a disability to learn to perform job functions may be a reasonable accommodation under certain circumstances. However, in *Riblett v. Boeing Co.* (1995), the Court upheld the termination, for poor performance, of a draftsman with visual learning impairments. The termination was found not to violate the ADA because the employer had provided a reasonable accommodation in allowing the employee almost two years to master the job functions. However, in *Peyton v. Fred's Stores of Arkansas* (2009), an indefinite leave of absence in order to treat cancer is not a reasonable accommodation.

SELECTING THE ACCOMMODATION

According to *Beck v. University of Wisconsin* (1996), the process of selecting a reasonable accommodation is an interactive one in which the employer and employee are to be responsive to reasonable inquiries from each other. The "interactive process" must take account of the parties who are interacting. In *Bultemeyer v. Fort Wayne Community Schools* (1996), the Court considered the case of a workplace custodian with mental illness and severe limitations who had previously received accommodations from the employer. In the current case, he made an ambiguous request for the accommodations previously given him. The employer concluded that he had made no request and fired him. The Seventh Circuit, following *Beck*, held that the employee had discharged his duty to request accommodations because, as part of the interactive accommodation process, which requires a great deal of communication between the employee and employer, the employer is obligated to seek clarification of the custodian's actions.

The interactive process works both ways. An employee may not refuse to accept a reasonable accommodation (if it truly is such) on the grounds that he or she would prefer another accommodation. In *Hankins v. The Gap, Inc.* (1996), the Sixth Circuit held that an employee is obligated to accept a reasonable accommodation offered by the employer and that the employee's refusal to accept available reasonable accommodations precluded her from arguing that other accommodations should also have been provided. In *Mathew v. Cardone Industries, Inc.* (1998) the Court held that a newly created job, offered by the employer but rejected by the employee, was a reasonable accommodation. The Court then said:

> Reasonable accommodations are therefore not accommodations based upon an individual's preferences, but upon those conditions which enable an individual to perform the essential functions of his position.

As noted in the discussion of academic accommodations, the ADAAA may bring about an increase in the number of individuals receiving reasonable accommodations.

LIMITATIONS ON THE DUTY TO ACCOMMODATE

No employer need provide an accommodation that would impose an undue hardship on the employer or create a danger to others. In *Allmond v. Akal Security, Inc., et al.* (2009), the Court considered a requirement of the U.S. Marshals Service, which is charged with providing security in U.S. courtrooms, that all candidates for employment be able to pass a hearing test without the assistance of a hearing aid, even though hearing aids were permitted on the job. The Court found that this requirement was a fundamental job requirement and justified by business necessity because marshals may be required to whisper to each other when confronting a threatening individual. Moreover, the consequences of a hearing aid failure could be catastrophic. The Court said:

> To benefit from the affirmative defense, an employer must prove that the pertinent qualification standard is job-related and consistent with business necessity. . . . Although this burden is generally quite high, it is significantly lowered when, like here, "the job clearly requires a high degree of skill and the economic and human risks involved in hiring an unqualified applicant are great . . . ." (*Hamer v. City of Atlanta*, 1989)

INDIVIDUALIZED INQUIRY

According to *Ward v. Skinner* (1991), legitimate job-related safety requirements may operate to bar an individual with disabilities from some employment. The ADA and the RA do not prohibit proper and reasonable restrictions where safety is concerned.

Both acts do, in general, require that each person with a disability be accorded an individualized inquiry to ensure that any rule limiting activities has a reasonable basis. See *School Board of Nassau County v. Arline* (1987) and *Traynor v. Turnage* (1988). (Note: Although both of these cases have been superseded by statutes, they are still appropriate for the points made in this text.)

Disclosure

No employee has an obligation to disclose a disability, and no employer has an obligation to provide accommodations for a disability that has not been disclosed. See *Morisky v. Broward County* (1996). To invoke the ADA, an individual must disclose his or her disability to the persons who have decision-making authority. In *Stevens v. Target Stores* (1997), the Court held that an employee with mild mental retardation was properly fired when she marked down a VCR to $20.00 and bought it herself. Although she told coworkers that she had a disability, she never told anyone in the "decision-making group." Therefore, the ADA did not apply to her. The "bottom line" is this: Disclose your disability only if you seek accommodations for it.

Documentation

Disclosure often involves documentation of the disability. The EEOC has given guidance. The EEOC's Enforcement Guidance on the Americans with Disabilities Act and Psychiatric Disabilities provides:

The determination that a particular individual has a substantially limiting impairment should be based on information about how the impairment affects that individual and not on generalizations about the condition. Relevant evidence for EEOC investigators includes descriptions of an individual's typical level of functioning at home, at work, and in other settings, as well as evidence showing that the individual's functional limitations are linked to his/her impairment. Expert testimony about substantial limitation is not necessarily required. Credible testimony from the individual with a disability and his/her family members, friends, or coworkers may suffice.

ENFORCEMENT

Rights are conferred on individuals with disabilities by the RA and the ADA. The RA may be enforced by several federal government departments and sometimes by private suits. The ADA may be enforced by various federal government departments and agencies and sometimes by private suits. Damages and injunctive relief are available remedies under both the RA and the ADA, except that Title III does not provide for damages as a remedy for violations of that title.

Government Agencies

Government agencies enforce the RA and ADA in two ways. First, they may use administrative proceedings to determine whether a federal aid recipient has complied with the duties imposed by the RA and whether the ADA has been violated. See *Alexander v. Sandoval* (2001) and *Lane v. Pena* (1996). The agencies most involved are the Department of Education's OCR, the Department of Justice, the Department of Labor, and the EEOC. The Department of Education is concerned primarily with education and the EEOC with employment. The Department of Justice may be involved with either. Second, these agencies may also seek injunctive relief to compel compliance with the RA/ADA or to prohibit violations of those statutes.

Private Suits/RA

The RA, 29 U.S.C. § 794, sometimes may be enforced by private civil suit—for example, when intentional discrimination against individuals with disabilities by an entity receiving federal funds can be shown. Damages and injunctive relief are available, according to 42 U.S.C. § 2000d-7(a)(2).

Private Suits/ADA

Title I (Employment)

A successful plaintiff will be entitled to injunctive relief and/or damages as the circumstances require.

Title II (States)

A successful plaintiff will be entitled to limited injunctive relief but not damages. Note that there is a serious issue as to the constitutionality of Title II under the ADAAA. The predecessor to the current Title II was found to be largely unconstitutional. See *Board of Trustees of the University of Alabama v. Garrett* (2001) and *Kiman v. N.H. Dep't of Corr.* (2002).

Title III (Places of Public Accommodation) (Includes Private Schools)

A successful plaintiff will be entitled to injunctive relief as the circumstances require but no damages.

Attorneys' Fees and Court Costs

No provision of the ADA authorizes damages for violation of this title. Attorneys' fees and court costs may be recovered by a prevailing private party under both the RA and

ADA. The government may not recover such fees and costs even when it is a prevailing party. See 29 U.S.C. § 794a and the ADA (42 U.S.C. §§ 12117, 12133, 12203[C], and 12205).

Dispute Resolution

Not every dispute need be resolved by litigation in court. There are a number of approaches short of going to court. The means of resolving disputes include: advocacy, mediation, arbitration, and formal filings with courts or governmental departments or agencies.

Advocacy

Advocacy is the first approach to resolving disputes without suing people. The discussion will be in the context of individuals with LD and ADHD, but the points have a broader application as well.

Five key areas in this process of taking responsibility and advocating successfully are:

1. Know yourself, your strengths and weaknesses.
2. Understand others by listening to what others say and watching facial expression and body language.
3. Select a good job or educational match, by knowing yourself and understanding all of the requirements of the academic program or career or particular job.
4. Use strategies (short-term and long-term goals) to promote success.
5. Familiarize yourself with applicable laws and regulations.

Be prepared to document your disability. Most documentation involves three steps: diagnosis, evaluation of impact, and recommendations. Together, they establish, for purposes of RA/ADA:

- A disability, which involves establishing the existence of an impairment and substantial limitation in a major life activity.
- The areas of functional impact and degree of impact resulting from the disability.
- The specific reasonable accommodations, required because of that disability, that will enable the individual to perform the essential job or program functions.

Advocacy takes place in various settings, ranging from an informal conversation to formal written presentations. The steps are:

1. Informal communication, such as a casual conversation.
2. Formal communication, such as a meeting called for a set purpose or a letter setting forth a position.

3. Negotiation between two parties in which there is a presentation of positions, involving a marshaling of facts and arguments based on those facts, in a structured meeting or in writing.
4. Alternative dispute resolution, which includes mediation and arbitration.
5. Litigation in court or formal filing of a complaint or charge with an appropriate government entity.

In each of these settings, we or our attorneys are seeking to persuade someone of the validity of our position. Initially, it is another party. Later, it may be an arbitrator, hearing officer, or judge.

Mediation

Mediation is a voluntary, structured process to facilitate dispute resolution. In mediation, the parties select a mediator who is a neutral person to facilitate resolution of the dispute. The mediator is paid on an agreed-on basis, which often is an hourly rate.

Once the mediator is selected, the mediation is scheduled for a mutually agreed-on day. Sometimes each party will submit a brief statement of position to the mediator prior to the scheduled mediation day. The mediator discusses the disputed issues with the parties jointly and then separately with each party. The content of private discussions is confidential and may not be disclosed to the other side without permission. The mediator seeks to facilitate the achievement of a settlement between the parties.

If the parties agree on terms of settlement, the common practice is to sign a brief written agreement reflecting the settlement terms.

Generally, statements and documents originating in the course of mediation may not be introduced as evidence if discussions do not result in settlement and arbitration or a court proceeding becomes necessary.

Arbitration

Arbitration is a private trial conducted by an arbitrator, who functions as a judge. The parties choose either a single arbitrator or, depending on the nature, dollar value, and complexity of the case, a panel of three arbitrators. The arbitrator will conduct a hearing, receive evidence, and decide the dispute. The arbitrator has only those powers provided by the arbitration agreement. If the arbitration agreement states that particular rules will apply, such as the employment rules of the American Arbitration Association, then such rules do apply to the arbitration.

The arbitrator receives a fee, which is agreed on by the parties. Often the fee is based on a daily or hourly rate. Some arbitration agreements provide for the recovery of the attorneys' fees and costs of the winning party. Administrative services (such as finding a suitable hearing location and collecting the arbitrator's fees) are often provided by the entity whose rules govern, such as the American Arbitration Association.

Arbitration proceedings are similar to court trials but are shorter, more simple, and less expensive. Evidence is presented through witness testimony and the introduction of documents, just as in court proceedings. However, technical rules of evidence are not strictly followed. Documentary evidence must be authentic and relevant. Oral testimony must be relevant. Affidavits may be permitted.

The decision of the arbitrator ordinarily is not lengthy. The decision will state: the result reached; the amount of money or other remedy awarded to the prevailing party: and who must pay the attorneys' fees, arbitration costs, and filing fees. Ordinarily, unless the agreement of the parties or a statute provides for shifting of attorneys' fees and costs, each party will bear his or her own attorney's fees and costs.

Arbitration awards are usually final and ordinarily may not be overturned by a court. As a result, arbitration is the fastest and least expensive method of presenting all the evidence that would be presented in a court proceeding.

Effective alternative dispute resolution depends on the availability and selection of qualified and neutral arbitrators and mediators who are knowledgeable about the applicable laws.

Litigation

When should one sue in court or file a formal complaint with a government department or agency? Timing is everything. Absent a strong legal position, generally it is not prudent to sue. Continue efforts to work out something, even if it is an agreement on how to exit your job or academic program. In many cases that are lost in court by a plaintiff alleging disability discrimination, a settlement was offered to a plaintiff and rejected. Then the plaintiff subsequently lost the case in court.

If the legal position is strong, you may get tough if (a) all efforts at persuasion have failed and/or (b) time constraints require immediate action.

An option is to file a complaint with an appropriate governmental entity, such as the OCR of the Department of Education or the EEOC. The complainant may proceed on his or her own or with the assistance of an attorney.

If suing in court, it would be prudent to consider retaining an attorney to write a lawyer's letter setting forth the demand. The retention and cost initially may be simply for that service, and not a retainer to conduct the entire litigation. The next step may be negotiations between the lawyer and the opposing party's lawyer. The next step may be the filing of a complaint. It is important to be clear at each stage what the lawyer is being retained to do and how and at what rate billing will be done.

CONCLUSION

The government of the United States is a limited one and has only that authority conveyed to it by specific provisions of the United States Constitution. The statutes with which we are concerned are authorized by the Commerce Clause, the Spending Clause, and the Fourteenth Amendment.

Establishing disability status requires a showing that the individual has a physical or mental impairment that substantially limits one or more major life activities, such as "caring for oneself, performing manual tasks, seeing, hearing, eating, sleeping, walking, standing, lifting, bending, speaking, breathing, learning, reading, concentrating, thinking, communicating, and working." The ADAAA goes further to specify that many body functions are themselves major life activities. The act provides that "a major life activity also includes the operation of major bodily function, including but not limited to, functions of the immune system, normal cell growth, digestive, bowel, bladder, neurological, brain, respiratory, circulatory, endocrine, and reproductive functions."

The limitation must be *substantial*, with the term "substantial" to be interpreted in a more broad and inclusive manner than the more strict manner that had prevailed in court cases. The impact of the impairment may be in broad areas of activity or just in one narrow area.

The RA and ADA do not fully protect all individuals with disabilities, only those who are "otherwise qualified" for the educational program, job, or license at issue. However, the very facts that establish disability status may also show that the individual is not otherwise qualified.

The RA and ADA protect individuals who meet the criteria set forth in the statutes. To invoke the protection of these statutes, an individual must establish that he or she is an individual with a disability.

Establishing disability status requires a showing that the individual has a physical or mental impairment that substantially limits one or more major life activities, such as learning, without taking into account the positive and negative effects of any medication and/or compensatory strategies. The impact of the impairment may be in broad areas of activity or just in one narrow area.

When a substantially limiting impairment has been shown, a disability within the meaning of the RA/ADA has been established. However, the individual must also show that he or she is capable of meeting the essential requirements of the educational program or employment with or without a reasonable accommodation and is thus a "qualified individual with a disability."

Reasonable accommodations must be requested. However, no educational institution or employer need modify the essential requirements of a program or a job.

The key to advocacy is documentation. Prepared by a professional, the documentation should address:

- The nature of the impairment, such as a learning disability or ADHD, and how it presents.
- The impact on a major life activity or bodily function.

- The individual's ability to meet the fundamental course or job requirements.
- The accommodation requested and how it will affect the individual's performance.

REFERENCES

29 U.S.C. § 794a.

28 CFR § 36.309(b) (1991).

Albertsons, Inc., v. Kirkingburg, 527 U.S. 555 (1999).

Alexander (1990) v. Sandoval, 532 U.S. 275 (2001).

Allmond v. Akal Security, Inc., et al., Docket No. 07-15561 (11th Cir., February 20, 2009).

Americans with Disabilities Act of 1990 (ADA), 42 U.S.C. §§ 12101, 12117, 12133, 12203(C), and 12205.

Barnes v. Gorman, 536 U.S. 181 (2002).

Bartlett v. New York State Bd of Law Exam'rs (S.D. N.Y., August 15, 2001).

Beck v. University of Wisconsin (7th Cir. 1996).

Board of Trustees of the University of Alabama v. Garrett, 531 U.S. 356 (2001).

Bombard v. Fort Wayne Newspapers, Inc. (7th Cir. 1996).

Bragdon v. Abbott, 524 U.S. 624 (1998).

Bultemeyer v. Fort Wayne Community Schools (7th Cir., November 18, 1996).

Bussey v. West (4th Cir. 1996).

Calef v. Gillette Co. (1st Cir. 2003).

City of Columbus v. Lowe (Ohio App. 1995).

Commeree v. Hantman, 1999 WL 1611325 (D.D.C. October 28, 1999).

Constitution, Art. I, § 8, Cl. 4.

Dazey v. Department of the Air Force, 54 M.S.P.R. 658 (M.S.P.B. 1992).

Detroyer v. Oakland Cmty College (Mich. Ct. App., August 24, 2001).

Dubois v. Alderson-Broaddus College, Inc. (N.D. W.Va. 1997).

EEOC v. Argo Distribution L.L.C., F.3d 2009 WL 95259 (5th Cir., January 15, 2009).

EEOC v. Chevron Phillips Chemical Co. Lp., Docket No. 07-20661 (5th Cir., June 5, 2009).

Ellis v. Morehouse Sch. of Med. (N.D. Ga. 1996).

Grinstead v. Pool Co. of Texas (E.D. La. 1994), aff'd, 26 F. 3d 1118 (5th Cir. 1995).

Guckenberger et al. v. Boston University, 974 F. Supp. 106 (D. Mass. 1997).

Hamer v. City of Atlanta, 872 F.2d 1521, 1535 (11th Cir. 1989).

Hankins v. The Gap, Inc. (6th Cir. 1996).

Hardy v. Sears, Roebuck & Co. (N.D. Ga., August 28, 1996).

Harris v. Polk County (8th Cir., December 31, 1996).

Hartman v. City of Petaluma (N.D. Cal. 1994).

Howell v. Michelin Tire Corp. (M.D. Ala. 1994).

Jackson v. Department of Veterans Affairs, 513 U.S. 1052 (1994).

Jackson v. Veterans Admin. (11th Cir. 1994), *cert. dismissed.*

Jenkins v. National Board of Medical Examiners, Docket No. 08-5371 (6th Cir., February 11, 2009).

Karracker et al. v. Rent-A-Center, Inc., Docket No. 02C2026 (7th Cir. 2005).

Kennedy v. Applause, Inc. (9th Cir. 1996).

Kiesewetter v. Caterpillar, Inc., No. 08-2140 2008 WL 4523595 (7th Cir., October 9, 2008).

Kiman v. N.H. Dep't of Corr. (1st Cir. 2002).

Lane v. Pena, 518 U.S. 187 (1996).

Leatherwood v. Houston Post Co. (5th Cir. 1995).

Letter of Findings Issued to Almont Community Sch. Dist. OCR Docket No. 15–96–(1996).

Letter of Findings Issued to Educational Testing Service. OCR Docket No. 02932027 (1993).

Letter of Findings Issued to Frostburg State University. Case No. 03952052 (1995).

Letter of Findings Issued to Golden Gate University. OCR Docket No. 09–96–2088–I (1996).

Letter of Findings Issued to Philadelphia College of Optometry. OCR Docket No. 03962024 (1996).

Letter of Findings Issued to St. Louis Community College at Meramec. OCR Docket No. 07912049 (1992).

Letter of Findings Issued to State University of New York. Case No. 02–93–2088 (1993).

Letter of Findings Issued to University of California, Los Angeles. OCR Docket No. 09–95–2204 (1996).

Letter of Findings Issued to Wingate University. OCR Docket No. 04962051. RES (1996).

Lyons v. Smith (D.C.C. 1993).

Mancini v. General Elec. Co. (D. Vt. 1993).

Mathew v. Cardone Industries, Inc. (E.D. Pa. July 1998).

Mathews v. Denver Post (10th Cir. 2001).

McAlindin v. County of San Diego, 192 F.3d 1226 (9th Cir. 1999).

Misek-Falkoff v. IBM Corp. (S.D. N.Y 1994).

Morisky v. Broward County (11th Cir. 1996).

Murphy v. United Parcel Service, Inc., 527 U.S. 516 (1999).

Peyton v. Fred's Stores of Arkansas, Inc., Docket No. 08-2346 (8th Cir., April 15, 2009).

Powell v. National Board of Medical Examiners (2d Cir. 2004).

Rehabilitation Act of 1973 (RA), 29 U.S.C.A. § 701 et seq.

Riblett v. Boeing Co. (D. Kan. 1995).

Ristrom v. Asbestos Workers Local 34 (8th Cir. 2004).

Robertson v. Neuromedical Ctr. (5th Cir. 1998).

Roe v. Cheyenne Mt. Conf. Resort (10th Cir. 1997).

Rohr v. Salt River Project Agricultural Improvement and Power District, Docket No. 06-16527, (9th Cir., February 13, 2009).

School Board of Nassau County v. Arline, 480 U.S. 273 (1987).

Shafer v. Preston Memorial Hospital Corporation (4th Cir. 1997).

Stern v. University of Osteopathic Med. and Health Sciences (8th Cir. 2000).

Stevens v. Target Stores (N.D. Ill., December 11, 1997).

Stutts v. Freeman (11th Cir. 1983).

Sutton v. United Air Lines, Inc., 527 U.S. 471 (1999).

Taylor v. Food World, Inc. (11th Cir. 1998).

Thompson v. Borg-Warner Protective Servs Corp. (N.D. Cal., March 12, 1996).

Toyota Motor Manufacturing, Kentucky, Inc., v. Williams, 534 U.S. 184 (2002).

Traynor v. Turnage, 485 U.S. 535 (1988).

Tyndall v. National Educ. Ctrs. (4th Cir. 1994).

Waites v. MCI (10th Cir. 1998).

Ward v. Skinner (1st Cir. 1991).

Wilder v. Southeastern Pub. Serv. Auth. (E.D. Va. 1994), *aff'd*, 69 F.3d 534 (4th Cir. 1995).

Wilson v. Phillips Petroleum Co. (N.D. Tex., December 8, 1998).

Wright v. CompUSA (1st Cir. 2003).

Wynne v. Tufts University School of Medicine (1st Cir. 1992).

PART

III

Treatment

11

Overview of Current Treatment Protocols

SAM GOLDSTEIN

I deally, assessment of Learning Disabilities (LD) and Attention-Deficit/Hyperactivity Disorder (ADHD) should lead directly to intervention. An increasing number of educational, vocational, and even medical options are available. For those in late adolescence or young adulthood, interventions usually focus heavily on transition. Transition from childhood to functional adulthood is a multiyear process. For those with LD and ADHD, this process must be tailored to the needs of each person. In school settings in accordance with the Individuals with Disabilities Education Improvement Act (IDEIA), formal transition teams are typically established composed of secondary school personnel, parents, and the student. The path to successful transition for those with ADHD and LD depends greatly on the knowledge and efforts of these professionals. In addition to educating people with LD or ADHD about their condition and options, professionals should work to provide family members, spouses, educators, and employers with a reasonable understanding of the strengths and weaknesses of the individual as well as strategies, ideas, and guidance. Over 20 years ago, Ginsberg and Gerber (1990) noted that understanding, acceptance, and actions are key activities in the lives of successful individuals with LD and ADHD.

The guidance, intervention, and transition process traditionally has focused on remediation of basic academic skills and the development of vocational skills and compensatory strategies necessary for adult living. However, it has increasingly been recognized that harnessing strengths and abilities as well as developing compensatory strategies are of equal if not of greater importance in the transition process (Goldstein & Naglieri, 2009). For individuals with LD and ADHD, this focus has emphasized the development of efficient problem-solving and daily life strategies with the aim of reducing impairment rather than teaching specific skills that may not generalize well (Deschler, Schumacher, Lenz, & Ellis, 1983).

The intervention chapters in the remainder of this edition are expanded from the first edition and offer a comprehensive overview of available scientific knowledge and practical clinical guidelines. Despite belief to the contrary in some circles, the treatment of late adolescent and adult ADHD and LD is strongly science based. In 1993, Lipsey and Wilson completed an expansive analytic review of the efficacy of psychological, educational, and behavioral treatments targeting the specific problems of people with LD and ADHD. Reporting on over 100 studies, these authors noted strong effect sizes in the majority of studies, including those reflecting computer-based education, individualized tutoring and assistance, perceptual/motor and visual strategies and supports, behavioral interventions, test taking and coaching strategies, as well as early intervention.

Millions of students with LD and ADHD have been appropriately served in elementary and secondary school settings since the inception of the Individuals with Disabilities Education Act of 2004 (IDEA). Despite the significant advances since the publication of the first edition of this volume, there continues to be a dearth of systematic scientific research identifying the college and vocational programs that are most effective in the long term for students with LD and ADHD. The heterogeneity of these populations suggest that such research will be detailed, lengthy, and difficult to complete. The Department of Education (DOE) undertook the first National Longitudinal Transition Study in 1987. This study was the first effort to document the experiences and outcomes of youth with disabilities. In 2001, the DOE launched its second National Longitudinal Transition Study (NLTS2). This 10-year study includes interviews with 12,000 students, ages 13 to 16, and their parents as well as surveys of their schools and teachers. The first NLTS2 report was issued in 2003 (Wagner, Cameto, & Newman, 2003). This report documents the extent and direction of differences in categories such as demographics, school achievement, and parent expectations between the populations of 15- to 17-year-old youth with disabilities in 1987 and those with disabilities in 2001. This initial report indicates that some experiences and outcomes for students using special education services have improved since 1987. For example, in 2001, more students with ADHD were being served. Many more students with LD were at the typical grade level for their age, and the average age at which students were first identified for LD was lower. In contrast, problem behavior was a larger issue in 2001 than in 1987, and the percentage of parents expecting their children to graduate from a 4-year college, though greater, was still very low. This report continued to document the lack of availability of specialized vocational, academic, and life skills programs for populations of students with these types of disabilities. This longitudinal transition study has just entered its final round of phone interviews. Final results of this study are slowly being disseminated (Newman, Wagner, Cameto, & Knokey, 2009).

In the meantime, clinicians must prepare students with LD and ADHD for post–high school educational and vocational training. They must also educate the professional community at large about available programs and the types of information college counselors and special educators require to work effectively with these student populations. In 1986, Rothstein noted that it was also the responsibility of clinicians to teach those with LD and ADHD to be assertive and not embarrassed about their disabilities. The responsibility of obtaining services falls on the shoulders of those with the condition. The responsibility of generating data so that appropriate services can be implemented falls on the shoulders of the clinician. Finally, the responsibility of developing and implementing appropriate programs falls on the shoulders of educators and vocational trainers.

A significant post–high school transition point for those with LD and ADHD is the decision to either enter college or seek competitive employment. Researchers traditionally have found that those accepted into a 4-year college with these conditions often suffer from less severe academic achievement problems and are more likely to come from enriched home environments and educational experiences (Gajar, Salvia, Gajria, & Salvia, 1989; Shaywitz & Shaw, 1988; Vogel, 1986). In 1986, Hoy and Gregg listed seven characteristics that appeared to increase the likelihood that a student with a learning disability would succeed in college:

1. High motivation
2. Willingness to experiment with new ideas
3. Verbal intellectual skills at a standard score of 90 or above (23rd percentile or better)
4. Ability to comprehend abstract language
5. Emotional maturity
6. Socially appropriate behavior
7. Career goals congruent with ability

Many clinicians, including school counselors, either know too little about LD and ADHD support services available at a college level or due to limited experience do not view these students as college material. Clinicians with these biases will not best serve the transitional needs of students with LD or ADHD. High school programs serving these students have become increasingly focused on developing transition plans and providing reasoned and reasonable guidance for students' post–high school experiences. Even with support, however, the choice is not easy, and a risk-benefit analysis for this decision is essential. Community colleges, for example, offer accessibility, less stringent admission requirements (if any), a wide variety of course work, basic educational courses, transition services, and often special education support. They are inexpensive because they are community supported. Funds that might otherwise have been spent on housing can be used to provide other special services. Such services can include accommodations under Section 504 of the Americans with Disabilities Act as well as remedial and compensatory interventions.

A remedial model of intervention for LD and ADHD focuses on improving basic academic skills, including reading, math, writing, and spelling, as well as basic executive skills, such as attention, planning, and organization. Remedial programs have a long and honorable history in the elementary and secondary educational literature. However, the benefits of these programs are difficult to measure long term. They may not be much more advantageous than programs focusing on strengths and compensation. Additionally, the short- and long-term results of cognitively based remedial programs for problems such as ADHD have had limited though increasingly promising results (Diller & Goldstein, 2006). It is not that students with these disabilities cannot learn how to plan, think, or solve problems; rather, they do not engage in these behaviors consistently in their daily lives.

Remediation traditionally has focused on organized, repetitive practice as a way to improve skills. In the LD arena, most advocates of remedial approaches emphasize the understanding of learning styles and multisensory teaching techniques as a way to facilitate the acquisition of educational material. In fact, some educators suggest that without knowledge of an individual's learning style, intervention is not going to be effective (Bingham, 1989). Proponents of the learning styles model characterized styles according to these four types:

1. *Visual.* The visual learner is comfortable with books and graphs.
2. *Auditory.* The auditory learner tends to think, memorize easily, perform poorly on group tests, and have poor perception of time and space.
3. *Kinesthetic.* The kinesthetic learner functions best by moving and touching.
4. *Tactile.* The tactile learner has trouble with one-to-one correspondence, rote computing, and sequencing at any level. This student requires concrete objects for learning and has difficulty learning abstract symbols. Diagrams and other illustrations are essential (Marsh & Price, 1980).

The second way of understanding the learning processes, as noted earlier in this volume, is to focus on the rote, conceptual, visual, or verbal skills necessary to perform a particular academic task. This model dovetails well with a learning styles approach. However, clinicians must keep in mind that much work in this area is based on theory and clinical practice rather than on firm scientific evidence.

The Planning, Attention, Simultaneous, and Successive theory (PASS; Naglieri & Das, 1997) is rooted in the work of A. R. Luria (1966, 1973, 1980). This theory provides a more modern means to appreciating and understanding the ability deficits driving symptomatic problems for individuals with ADHD and LD. Luria's research examined the functional aspects of brain structures and formed the basis for his theory (Das, Naglieri, & Kirby, 1994). Das and Naglieri and their colleagues used Luria's work as a blueprint for defining the important components of human intelligence and abilities (Das et al., 1994). This work represents the first time that a specific research-based neuropsychological theory was used to conceptualize human intelligence and abilities. Luria defined four abilities as providing an explanation and understanding for the symptomatic and related problems individuals with developmental disabilities such as LD and ADHD experience:

1. *Planning*. Planning is a frontal lobe function. It is associated with the prefrontal cortex and is one of the primary abilities distinguishing humans from other primates. Planning helps individuals achieve through the selection or development of plans or strategies needed to complete tasks for which a solution is required and is critical to all activities where the child or adult has to determine how to solve a problem. This process includes generation, evaluation, and execution of a plan as well as self-monitoring and impulse control. Planning deficits have been very clearly associated with youth suffering from LD as well as ADHD (Goldstein & Naglieri, 2010).

2. *Attention*. Attention is a mental process that is closely related to the orienting response. The longer attention is required, the more the activity demands vigilance. Attention is likely directed by the right prefrontal cortex as well as the base of the brain. Attention is controlled by intentions and goals and involves knowledge and skills as well as the other three PASS processes.

3. *Simultaneous processing*. Simultaneous processing is essential for organization of information into groups or a coherent whole. The parietal-occipital-temporal region of the brain provides a critical ability to see patterns as interrelated elements. Simultaneous processing is not limited to nonverbal content, as illustrated by the important role it plays in the grammatical components of language and comprehension of word relationships, prepositions, and inflections.

4. *Successive processing*. Successive processing involves the use of stimuli arranged in a specific serial order. Whenever information must be remembered or completed in a specific order, successive processing is involved. Successive processing has been demonstrated to be a critical ability in the development of early phonemic awareness (Boden & Kirby, 1995; Naglieri, 1999, 2000, 2001; Naglieri & Pickering, 2010; Naglieri & Rojahn, 2004).

One of the advantages of the utilization of this theory is once weak abilities or processes leading to symptomatic problems are identified, they can be used to develop and direct strategic interventions that can improve basic abilities and thus reduce symptomatic problems and functional impairments (Naglieri & Das, 2002; Naglieri & Pickering, 2010).

Once an individual's academic strengths and weaknesses are identified, the remedial approach concentrates on improving weaknesses necessary to perform academic tasks competently. Four traditional approaches used for education or remediation of reading skills, for example, have been:

1. Traditional phonics.
2. Sight word reading.
3. Word pattern approach (teaches decoding and relies on the ability to rhyme ending sounds).
4. Language experience or the whole language approach.

Despite the popularity of this model, limited research data exist to suggest that it is a better intervention that offers greater understanding of individuals than other available models. This model simply appears to make sense and thus is attractive to many educators. Caution is required, not so much because these interventions are ineffective as because they are untested.

Many university administrators are not fully responsive to the needs of students with disabilities, especially those with LD and ADHD. Graduate school administrators have been reported to be even less responsive (Booren & Hood, 2007; Parks, Antonoff, Drake, Skiba, & Soberman, 1987). At the administrative level, modifications made are based on available funding and legal requirements rather than on the actual needs of the student population. These issues are addressed in depth in Chapter 10.

At a university level, emphasis has been on identifying the specific needs of students with LD or ADHD and providing them with accommodations. For example, the next set of teaching accommodations has been suggested for college students with LD or ADHD. As with others strategies, these interventions may not reflect the culmination of science but are at first blush practical. In fact, many of these suggestions would be beneficial for all students and constitute good teaching:

- Making the syllabus available 4 to 6 weeks before the beginning of the class, and when possible, being available to discuss it with students considering taking the course.
- Beginning lectures with a review of the previous lecture and an overview of topics to be covered that day or an outline of the lecture.
- Using a chalkboard or overhead projector to outline and summarize lecture material. Being mindful of legibility and the need to read aloud what is written.
- Explaining technical language, specific terminology, or foreign words.

- Emphasizing important points, main ideas, and key concepts orally or in lecture or highlighting them with colored pens on an overhead computer projector.
- Speaking distinctly and at a relaxed pace, pausing occasionally to respond to questions, offering students the chance to catch up in their note taking.
- Noticing and responding to nonverbal signs of confusion or frustration in students.
- Trying to diminish if not eliminate auditory and visual classroom distractions, such as hallway noise or flickering florescent lights.
- Leaving time for a question-and-answer period and/or discussion periodically at the end of each lecture.
- Trying to determine whether students understand the material by asking volunteers to offer an example, summarize, or respond to a question.
- Providing periodic summaries during lectures and emphasizing key concepts.
- Offering assignments in writing as well as orally and being available for clarification.
- Providing a suggested timeline when making long-range assignments and suggesting appropriate check points.
- Being available during office hours for clarification of lecture material, assignments, and reading.
- Selecting a textbook with a study guide if available; offer questions and answers to review in quiz sections.
- Helping students find study partners and organizing study groups. Providing study questions for exams that demonstrate the format to be used as well as the content.
- Asking the student how the instructor can facilitate his or her learning.
- Discussing in private with students suspected of having these conditions, describing what was observed and, if appropriate, referring the student for available support services.

It has also become increasingly popular for technology to be considered as a valuable asset in the education and vocational training experiences of individuals with ADHD and LD. As defined by the Technology Related Assistance for Individuals with Disabilities Act of 1988, an "assistive technology device" is "any item, piece of equipment or product system whether acquired commercially, off the shelf, modified or customized that is used to increase, maintain or improve functional capabilities of individuals with disabilities." This act was amended in 1998. States can receive discretionary grants to assist them in developing and implementing state-wide programs for technology-related assistance for individuals of all ages who have disabilities. This technology is not intended to teach or instruct but is used to increase access to instruction consistent with the Americans with Disabilities Act (ADA). Assistive technology has demonstrated the potential, though research is still limited, to help adults with LD or ADHD compensate for their problems. Assistive technology includes word processing software (with spelling and grammar checkers), voice-activated word processors, personal data managers, listening aids, and a whole host of portable electronic devices. These devices are touted as beneficial with some limited research supporting their advantages (Bogart, Kintsch, Visvader, Clark, & Riordan, 2005; Raskin, 1993). A list of everything from personal tape recorders to electronic date planners and other electronic devices continues to be suggested as helpful to those with LD and ADHD.

It has been well documented that individuals with LD and ADHD typically enter the workforce at lower levels and have fewer job promotions and more job changes (Barkley & Murphy, 2005; Herzog & Falk, 1991; Shapiro & Lentz, 1991). Additionally, it has been demonstrated that even 2 years after high school graduation, these individuals hold near–minimum wage jobs. Unemployment rates for dropouts, whether with these conditions or not, are twice as high as for high school graduates (Alliance for Excellent Education, 2009). Not only do high school dropouts earn less when they are employed, but they are also much more likely to be unemployed during economic recessions. According to the report of the Alliance for Excellent Education in July 2009, the unemployment rate for high school dropouts was 15.4% compared to 9.4% for high school graduates, 7.9% for individuals with some college credits or an associate's degree, and 4.7% for those with a bachelor's degree or higher. Although data are scarce, the logic is difficult to deny. If appropriate vocational educational programs are not provided to students with LD and ADHD before they leave school, it is likely that they will struggle vocationally and experience chronic if not lifetime impairments in adulthood. Although the scientific data may be limited, problems with social skills, memory, organization, linguistic weaknesses, or academic abilities and problems with executive functioning are all recognized as potential contributors to poor vocational performance and outcome. Some have suggested that those with LD and ADHD experience few problems in the workplace (Felton, 1986). By far the data are much stronger suggesting that this is not the case (Barkley 2005; Hoffman et al., 1986).

A number of variables are critical in predicting successful vocational outcome for adults with these conditions. Nearly 20 years ago, in their review of the literature, Vogel and Adelman (1993) identified 10 employment issues for adults with LD and ADHD:

1. Assisted transition into the workplace
2. Obtaining employment
3. Type of employment
4. Rate of employment
5. Wages

6. Job satisfaction
7. Job success
8. Effect of condition on vocational performance
9. Development of compensatory strategies
10. Employer perceptions of disability

These authors concluded that despite "considerable evidence that some adults with LD's achieve success in the work place, they still experience a disproportion of unemployment and underemployment (Vogel & Adelman, 1993, p. 230). In particular, it appears that females with histories of these conditions are underrepresented in the workforce. Furthermore, individuals with these conditions, even after several years of employment, are found overwhelmingly in entry-level positions and earning near–minimum wage salaries (Barkley & Gordon, 2002; Mannuzza, Gittelman-Klein, Bessler, Malloy, & LaPadula, 1993). Which of these two groups with LD and ADHD are composed of individuals with lower cognitive skills rather than true disabilities has yet to be determined. Adelman and Vogel (1993) reported that a major factor differentiating successful from unsuccessful individuals is a match between career and ability. Finally, limited data continue to be available concerning the difference in vocational outcome for adults with these conditions when those completing college programs are compared with those who simply enter job training. In fact, limited data suggest that students with LD who graduate from college find employment equal to college graduate peers in the workplace. There is a small but growing body of research about successful programs providing occupational skills training to those with these disabilities. These programs fall into two broad categories: those that help the individual to understand and develop compensatory strategies and those that attempt direct remediation. As noted, a third alternative, one that has become increasingly popular, is to build on assets and strengths, trying to find a match between best abilities and vocational demands.

Over 30 years ago, it was reported that family-friend networks were perhaps the most successful way for individuals with LD or ADHD to find employment (Haring, Lovett, & Smith, 1990; Taymans, 1982). Further, in 1991, D'Amico reported that certain demographic factors, including low socioeconomic status and urban residence, place those with these conditions at risk for greater vocational challenges. Minskoff and DeMoss (1993) proposed a structured model for the skills needed for success in the workplace for these transitioning youth. These authors developed the Trade-Related Academic Competencies (TRAC) model to assess and develop the basic academic skills necessary for 26 vocational and education programs. The model was designed to be used by special education teachers in conjunction with vocational educators. It was intended to provide a positive first experience for students with disabilities in the transition to adult vocation. Another model was developed as part of an LD training program (Dowdy, 1990). It focused on compensation, accommodations, modifications, and strategies (CAMS) for this population entering the workforce.

In 1991, in response to the increasing volume of information about vocational training for those with LD, the U.S. Department of Labor recommended a number of goals, which still are relevant today:

- *Incorporate appropriate instructional strategies into job search training and pre-employment components.* Since a larger proportion of Job Training Partnership Act (JTPA) adults who are reading below the seventh-grade level may be learning disabled, even if a program does not routinely screen for LD, it makes sense to integrate into group components some of the simpler instructional techniques (e.g., small groups, video, computer-based and verbal material rather than just written manuals, verbal and untimed tests) that work well for those with LD and ADHD.
- *Combine basic skills instruction with functional occupational skills instruction.* Learning disabled persons benefit from a training program integrating basic education with applied functional skill development. Such training can be done in a traditional classroom, in a vocational training setting, or in the work place on the job.
- *Avoid arbitrary referral of persons with low reading skills to possibly inappropriate remediation programs.* Many JTPA and Job Opportunities and Basic Skills Training (JOBS) programs refer persons with low reading levels to adult education programs. However, one reason for the high dropout rate from traditional education or, for that matter, remedial programs may be that the classes are not designed to accommodate those with LD or ADHD. Some screening system needs to be developed to identify those at risk due to these conditions and to refer them for appropriate assessment and service.

The U.S. Department of Labor also recommended that at a national level:

- *An interagency work group on adult LD should be established.* This group should include representatives from JTPA, Vocational Rehabilitation, Adult Education, JOBS, and Vocational Education. The purpose of the group would be to improve the quality of services to the adult LD and ADHD population. A coordinated federal agency effort at sharing knowledge and experience could encourage the development of integrated policy guidelines for various programs, joint research, and technical assistance.
- *The Department of Labor should review the need for a department research and technical assistance agenda to examine the LD population and current practices for serving them.* This should include:

1. Research on the size and characteristics of the LD and ADHD populations.
2. Studies to examine different employment-related problems and service needs for subgroups within these populations.
3. A review of various assessment tools in the development of a technical assistance package for use by program operators.
4. Research on the current practices and extensive services for LD and ADHD adults by JTPA, JOBS, Vocational Rehabilitation, community colleges, and other entities. Once more knowledge has been accumulated, it will be useful to conduct studies to identify and document exemplary service models and establish pilot and demonstration products.

Although educational training and vocational development have been the traditional foci of transition planning for those with these conditions, emphasis has over the past 10 years shifted to the development of strengths and abilities, general life skills, interpersonal relations, and stress management. To date, many of the interventions most highly touted currently have been the least researched or understood in terms of their potential benefits to those with LD and ADHD. However, as Halperin noted in 1993, these may be the very phenomena on which vocational or academic success hinges.

Finally, clinicians may be interested in a categorical organization offered by Barton and Fuhrman (1994) concerning the impact of LD or ADHD on an adult life. Their four categories were:

1. Stress and anxiety resulting from being overwhelmed by the complexity of daily life demands.
2. Low self-esteem and feelings of incompetence.
3. Unresolved grief.
4. Helplessness resulting from limited understanding of abilities and disabilities.

When they experience problems with emotional adjustment, adults with histories of LD or ADHD bring a unique set of needs and problems to the therapy setting. Regardless of therapists' theoretical perspectives, it is critical that they understand that although individuals with LD and ADHD share most characteristics and life experience with others, they also possess a unique set of experiences that sets them apart in their thinking and worldview.

The science of medicines to help adults with LD and ADHD still remains in its infancy, even now with the publication of the second edition of this volume. Much of the available literature continues to focus on the use of stimulant medications for the treatment of childhood ADHD with an increasing number of studies focusing on late adolescent and adult ADHD (Barkley, Murphy, & Fischer, 2008). For those with

ADHD, the emerging data are clear. Medications offer an important component of treatment for this population. In regard to medicines that might facilitate learning, the literature is less clear although it is promising in regard to assisting in the strengthening of basic associational learning and memory.

REFERENCES

Adelman, P. A., & Vogel, S. A. (1993). Issues in the employment of adults with learning disabilities. *Learning Disability Quarterly, 16,* 219–232.

Alliance for Excellent Education (2009). The high cost of high school drop outs. *Public Education Policy and Progress, 9*(17), 1–7.

Barkley, R. A. (2005). *Attention Deficit Hyperactivity Disorder: A handbook for diagnosis and treatment* (3rd ed.). New York, NY: Guilford Press.

Barkley, R. A., & Gordon, M. (2002). Research on comorbidity, adaptive functioning and cognitive impairments in adults with ADHD: Implications for a clinical practice. In S. Goldstein & A. T. Ellison, *Clinician's guide to adult ADHD: Assessment and intervention* (pp. 43–69). New York, NY: Academic Press.

Barkley, R. A., & Murphy, K. R. (2005). *Attention deficit hyperactivity disorder: A clinical workbook.* New York, NY: Guilford Press.

Barkley, R. A., Murphy, K. R., & Fischer, M. (2008). *ADHD in adults: What the science says.* New York, NY: Guilford Press.

Barton, R. S., & Fuhrman, B. S. (1994). Counseling and psychotherapy for adults with learning disabilities. In P. J. Gerber & H. B. Reiff (Eds.), *Learning disabilities in adulthood* (pp. 82–92). Stoneham, MA: Butterworth-Heinemann.

Bingham, M. B. (1989). *Learning differently: Meeting the needs of adults with learning disabilities.* Knoxville, TN: University of Tennessee, Center for Literacy Studies.

Boden, C., & Kirby, J. R. (1995). Successive processing, phonological coding and the remediation of reading. *Journal of Cognitive Education, 4,* 19–31.

Bogart, R., Kintsch, A., Visvader, P., Clark, R., & Riordan, J. (2005). Virtual ramps for invisible disabilities: One district's approach to assistive technology for students with learning disabilities. *Closing the Gap, 24,* 1–4.

Booren, L. M., & Hood, B. K. (2007). Learning disabilities in graduate school: Closeted or out in the open. *Observer: Journal of the Association for Psychological Science, 20*(3), 28–29.

D'Amico, R. (1991). The working world awaits: Employment experiences during and shortly after secondary school. In M. Wagner, L. Newman, R. D'Amico, E. D. Jay, P. Butler-Nalin, C. Marder, & R. Cox, *Youth with disabilities: How are they doing? The first comprehensive report from the National Longitudinal Transition Study of Special Education Students* (pp. 8-1–8-55). Menlo Park, CA: SRI International.

Das, J. P., Naglieri, J. A., & Kirby, J. R. (1994). *Assessment of cognitive processes.* Needham Heights, MA: Allyn & Bacon.

Deschler, D. D., Schumacher, J. B., Lenz, B. K., & Ellis, E. (1983). Academic and cognitive interventions for LD adolescents (pt. 2). *Journal of Learning Disabilities, 17*, 170–179.

Diller, L., & Goldstein, S. (2006). Science, ethics and the psychosocial treatment of ADHD. *Journal of Attention Disorders, 9*, 571–574.

Dowdy, C. (1990). *LD characteristics checklist*. Birmingham, AL: University of Alabama at Birmingham.

Felton, R. (1986, November). *Bowman-Gray follow-up study*. Paper presented at the Orton Dyslexia National Conference, Philadelphia, PA.

Gajar, A., Salvia, J., Gajria, M., & Salvia, S. (1989). A comparison of intelligence achievement discrepancies between learning disabled and non-learning disabled college students. *Learning Disabilities Research, 4*, 199–124.

Ginsberg, R., & Gerber, P. (1990, April). *Conquering success: Patterns of highly successful learning disabled adults in the workplace*. Paper presented at the annual meeting of the American Educational Research Association, Boston, MA.

Goldstein, S., & Naglieri, J. (2009). Defining the evolving concept of impairment. In S. Goldstein & J. A. Naglieri (Eds.), *Assessing impairment: From theory to practice* (pp. 1–4). New York, NY: Springer.

Goldstein, S., & Naglieri, J. (2010). *Autism Spectrum Rating Scales: Technical manual*. North Tonawanda, NY: Multi-Health Systems.

Haring, K. A., Lovett, D. L., & Smith, D. D. (1990). A follow-up study of recent special education graduates of learning disabilities programs. *Journal of Learning Disabilities, 23*, 108–113.

Herzog, J. E., & Falk, B. (1991). A follow-up study of vocational outcomes of young adults with learning disabilities. *Journal of Postsecondary Education and Disability, 9*, 219–226.

Hoffman, F. J., Sheldon, K. L., Minskoff, E. H., Sautter, S. W., Steidle, E. F., Baker, D. P., . . . Echols, L. D. (1987). Needs of learning disabled adults. *Journal of Learning Disabilities, 20*, 43–52.

Hoy, C., & Gregg, N. (1986). Learning disabled students: An emerging population on college campuses. *Journal of College Admissions, 112*, 10–14.

Lipsey, W. E., & Wilson, D. B. (1993). The efficacy of psychological, educational, and behavioral treatment: Confirmation from meta-analysis. *American Psychologist, 48*, 1181–1209.

Luria, A. R. (1966). *Human brain and psychological processes*. New York, NY: Harper & Row.

Luria, A. R. (1973). The origin and cerebral organization of man's conscious action. In S. G. Sapir & A. C. Nitzburg (Eds.), *Children with learning problems* (pp. 109–130). New York, NY: Brunner/Mazel.

Luria, A. R. (1980). *Higher cortical functions in man* (2nd ed.). New York, NY: Basic Books.

Mannuzza, S., Gittelman-Klein, R. G., Bessler, A. A., Malloy, P., & LaPadula, M. (1993). Adult outcome of hyperactive boys: Education achievement, occupational rank, and psychiatric status. *Archives of General Psychiatry, 50,* 565–576.

Marsh, G. E., & Price, B. J. (1980). *Methods for teaching the mildly handicapped adolescent.* St. Louis, MO: Mosby.

Minskoff, E. H., & DeMoss, S. (1993). Facilitating successful transition: Using the trace model to assess and develop academic skills needed for vocational competence. *Learning Disability Quarterly, 16,* 161–170.

Naglieri, J. A. (1999). *Essentials of CAS assessment.* New York, NY: Wiley.

Naglieri, J. A. (2000). Can profile analysis of ability test scores work? An illustration using the PASS theory and CAS with an unselected cohort. *School Psychology Quarterly, 15,* 419–433.

Naglieri, J. A. (2001). Using the Cognitive Assessment System with learning-disabled children. In A. S. Kaufman, & N. L. Kaufman (Eds.), *Specific learning disabilities and difficulties in children and adolescents: Psychological assessment and evaluation* (pp. 141–177). New York, NY: Cambridge University Press.

Naglieri, J. A., & Das, J. P. (1997). Intelligence revised. In R. Dillon (Ed.), *Handbook on testing* (pp. 136–163). Westport, CT: Greenwood Press.

Naglieri, J. A., & Das, J. P. (2002). Practical implications of general intelligence and PASS cognitive processes. In R. J. Sternberg & E. L. Grigorenko (Eds.), *The general factor of intelligence: How general is it?* (pp. 855–884). New York, NY: Erlbaum.

Naglieri, J. A., & Pickering, E. B. (2010). *Helping children learn: Intervention handouts for use in school and at home* (2nd ed.). Baltimore, MD: Brookes.

Naglieri, J. A., & Rojahn, J. R. (2004). Validity of the PASS theory and CAS: Correlations with achievement. *Journal of Educational Psychology, 96,* 174–181.

Newman, L., Wagner, M., Cameto, R., & Knokey, A. M. (2009). *The post-high school outcomes of youth with disabilities up to 4 years after high school: A report from the National Longitudinal Transition Study-2* (#NCSER 2009-3017). Menlo Park, CA: SRI International.

Parks, A. W., Antonoff, S., Drake, C., Skiba, W. F., & Soberman, J. (1987). A survey of programs and services for students with learning disabilities in graduate and professional schools. *Journal of Learning Disabilities, 20,* 181–188.

Raskin, D. M. (1993). Assistive technology and adults with learning disabilities: A blueprint for exploration and advancement. *Journal of Learning Disabilities, 16,* 16–28.

Rothstein, L. (1986). Section 504 of the Rehabilitation Act: Emerging issues for colleges and universities. *Journal of College and University Law, 13,* 229–265.

Shapiro, E. S., & Lentz, F. E. (1991). Vocational-technical programs: Follow-up of students with learning disabilities. *Exceptional Children, 58,* 47–59.

Shaywitz, S. E., & Shaw, R. (1988). The admissions process: An approach to selecting learning disabled students at most selective colleges. *Learning Disabilities Focus, 3*, 81–87.

Taymans, J. M. (1982). Career/vocational education for handicapped students: A joint venture through the school years. *Pointer, 26*(4), 13–17.

U.S. Department of Labor. (1991). *The learning disabled in employment and training programs.* (Research and Evaluation Report No. 91-E.) Washington, DC: U.S. Government Printing Office.

Vogel, S. A. (1986). Levels and patterns of intellectual functioning among LD college students: Clinical and educational implications. *Journal of Learning Disabilities, 19*, 71–79.

Vogel, S. A., & Adelman, P. B. (1993). *Success for college students with learning disabilities.* New York, NY: Springer.

Wagner, M., Cameto, R., & Newman, L. (2003). *Youth with disabilities: A changing population; A report of findings from the National Longitudinal Transition Study (NLTS) and the National Longitudinal Transition Study-2 (NLTS2).* Menlo Park, CA: SRI International.

12

Treatment Effectiveness for LD and ADHD

Anastasia L. Betts

Treatment effectiveness for any condition is a measure of how well methods used to deal with or manage that condition result in the desired outcomes. At their most effective, treatment interventions are based on sound theory, verified by empirical evidence, carried out with fidelity to the original design, and result in efficient improvement of participant outcomes (Mostert & Kavale, 2001). Many different interventions have been designed to improve learning outcomes in children and students with disabilities, but there is little empirical evidence that these interventions translate to effective treatments outside the academic environment or with adolescents and adults rather than children (DuPaul & Stoner, 1994; Marks, 2004; Murphy, 2005). Establishing the relative effectiveness of these treatment interventions can be daunting because of the enormous number of studies (Lloyd, Forness, & Kavale, 1998), the conflicting results generated by some investigations (Varhely, 2006), and the need to extrapolate information describing children to the treatment of adults (Murphy, 2005).

Literally hundreds of methods and techniques to treat learning disabilities, hyperactivity, or lack of attention have been introduced over the last 100 years (Arnold, 2001; Lloyd et al., 1998). Treatments include dietary changes (Boris & Mandel, 1994;

As an inexperienced writer and graduate student, I was thrilled to receive an invitation from my professor and mentor, Dr. Ken Kavale, to collaborate on a chapter discussing treatment effectiveness. We discussed the steps I should take to begin the effort over the phone on a Tuesday. Four days later, I received a much sadder phone call to inform me that my friend and mentor had passed away.

Ken was the perfect choice to author a chapter on treatment effectiveness. As a recognized leader in the field of specific learning disabilities and meta-analysis, his knowledge of types of treatments, history of reviewing treatments, and in-depth understanding of what elements determine the effectiveness of specific treatments was just the combination necessary to provide an excellent contribution to this book.

I have endeavored to write alone the chapter we would have authored together. I only hope Ken would have been proud to have his name attached to it.

Jacobson, Schardt, & Center for Science, 1999; Lavoie, 2009; Schnoll, Burshteyn, & Cea-Aravena, 2003), specific instructional techniques (DuPaul & Eckert, 1997; Kavale & Forness, 1995; Lipsey & Wilson, 1993), self-regulation techniques (Reid, Trout, & Schartz, 2005), neurofeedback (Jacobs, 2005), hypnosis (Barabasz & Barabasz, 2000), and cognitive behavioral therapy (Ramsey & Rostain, 2006;). Determining which of these treatments are most effective requires attention to the type of treatment and desired outcome and the individual characteristics of the subject of the intervention.

TREATMENT CATEGORIES

The key to understanding the effectiveness of treatments is to delineate clearly the expected outcome of the treatment. Until recently, both Learning Disabilities (LD) and Attention-Deficit/Hyperactivity Disorder (ADHD) were considered childhood disorders that dissipated during adolescence, self-curing with maturity (Marks, 2004). Although research evidence belies this view, if one is under the impression that LD or ADHD can be cured, treatment effectiveness implies an *elimination* of symptoms of learning difficulties, distractibility, or impulse control. However, if one holds the view that LD and ADHD are lifelong, chronic conditions that may be managed or improved, treatment effectiveness implies progress toward appropriate management of one's condition.

Types of treatments applicable to adolescents and adults with ADHD and LD may be loosely grouped as academic, behavioral, social, transitional, or self-regulated treatments. Multimodal treatments that combine pharmacological, behavioral, and transitional interventions have been well received and are more prevalent than single-mode treatments. Determining effectiveness of multimodal treatments involves understanding not only the effectiveness of the component interventions but also how and in what order the interventions combine in a comprehensive whole to increase positive results (Hoza, Kaiser, & Hurt, 2007; Majewicz-Hefley & Carlson, 2007; Swanson et al., 2008).

Focus on Children

For children and students, academic outcomes may relate to expected increases in academic skills, learning strategies, specific content knowledge, higher-order processing capabilities (e.g., Bloom's taxonomy [Bloom, 1956]), problem-solving skills, technological competency, autonomy in learning, self-efficacy, self-responsibility for learning, or scores on ubiquitous standardized tests (DuPaul & Eckert, 1997; Lloyd et al., 1998; Swanson, 1999; Vaughn, Gersten, & Chard, 2000). For individuals with LD, Swanson (1999) indicated that interventions are more effective when they include cognitive strategy instruction or direct instruction but only a few specific components of instruction increase treatment effectiveness. In addition, treatments are generally more effective for low-achieving students (i.e., those with low reading and low IQ scores) than for those with a discrepancy between normal to high IQ and low achievement.

Although ADHD has traditionally been researched from a behavioral rather than an academic point of view, desired outcomes include academic improvement. Academic outcomes are generally poorer for students with ADHD than for students without ADHD (Barkley, 1998; Cantwell & Baker, 1991), and researchers tend to suggest that these academic deficits are the result of ADHD-related behavioral characteristics in the classroom, such as difficulties in following directions, maintaining attention to tasks, and organizing materials and activities (Trout, Lienemann, Reid, & Epstein, 2007).

Behavioral interventions in research with students with disabilities may be categorized as school-based or individual-based interventions (DuPaul & Weyandt, 2006). School-based treatments may either be school-wide reforms, such as token economies or "attaboy" programs, often designed to reduce behavior referrals and incidents, or school-based classes for specific individuals, groups of students working with counselors, peer-focused interventions, or individual behavior plans. Effective interventions target specific behaviors (Harlacher, Roberts, & Merrell, 2006), utilizing techniques such as functional behavior analysis to identify antecedents to and consequences of the behavior. The intervention is designed to replace the undesirable behavior with an acceptable alternative that fulfills the same need for the student.

For example, a meta-analysis conducted by Robinson, Smith, Miller, and Brownell (1999) examined cognitive behavioral modification (CBM) techniques of reducing hyperactive-impulsive and aggressive behaviors in children and adolescents. The overall effect size of 0.74 suggested that CBM is efficacious in reducing these behaviors. This specifically targeted behavior modification is distinct from counseling such as "talk therapy" or cognitive techniques designed to understand the "why" behind the antecedent. Behavioral modification is more effective when it is designed for the individual rather than school-wide, and individual behavior modification is a significant element of multimodal treatment for ADHD at all ages (DuPaul & Eckert, 1997; Harlacher et al., 2006).

Social skills training, sometimes considered a subset of behavioral interventions, is intended to remediate the social skills deficits of children with disabilities. The social behaviors of students with LD and ADHD often result in poor peer acceptance or peer rejection of these youngsters (Gresham & Elliott, 1989). In fact, these deficits in social skills correlate to students with LD so often that the revised definition of learning disabilities includes social skills as a primary learning disability on its own (IDEIA, 2004). Many authors, however, dispute the conception that the rate of social skill deficits in the population with disabilities is significantly different from that of their peers without disabilities (Coleman & Minnett, 1992; Forness & Kavale, 1991;

Gresham & Elliott, 1989), and repeated analyses, meta-analyses, and reviews identify a minimal effect of social skills training on social competency of students.

Social skills training, as it stands, is not an effective intervention for the development of social competence in students with LD and ADHD (effect size [ES] = 0.211; Forness & Kavale, 1996). However, the need to train socially rejected and neglected students in social skills in order to limit negative outcomes such as crime, poor self-concept, and school dropout rates has been substantiated (Parker & Asher, 1987). The challenge to both researchers and providers is to develop effective training, good research designs, and key practices to establish and effect appropriate social skill development in individuals with LD and ADHD.

Focus on Adolescents

Empirical evidence for the effectiveness of academic, behavioral, and social interventions focuses on children and students. Interventions designed to produce positive outcomes for adolescents tend to focus on skills and knowledge considered necessary for the transition from school to adulthood. Treatment outcomes for transitional interventions include self-advocacy and self-determination skills, preparation for independent living (money and time management, household skills), accountability, understanding of the disability, understanding of one's rights under the Americans with Disabilities Act (ADA), and goal planning and implementation. Alternatively, transition skill development has been approached as a remedial training treatment program, including remediation in academic skills, vocational skills, or compensatory strategies for dealing with LD or ADHD on the job or in adult life.

As an example of the transition challenges facing adolescents with ADHD, consider the case of Joe (Murphy, 2007). Joe is a young man with severe ADHD. At 25 years of age, he lives with his parents because he is unable to organize his finances or maintain employment. Joe dropped out of school after 11th grade, rarely participates in household upkeep, and is addicted to tobacco, alcohol, and computer games. In order to maintain employment, move from his parents' home, and reduce impulsive spending and behavior, Joe requires transition services. The effectiveness of these treatments, according to Ramsey and Rostain's comments on the case (Murphy, 2007), will be based on Joe's readiness for therapy, his family's ability to change its own behavior patterns, and Joe's concommitant diagnoses of dyslexia and substance abuse. Recommendations for Joe's treatment include education about adult ADHD symptoms, skills for coping with challenges, continued pharmacotherapy, and cognitive behavioral training.

Focus on Adults

Counseling strategies for adults with LD and ADHD are designed to increase self-regulation of behavior and coping skills. Outcome measurements of these treatments may include: self-control, self-monitoring, and self-reinforcement abilities, client knowledge of his or her disability, attention management skills, interpersonal and social skills, stress and time management skills, anger management skills, or problem-solving skills (Jackson & Farrugia, 1997). Effectiveness of these treatments is often extrapolated from similar studies with children rather than based on empirical evidence of effectiveness with the adult population. Thus, measurements of treatment effectiveness encounter generalizability issues, and researchers must also consider the appropriateness of treatments to the different symptomology of adults with LD and ADHD as opposed to the symptoms encountered in children.

Complementary and Alternative Treatments

A number of alternatives to pharmacological and behavioral interventions have been proposed and adopted, due in part to aversion to the use of medication and in part to the popularity of complementary and alternative medicine (Arnold, 1999, 2001; Rojas & Chan, 2005). Claims have been made for the effectiveness of diet and/or exercise, including the Feingold diet (Feingold, 1975) and a restricted sugar diet. Other alternative medical suggestions include chiropractic care (Giesen, Center, & Leach, 1989), meditation and biofeedback (Ramirez, Desantis, & Opler, 2001), acupuncture, homeopathy, massage, or spiritual healing (Arnold, 1999, 2001; Rojas & Chan, 2005), and even a refusal to believe in the existence of ADHD and LD, naming both disorders as social or cultural constructs (Stolzer, 2009). These alternatives to medication and behavioral modification therapies lack empirical support, often basing their claims on partial evidence (Rojas & Chan, 2005), and their comparative effectiveness in changing academic and behavioral outcomes are limited. However, each of these alternatives has also been promoted as a therapy to reduce stress and increase affective or cognitive self-regulation skills. Perhaps an increase in overall health and a reduction of associated frustration (when determined to be the desired treatment outcome) would be served by the use of these types of techniques. In general, however, treatment effectiveness is determined by academic, transition, or social skill outcome measures, rather than measures of health-related outcomes.

TREATMENT DECISIONS

In order to determine if a treatment is effective for adolescents or adults with ADHD or LD, consider these seven questions:

1. How was the effectiveness measured? (Does the outcome measure match the treatment, and was this a single study or a synthesis of studies?)
2. Is the intention of the treatment to "cure" the disorder, or does it propose to improve select outcomes?
3. What are the expected outcomes of the treatment, and are these outcomes developmentally appropriate and important in the lives of the participants?

4. Does the treatment match the diagnosis (ADHD, LD, both or neither, other comorbid conditions)?
5. Is the treatment designed for individuals who have a childhood history of similar treatments or for those diagnosed in adulthood, and how may this treatment interact with past treatments?
6. Has the treatment been designed and tested for adults or only for children?
7. Does the treatment rely on knowledge or abilities not yet acquired by the participants?

Practitioners may find answers to these questions through consideration of the contributing effects of several factors in the individual with disabilities, including personal, environmental, and medical factors, and in the treatment design, including research and interaction features.

TREATMENT FACTORS

When the expected treatment outcome is right for the subject (personal and environmental factors), the outcome derives cleanly from the treatment and the treatment derives from solid theory (research factors), the theory is sound in the first place (medical factors), and there are no blocks (interaction factors), the treatment is likely to be highly effective for the individual. An individualized treatment plan includes careful evaluation of each factor for each patient.

Research Factors

Research factors that affect treatment effectiveness may include the type of research design used in the study or, in the case of syntheses, both the type of synthesis and the type of studies included or excluded from the synthesis. Generalizability of findings, comparability of different studies to one another, and the percentage of research focused on any particular area must also be of concern when making effectiveness determinations. Highly effective interventions, based on sound theory, standards of evidence, and replicability, may be general instructional strategies, such as identifying similarities and differences (ES $d = 1.61$; Marzano, 2003) or mnemonic strategies (ES $d = 1.62$; Kavale & Mostert, 2004). They may also be specific instructional strategies, such as phonics programs for reading (ES $d = 0.41$; Ehri, Nunes, Stahl, & Willows, 2001) or strategies for understanding and changing behavior, such as functional behavioral analysis (Ervin et al., 2001). Empirically based and tested through experimental or quasi-experimental means, treatments with the highest effectiveness have strong underlying concepts, appropriate sampling procedures, clearly described implementation and outcome measures, and appropriate data analysis (Gersten et al., 2005).

Effective interventions may also be empirically supported by other means. Single-subject research with precisely defined and described participants, settings, dependent variables, independent variables, and baseline measurements offers evidence on which to base a judgment of effectiveness and best practice, provided internal, external, and social validity are supported and treatment fidelity is maintained (Horner et al., 2005). Likewise, correlational research may inform practice when: reliability coefficients are reported; the research has statistical, practical, and clinical significance; and the study and statistical design are well constructed based on sound theory (Thompson, Diamond, McWilliam, Snyder, & Snyder, 2005). For an intervention to be identified as effective does not necessarily require a large effect size but does imply the existence and measurement of a significantly positive effect size supported by careful research. Additionally, the effect associated with the intervention should by definition be the best positive effect size of similar or related interventions.

To empirically determine effectiveness, available methods must be defined, tested, and replicable, and measures of the outcomes must be logical, reliable, and related to the treatment itself. The sample tested must be representative of the target population, and treatment integrity must be maintained (Gersten et al., 2005). Overall judgments concerning the effectiveness of any treatment must take into account results from all or most studies related to that treatment.

Intervention research in children and students sometimes produces conflicting findings, and sometimes becomes controversial, as when an intervention based on intuitively appealing ideas (rather than empirical data) is shown to be less effective than hoped (Lloyd et al., 1998). In order to make sense of the disparate findings, various methods of research synthesis are used to develop recommendations and guide treatment choices. This is often accomplished through meta-analysis for experimental and quasi-experimental studies; through narrative review and the use of percentage of non-overlapping data (PND) for single-case studies; and through systematic narrative synthesis for correlative, qualitative, and mixed studies.

Research Designs

Meta-analysis, or research in which the study is the unit of analysis, has been used extensively in the field of education. The effectiveness of meta-analysis is in its quantitative scrutiny and systematic process, designed to reduce subjective bias often found in other types of analysis. The advantages of using meta-analysis are: the use of quantitative, statistical methods; the elimination of study selection bias; the use of all information in each study; and the method's ability to detect interactions (Kavale, 2001). It accounts for different magnitudes and power among studies and enables a research synthesizer to examine a large number of studies at one time (Lipsey & Wilson, 2001), examines characteristics of studies as if those characteristics were variables (Wolf, 1986), and takes into account studies with nonsignificant findings (Rosenthal & DiMatteo, 2001).

Meta-analysis combines the results from studies in a specific area by converting each study's result into an effect size and combining or comparing ESs to determine overall effectiveness (Glass, McGaw, & Smith, 1981). The ability of meta-analysis to identify features of the study or the population that may have an effect on the outcome can be invaluable; however, the converse is also true: Features of the studies and populations included in a meta-analysis vary considerably, and evaluation of effect sizes based on comparisons to different control interventions may be problematic (Lipsey & Wilson, 2001).

The PND between baseline and treatment phases is an outcome metric for single-subject design research. When data from both phase types are plotted in a graphic display, in general, less overlap between the two phases indicates a greater treatment effect (Scruggs & Mastropieri, 1998, 2001). PND scores of over 90, indicating that 90% of treatment observations exceed the highest baseline observation, are considered very effective. Scores between 70 and 90 are effective, scores between 50 and 70 are questionable, and scores below 50 are considered ineffective. However, in common with most systematic reviews, PND information cannot compensate for unidentified variables, specific study design elements, or lack of treatment integrity in the original studies.

A thorough and systematic narrative review may bring together studies from disparate fields, including medicine, husbandry, education, sociology, psychology, and anthropology, yet still follow the same steps as in a meta-analysis: determining the problem and question to be reviewed, selecting the studies, identifying exclusion criteria, and conducting as unbiased a review of the primary studies as possible (Mostert, 2001). A systematic synthesis describes "characteristics of studies and the general direction of results using extensive tables and text" (Shadish, Cook, & Campbell, 2002, p. 422). Indeed, it most closely approximates meta-analysis without a calculated effect size. The most significant difference is that narrative synthesis includes both qualitative and quantitative primary studies; therefore, a single analysis may systematically and logically incorporate diverse studies.

Qualitative research emphasizes understanding and explains specifics. It is well suited for developing theory rather than for generalizing intervention methodology or determining comparative efficacy (Mostert & Kavale, 2001). However, as a consequence of bias and the manner in which narrative studies are designed, qualitative research in education generally results in positive findings (Davies, 2000; Shadish et al., 2002). Only when these qualitative findings are then supported by empirical evidence may one begin to rely on their determination of effectiveness.

There are negative aspects of each type of research synthesis. Most notably (borrowing a phrase from the field of information technology), garbage in equals garbage out (Rosenthal & DiMatteo, 2001). A research synthesis relies on the information provided in the primary studies; if the initial information is incomplete, misunderstood, or not comparable to similar studies, any small errors or omissions are compounded in the synthesis. Like meta-analysis, narrative synthesis is only as good as the studies that comprise it, the transparency of exclusion criteria, and the expertise of the synthesizer (Shadish et al., 2002). Similarly, differences in the definition of the condition, the definition of management, the population in question, the identification of desired outcomes, or the measurement of those outcomes are significantly amplified by inclusion of the studies in the research synthesis.

Conversely, widespread elimination of otherwise relevant studies poses a problem with bias (Lipsey & Wilson, 2001; Wolf, 1986), and may result in inaccurate determinations of effective practice. Thorough syntheses include indicators of evidence reliability, methods to compensate for research quality of primary studies, and discussion of study features and differences that may have acted as barriers to a determination of treatment effectiveness (Lloyd et al., 1998; Mostert, 2001).

Measuring Treatment Outcomes

As previously mentioned, outcome measures, and the treatments that generate them, generally fall into one of several categories: academic, behavioral, social, transitional, or self-regulatory. Lipsey and Wilson (1993) and Kavale and Mostert (2004) provide excellent summaries of ESs of different academic and behavioral treatment programs. These reviews clearly indicate that well-designed treatments with effective outcomes exist. What is not clear, however, especially in meta-analyses, is whether the primary outcome measures used to determine effect size were similar and whether outcome measures were congruent with treatment techniques. When several different outcome measures are combined to form a single effect size, determination of the priority of one specific outcome over another is subjective, suggesting that the weighting of each type of outcome in any synthesis is a result of researcher bias (Davies, 2000).

Thus, the onus is on the clinician or educator, in partnership with the adolescent or adult with ADHD or LD and his or her caretaker, family, or employer, to identify the most desirable outcome measures on an individual basis, taking into account the age, vocation, and environmental factors of the patient with ADHD or LD. Following the identification of desired outcome, the empirical basis of an effect size should be reviewed for consistency with intervention techniques. Reporting an effect size of an academic achievement outcome (such as an assessment) from a behavior intervention (such as a classroom-based positive reinforcement contingency program), although not incorrect, clouds an already complex picture of individuals and symptoms.

ESs comparisons should not be used as "cookbooks" to determine curricula or methods. The act of picking and choosing parts of an effective program runs the risk of missing the crucial element, and combining several interventions can moderate the positive effects of any or all of the treatments (Marzano, 2003). The key to effective treatment is careful consideration of the desired outcome and attention to each aspect of the intervention most likely, based on available empirical evidence, to produce the expected results.

Finally, the effectiveness of a treatment or lack thereof may result from treatment integrity, the degree to which the treatment has been correctly applied by the practitioner, and the degree to which the recipient has complied with treatment protocol. Unfortunately, measures of treatment integrity have been included as a standard requirement in study reports only within the last few years. Consequently, few analyses of effectiveness investigate whether participants have received the exact treatment described, complied with each component of the treatment, or even had knowledge and skills prerequisite to participation in the treatment.

Personal Factors

Personal factors that may affect treatment effectiveness may include changes in desirability of specific outcomes, self-knowledge, and personal responsibility as an individual transitions from childhood through adolescence and into adulthood.

Treatment effectiveness when applied to adults and adolescents with ADHD and LD takes on several connotations not necessarily applicable to children with the disorders. For example, until the Individuals with Disabilities Education Act (IDEA) was reauthorized in 2004 (renamed the Individuals with Disabilities Education Improvement Act, or IDEIA), students with LD were identified almost solely by a discrepancy model, in which a significant discrepancy between expected academic achievement based on measures such as IQ and actual academic achievement was the basis for a diagnosis of LD. Since the IDEIA, response to intervention (RTI) techniques have been used in addition to or in place of the discrepancy model to diagnose LD, yet both methods rely on deficits in academic achievement outcomes to define the existence of a learning disability (Learning Disabilities and Young Children, 2007). Consequently, treatment methods for children focus most often on the improvement of *academic* outcomes, especially with the advent of No Child Left Behind (NCLB, 2001) and the national priority of standardized test scores. A great deal of research, however, has also been conducted on concomitant social and behavioral deficits often found in students with LD, and interventions have been developed to improve social and behavioral outcomes for students with LD.

Parents and teachers often monitor children's development through academic outcomes, children's lives tend to center around school and academic pursuits, and parents and teachers provide an academic definition of what constitutes a positive result of treatment. As students leave school and enter adulthood, however, teachers and parents no longer shape goals and definitions. Knowledge of one's rights under the ADA, how and what to reveal in the workplace or classroom, and personal coping techniques or methods to alter the working environment are up to the individual rather than those around him or her. Not only does primary responsibility for treatment shift; so do the types of treatment outcomes desired. Young adults in the workforce are generally no longer concerned with improving academic outcomes; rather they strive to improve *social* outcomes. The effectiveness of interventions with academic outcomes becomes a meaningless measure; true effectiveness of treatments for the symptoms of LD and ADHD are no longer measured by standardized test scores or grade point average but by social measures of job stability and relationship stability or by self-measures of happiness, ability to cope, and self-regulation.

Additionally, the nature of the symptomology faced by individuals with LD and ADHD changes with age (Faraone, Biederman, & Mick, 2006; Kavale & Forness, 1996). Physical hyperactivity generally decreases, and the effects of disorganization and impulsivity on time management and planning often present as psychosocial issues rather than academic ones (Murphy, 2007; Solanto, Marks, Mitchell, Wasserstein, & Kofman, 2008). Understanding treatment effectiveness for adults and adolescents with ADHD and LD is rendered quite complex by differences in definitions, populations, and desired outcomes, yet the effective treatment of ADHD and LD in adults and adolescents relies on a clear understanding of desired outcomes and of the characteristics of those treated. Although there has been a great deal of empirical research on children with ADHD and LD, very little empirical research relates specifically to adults and adolescents, and most treatments have been extrapolated from what has been shown to be effective for children.

Self-understanding, self-concept, and a sense of personal responsibility develop with increased maturity, although at a slower pace than that of peers without disabilities. When self-understanding includes personal knowledge of one's disability, strengths, and weaknesses (an important aspect of transition interventions is to teach students with ADHD and LD to understand their disability and their abilities), an individual is in a better position to learn which vocations are most suitable for his or her personality and development. Similarly, training that helps an adolescent or adult to understand the meaning of social indicators and to respond with appropriate social behaviors is likely to help an adult in the workforce determine when and to what extent he or she should disclose a disability to supervisors or workmates.

In the workplace, specifically, adults with ADHD and LD benefit from skills in three critical areas: knowledge of the ADA, how to navigate workplace self-disclosure and accommodations, and self-determination (Madaus, Gerber, & Price, 2008). Self-determination is a set of skills, attitudes, and beliefs that enable an individual to engage in goal-directed and autonomous behavior (Wehmeyer & Powers, 2007).

Environmental Factors

Environmental factors that may affect treatment effectiveness include changes in symptomology, expectations of others, and legal rights and responsibilities as an individual transitions from childhood through adolescence and into adulthood. Although similar to personal factors, environmental factors describe the expectations of others rather than internal changes or measures of self-understanding.

Appropriateness of Treatment Outcomes

The expected outcomes of any specific treatment are based not only on the particular intervention method but also on the age and development of the participants. In addition, how an outcome is measured influences the size and even the direction of any particular effect (Hoza et al., 2007).

Children

As previously discussed, children with LD and ADHD are primarily treated with techniques designed to increase academic achievement outcomes. Access to special education services for students with LD and those with ADHD whose academic achievement is adversely affected by their disability is determined through academic discrepancy or RTI models (IDEIA, 2004). Without going into extensive detail about the controversy surrounding the best method of determination, if special education services are warranted, they are delivered along a continuum of placement options. Children may receive interventions through accommodations in the regular classroom, through placement in a special school, or in a situation between these two extremes. Students with LD and/or ADHD but without other complications are often placed in the general education classroom or in special resource or "pull-out classes," where they receive academic and/or behavioral interventions to treat their disability.

Educational interventions with academic outcome measures closely related to the treatment may have high effectiveness, but it is difficult to separate specific outcome effects applicable to all students from those more specifically targeted to students with ADHD. In a meta-analysis conducted across the 1990s, Purdie, Hattie, and Carroll (2002) describe the importance of outcome measures specifically tied to the treatment. Out of 74 studies with 1,497 associated effect sizes, only 8 studies assessed the effectiveness of educational interventions on academic achievement measures. Most studies assessed the effects of pharmacological interventions on behavioral outcomes and suggested that reduction in behavior problems can be generalized to an overall improvement in educational outcomes. In fact, school-based interventions are effective in behavioral improvements because they are behaviorally based, yet those same interventions do not generalize to academic improvements with a similar magnitude (DuPaul & Eckert, 1997).

The overall weighted effect size of educational interventions on academic achievement measures in Purdie and her colleagues' study was .28, a small to medium ES (Cohen, 1988). However, the average ES of learning strategy interventions across all students is .61 (as reported by Purdie et al., 2002), suggesting that education interventions such as direct instruction of learning strategies may have an important outcome for all children, including those with ADHD and LD. In other words, educational interventions that have been empirically validated for all children should be considered as likely to be effective for students with ADHD and LD as for their peers without ADHD or LD. Additional academic treatments specifically targeted for students with ADHD must also take into account the direction and intensity of effects of general education techniques.

The effectiveness of educational treatments for students with LD has a larger research base, based on the relative priority of academic achievement over behavioral issues in LD research as compared to ADHD research. In a mega-analysis of 18 meta-analyses, Forness, Kavale, Blum, and Lloyd (1997) separated a number of medical, social, behavioral, and educational approaches for mitigating LD by relative effectiveness. Those with negligible or modest ESs included the Feingold diet, perceptual-motor training (including modality instruction and learning styles), and social skills training (ES = .16 with teacher ratings, .24 with student self-ratings). Those with good effect sizes included antidepressant medication and other psychotropic drugs (ES = .30), reduced class size (ES = .47 when controlling for attitude toward school), psycholinguistics training (including phonics training, ES = .39), peer tutoring (ES = .48), and stimulant drugs (ES = .80 on behavioral outcomes and .38 on cognitive measures). Finally, interventions with convincing effect sizes included formative evaluation (ES = .70), behavioral modification (ES = 1.57 for academic improvement), and the use of mnemonics and systematic reading comprehension strategies (ES > 1.0).

Because meta-analysis is generally confined to experimental and quasi-experimental studies, it is worthwhile to compare a synthesis of single-subject research. Swanson and Sachse-Lee's (2000) review of single-subject intervention research for students with LD indicated that interventions with high ESs generally included instructional components such as drill-repetition-practice-review, segmentation, small interactive groups, and the use of strategy cues, components that have empirical support for increasing achievement outcomes in all students. Interventions that included elements of direct strategy instruction (more effective for students with a small discrepancy between reading level and IQ) were found to be the most effective for increasing educational outcomes.

Adolescents

Adolescents occupy a unique position between childhood and adulthood. The symptomology of ADHD in adolescents encompasses both symptoms typically found in childhood, such as the inability to stay in one's seat, and those more often associated with adult ADHD or LD, such as reduced self-confidence and disorganization (Wolraich et al., 2005). ADHD research in adolescents is also complicated by the effects of puberty and its associated hormonal surges (especially as related to sleep; Wolraich et al., 2005) and the effects of changes in the school environment (increased cognitive demands and reduced adult supervision).

Treatments for adolescents with ADHD include self-advocacy and self-regulatory skill training, skill development to prepare for independence, medical supports, and behavioral therapy (Murphy, 2005). Adolescents with LD often receive training in self-determination skills (Madaus et al., 2008; Wehmeyer & Powers, 2007), transition planning (Carter, Trainor, Sun, & Owens, 2009), and academic remediation to support work-related skills. The main goal of treatment in the adolescent years is to lessen the associated distress of managing a disability and to increase the quality of life and independence of the resulting young adult. Therefore, treatment often focuses on transition skills as students move from the academic sphere to independence in postsecondary or vocational life pursuits. Treatments specifically oriented to academic outcomes or vocational outcomes tend to have less effective results for adolescents than those treatments designed to manage the changes occurring in their lives (Cobb & Alwell, 2009; Wolraich et al., 2005).

Student-focused planning, student development, interagency planning, family involvement, and program structure are vital components of transition intervention services (Cobb & Alwell, 2009). Student-focused planning—in which each student is treated as an individual, with an individual transition plan and the opportunity to contribute to the development of that plan—is reported as highly effective (ES = 1.47). Several promising branded intervention packages are available for transition planning and student development, although they currently lack qualitative, empirical research support.

Adults

In contrast to the hyperactivity of children, adult symptoms of ADHD reflect poor self-regulation of mood, arousal, and behavior (Wadsworth & Harper, 2007). The inability to follow directions may result in loss of employment, financial disaster, and marital discord (Harvard College, 2009). Additionally, more than 80% of adults with ADHD meet the *Diagnostic and Statistical Manual of Mental Disorders* (4th ed.; *DSM-IV-TR*) criteria for at least one other psychiatric disorder, including Anxiety Disorder, Depressive Disorder, Dysthymic Disorder, Antisocial Personality Disorder, Oppositional Defiant Disorder, Conduct Disorder, and Substance Abuse (Harvard College, 2009; Jackson & Farrugia, 1997; Wadsworth & Harper, 2007). Clearly, the characteristics and concerns of adult ADHD are not comparable to those of childhood, yet most treatment plans are generalized from those offered to students.

Characteristics of adults with learning disabilities are similar to those of younger persons. However, desired treatment outcomes do not necessarily remain the same. After leaving high school, individuals with LD are no longer simply seeking academic outcomes; they require educational interventions to learn more about their disabilities and their rights under ADA, cognitive behavioral interventions to learn to cope with their weaknesses and accentuate their strengths, and, often, remedial vocational training to support their choice of occupation. Adults with LD also commonly meet the criteria for other psychiatric disorders, especially Mood Disorders and ADHD.

Treatment needs in adults with LD and ADHD reflect the change in environmental situation as well as comorbid pathologies. Take, for example, the case study of Ralph, as reported by Rosenfield, Ramsay, and Rostain (2008): Ralph was diagnosed with ADHD and treated with medications in childhood. However, his symptoms in adulthood led to several crises that resulted in his self-referral to an evaluator at the behest of his wife. At 30 years old, Ralph had been fired from nine jobs in less than 5 years and had been employed for the 2 years previous to his evaluation. His wife frequently complained about his irresponsibility and social awkwardness.

In the working world, Ralph tended to respond defensively, make excuses, and blame others. This stubbornness with superiors, in addition to his inability to follow rules and tendency to misinterpret social cues, compounded his difficulties with procrastination, poor task focus, and task incompletion. Additionally, Ralph refused to disclose his condition to his employers. Assessment indicated ADHD with comorbid mild depression, and treatment for Ralph consisted of ongoing medication, cognitive behavioral therapy, and marital therapy. In this particular case, the effectiveness of his multimodal treatment resulted in Ralph's ability to maintain employment and repair his marriage.

Had the evaluators not recognized the results of ADHD in Ralph's life, it is likely that his treatment may have been inadequate or incomplete. Treatment for his depression and/or marital therapy alone would not have addressed the underlying condition (ADHD) causing the problems. Conversely, medical treatment alone would not have addressed his behavioral functioning (time management, organization, and social skills). The need for individualized multimodal treatments for adults with ADHD and LD is apparent in Ralph's case (Rosenfield et al., 2008).

Medical Factors

As seen in Ralph's case, both personal diagnostic issues and the changes in medical diagnostic understanding over the course of lifelong treatment may be factors in the determination of treatment effectiveness. An adult with ADHD or LD (or both) may have been diagnosed and treated as a child or diagnosed as an adult. Effectiveness may therefore be examined as a measure of childhood treatment on adult outcomes, adult treatment on adult outcomes, or a combination of treatment effects throughout the life span. Those diagnosed and treated while still children or teens may be continuing treatment or have ended treatment. Differences in receptivity to further treatment in the adult years may arise from the personal choices of individuals and their teachers and caregivers during adolescence, especially decisions to discontinue medication.

A major difficulty in the treatment of individuals with LD and ADHD is the heterogeneity of the disability categories, especially specific learning disabilities. In schools, where an initial determination as to the need for services is most often made, a battery of assessments are utilized to decide whether a student is eligible for special education services. These assessments may, but are not required to, include a diagnosis based on *DSM-IV-TR* or similar criteria. Instead, decisions may be based on a student's response to previous intervention techniques (e.g., RTI; Kavale, Holdnack, & Mostert, 2006), the discrepancy between a student's expected achievement level based on intelligence assessments and actual performance (Peterson & Shinn, 2002), both cognitive and response indices (Hale, Kaufman, Naglieri, & Kavale, 2006), and/or the experience of the special education team (Learning Disabilities and Young Children, 2007; Scruggs & Mastropieri, 2002). The category of specific learning disability (SLD) is too often a catchall category for students who are low achievers, classified at risk, or who should fall under another category, such as intellectual disability or emotional/behavioral disability, but whose caregivers are more comfortable with what they perceive as a less negative label. Regardless of the intent of the law, well-meaning school officials may inadvertently make determination of the actual nature of a disability even more difficult by working to gain special services for students who appear to be in need of additional help yet do not meet the specifications for a specific learning disability. The category of other health impairment (OHI) serves a similar function as SLD, especially for students with ADHD.

In addition to special education services serving students determined to be in need under IDEIA, American schools provide services to students for whom English is a second language, students at risk under Title I determinations, gifted students, and students with temporary issues (e.g., traumatic events or temporary homelessness) that interfere with schooling. As these students grow into adults, they may remember they had special services but not know whether they were diagnosed with LD or ADHD. Those who know for certain that they were diagnosed and remember their educational services as a negative experience may avoid any situation that similar in postsecondary school or job training.

Even eliminating questionable determinations of SLD and OHI in the schools, the definitions provided by IDEIA cover a large number of neurological and psychological aspects of learning disabilities. The largest category of disability under the IDEIA— specific learning disabilities—may manifest as perceptual disabilities, brain injury, minimal brain dysfunction, dyslexia, or developmental aphasia (IDEIA, 2004). The sheer number of different symptoms and difficulties encountered by students cloud treatment effectiveness measures; different underlying problems react differently to treatment, and treatment studies (with the possible exception of those focused on improving reading outcomes) rarely separate out subgroups of LD limitations for comparison.

Diagnosing adults with ADHD is also complicated by the *DSM-IV-TR* criterion that symptoms be present before the age of 7. Self-reports of adults about events prior to age 7 may be poorly remembered. Furthermore, the incidence of comorbidity of ADHD with other psychiatric disorders, most commonly LD, Oppositional Defiant Disorder, Anxiety Disorder, Depressive Disorder, and Borderline Personality Disorder, create a cornucopia of symptoms that require careful separation in order to predict effectiveness of targeted interventions.

Interaction Factors

Interactions of one treatment with another or the consequences of repeated treatment failure may take a psychosocial toll on the adult with ADHD or LD (Rosenfield et al., 2008). Interaction factors that alter treatment effectiveness may include age at diagnosis, treatment buildup or past conditioning to treatment types and styles, concomitant diagnoses and masking effects, attention and maturation effects, and similar threats to study validity (Campbell & Stanley, 1963). Future research is needed to focus on interaction effects of specific treatments at different points in the life span to determine how past treatments may affect current treatment options, as there is little or no research to date on this area of ADHD and LD study.

PROMISING PRACTICE IN THE TREATMENT OF ADULTS AND ADOLESCENTS

Currently, the most promising treatment for adults with LD begins with systematic academic and social support in postsecondary education or in vocational training (Hock, Deschler, & Schumaker, 1993; Kavale & Forness, 1996), specifically in higher-order processing skills (Swanson, 1999). In combination with academic and social support, adults with LD require education about specific disabilities and recognizing their strengths and weaknesses (Kavale & Forness, 1996), including guidance to increase self-determination (Madaus et al., 2008; Wehmeyer, 1996). Finally, an effective treatment should include education about ADA, the rights and responsibilities of individuals with disabilities, and education and counseling to determine when and how to disclose a disability to an employer (Madaus et al., 2008). Adolescents with LD should be provided with transition programs that emphasize the development of self-determination and of knowledge and skills pertaining to disabilities and the realities of disabilities in postsecondary school, the workplace, and life.

The most promising treatment of adults with ADHD, however, begins with pharmacological interventions in conjunction with patient education and specific behavioral modification strategies (Murphy, 2005; Rostain & Ramsay, 2006). Depending on the circumstances of the individual presenting for treatment, additional therapies (e.g., cognitive behavioral, marital, or vocational) may be warranted (Resnick, 2005).

Jackson and Farrugia (1997) identified seven particularly helpful strategies for therapeutic treatment for adults with ADHD:

1. Educating clients about the disorder
2. Developing attention management skills
3. Developing self-management skills
4. Developing interpersonal and social skills
5. Developing stress management skills
6. Developing anger management skills
7. Developing problem-solving skills

Prioritizing treatment of comorbid disorders may require additional counseling or pharmacological treatments prior to implementation of the ADHD treatment regimen (Harvard College, 2009; Marks, 2004). Additionally, investigation into the generalizability of patient response to treatment among children, adolescents, and adults is lacking. Multimodal treatments have become the norm for children with ADHD (Hoza et al., 2007), yet it remains to be determined which components of these treatment packages, in what order, are most critical to successful outcomes for adults and adolescents.

REFERENCES

Arnold, L. (1999). Treatment alternatives for attention-deficit/hyperactivity disorder (ADHD). *Journal of Attention Disorders, 3*, 30–48.

Arnold, L. (2001). Alternative treatments for adults with attention-deficit hyperactivity disorder (ADHD). In *Adult attention deficit disorder: Brain mechanisms and life outcomes* (pp. 310–341). New York, NY: New York Academy of Sciences.

Barabasz, A., & Barabasz, M. (2000). Treating AD/HD with hypnosis and neurotherapy. *Child Study Journal, 30*, 25–42.

Barkley, R. A. (1998). *Attention deficit hyperactivity disorder: A handbook for diagnosis and treatment*. New York, NY: Guilford Press.

Bloom B. S. (1956). *Taxonomy of educational objectives, handbook I: The cognitive domain*. New York, NY: David McKay.

Boris, M., & Mandel, F. (1994). Foods and additives are common causes of the attention deficit hyperactive disorder in children. *Annals of Allergy, 72*, 462–468.

Campbell, D. T., & Stanley, J. C. (1963). Experimental and quasi-experimental designs for research on teaching. In N. L. Gage (Ed.), *Handbook of Research on Teaching*. Chicago, IL: Rand McNally.

Cantwell, D. P., & Baker, L. (1991). Association between attention-deficit hyperactivity disorder and learning disorders. *Journal of Learning Disabilities, 24*, 88–95.

Carter, E. W., Trainor, A. A., Sun, Y., & Owens, L. A. (2009). Assessing the transition-related strengths and needs of adolescents with high-incidence disabilities. *Exceptional Children, 76*, 74–94.

Cobb, R. B., & Alwell, M. (2009). Transition planning/coordinating interventions for youth with disabilities: A systematic review. *Career Development for Exceptional Individuals, 32,* 70–81. doi: 10.1177/0885728809336655

Cohen, J. (1988). *Statistical power analysis for the behavioral sciences.* Hillsdale, NJ: Lawrence Erlbaum.

Coleman, J. M., & Minnett, A. M. (1992). Learning disabilities and social competence: A social ecological perspective. *Exceptional Children, 59,* 234–246.

Davies, P. (2000). The relevance of systematic reviews to educational policy and practice. *Oxford Review of Education, 26,* 365–378.

DuPaul, G. J., & Eckert, T. L. (1997). The effects of school-based interventions for attention deficit hyperactivity disorder: A meta-analysis. *School Psychology Review, 26,* 5–27.

DuPaul, G. J., & Stoner, G. (1994). *ADHD in the schools: Assessment and intervention strategies.* New York, NY: Guilford Press.

DuPaul, G., & Weyandt, L. (2006). School-based intervention for children with attention deficit hyperactivity disorder: Effects on academic, social, and behavioural functioning. *International Journal of Disability, Development & Education, 53,* 161–176.

Ehri, L. C., Nunes, S. R., Stahl, S. A., & Willows, D. M. (2001). Systematic instruction helps students learn to read: Evidence from the National Reading Panel's meta-analysis. *Review of Educational Research, 71,* 393–447.

Ervin, R. A., Radford, P. M., Bertch, K., Piper, A. L., Ehrhardt, K. E., & Poling, A. (2001). A descriptive analysis and critique of the empirical literature on school-based functional assessment. *School Psychology Review, 30,* 193–210.

Faraone, S. V., Biederman, J., & Mick, E. (2006). The age-dependent decline of attention-deficit hyperactivity disorder: A meta-analysis of follow-up studies. *Psychological Medicine, 35,*159–165. doi:10.1017/S003329170500471x

Feingold, B. E. (1975). *Why your child is hyperactive.* New York, NY: Random House.

Forness, S. R., & Kavale, K. A. (1991). Social skills deficits as a primary learning disability: A note on problems with the ICLD diagnostic criteria. *Learning Disabilities Research and Practice, 6,* 44–49.

Forness, S., & Kavale, K. (1996). Treating social skill deficits in children with learning disabilities: A meta-analysis of the research. *Learning Disability Quarterly, 19,* 2–13.

Forness, S. R., Kavale, K. A., Blum, I. M., & Lloyd, J. W. (1997). Mega-analysis of meta-analyses: What works in special education and related services. *Teaching Exceptional Children, 29,* 4–9.

Gersten, R., Fuchs, L. S., Compton, D., Coyne, M., Greenwood, C., & Innocenti, M. S. (2005). Quality indicators for group experimental and quasi-experimental research in special education. *Exceptional Children, 71,* 149–164.

Giesen, J. M., Center, D. B., & Leach, R. A. (1989). An evaluation of chiropractic manipulation as a treatment of hyperactivity in children. *Journal of Manipulative Physiological Therapy, 12,* 353–363.

Glass, G. V., McGaw, B., & Smith, M. L. (1981). *Meta-analysis in social research.* Beverly Hills, CA: SAGE.

Gresham, F., & Elliott, S. (1989). Social skills deficits as a primary learning disability. *Journal of Learning Disabilities, 22,* 120–124.

Hale, J. B., Kaufman, A., Naglieri, J. A., & Kavale, K. A. (2006). Implementation of IDEA: Integrating response to intervention and cognitive assessment methods. *Psychology in the Schools, 43,* 753–770.

Harlacher, J., Roberts, N., & Merrell, K. (2006). Classwide interventions for students with ADHD. *Teaching Exceptional Children, 39,* 6–12.

Harvard College President & Fellows. (2009). Recognizing and managing ADHD in adults. *Harvard Mental Health Letter, 26*(5), 1–4.

Hock, M. F., Deshler, D. D., & Schumaker, J. B. (1993). Learning strategy instruction for at-risk and learning-disabled adults. *Preventing School Failure, 38,* 43–57.

Horner, R. H., Carr, E. G., Halle, J., McGee, G., Odom, S., & Wolery, M. (2005). The use of single-subject research to identify evidence-based practice in special education. *Exceptional Children, 71,* 165–179.

Hoza, B., Kaiser, N. M., & Hurt, E. (2007). Multimodal treatments for childhood attention-deficit/hyperactivity disorder: Interpreting outcomes in the context of study designs. *Clinical Child and Family Psychologocal Review, 10,* 318–334. doi: 10.1007/s10567–007–0025–5

Individuals with Disabilities Education Improvement Act of 2004 (IDEIA), Publ.No. 108–446, 118 Stat. 2647 (2004), amending 20 U.S.C. §§ 1400 et seq.

Jackson, B., & Farrugia, D. (1997). Diagnosis and treatment of adults with attention deficit hyperactivity disorder. *Journal of Counseling and Development, 75,* 312–319.

Jacobs, E. H. (2005) Neurofeedback treatment of three adults with attention deficit hyperactivity disorder and related conditions. *Insights on Learning Disabilities, 2,* 23–41.

Jacobson, M., Schardt, D., & Center for Science in the Public Interest (1999). *Diet, ADHD & behavior: A quarter-century review [and] A parent's guide to diet, ADHD & behavior.* Retrieved from ERIC.ed.gov

Kavale, K. A. (2001). Meta-analysis: A primer. *Exceptionality, 9,* 177–183.

Kavale, K. A., & Forness, S. R. (1995). *The nature of learning disabilities: Critical elements of diagnosis and classification.* Mahwah, NJ: Lawrence Erlbaum Associates.

Kavale, K. A., & Forness, S. R. (1996). Learning disability grows up: Rehabilitation issues for individuals with learning disabilities. *Journal of Rehabilitation, Jan-Mar 1996,* 34–41.

Kavale, K. A., Holdnack, J. A., & Mostert, M. P. (2006). Responsiveness to intervention and the identification of specific learning disability: A critique and alternative proposal. *Learning Disability Quarterly, 29,* 113–127.

Kavale, K. A., & Mostert, M. P. (2004). *The positive side of special education: Minimizing its fads, fancies, and follies.* Lanham, MD: Scarecrow Education.

Lavoie, T. (2009). Holistic treatment approaches to ADHD: Nutrition, sleep, and exercise. *Exceptional Parent, 39*, 46–47.

Learning Disabilities and Young Children: Identification and Intervention. A Report from the National Joint Committee on Learning Disabilities. October, 2006. (2007). *Learning Disability Quarterly, 30*, 63–73.

Lipsey, M. W., & Wilson, D. B. (1993). The efficacy of psychological, educational, and behavioral treatment. *American Psychologist, 48*, 1181–1209.

Lipsey, M. W., & Wilson, D. B. (2001). *Practical meta-analysis: Applied social research methods series, volume 49.* Thousand Oaks, CA: SAGE

Lloyd, J., Forness, S., & Kavale, K. (1998). Some methods are more effective than others. *Intervention in School and Clinic, 33*, 195–200.

Madaus, J. W., Gerber, P. J., & Price, L. A. (2008). Adults with learning disablities in the workforce: Lessons for secondary transition programs. *Learning Disabilities Research & Practice, 23*, 148–153.

Majewicz-Hefley, A., & Carlson, J. (2007). A meta-analysis of combined treatments for children diagnosed with ADHD. *Journal of Attention Disorders, 10*, 239–250. doi: 10.1177/ 1087054706289934

Marks, D. J. (2004). ADHD in adults: Assessment and treatment considerations. *Behavioral Health Management.* May, 2004. Retrieved December 01, 2009, from http:// www.highbeam.com

Marzano, R. J. (2003). *What works in schools: Translating research into action.* Alexandria, VA: Association for Supervision and Curriculum Development.

Mostert, M. P. (2001). Characteristics of meta-analyses reported in mental retardation, learning disabilities, and emotional and behavioral disorders. *Exceptionality, 9*, 199–225.

Mostert, M. P., & Kavale, K. A. (2001). Evaluation of research for usable knowledge in behavioral disorders: Ignoring the irrelevant, considering the germane. *Behavioral Disorders, 27*, 53–68.

Murphy, K. (2005). Psychosocial treatments for ADHD in teens and adults: A practice-friendly review. *Journal of Clinical Psychology In Session, 61*, 607–619. doi: 10.1002/ jclp.20123

Murphy, K. (2007). Treatment strategies for a case of severe ADHD. *Journal of Attention Disorders, 11*, 407–409. doi: 10.1177/1087054707308432

No Child Left Behind (2001). *Executive summary of the No Child Left Behind Act.* Available from www.ed.gove/print/nclb/overview/intro/execsumm.html

Parker, J., & Asher, S. (1987). Peer relations and later personal adjustment: Are low-accepted children at risk? *Psychological Bulletin, 102*, 357–389.

Peterson, K. M., & Shinn, M. R. (2002). Severe discrepancy models: Which best explains school identification practices for learning disabilities? [Electronic version]. *School Psychology Review, 31*.

Purdie, N., Hattie, J., & Carroll, A. (2002). A review of the research on interventions for attention-deficit hyperactivity disorder: What works best? *Review of Educational Research, 72,* 61–99. doi: 10.3102/00346543072001061

Ramirez, P., Desantis, D., & Opler, L. (2001). EEG biofeedback treatment of ADD: A viable alternative to traditional medical intervention? *Annals of the New York Academy of Sciences, 931,* 342–358.

Ramsay, J. R., & Rostain, A. L. (2006). Cognitive behavior therapy for college students with attention-deficit/hyperactivity disorder. *Journal of College Student Psychotherapy, 21,* 3–20. doi: 10.1300/J035v21n01_02

Reid, R., Trout, A. L., & Schartz, M. (2005). Self-regulation interventions for children with attention deficit/hyperactivity disorder. *Exceptional Children, 71,* 361–377.

Resnick, R. J. (2005). Attention deficit hyperactivity disorder in teens and adults: They don't all outgrow it. *Journal of Clinical Psychology In Session, 61,* 529–533. doi: 10.1002/jclp.20117

Robinson, T. R., Smith, S. W., Miller, M. D., & Brownell, M. T. (1999). Cognitive behavior modification of hyperactivity-impulsivity and aggression: A meta-analysis. *Journal of Educational Psychology, 91,* 195–203.

Rojas, N., & Chan, E. (2005). Old and new controversies in the alternative treatment of attention-deficit hyperactivity disorder. *Mental Retardation And Developmental Disabilities Research Reviews, 11,* 116–130. doi: 10.1002/mrdd.20064

Rosenfield, B. M., Ramsay, J. R., & Rostain, A. L. (2008). Extreme makeover: The case of a young man with severe ADHD. *Clinical Case Studies 2008, 7,* 471–490. doi: 10.1177/1534650108319912

Rosenthal, R., & DiMatteo, M. R. (2001). Meta-analysis: Recent developments in quantitative methods for literature reviews. *Annual Review of Psychology, 52,* 59–82.

Rostain, A., & Ramsay, J. (2006). A combined treatment approach for adults with ADHD—Results of an open study of 43 patients. *Journal of Attention Disorders, 10,* 150–159. doi: 10.1177/1087054706288110

Schnoll, R., Burshteyn, D., & Cea-Aravena, J. (2003). Nutrition in the treatment of attention-deficit hyperactivity disorder: A neglected but important aspect. *Applied Psychophysiology & Biofeedback, 28,* 63–75.

Scruggs, T. E., & Mastropieri, M. A. (1998). Summarizing single-subject research: Issues and applications. *Behavior Modification, 22,* 221–242. doi: 10.1177/01454455980223001

Scruggs, T. E., & Mastropieri, M. A. (2001). How to summarize single-participant research: Ideas and applications. *Exceptionality, 9,* 227–244.

Scruggs, T. E., & Mastropieri, M. A. (2002). On babies and bathwater: Addressing the problems of identification of learning disabilities. *Learning Disability Quarterly, 25,* 155–168.

Shadish, W. R., Cook, T. D., & Campbell, D. T. (2002). *Experimental and quasi-experimental designs for generalized causal inference*. Boston: Houghton Mifflin.

Solanto, M. V., Marks, D. J., Mitchell, K. J., Wasserstein, J. & Kofman, M. D. (2008). Development of a new psychosocial treatment for adult ADHD. *Journal of Attention Disorders, 11*, 728–736. doi: 10.1177/1087054707305100

Stolzer, J. M. (2009). Attention deficit hyperactivity disorder: Valid medical condition or culturally constructed myth? *Ethical Human Psychology & Psychiatry, 11*, 5–15. doi: 10.1891/1559-4343.11.1.5

Swanson, H. L. (1999). Intervention research for adolescents with learning disabilities: A meta-analysis of outcomes related to higher-order processing. In *Two decades of research in learning disabilities: Reading comprehension, expressive writing, problem solving, self-concept. Keys to successful learning: A National summit on research in learning disabilities*. New York, NY: National Center for Learning Disabilities.

Swanson, H. L., & Sachse-Lee, C. (2000). A meta-analysis of single-subject design intervention research for students with LD. *Journal of Learning Disabilities, 33*, 114–136.

Swanson, J., Arnold, L., Kraemer, H., Hechtman, L., Molina, B., Hinshaw, S., ...Wigal, T. (2008). Evidence, interpretation, and qualification from multiple reports of long-term outcomes in the Multimodal Treatment study of children with ADHD (MTA): Part I: Executive summary. *Journal of Attention Disorders, 12*, 4–14.

Thompson, B., Diamond, K. E., McWilliam, R., Snyder, P., & Snyder, S. W. (2005). Evaluating the quality of evidence from correlational research for evidence-based practice. *Exceptional Children, 71*, 181–194.

Trout, A. L., Lienemann, T. O., Reid, R., and Epstein, M. (2007). A review of non-medication interventions to improve the academic performance of children and youth with ADHD. *Remedial and Special Education, 28*, 207–226.

Varhely, K. S. (2006). *Direct comparison of treatment modalities for childhood disorders: A meta-analysis* (Doctoral dissertation, Adler School of Professional Psychology). Retrieved December 5, 2009, from Dissertations & Theses: Full Text. (Publication No. AAT 3223084)

Vaughn, S., Gersten, R., & Chard, D. J. (2000). The underlying message in LD intervention research: Findings from research syntheses. *Exceptional Children, 67*, 99–114.

Wadsworth, J. S., & Harper, D. C. (2007). Adults with attention-deficit/hyperactivity disorder: Assessment and treatment strategies. *Journal of Counseling & Development, 85*, 101–108.

Wehmeyer, M. L. (1996). Self-determination as an educational outcome: Why it is important to children, youth, and adults with disabilities? In D. Sands &

M. Wehmeyer (Eds.), *Self-determination across the lifespan: Independence and choice for people with disabilities* (pp. 17–36). Baltimore: Brooks.

Wehmeyer, M., & Powers, L. (2007). Self-determination. *Exceptionality, 15,* 1–2.

Wolf, F. M. (1986). *Meta-analysis: Quantitative methods for research synthesis.* Newbury Park, CA: SAGE.

Wolraich, M. L., Wibbelsman, C. J., Brown, T. E., Evans, S. W., Gotlieb, E. M., Knight, J. R., . . . Wilens, T. (2005). Attention-deficit/ hyperactivity disorder among adolescents: A review of the diagnosis, treatment, and clinical implications. *Pediatrics, 115,* 1734–1746.

13

Building Resilience
by Shaping Mindsets

ROBERT B. BROOKS

I have been a clinical psychologist for more than 40 years and have seen hundreds of children, adolescents, and adults in therapy, a significant number of whom were diagnosed with a Learning Disabilities (LD) and/or Attention-Deficit/Hyperactivity Disorder (ADHD).* I also served as principal of a school in a locked door unit of the child and adolescent program of a psychiatric hospital and found that while many of the hospitalized youth were diagnosed with a conduct disorder or anxiety or depression, it was not unusual to discover that they were also burdened with significant learning and attention problems.

I have witnessed the response of parents as I reviewed my assessment findings of their child, findings that prompted me to give a diagnosis of LD or ADHD. On numerous occasions one of the parents exclaimed, "I know you're describing your test results for my son/daughter, but you're also describing me. From the time I was a little kid I thought I was dumb and stupid, but now there's an explanation for my problems. I only wish I had known this years ago."

RESILIENCE AND THE POWER OF MINDSETS

As a clinician my interventions with children, adolescents, and adults with LD or ADHD have focused on the impact that their learning and attention struggles have on their self-perceptions, self-esteem, coping strategies, and interpersonal behaviors (Brooks, 1987, 1999, 2001a, 2002). One of the early roots of my interest in the

---

*Some individuals have a diagnosis of both LD and ADHD while many others have only one of these diagnoses. For the sake of simplifying the writing style, I will be referring to LD *or* ADHD rather than LD *and/or* ADHD throughout the chapter. However, I recognize that in some of the case illustrations, both diagnoses apply to the same person.

concept of resilience was triggered by my work with individuals with LD or ADHD. I was intrigued with the question: What factors led some of this group to cope more optimistically and effectively with their struggles while others remained depressed and pessimistic, assuming a victim-like stance?

This last question served as a catalyst for me to introduce the concept of "mindsets" in my work. This concept has become an increasingly prominent area of study, especially with the emergence of the field of positive psychology. As examples, Carol Dweck authored a book titled *Mindset* (2006) in which she distinguished between a "fixed" and a "growth" outlook; the research and writings of Martin Seligman and his colleagues about "learned helplessness" and "learned optimism" as well as resilience (Reivich & Shatte, 2002; Seligman, 1990) have roots in attribution theory, which is basically a theory about mindsets, examining how we understand the reasons for our successes and setbacks (Weiner, 1974).

A major focus of my collaboration with my close friend Dr. Sam Goldstein has been to elaborate on the concepts of both mindsets and resilience (Brooks & Goldstein, 2001, 2004, 2007; Goldstein & Brooks, 2005, 2007). In our book *The Power of Resilience: Achieving Balance, Confidence, and Personal Strength in Your Life*, we write that all people possess a set of assumptions about themselves and others that influence their behaviors and the skills they develop. In turn, these behaviors and skills influence this set of assumptions so that a dynamic process is constantly operating. We label this set of assumptions a *mindset* and highlight the features of the mindset possessed by hopeful, resilient people, including:

- Feeling in control of one's life
- Being empathic and displaying effective communication and other interpersonal skills
- Possessing solid problem-solving and decision-making skills
- Establishing realistic goals and expectations
- Learning from both success and failure
- Being a compassionate and contributing member of society
- Living a responsible, self-disciplined life based on a set of thoughtful values

Possessing a resilient mindset does not suggest that one is free from stress, pressure, and conflict, but rather that one can cope effectively with problems as they arise.

Examples of Contrasting Mindsets

Many individuals with LD or ADHD from childhood are at a disadvantage of developing a resilient mindset. The very nature of their learning problems serves as a barrier for experiencing success in key areas of their lives. Yet others, beset with similar struggles, move forward, slowly nurturing a more optimistic, hopeful perspective that contributes to their navigating life's challenges with greater self-assurance. The next two case examples illustrate widely different mindsets in two men with ADHD.

Several years ago I received a poignant letter from a man in his mid-40s who knew that I was collecting life stories from children and adults with ADHD. He was diagnosed with ADHD as an adult and noted, "When I found out about my ADHD I felt no relief. The depth of my anger and hurt surprised my therapist. . . . I've had lots of rejections: loves lost, great jobs blown. I take all of this personally so all these rejections mean they're my fault. Then the diagnosis comes, and it confirms what others have said about me: that something was wrong, that I'm defective, or just plain no damn good."

He continued, "My time has passed. . . . I wish you well on your research. You can't help me but I'm willing to be used as a 'bad example' for those younger than me. . . . Because for them, perhaps, there's still some hope."

The pain, the distress, the feelings of hopelessness, and the honesty of this man were evident throughout his letter.

In contrast, I worked with an adolescent with ADHD. He described his condition in this way:

I sat in the red chair, listening behind the old unbreakable desk, while the teacher rambled out our next in-class assignment, listening, focusing on the words as they came from her lips. Her lips stopped, and I reached for my math book, setting it down on my desk, my pencil in my right hand, ready to work. But wait a minute! What was the assignment? I turned to the classmates on both sides, but they were already working away, scratching the graphite into numbers on the standard gray sheet of paper.

ADD haunted me in everything I did. I did not know how to react to the situations around me. . . . In fifth grade the kids would slide down the ice-covered hill, like toboggans on the slope. I would join in, but what at first seemed to be fun turned into an abusive and painful experience. The kids would try to hit me as they slid down, their bodies crashing into mine, knocking the wind out of me, leaving me gasping for breath amongst my assailants, frozen in fear against the next onslaught. Yet each day, I returned. . . . Yet these experiences of pain have led me to my interest in others. Whenever I see a child being teased, I remember. I want to rush in and defend, to annihilate the inhumanity of harassment.

The young man who wrote these words, who committed himself to helping others, who turned despair into optimism, realized his dream and is a physician today.

Two men, each diagnosed with ADHD, yet each views himself and the world so differently. Each possesses a different mindset—or assumptions about his condition and his future. One is filled with hope, the other with hopelessness and despair. One is resilient; the other cannot even entertain the notion that things might improve.

What factors contribute to these very different mindsets? The answer is complex. One consideration is that simply because two people share the same diagnosis does not suggest they face the same hurdles. There are different kinds and degrees of learning disabilities, some impacting in a more negative, comprehensive way than others. There are different levels of intensity in the manifestation of the symptoms of ADHD. There are noticeable differences in the ways in which significant others respond to the learning or attention problems of a child, adolescent, or adult, and those responses will influence the extent to which a resilient mindset may be forged.

In this chapter I review how the major characteristics of adolescents and adults with LD or ADHD, evident since childhood, shape the mindset of these individuals, a mindset for many that is vulnerable to and permeated with negative thoughts and feelings. I examine how this negative mindset may prompt coping behaviors that turn out to be counterproductive and self-defeating, intensifying rather than relieving sadness. Finally, I describe the features of a positive, resilient mindset and the interventions we can use as clinicians to reinforce these features in adolescents and adults with LD or ADHD.

A major goal in this chapter is to articulate therapeutic strategies that clinicians can apply for changing negative into resilient mindsets. I do not address certain forms of treatment, such as pharmacological interventions, since that is not my focus. However, the use of medication is not mutually exclusive from the strength-based approach I advocate and should be considered, especially for individuals with ADHD as well as for those with LD who have comorbid conditions such as anxiety and depression.

Before turning to the theme of mindsets, coping behaviors, and therapeutic strategies, I believe it is necessary to address a controversy related to LD and ADHD.

LD AND/OR ADHD: A GIFT OR A DISORDER?

Many individuals, including clinicians, have argued that diagnoses such as LD or ADHD, which emphasize the words "disabilities" and "disorder," pathologize a situation that should not be viewed as a disability, disorder, or deficit but rather as a *different* way of absorbing information and perceiving the world. Some take this position a step further and advocate that LD or ADHD should be seen as a gift, providing the holder with a more creative or intuitive mind than those who do not share these learning and behavioral styles. Others do not view these conditions as a gift but rather as symptoms that make it more difficult for individuals with these diagnoses to meet the typical challenges of childhood and adulthood. These contrasting views are captured in many writings (Barkley, Murphy, & Fischer, 2008; Brooks, 2001b; Glenn, 2007; Hallowell & Jensen, 2008; Hartmann, 2003; Healey & Rucklidge, 2008; Honos-Webb, 2005; Langston, 2010; Solden, 2002).

Daniel Pink, in his thought-provoking book *A Whole New Mind: Why Right-Brainers Will Rule the Future* (2005), reports one study that found self-made millionaires were four times more likely than the rest of the population to have been diagnosed with dyslexia. He contends:

> Why? Dyslexics struggle with L-Directed (left brain) Thinking and the linear, sequential, alphabetic reasoning at its core. But as with a blind person who develops a more acute sense of hearing, a dyslexic's difficulties in one area lead him to acquire outsized ability in others. As Sally Shaywitz, a Yale neuroscientist and specialist in dyslexia, writes, "Dyslexics think differently. They are intuitive and excel at problem-solving, seeing the big picture, and simplifying. . . . They are poor rote reciters, but inspired visionaries" (Shaywitz, 2003, p. 366). Game-changers such as Charles Schwab, who invented the discount brokerage, and Richard Branson, who has shaken up the retail music and airline industries, both cite their dyslexia as a secret to their success. (p. 141)

One may argue that even if self-made millionaires were four times more likely than the rest of the population to have been diagnosed with dyslexia, dyslexia in itself is not a precondition for success. Perhaps a more accurate indicator would be following children with and without LD or ADHD into their adolescent and adult years and comparing their level of success on different measures. Studies indicate that children with LD and ADHD diagnoses do not fare as well as their peers (Barkley & Fischer, 2005; Barkley, Murphy, & Fischer, 2007; Daniel, Walsh, Goldston, Arnold, Reboussin, & Wood, 2006). Thus, more pertinent questions might be: What are the factors that assist children, adolescents, and adults with LD or ADHD to become more successful and resilient? What contributed to the success of a Charles Schwab and Richard Branson while others with dyslexia were not very successful in their personal and professional lives as adults?

Solden (2002) examines the issue of gift versus disability for adults with ADHD. Similar questions can be raised for individuals with LD. Solden asserts:

> I have written this book to address what seems to me the growing polarization in the field of adult AD/HD. The following questions speak to that divide. Is AD/HD a curse or a blessing? Is AD/HD to be judged only by external, measurable symptoms or by inner experiences as well? When people who have AD/HD are successful, is it because or in spite of their difficulties? Is AD/HD the province of research scientists or clinicians? (p. xiv)

Solden attempts to answer these questions by advancing this view:

> I believe we must bring humanism and science together. The challenge at this point in the field of adult AD/HD, when so many have now been diagnosed for several years, is to expand the focus on biochemistry to include an examination of how living with a particular brain function affects the development of one's view of self. Working on the self is not just a "feel-good" piece of the AD/HD puzzle.

On the contrary, it is often the critical link, which in the long run makes the difference between those adults who are able to utilize all the medical and scientific advances and those who are not. (p. xv)

Earlier I questioned the notion of ADHD (or LD) being perceived as a "gift" (Brooks, 2001b). However, I believe that one need not view ADHD as a gift and still subscribe to a strength-based approach that focuses on reinforcing each individual's strengths or "islands of competence." I state:

When we accept the difficulties inherent in AD/HD, and appreciate the pain and distress many of these youngsters experience day in and day out, we can consider realistic treatment goals. When we reflect on guideposts directing our treatment, we will learn that "fixing" deficits plays an important, daily role, but that the most impressive, long-lasting changes will result from using each child's islands of competence to nurture a resilient mindset. This is the true "gift" we give to our children. (p. 5)

Thus, rather than engaging in an ongoing debate about "gifts" versus "disorders," I think it is more fruitful to expend our time and energy to understand the different ways in which each individual processes information and learns and the unique strengths and weaknesses we all have. As I discuss later in this chapter, we must make certain that children, adolescents, or adults with LD or ADHD do not experience themselves as failures. Unfortunately, a large number do believe that something is wrong with them, given their ongoing struggles to manage the typical developmental demands that one faces at different points in one's life.

In our offices we must focus on changing negative into resilient mindsets. However, if we are to have greater success with our patients in high school or college, we must work closely with their teachers so that the latter group is increasingly knowledgeable about educating them in ways they learn best. In addition, we must guide and encourage adolescents and adults with LD or ADHD to engage in activities that will permit them to harness their unique abilities; this includes the vocation or profession they choose. As Gardner (1983) has written, we all possess "multiple intelligences" and display varying levels of strength in each. In my experience, people are more content and motivated and their self-esteem is enriched when they are involved with tasks that tap their interests and strengths.

CHARACTERISTICS OF ADOLESCENTS OR ADULTS WITH LD OR ADHD

Adolescents and adults with the diagnosis of LD or ADHD are not a homogeneous group. Their cognitive style, thoughts, and behaviors that led to these diagnoses do not define their entire functioning or existence. However, there are certain core behaviors that many possess that distinguish them to a greater or lesser extent from individuals without LD or ADHD. These core behaviors elicit responses from others, responses that contribute to the formation of their mindset. Unfortunately, as noted earlier, in many instances the mindset of individuals with LD or ADHD is filled with negativity. A selected list of those behaviors that I believe have some of the strongest impact on their mindset and lives:

- Impulsivity
- Low frustration tolerance
- Depression
- Disorganization
- Rigidity, inflexibility, and insatiability
- Limited empathy

Impulsivity

One of the most prominent characteristics of individuals with ADHD and a number with LD is their impulsivity. They are often described as acting before they think, of failing to consider the consequences of their behaviors. As children, they are likely to blurt out answers in a classroom, or push their peers out of the way to be first in line, or place their finger in a light socket to see what happens, or climb a tall tree without considering the dangers. Just as they may have trouble learning to read and comprehend words, they also have difficulty slowing down and "reading" the cues and reactions of others. Educator Rick Lavoie captures the problems individuals with LD have with social interactions in his aptly titled book *It's So Much Work to Be Your Friend* (2005).

Others will inform impulsive kids and adults how to behave in certain situations, and they will agree with the suggestions. However, moments later, they seemingly forget what they have just been taught, behaving in ways that are in stark contrast to what they have been told. It is easy to interpret their behaviors as manipulative or oppositional, but as Barkley (1995, 2009) and others have taught us, it is not that they do not know what to do but rather they are so impulsive that they do not use what they know.

It is not unusual to find that the impulsivity of childhood and adolescence continues to be manifested in the behaviors of adults with LD or ADHD. They may rush through tasks, or fail to demonstrate social skills by saying things that others experience as abrasive, or engage in risk-taking activities. Pera (2008) skillfully describes how impulsivity and other behaviors associated with ADHD can increase tension and discontent in the relationship that a couple has with each other. I recall a couple I saw in therapy. The husband constantly interrupted his wife because "he had important things to say." At the beginning of one session, his wife was furious. Earlier that day he had impetuously quit his job when his supervisor asked him to make some modifications on a project. Apparently, he told his supervisor that he knew more than the supervisor and that the latter should "get off his back or he would quit." The supervisor accepted his offer to quit.

As this last example suggests, impulsivity is often reflected in a lack of self-discipline or self-control. Self-discipline is an essential component of resilience (Brooks & Goldstein, 2007). Goleman (1995) has highlighted self-discipline as a major ingredient of emotional intelligence, which he defines as "being able to motivate oneself and persist in the face of frustrations; to control impulse and delay gratification; to regulate one's moods and keep distress from swamping the ability to think; to empathize and to hope" (p. 34). Goleman's definition of emotional intelligence has direct bearing on other features of adults with LD or ADHD.

Low Frustration Tolerance

Closely linked to an impulsive style is how quickly adolescents and adults with ADHD become frustrated and angry, a feature also seen in numerous individuals with LD. This frustration is evident in many situations. If a task is difficult and not very interesting to them, they are quick to give up. If someone does not respond to what they want, they are quick to show their anger. A woman reported yelling at a coworker, blaming the latter for her own difficulty in finishing a challenging task. A man with ADHD had a 10-year-old son with the same disorder. Instead of being empathic and appreciating his son's struggles with homework, he would shout, "Just try harder! You always give up! Do you want to be a loser in life?"

Adolescents and adults with LD or ADHD often have difficulty tolerating their own shortcomings as well as the shortcomings of others. It is not unusual for them to cast blame on others when things do not go well. They expect others to change but may not be as willing to change themselves. On the surface this unwillingness may appear as a statement that they are right and others wrong, but often their reluctance to change is rooted in feelings of helplessness. As one woman with ADHD told me, "I just felt I couldn't change my angry outbursts at my kids. I felt terrible but I blamed them and told them that if they met their responsibilities and treated me with more respect, I wouldn't have to shout at them or spank them. But I didn't take any responsibility for my own behavior." Her insight was to be the first step toward change.

Depression

A number of individuals with LD or ADHD are burdened by depression or fluctuations in mood. Some feel sad much of the time while others may experience moments of happiness only to have feelings of sadness dominate within a short period of time.

Some clinicians contend that the depression is primarily biologically based while others feel that it is in response to years of frustration and failure. As with any affective disorder, most likely both biology and environment interact to different degrees with different individuals to contribute to moodiness and depression.

Depression or shifts in mood are burdensome not only to adolescents and adults with LD or ADHD but also to those who interact with them. As one 9-year-old boy told me about his father with ADHD, "I never know how he's going to feel or act. It's scary sometimes." A 30-year-old woman with significant reading and organizational problems reported in therapy, "When I accomplish a task at work I feel so good, but I know that feeling is only going to last briefly, just until I have trouble understanding my next task. When that happens I wonder if I'm smart enough to hold a good job. It's hard for me to shake these feelings of doubt."

The frustration and sadness of youth with LD can be very intense. For instance, Daniel et al. (2006) found that adolescents with poor reading ability were more likely to experience suicidal ideation or engage in suicidal behaviors and more likely to drop out of school than peers without reading disorders, even controlling for sociodemographic and psychiatric variables. Their findings are consistent with earlier investigations examining the relationship between learning disabilities and depression and suicidality (e.g., Hayes & Sloat, 1988; Huntington & Bender, 2001).

Lackaye and Margalit (2006) highlighted the negative mood and social-emotional ramifications faced by young adolescents with LD. They note:

> The current study demonstrated the uniqueness of the social-emotional self-perceptions of students with LD. Their distressed experiences of loneliness, negative mood, and academic failure may interfere with future effort and may even interfere with their recognition of success when it does happen. (p. 444)

Disorganization

One of the most frequent complaints I hear from individuals with ADHD as well as from a number with LD is their difficulty in becoming organized. As children and adolescents, they are the ones whose desks in school look as if a tornado has struck, whose three-ring binders that appeared so neat the first day of school quickly fall prey to different subjects being mixed together, who fail to do homework assignments, who finally finish assignments that somehow are lost or misplaced on the way from home to school (for many of these children it seems that a black hole exists between home and school, sucking up assignments and papers with great regularity), and who constantly search for lost socks, shoes, coats, and bookbags.

This pattern typically follows them into their adult years. They lose things, forget where they placed their keys, cannot locate bills to pay, neglect to jot down an important appointment in their book, or fail to complete a project at work because they have misjudged the time required or have become distracted with two other projects. Needless to say, their time management skills leave much to be desired. As one man with ADHD sadly related, "I feel I have no control of my life. I can't keep track of things. I can't keep track of my schedule. I spend all of my energy trying to keep things in order but you would never know it from the outcome."

A college student informed me that she could not locate one of her two credit cards, a situation made even more frustrating since she had lost the other card a month earlier. In an exasperated tone she stated, "I start off each day telling myself to pay close attention to what I have to do that day. I even make a list. And guess what? Sometimes I can't find the list."

Rigidity, Inflexibility, and Insatiability

The other side of the coin of impulsivity and disorganization is the lack of flexibility that many adolescents and adults with LD or ADHD demonstrate. Someone observing their behavior might be puzzled by how a person can be so impulsive and disorganized at one moment and so rigid the next. On one hand this rigidity may exemplify, in part, a desperate attempt to cope with the disorganization and lack of control in one's life, but it also seems to be another example of a failure of self-regulation.

Children and adolescents will manifest this pattern by having difficulty with transitions. Thus, in school they take a great deal of time to get started with an activity. When the teacher informs the class it is time to stop this activity and begin a new one (e.g., shifting from reading to math), they will not want to stop the first activity until they have completed it. If they are involved with a game or task at night, they do not want to go to bed until they have finished it, much to the frustration of their parents. Relatedly, I recall a number of youngsters with ADHD whom I would remind with at least 10 minutes left in our therapy session that our meeting would be over in 10 minutes. Even with this reminder, some would plead or argue for another few minutes to finish a drawing or a game.

This characteristic of inflexibility frequently will be manifested in the difficulty youth with ADHD have in accepting no as an answer to a request (or demand) they have made. Their cognitive style does not leave room for compromise. They believe that their requests are reasonable and that when adults do not comply, the adults are being unfair and arbitrary. They frequently perceive only one solution to the problem, namely, that others comply with their wishes and when this does not occur they often experience meltdowns with accompanying tantrums (Greene, 1998). I have observed this same pattern in my adult patients with LD or ADHD. They have difficulty compromising, often viewing situations in black-and-white terms, a situation that impacts on their families and in the workplace.

A feature closely linked to inflexibility and a failure to compromise is what might be labeled "insatiability." I have been impressed with the number of parents who have described their children as "impossible to please." One mother tearfully said, "From the moment my son was born, I felt I could not satisfy him. He always seemed to want more and more and more. As he got older, no toy was good enough for him even if we had given him a choice of what toy he could buy. Now, as a teenager, he won't take no as an answer, always arguing to get what he wants. I thought I must have done something really wrong to have a child who never seemed satisfied or grateful."

This inborn feeling of insatiability, which is not easily quenched, leads to the perception that the world is unfair. When insatiability, inflexibility, and rigidity become interwoven into a cognitive and emotional tapestry, which is not unusual in children with ADHD, the end result are children who are demanding, unhappy, difficult to soothe, and unable to compromise. Although this may seem an overly bleak picture, it is found in many youngsters with so-called difficult temperaments (Brooks & Goldstein, 2001; Chess & Thomas, 1987). Children and adolescents with ADHD as well as a number with LD typically fall under the category of temperamentally "difficult."

In adults, insatiability and inflexibility are displayed in many aspects of their lives. They may fail to experience satisfaction even when they succeed at something. Enjoyment is fleeting at best. In couples therapy, where one member of the couple has ADHD, it is not surprising to hear the other describe his or her spouse as difficult to please, as unhappy, as always seeing the glass as half empty, as possessing an intense need to be right, as perceiving compromise as giving in, and as not paying attention. Often the spouse with ADHD minimizes these descriptions by saying he or she would feel fine if other people were more giving and considerate. In their parenting roles, the inflexibility may be expressed in an authoritarian style replete with anger. It is little wonder that tension and friction become dominant features of families where one or more members have LD or ADHD.

Limited Empathy

Many individuals with LD or ADHD struggle with being empathic. While this difficulty with empathy is closely linked to the characteristics associated with LD or ADHD I have already described, I believe that given its importance in our day-to-day interactions it deserves special mention. As noted earlier, Goleman (1995) has highlighted empathy as a major ingredient of emotional intelligence.

In simple terms, "empathy" may be defined as the capacity to put oneself inside the shoes of other people and to see the world through their eyes. Empathic people are able to take the perspective of others even when they disagree with these others. They attempt to understand how their words and deeds are experienced and how others would describe them. They reflect on and take responsibility for their behavior. They are able to realistically assess and appreciate the "social scene."

Both cognitive and affective skills are necessary for empathy to develop. If one examines the characteristics of children and adults with LD or ADHD, one can appreciate why empathy is often compromised. It is a struggle to assume the perspective of another when we have trouble "reading" social cues; when we are impulsive, frustrated, or moody; when we quickly interpret the actions of others as withholding or unfair; when we believe that others are not listening to us; and when we feel we are being cheated. A patient I saw with ADHD summed up his improvement with this insightful statement: "It wasn't until I could slow down and realistically separate what I was feeling from the intention of others that I could become a more empathic person."

In contrast to this comment was one offered by a young adult with LD and ADHD during a discussion of empathy. He argued, "Why should I really care about how I come across to others or how others see me? If I think too much about that, if I act too nice, they might take further advantage of me." This young man's definition of empathy was much different from mine. He viewed empathy as a weapon for manipulation rather than as a skill to foster more satisfying relationships. As long as he maintained this perspective, it would be difficult for him to engage in comfortable, satisfying relationships.

UNFORTUNATE MINDSET OF INDIVIDUALS WITH LD OR ADHD

If impulsivity, low frustration tolerance, depression and/or moodiness, disorganization, rigidity, inflexibility, insatiability, and a lack of empathy are possible manifestations of the biological underpinnings of LD or ADHD, as we have already seen, these characteristics will impact on almost all aspects of a person's life. They will serve as a major influence in determining the ways in which we respond to others and they respond to us as well as how successful we are in the many personal and professional activities in which we are engaged.

From childhood, the particular style of a number of individuals with LD or ADHD results in poor interpersonal relationships as well as compromises in school and then work performance. Slowly, negative assumptions or perceptions about oneself and others take shape, becoming an integral part of an individual's mindset. In turn, this mindset plays a powerful role in determining one's behaviors in a wide spectrum of situations, generating a cycle of negative beliefs, a loss of hope, and self-defeating behaviors.

The next subsections present several of the main interrelated features of this negative mindset with suggestions at the end on ways that clinicians might assess this mindset via interview questions. Also, tests such as Seligman's (1990) "learned optimism" scale may be used in conjunction with interview material to evaluate the positive or negative qualities of the mindset.

I Do Not Have a Great Deal of Control of My Life

One of the hallmarks of a positive mindset is feeling a sense of control over what transpires in one's life together with a realistic appraisal of those areas over which one has control and those that are beyond one's influence. As Covey (1989) has eloquently noted, all people have "circles of concern," but effective people recognize and use their time and energy to focus on their "circles of influence"; that is, they are proactive rather than reactive. Stress is frequently linked to the belief "I have little say or control over the important things that occur in my life."

The very nature of the characteristics of LD and ADHD contribute to a feeling of not being in control. For example, if one behaves impulsively without considering the consequences, negative results are likely to follow that are often interpreted as a lack of control of one's actions. As one woman told me, "I always yell at my kids. I tell myself not to but then when they don't do what I want them to do I get so frustrated so quickly that I scream. I feel terrible afterward." A man with ADHD said, "No one really listens to me. Nothing I do seems to work."

Or as another example, if one is insatiable, constantly seeking unobtainable gratification, then continued hunger and frustration are the likely outcome as is the feeling that "nothing I do is enough to get what I want" or "people won't give me what I deserve."

It is not surprising that Gerber, Ginsberg, and Reiff (1992) found that possessing a sense of control over events in their lives was the most significant factor in distinguishing adults with LD who were successful compared with those who were pessimistic and experienced little, if any, success.

When I Am Successful It Is Based on Luck or Chance

Whether we are aware of it or not, when we succeed or fail at things in our life we offer ourselves different explanations for these successes and failures. As attribution theory, initially proposed by Weiner (1974), suggests, these explanations are linked to our self-esteem and sense of optimism. A great deal of research pertaining to attribution theory has studied individuals with LD or ADHD as a target population (Brooks, 1999; Canino, 1981; Licht, 1983).

This research indicates that children, adolescents, and adults with high self-esteem perceive their successes as based in great part on their own efforts or abilities. These individuals assume realistic ownership for their achievements. They believe they are active participants in their own success.

In contrast, individuals with low self-esteem typically attribute success to things outside of their control, such as luck or chance or fate. One child with ADHD told me that his good grade on a test was "pure luck." An adolescent with LD was convinced that "the teacher made the test easy." An adult with ADHD vividly said that her success in life was like "a house made out of cards." She added, "I feel that if any kind of wind comes along, my entire façade of success will crumble."

If you believe that your success is not rooted in your resources and effort but rather in luck or chance or things beyond your control, then it is difficult to be confident about experiencing success in the future. In such a case, a loss of hope becomes a dominant feature of one's life.

Failure Indicates My Inadequacy as a Person

Just as attribution theory highlights differences in how individuals understand the successes in their lives, so too does it clarify how failure is perceived. Children, adolescents, and adults with high self-esteem typically believe that mistakes are experiences from which to learn rather than feel defeated. Mistakes are attributed to variables that can be modified, such as a lack of adequate effort when engaged in reaching a realistically attainable goal or the use of ineffective strategies when studying for a test. A teenager requesting assistance to learn the strategies involved in solving geometry problems or an adult registering for a computer course in response to struggles to master the computer represent examples of taking positive action to confront mistakes.

In contrast, individuals with low self-esteem, which is often a concomitant of LD or ADHD, are vulnerable to thinking that they cannot correct the situation or overcome the obstacle. They view mistakes as a consequence of factors that are not modifiable, such as a lack of ability or intelligence, and this belief breeds a feeling of helplessness and hopelessness (Brooks, 2001; Mather & Ofiesh, 2005). They begin to believe regardless of what they do, few, if any, positive outcomes will result. The probability of future success is diminished because these people expect to fail and thus, retreat from the challenges at hand. I have seen this pattern with a number of adults with LD or ADHD.

I'm Less Worthy than Others

If one encounters many failure situations, it is not difficult to understand how self-esteem is adversely affected. True self-esteem, or what Lerner (1996) calls "earned self-esteem," is based on realistic accomplishment. Each success serves as a step up the ladder of future success. However, when mistakes, failure, and negative feedback are major parts of a person's landscape, there is little room for high self-esteem or confidence.

Self-doubts appear early in the lives of many children with LD or ADHD and continue into their adulthood. Sentiments such as "I can't do that, it's too tough" or "This is stupid" (the child in fact feels stupid) are voiced by children as young as 5 and 6. Just as each success serves as the foundation for future success, so too does each setback serve as a reinforcement of the idea "I am not very capable."

A man with ADHD said to me, "If I have any doubts about my ability to do something, these doubts quickly multiply and interfere with my ever being able to succeed.

I see myself as klutzy and I have trouble concentrating. The other day I went to assemble a toy we had bought for my son. The moment I saw the number of parts and the directions I told myself, 'I'll never be able to do that. I can't understand directions. I bet I'll have pieces left over.' And guess what? When I finished, the toy didn't work and I had pieces left over." With much insight he added, "The moment I told myself I couldn't do it, the outcome was no longer in question."

The man with ADHD mentioned at the beginning of this chapter described these feelings of low self-worth when he wrote to me, "Then the diagnosis comes, and it confirms what others have said about me: that something was wrong, that I'm defective, or just plain no damn good."

Veronica Crawford (2002) in her autobiography poignantly describes her sense of incompetence as a result of her learning problems and the desperate ways in which she attempted to avoid her sense of humiliation and despair. She writes:

I couldn't even understand what I was reading; I couldn't remember any of what the teachers taught us. I wanted it to end. I would run away in my mind to a place that was safe, my own world in which I was the winner, in which I was recognized for what I could do. NO MORE BOOKS! With the tears streaming down my face, I would still pretend to read, but I knew the truth; I knew it was useless. I'd give up, go find a television, watch cartoons, and pretend I was still a young child. (p. 71)

As we shall see, negative feelings of low self-worth often trigger coping strategies that exacerbate rather than improve the situation.

The World Is Unfair

Individuals with LD or ADHD are vulnerable to believing that situations and people are unfair. The characteristics noted earlier such as insatiability, inflexibility, and low frustration tolerance reinforce the feeling that things are not fair. This belief was vividly and directly captured by a boy who wrote to me, "Why did I have to be born with ADHD? It's not fair."

The sense of unfairness is manifested in other ways during one's youth. One middle school boy with ADHD was angry with a teacher who gave him a D grade for the semester. On five tests he had received 3 Fs, 1 D, and 1 B. In actuality, the teacher might have been justified in giving him a failing grade. The boy complained that he deserved a B as a grade since one of his test scores was a B. When I pointed out that the teacher was probably basing the grade on all five tests, the boy persisted, "But I got a B on a test!"

At first I thought that he realized that he did not deserve a B but was attempting to convince himself or me that he did. However, I soon appreciated that his seeming distortion of the situation actually reflected a couple of the characteristics associated with ADHD: (1) He was conditioned to perceive things as unfair when he did not get what he wanted, and (2) his cognitive style was to view situations in a rigid, black-and-white fashion, not allowing him to assume another perspective. Once he felt he deserved a B, there was no room to entertain a different view.

Another teenager with LD failed his test for a driver's license because he turned left when the person giving the test requested he turn right. Unfortunately, he often confused left with right. After failing his test he complained, "It's unfair. Why do I have to have learning problems? Why can't I remember left from right?"

This feeling of unfairness, which becomes an ongoing, emotional strain, is also apparent in adults with LD or ADHD. They harbor constant complaints about employers, spouses, and salespeople whom they believe are not fair. Although at times there may be justification to these complaints, frequently they represent anger at feeling misunderstood and not having demands met.

People Seem Angry with Me

Closely related to this last point but deserving separate mention is the sense that others are angry or disappointed with you. This perception, although exaggerated at times, does have some basis in reality. Many people find it exhausting and troubling to be with someone who comes across as self-centered or self-deprecating, demanding, and impulsive. People do not want to interact with someone who constantly complains or blames others. Annoyance and frustration often pervade these relationships, contributing to the feeling that the other people are angry with the person. Unfortunately, if empathy is lacking, the response to this feeling is to become angry in return rather than attempt to resolve the conditions that are reinforcing the anger.

A woman with ADHD told me that her brother and sister were always "ganging up" on her and calling her "inconsiderate" and "selfish." She said that she let them know in "no uncertain terms" that they were the selfish ones and should go see a therapist. She was unable to consider the possibility that her siblings were accurate about her behavior, instead feeling that they were angry because of their "personality problems" and their "jealousy" of her talents.

A teenager with LD frequently blamed "poor" teachers for his difficulty learning. Although the teachers, in fact, did bear some responsibility for his not succeeding at school since they did not appreciate the magnitude of his LD and exhorted him to "try harder," his angry outbursts at them prompted their annoyance.

I Have Little, if Anything, to Offer the World

Self-esteem and dignity are nurtured when individuals feel that they are making a contribution to their world, that their actions make a positive difference (Brooks, 1991;

Brooks & Goldstein, 2001). This belief was supported by research I conducted when I asked adults to identify one of the most positive moments they ever had in school. The most frequent answer I received concerned when they were asked to help out in some manner (e.g., painting a mural on the wall, watering plants, tutoring younger children). The act of assisting others typically reinforces the belief "I am worthwhile. I have something positive to offer others." The second man with ADHD I described at the beginning of this chapter is an example of someone who found a way of turning his hurt into helping others, namely, by becoming a physician.

Many adults with LD or ADHD who possess a negative mindset view themselves as adding little, if anything, to the lives of others. The first man I mentioned at the beginning of this chapter who gave me permission to use his story as an example to others emphasized the negative in doing so ("My time has passed. . . . I wish you well on your research. You can't help me but I'm willing to be used as a 'bad example' for those younger than me. . . . Because for them, perhaps, there's still some hope").

The belief that one has little to contribute to others lessens feelings of competence and a sense of worth and dignity. One man with ADHD summed up his feelings when he told me with great honesty, "I think the only thing I have ever given others is heartache." A woman with LD echoed this sentiment when she expressed the belief, "I feel that I have disappointed people all of my life and that if I disappeared tomorrow no one would really miss me."

I Am Pessimistic that Things Will Improve

This feature of a negative mindset is understandable, given the other beliefs that many individuals with LD or ADHD hold. It is difficult to be optimistic when people feel little control of their lives, when they have difficulty taking ownership for success, when they believe others are unfair and angry, and when they are unable to see any ways in which they make a positive difference in their world. Pessimism about future success and happiness often results in a self-fulfilling prophecy for failure. If you expect that you will continue to experience unhappiness and failure, subtly or not so subtly your actions will lead to these expectations being realized. An ongoing cycle of expected failure and actual failure is a very powerful force in contributing to a pessimistic outlook that is devoid of a sense of hope.

This sense of pessimism and loss of hope was poignantly reflected in the writings of a young man with ADHD explaining why he dropped out of high school. "My alarm goes off and I awake to a new day. At 7:00 in the morning my stomach is queasy and my head hurts. 'Oh God, another day of school.' Too sick to eat breakfast, I stand in the shower saying 'Maybe it will be a good day,' but deep inside I know it will be the same." Given these strong beliefs, it is little wonder that he perceived that his only way of coping was to leave school.

ASSESSING THE MINDSET OF INDIVIDUALS WITH LD OR ADHD

It is important to emphasize that not all adolescents and adults with LD or ADHD develop these characteristics of a negative mindset. However, many do, and, of course, as clinicians we are likely to see in our practices those with a more pessimistic outlook. Before examining the coping strategies used by this population with LD or ADHD and the ways in which a clinician can help replace a negative mindset with a mindset that is filled with more positive and resilient beliefs, it may be helpful to articulate the kinds of questions that clinicians can raise to assess the mindset of individuals with LD or ADHD.

Although paper-and-pencil procedures have been developed to evaluate a person's self-esteem, sense of competence, and optimism or pessimism, as a clinician, I have found that interview questions remain the best resource for obtaining revealing information. Interview questions permit a more in-depth view of an individual's perspective, and they allow you to follow-up and elaborate on particular points. The next list represents a sample of questions that may be raised. It is important to remember that many of these questions serve as a springboard to further questions and discussion, helping us to understand the mindset of adolescents and adults with LD or ADHD:

How does having LD or ADHD affect your life?

What do you perceive to be both the negative and positive aspects of having LD or ADHD?

What things would you like to see changed in your life?

What have you attempted to do to change any of these things?

In what areas have you been successful?

Why do you believe you have been successful?

In what areas have you been unsuccessful?

What do you think has contributed to your not being successful?

When you are not successful at a certain task, what is your usual response? Give a few examples.

Are there people who are trying to be of help to you?

Who are they?

How do you know they are trying to be of help?

What is one of the most helpful things someone said to you or did for you?

Are there any people who actually seem to be interfering with your chances for success?

In what way are they behaving to keep you from being successful?

What is one of the least helpful or even hurtful things someone did to you?

If you could change one or two things about yourself beginning tomorrow, what would they be?

How would you start?

Looking a year or two ahead, how do you see your life changing?

For things to improve, do you think others have to become more tolerant of your having LD or ADHD, or do you feel you have to begin to make some changes, or is it a combination of the two?

All of these questions tap into the views that people have of themselves, of others, of their competencies and vulnerabilities, of their relationships, of their sense of responsibility, of their hopes for the future, of their beliefs of whether they can bring about change. In essence, the answers to these questions represent a mindset or a set of assumptions about oneself and others.

COPING STRATEGIES: HELPING OR EXACERBATING THE PROBLEM?

We all rely on a variety of coping strategies to deal with stresses and challenges in our lives. Some coping strategies appear to be effective, helping individuals to deal successfully with the challenges they face. Other coping behaviors may afford temporary or illusory relief but not only do they fail to resolve the problem, they actually worsen the situation. One of the questions raised in the last section—When you are not successful at a certain task, what is your usual response? Give a few examples—is an attempt to gather information about the ways in which a person copes.

The question of what differentiates an effective from an ineffective coping strategy does not always invite an easy answer. Paradoxically, what I might consider to be an ineffective coping strategy may actually diminish stress for at least a certain period of time more than what I would perceive to be an effective coping strategy. As one illustration, imagine if you were invited to give a presentation at a local organization and you are very fearful of public speaking. One way of coping with the anxiety would be to offer the excuse that you are busy and not able to accept the offer. The immediate feeling is typically relief. One might argue that this way of coping was effective since it lessened stress. However, as a clinician I have found that eventually what replaces this relief is regret—regret at having fled away from a challenge.

For example, a woman with LD and ADHD whose main coping behavior was to avoid situations that she felt could lead to mistakes and embarrassment came to see me. She said that she was constantly telling her two children to "stick with things and not give up" but she felt like "a hypocrite" since she had spent much of her life "running away from things that might lead to failure and humiliation." She noted, "When I say no to a certain request, I feel okay for a few minutes but then I hate myself for being so scared and always avoiding tough things. But then I keep running from things."

Now imagine if instead of immediately offering an excuse not to speak, this woman said yes and then considered ways to cope with the anxiety she was experiencing. She listened to a tape or read a book about lessening the anxiety of public speaking. She practiced her speech using a tape recorder or in front of a trusted friend or relative. As she coped in this way, she might remain anxious but most likely her preparation would lead to a more than satisfactory performance. The fact that she did not back away from the challenge but rather faced it directly would be one of the strongest determinants of feeling a sense of self-dignity. If she took this route, although her coping behavior might not diminish her distress at first, I believe that eventually it would, since she faced rather than fled from a problematic event.

A coping behavior may be deemed effective when individuals confront challenging situations rather than retreat from them, when coping leads to emotional growth and greater feelings of self-worth, and when coping helps people to experience a sense of control of their own lives, that they are masters of their own fate. The factors that contribute to whether an individual uses effective or ineffective ways of coping appear to be based on an ongoing, dynamic interaction between inborn temperamental factors and environmental conditions (Brooks, 1984).

Since a major feature of the mindset of many individuals with LD or ADHD is their belief that they are not very competent, that they are destined to fail and that they do not control their own destiny, they are likely to recruit coping strategies that prove self-defeating and do not result in emotional growth or in success.

I have observed some common ineffective coping strategies with adolescents and adults with LD or ADHD. As clinicians, we must remember that these strategies, although self-defeating, originally served a protective purpose. They were called on in an attempt to avoid the possibility of further failure, humiliation, and embarrassment. If we keep this purpose in mind, we will recognize that our task is to help individuals with LD or ADHD feel less vulnerable so that they are more secure and capable of replacing ineffective means of coping with effective strategies. Some of these self-defeating coping behaviors, several of which can occur at the same time, are discussed next:

- Avoiding
- Quitting
- Rationalizing
- Controlling
- Being aggressive
- Being impulsive and rushing through things

Avoiding

The avoiding coping behavior is represented by the actions of the woman described earlier who turned down a speaking request. People usually avoid a task that they believe will lead to failure. I worked with one man with ADHD who described himself as "klutzy and unathletic." When friends asked him to join in a relatively noncompetitive local softball or basketball game, he always said "no." Yet a number of other people who also were not athletically inclined did participate. In the course of therapy, this man reflected, "I spend more time and energy avoiding things than I do trying things. I guess I'll never know what I'm capable of doing, but I hate to look foolish."

Quitting

The quitting coping style is similar to avoiding but is used to describe people who begin a task but quit as soon as they encounter difficulty. Often this pattern is established early in children's lives, continuing into their adulthood. I have heard many examples of children with LD or ADHD who start a musical instrument or join a sports team, only to leave in a short time with some excuse. A woman I knew quit college believing that she was "too dumb to succeed." When she returned several years later to take courses, her style was to drop certain courses, either saying they were boring or required too much work, given her busy schedule. However, her quitting was truly rooted in her feeling that she could not succeed at the task.

Rationalizing

The rationalizing strategy is frequently used by individuals with LD or ADHD. It involves offering excuses for perceived difficulties and failure rather than accepting responsibility. The woman in the last example who quit college because the courses were too "boring" provides an example of the use of rationalization. A man I saw in therapy refused to go for a job interview for a new position, saying he was certain it would not be a challenge. He offered this opinion even before he had obtained all of the details of the new job. In fact, he was quite frightened of taking on new challenges, which he saw as eventuating in failure.

At times, rationalization assumes the form of "externalizing"—that is, blaming other people or external events for unsatisfactory outcomes. Examples include a woman with ADHD who explained her poor interpersonal relations by contending that other people were unfair to her for no reason or a man who blamed his boss for his own poor work performance. He told me, "My boss knows I have ADHD but yet he gives me very detailed work to do, more detailed than my coworkers get." When I wondered why his boss would do this, he answered, "He just doesn't like me. He's unfair." However, as our therapy work progressed, he was able to acknowledge that the work his boss expected of him was no different from that of other employees. He was able to see that blaming his boss was a way of coping with his own feelings of inadequacy and also represented the mindset that the world is unfair.

Controlling

As noted earlier, a number of adolescents and adults with LD or ADHD feel little, if any, control of what occurs in their lives; a sense of helplessness is not an uncommon result. In response, some individuals attempt to take command and become dictatorial, telling others what to do or how to run their business or their lives. This coping behavior is typically reinforced by problems with empathy and poor social skills. A man with ADHD lost several jobs as he fell into the pattern of telling his manager how the department should be run. On a couple of occasions he did not fulfill certain responsibilities that he felt "made no sense." He also was free with advice to his colleagues about how they might do a better job.

A woman with LD and ADHD who felt "overwhelmed" by the requirements of parenting resorted to micromanaging everything her 10- and 8-year-old sons did. Her need to control their lives was based, in part, on her feelings of inadequacy as a parent as well as a need to "keep the household in order."

Being Aggressive

Closely tied to several other counterproductive coping behaviors such as externalizing and controlling is being aggressive and striking out at others. If people feel that others are unfair or that the task is too difficult, some may respond by avoiding the situation; others may resort to angry outbursts bordering on bullying. The specific coping behavior that is used often is influenced by an individual's temperament as well as life experiences. I have found that a number of adults with ADHD will manifest being aggressive with a heavy dose of rationalization; that is, they will rationalize their aggressive behavior by arguing that their actions were justified, given the ways in which the other person behaved toward them.

A rather driven president of an engineering company was diagnosed with ADHD. Although brilliant in his scientific work, he had difficulty accepting vulnerabilities in himself or in others; his ability to be empathic was limited at best. He had an intense need to be in control, which his position in the company permitted him to do. He left college after his junior year with a transcript filled with incompletes, asserting that many of the requirements to complete a class were "stupid." He then quit his first two jobs after arguments with his supervisors. He began his own company to "show his professors I don't need a college degree to be successful" and to show his former employers that if they "listened to me, their companies would be much more successful."

A downturn in his own business resulted in anxiety, and he was referred to a psychiatrist for a medication consultation. The psychiatrist did an evaluation and made a diagnosis of ADHD as well as an anxiety disorder. This man was placed on medication and referred to me. As he became more comfortable in therapy, he shared his disappointment at not having finished college and added, "It's not a good example for my teenage son and daughter."

He then discussed his relationship with his employees, especially since many of his middle managers were leaving the company. As he described his interactions, it was obvious that he demanded perfection, prompted, in part, by a driving need to prove his professors and former employers wrong. When something did not work out, rather than discuss it rationally with his staff, he would become angry and say some hurtful things. At one meeting, he shouted, "What a dumb thing to do!" while at another he asked one of his managers, "Are you using your brains?" He justified these outbursts by saying "I get angry when people fall short of what their performance should be, and it's good to let them know how disappointed I am."

Given his lack of empathy and his need to be in control, he had little awareness of how this form of motivation was counterproductive; it basically motivated his staff to avoid him or leave the company. Much of the emphasis of our therapy was to help him become more accepting of his own vulnerabilities and more empathic toward other people in his life.

Being Impulsive and Rushing through Things

Although impulsivity is a major characteristic of ADHD, it may also represent a way of coping in individuals with either LD or ADHD. It is not unusual for some adults to want to finish a challenging task or burdensome chore as quickly as possible "to get it over with." The obvious problem is that the more quickly and impulsively the task is done, the more likely that the final product will be riddled with mistakes and flaws. A negative cycle is established since such mistakes reinforce for these individuals that they are not very competent. To deal with these feelings, they resort to one or several of the self-defeating coping behaviors that have been described in this section. Success becomes more and more elusive while a negative mindset becomes increasingly entrenched.

STEPS FOR CHANGING NEGATIVE INTO POSITIVE MINDSETS

As clinicians, one of our main roles when working with individuals with LD or ADHD who are burdened by a negative mindset and accompanying self-defeating coping behaviors is to help them to replace their negative feelings and thoughts with an optimistic, positive outlook and more adaptive ways of managing stress and pressure. We must serve as a catalyst to generate a positive cycle in which the individual engages in activities that lead to fulfillment, satisfaction, and success. As each success chips away at negative feelings, realistic risk taking and the confronting of challenges are likely to follow. As noted earlier, success breeds success. The following represent three major features of replacing negative with more optimistic, positive mindsets:

1. Demystifying mindsets
2. Defining the main components of a positive, resilient mindset
3. Developing a plan of action for change

Step 1: Demystifying Mindsets

An initial step in changing negative mindsets is to help our patients define and understand (a) the assumptions that they have about themselves (including their LD or ADHD) and others and (b) how these assumptions prompt certain behaviors and coping strategies that may be self-defeating. In essence, this first step emphasizes the strengthening of self-awareness, which Goleman (1995) views as a basic component of emotional intelligence.

As examples, the two men described at the beginning of this chapter had different understandings of ADHD. The first man, who was diagnosed as an adult with ADHD, had already suffered years of humiliation and failure. In his case, the despair and hopelessness were apparently such entrenched features of his mindset that the diagnosis did not help to demystify what had occurred all of these years. Rather, the diagnosis was quickly incorporated into his negative mindset as a confirmation "that something was wrong, that I'm defective, or just plain no damn good."

In contrast, the man who became a physician learned of his ADHD earlier in his life. His parents and doctors explained what it meant and how it manifested itself. Understanding his condition helped to demystify it so that it was not as threatening. Although he experienced pain and rejection, he also was helped to see that one could learn ways of coping with ADHD, that it was not a sentence for lifelong misery. Even when upset, he could see a light at the end of the tunnel and could appreciate that he could learn from his experiences. He could harness the pain into a positive force of understanding and helpfulness, eventuating in his becoming a physician.

Similarly, when I gave feedback to a teenage girl I had evaluated and I carefully described both her learning strengths as well as the areas in which she had difficulty, she felt relieved in having an understanding of her learning style. Her relief was heightened when I also explained that there were strategies that she could apply to learn more effectively.

The questions I outlined earlier to assess the mindset of adolescents and adults with LD or ADHD can serve as the catalyst for demystifying these conditions and promoting greater self-awareness. As an example, when I asked a man with ADHD to describe both a successful and unsuccessful experience from his life, his answers were very revealing. It was almost as if he had read and decided to adhere to the tenets of attribution theory. The successful experience he recounted was of a tennis match against a friend who was a good tennis player. My patient won the match and told me in therapy, "I was lucky. My friend didn't play at his best. I even wondered if he was trying to let me win since he had beaten me so often."

As an unsuccessful experience, he recalled an incident from college when he failed the initial exam given in a mathematics course. His first thought was "I'm really stupid in math. I'll never pass." He dropped the class. He then confided in me, "After I dropped the class, I started to blame the teacher and thought, 'If the teacher were a better teacher, I would have been able to handle the material in the class and pass it.'" He used two main coping strategies to deal with his sense of failure: quitting and rationalizing/externalizing.

Although it may seem very obvious to the reader that this man possessed a negative mindset, that he was unable to take credit for his success and felt as if he would never learn from his failure, he was unaware of the power of these assumptions and how they affected his life. To him they were not assumptions but reality. In therapy he offered a number of other examples of this way of thinking. To assist him to become more cognizant of these negative assumptions and to begin to challenge him to change, I borrowed a technique described by solution-oriented therapists, namely to elicit "exceptions" to typical ways of behaving and thinking. Exceptions pertain to situations in which certain problems do not occur or occur less frequently (de Shazer, 1991; Murphy, 1997).

I have modified to some extent the "exception" technique by asking my patients to think of times that they were successful in a certain domain rather than focusing on when the problem did not occur. Concerning this particular man with ADHD, I asked him to reflect on times that he was successful and attributed his success to his own resources and of times he made mistakes and was able to learn from these mistakes.

He struggled at first to think of examples but with some encouragement was able to do so. Both illustrations involved the actions of a coach. He recalled as a young teenager playing in a youth basketball league; he almost single-handedly won a playoff game by making two steals and three baskets in the last minute. "When the game was over and my coach congratulated me, I said, 'I was really lucky.' My coach said really strongly, 'It wasn't luck, it was your determination and skill.' The way he said it made me believe him."

He also recalled that from the first day of practice, this coach actually told the team that if they thought their success was based on luck, they did not realize the benefits of practice, hard work, and teamwork. "I also remember when I had a bad game and was really feeling down. The coach put his hand on my shoulder and said even the pros have bad games. He reminded me of my good games and then pointed out how I wasn't following through on my shot. I wish I could have remembered this coach's lessons. During the year he was my coach I felt more confident than ever before, but unfortunately the feeling didn't last long."

He then described the coach he had the following year who "believed in sarcasm and putdowns and never seemed to offer encouragement." He continued, "I remember a game that we were losing by one point. A teammate threw the ball to me with a few seconds to go and it went off my hands and out of bounds. We lost the game. I don't know if the throw to me was too hard or I was just too anxious to get it and shoot. I felt terrible and then even worse when the coach said in front of everyone that I missed the ball because 'I didn't have good hands.' Can you imagine that? I wasn't that secure to begin with, and his remark made me feel like I would never be good. After that, anytime someone threw the ball to me, I felt uncomfortable. I'm still upset with myself that I let his remark have such a negative impact on me."

These examples, especially the "exceptions" to his current mindset, helped him to appreciate and understand the assumptions that directed his way of thinking and behaving and set the stage for the second step involved in developing a more positive mindset: articulating the components of this mindset. This articulation provides clinicians with a compass in guiding interventions to nurture a resilient mindset.

Step 2: Defining the Main Components of a Positive, Resilient Mindset

In many ways, the features of a positive mindset are the mirror image of the earlier description of a negative mindset. They include:

1. I will learn to distinguish what I have control over from that which I do not and focus my time and energy over those things over which I have control.
2. I can base success on my own strengths and resources.
3. I have "islands of competence."
4. I believe that mistakes are opportunities for learning and growth.
5. I make a positive difference in the world.

I Expend Time and Energy on those Things over which I Have Control

I will focus my time and energy over those things over which I have control since I am the author of my own life. As was noted earlier, one of the hallmarks of effective people is their belief that they are masters of their own destiny. Research focusing on successful adults with LD or ADHD found that they did not adhere to a martyr role. They never asked, "Why me?" but instead believed, "I had no control of being born with LD or ADHD, but what I do have control over is how I deal with this condition."

Gerber et al. (1992), who have studied the ways in which successful adults with learning disabilities view themselves (the same is true for adults with ADHD) emphasize the importance of feeling in control when they write: "Control is the key to success for adults with learning disabilities. . . . Control meant taking charge of one's life and adapting and shaping oneself in order to move ahead. . . . Control was the fuel that fired their success" (p. 479).

The sense of being in control is associated with the attitude that if changes are to occur in my life, I must take responsibility for these changes and not wait for others to come to my rescue or immediately satisfy my needs. Such a perspective not only lessens the sense that the world is unfair and ungiving but also places responsibility for change within oneself. People will feel more in control if they have an understanding of their learning and attention problems and appreciate there are steps they can take to overcome these problems.

Researchers at the Frostig Center, an organization that specializes in working with children with LD in Pasadena, California, have conducted a long-term research project to identify those qualities that lead this population of youngsters to be successful as adults (Goldberg, Higgins, Raskind, & Herman, 2003; Raskind, Goldberg, Higgins, & Herman, 2002). Included among the six attributes they have identified are two related to what I have just described: *self-awareness*, which is tied to demystification and understanding one's strengths and vulnerabilities, and *proactivity*, which overlaps with feeling in control and taking appropriate action to improve one's situation. The other four attributes also relate to features of a resilient mindset I have discussed or will examine below. They are: perseverance, goal-setting, the presence and use of effective support systems, and using adaptive emotional coping strategies.

Success Can Be Based on My Own Strengths and Resources

This feature of a resilient mindset is closely aligned with feeling a sense of control of one's life and is one of the dimensions studied in attribution theory. Although effective people will give credit to individuals who contributed to their success, they also believe that their success rests largely on their own efforts. In essence, they assume ownership for what occurs in their lives.

A woman with ADHD constantly downplayed any of her accomplishments, an attitude that not only diminished her enjoyment when she succeeded but also lessened the probability of future achievement. Adhering to a negative script, she had this knee-jerk reaction to success: "I was lucky this time. It probably won't happen again." Each success elicited the same thoughts. In her case, she segregated one success from the next, so that they did not build on each other to change her negative mindset. As she became more aware of this self-defeating attitude, she was able to adopt a realistic outlook in which she could say "I did well because I planned what I was going to do and worked hard."

As a therapist, I am acutely aware of conveying statements that reinforce my patients accepting credit for their successes. If patients finish therapy with me believing their success is based primarily on my skills as a therapist, then I have not reinforced a very important message. I want them to feel that although I was helpful, their success is based in great part on their own initiative and efforts. A teenager with ADHD summed it up best when he thanked me during our last therapy session and observed, "You really helped me, Dr. Brooks, but if it wasn't for me, none of this would have been possible." This was not said in a bragging manner. I reinforced his belief by replying "I'm glad I was of some help, but you are right. It was your insight and courage to change that made all that you have accomplished possible."

I Have "Islands of Competence"

We all have areas of strength, or what I call "islands of competence." However, as we have seen, a number of adolescents and adults with LD or ADHD fail to acknowledge or appreciate their strengths. People with a more positive, resilient mindset are able to identify their islands of competence. It is for this reason that in my clinical work I directly ask my patients to tell me what they view as their strengths and how do they use these strengths in their daily lives. It is also why I use the technique of searching for "exceptions" when people respond that they don't feel they are very good at anything. I want to begin to plant the seeds that will flower into areas of competence.

On a number of occasions, patients have responded that they cannot think of any strength that they have. If they say this, I typically rephrase the question and ask, "What do you enjoy doing, what are your favorite activities?" Although most can tell me about activities they enjoy, some still have difficulty. If that occurs, I respond, "As I work with you, I'd like to figure out what you enjoy doing and what you think you're pretty good at doing."

A high school boy with ADHD struggled in school. His parents, both of whom had master's degrees, were upset when he informed them that he did not wish to go to college. His island of competence was that he loved working with his hands and doing carpentry. After some initial reservations from his parents, they supported his becoming an apprentice with a carpenter the family knew. He helped to renovate houses and with his mentor's encouragement began his own business. Several years after he graduated from high school, his mother contacted me to let me know that his business was very successful. With some pride she announced, "He makes more than my and my husband's salaries combined, but even more important than what he is earning is that he seems so happy and always has a smile." She added that he had more than 20 people working for him. Since he was somewhat disorganized, she anticipated what was on my mind by saying with some levity, "And he wisely hired a very good administrative assistant who takes care of all the financial details of the business."

I Believe that Mistakes Are Opportunities for Learning and Growth

No one is really thrilled when they make mistakes or fail. However, as clinicians, we recognize that one of our most important tasks is to help people feel less intimidated by mistakes. When mistakes are viewed as situations from which to learn, people are more willing to take realistic risks rather than backing away from challenges. They do not expend an inordinate amount of time and energy fleeing from possible setbacks. Rather, their efforts are directed toward developing plans of action to succeed; if they do not succeed, they reflect on what they have learned and what they can differently next time. Their outlook is optimistic.

I Make a Positive Difference in the World

A basic component of emotional well-being appears to be the belief that one's actions benefit others (Brooks & Goldstein, 2001, 2004). As a therapist, I have witnessed countless examples of individuals, many with LD or ADHD, who engage in activities that make a positive difference (e.g., being involved in a charity, serving as a coach in a youth sports league, helping at a senior citizens' center); in the process their own sense of dignity and self-worth is enhanced and the roots of a resilient mindset are secured.

Step 3: Developing a Plan of Action for Change

Once clinicians help adolescents and adults with LD or ADHD to identify the assumptions that characterize their current mindset and guide their behaviors, the next step is to articulate a problem-solving model for change. The model on which I predicate my interventions was developed by psychologist Myrna Shure for children and adolescents, but is equally relevant for adults (Shure, 1994, 2000). My modification of Shure's basic model includes eight components, all of which I believe have a realistic, achievable quality to them:

1. Articulate both short-term and long-term goals for change.
2. Select a couple of goals to address.
3. Develop realistic, achievable plans to reach the designated goals.
4. Have criteria for evaluating the success of a plan of action.
5. Consider possible obstacles to the goals being achieved as well as how these obstacles will be handled.
6. Change the goals if repeated efforts at success do not work.
7. As goals are reached, add new goals to reinforce a positive mindset and be aware of the negative thoughts that may serve as obstacles to future growth.
8. As new goals are added, continue to develop more effective ways of coping that will help to maintain a positive mindset and strengthen the gains that have been made.

Articulate Both Short-Term and Long-Term Goals for Change

If adolescents or adults with LD or ADHD have developed a negative mindset that offers little hope for the future and we have helped them to understand that mindsets can be changed, a first step is to have them begin to articulate the changes they would like to see occur in their lives. It is often helpful to divide these changes into short-term and long-term goals, with the short-term goals contributing to the realization of the long-terms goals.

Select a Couple of Goals to Address

I have discovered that although some individuals with LD or ADHD struggle to articulate goals (as therapists, we can help them to do so), others are able to generate a long list. However, sometimes their impulsivity and low frustration tolerance prompt them to begin to work on all of these goals at once, which is almost a certain prescription for failure. Instead, as therapists, we must assist them to prioritize their goals and to select one or two on which to give initial focus (O'Hanlon, 1999). We want to maximize the probability that the goals they have selected are achievable so that success will be more likely. Once we have selected the areas they wish to address, we can help to articulate both the short-term and long-terms components of these goals.

As an example, in my sessions with patients with LD or ADHD, I take out a sheet of paper and ask them what they would like to see change in their lives. We write down their responses and then select one or two areas on which to focus. The very exercise of examining and selecting these one or two areas serves several purposes. It helps to define precise and realistic goals. In addition, it serves to challenge and modify various components of a negative mindset, such as feelings of low self-esteem and not having control over one's life.

I worked with a man with ADHD who defined as two of his goals "strengthening his marital relationship" and "focusing on his physical health" (he was overweight). We discussed both of these goals, which at first were cast in somewhat general terms. While describing his marital relationship, aspects of a negative mindset were immediately apparent. He initially placed responsibility for change on his wife, contending that "she was not as supportive and loving as she could be." He also felt that she was unfair in what she expected him to do around the house.

The characteristics of a negative mindset, especially the sense that he had little, if any, control of his life, were also operating when we discussed the issue of his physical health. He complained that he had a "poor metabolism," contending "I can just smell food and I put on weight." He also said that his job demands made it almost impossible to engage in a regular exercise routine.

In essence, he was erecting obstacles to the achievement of goals before they were well defined and planned. He externalized responsibility by arguing his wife needed to be more supportive and that she should not expect too much of him since he had ADHD; he blamed his poor fitness on his metabolism and job schedule. Although there might be some truth in all of these assertions, if he continued to adhere to these obstacles to success, it would keep him from asking this question: Even given these obstacles, what is it that I can do to slowly begin to deal with the problems at hand?

In my role as a therapist, I pointed out in an empathic style the self-defeating patterns he had established so that we could reframe his goals in this way:

- Long-term goal: Improve his marital relationship. Short-term goals: Spend more time with his wife, be less critical of her, and fulfill two designated household responsibilities on a regular basis.
- Long-term goal: Improve his physical fitness. Short-term goals: Go on a healthy diet, begin exercising on a regular basis, and lose 1 pound each week until he had shed 20 pounds.

A man with LD and ADHD was successful in graduating from college and starting a small business. Although these achievements promoted a sense of accomplishment, he voiced feelings of loneliness. He felt that he had devoted so much time and energy to his academic and work pursuits that he had neglected interpersonal relationships, especially with women. His short-term goal was to meet people, while his long-term goal was to meet a woman with whom he could share his life. As we examined actions he could take to meet his goals, he explained, "I'm not into the bar scene." I asked what activities he enjoyed that might set the stage for his meeting new people. Since he was fascinated by politics, he decided to volunteer on the campaign of a local state representative. Although he did not meet a future wife, he cultivated several friendships that led to his going out with them to a restaurant or to a movie. This companionship lessened his sense of loneliness.

Although he had LD and ADHD, which for some people might serve as a barrier to reading books, he developed a love of reading. He acknowledged that it took him longer to read a book than most people, but that did not deter him from engaging in this activity. Given his love of books, he discovered that a local bookstore had readings by different authors, which he began to attend. At one reading he met a woman with many interests common to his. Today they are in a long-term relationship.

Develop Realistic, Achievable Plans to Reach the Designated Goals

Given the impulsivity, poor planning skills, and low frustration tolerance of many adolescents and adults with LD or ADHD, the importance of designing a realistic plan of action is of paramount importance. For example, I worked with a woman with ADHD, who similar to the man in an earlier example, wanted to lose weight through diet and exercise. However, she was in such a "rush" to do so that she went on what could be seen as a starvation diet and immediately engaged in doing several hours of exercise a day, although she had done little exercise previously. She began to lose weight quickly, but her initial exuberance and feeling of success were soon replaced by exhaustion and not feeling well physically. Before long, she resorted to her old habits, asserting "This diet and exercise stuff really doesn't work." As obvious as it may appear to the reader that this woman's approach was doomed to failure, the possibility of failure was not at first evident to her.

Returning to the man whose goals were to develop a better relationship with his wife and to become more physically fit, once he accepted his role in making changes, we explored actions he could take to reach his goals. We discussed sharing with his wife his wish to spend time with her and their setting aside a time each week to be together with no distractions. Although some may wonder why this couple could not just discuss things on a spontaneous basis, time management for many adolescents and adults with LD or ADHD is poor. Thus, establishing a set time to chat was important for this man.

We also considered different topics that he wanted to discuss with his wife. As he described them to me, many seemed critical of her and were certain to lead to increased tension in their relationship. I wondered how often he gave his wife positive feedback; it was not easy for him to offer an example. Consequently, we discussed his finding opportunities throughout the week (not just at a "scheduled" meeting) to compliment his wife. In essence, we were searching for ways for him to change the "negative scripts" that had become entrenched in his style of relating (Brooks & Goldstein, 2004).

Concerning the goal of becoming more fit, he thought it would be easier if he and his wife consulted with a nutritionist. He felt it was important for his wife to be present since she often bought the food and prepared the meals in the house. He told me, "Her support will be crucial." In addition, he joined a local health club, but before he started an exercise regimen, he met with one of the staff and they developed a realistic and achievable plan for him. A course of action that may come easily for an adolescent or adult without LD or ADHD often requires specific input and feedback for adults with these conditions.

Have Criteria for Evaluating the Success of a Plan of Action

Another key issue involved when developing a strategy to reach one's stated goals is the criteria used to assess whether the plan is working effectively. In some instances, the criteria are very concrete, such as weight loss and greater fitness (e.g., losing a certain amount of weight in a specified time period or being able to jog 2 miles within a month). In other instances, an assessment of effectiveness may require more work in defining criteria for success, such as when the goal is "an improved relationship with one's spouse." This man did monitor that he and his wife were meeting at the time they had agreed on and that they were discussing issues in the marriage that both judged to be important; he even found it helpful to keep a record for himself of the number of times he complimented his wife. He said, "At first I thought it would seem artificial, but it soon became a more natural part of my 'new script.'" The evaluation of the effectiveness of any intervention should also include realistic time limits.

Consider Possible Obstacles to the Goals Being Achieved as Well as How These Obstacles Will Be Handled

In addition to developing criteria to assess the effectiveness of different strategies, I have found that it is important to discuss openly the possibility that a plan may not work. It is not unusual for me to say after we have considered a plan, "What if it doesn't work?" This comment is not offered as a self-fulfilling prophecy for failure since I then add, "Some plans seem great in my office but they don't work outside the office. So let's think of possible back-up plans should the first one prove ineffective."

I believe that is it essential to acknowledge in advance that some courses of action will prove ineffective but that we can learn from them. I found that when I did not discuss the possibility of failure, the reaction of many adolescents and adults with LD or ADHD to a plan that proved unsuccessful was to view it as another indication of their ineffectiveness. It lowered even further their sense of self-worth, triggered feelings of sadness, prompted anger toward themselves or me as their therapist, and reinforced a more pessimistic view of what they could accomplish to change their lives. However, by proactively considering possible obstacles as well as subsequent strategies, these adults were less vulnerable to feelings of failure and better equipped to handle disappointments. By possessing backup plans, they also felt more in control of their lives rather than victims and martyrs.

The man we have been discussing learned that if at times his wife did not want to talk, instead of getting angry at her, he would simply say "That's okay, we can find another time." In terms of exercising regularly, when he began to find it "boring" to go to the gym, he made plans with a friend who was using the same gym to go together, in effect, supporting and encouraging each other. (Apparently his friend also struggled with following through on things.)

Given the negative mindset of many adolescents and adults with LD or ADHD—a mindset that frequently assumes the worst and interprets each failure as an indication of how unworthy they are—it is critical to build in this step of anticipating that some interventions will not be successful and designing alternative strategies.

Change the Goals If Repeated Efforts at Success Do Not Work

If our strategies to reach particular goals continue to lead to failure, it is often a signal that the goals may need to be changed. Goals that appear reasonable actually may turn out to be too ambitious, or other unanticipated factors may interfere with their success. When this occurs, it is important to review and modify the original goals.

A woman with ADHD set as one of her goals spending a half-hour each evening playing the piano, an activity she not only enjoyed but helped to relax her. In our sessions she decided that if this goal of playing piano a half-hour each evening did not work, her backup plan was to practice every other evening. Given her other responsibilities, she found it difficult to set aside a half-hour every evening to play piano. She resorted to the backup plan, namely, to practice every other evening. Much to her dismay, she discovered that she began to miss some of her practices every other evening. She said to me, "Another example of my not being able to follow through on things."

I asked what she thought would help her find time to play the piano, especially since it was an activity that brought her enjoyment. At first she fell prey to a negative mindset and contended, "Probably nothing would work. I can't even succeed at something I enjoy doing." However, with some encouragement, she offered an interesting observation together with a revised goal. "A half-hour doesn't seem like much but maybe it is. I wonder what would happen if I began by setting aside 15 minutes each evening."

Although some may judge this modification of a goal as simplistic, I viewed it as a major step forward in terms of indicating that she was altering her negative mindset. The very task of contemplating and implementing a new goal was a reflection that she was moving beyond the feeling that she was helpless, that the situation was hopeless, and that she did not have the resources to find an alternative solution. She discovered, much to her delight, that 15 minutes a night of practice was achievable for her. Not surprisingly, she frequently extended the 15 minutes to 20 or 25 minutes once she was seated at the piano—she perceived this additional time as a "bonus."

As Goals Are Reached, Add New Goals to Reinforce a Positive Mindset

After one month of practicing piano for 15 minutes, she moved to her next goal: playing 20 minutes each evening. The seemingly small accomplishment of playing 15 minutes a night was like climbing Mount Everest for her. She found that true success is based on realistic accomplishment and that each success reinforces a positive mindset thereby, setting the stage for future success. Feeling more confident, she added a new goal: taking piano lessons once a week to strengthen her skills. She felt that she had achieved a certain level of discipline and commitment to take these lessons.

I will never forget the session we had when she came in and said, "My piano teacher feels I have real talent." In the past, she might have added, "I think the teacher is just saying this to be nice." However, her attributions about success had changed. She could now accept the piano teacher's appraisal. Given her greater self-assurance,

I could even joke and ask, "Now, you're certain that your accomplishments are not just because of luck or that somehow your fingers just moved across the piano without any direction from you?" She laughed and said, "No, it's me in charge." That statement had great meaning on both a figurative and literal level. For one of the first times in her life, she felt a sense of ownership for her accomplishments.

As New Goals Are Added, Continue to Develop More Effective Ways of Coping that Will Help to Maintain a Positive Mindset

Replacing a negative mindset takes ongoing work and effort. As a clinician, I have discovered that until a more positive mindset is firmly rooted, there will be many occasions when the old mindset rears its ugly head and begins once again to be a dominating force.

It is for this reason that I spend time helping adolescents and adults with LD or ADHD to recognize four things:

1. The feelings and beliefs that signal the possibility that a negative mindset is taking hold (e.g., believing "I am stupid" or "I am worthless" or "I will always fail" or as the woman I described earlier told me that her success in life was like "a house made of cards. I feel that if any kind of wind comes along, my entire facade of success will crumble")
2. The different coping strategies that are being used to manage these feelings and which ones are actually counterproductive
3. The need for more realistic goals and plans of action
4. The acceptance of one's strengths and vulnerabilities

CONCLUDING THOUGHTS ABOUT TWO MEN

Returning to the stories of the two men at the beginning of this chapter, I believe that the one who went on to become a physician was aided by an early diagnosis, by ongoing support from his parents and therapists, by discovering his islands of competence (e.g., helping others), and by learning as much as he could about ADHD. (He even volunteered as a research assistant during one summer on a project related to ADHD.) He increasingly gained a feeling of control over his life.

In contrast, the other man did not "discover" his condition until he was in his 40s. Unfortunately, by then, his negative mindset was so entrenched and so hardened that all of his life experiences were filtered through this mindset. The pain of continuous failure made it difficult for him to find a new path, although I believe even individuals trapped in such a negative mindset can change. They typically need the input and support of therapists and others who can help them to learn about and follow the ideas outlined in this chapter.

As clinicians, we must be empathic and understand the world of adolescents and adults with LD or ADHD. We must provide realistic hope by offering strategies for success. We must strive to replace a negative mindset with a mindset filled with optimism and promise. This is one of our greatest gifts to our patients with LD or ADHD. When this gift is realized, it offers us a great source of satisfaction.

REFERENCES

Barkley, R. A. (1995). *Taking charge of ADHD: The complete, authoritative guide for parents*. New York, NY: Guilford Press.

Barkley, R. A. (2009). *ADHD in adults*. Boston, MA: Jones & Bartlett.

Barkley, R. A., & Fischer, M. (2005). Suicidality in children with ADHD, grown up. *ADHD Report, 13*, 1–6.

Barkley, R. A., Murphy, K. R., & Fischer, M. (2007). Adults with ADHD: Clinic-referred cases vs. children grown up. *ADHD Report, 15*, 1–7 & 13.

Barkley, R. A., Murphy, K. R., & Fischer, M. (2008). *ADHD in adults: What the science says*. New York, NY: Guilford Press.

Brooks, R. (1984). Success and failure in middle childhood: An interactionist perspective. In M. D. Levine & P. Satz (Eds.), *Middle childhood: Development and dysfunction* (pp. 87–128). Baltimore, MD: University Park Press.

Brooks, R. (1987). Storytelling and the therapeutic process for children with learning disabilities. *Journal of Learning Disabilities, 20*, 546–550.

Brooks, R. (1991). *The self-esteem teacher*. Loveland, OH: Treehaus Communications.

Brooks, R. (1999). Fostering resilience in exceptional children: The search for islands of competence. In V. Schwean & D. Saklofske (Eds.), *Handbook of psychosocial characteristics of exceptional children* (pp. 563–586). New York, NY: Kluwer Academic/Plenum.

Brooks, R. (2001a). Fostering motivation, hope, and resilience in children with learning disorders. *Annals of Dyslexia, 51*, 9–20.

Brooks, R. (2001b). Nurturing islands of competence: Is there really room for a strength-based model in the treatment of ADHD? *ADHD Report, 9*, 1–5.

Brooks, R. (2002). Changing the mindset of adults with ADHD: Strategies for fostering hope, optimism, and resilience. In S. Goldstein & A. Teeter (Eds.), *Clinician's guide to adult ADHD: Assessment and intervention* (pp. 127–146). San Diego, CA: Academic Press.

Brooks, R., & Goldstein, S. (2001). *Raising resilient children*. New York, NY: McGraw-Hill.

Brooks, R., & Goldstein, S. (2004). *The power of resilience: Achieving balance, confidence, and personal strength in your life*. New York, NY: McGraw-Hill.

Brooks, R., & Goldstein, S. (2007). *Raising a self-disciplined child*. New York, NY: McGraw-Hill.

Canino, F. J. (1981). Learned-helplessness theory: Implications for research in learning disabilities. *Journal of Special Education, 15*, 471–484.

Chess, S., & Thomas, A. (1987). *Know your child*. New York, NY: Basic Books.

Covey, S. R. (1989). *The 7 habits of highly effective people*. New York, NY: Simon & Schuster.

Crawford, V. (2002). *Embracing the monster: Overcoming the challenges of hidden disabilities*. Baltimore, MD: Brookes Publishing.

Daniel, S. S., Walsh, A. K., Goldston, D. B., Arnold, E. M., Reboussin, B. A., & Wood, F. B. (2006). Suicidality, school dropout, and reading problems among adolescents. *Journal of Learning Disabilities, 39*, 507–514.

de Shazer, S. (1991). *Putting difference to work*. New York, NY: Norton.

Dweck, C. (2006). *Mindset: The new psychology of success*. New York, NY: Random House.

Gardner, H. (1983). *Frames of mind*. New York, NY: Basic Books.

Gerber, P. J., Ginsberg, R., & Reiff, H. B. (1992). Identifying alterable patterns in employment success for highly successful adults with learning disabilities. *Journal of Learning Disabilities, 25*, 475–487.

Glenn, B. (2007). *Simply special: Learning to love your ADHD*. Carmel, IN: A Chalkguy Publishing Book.

Goldberg, R. J., Higgins, E. L., Raskind, M. H., & Herman, K. L. (2003). Predictors of success in individuals with learning disabilities: A qualitative analysis of a 20-year-longitudinal study. *Learning Disabilities Research & Practice, 18*, 222–236.

Goldstein, S., & Brooks, R. (2007). *Understanding and managing children's classroom behavior: Creating resilient, sustainable classrooms*. New York, NY: Wiley.

Goldstein, S., & Brooks, R. (Eds.) (2005). *Handbook of resilience in children*. New York, NY: Springer.

Goleman, D. (1995). *Emotional intelligence*. New York, NY: Bantam.

Greene, R. (1998). *The explosive child*. New York, NY: Harper/Collins.

Hallowell, E. M., & Jensen, P. S. (2008). *Superparenting for ADD: An innovative approach to raising your distracted child*. New York, NY: Random House.

Hartmann, T. (2003). *The Edison gene: ADHD and the gift of the hunter child*. Rochester, VT: Park Street Press.

Hayes, M. L., & Sloat, R. S. (1988). Preventing suicide in learning disabled children and adolescents. *Academic Therapy, 24*, 221–230.

Healey, D. M., & Rucklidge, J. J. (2008). The relationship between ADHD and creativity. *ADHD Report, 16*, 1–5.

Honos-Webb, L. (2005). *The gift of ADHD: How to transform your child's problems into strengths*. Oakland, CA: New Harbinger.

Huntington, D. D., & Bender, W. N. (2001). Adolescents with learning disabilities at risk? Emotional well-being, depression, suicide. *Journal of Learning Disabilities, 26*, 159–166.

Lackaye, T. D., & Margalit, M. (2006). Comparisons of achievement, effort, and self-perceptions among students with learning disabilities and their peers from different achievement groups. *Journal of Learning Disabilities, 39*, 432–446.

Langston, R. W. (2010). *The power of dyslexic thinking: How a learning disability shaped six successful careers*. Austin, TX: Bridgeway Books.

Lavoie, R. (2005). *It's so much work to be your friend: Helping the child with learning disabilities find social success*. New York, NY: Simon & Schuster.

Lerner, B. (1996). Self-esteem and excellence: The choice and the paradox. *American Educator, 20*, 14–19.

Licht, B. G. (1983). Cognitive-motivational factors that contribute to the achievement of learning-disabled children. *Journal of Learning Disabilities, 16*, 483–490.

Mather, N., & Ofiesh, N. (2005). Resilience and the child with learning disabilities. In S. Goldstein & R. Brooks (Eds.), *Handbook of resilience in children* (pp. 239–255). New York, NY: Springer.

Murphy, J. J. (1997). *Solution-focused counseling in middle and high schools*. Alexandria, VA: American Counseling Association.

O'Hanlon, B. (1999). *Do one thing different and other uncommonly sensible solutions to life's persistent problems*. New York, NY: Morrow.

Pera, G. (2008). *Is it you, me, or adult A.D.D.? Stopping the roller coaster when someone you love has attention deficit disorder*. San Francisco, CA: Alarm Press.

Pink, D. H. (2005). *A whole new mind: Why right-brainers will rule the future*. New York, NY: Riverhead Books.

Raskind, M. H., Goldberg, R. J., Higgins, E. L., & Herman, K. L. (2002). Teaching "life success" to students with learning disabilities: Lessons learned from a 20-year-old study. *Intervention in School and Clinic, 37*, 201–208.

Reivich, K., & Shatte, A. (2002). *The resilience factor: 7 keys to finding your inner strength and overcoming life's hurdles*. New York, NY: Random House.

Seligman, M. (1990). *Learned optimism: How to change your mind and your life*. New York, NY: Pocket Books.

Shaywitz, S. (2003). *Overcoming dyslexia*. New York, NY: Knopf.

Shure, M. B. (1994). *Raising a thinking child*. New York, NY: Holt.

Shure, M. B. (2000). *Raising a thinking preteen*. New York, NY: Holt.

Solden, S. (2002). *Journeys through ADDulthood*. New York, NY: Walker Publishing.

Weiner, B. (1974). *Achievement motivation and attribution theory*. Morristown, NJ: General Learning Press.

14

Using Neurocognitive Psychotherapy for LD and ADHD

Carol Ann Robbins
Judith M. Glasser

Although Attention-Deficit/Hyperactivity Disorder (ADHD) is the most researched childhood psychiatric disorder, most of that research continues to focus on children. Early recognition that perhaps ADHD does not end with childhood was reflected in the publication of books such as *Hyperactive Children Grown Up* (Weiss & Hechtman, 1993); however, this title is notable for reflecting our continuing focus on ADHD as a childhood disorder. In the mid-1990s, recognition of ADHD as a life span disorder, affecting individuals at every phase of development, came into broad acceptance. Public awareness of ADHD in adults began with the publication of *Driven to Distraction* in 1995, a nationwide best-seller coauthored by psychiatrists Ned Hallowell and John Ratey. CHADD, the largest national advocacy organization for those affected with ADHD, officially changed its name to Children *and Adults* with Attention Deficit Disorder in1994.

In the intervening years, a number of books have been published addressing the treatment of adolescents and adults with ADHD. These approaches recognize that traditional psychotherapy in combination with stimulant medication was not adequate to help adolescents and adults cope with the multiple challenges of ADHD. Several studies of the efficacy of cognitive behavioral therapy (CBT) have been conducted with encouraging results (e.g., Ramsey & Rostain, 2008; Safren, Otto, Sprich, Wilens, & Biederman, 2005). As so often happens, clinical experience precedes research to document the efficacy of treatment approaches that are reported anecdotally to show positive results. This is the case with the treatment approach that we present in this chapter, which was originally developed by Kathleen G. Nadeau, Ph.D., an internationally recognized expert in the field of attention and learning disorders, and is used extensively at the Chesapeake ADHD Center in Silver Spring, Maryland, where we practice under the clinical direction of Dr. Nadeau (www.chesapeakeadd.com). Our approach, called neurocognitive psychotherapy, has developed pragmatically and incrementally since the early 1980s (Nadeau, 1995; Nadeau in Goldstein & Ellison, 1992). Its name was chosen to emphasize the neurological basis of ADHD and Learning Disabilities (LD), reminding the clinician that ADHD and LD cannot be treated effectively if only the emotional and interpersonal sequelae are addressed without also directly addressing ways to improve underlying brain functioning.

Recent trends in the mental health field have focused more extensively on the intersection of neuroscience and psychology, such as described by Louis Cozolino (2002) and Daniel Siegel (1999) in their groundbreaking books. More recently, a Swedish neuropsychologist, Barry Karlsson, has begun to organize an international network of professionals to further explore neurocognitive disabilities and attempt to understand the combined effect of intellectual disability, cognitive deficits, and problem-solving strategies.

ADHD is a psychiatric condition that has received much attention from a range of professions, including medicine, psychology, and education, as well as the newly emerging profession of ADHD coaching. Each of these communities, predictably enough, has tended to approach ADHD with the tools already favored by their trade. The medical community has strongly emphasized medication as the primary treatment approach. The educational community has focused on educational and behavioral approaches to improve classroom behavior and academic achievement. The field of psychology, adhering to what it knows best, has primarily offered psychoeducation, behavioral, and cognitive behavioral approaches to treating ADHD. The newly emerging profession of ADHD coaching has emphasized the pragmatics of daily living, habit building, and goal achievement.

In a parallel universe that rarely intersects with the medical, educational, or mental health community is the field of cognitive rehabilitation or cognitive retraining. Many of their treatment approaches, developed to assist those with Traumatic Brain Injury, seem easily adapted to the treatment of ADHD and LD. Much of cognitive rehabilitation is designed to improve executive functioning skills and daily life management, issues that are among the core struggles for those with ADHD/LD. However, there has been very limited contact between those in cognitive rehabilitation and other professions that are focused on treating ADHD/LD. Much like the parable of the blind men and the elephant, each profession has taken a narrow view of ADHD, derived from its particular training and perspective, and promotes an approach to treating it that may have merit but fails to take the broad and complex nature of ADHD and LD into account.

ADHD frequently co-occurs with LD and both persist into adolescence and adulthood. Estimates of the co-occurrence rates vary; however Tannock and Brown (in

Brown, 2009) report that approximately 25% to 40% of people with ADHD also have a specific learning disability. The most well-researched form of learning disability is dyslexia. Like ADHD, dyslexia has been found to be genetically linked and brain based. However, individuals with ADHD can have slow reading speed and problems with reading comprehension even in the absence of a specific learning disability. Recent research conducted by Sally Shaywitz and Bennett Shaywitz (2008) has highlighted the role of attentional mechanisms in reading difficulties. Their research has also demonstrated that medications used to treat ADHD can be helpful in improving reading in people with dyslexia. Mathematics disorders are less well understood, although recent neuroimaging research is shedding light on this important topic. However, it is clear that problems with attention and with working memory can have a huge impact on a person's ability to perform mathematical problems. Disorders of written expression can be due to impairments in the brain's language system, visual-motor system, executive functions, or to all of these. Speech and language disorders often co-occur with ADHD. The term "speech disorders" refers to problems with articulation, fluency, and rate of speech. The term "language disorders" refers to problems in understanding the meaning of words (receptive language) or in being able to put thoughts into words in a meaningful way (expressive language). Estimates of the overlap between these communication disorders and ADHD vary from 8% to 90% (Brown, 2009).

It is very clear that in order to treat the whole person, we are remiss if we do not evaluate and treat comorbid LD. These problems combine in a way that often creates extraordinary and chronic stress as well as secondary emotional difficulties. Often individuals who do not do well in school develop a profound sense of shame that remains with them into adulthood, undermining their confidence and sometimes making them feel like an imposter.

The approach that we outline in this chapter reflects our efforts over the past many years to develop an integrative, brain-based approach that borrows the most effective aspects of treating ADHD/LD from the fields of psychiatry, psychology, education, nutrition, exercise physiology, coaching, and cognitive rehabilitation. As such, it is an approach that requires practitioners of neurocognitive psychotherapy to stretch their professional skills in many directions, expanding their knowledge base and skill set. Due to space limitations within a single chapter, we will be able to touch on only a number of critical topics, but we cite resources that can provide more in-depth information about each aspect of our integrative approach.

A BRAIN-BASED APPROACH

Recent exciting trends in psychology have furthered a conceptual integration of the "psychological" and "neurocognitive" into a unified theory of psychology in which "psychological" events (i.e., interpersonal and intrapersonal events) affect brain structure, growth and development; conversely, brain functioning mediates psychological functioning. In other words, the field of psychology is rapidly moving away from dichotomous thinking of mind/body and mind/brain dichotomy toward a unified view of humans as organisms that feel, think, emote, and react in a completely integrated manner throughout our bodies. As more psychologists embrace this view, it will become clearer that all psychological treatments should be brain based. But let us begin with a more modest proposal, that ADHD and LD, in particular, should be treated using a brain-based approach.

A brain-based approach to treating ADHD/LD does not imply, however, that medication is, therefore, the treatment of choice—a view increasingly popular over the past several decades during the explosive growth of effective psychotropic medications. What we now know is that a multitude of factors influence the neurochemistry of our brains and that we must understand and address those factors rather than relying predominantly on a "chemical cure." The chemistry and electrical activity of our brains is fluid and is impacted by events and interactions around us on a minute-by-minute basis. Our brain chemistry and electrical activity is influenced in a highly reactive, moment-by-moment basis by the nutrients we ingest, by exercise, by stress, by sleep (or lack of sleep), by our thoughts and emotions, and by the interpersonal interactions that we experience. Recent research demonstrates that aerobic exercise increases brain chemicals that promote the growth of new neurons as well as the growth of dendritic connections between existing neurons (Ratey & Hagerman, 2008). Research now shows us that we can even bring about structural changes in the brain, can literally exercise and "grow" areas of our brains, through repetitive practice. Stress and trauma have been demonstrated to interrupt and block the smooth collaborative functioning between areas of the brain, leading us to become caught in repetitive emotionally reactive loops, unable to use calm judgment to engage in constructive problem solving. Research confirms that our thoughts strongly influence our feelings—the basis for CBT that has become so widespread in recent years.

As we learn of all of these influences on our brain, it is incumbent on us to broaden our approaches beyond "talk therapy" to include an informed, integrative approach to helping our clients feel and function better in their lives. The core of our approach in neurocognitive psychotherapy is an effort to develop an integrative, brain-based approach that we outline in this chapter. Neurocognitive psychotherapy borrows from different treatment modalities to build an approach that attempts to address the broad range of challenges often associated with ADHD. This form of therapy integrates evidenced-based treatments from different fields, including cognitive retraining and CBT.

Cognitive Rehabilitation

Cognitive retraining (earlier referred to as cognitive rehabilitation) is a set of systematically applied interdisciplinary services that are provided with the goal of improving functioning in the areas of attention, memory, language, and/or executive functioning for people who have sustained a brain injury. People who suffer from brain injuries often have subsequent difficulty with arousal, attention, memory, and decision making that makes it hard for them to function in everyday life. They also often have difficulty with emotional and behavioral regulation as well as with social relationships. These are the same issues that our ADHD/LD clients face.

Cognitive retraining typically focuses on two combined approaches: restoring cognitive skills that have been lost due to brain injury, and learning to use strategies to compensate for the impaired abilities. A neuropsychological evaluation usually is conducted initially, which helps to identify the person's specific strengths and weaknesses that become the focus of therapy. The first part of cognitive retraining, restoring skills, can be compared to rebuilding a weakened muscle. Exercises used in retraining programs may work to rebuild cognitive skills such as attention, concentration, memory, organization, perception, judgment, and/or problem solving. Exercises can include computer programs designed to improve visual-perceptual processing, reaction time, memory, and attention. The second component of cognitive retraining is learning to use strategies or compensatory techniques to cope with weaker areas of function. Strategies are designed for each patient using his or her areas of strength to compensate for weaker skill areas (see American Brain Tumor Association, www .abta.org; Cognitive Retraining). Concrete tasks of daily living are often the focus of cognitive retraining. For example, exercises involving common multistep activities, such as meal preparation and ordering from a restaurant menu, sometimes are used as tasks to improve executive functions. Role playing is used as patients work to improve skills in working memory that are necessary for socialization. Concrete suggestions are made to work on improving organization, time management, attention, and memory. These can include ideas about making lists, setting alarms, and using personal digital assistants (PDAs) or day planners. "The benefits of cognitive rehabilitation have been discussed in more than 700 published research studies and are evident in positron emission tomography (PET) scans and other neuroimaging techniques," claims Dr. Douglas I. Katz, Brain Injury Programs Medical Director at Braintree Rehabilitation Hospital in Braintree, Massachusetts, and first author of the Brain Injury Association of America (BIAA)'s position statement (Katz, Ashley, O'Shanick, & Connors, 2006).

Research has demonstrated that the brains of people diagnosed with ADHD/LD are different from those of normal controls in areas that are involved in important cognitive functions (Biederman, 2005). People diagnosed with ADHD often experience cognitive challenges, although less severe than those that have experienced brain injury. Therefore, there is reason to expect that principles of cognitive retraining would apply to people with ADHD as well.

There is clear evidence that ADHD is a disorder of the brain's executive functions that is associated with lifelong impairments (Barkley, 2006, 2008). Denkla (in Brown, 2009) defined the executive functions in this way:

> These underlying neural control functions typically include selective and sustained attention, initiation and/or inhibition and/or shifting of responses, verbal and/or visual working memory, emotion regulation, self-monitoring, and sequencing of complex behaviors, as well as management of time and space. (p. 242)

In adults, the clinical picture of ADHD is marked more by inattentiveness than by hyperactivity or impulsivity. Adults may have difficulty with procrastination that interferes with work performance; may be easily distracted; may have poor task completion; and may be forgetful, disorganized, and prone to frequently misplacing personal items. Executive function impairments can be more problematic for adults than for children due to the increased expectations and demands on adults. Although medication can be very effective in improving symptoms of ADHD, including executive function, medication alone is not sufficient to improve overall functioning. New skills must be learned as well.

Cognitive Behavioral Therapy

Another important facet of neurocognitive psychotherapy incorporates aspects of CBT, which has been widely used for more than 30 years. CBT was originally based on the idea that thoughts could be treated like behaviors and modified using behavioral techniques. In recent years, several researchers have investigated the use of CBT specifically for ADHD (Branham, 2009; Ramsay & Rostain, 2008; Safren et al., 2005). Research has supported the use of CBT for ADHD clients to provide psychoeducation, to teach coping strategies for managing symptoms, and to work on changing core beliefs and faulty thinking that developed due to having grown up with ADHD.

A key aspect of neurocognitive psychotherapy is psychoeducation. A fundamental change can occur when people begin to see that the way they have been their whole lives has been due to an underlying neurobiological problem rather than to a character flaw. Often the diagnosis itself is very therapeutic as it provides a brain-based explanation for the struggles many have experienced thus far in their lives. It allows clients to re-create their life story through the lens of having ADHD and no longer engage in self-blame, attributing their failures to character flaws such as laziness, stupidity, or "spaciness." In addition to helping clients explain their struggles in terms of a neurobiological difference, it is also very important to help clients redefine themselves by their strengths rather than their weaknesses. Decreasing symptoms and building strengths can then become the focus of treatment, with an emphasis on problem solving rather than self-blame.

PUTTING NEUROCOGNITIVE PSYCHOTHERAPY INTO PRACTICE

The primary goals of neurocognitive psychotherapy are to optimize cognitive functioning, to restructure the client's environment (including home, school, work, and social environments) in support of improved functioning, and to help the client develop effective compensatory strategies. We teach clients to improve their cognitive functioning by helping them to manage their medication, to develop brain-changing behavioral habits (sleep, exercise, nutrition, meditation), and to engage in brain training activities.

Medication Management to Improve Cognitive Functioning

Active medication management is an essential part of treating individuals with ADHD. As clinicians treating individuals with ADHD, we must be knowledgeable about the typical medications used with this population, including their efficacy, side effects, dosing, and contraindications. It is imperative to review regularly the efficacy of the client's current medication regimen, with regard to managing both the symptoms of ADHD as well as managing commonly occurring comorbid conditions such as Generalized Anxiety Disorder, Obsessive-Compulsive Disorder, Major Depressive Disorder, Dysthymic Disorder, Post-Traumatic Stress Disorder, and Bipolar Disorder. Careful and regular coordination with the client's prescribing physician is vital, as the ADHD specialist is often in the position of recommending medications to physicians who may not be well versed in treating adolescents or adults with ADHD. Because the clinician typically has much more time to observe the client, it is incumbent on us to assist the physician in monitoring response to medication: side effects, timing of doses, attaining adequate length of coverage, and achieving clinical efficacy. In the ideal situation, we develop a close working relationship with the treating physician so that treatment can be well coordinated. We also need to help our clients develop habits that support consistently taking medication as prescribed (remembering to take it, keeping it in multiple locations, setting reminders, pairing it with existing habits, etc.).

One of the most common issues in effective medication management for both adolescents and adults with ADHD stimulant medication is the tendency of physicians to undermedicate, thereby not allowing the client to experience optimal clinical efficacy. Clients may then be led to believe that medications do not work for them and perhaps erroneously conclude that they must not have ADHD after all. We need to be aware that rate of response often increases with higher doses and that adults may need as much as 1.0 mg per kg of body weight (Prince & Wilens, in Nadeau & Quinn, 2002).

Another important factor that needs to be taken into consideration is the metabolism rate of the individual client. Fast metabolizers will effectively "burn through" the medication much more quickly than average, necessitating higher and more frequent dosing. These fast metabolizers may require off-label dosing as they often need 2 daily doses of long-acting formulations prescribed at a higher per dose level than recommended by manufacturers. Ideally, the prescribing physician will allow the client to titrate the dose upward until clinical efficacy is achieved, with close monitoring by the ADHD clinician. Because many physicians have little experience in prescribing stimulant medication to adolescents and adults, referrals may need to be made to physicians who are more experienced at effectively managing these medications.

It is important for the clinician to be aware of the interaction between hormonal fluctuations in women and their response to stimulant medication. Varying levels of estrogen can affect attention, memory, and mood. The efficacy of stimulants varies not only in different phases of the menstrual cycle but also in perimenopause and menopause.

Stress, depression, and lack of sleep may also decrease the clinical efficacy of stimulant medication for all clients. Although stimulants can cause insomnia for some, other clients may need a late dose to "turn down the noise" in their brain in order to go to sleep at night.

For clients who struggle to get out of bed in the morning or are in a fog, the psychotherapist might suggest having them take the stimulant an hour or so before wake-up time by setting an initial alarm, taking the medication (left by their bedside), and then going back to sleep until the final alarm time to get out of bed. This way the medication will already be in their system when they arise, enabling them to be much more efficient in their morning routine prior to departure for work or school.

It is wise to suggest that clients decrease or eliminate their caffeine intake while initially trying stimulant medication, as the combination may overstimulate the nervous system, resulting in jitteriness.

Other medication management concerns to consider include the fact that all citrus juices lessen the effect of amphetamines (Adderall, Dexedrine, Vyvanse), as they acidify urine, resulting in more excretion of the medication. Taking pseudophedrine with stimulants may potentiate the effects of both medications, resulting in the development of a rapid pulse or high blood pressure. Antihistamines may diminish the effectiveness of the medication and cause crankiness or hyperactivity.

Improving Cognitive Functioning through Lifestyle Management

Chronic sleep deprivation is often the most significant issue in self-care for individuals with ADHD, followed by stress management, nutrition, and exercise. Cognitive functioning is adversely affected by lack of sleep, stress, an improper diet, and hormonal changes.

Sleep

Lack of sleep adversely affects executive functioning, energy level, and mood. Disturbed sleep patterns are quite common in this population and include delayed sleep phase syndrome (night owl sleep patterns), difficulty waking, being "in a fog" in the morning, and having racing thoughts that can interfere with sleep onset. It is imperative that we help our clients to develop healthful sleep habits, including ensuring that they maintain a schedule which allows them to obtain optimal sleep for their body (which typically ranges from 7 to 9 hours). We must teach them to avoid overstimulation 1 to 2 hours before bed—television shows, news, internet, video games, engaging books, active play. Many people are not aware that the blue light emitted by computer monitors and television sets actually stops melatonin production in the brain, the naturally occurring hormone that causes sleep onset (Brainard, 2001; Thapan et al., 2001). Encourage clients to accept a 1-week challenge of turning off their "blue light" devices 90 minutes before bedtime and then reporting back at their next session regarding sleep quality during that week. We have found that many clients have the long-standing habit of watching television right up until bedtime, and some even fall asleep to it, yet they typically come back after this challenge reporting that they have never slept better in their lives. This practice has the added benefit of creating time before bed for engaging in more meaningful activities, including quality interactions with one's significant other.

Other sleep strategies that may be helpful to our clients include taking melatonin (an over-the-counter supplement) half an hour before bedtime, drinking warm milk with honey and vanilla or herbal bedtime tea, listening to soothing music, using white noise (a fan, sound machine, or nature sounds), doing meditation, or taking a relaxing bath. We must help clients to make getting adequate sleep a top priority by encouraging them to create daily routines to support it.

Exercise

Exercise is essential for a healthy brain and body. It boosts blood flow to the brain and increases seratonin, dopamine, and norepinephrine availability, creating new receptors. As Ratey and Hagerman pointed out in their book *Spark: The revolutionary new science of exercise and the brain* (2008), "Exercise is the single most powerful tool you have to optimize your brain function." Research (Ratey & Hagerman, 2008, p. 245) has shown that exercise significantly improves academic performance, test scores, cognitive flexibility, and executive functioning. There is a strong relationship between movement and attention (they share overlapping pathways), and the area of the brain that controls movement (the cerebellum) also coordinates the flow of information to the prefrontal lobes.

Ratey and Hagerman (2008) explain that the best exercises are complex and structured, such as martial arts, ballet, figure skating, and gymnastics, because paying attention to learn new movements engages and trains both movement and attention networks. Exercise helps regulate the amygdala and improves the tone of the locus coeruleus, which blunts hair-trigger reactivity, rage reactions, and reduces irritability. A recent study (Kramer, 2006) demonstrated through magnetic resonance imaging scans that walking 3 days a week for 6 months increased the volume of the prefrontal cortex in older adults and improved their working memory, cognitive switching between tasks, and screening out irrelevant stimuli. Exercise helps normalize the activity of the cerebellum, which is overactive in fidgety children, and it significantly helps manage depression and anxiety as well. Optimally, it is recommended that people exercise 6 hours a week (Ratey & Hagerman, 2008); however, 30 to 45 minutes at least 3 to 5 times per week is a good goal. The goal is to achieve fitness—normal body mass index and robust cardiovascular system optimizes the brain.

Exercise compliance is often very difficult for our ADHD clients, even when they understand and experience the benefits. Some may maintain a new regimen for a week or two only to abandon it due to some change in their schedule, mood, or energy level. As therapists, we must help clients problem-solve to improve adherence and reduce obstacles to compliance. Building in structure, accountability, and support is often essential. Suggestions to enhance compliance include using an exercise buddy or personal trainer, attending regularly scheduled exercise classes (prepaid), going to Curves (30-minute circuit training for women), adding movement during the day (using the stairs, parking far away, dancing around house to favorite music), taking brisk walks, playing a fun sport, using a pedometer, and engaging in group activities. Finding a way to make exercise enjoyable and convenient are key factors in compliance.

Nutrition

Nutrition is another important aspect of good brain health and improved cognitive and behavioral functioning that needs to be addressed with clients. Generally, a higher-protein, lower-carbohydrate diet enhances energy and concentration. Protein contains the amino acid building blocks for dopamine and other important neurotransmitters and is essential to a "concentration" diet.

Impaired glucose function, or the inability to properly process carbohydrates (sugars) in the body, is also common in this population, causing them to crave sugars and simple carbohydrates. These foods cause the pancreas to release more insulin in response to higher blood sugar levels, which paradoxically causes an overproduction of insulin, resulting in low blood sugar—causing the affected individual to feel tired, sluggish, and inattentive. Fiber and protein stabilize blood sugar levels, sustaining energy and focus and raising dopamine levels.

Common nutritional issues for individuals with ADHD include problems with digestion, absorption, food intolerances and reactions; nutritional deficiencies in vitamins (B, A, and D), omega-3 fatty acids, and minerals (zinc, magnesium, iron selenium); and the presence of toxic metals (mercury, lead, cadmium, arsenic, aluminum) Compart, & Laake, 2007). These biochemical imbalances have been found to play a significant role in manifesting behavioral disorders (Walsh, 2000) and need to be assessed through referral to an appropriate nutritionist or holistic/alternative medicine physician.

As Phyllis A. Balch tells us in *Prescription for Nutritional Healing*:

When you are dealing with AD/HD, it is best to think of the diet as feeding the brain rather than the stomach. Many researchers believe that if the contributors are removed from the diets, and the right nutritional supplements are added, numerous symptoms often disappear, and medications used to treat can often be eliminated (p. 204).

Several promising research studies support these claims (Bryan et al., 2004; Eilander et al., 2010; Harding, Judah, & Grant, 2003). In one study, children who had sodium benzoate and artificial coloring removed from their diet, and later added back in as a cross-over challenge, were rated as less hyperactive off of these additives than on them, regardless of their ADHD diagnosis (Bateman et al., 2004). In another study (Harding et al., 2003), food supplementation was found to be equally effective as Ritalin in improving attention and self-control.

Enhancing Cognitive Functioning through Meditation, Neurofeedback, and Nature

The benefits of meditation practices have been well accepted in Eastern traditions for centuries; however, more westerners have been studying these practices over the past 30 years and have made them accessible to all of us through their teachings, research, and books. Meditation has been successfully used to treat depression, anxiety disorders, emotional regulation, and pain management, among other conditions. Brain scans and other research studies have demonstrated the brain-related benefits of these practices, including the physiological changes that occur in the brain as a result of meditation: modification of attentional networks, changes in dopamine levels, modulation of electroencephalogram (EEG) patterns, and changes in neuronal activity.

Mindfulness meditation, as taught by Jon Kabat-Zinn, Tara Brach, Jack Kornfield and many others, has the potential to regulate brain functioning and attention by exercising the brain through training in the intentional focus of awareness. A recent study

(Zylowska et al., 2008) of mindfulness meditation for the treatment of adolescents and adults with ADHD found that 78% of participants reported reductions in total ADHD symptoms, even though most of them were already being treated with medication, and that there were significant improvements on several neuropsychological measures. The adults also reported significant reductions in depression and anxiety symptoms. Daniel Siegel writes extensively about the brain-based changes in attention regulation, neural integration, and emotional regulation found with mindfulness meditation in his recent book, *The Mindful Brain* (2007). Transcendental meditation and contemplative prayer are alternative practices which positively impact the same regions of the brain. Although more controlled research is needed regarding the efficacy of meditation for the treatment of ADHD, it is an extremely promising alternative treatment to medication that has been found to be clinically effective for improving focus and symptoms of anxiety, depression, and stress.

A number of brain-training programs have been developed over the past few years that seem reasonably effective in enhancing cognitive functioning and reducing ADHD symptoms. The most widely researched of them is Cogmed (www.cogmed. com), an Internet-based working memory training program that is conducted at home with supervision from parents and telephone coaching from a trained Cogmed professional. Cogmed offers programs for preschoolers through adults.

EEG neurofeedback is another form of brain training that has been researched over the past 20 years, but only more recently as a form of treatment for ADHD (Monastra, Lubar, Rossiter, etc.). It involves training individuals to alter their brain wave patterns (regulating the activation of the frontal lobe and/or sensorimotor cortex) with real-time feedback so as to enhance attention and executive function as well as reduce other targeted symptoms (anxiety, depression, etc.). Although typically administered in a clinician's office, several home-based versions have been developed, although their effectiveness is not as well documented. A recent meta-analysis conducted on all published research (15 studies) about neurofeedback treatment for ADHD concluded that neurofeedback can be considered an evidence-based treatment for ADHD (Arms, de Ridder, Breteler, & Coenen, 2009). Neurofeedback treatment, the results show, has large and clinically significant effects on impulsivity and inattention, with more moderate improvement of hyperactivity.

Exposure to nature has been found to be very beneficial in managing symptoms of ADHD. Research has demonstrated that green outdoor settings appear to reduce ADHD symptoms in children (Kuo & Taylor, 2004) and improve concentration (Taylor & Kuo, 2009). We often recommend that clients take "green breaks" when possible during the work or school day and that they surround themselves with plants when they are in indoor settings. Exercising outdoors gives the double benefit of exposure to nature while gaining the benefits of aerobic exercise.

Stress Reduction and Management

For our purposes in this chapter, what is important for the clinician to recognize is that living with undiagnosed or inadequately managed ADHD leads to high levels of daily stress, anxiety, and often depression. It is critical that clinicians are aware of the circular negative effects of stress on ADHD. Those with ADHD experience multiple daily stressors (criticism by others due to unmet commitments; embarrassment related to social missteps; perpetual rushing due to chronic lateness; missed deadlines; lost personal items; difficulty finding necessary paperwork; parking tickets; overdue bills) that impact brain functioning, leading in a downward spiral to an increase in ADHD symptoms.

A key goal of neurocognitive psychotherapy is to help the individual identify, eliminate, or reduce the significant stressors in his or her life, whenever possible. Due to memory problems and dysfunctional thought patterns, it can be very helpful to identify concretely and list stressors with the client and then engage in problem solving to systematically reduce the client's stress level. Common stressors include: conflicts in primary relationships, school failure, underfunctioning in the workplace or job loss, poor money management, chronic overcommitment, parental stress (especially when children also have ADHD), poor time management, missed deadlines, poor planning ability, difficulty prioritizing, escape and avoidance activities, and health problems.

In helping to identify and reduce stressors, the clinician needs to develop an array of skills to guide clients to improve a broad array of executive functioning, life management, and relationship skills.

Taking Charge of ADHD: Teaching Compensatory Strategies and Life Management Skills

Impaired executive functioning often results in underdeveloped life management skills, typically causing ADHD clients to feel overwhelmed and out of control. We use a comprehensive solution-focused approach that involves working with them to problem-solve areas of difficulty, helping clients develop systems and strategies to manage paper, belongings, and processes of daily life, and suggesting specific environmental changes they can make to enhance their functioning.

It is essential that we address daily management strategies with our ADHD clients, many of whom struggle mightily with the management of time, household tasks, and money. We need to be aware of the various technologies and assistive devices available to help them become better organized—computer software programs, online banking, electronic reminders, and time management systems—and sometimes even teach them how to use these programs in the sessions. No one system fits everyone, which necessitates our collaboratively exploring the best options for each client and often learning from clients about technologies that they have discovered. One very comprehensive organizational tool that we recommend that clients take a look at is Skoach (www.skoach.com), a Web-based time and task management program with a built-in coaching component specifically designed with individuals with ADHD in mind by our clinical director, Kathleen G. Nadeau, based on her book *ADD-Friendly Ways to Organize Your Life* (Kohlberg & Nadeau, 2002). It is often helpful to have clients explore these tools in our offices, if possible, so that we can provide them with some hands-on support and ensure that they will make the time to follow-through. Time and task management, goal setting, planning and organizing, and carrying out projects are all skill sets that many of our clients still struggle with in their home and work environments. As ADHD therapists, we must expand our clinical skill set in order to help clients to develop these executive functions, providing them with structure, strategies, and support.

There are three levels of structure and support that we can work on developing with our clients, depending on their needs and the severity of their impairment. One level is to enable the client to function independently to perform the task; the second level is to use a buddy or spouse for support in the process; and the third level is to incorporate the services of an ADHD coach or professional organizer. The level of support is matched to the challenge of the task and may be reduced over time as clients build habits (Kohlberg & Nadeau, 2002).

Time and task management is often addressed first when we work with clients, as developing these skills will better allow them to organize their lives more efficiently and productively. The first step is to assist clients to find a calendar system that works for them, whether it is Web based, a software program, a hand-held electronic device, or in notebook/paper form. It must be convenient and accessible for them, as they will need to learn to consistently use it for planning, scheduling, and making to-do lists to manage tasks. One important habit to help clients develop is to do a daily planning session. This involves looking at the scheduled activities for the next day and then creating a doable prioritized daily task list for that day, incorporating items from their master task list (a compilation of all tasks), and including not only the immediate time-critical tasks but also the important (but less urgent) items that tend to get put off. Time management skill development also involves the ability to be on time, to remain aware of the passage of time, and to accurately predict the time needed to complete a given task. Task or "to-do" management involves improving prospective memory—the ability to keep in mind and recall at the appropriate time specific acts that need to be done (remembering to go to an appointment, take medication, or bring necessary papers to the office). We need to problem-solve the use of reminders, alarms, and supports to assist them in doing this.

Keeping track of essential personal items is another executive function challenge that our clients typically face and require our assistance to manage. Many of them respond positively to the idea of creating a "launch pad" in their house, a specific location to place all critical items (keys, wallet, cell phone, planner, etc.) that need to go with them when they "launch" into their day. We need to work with clients to develop the habit of consistently using the launch pad, engaging in creative problem-solving with them when they encounter difficulties in consistency.

Therapists should also be active in helping their ADHD clients to develop systems and schedules for managing money, paying bills, and keeping records. Computer software programs, such as Quicken, can be helpful, as can be using automatic bill paying, online banking, and direct deposits when possible. Budgeting and credit card management are related issues that may need to be addressed as well.

Mail and paper management are often difficult for those with ADHD. Many adults with ADHD develop avoidance patterns as detailed paperwork is difficult for them, and unpaid bills increase already high anxiety levels. We work to help clients to develop effective sorting and organizing strategies. For those who are highly anxious or overwhelmed, we may suggest hiring an ADHD coach or organizer to help them create good systems to manage their paperwork and finances. For some, ongoing assistance may be necessary, while others may be able to develop more functional habits and learn to manage their paperwork independently—or be able to delegate it to others (spouse, administrative assistant, etc.).

Other daily tasks requiring good executive functioning that we assist our clients in developing systems for include food preparation and shopping, meal planning, and laundry management. Many of these strategies are described in *ADD-friendly Ways to Organize Your Life* (Kohlberg & Nadeau, 2002), which we often recommend to clients. These skills will need to be practiced over a period of months, often with additional support and reminders, before they develop into consistent habits.

Positive Habit Development

Positive habit development is a crucial aspect of treatment for adolescents and adults with ADHD. Healthy new habits typically are difficult for individuals with ADHD to develop, as some might say: "If it weren't for bad habits, I wouldn't have any habits at all." They need more structure and support to develop new habits, which includes building in accountability, reminders, and repetition. Consistent practice in developing new habits creates connections that increase the likelihood of the continuation of the habit. It is best if the new behavior can be paired with an existing habitual behavior. For example, if people need to remember to take medication before going to bed each night, they can try pairing that new behavior with the already established routine of brushing their teeth. Their medication bottle can even be stored in the bathroom glass they use after cleaning their teeth, serving as a visual reminder to them. The new habit needs to be as easy or convenient as possible, using a location or behavioral sequence that makes sense for clients and is hard to ignore. Certainly reminders will be needed (alarms, Post-it notes), and clients may benefit from practicing the habit, visualizing themselves doing it, and rewarding themselves when they do it for a certain period of time.

When assisting a client to develop a new habit, the therapist's goal is to provide structure and support for at least the first month and then to check in periodically after that to ensure that the behavior is being maintained effectively. Doing this involves having clients establish daily reminders (setting alarms or electronic reminders), building in accountability through e-mail reports to the therapist, keeping a log, or leaving voicemail messages for the therapist reporting on daily behaviors. The therapist and client problem-solve together to resolve any difficulties in establishing the habit at each session. Structure and support may also be needed from friends and family, at least initially.

One specific example illustrating how we put this process into practice involves helping clients develop the habit of remembering to charge their cell phones, a common challenge for our ADHD clients. First, you try to help your clients tie the new behavior to an existing one and make it convenient for them to incorporate into their daily routine. If clients already have an established place to put their cell phone once they get to their home, you can suggest that they place the charger at that location. Seeing it there when they put down their pocketbook, briefcase, bookbag, or empty their pockets at the end of the day will more likely trigger them to plug it into the charger. To make it harder to ignore, they can put something bright and colorful on the charger to draw their attention to it, or be forced to have to move the charger to place their bag down. A colorful Post-it note can be placed there as well, and an alarm can be set on the cell phone with a reminder to "plug me in." You can have clients visualize doing this when they get home that day and reward themselves if they manage to remember to do it.

Until the habit is well established, the issue will need to be addressed at each session, and any problems in executing the plan will need to be creatively problem-solved. Ideally, any potential pitfalls to the plan will be discussed in advance and problem-solved initially, but often adjustments may need to be made along the way to enhance compliance. The additional assistance of an ADHD coach to provide more structure and accountability in developing good habits, maintaining progress toward short-term goals, and managing time is often a very useful (at times essential) adjunctive aspect of effective treatment.

Creating an ADHD-Friendly Environment and Lifestyle

This important aspect of the cognitive rehabilitation or retraining approach involves restructuring the physical and social environment to maximize functioning. Due to the neurological underpinnings of the challenges they face, adolescents and adults with ADHD need more assistance than their same-age counterparts without ADHD to effectively manage their daily lives, at home, at school, and in the workplace. We need to guide them in simplifying their lives as much as possible, both in regard to taking on too much in the way of time commitments (events, committees, activities, long commutes) and in regard to having too much clutter and distraction in their living environments. The use of a professional ADHD organizer, who comes into the homes and/or workplace, can be very effective in assisting clients to create more stream-lined and ADHD-friendly ways to organize their environments.

As ADHD specialists, we need to help clients examine their life choices (size of home, number of children, type of job, commute) and social environments so as to reduce stress and enhance manageability. To do so, we really must know ADHD and what it is like to live with it firsthand. Most of us in the field either have ADHD our-selves or have family members with it, which allows us to more fully comprehend our clients' struggles and needs.

Social support is essential for individuals with ADHD, as they are so often misun-derstood, maligned, and rejected by others, both within their own families and in the community at large. We need to help them to educate those close to them about their ADHD and to make proactive choices about surrounding themselves with people who appreciate their strengths and can tolerate or understand their ADHD-related behav-ioral patterns (tardiness, forgetfulness, disorganization, interrupting).

ADHD Plus: Treating Comorbid Conditions

Many individuals with ADHD develop secondary psychiatric disorders, such as anxi-ety and depression, from the stress of living with undiagnosed and untreated ADHD as well as from the negative impact of difficult early life experiences growing up with ADHD. Countless adults with undiagnosed ADHD have complained to their physi-cians about feeling overwhelmed and stressed, leading to their being treated medically for anxiety or depression, without any regard to the underlying ADHD/LD at the root of the problem. Often, once the ADHD is identified and treated effectively, these secondary conditions remit or at least improve significantly. Treating low self-esteem, along with demoralization, self-blame, and a sense of shame, is often an important aspect of therapy for clients with ADHD/LD, as many develop negative core beliefs and ineffective coping strategies, contributing to their secondary symptoms.

There are also a high degree of primary coexisting conditions in the ADHD popu-lation. Research demonstrates that an adult with ADHD is 6 times more likely than an adult without this diagnosis to have at least one other psychiatric disorder during their lifetime (Kessler et al., 2006), and the risk of comorbid conditions increases with age (Hechtman in Brown, 2009, p. 88). ADHD often coexists with LD, anxiety or mood disorders (depression, Seasonal Affective Disorder, Bipolar Disorder, Obsessive-Compulsive Disorder, Generalized Anxiety Disorder, Social Anxiety Disorder, Posttraumatic Stress Disorder), Eating Disorders, or other childhood disorders (Oppositional Defiant Disorder, Conduct Disorder, Tourette's, Asperger's, Autism).

Substance Use Disorders (SUD) are also common in the ADHD population, especially marijuana, alcohol, and cocaine abuse. Dr. Tim Wilens suggests, based on his review of the research, that both genetic as well as self-medication factors may be operational in the development of SUD in people diagnosed with ADHD (in Brown, 2009). Another important potential comorbidity to consider is Lyme disease, as the symptoms of this tickborne illness can mimic the cognitive impairments found with ADHD/LD.

Due to the high incidence of comorbidity of many disorders, both secondary and primary, therapists are advised to perform a thorough clinical assessment during the initial stages of treatment, bearing in mind that many symptoms of ADHD overlap with other psychiatric disorders. A thorough neuropsychological evaluation at the onset of treatment can be extremely useful in clarifying the diagnosis and any potential coexisting conditions.

ROLE OF THE NEUROCOGNITIVE PSYCHOTHERAPIST: STRUCTURING THE SESSION

Therapists must learn to provide a structured framework for each session during which multiple components of treatment are interwoven. Treatment needs to constantly interweave the practical and psychological, functioning and feelings using a directive, hands-on approach. The therapy session is a microcosm of life. Rather than using a looser free association format, we need to address cognitive challenges directly by providing and modeling the structure required to help clients get back on track and function in a more organized manner. Clients will need to devote a notebook to therapy in which to take notes, record the action plan, list their homework assignments, and keep track of other suggestions, strategies, or references discussed during the session. They may also wish to record the session to assist with memory issues. Clients should be encouraged to bring an agenda to the session so that we can help them to stay on track and focus on the most pressing issues. If the client is unable to provide an agenda, we need to assist them in developing one during the session as a way of modeling executive functioning. We want to support positive habit development and maintenance, establish short-term goals, and problem-solve regarding any potential impediments to following through on the action plan.

It is helpful to encourage clients to take action during the session itself, such as by making an important phone call that they have procrastinated on (e.g., making an appointment to obtain more medication), looking something up online that they need to take action on, or setting up a planner with their schedule for the week. There is a lot of skill-teaching and building involved in the sessions, including how to set up and maintain a planner or organizer (whether in paper format or electronic). Electronic organizing systems have the added benefit of providing built-in reminders and alarms for scheduled tasks or appointments and often can be accessed through cell phones.

We must help clients develop the habit of scheduling daily planning sessions to manage tasks, appointments, and goals.

The session ends with a summary of issues discussed during the session and a review of the specific homework goals and tasks (or action plan) that were assigned and agreed on. Often it is helpful to have clients check in midweek between sessions by e-mail, text message, or voicemail to report progress toward goals. Therapists must check on homework progress in subsequent sessions as the goal is to build in accountability to others and the therapist.

The neurocognitive psychotherapist also serves as an active case manager. Coordination among service providers is essential with this population. We must maintain close communication throughout treatment with the medicating physician, ADHD organizer and/or coach (if on board), and potentially with other professionals, such as the neuropsychological testing provider, neurofeedback provider, financial manager, supervisor, teacher, tutor, or guidance counselor.

So, you might be asking, how *do* we weave all of these treatment elements together in the course of a therapy session? We need to focus initially on the most clinically urgent presenting issue(s) while developing a relationship with the client, plus addressing ADHD behaviors that impact his or her life and relationships. We help clients to develop specific behavioral strategies to reduce ADHD-related problems while concurrently working toward good habit development and self-care strategies. Keeping the session structured and practical, we evaluate medication management as needed, review and assign homework, and make sure to review the session at the end. A focus on emotional and relational issues is critical as well, as ADHD tends to impact self-esteem, emotional control, and many aspects of relationships. Adjunctive referrals are made as needed (support group, couples counseling, ADHD coach, organizer, psychiatrist, etc.). Neurocognitive psychotherapy must be comprehensive and coordinated, addressing all aspects of life affected by ADHD, including secondary psychological issues and coexisting conditions.

TREATING ADHD ACROSS THE LIFE SPAN
Transition to Young Adulthood and College

As adolescents mature and move toward independence, they experience decreasing support and structure from their environment, coupled with increasing demands. Parents and teachers are no longer as involved in maintaining daily routines and providing structure or oversight. Due to the typical ADHD pattern of delayed maturity, young adults with ADHD are often not well equipped to manage themselves effectively at school, in the workplace, or at home, where the demands for judgment, self-control, organization, and planning are ever increasing. Managing money, job applications and duties, leases and insurance, routine activities of daily living, and self-care are often very challenging to handle on their own. Adolescents with ADHD will need help in managing this transition and in building appropriate supports, structure, and routines into their lives. Unlike in traditional psychotherapy, helping adolescents sometimes involves working with their parents in therapy as well, as they may help provide some of the needed scaffolding from which young adults can launch themselves. Some parents may need help in setting realistic and appropriate expectations for their "adult" child with ADHD/LD and guidance in establishing an optimal level of support for them.

Some may need to delay college and work for a while first or choose more hands-on learning experiences and job opportunities. This is an important time of life in which to intervene in guiding young adults with ADHD to make informed, ADHD-friendly life choices for their future, (type of partner, parenting decisions, career path, money decisions, etc.). The strain of young adulthood with ADHD often leads to patterns of self-medication to reduce anxiety and stress. Therapists can help young adults identify and, it is hoped, minimize tendencies towards self-medication with alcohol, marijuana, nicotine, excessive caffeine or carbohydrates, and other substances before very destructive addictions and dependencies develop. Research shows that appropriate medication for ADHD may reduce the likelihood of substance abuse. Other addictive patterns that the ADHD clinician may need to address in working with young adults involve dangerous or problematic patterns of self-stimulation and addictive behaviors, such as excessive risk taking, out-of-control spending, Internet pornography, binge eating, or addictive gaming (computer games, Sudoku, crosswords, etc.).

For those who decide to go on to higher education, the transition to college can be a significant challenge for many adolescents with ADHD. One young man put it this way about his own experiences:

> It [life in college] required providing structure for myself. In high school there was a set schedule of classes and homework was done in the evenings. However in college there is no set schedule and no clear time to do homework. It also meant providing initiative to get started on things, and prioritizing what needed to be done when. I also needed to learn to manage my life. My mom used to do all those things for me.

College places high demands on executive functions, both inside and outside of the classroom, and few students with ADHD will transition smoothly without careful planning and preparation. To begin with, many students will need assistance with college selection, and considering factors such as size, location, proximity to home, availability of disability support services, and whether to request formal accommodations or not.

Accommodations can include preferential scheduling (priority registration), notetaking services, and test-taking accommodations (extra time on tests, separate location, oral administration, etc.). Psychoeducational testing may need to be updated to qualify for formal accommodations, since most colleges require testing to be done within 3 years of college entry. It is very important that students understand the nature of their particular strengths and weaknesses so that they can advocate for themselves with their professors, proactively introducing themselves early in the semester as students with a disability. It is best to have students (and their parents) meet with someone in the office of disability services at their college or university before classes even begin, so as to familiarize them with the available services (including use of the writing center, math assistance, tutoring, coaching, etc), help them with course selection, and arrange for accommodations.

When selecting classes, students need to take into account the time of the class (early morning versus midday or evening), its duration (several shorter class periods per week versus fewer longer ones), the teaching style of the professor (rigid versus flexible, engaging versus monotonous, etc.) and the manner in which the material will be graded (papers versus multiple-choice exams versus take-home exams versus projects). The clinician can help guide college students to select supportive and engaging professors, whenever possible, to carefully balance courses that require several papers with others that do not, and to seek support before crisis sets in late in the semester. Most students with ADHD/LD are better able to succeed by taking a reduced course load and strategically taking especially demanding courses individually, during the summer term, with tutoring support. Study skills and time management classes are frequently offered on campus, and students should be encouraged to take advantage of them, as well as the use of tutors, coaches, and ADHD support groups. Medication needs to be managed carefully, and students need to understand the risks involved in sharing their medication with others or misusing it to stay up late to study.

Many students, however, do not approach college welcoming the available support but rather prefer to try to make it on their own, often without even the benefit of medication. They often fall into the trap of socializing too much, staying up too late, and not getting up to attend classes, causing them to fall further and further behind academically.

Gifted students with ADHD/LD may face their own special challenges in college because they have never learned how to study. They may have gotten through high school with little effort, relying only on their native intelligence. College, however, often demands more of them, and they may not have the skills to cope. This can lead to the crash-and-burn syndrome, in which students let things slide until they are placed on academic probation or fail and must return home.

In addition to the academic challenges inherent in the transition to college, students must now take responsibility for themselves, without much parental supervision or oversight. They must learn to balance the academic demands with daily life management tasks such as laundry, shopping for and preparing meals if they live in an apartment, managing money and paying bills (cell phone, books, fees, sometimes rent and food or utilities), and getting proper sleep and exercise. Therapy with this population needs to focus on learning from one's mistakes, working through the negative beliefs that have developed, assisting with understanding strengths and weaknesses, problem solving and skill development (time management, organization, study skills), and self-management (sleep, exercise, nutrition, daily routines).

Many students who have fallen into a failure cycle in college benefit from a break from school to develop better daily life management skills before they return to focus on academics. Alternatively, other students benefit from living at home while attending college, eliminating the simultaneous demands for academics and life management skills.

Workplace and Career Issues

In working with the ADHD population, it is critical that we develop the skills needed to address a range of workplace and career-related issues. Just as child ADHD specialists need to be intimately familiar with the challenges children with ADHD face at school, adult ADHD specialists need to be well versed in the workplace challenges faced by the adult population. We must become familiar with a variety of helpful accommodations that we can encourage our clients to request, whether informally or as part of a more formal disability disclosure process. Some clients will be placed on performance improvement plans (PIPs) due to their ADHD issues in the workplace and will need our help in developing appropriate strategies, habits, and supports, including environmental changes, to optimize their functioning in the workplace. We need to be able to advise our clients about ADHD-friendly career and workplace choices and to help them to find a better match for their pattern of strengths and weaknesses. Dr. Nadeau's book entitled *ADD in the Workplace* (1997) is a very helpful guide for clients and therapists alike, as it provides useful information pertaining to career guidance, disclosure issues, workplace accommodations, and enhancing workplace functioning.

Family and Parenting Issues

Almost everyone finds parenting to be challenging; however, in the families that we treat, parenting is often exponentially more difficult. Typically several members of the family (or even all the members) have ADHD/LD. When both parents and children have ADHD, the result can be a very chaotic household. Many parents with ADHD do not plan well and may have more children than they can effectively handle. They have the tendency to take on too many activities and commitments, either due to a difficulty in saying no or to stimulation seeking. The resulting overcommitment can intensify difficulties with time management, disorganization, and forgetfulness, and leaves little down time to recuperate from life's daily stressors.

We need to help parents to develop daily routines to manage the household and to support a predictable and organized ADHD-friendly environment for themselves and their children. Often parents will need to be treated for their own ADHD before they can provide consistent structure for their family, even when the child or adolescent is the identified client. Educating parents about managing their child's ADHD is important, as the child's developmental delays can be frustrating for them. The clinician's role is to help parents adjust their expectations appropriately and to help them learn suitable disciplinary or behavioral management approaches.

Relationship Issues

The neurological underpinnings of the disorder often contribute to the development of poor social and communication skills and can lead to a lifetime of relationship difficulties. Most ADHD/LD individuals experience some relational challenges with partners, children, friends, colleagues, and employers. Their ADHD-related behaviors may annoy, hurt, or frustrate others. Many individuals with ADHD have suffered from social isolation or rejection due to having had their ADHD behaviors misattributed to selfishness, lack of caring, thoughtlessness, laziness, stupidity, or craziness. For example, when an individual with ADHD is late, others tend to attribute this to a lack of caring or selfish disregard rather than understanding that time management is a chronic problem for many people with ADHD. Another issue for many is that low self-esteem can lead to poor partner selection. ADHD clinicians need to work with adults to enhance good communication skills and to strengthen relationships.

Imago Relationship Therapy (IRT), developed by Harville Hendrix, is a brain-based approach that is highly compatible with ADHD. It facilitates healthy communication by slowing down the process, providing structure, and containing reactivity, so that the participants can fully hear one another. It encourages the development of stronger listening skills and better self-control to enhance understanding and problem solving. This approach can be used with parent-child dyads as well as in other settings. However, there are no controlled outcome studies using Imago Relationship Therapy with ADHD clients.

Often adults with ADHD are so overwhelmed by daily demands that they may appear insensitive and uncaring to their partners. It can be very helpful to coach ADHD clients to perform caring/loving behaviors for their partners, such as calling them at lunchtime, massaging their feet, or bringing them coffee. Going on regular dates together and finding ways to laugh and have fun together are also very important as a counterbalance to the inevitable higher stress level that exists in ADHD families. Giving each other surprises, such as flowers, goodies, love notes, or tickets to a favorite event, also enhances relationships. Couples and parents are encouraged to express appreciation daily, acknowledging the efforts of loved ones and thanking their spouse or children for performing certain task/behaviors, and complementing one another. Finally, it is important for individuals with ADHD to take responsibility for managing their ADHD by taking prescribed medications faithfully, exercising regularly, and maintaining an ADHD-friendly lifestyle, in order to reduce the impact of the disorder on their loved ones when possible. We need to help them to become aware of how their ADHD behaviors may impact others and to develop effective strategies to manage them, both at home and in the workplace. Spouses of individuals with ADHD must also educate themselves about the disorder to avoid misinterpreting their partner's behavior or contributing to the creation of an ADHD-unfriendly environment for them. Keeping these strategies in mind, therapists can play an important role in assisting individuals with ADHD in enhancing their relationships and building new communication skills for life.

Women with ADHD

Women often experience a different trajectory across their life span regarding the impact, age of onset, and syptomology of their ADHD in contrast to their male counterparts, due to both the hormonal influences on the brain and differing societal expectations and demands. Many women with ADHD are not diagnosed until later in life, and many have been misdiagnosed (depression, bipolar, anxiety) based on associated or secondary features that may resemble mood or anxiety disorders. Often girls miss being diagnosed earlier in life due to differences in their symptom profile (less disruptive), multiple protective factors (high IQ, good social skills, supportive environment), their efforts to hide their struggles or compensate for them, and their desire to please teachers and parents (Nadeau & Quinn, 2002; Solden, 1995).

Women with ADHD tend to experience feelings of shame and inadequacy as they struggle to fulfill the gender role expectations of mothers, wives, and homemakers, often exhausting themselves trying to meet these daily demands on their executive functioning. We must help them to create ADHD-friendly routines, strategies, and supports to better manage themselves, their children, and their households, and help to reduce their shame through educating them and their significant others about ADHD. Other gender-specific issues that women with ADHD face include the impact of premenstrual syndrome (PMS), perimenopause, and menopause on their cognitive functioning. At times PMS may need to be treated as a comorbid disorder. Some women may benefit from hormone treatments to help regulate emotional and cognitive symptoms.

SUMMARY

Neurocognitive psychotherapy is a comprehensive and integrative form of treatment for adolescents and adults with ADHD and LD developed by Kathleen G. Nadeau that expands on the principles of cognitive retraining and cognitive behavioral therapy and integrates evidenced-based treatments from a number of different fields. This is a brain-based approach in which therapists must be directive, practical, hands-on, and structured. Emphasis is placed on optimizing brain functioning, teaching skills and compensatory strategies, and structuring the environment to support a more ADHD-friendly lifestyle. It is a solution-focused process involving direct problem solving and skill building to enhance executive functioning. The neurocognitive approach requires ADHD specialists to stretch their professional skills in many directions, expanding their knowledge base and developing new specialized skill sets in order to serve this population more effectively.

REFERENCES

Arns, M., de Ridder, S., Breteler, M., & Coenen, A. (2009). Efficacy of neurofeedback treatment in ADHD: The effects on inattention, impulsivity, and hyperactivity: A meta-analysis. *EEG and Clinical Neuroscience, 40*(3), 180–189.

Balch, P. (2006). *Prescription for nutritional healing* (3rd ed.). New York, NY: Penguin Group, Inc.

Barkley, R. (2006). *Attention-Deficit Hyperactivity Disorder: A handbook for diagnosis and treatment* (3rd ed.). New York, NY: Guilford Press.

Barkley, R., Murphy, K. R., & Fischer, M. (2008). *ADHD in adults: What the science says.* New York, NY: Guilford Press.

Bateman, B., Warner, J., Hutchinson, E., Dean, T., Rowlandson, P., Gant, C., . . . Stevenson J. (2004.) The effects of a double blind, placebo controlled, artificial food colourings and benzoate preservative challenge on hyperactivity in a general population sample of preschool children. *Archives of Disease in Childhood, 89,* 506–511.

Biederman, J. (2005). Attention-Deficit/Hyperactivity Disorder: A selective overview. *Biological Psychiatry 57,* 1215–1220.

Brainard, G. (2001). Action spectrum for melatonin regulation in humans: Evidence for a novel circadian photoreceptor. *Journal of Neuroscience, 21*(16): 6405–6412.

Branham, J. et al. (2009). Evaluation of group CBT of adults with ADHD. *Journal of Attention Disorders, 12*(5), 434–441.

Brown, T. E. (Ed.). (2009). *ADHD comorbidities: Handbook for ADHD complications in children and adults.* Washington, DC: American Psychiatric Press.

Bryan, J., Osendarp, S., Hughes, D., Calvares, E., Baghurst, K. & Willem van Klinken, J. (2004). Nutrients for cognitive development in school-aged children. *Nutrition Reviews, 62*(8), 295–306.

Compart, P., & Laake, D. (2006). *The kid-friendly ADHD and autism cookbook: The ultimate guide to the gluten-free, casein-free diet.* Gloucester, MA: Fair Winds Press.

Cozolino, L. (2002). *The neuroscience of psychotherapy.* New York, NY: Norton.

Eilander, A., Gera, T., Sachdev, H., Transler, C., van der Knaap, H., Kok, F., & Osendarp, S. (2010). Multiple micronutrient supplementation for improving cognitive performance in children: Systematic review of randomized controlled trials. *American Journal of Clinical Nutrition, 91*(1):115–130.

Goldstein, S., and Ellison, A. T. (1992). *Clinician's guide to adult ADHD: Assessment and intervention.* San Diego, CA: Academic Press.

Hallowell, E., & Ratey, J. (1994). *Driven to distraction: Recognizing and coping with Attention Deficit Disorder from childhood through adulthood.* New York, N.Y.: Pantheon Books.

Harding, K., Judah, R., & Grant, C. (2003). Outcome-based comparison of Ritalin versus food-supplement treated children with AD/HD. *Alternative Medicine Reviews* 2003(8): 319–330.

John Carroll University. (2007, November 14). Blue-blocking glasses to improve sleep and ADHD symptoms developed. *Science Daily.* www.sciencedaily.com/releases/2007/11/071112143308.htm

Katz, D. I., Ashley, M. J., O'Shanick, G., J., & Connors, S. H. *Cognitive rehabilitation: The evidence, funding and case for advocacy in brain injury.* McLean, VA: Brain Injury Association of America, 2006.

Kessler, R. et al. (2006). The prevalence and correlates of adult ADHD in the United States: Results from the National Comorbidity Survey replication. *American Journal of Psychiatry, 163: 716–723.*

Kolberg, J., & Nadeau, K. (2002) *ADHD-friendly ways to organize your life.* New York, NY: Brunner/Routledge.

Kramer, A. et al. (2006). Aerobic exercise training increases brain volume in aging humans. *Journal of Gerontology Series A. 61* (11): 1166–1170.

Kuo, F., & Taylor, A. (2004). A potential natural treatment for Attention Deficit/Hyperactivity Disorder: Evidence from a national study. *American Journal of Public Health, 94*(9), 1580–1586.

Maarit Virta Rinnekoti Research Centre, Finland, Vedenpää, A., Grönroos, N., Chydenius, E., Partinen, M., Vataja, R., . . . Iivanainen. M. (2008). Adults with ADHD benefit from cognitive-behaviorally oriented group rehabilitation. *Journal of Attention Disorders,12*(3), 218–226.

Monastra, V. (2004). EEG and neurofeedback findings in ADHD: An empirical response. *The ADHD Report, 12*(1), 5–8.

Monastra, V., Lynn, S., Linden, Ms, Lubar, J. Gruzelier, J., & LaVaque, T. (2005). Electroencephalographic biofeedback in the treatment of attention-deficit/hyperactivity disorder. *Applied Psychophysiology and Biofeedback, 30* (2): 95–114.

Nadeau, K., & Quinn, P. (Eds.). (2002). *Understanding women with AD/HD.* Silver Spring, MD: Advantage Books.

Nadeau, K. G. (1997). *ADHD in the workplace.* New York, NY: Brunner/Mazel.

Nadeau, K. G. (Ed.). (1995). *A comprehensive guide to attention deficit disorder in adults: Research, diagnosis and treatment.* New York, NY: Guilford Press.

Ramsay, R., & Rostain, A. (2008). *Cognitive-behavioral therapy for adult ADHD: An integrative psychosocial and medical approach.* New York, NY: Routledge Taylor and Francis Group.

Ratey, J., & Hagerman, E. (2008). *Spark: The revolutionary new science of exercise and the brain.* New York, NY: Little, Brown.

Rostain, A., & Ramsay, R. (2006). A combined treatment approach for adults with ADHD—Results of an open study of 43 patients. *Journal of Attention Disorders, 10,* 150–159.

Safren, S., Otto, M., Sprich, S., Winett, C., Wilens, T., & Biederman, J. (2005). CBT for ADHD in medication-treated adults with continued symptoms. *Behavior, Research and Therapy, 43*(7), 831–842.

Safren, S., Sprich, Perlman, C., & Otto, M. (2005). *Mastering your adult ADHD: A cognitive-behavioral treatment program.* New York, NY: Oxford University Press.

Siegel, D. (1999). *The Developing Mind: How relationships and the brain interact to shape who we are.* New York, NY: The Guilford Press.

Siegel, D. (2007). *The mindful brain: How relationships and the brain interact to shape who we are.* New York, NY: Norton.

Shaywitz, S. E., & Shaywitz, B.A. (2008). Paying attention to reading: The neurobiology of reading and dyslexia, *Development and Psychopathology, 20,* 1329–1349.

Solden, S. (1995). *Women with attention deficit disorder: Embrace your differences and transform your life.* Nevada City, CA: Underwood Books.

Thapan, K. et al. (2001). An action spectrum for melatonin suppression: Evidence for a novel non-rod, non-cone photoreceptor system in humans. *Journal of Physiology, 535,* 1, 261–267.

Taylor, A., & Kuo, F. (2009). Children with attention deficits concentrate better after walk in the park. *Journal of Attention Disorder, 12*(5), 402–409.

Walsh, W. (2000). *Food allergies: The complete guide to understanding and relieving your food allergies.* New York, NY: Wiley.

Weiss, G., & Hechtman, L. (1993). *Hyperactive children grown up: ADHD in children, adolescents, and adults* (2nd ed.). New York, N.Y.: Guilford Press.

Zylowska, L., Ackerman, D., Yang, M., Futrell, J., Horton, N., Hale, T., Pataki, C., & Smalley, S. (2008). Mindfulness meditation training in adults and adolescents with ADHD. *Journal of Attention Disorders, 11,* 737–746.

15

Strategic Coaching for LD and ADHD

NANCY RATEY
JODI SLEEPER-TRIPLETT

INTRODUCTION

Research and clinical experience suggest that Learning Disabilities (LD) and Attention-Deficit/Hyperactivity Disorder (ADHD) lead to significant educational, occupational, and family dysfunction and contribute to a wide range of social, economic, and health-related problems.

As researchers and clinicians better understand the causes and effects of LD and ADHD, it has become clear that traditional methods of treatment—medication, behavioral or psychological therapies, and education, or workplace accommodations alone—are not effective for all individuals. Different interventions and services are needed.

Anecdotally, we know that coaching aims to increase an individual's ability with ADHD to improve and bridge gaps in executive functions, self-manage, maintain motivation, and sustain attention long enough to reach desired goals on a consistent basis.

However, for ADHD coaching to be taken seriously in the medical community, it must be validated by research. Recently, several preliminary studies have shown promising results. These studies have demonstrated that coaching has a positive effect on client's executive functions. It is clear more research needs to be done. Other, more in-depth studies are currently in place to expand on some of these studies and aim to demonstrate the same results.

WHAT IS COACHING?

Coaching is based on a wellness model that assumes the client is whole and does not have serious issues that need to be "fixed." Clients have an idea of what their struggles are and are ready to devote time and effort to work on them. Clients hold themselves accountable to the coach for each step of the process until desired goals are reached. Although this new, evolving profession overlaps with other self-improvement services—counseling, mentoring, therapy, and tutoring—coaching focuses on motivating a client to take action and measures the outcomes of those actions. Because coaching is client centered and client driven, it is the client's job to create a productive alliance with the coach to forward his or her own agenda.

Coaches facilitate this by establishing a nonjudgmental relationship and environment for clients to reflect on and question their behaviors. Through the coach's gentle but insightful questioning, clients discover which strategies will help them cope successfully with life's demands and challenges. When these strategies are formulated, the coach and client work together to figure out effective ways to hold the client accountable to the plan of action. In short, the coach fosters a climate of support and encouragement so that clients can discover for themselves how to replace negative, defeating behaviors with positive patterns of success.

Coaching is holistic. When working with a coach, clients develop a comprehensive plan to compensate for their symptoms of LD and ADHD. Doing this involves working on many facets of the individual's life. It means understanding that lifestyle choices—what one eats, how much sleep one gets, how strong one's social network is, whether one has a spiritual life, one's satisfaction with a job—affect how well, or not, a client functions.

Coaching is a process of exploration that happens over time. Clients must be ready for coaching before they commit to the process. How will clients know if they are ready to work with a coach? When they admit that they have a problem, agree to spend the time necessary to create strategies to improve their behavior, and work hard to stick with those strategies. If clients with LD and ADHD are not ready to commit to the process, then they will not benefit from coaching.

BENEFITS OF COACHING

The coaching partnership provides support, encouragement, and accountability, as clients learn to recognize and address their problems and challenges. The goal is to prepare clients to be independent and to empower them to manage challenges, small and large. Coaching builds hope by educating clients about how LD and/or ADHD affect their daily lives. A coach works with them to develop systems and strategies they can use to dramatically improve their lives.

Coaching enables clients to:

- Consider consequences of actions.
- Set goals and priorities and follow through on them.
- Break things down into small tasks and sequencing.
- Create and stick to timelines.

- Improve organizational skills.
- Build self-esteem and self-acceptance.
- Increase self-awareness and the ability to self-regulate.
- Improve interpersonal skills .
- Identify positive characteristics in themselves and recognize their strengths.
- Increase understanding of LD and ADHD.
- Identify and create customized systems based on their strengths.
- Improve executive functioning and critical thinking skills.
- Develop accountability and promote action.
- Improve self-advocacy skills.

Coaches motivate clients to compensate for their brain differences by working with them to develop strategies for meeting their goals and providing an objective perspective on their internal inconsistencies. By partnering with a coach, clients discover ways to succeed. For example, college students with LD and ADHD may or may not be aware of the need to design their environment in order to be productive and have proper reminders for success.

Coaching helps these students learn techniques for maintaining focus, staying on task, improving time management and organizational skills, and advocating for necessary accommodations at college.

Distinguishing Coaching from Other Services

Due to the performance-based nature of LD and ADHD, people with these conditions often seek the services of a variety of professionals. Help is generally sought in several areas.

Skill Building

Clients approach skill building to improve academic or language skills by working with a tutor, educational therapist, speech pathologist, or a social-skills specialist.

Psychological Services

Clients utilize psychological services to understand and change behaviors and emotion-based conduct. Working with a counselor, psychotherapist, or cognitive behavioral therapist enables clients to learn how to cope with stress and find new ways to identify, and move beyond, destructive emotional blocks.

Medical/Neurological Professionals

Many people with ADHD take medication to manage the biological/medical symptoms, or to treat associated disorders like depression, Obsessive-Compulsive Disorder, or anxiety-based disorders.

Organizational Services

People with ADHD who have executive dysfunction often take time management classes to learn organizational skills or hire a professional organizer to help with clutter at home or in the workplace.

Tutoring

Tutors work on the short-term focus of reteaching content and on academic-specific skill building. A tutor might "coach" a student by acting as a cheerleader or by helping him or her develop time management strategies to improve academic performance: setting up an organized study space, marking due dates on a calendar, or other practical aids for achieving goals at school.

COACHING VERSUS THERAPY

Coaches and therapists share some similarities. Both work to help clients better understand, accept, and work constructively with their LD and ADHD symptoms. Both work to help clients improve their quality of life and build their self-esteem. Both are supportive and encouraging, and both have the client's interest as their top priority. Each professional, however, uses different methods and tools to help clients achieve progress in these areas, and each brings different training and perspectives to treatment.

Therapy differs from coaching in terms of logistics. Therapy is done in "neutral territory," in a setting without emotional triggers for clients. A coach, however, may go "on site," working with clients in their offices or homes. Therapy typically takes place in face-to-face sessions that run from 45 to 60 minutes. Sessions are weekly or less frequent. Coaching has no set model. Sessions can be face-to-face, over the phone, or via e-mail. Depending on which approach works best for clients, the sessions can last 30 minutes or less once a week by telephone or they can be weekly, hour-long, one-on-one meetings. This logistical flexibility allows the coach and client to focus on strategies and client accountability.

Therapy also has different goals. Therapists sometimes help clients understand the impact of their behaviors and emotions on their daily life. Cognitive behavioral therapists, for instance, develop strategies to turn that understanding into a structured plan of action. Typically, though, therapy is less structured than coaching. A coach pushes clients to follow through on a structured plan of action, whether that plan is developed by the therapist or by the coach.

Coaching is highly structured, providing a framework of routines that is consistent and predictable. While therapy may involve goal setting, coaching centers on it as well as on implementing the actions, strategies, and practical solutions for achieving those goals. Coaches do not address medical issues. A coach cannot diagnose ADHD or write prescriptions, but a coach can help clients create systems that monitor and evaluate the effects of medications and to be able to report this information to their doctor.

Coaching and LD

Although there are tutors who are trained to work with the LD population, ADHD coaches are specialized in working primarily with people with ADHD. However, in light of the high percentage of overlap between LD and ADHD in many individuals, coaches must be knowledgeable about LD and its impact on various areas of the client's life. The coach, for example, explores with clients how their LD affects their learning and processing ability and considers such questions as: How does the LD impact the ability of my client to learn effectively (in the coaching relationship and beyond)?

Although the desired outcomes in coaching either population is the same—helping clients to develop methods to bridge gaps in performance—the coaching techniques may vary. Coaching people with LD would involve engaging clients in a more tactical and strategic process about developing specific compensatory strategies tailored specifically to their particular processing disability. For example, phone coaching might not work as well for the clients.

Coaching and LD/ADHD

Clients with LD/ADHD often present a combination of challenges. A coach must have working knowledge of LD and ADHD and the varying symptoms, *and* be familiar with the symptoms of comorbid conditions, such as Obsessive-Compulsive Disorder, addictions, anxiety, or depression. Many clients also have emotional challenges—damaged self-esteem due to years of lack of success, frustration, and defeat. A coach needs to identify when such problems hinder clients in attaining goals. Coaches address all of these issues based on how these issues impact clients' level of performance in the coaching process. The focus is on recognizing clients' problems other than ADHD and referring clients to and/or collaborating with appropriate professionals. The ADHD coach plays a more specialized role than a therapist—he or she works on moving clients forward, despite their issues, and does not address the whys of client behavior.

In sum, a coach helps individuals with LD and ADHD discover their current needs by asking clarifying questions. A coach directs clients to the appropriate professional—medical doctor, specialized tutor, therapist, or counselor who can help with other challenges—while continuing to work with clients on making concrete, tangible steps forward.

COACHING PROCESS

The coach is uniquely positioned to observe clients' everyday problems. The coach often points out areas where clients are blocked or stuck. Coaches do not concern themselves, however, with why these problems occur. Instead, they ask questions that will elicit strategies and action from client: "What can you do about it?" "How can you motivate yourself to take action toward this goal?" "When must this action be completed?" Coaches focus on what, how, and when—never why.

Coaches provide encouragement, recommendations, feedback, and practical techniques, such as reminders, questions, and calendar monitoring. They develop strategies to address time management, to eliminate clutter in the home or office, and to become more effective in one's personal and professional life. ADHD coaching is not therapy.

Regular meetings and check-ins are an essential part of the coaching process. These sessions can be done in person, by telephone, fax, or e-mail, whichever clients prefer. However, before coaching begins, client and coach should have an in-depth, 1- to 2-hour initial meeting, called the initial intake, to develop step-by-step plans for achieving goals.

Initial Intake

The purpose of the initial intake is threefold.

1. It enables the coach to assess a client's readiness to be coached.
2. It addresses administrative issues associated with the partnership.
3. It starts the process of defining the coaching partnership.

The initial intake is best done in person. If the client is not within reasonable driving distance of the coach's office, then the initial intake is done over the phone. Because there is so much ground to cover in this session, it may be divided into two shorter, 1-hour sessions. There are no set rules for how these sessions are structured, as long as the important issues are explored and covered.

Designing the Partnership

The bedrock of the coaching partnership is making sure clients understand what coaching is, how it is done, and its potential benefits. Doing this involves a discussion of general administrative issues, along with an agreement about the role of the coach in their life. Ideally, coaches define these parameters in a "Coaching Service Agreement," which should be reviewed in the beginning of the initial interview. These points should be covered in a Coaching Service Agreement:

- Issues that coaching will and will not cover
- Maintaining client confidentiality
- Need for client honesty and openness
- Need for coach and client to work together
- Keeping open lines of communication between client and coach
- Establishing the rate for the coach's services and the billing procedures
- Establishing the policy for missed appointments

- Making it clear, in writing, that coaching holds no guarantees, that the client is responsible for his or her own outcomes, and that the client takes responsibility for his or her actions or lack of action

Assessing Client Readiness and Identifying Goals

The coach should understand the client's background and history. Taking a history uncovers patterns of behavior and enables the coach to evaluate the client's current level of functioning as well as awareness of his or her issues. The next questions typically are used to get information from which to construct a plan:

Educational, Vocational, Avocational
- What do you do well—and not well?
- What challenges do you experience in life and at the job?
- What do you enjoy doing?
- Do you observe patterns in your life?

Medical History
- What is your diagnosis, date of diagnosis, symptoms of disability?
- What medications are you taking?
- What other professionals are you seeing?
- Have you discussed working with a coach with them?

Health and Social Well-being
- What supports are in place in your life?
- What are your sleep patterns? Eating habits? Do you exercise?
- What other habits, routines, or rituals do you keep?
- What stressors are present in your life?

MODEL FOR COACHING

Successful coaching depends on the client's commitment to the process. Coaching depends on partnership: The coach guides the process but does not drive it; provides structure by imposing it; and asks questions without judgment. The three core components of ADHD coaching are

Partnership: Client and coach co-engineer the relationship to benefit the client.

Structure: Client and coach co-create strength-based strategies to provide internal and external structure in the client's life.

Process: The coach guides the client in self-exploration and education about himself and his condition.

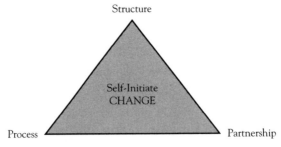

Figure 15.1 How Does Coaching Work?
Source: Nancy E. Ratey, Ed.M., MCC

Coaching is a dynamic methodology that nurtures clients' ability to initiate change on their own. Only when these three core components mentioned above are present, and working optimally, can coaching achieve its desired ends (See Figure 15.1).

Partnership: A Team Effort

The client is responsible for developing the coaching *partnership* to meet specific needs. The parameters of the relationship are co-created, or co-engineered, by coach *and* client. It is an ongoing, collaborative process that moves clients forward as they learn strategies to become more productive in their daily lives. This process requires clients to identify and use their own strengths to develop a user-friendly environment, giving them a safe place to change their ADHD behaviors. Through this method of self-help, clients learn to build on essential life skills: acquiring a deeper understanding of their own disability; isolating and altering old patterns; articulating, identifying, and clarifying needs; and learning how to motivate themselves.

Clients often call a coach on a loved one's recommendation. For coaching to work, however, the motivation for change must come from the clients. Clients also need to understand that coaching is a process that works over time. It involves a financial commitment. Clients should know what coaching will offer them (structure, support, and encouragement) and honestly assess their commitment to making changes.

Based on the initial contact, coach and client should decide if they want to work together. Coaches should evaluate whether they can help the specific client and whether they can work with him or her. If coaches decide they cannot, they should refer the client to another coach, who might be a better match. If the client is working with, or was referred by, a therapist, the coach may confer with the therapist beforehand (with the client's prior written consent) to decide if the therapist and coach are in agreement with the client's goals.

Clients should be able to tell the coach where they need help, so that the coach can tailor services and strategies to encourage and motivate them. The coach requires clients to "program the coach," or define ways to hold clients accountable for achieving goals. Doing this helps clients take responsibility for their own actions. Over time, clients will learn what motivates them and what does not and to tweak the process with the coach, if needed. This is important, since most clients hire an ADHD coach because they are caught up in a "start-stop" syndrome—they start a project but lose motivation or are diverted from the goal. As a result, they never finish what they started.

Structure: Leveraging the Strengths of the Client

The coach must provide *structure*. Identifying and setting up structures will help clients succeed. Coaches develop structure through consistency (scheduled coaching sessions), building predictability into coaching sessions, and enabling clients to recognize the need for structure in their daily lives. Regularly scheduled check-ins help the coach hold clients accountable for their actions *and* measure their progress in small, achievable increments. A history of small successes gives clients the confidence to take charge of their lives. In addition, clients can draw on these successes later in the process to motivate themselves to keep moving forward. Eventually, clients will internalize the structure, so that they can change habits and achieve goals.

Most people with ADHD have a love-hate relationship with structure. To them, schedules and lists force them to do tasks they do not like or that do not suit them. A successful coach works with clients to build structures that *do* suit them, structures that work with their strengths and preferences, not against them. By working with clients' strengths, scheduling less desirable tasks at optimal times, and teaching clients to reward themselves with pleasurable activities after completing difficult tasks, the structures agreed to by the coach and client become guideposts to achievement.

Similar to blinders that prevent a racehorse from being distracted or spooked by the activity around it, structures are blinders to direct clients' energy and prevent symptoms of ADHD from sending them off course. For instance, some clients with ADHD find it hard to gauge time, which hinders them from making and keeping schedules or managing projects. External structures provide ways that help make time more "tangible." Eventually, clients acquire their own built-in sense of how to measure time accurately. They can use that skill to achieve other goals.

Once coach and client understand a client's learning style, the coach should identify organizational tools that match the client's strengths. This compatibility will increase the likelihood that a client will use the tools. Examples of commonly used organizational tools include calendar systems, sticky notes, color-coded files, and electronic and voice organizers. These are instrumental in reducing clutter and chaos and allow clients to prioritize and sustain attention on achieving goals. Another part of structure is helping clients integrate these tools into their lives.

Process: Using Guided Self-Exploration

The power of coaching lies in the *process* itself. The coach guides clients through a process of self-exploration, helping them develop and increase self-awareness. The coach must listen closely to their clients while remaining emotionally detached. A coach should ask questions in a nonjudgmental, nonthreatening tone. This provides a secure environment for exploring client needs, identifying possible actions for meeting those needs, and determining the next steps. The coach offers space and detachment, along with continuous feedback and discussion of plans and ideas. Doing this allows the coach to "mediate" between clients and their desired actions. The coach's focus is on problem solving through guided discussion, so he or she carefully selects words and questions in order to draw solutions from clients. Because clients come up with their own solutions, they will readily take ownership of their actions. Clients must look inward to identify and articulate needs on an ongoing basis.

The coach avoids asking questions about why clients took a certain action. Asking a question such as "Why did you do that?" hinders progress, because clients have to look back and assign blame rather than look forward toward solutions. It is more constructive to ask such questions as "How are you going to approach this problem? What options do you have?" Eventually, clients will internalize these questions and ask them on their own.

How people with LD and ADHD talk to themselves has a powerful effect on how they feel about themselves and governs many of their actions and decisions in life. Their differences have often caused them to be misunderstood as "stupid," "ditzy," or "irresponsible." In order for clients to succeed, they need to believe they *can* succeed. Therefore, it is necessary for the coach to discourage negative self-talk—or "negative scripts"—that hold clients back. Guided self-exploration enables clients to reframe their disability. By separating themselves from their negative scripts, clients are able to look at themselves more objectively. They can now choose how to respond to their challenges.

COACHING ADULTS

Meet Alison

When Alison started working with a coach, she was treated for mild depression, anxiety, and ADHD. She was suffering from low-self esteem and was frustrated that she "couldn't get out of her own way." She is a mother of five children, ranging from 5 to 16 years of age, and works at home taking care of the house and kids.

In her initial consult with her coach, Alison said, "I often feel like I am missing out on life because of my inability to prioritize the details that make up my life. I find it hard to sort through the tasks and ideas that arise during a day or week. I think about everything—all the time. I seem to have two speeds: really on and really off. I cannot believe that I am still saying it but I frequently tell myself 'If I just tried a little harder to get organized, my life would be much more manageable.' When I try to do everything at the same time, I never finish anything. Worse, I don't do the things that are the most important to me. I need help in structuring my days."

Alison is also dyslexic and told the coach that the disability, along with ADHD, have taken a toll on her 20-year marriage. "My husband and I had a magical start to our relationship, and now all I can say is that it is a miracle we are still married. The stress and chaos caused by my disabilities gets between us. He doesn't understand how I can be so inconsistent, take so long to complete a task, lose my keys as often as I do, or be late all the time."

She fought back tears as she talked about her reading journal entries from 15 years ago and realized she is struggling with the same issues today. She knew what she needed to do but wasn't able to figure out *how* to accomplish it. Her feelings of shame and guilt, of feeling like a failure as a mother and wife, she said, often paralyzed her.

How Coaching Helped Alison

Feeling that she and the coach could work productively together, Alison made an appointment for an initial intake. In the meeting, the coach confirmed that Alison saw a psychiatrist to monitor her medication and a therapist to treat depression. They reviewed information from the intake forms—which included a history of how dyslexia and ADHD affected her life, identification of strengths and weaknesses, and a list of initial goals.

Alison and her coach then took a closer look at the goals that she would like to achieve. They included maintaining health, balancing family life, restoring order to a messy house, and making time for herself as well as for her family and husband.

Many clients have too many goals. The coach needs to help clients categorize and prioritize goals, and pinpoint what is preventing them from reaching those goals. The coach also works with clients to formulate strategies that will help them move forward as well as plans for when they run into problems. For instance, Alison spent hours beating herself up over not knowing how to start a task. Her negative self-talk prevented her from taking action, and she would give up. Alison also consistently overestimated what she could accomplish in a certain time. She would get overwhelmed and leave unfinished what she started. The end result? Feelings of guilt and shame.

Alison opened up to the coach and shared her patterns of being overwhelmed and frustrated. The two worked out a system by which the coach would point out when

Alison had too much on her plate or when negative thoughts impeded her progress. By codesigning the relationship and agreeing with the coach on how they would work together, Alison remained in control and responsible for her actions during the coaching process.

A coach needs to figure out the cause of clients' problems and to understand when they result from certain symptoms associated with dyslexia and ADHD and not from willful behavior or character flaws. Alison was not able to realize how her disabilities were preventing her from achieving her goals. She could only see the negative results. Without understanding and accepting the cause of her problems, it was hard to create strategies to help her move forward.

Alison and her coach pinpointed two areas that were preventing her from reaching her goals: the inability to organize and prioritize and the inability to measure and estimate time.

Organize and Prioritize

Alison was adversely affected by her disorganized house. In addition, orchestrating the activities and schedules of five children confused her and caused excessive anxiety. To her, every chore seemed equal and pressing. Living with five children is challenging for anyone. For someone with Alison's disabilities, making it through the day was a Herculean task. By understanding that her brain processes information differently, Alison was able to take a step a back, avoid blaming herself, and work on solutions.

The first line of action was hiring a professional organizer, who helped Alison set up systems in the house for doing laundry—placing two bins in each child's room, one for colored clothes and the other for whites—creating a family calendar, starting a chore notebook, and so on.

Alison and her coach created accountability standards that would enable Alison to follow through and stick to the systems. They set up routines and rituals for doing laundry and grocery shopping on specific days of the week.

She and her coach also examined Alison's weekly schedule and marked down her regular obligations. This way, they both could see where she had "open zones." In these zones, she and her coach plugged in times for her weekly priorities and goals—exercising, socializing, and spending down time with her husband and children.

Measure and Estimate Time

Alison spent hours on the Internet, got distracted by the family dogs or by the large piles of laundry. By the end of the day, she wondered where the time went. To help Alison measure time and manage her ADHD symptoms, she and her coach designated specific start-and-stop times for working on her priorities. Alison programmed her cell phone to beep and created a "time card" that allowed her to clock in to work and clock out when she completed a task.

Alison also programmed a sports watch to beep every hour, so she could "hear" the passage of time. She agreed with her coach to stop for 30 seconds when the watch beeped to take stock of what she was doing at the moment and to ask herself a series of questions: "Am I on task or off task? If not, what can I do to get back on track? Have I been realistic in my plans today? If not, what can I change to accomplish my top priority for the day?"

By assessing actions and plans—what worked, what did not work—two times a week over the phone, Alison was better able to identify and remember her major priorities for each day. She increased her ability to follow through on tasks by breaking them down into smaller pieces and by creating accountability with her coach to complete the task. Alison e-mailed and text-messaged her coach as she finished a small part of a large task. The digital check-ins allowed her to reach goals. Encouragement from the coach motivated Alison and sustained her momentum.

To avoid being late, Alison suggested to her coach that she keep a journal and write down events in which she had gone off track and made bad choices. For example, Alison tried to fit in several errands on the way to pick up her daughter at school when she was already an hour late. The journal encouraged Alison to observe herself in action. By analyzing her miscues, Alison was able to reflect on and talk through alternative actions. Alison also asked the coach to remind her about the "pain of the past," of repeating the same mistakes—specifically, convincing herself that she could do more than she could in a set time frame. At appropriate times, the coach mentioned to her: "Remember, Alison, you tend to fool yourself into thinking that you can do everything all at once. How can you be more realistic?"

Coaching worked for Alison. She was better able to develop ways to assign and direct her attention to accomplish important tasks each day—and not veer off course. The coaching partnership, along with developing strategies that worked with Alison's strengths, holding her accountable for carrying out the actions, and talking over problems when she did not, turned her life around. Coaching helped Alison move beyond repeating the same mistakes she had made for over 15 years. She became more confident and had a more balanced, happy life.

COACHING ADOLESCENTS WITH LD AND ADHD

When coaching adolescents with LD and ADHD, the coach shifts to a more directive approach, weaving brainstorming and strategic thinking into the coaching process to accommodate for the young client's lack of skill and self-direction. With adolescents and young adults, self-initiated change takes a longer time to establish, and coaching can help "drive" that process.

Unlike adults, adolescents with LD and ADHD do not have the internal motivation to make changes independently. Moving the process forward often requires more direction from the coach. There is usually a team approach to the coaching process, involving parents, therapists, teachers, and tutors. The coach and client set up a plan that allows for support from the team while honoring the confidentiality of the relationship between the adolescent and the coach. The coaching process may include parents directly in coaching sessions or indirectly through open e-mail exchanges in support of the client's efforts. Each client is unique. Therefore, as with adults, the coaching plan is designed to meet the needs of the individual. For example, a teenage client with short-term memory issues may need parents and teachers to confirm completion and receipt of homework assignments and require the teen to get a grade sheet signed each week. This process is supported by the coach as part of the coaching plan.

It is important to note that the coach's focus is not limited to academics. As with adults, the focus should be on the whole person. This is a critical difference that distinguishes the field of coaching from that of other professionals. Some coaches are trained to focus only on academics, and many do double as tutors. An ADHD coach focuses on all life areas, from social skills, self-advocacy, health and well-being, life balance, career exploration, and academics. When LD issues are prominent, the ADHD coach will support the young client with structure and a specific plan of accountability designed to help the client choose, and use, the most effective strategies to overcome the learning issues.

Typically, adolescents do not seek out a coach; the parents usually request and pay for services. Nonetheless, it is important for the teen to be involved from the beginning. In fact, prospective teen clients should interview a coach before the process begins. Teens are drawn to coaching when they understand that a coach is a partner in the process, not an authority figure.

The fact that the teen is the client is to be clearly stated at the outset of the coaching relationship. It is therefore essential that the coach develops a good rapport with the teen. A trusting and comfortable connection between coach and client, of any age, and particularly a teen, is essential for coaching to be a success. This process is called co-creating the relationship: The coach establishes trust and intimacy with the client. As part of the coaching agreement, the coach, teen, and parents must agree to terms that will work for everyone.

Steven's Story

"But, Mom, I did study! Why don't you ever believe me?" Steven looked at the floor and stomped out of the room. He was frustrated and angry with his teacher, his parents, and himself. Even though he put time into studying for the English test and felt confident about his level of knowledge, Steven got another D.

"Why am I so stupid?" Steven asked himself. "All my friends do less work and get better grades. They must all be smarter than me." Steven, age 16, was a junior in high school. He was always thinking about getting good grades and getting accepted to a top-notch college. He always felt pressure to do well but just could not seem to make that happen.

At age 11, Steven was diagnosed with ADHD, predominantly Inattentive Type, with a visual memory learning disability. According to the psychoeducational testing, Steven had an above-average IQ. However, he had deficits in reading comprehension and trouble remembering number sequences (long division, phone numbers, complex football plays).

To improve Steven's test scores, his parents hired tutors in middle school to work with him on reading and math. It seemed to help but now, at 16, Steven did not want help and told his parents he would figure it out on his own. Today, Steven once again found that his efforts alone would not cut it. At the request of his parents, Steven tried stimulant medication for his ADHD. It helped a bit before tests and when reading books, but now the medications alone are not getting him closer to academic success.

When Steven got to his room, he sat down at his desk. "What's the point?" he wondered. "I don't know what I did wrong and why I messed up so badly." He pulled out his English test and saw that the teacher had made notes in the margins. She indicated that Steven's answers were too short and in some cases dead wrong. As he went through the test pages, Steven was really confused. He could see where he messed up but did not remember doing that during the test. This was so frustrating!

That evening, Steven's parents called a family meeting at the kitchen table. They were very concerned and, to Steven, seemed kind of angry. Steven was expecting to get grounded or have his weekend privileges taken away. When his parents mentioned ADHD coaching, he was surprised. They told him that someone recommended a coach who could help him to figure out what was not working at school, at home, and even on the football field. His mom reminded Steven that the issues were not just poor grades but also his inability to stay on track in football practice and games. Steven loved football and wanted to be a better player, so that piqued his interest.

When Steven and his family met with the ADHD coach, they shared their observations and concerns. Steven had an equal voice in the discussion and felt supported. He learned that the problems he faced are common and that, by learning and implementing new strategies with the support of his coach, he could make positive changes in his life.

After the initial intake session with Steven and his parents, the coach met one-on-one with Steven to review his areas of difficulty and discuss his goals and his willingness to work in partnership with the coach. It is important for coaches to reaffirm the new client's commitment to the coaching process out of earshot of the parents. When a client is unwilling or unready to move forward, coaching is not the best intervention; in such cases, the coach may be putting forth the effort and energy that needs to come from the client. Adolescents and young adults benefit from a solid review of what coaching is, and is not, before they move forward with the coaching plan.

How Coaching Helped Steven

Steven's difficulties with short-term memory resulted in his forgetting what he studied. He also had problems following plays his football coach reviewed during practice. When Steven hit the football field, he was not always clear on the game plan. His inattentiveness made him distractible—teachers and coaches thought he just was not listening or was not interested enough to learn.

Steven and his coach worked together to formulate a plan of action.

Learn Self-Advocacy Skills

Steven and his coach role-played and brainstormed strategies to help Steven learn how to ask for accommodations and assistance from his teachers and football coach. As Steven became more articulate and comfortable explaining his problems and his needs, he grew more confident in advocating for himself. Steven talked with his parents about letting go of some of the daily contact with the school, so that he could step in and advocate for his needs with the teachers.

Learn Strategies for Improving Focus/Decrease Distractibility

Steven told his coach that he did not think that his medication was working effectively and that he did not bother taking it all the time. He agreed to take the medication every day and report back to his coach on the positive and negative effects. Steven and his coach discussed strategies for increased focus, including: taking breaks during homework and study time; requesting a seat on the end of the row in his classes to allow him to stretch his legs without disturbing others; and using a tape recorder for class lectures to capture information he may have missed.

Use Compensatory Strategies to Help with Short-Term Memory Issues

When Steven worked with his tutor in middle school, he was taught how to break up his work into small chunks and reread to increase comprehension. When he started high school and life got busier, Steven stopped using those strategies. He agreed to work on his short-term memory problems independently and report his progress to his ADHD coach.

Steven asked his teachers to provide notes from the lectures for review after class. This, in addition to the recorded lectures, allowed Steven to have all the data he needed to review materials and retain the information.

Steven found coaching to be helpful. Over time, he was able to confidently communicate his needs to his parents, teachers, and his football coach. He learned how to stick with the plan created in coaching to improve his focus and study skills to compensate for his short-term memory deficits. Steven's coach encouraged him to stick with the coaching plan and communicate openly and honestly about his progress, backslides, and frustrations. The coach frequently reminded Steven and his parents that coaching is not a quick fix—it is a slow, steady process that requires patience, support, and encouragement along the way.

POWER OF COLLABORATION

One of the most effective ways to help clients with LD and ADHD is for the coach to collaborate with other professionals. When medical or academic issues arise, or clients struggle with a complex emotional problem, the coach should refer them to professionals who can address those problems. Indeed, it is the coach's job to distinguish between these issues and those that he or she can solve.

Collaboration facilitates professionals from different disciplines to share important information about clients. This synergy has a powerful effect on a client's treatment outcome—and success. For instance, when a person is evaluated for ADHD by a psychiatrist, physician, or mental health professional specializing in ADHD, he or she often needs help from a coach for organizational challenges and a lack of follow-through. If the client is prescribed medication to manage LD and ADHD symptoms, the coach can make sure the client takes the medication as prescribed by holding him or her accountable.

Some psychotherapists are limited in helping clients with LD and ADHD because of the clients' time management and organizational challenges. If clients forget about their therapy appointments, cannot get to them on time, or cannot recall the goals that were set in the last session, then therapy is unlikely to be effective. A coach can develop strategies to deal with these problems, helping clients to derive benefit from psychotherapy.

For example, a skilled professional organizer who is knowledgeable about ADHD might refer a client to a coach to hold the client accountable for organizing his house or office. If a client is a high school or college student and finds it difficult to manage time and to write papers, she may need to work with a coach *and* a writing tutor. Or, in therapy, she might explore emotional issues hampering her success.

Ideally, all professionals treating a client should consider themselves a team, providing feedback to each other to facilitate treatment success. It is important that team members understand the types of problems addressed and the methods used by other professionals on the team. Some therapists, for instance, do not know what a coach does. If this is the case, it is the coach's job to inform the therapist of the scope of the coaching relationship, the challenges being addressed, and the methods used to address them.

Coaching Is Never a Substitute for Therapy

Many individuals with LD and ADHD also struggle with significant emotional challenges. These challenges should not be ignored or downplayed. Coaches and therapists work most effectively by staying in regular contact and working in partnership to help their clients feel and function better. For example, a coach can make therapy more productive by working with clients to develop a system—a notebook, for example—in which to jot down thoughts they want to discuss in therapy. Therapists can enhance the effectiveness of coaching by treating the emotional challenges that can sabotage the best coaching plan.

Issues that Complicate the Coaching Process

Some clients' challenges are so severe that a coach should refrain from coaching them. In these cases, the coach may put the coaching relationship on hold and refer the client to another professional. Not all of the next scenarios preclude coaching, but they do call for a referral to a qualified professional. Some of these occur when:

- Medical or psychodynamic issues are discovered. These are not always apparent at the start of a relationship, but if coach does uncover them, the client should be referred to a medical doctor.
- The client continually resists using simple self-management and/or organizational strategies to obtain goals, despite the coach's resources and reminders.
- Comorbid issues—Anxiety Disorder, Depression, Anger Disorder, rapid mood swings, and self-defeating thoughts—are present on a repeated basis. These issues obstruct progress toward goals.
- The coach discovers that the client needs emotional or psychological support because of a death in the family, marital separation, divorce, or serious illness.
- The designated goals are not realistic and need to be reworked.

When coaching adolescents, these scenarios may complicate the coaching process:

- The parents drive the coaching agenda, and the adolescent is not committed to the coaching process. In such cases, the coach may work on parenting skills with the adults while the adolescent works with a therapist or an educational specialist.
- The adolescent does not understand the coaching process or how to work in partnership with a coach because of emotional immaturity or underdeveloped cognitive ability.
- Lack of motivation results from repeated failure, low self-esteem and self-confidence, and difficulty envisioning success. In this case, therapy may be advisable in addition to coaching—or, based on the coach's judgment, coaching should be put on hold while the adolescent receives counseling to resolve issues.

FINDING AND CHOOSING A COACH

Increasingly, more people with LD and ADHD are turning to coaching to improve their lives. As a result, coaching seems to have become a cottage industry overnight. How can prospective clients navigate the maze of information on the Internet to find a coach that is right for them?

Although coaching is still in its infancy, the field has created some standards and credentialing procedures. No matter which type of training a coach has received, a person with LD and ADHD should seek out coaches who are in credentialed in treating ADHD. For this reason, the Institute for the Advancement of ADHD Coaching (IAAC www.adhdcoachinstitute.org) was developed. The goal of the institute is to develop universal standards of excellence, training, continuing education, and ethical behavior. These standards are essential to the credibility of the coaching profession, and they safeguard the consumers. A coach credentialed by the IAAC has received rigorous training in working with people with ADHD.

Other organizations also credential coaches. In the end, though, the consumer must research a prospective coach's training and background. Some organizations that list directories of ADHD coaches include:

ADHD Coaches Organization (ACO): www.adhdcoaches.org
Attention Deficit Disorder Association (ADDA): www.add.org
Children and Adults with Attention Deficit Disorder (CHADD): www.chadd.org
International Coaching Federation (ICF): www.coachfederation.org

Creating the Right Match

Because coaching is a relatively new profession, clients should consider many factors, in addition to training, when choosing a coach—for example, knowing one's needs, being able to articulate them, and determining whether one can work successfully with the coach.

Before interviewing a prospective coach, clients should *assess their needs* by asking themselves these questions:

- Do I prefer face-to-face coaching sessions? If so, the client should look for a coach who is nearby or within driving distance who offers one-on-one sessions. Many coaches conduct the initial session in person and follow up with weekly check-ins by phone and/or e-mail. If in-person contact is not important, the client can look for a coach anywhere in the country.
- Is the gender of the coach important? Would I prefer to be coached by a man or woman?
- Will I benefit more by working with a coach who has a background in business, academia, gender issues, or some other specialty?

- Am I looking for someone with a specific expertise—clutter management, family issues, academic-related challenges, or school issues?
- Do I want to work with a coach who is outgoing and who cheerleads my successes or one with a more subtle, low-key approach?
- How important is a sense of humor to me? Or would a serious approach make a better match?

When interviewing a coach, clients should determine the professional's involvement in and commitment to the field of ADHD coaching. Because coaching is a developing field, coaches need to continue their education in order to keep their skills sharp. Clients should ask:

- What coach training courses have you completed, and when?
- How many clients with ADHD have you coached? Parents of an adolescent should ask: How many teen clients (not relatives) with ADHD have you coached?
- How long have you been providing ADHD-specific coaching services?
- What is the age range of your clients and past clients?
- What are your professional coaching and ADHD affiliations, memberships, and credentials?

Clients should interview at least two prospective coaches and ask about experience, training, client references, and affiliation with LD, ADHD, and coaching organizations. In addition, clients should ask for referrals from allied professionals—therapists, psychiatrists, and responsible organizations that regularly offer services to people with LD and ADHD. For adolescent clients, parents often conduct the first interview, after which time the adolescent needs to interview the coach directly to ascertain if he or she is a good match.

Qualities to Look for When Choosing a Coach

A coach should have these qualities:

Be Knowledgeable about LD and ADHD

An ADHD coach must have some educational background or experience in working with persons with LD and ADHD. They must be familiar enough with symptoms and their effects to give clients a deeper understanding and appreciation of their condition. A skilled coach will foster a client's acceptance of, and an ability to forgive, him- or herself. The coach enables clients to draw more from their strengths and to learn ways to build bridges over their weaknesses.

Be Effective

A client can gauge the effectiveness of a prospective coach by how well the coach understands, or "gets," the client on that first call. Client should ask themselves:

- Does the coach use an approach I feel comfortable with?
- Is the coach able to listen to me and identify my needs?
- Does the coach ask questions that clarify issues and make me feel more
- empowered?
- Is the coach intuitive? Can she pick up on what I am saying and move me along in the conversation?
- Is the coach skilled at creating rapport with adolescents?

It is the coach's job to educate the client about the coaching process and to determine whether the client is ready to undertake it.

Be a Good Listener

The coach should be able to "hear" and understand the client's frustrations and struggles. He or she must be able to untangle the complex patterns of thought and behavior that hold the client back.

Be Nonjudgmental

It is essential that the coach make the client feel safe and accepted. If the coach cannot, then the client will avoid speaking freely for fear of being judged. This will short-circuit the coaching process.

Work on the Client's Agenda

A coach must support the client in establishing his or her goals and in working toward them. The coach should not allow his or her own values or goals to influence the coaching process.

Encourage the Client

Most clients who decide to work with a coach are frustrated and have experienced failure. The coach should celebrate their success and motivate them to try again when they struggle or stumble.

Provide Direction

When a client needs direction, the coach should offer suggestions while holding the client accountable for sticking with the game plan. The client should not be overwhelmed by the coach's direction and advice. Good direction from a coach focuses clients and gets them back on track.

Empower Clients

At one time or another everyone thinks, "I can't do that" or "Nothing ever goes right for me." For people with ADHD, these negative judgments are often pervasive. The coach should point out these negative scripts and offer positive ones in their place. Affirmations like "Good for me for trying!" Or "I'm doing better now than before" are typical examples.

Keep Clients on Track

Coaches refer to this as "forwarding the action." A coach develops strategies that clients learn to implement on their own when they get stuck.

CONCLUSION

The field of personal and professional coaching is gaining recognition as a treatment option that empowers individuals to be more purposeful and proactive in today's fast-paced world. Coaching has become an indispensable tool in the arsenal of LD and ADHD treatment. The coach and the client develop a partnership that motivates the client to move forward in a deliberate and structured way. It puts the client in the driver's seat to take responsibility for his or her action—or inaction.

Many people with LD and ADHD also work with professionals in other disciplines. Each professional (therapist, medical doctor, tutor, professional organizer) addresses a specific area of difficulty (mental, medical, academic, organizational) for the client. Coaches, however, focus on solving problems and achieving goals; they do not address the whys of the client's behaviors but the whats, hows, and whens. Coaches ask their clients pointed, insightful questions—What are the areas of difficulty in your daily life? What goals can you set to work around those difficulties? How are you going to motivate yourself to get to your appointments on time? When would it be reasonable for you to accomplish your goals?—to help them better understand themselves.

Although each care provider brings his or her own set of valuable skills to the treatment process, collaboration among providers is the most powerful approach in helping persons with LD and ADHD lead a fulfilling life. Coaching can be an excellent adjunct to the treatment plan for adolescents and adults with LD and ADHD.

BIBLIOGRAPHY

Heininger, J. E., & Weiss, S. K. (2001). *From chaos to calm: Effective parenting of challenging children with ADHD and other behavior problems*.New York, NY: Berkley.

Jaksa, P., & Ratey, N. (1999). Therapy and ADD coaching: Similarities, differences and collaboration. *Focus, 3*, 10–11.

Levine, M. (2005). *Ready or not, here life comes*. New York, NY: Simon & Schuster.

Quinn, P. O., & Ratey, N. A. (Eds.). (2003). *ADHD throughout the life-span: Research, diagnosis and treatment.* [30-hour curriculum]. Easton, MA: S.C. Publishing.

Quinn, P. O., Ratey, N. A., & Maitland, T. L. (2001). *Coaching college students with ADHD: Issues and answers.* Bethesda, MD: Advantage Books.

Ratey, N. A. (2001). Life-style habits for success. In P. O. Quinn (Ed.), *ADD and the college student: A guide for high school and college students with Attention Deficit Disorder* (rev. ed.; pp. 91–98). Washington, DC: Magination Press.

Ratey, N. A. (2002). Life coaching for adult ADHD. In S. Goldstein & A. T. Ellison (Eds.), *Clinician's guide to adult ADHD: Assessment and intervention.* London, UK: Academic Press.

Ratey, N. A. (2003). ADHD and coaching." In P. Quinn & N. A. Ratey (Eds.), *ADHD throughout the lifespan: Research, diagnosis and treatment* (pp. 1–14). Easton, MA: S.C. Publishing.

Ratey, N. A. (2008). *The disorganized mind: Coaching your ADHD brain to get control of your tasks, time, and talents.* New York, NY: St. Martin's Press.

Ratey, N. A., & Jaksa, P. (Eds.). (2002). *The ADDA guiding principles for coaching individuals with attention deficit disorder.* Highland Park, IL: Attention Deficit Disorder Association.

Ratey, N. A., & Maitland, T. (2001). Working with an ADD coach." In P. O. Quinn (Ed.), *ADD and the college student: A guide for high school and college students with Attention Deficit Disorder* (rev. ed.; pp. 99–106). Washington, DC: Magination Press.

Sleeper-Triplett, J. (2008). The effectiveness of coaching for children and teens with ADHD. *Pediatric Nursing, 34*(5), 433–435.

Sleeper-Triplett, J. (2009, October). Coach-assisted transitioning to college and independence. *Learning Disabilities Association of Utah Newsletter* (pp. 1–4).

Sleeper-Triplett, J. (2010) *Empowering Youth With ADHD. Your Guide to Coaching Adolescents and Young Adults for Coaches, Parents, and Professionals.* Plantation, FL: Specialty Press.

16

College Programs and Services

Kevin Hills
Ian Campbell

TRANSITION FROM K–12 TO COLLEGE

High school students with disabilities who plan to go to college should start planning early. Under the Individuals with Disabilities Education Act (IDEA), discussions about student's transition from high school must begin no later than age 14 and should begin being implemented no later than age 16. Students who plan to attend college and their parents need to understand that in order to receive accommodations for disabilities at the college or university level, they must provide current documentation of their disability. In most cases, Disability Supports Service (DSS) providers need to have an adult-level assessment that was conducted on the student after 16 years of age. Be sure to request an updated assessment for college-bound students before they graduate and specifically ask for retesting; otherwise you could end up paying for a private assessment out of pocket. Although some colleges and universities provide assessments for their students at a reduced rate, most do not, and a private assessment can cost upward of $2,000. Many high school counselors and special education teachers are under the impression that it is better to transition students out of special education before they go to college. Nothing could be further from the truth! If students are determined ineligible for services in high school, then why would they qualify in college? Even if a student chooses not to seek accommodations in college, it is better to have the option if the need should arise. You may also be advised, at the high school level, that students with disabilities do not need to take the SAT or ACT or that if they take, it they cannot receive accommodations, such as extra time. Also not true! High schools do not have the authority to adjust the admission standards at colleges and universities. If the schools you plan to attend requires the SAT or ACT, you must take it and score high enough to meet the index of that school. Students who require accommodations on the SAT or ACT need to contact the testing agency to request nonstandard accommodations for disability and must provide documentation. Students who are unable to meet the admission criteria for more selective institutions can begin their college career at a number of community colleges or private schools with lower indexes. Once you have earned an AA transfer degree, you can enter most universities as a junior. Some schools even take no degree holding students once they have earned approximately 1 year's worth of credits; usually a minimum GPA of 2.0 is also required. As parents, we tend to want to do everything for our children. This transition period is a good time to have them start making the necessary contact and arrangements while we are still close by to add assistance.

DIFFERENCES BETWEEN PROGRAMS AND THE IMPORTANCE OF SHOPPING

All colleges and universities are required to provide DSS under the Americans with Disability Act, but the level of commitment by the administration may vary from one school to the next. It is important for prospective students and their parents to shop around and choose the school that best suits their needs. Many DSS programs are largely self-contained and provide accommodations in-house with little interaction with faculty; others follow a more collaborative model, relying more on faculty and other departments to assist in providing accommodations. Other schools are adopting the concept of universal access by educating faculty and staff about creating an environment that truly removes barriers and reduces the need for accommodation because the programs are accessible to all students regardless of disability. When touring schools, visit the DSS office and meet with the director or the person in charge of accommodations. Ask questions:

- How many students do you serve?
- How many staff work in the DSS office?
- How accommodating are the faculty?
- How are specific accommodation provided—that is, extra time on tests, how much time is allowed, where are tests taken, and so on?

Keep in mind that the largest program is not always the best match for the student. Many DSS programs are one-person operations and they provide exceptional service; others may have multiple staff members and resources but lack the working relationship with faculty, staff, and students needed to be effective. Each student is an individual and not all programs fit all students. Be aware of your needs and seek a program that best meets those needs. No matter how committed to student success a program is, the responsibility for success falls on the student. Most DSS programs are able to accomplish amazing success, but no one can read minds or see into the future. It is up to the student to make DSS aware of problem situations as early as possible, so they can assist. Students who try to ignore situations and avoid asking for help usually find themselves facing academic or financial probation or suspension. Often these situations can be avoided by contacting DSS early in the term when problems first appear. Just as in transition planning, it is important to have students take the lead role when college shopping, as they will need to continue to assume this responsibility as they progress through school and throughout life.

DOCUMENTATION

Currently there is no documentation standard that all schools must follow. Some colleges require less information in their documentation than others. The guidelines listed here should provide you with the necessary components to meet the documentation requirements at the majority of institutions. The documentation requirements provided are for Eastern Washington University, as adopted from guidelines and recommendations from the Washington Association on Postsecondary Education and Disability and the Association of Higher Education and Disability.

Documentation should show impact of the disability at age 16 years or older and should include:

1. A statement of diagnosis of the learning disability in the nomenclature used by the *DSM-IV-TR* or successive editions.
2. Tests administered to determine this diagnosis. Learning disability assessment must be specific, comprehensive, and include:
    a. Aptitude: The Wechsler Adult Intelligence Scale III (WAIS III) with subtests scores in preferred. The Woodcock-Johnson Psycho-Educational Battery Revised: Test of Cognitive Ability is acceptable. The Leiter International Performance Scale or the Comprehensive test of Non-Verbal Intelligence (C-TONI) is accepted when cultural bias or hearing loss is a concern.
    b. Achievement: Current level of functioning in reading, mathematics, and written language are required. Acceptable instruments include the Woodcock-Johnson Psych-Educational Battery-Revised: test of achievement; Stanford Test of Academic Skills (TASK); or specific achievement tests such as the Test of Written Language-2 (TOWL-2), Woodcock Reading Mastery Tests-Revised, or the Stanford Diagnostic Mathematics Test. Please note: The Wide Range Achievement Test Revised is NOT a comprehensive measure of achievement and, therefore, is not suitable.
    c. Information Processing: Specific areas of information processing (e.g., short and long term memory; sequential memory; auditory and visual perception/processing; processing speed) must be assessed. Use of subtests from the WAIS-R or the Woodcock-Johnson Test of Cognitive Ability are acceptable.

NOTE: The above are not intended to be exhaustive lists or to restrict assessment in other pertinent and helpful areas such as vocational interest and aptitudes.

d. Raw Data and Interpretation.

e. Specific recommendations based on interpreted tests. These recommendations can be based on or taken from a copy of school I.E.P. but must identify specific learning disability and reflect the individual's present level of functioning in intelligence, achievement, and processing.

f. Tests need to be current. In most cases an adult level assessment that was administered after 16 years of age is required and in some cases institutions may require an assessment after 18 years of age.

Suggestions for reasonable accommodations with supporting evidence can be included. The final determination for providing appropriate and reasonable accommodations rests with the college or university the student plans to attend. The DSS office reserves the right to obtain clarification regarding the documentation if necessary.

It is important to discuss with your school districts special education coordinator the importance of retesting as part of the transition planning process before the student graduates. Contact the DSS office at all schools you plan to apply to and request copies of their documentation policies. You should provide them to your district education specialist, as part of the retesting process.

DOCUMENTATION POLICIES FOR ATTENTION DISABILITIES

1. Documentation must be prepared by a professional who has comprehensive training in differential diagnosis and direct experience working with adolescents and adults with ADHD. Such professionals may include clinical psychologists, neuropsychologist, psychiatrists, and other relevantly trained medical doctors.

2. Documentation should be current; the provision of all reasonable accommodations and services is based on the assessment of the current impact of the disability on academic performance. This means that the diagnostic evaluation should show the current level of function and impact of the disability.

3. Documentation must be comprehensive and should address the next areas:

a. *Evidence of early impairment.* Due to the fact that ADHD is, by definition in the fourth edition of the first *Diagnostic and Statistical Manual of Mental Disorders (DSM-IV-TR),* exhibited in childhood and manifests itself in more than one setting, a comprehensive assessment should include a clinical summary of objective historical information garnered from sources such as transcripts, report cards, teacher comments, tutoring evaluations, past psychoeducational testing, and third-party interviews when available.

b. *Evidence of current impairment.* Diagnostic assessment should consist of more than a self-report. Information from third-party sources is critical in the diagnosis of ADHD. Information from a variety of sources should include history of presenting attentional symptoms, developmental history, family history for presence of ADHD, relevant medical and medication history, relevant psychosocial history, any relevant interventions, academic history, review of prior psychoeducational test reports, relevant employment history, and relevant history of prior therapy.

Alternative diagnoses or explanations should be ruled out, including medical, psychiatric disorders, and educational or cultural factors affecting the individual that may result in behavior mimicking ADHD, should be explored.

Testing must be relevant. Test scores or subtest scores alone should not be used as a sole measure for the diagnostic decision regarding ADHD. Selected subtest scores from measures of intellectual ability, memory functions tests, attention or tracking tests, or continuous performance tests do not in and of themselves establish the presence or absence of ADHD. Checklists and/or surveys can serve to supplement the diagnostic profile, but by themselves are not adequate for the diagnosis of ADHD.

If applicable, present a specific diagnosis of ADHD based on the *DSM-IV-TR* diagnostic criteria. The diagnostician should use direct language in the diagnosis of ADHD, avoiding the use of such terms as "suggests" "is indicative of" or "attention problems."

Provide a comprehensive interpretive summary synthesizing the evaluator's judgment for the diagnosis. The reports should include:

- All quantitative information in standard scores and or percentiles.
- All relevant developmental, familial medical, medication, psychosocial, behavioral, and academic information.
- A clear identification of the substantial limitation of a major life function presented by the ADHD.

Suggestions for reasonable accommodations with supporting evidence can be included. The final determination for providing appropriate and reasonable accommodations rests with the college or university the student plans to attend. DSS offices may reserve the right to obtain clarification regarding the documentation, if necessary.

COORDINATION OF SERVICES

Equally as important as the type of services available to the student is how services are provided and who is responsible to make sure that accommodations are provided. The DSS programs of many institutions are largely self-contained, providing all of the students' accommodations within the DSS office. For example, they provide testing rooms, paid note takers, and academic advising, just to name a few. Others DSS programs rely on the institution as a whole to meet the needs of students by asking the faculty to take an active part in providing accommodations, such as allowing testing within the department, helping to identify fellow students who can share notes, and having students advised by general undergraduate or departmental advisors. Both types of programs have their strengths. Although more self-contained DSS programs are able to better monitor their students' accommodations and avoid students being unserved, programs that rely on the entire institution tend to place more responsibility on students to communicate with all parties involved and therefore allow students to become more self-sufficient and empowered in the future. Students both with and without disabilities who take a more active role in their education tend to be more successful, both in school and after graduation, than passive students.

TECHNOLOGICAL ACCOMMODATIONS IN POSTSECONDARY EDUCATION

The accommodation process in postsecondary education is becoming increasingly technological for a number of reasons. Over time, these assistive technologies are being used by larger populations, which has generated increased research and development investment by software companies to make these products more user friendly and functional. Another factor that has increased the usage of these applications is that more DSS providers are becoming aware of the effectiveness of these programs. Also, a growing number of states have passed legislation that mandates increased provision of educational media that can be accessed through assistive technology. Many of the accommodations that are granted in postsecondary education are human-based services that will not follow students as they transition into employment. In contrast, technological accommodations are not dependent on human services; therefore, they are more accepted in the employment world. The three types of assistive technology that are commonly utilized to accommodate learning disabilities and ADHD are text-to-speech software, voice recognition software, and mind mapping software. A brief overview of these technologies is given in the next sections.

Text-to-Speech Software

Text-to-speech software, or literacy software, consists of computer programs that process digitized text into computer-synthesized speech. Users of these applications are able to scan text into a computer using a document scanner, and a speech engine can convert the text into its phonetic equivalent. This phonetic equivalent is then voiced through computer speakers or headphones in the form of computer-synthesized speech. In summary, the computer is able to read electronic text to the user. Because of the amount of reading required in postsecondary education, it is recommended that users spend a considerable amount of time researching different text-to-speech software packages in order to find one that contains features that will benefit them.

Popular features include the ability to select from multiple speech synthesizers, allowing users to choose between different-sounding voices. Popular synthesizers include both male and female voices, different languages, and multiple accents of U.S. English. Some text-to-speech software applications allow students to make adjustments to speech output, such as reading speed and variable speech inflection.

Text-to-speech programs offer differing levels of adjustment to visual settings as well. Some programs allow students to adjust font size to make the text easier to see. While reading, some applications allow for "spotlighting" of text that allows users to easily follow along with the synthesized voice. Many applications allow students to enable spotlighting by word, line, sentence or paragraph. Another very popular visual setting in text-to-speech programs is the ability to change the background color of the text. Students report that customizing the background color allows them to use speech-to-text software for longer periods of time.

Another increasingly popular feature is the ability to output to digital audio files, such as MP3 and WAV files. This feature allows students to convert digitized text into a compatible format that can be played by a digital audio player. Many students are now converting texts into formats that are playable on cell phones that feature digital audio players.

A noncomprehensive list of popular text-to-speech applications includes:

ClaroRead
CWU Portable Textbook Reader
Kurzweil 3000/1000
NaturalReader
Read &Write Gold
ReadPlease
Read:OutLoud
TextAloud
Wynn Wizard/Reader

Voice Recognition Software

Voice recognition software is software that allows students to speak to the computer and the computer records their voice into text. Voice recognition software almost entirely replaces the need to input text into a computer using a keyboard. This can be extremely advantageous for students with LD and ADHD for a number of reasons. Students with LD that affect written expression and spelling experience functional limitations in their ability to word process, and many such students report increased comfort expressing themselves orally rather than in written format. Students diagnosed with ADHD commonly report that they experience difficulties staying seated and remaining on task during word processing. They also report that their thoughts race, making it difficult to stay on topic while word processing. Voice recognition allows students with ADHD to record their thoughts in less time, therefore enabling them to word process at a pace that is more natural for them.

Voice recognition software requires each user to create a profile that allows the computer to recognize the speaker's voice. This profile is created by reading a predefined set of text to the computer for approximately 15 minutes. Postsecondary educational institutions have a responsibility to provide assistive technologies and offer adequate training to students. When shopping for a school, it is strongly recommended that students who will be using assistive technologies ask the DSS office how it facilitates the training of such applications. It is very common for trainers to work with students for multiple training hours before the students independently use voice recognition software.

The idea of voice recognition software seems extremely attractive to most students. The reality is that certain students are extremely effective at using the keyboard for word processing functions. These students struggle to make the transition into utilizing voice recognition software as a primary input method. These students usually find that transitioning to voice recognition software delays the time required to word process.

Voice recognition software has been widely utilized as a technological accommodation for students with disabilities since the mid-1990s. Many users who have not received effective training complain about the accuracy of the recognition process. It is essential that users of voice recognition software receive adequate training.

A noncomprehensive list of popular voice recognition programs includes:

Dragon Naturally Speaking
IBM ViaVoice
MacSpeech
Microsoft Windows Speech Recognition

Mind/Concept Mapping Software

Mind mapping or concept mapping software is an invaluable organizational tool for students with learning disabilities and ADHD. Mind mapping software allows students to organize their thoughts in a dynamic graphical environment. The most common use of mind mapping software is to organize thoughts prior to writing, but it is also used to organize concepts for other complex processes, such as presentations and debates.

Students with ADHD and LD frequently report experiencing symptoms of writer's block. These students report experiences of sitting in front of a computer and struggling to find appropriate sequencing of their thoughts and also lacking effective prose to transition from thought to thought. Mind mapping software allows them to start with a main topic and brainstorm many subtopics without having to be concerned with sequencing of the subtopics early in the writing process. After brainstorming, students are able to visually see all of the topics that they are interested in writing about and associate graphics or images with these topics.

The following is a noncomprehensive list of popular mind/concept mapping programs:

FreeMind
Inspiration Software
Microsoft Visio
MindGenius
MindMapper
Semantica

PROVISION OF PRINT MATERIALS IN ALTERNATIVE FORMAT

The Americans with Disabilities Act and Section 504 of the Rehabilitation Act are examples of federal legislation that mandate that postsecondary educational institutions accommodate people with disabilities by providing accessible educational materials. Since the passage of these laws, multiple states across the nation have also passed legislation that mandates that postsecondary educational institutions provide students with disabilities with print materials in alternative format. Some of these laws target publishing companies, stating that if a company is producing educational materials for an institution of higher education, it must also produce formats that are accessible for students with disabilities. Unfortunately, many of the alternatively formatted materials that are distributed by publishing companies are not of adequate quality for distribution to students with disabilities. Institutions of higher education are left with the burden of processing such materials into adequate formats that coincide with the functional limitations of the students with disabilities. Not all higher educational institutions are able to process and provide advanced levels of print materials in the alternative format. This should be a key consideration for prospective students to look at when shopping for an institution of higher education especially if students are considering seeking degrees in science, technology, engineering, and mathematics.

The initial discussion around print materials in alternative format was surrounding the needs of students with visual impairment. This has since changed. Now these conversations are focused primarily on students with print access LD. This is because the number of students with print access LD is far greater than the number of students with visual impairment. The vast majority of alternative formats that are distributed in postsecondary education is for students with LD; the needs of that population now define the national dialogue regarding print materials in alternative format.

Students with ADHD should cautiously review a prospective school's policy on distribution of print materials in alternative format. Many schools provide this accommodation only to students with print access LD, and ADHD is commonly not classified as a print access disability. Other schools offer less restrictive access to this accommodation. For students with ADHD who struggle to access printed materials, this should be a strong consideration when choosing a postsecondary educational institution.

In best practice, DSS professionals should engage in an interactive process with students who qualify for print materials in alternative format. This interactive process should determine what method the student will use to read the alternative format and thus determine what format is most appropriate for the student. Different text-to-speech programs have varying levels of ability to utilize different file formats. Common formats include DAISY files, Microsoft Word document files, and text-selectable PDF files.

CONNECTEDNESS AND SOCIALIZATION

Research indicates that the more connected students feel to an institution, the more likely they are to be retained, matriculate, and ultimately graduate. Students with disabilities are no different, in that respect. Encourage students to pursue their nonacademic interests as well as their studies. Students should seek membership in campus clubs and organizations and should be encouraged to participate in intramural sports and athletic events, guest speaker events, concerts and students activities. Students who obtain campus employment often find that working at the school develops a number of skills that are not normally addressed in the classroom. In some cases, student employment can lead to jobs after graduation and even long-term careers in higher education.

EMPOWERMENT AND SELF-ADVOCACY

Applying the strength-based perspective to students to help them identify their own strengths and assisting them in developing appropriate strategies for self-advocacy will empower them and help them be more successful after graduation when they enter the workforce. Often the working environment is not as supportive as the educational setting. Students who practice advocating for themselves in school are much more likely to be strong self-advocates in the future.

17

Classroom and Instructional Strategies

Robert J. Volpe

R. Julius Anastasio

George J. DuPaul

Attention-Deficit/Hyperactivity Disorder (ADHD) is a psychiatric diagnosis typified by developmentally inappropriate levels of inattention, impulsivity, and overactivity that result in functional impairment in more than one setting (American Psychiatric Association, 2000). Problems with inattention are marked by frequent daydreaming, inconsistent work completion, and difficulties following task-related directions. Impulsive behaviors often include talking without permission, carelessly completing assigned work, and taking risks in social situations. Although high levels of gross motor activity may not be as prominent as found among children with ADHD (Barkley, 2005), adolescents with this disorder may frequently exhibit fidgetiness and report feeling a high degree of internal restlessness (Barkley, 2006; Weyandt et al., 2003) and continue to exhibit high levels of inattentive symptoms (e.g., Frazier et al., 2007). An increasing body of evidence suggests that the inattentive symptoms of ADHD produce the most extensive impairment in the transition to young adulthood and significantly impact employment, and familial and social relationships (Achenbach et al., 1995; Barkley, 2006; Stimmel, 2009). Students with ADHD are highly likely to display symptoms of comorbid disorders, such as Oppositional-Defiant Disorder (ODD) and Conduct Disorder (CD), so they may engage in aggressive, non-compliant, and antisocial behaviors in school settings.

ADHD symptoms often are associated with significant academic impairment including failing grades and below-average academic achievement in most subject areas (Barkley, Anastopoulos, Guevremont, & Fletcher, 1991). Academic difficulties associated with ADHD often begin in early elementary school and continue through high school and college (Barkley, Fischer, Edelbrock, & Smallish, 1990; Barkley, Murphy, & Fischer, 2008; Mannuzza, Gittelman-Klein, Bessler, Malloy, & LaPadula, 1993). Therefore, it is not surprising that adolescents with ADHD are more likely than their non-ADHD peers to be retained in one or more grades, placed in special education for learning and/or behavior difficulties, drop out of high school (Fischer, Barkley, Smallish, & Fletcher, 2002; Wilson & Marcotte, 1996) and be suspended and expelled from school, particularly when they exhibit comorbid CD (Wilson & Marcotte, 1996). Fewer adolescents with ADHD attend college, and of those who do, fewer complete degree programs relative to the non-ADHD population (Barkley et al., 2008).

Several studies have demonstrated that students with ADHD are at higher than average risk for comorbid Learning Disabilities (LD) and vice versa; however, prevalence estimates have varied widely between studies, and the association between the two disorders is decidedly less than perfect (see Willcutt & Pennington, 2000). The inattentive and impulsive characteristics of ADHD make it difficult to determine if a student's academic difficulties are the result of LD or a consequence of attentional deficits (Semrud-Clikeman et al., 1992). Although ADHD symptoms appear to impact all core academic content areas, a meta-analysis of studies examining the association between ADHD and academic problems found that effect sizes were greatest in the area of reading, followed by math and then spelling, with each difference being statistically significant. One possible explanation of this finding is that errors in reading may be more difficult for students to monitor, whereas because tasks in math and spelling typically involve writing, errors may be more easily identified. Likewise reading may be more heavily dependent on working memory. In addition, the same study found that the relationship between ADHD and academic problems was highest for children, followed by adolescents, with the relationship being the least pronounced in adults (Frazier, Youngstrom, Glutting, & Watkins, 2007). This finding stands in contrast to several studies documenting that students who are poor readers in the first grade rarely become at-least average readers (Francis, Shaywitz, Stuebing, Shaywitz, & Fletcher, 1996; Torgesen & Burgess, 1998). One possible explanation for the findings of Frazier et al. is that students with ADHD and LD may not have been adequately represented in adolescent and adult samples.

Adolescents with ADHD and/or LD must exert great effort academically, emotionally, and socially to compensate for their learning deficits. This strain leaves them more susceptible to emotional maladjustment, negative attitudes toward school, atypicality, and depression (Martinez & Semrud-Clikeman, 2004), further impeding academic achievement. Students with LD or low achievement in reading are approximately 3 times more likely to drop out of school than their typically developing peers (U.S. Department of Education, 2007), and far fewer students with learning problems attend college. Although more than 50% of students in general education go on to postsecondary programs within 2 years of high school graduation, only 11% of students in special education do so (National Longitudinal Study II, 2003). Students with ADHD and/or LD who do go on to attend college report much higher rates of adjustment difficulties than their peers. Throughout their college careers, students with LD also perform significantly worse in areas such as adaptability, writing speed, note-taking ability, and organizational skills than their peers (Hughes & Suritsky, 1994). Follow-up studies have revealed that adolescents with LD do not fare as well as their peers in achieving successful employment, living on their own, engaging in social activities, managing academic and nonacademic obligations, or effectively using community resources (Lewis & Taymans, 1992).

It is clear that many adolescent students with ADHD and/or LD demonstrate academic and behavior problems in the school setting that impact their daily functioning and are associated with a host of negative long-term outcomes (Barkley, 2006; Bender, 2008). A comprehensive review of classroom academic and behavioral interventions for adolescents and adults with these problems is well beyond the scope of this chapter. Instead, unique challenges in working with these populations in secondary and post-secondary school settings are discussed, and a set of interventions are reviewed with the intent of addressing these barriers.

INTERVENING WITH ADOLESCENTS WITH ADHD AND LD

The development and implementation of interventions for adolescents with ADHD and LD must take into account several factors unique to this age group. Specifically, compared to younger children, adolescents typically experience a greater number of transitions between classrooms and teachers, decreases in adult contact and monitoring, and additional social pressures (see Schultz, Evans, & Serpell, 2009). These contextual issues can be greatly compounded for adolescents with ADHD and/or LD, many of whom experience long-standing academic problems (Gresham, MacMillan, & Bocian, 1997), peer rejection (Kuhne & Wiener, 2000), social isolation (Margalit, 1998), and poor organizational skills. Uncurbed, these issues can contribute to negative self-attribution and learned helplessness, which contribute to later academic failure. Furthermore, in adolescence, impairments associated with ADHD and LD may have an impact on an expanded set of domains, such as driving, romantic relationships, vocational performance, and the use/abuse of controlled substances (Barkley et al., 2008; Bender, 2008; Evans, Serpell, Schultz, & Pastor, 2007).

Increased Transitions and Reduced Adult Contact

Adolescent development is marked by a general increase in independence and significant decreases in adult contact. These adult interactions are replaced by peer exposure and decreasing adult influence on adolescent behavior.

The transition from elementary to middle school marks a dramatic increase in student transitions throughout the school day. Consistency and follow-through in the school setting is affected both by an increase in the number of teachers and number of classrooms and by shifting schedules. Moreover, the limited time teachers spend with any particular child may limit the time and energy they are willing to expend to address the individual needs of any one student. This must be considered in the design of interventions (Evans, Vallano, & Pelham, 1995) and procedures for assessing the effects of intervention effects (Evans, Allen, Moore, & Strauss, 2005; Evans, Langberg, Raggi, Allen, & Buvinger, 2005; Molina, Pelham, Blumenthal, & Galiszewski, 1998).

Developmental Considerations

Many commonly accepted classroom intervention strategies may not be appropriate for use with adolescents. Peer group interaction is an increasingly crucial matter for adolescents and a qualitatively more significant aspect of adolescent life (Ausubel, 2002). During a time when egocentrism and identity formation take the forefront, there is a heightened sensitivity to being singled out for both positive and, especially, negative reasons. The importance of social peer recognition and acceptance can elicit more negative reactions to interventions during adolescence than in childhood. Hence, care is warranted in the application of any kind of contingency that can be readily observed by peers (e.g., a token economy) or where contingencies for the student's disruptive behavior could have a negative effect on peers (e.g., a group contingency). In addition, physically oriented strategies, such as time-out procedures and mild restraint, are poor options in general, but even more so when dealing with defiant adolescents who may be physically larger than intervening adults (Evans, Pelham, & Grudberg, 1995).

Implications for Treatment

Intervention efficiency and the developmental level of students are important considerations in designing intervention packages for adolescents with ADHD and/or LD. Moreover, interventions should focus on socially valid objectives (e.g., improvement in academic grades, decrease in verbal confrontations and physical fights with peers and adults) that diminish emotional distress and support areas of social and academic impairment. As adolescents approach adulthood, a focus on building independence is particularly important. Thus, it is critical for adolescents to be directly involved in the design and implementation of interventions, whenever possible.

In light of these considerations, several interventions are reviewed in this chapter that have these three features in common:

1. They require minimal teacher time.
2. They target functionally relevant skills.
3. They help students develop self-regulatory skills.

The interventions to be reviewed include self-monitoring (Reid, Trout, & Schartz, 2005), daily report cards (Evans & Pelham, 1991), check-in/check-out (Filter et al., 2007), and several academic interventions including training in effective note taking (Evans et al., 1995).

SELF-MONITORING

Description

Frequent transitions between classrooms and teachers, and the relatively unmonitored storage of textbooks, folders, notebooks, gym gear, and the like in a locker outside of the classroom necessitate organizational skills and independence not required in typical primary grade settings. Middle school students increasingly are required to work independently to keep track of homework and belongings. Moreover, punctuality, classroom preparedness, and completing assignments on time increasingly are expected (Gureasko-Moore, DuPaul, & White, 2006). Teachers often are not inclined to make classroom modifications or specifically teach classroom preparation skills. For adolescents with ADHD and/or LD, organizational skills, independent work habits, transitional capability, behavior regulation, and classroom preparedness all are areas of particular difficulty. Such students often enter class unprepared for the day's activities, in part due to a failure to write down assignments and to bring with them the materials required for in-class learning activities (e.g., notebooks, protractors, calculators). In addition, students often fail to complete homework assignments or to complete them on schedule (DuPaul & Stoner, 2003).

Self-monitoring interventions can help students learn to manage their time and organize their materials (Pfiffner, Barkley, & DuPaul, 2006; Shimabukuro, Prater, & Jenkins, 1999). Self-monitoring can also assist students to manage classroom transitions effectively (Stecker, Whinnery, & Fuchs, 1996). Managing classroom transitions can be particularly important for students with ADHD and/or LD, as they often miss class time for remedial instruction. This intervention approach involves training students to observe and record their own behavior. The act of recording one's own behavior can serve as immediate feedback, which can have a positive influence on future behavior (e.g., Mace, Belfiore, & Hutchinson, 2001). For example, students can be taught to use a checklist to ensure they bring home the materials necessary to complete their homework. Such a procedure can be used alone or in combination with a self-reinforcement procedure (Barkley et al., 1990). Self-monitoring interventions have three advantages.

1. The intervention approach fosters student awareness and helps to develop self-regulated behavior.
2. Because the intervention is maintained by the student, it is less demanding of teachers whose time with individual students is limited (Cole, 1992).
3. Self-monitoring allows for increased mobility, developing skills that generalize across school settings.

Intervention Procedures

A self-monitoring intervention begins with an evaluation of the student's problem behaviors. Target behaviors are selected and specifically defined to facilitate monitoring (e.g., homework or task completion, classroom readiness). Target behaviors then are positively worded on a self-monitoring checklist. (See Figure 17.1.) These target behaviors must be well-defined to allow explicit behavioral measurement and to ensure consistent follow-through (Power, Karustis, & Habboushe, 2001). In self-management (a variant of self-monitoring), student ratings are compared against a criterion. Here, teachers complete the same checklists as students, and the student receives regular feedback on the accuracy of recording.

An initial meeting between the student and consultant should identify and discuss the importance of the behaviors being targeted. In this session, the checklist should be

---

Classroom Preparation Behavior Checklist for: Tommy

Date: 11/3/11   **Class:** Math

	Yes	No
Was I in my seat when the bell rang?	■	☐
Did I have a pencil and paper on the desk?	■	☐
Did I have my textbook on the desk and open at the beginning of the lesson?	■	☐
Did I turn in my homework?	☐	■
Did I answer each item on the homework assignment?	☐	■

Classroom Preparation Behavior Checklist: Tommy

Date: 11/3/11   **Class:** Science

	Yes	No
Was I in my seat when the bell rang?	■	☐
Did I have a pencil and paper on the desk?	■	☐
Did I have my textbook on the desk and open at the beginning of the lesson?	☐	■
Did I turn in my homework?	☐	■
Did I answer each item on the homework assignment?	■	☐

Classroom Preparation Behavior Checklist: Tommy

Date: 11/3/11   **Class:** Social Studies

	Yes	No
Was I in my seat when the bell rang?	■	☐
Did I have a pencil and paper on the desk?	■	☐
Did I have my textbook on the desk and open at the beginning of the lesson?	☐	■
Did I turn in my homework?	■	☐
Did I answer each item on the homework assignment?	■	☐

Figure 17.1   Self-Monitoring Checklist Example

introduced and explained, citing specific examples for each item. It is especially important for both student and consultant to agree on the behaviors being monitored; failing to do so will decrease ownership and consistent execution of the intervention. The student's teachers should be notified before the start of the intervention and informed of their role in comparing the student's checklist with their own.

Initially, the consultant should meet the student daily to assess the student's implementation of the checklist. The consultant should comment on the student's conformity to desired behaviors by comparing student and teacher ratings, commending the student on compliance with goals and offering suggestions in areas where the goal was not met. These meetings should continue until the student is capable of demonstrating all of the target behaviors at least 80% of the time. Once this criterion has been achieved, meeting frequency can decrease to alternate days, then once a week. Although rewards contingent on behavioral improvement may help reinforce positive behavior during self-monitoring (Creel, Fore, & Boon, 2006), similar levels of academic and behavioral improvement have been found to occur without the presence of such rewards (Shimabukuro et al., 1999).

Outcomes

Although few studies have addressed the effectiveness of self-monitoring for adolescents with ADHD and/or LD, the overall academic and behavioral findings are promising (for review, see Reid, Trout, & Schartz, 2005). Adolescent self-monitoring intervention studies involving groups of three to four 12-year-old students (Creel et al., 2006; Gureasko-Moore et al., 2006; Shimabukuro et al., 1999; Stecker et al., 1996) and eight 13- to 16-year-olds (Trammel, Schloss, & Alper, 1994) have targeted classroom preparedness (Creel et al., 2006; Gureasko-Moore et al., 2006, Trammel et al., 1994), academic accuracy, productivity, on-task behavior (Shimabukuro et al., 1999), and transition time (Stecker et al., 1996). Trammel et al. (1994) found that self-monitoring increased homework completion from 0–2 to 4–6 assignments turned in per day. Shimabukuro et al. (1999) found that using this intervention with adolescents with ADHD and LD improved academic performance, doubling academic productivity and increasing work accuracy from 47–67% to 71–89%. Self-monitoring interventions have also produced immediate and sustainable reductions in the classroom transition times of these students (Stecker et al., 1996). Students with ADHD also indicated that self-monitoring allowed them to realize the importance of coming to class prepared (Creel et al., 2006). Teachers consistently reported that self-monitoring was easy to implement, particularly because doing so required little time (Creel et al., 2006; Shimabukuro et al., 1999).

These dramatic increases in classroom preparation and organizational skills occurred almost immediately after the intervention was implemented and have been found to be readily maintained even after all aspects of the intervention were systematically faded out over time (Creel et al., 2006; Gureasko-Moore et al., 2006). The intrinsic rewards of classroom success appear to promote students' continuation of strategies for productivity and preparedness (Creel et al., 2006).

Limitations

Although the empirical evidence for self-monitoring interventions for students with ADHD is encouraging, to our knowledge all studies have focused only on young adolescent males, making generalizations to older and female students tenuous. Moreover, the majority of studies has involved small numbers of three to four students (Creel et al., 2006; Gureasko-Moore et al., 2006; Rogevich & Perin, 2008; Shimabukuro et al, 1999) or have been conducted in atypical school populations or environments (Rogevich & Perin, 2008). Although time required for initial and assessment meetings is relatively minimal (occurring for several minutes a day at its peak), the amount of time still may constitute a barrier for overextended or reluctant teachers or support staff.

DAILY REPORT CARDS

Daily report cards have a long history in the treatment of ADHD (DuPaul & Eckert, 1997; Pelham, Wheeler, & Chronis, 1998). The daily report card itself consists of a list of clearly defined behaviors targeted for intervention, which can be rated by teachers on a scale (e.g., Riley-Tillman, Chafouleas, & Briesch, 2007). In some versions specific goals are listed for each behavioral target (e.g., follows directions with fewer than 2 reminders), and teachers complete a checklist to record whether each daily goal has been reached or not (e.g., Fabiano et al., 2010), although Likert-type scales and/or frequency counts also have been used (see Chafouleas, Riley-Tillman, & McDougal, 2002). In typical daily report card interventions, teachers provide immediate feedback to students for each target behavior and administer liberal praise to students for working toward goals. The daily report card can be carried by the student from class to class and is taken home to be reviewed and signed by parents. Parent signatures record that the student followed the procedure. Finally, parents provide the student with rewards contingent on the attainment of daily goals (e.g., time on the Internet).

Although no studies have examined the use of daily report cards specifically for adolescents with ADHD or LD, the intervention offers four potential advantages for this population worthy of consideration.

1. The procedure is flexible, enabling students to receive regular feedback from teachers regarding their performance in several areas of classroom functioning.
2. Parents receive daily information about student classroom performance, which provides an ongoing forum for teacher-parent communication. Because adolescents with ADHD and/or LD often experience significant problems in classroom

behavior and academic progress, this schedule of communication is preferable to waiting for a parent-teacher conference or an end-of-the-term report card.

3. Daily report cards address some of the developmental and practical considerations mentioned earlier because the procedure involves limited teacher time. In addition, reinforcement for appropriate school behavior is provided in the home as opposed to the school setting, thereby bypassing the need to single the student out in front of peers.

4. The data provided by teachers on the daily report card can serve as a measure of student response to the intervention (Pelham, Burrows-MacLean et al., 2005; Pelham, Fabiano, & Massetti, 2005; Riley-Tillman et al., 2007).

Several online resources are available to assist in the design and implementation of daily report cards (e.g., http://ccf.buffalo.edu; www.directbehaviorratings.com; www.interventioncentral.org).

Outcomes

To our knowledge, no studies of daily report cards have focused solely on adolescents with ADHD or LD. Most studies have focused on children with ADHD and have examined daily report cards as one part of multicomponent interventions (parent training, summer treatment, or classroom management) (Pelham et al., 1998). However, given the positive findings associated with daily report cards and their ease of use, they have been recommended as first-line intervention for students presenting with ADHD (Pelham & Fabiano, 2008) and make sense as an intervention component for students with learning problems, particularly those who demonstrate classroom behavior problems.

Recently, Fabiano et al. (2010) examined the effectiveness of daily report cards in a randomized controlled clinical trial of 6- to 12-year-old children with ADHD receiving special education services. In this study students' Individualized Education Plan (IEP) goals and objectives were utilized to develop targets for intervention, and effects were examined over one year of intervention. Dependent measures were administered to 33 students receiving the daily report card intervention and 30 control students. Results indicated significant effects favoring the daily report card group on progress toward IEP goals and measures of classroom behavior, and academic productivity. Unfortunately, effects on standardized tests of academic skills were not statistically significant.

Limitations

Although daily report cards offer much promise as a feasible and efficient intervention, the lack of data examining the effectiveness of the intervention in isolation in adolescent populations is a significant limitation. Several features enhance the probability of success with a daily report card system. Between 3 and 8 attainable behavioral goals should be specified that are linked to the needs of an individual student (e.g., inter-actions with classmates may be targeted if the child is prone to arguing and fighting with peers). These behavioral targets should be operationally defined, include the goal for intervention, and be readily observable for the teacher(s) who are to complete the forms. The student should be involved in the process of identifying target behaviors to enhance motivation toward goal attainment. Likewise the student should be involved in the selection of daily and weekly reinforcers in order to identify the most salient reinforcers and to encourage him or her to cooperate with the intervention. To ensure positive behavior change, a home token reinforcement program can be arranged to enable the "purchase" of backup reinforcers (e.g., household privileges, television time, spending a night at a friend's home).

The complexity of secondary schools compared to elementary schools makes this intervention more difficult to implement with adolescents than with young children. The presence of multiple teachers for each child and the ability of adolescents to defy and sabotage systems such as these require those attempting to use daily report cards to address many practical obstacles. Selecting individual teachers who report problems and are willing to follow the procedures consistently is recommended over trying to implement a daily report card system for all of a student's teachers. Finally, in cases where students cannot be relied on to bring the daily report card to and from school, e-mail or telephone communication directly to the parents may be a necessary adaptation.

CHECK-IN/CHECK-OUT

Description

Check-in/check-out (CICO) has received support as a targeted intervention embed-ded within schools implementing school-wide positive behavior support. The method focuses on the development of student self-regulation and shares elements with both self-monitoring and daily report cards. It may be well suited for adolescents with ADHD and/or LD who may not yet have developed levels of self-regulation necessary to be successful in the aforementioned self-monitoring intervention. CICO involves a teacher or staff member providing ongoing coaching, monitoring, and feedback in an effort to develop the students' ability to independently monitor their own activi-ties (Pfiffner et al., 2006). As students progress in the intervention, support is gradually faded, and monitoring shifts from adult to student. CICO consists of three components:

1. A short meeting with the coordinating adult at the beginning of the day to set daily goals and at the end of the day to review behavior
2. A point card on which teachers award points for attaining goals and provide feedback to the student
3. Rewards for earning a predetermined number of points (Crone, Horner, & Hawken, 2004)

Intervention Procedures

CICO can be designed to address any number of academic issues for adolescents with ADHD and/or LD, but existing literature has focused on either organization (Fischer & Barkley, 2006) or academic behavioral outcomes (Crone et al., 2004). Both variations center around one of the adolescent's teachers or a specific staff member acting as a coordinator to provide brief contact and feedback throughout the day.

Organization Check-in/Check-out

Organizational skills, which many teachers assume to be implicit, are a particular difficulty for many adolescents with ADHD transitioning into middle school (Campbell & Anderson, 2008). CICO addresses these skill deficits by having a coordinator serve as a mentor, or "coach," meeting for 3 to 5 minutes 3 times each day to help keep the adolescent organized (Barkley, 2006). Meetings serve the purpose of helping with student organization; mentors make sure students have the books and assignments needed for classes and check whether any homework assignments have been copied down. At the end of the day, the mentor makes sure students have all the necessary books and assignments they need to bring home with them.

Behavioral Check-in/Check-out

Adolescents with ADHD frequently transition into middle or high school with histories of behavioral difficulties resulting from academic failure. CICO can target disruptive behaviors by utilizing brief meetings throughout the day involving the coordinator monitoring and providing feedback regarding the adolescent's behavior goals. This intervention consists of five steps:

1. The coordinator and adolescent meet to establish the current areas of concern involving behavioral issues that may be affecting the student's academic performance. The coordinator and student define behavioral goals that the student can work to achieve in order to help produce a successful school day. The coordinator establishes with the student when and where future meetings will occur throughout the day, and introduces a behavior rating sheet (see Figure 17.2). Students can use this sheet to rate how they feel they did throughout certain periods of the day.

2. Short, positively focused meetings with the CICO coordinator occur throughout each day. Behavior goals should be set in a meeting at the beginning of each day, and outcomes should be reviewed at the end of the day. Additional meeting times throughout the day can be added if the adolescent's behavior initially requires more frequent evaluation.

3. During these predetermined times, the coordinator can allot points for meeting defined behavior goals and also provide feedback to the student.

CICO Record

Name: *Tyrone*   Date: *10/15/11*

3 = great, 2 = okay, 1 = hard time

Check-In				Science			
Safe	③	2	1	Safe	3	②	1
Responsible	3	②	1	Responsible	3	②	1
Respectful	3	②	1	Respectful	3	②	1

French				At Check-Out			
Safe	③	2	1	Safe	③	2	1
Responsible	3	2	①	Responsible	③	2	1
Respectful	3	2	①	Respectful	③	2	1

Today's point goal: 25

Today's total points: 27

___X___ I met my goal today _____ I had a hard day

One thing I did really well today was: ___I made it to classes on time___

Something I will work on tomorrow is: ___Not talking back to my teachers___

Comments:

Figure 17.2   CICO Behavior Sheet Example

4. Tangible and intangible rewards can be given for earning a predetermined number of points. A reward criterion of achieving 80% or more of the daily total possible points has been shown to have positive outcomes (Hawken & Horner, 2003).

5. Frequency of checks throughout the day can be reduced gradually as the adolescent shows behavioral improvement, eventually leading to complete behavioral self-monitoring (Crone et al., 2004).

Effective feedback and communication between coordinator and student is a key component to the success of behavioral CICO. Effective implementation of this intervention has been shown to both decrease disciplinary referrals (Filter et al., 2007) and reduce overall problem behaviors in the classroom (Hawken & Horner, 2003).

Outcomes and Limitations

CICO has been shown to decrease classroom problem behavior and increase academic engagement primarily in elementary school children (Filter et al., 2007). The intervention has yielded modest reductions in middle school students' classroom problem behaviors (Hawken & Horner, 2003), but empirical evidence for CICO's effectiveness during late adolescence is minimal. Unfortunately, empirical evidence specifically supporting the implementation of CICO for adolescents with ADHD is virtually nonexistent. Anecdotal accounts of CICO in similar settings suggest that providing ongoing coaching, monitoring, and feedback will aid adolescents with ADHD in developing the behavioral and/or organizational skills they need for academic success.

CICO focuses adult attention toward appropriate behavior, making it most successful for students who enjoy positive interactions with adults, or whose problem behavior is maintained by peer or adult attention and who find adult attention reinforcing. This intervention would likely be less effective for adolescents who have problems with task avoidance (Campbell & Anderson, 2008) or do not find adult attention reinforcing (Hawken & Horner, 2003).

ACADEMIC INTERVENTIONS

Medication studies have demonstrated short-term academic gains for adolescents taking stimulant medication (Evans et al., 2001), but these reports reveal that medication alone typically is inadequate and some adolescents show little or no gains. Unfortunately, even though adolescents with ADHD may qualify for special education plans that are supposed to include evidence-based interventions, there has been very little intervention research concerning the efficacy of academic interventions for this population.

Given the scarcity of academic intervention studies focusing on adolescents with ADHD, it is necessary to consider upward extensions of interventions that have been successful in younger populations. We briefly review several such interventions, address potential barriers to their implementation with adolescents, and provide considerations for addressing them.

Class-wide peer tutoring (Greenwood, Delquadri, & Carta, 1988) involves providing instruction to all students in a classroom about the role of a tutor and tutee in the practice of an academic task. Then students take turns completing tasks (e.g., reading passages, math problems) and providing encouragement and corrective feedback. Students with ADHD participate in the same way as the rest of their classmates. Using an ABAB reversal design (where A represents baseline phases and B represents intervention phases), DuPaul, Ervin, Hook, and McGoey (1998) evaluated this technique and reported improvements in test scores for elementary school age children with and without ADHD. Although initial findings are encouraging, additional research is needed to refine procedures and identify potential moderators and mediators of treatment response. Furthermore, there is a need to adapt and evaluate peer tutoring in secondary school settings. One important consideration in secondary school is that as children age, the achievement gap between students with and without learning problems tends to grow (Stanovich, 1986). Wide differences in achievement levels across the classroom may reduce the acceptability of the intervention for both students and teachers. One way to address this concern is to group for instructional level or to use class-wide peer tutoring to practice newly introduced skills. In any event, adolescents may be particularly sensitive to peer awareness of their academic difficulties, and so care must be taken in the application of this peer-mediated intervention.

Other techniques such as computer-assisted instruction and a variety of modifications to teacher instruction have received some research attention at the elementary school level. However, the evidence supporting them tends to be inconsistent, minimal, or not directly transferable to secondary schools (Raggi & Chronis, 2006).

One technique that has been evaluated with an adolescent sample is the application of a note-taking procedure to secondary school classrooms. Specifically, Evans, Pelham et al. (1995) adapted the Directed Notetaking Activity (Spires & Stone, 1989) for use with adolescent children with ADHD. Two studies were conducted in two successive years in the Summer Treatment Program (Pelham & Hoza, 1996) with middle school students diagnosed with ADHD in the context of an American history class that met for 1 hour 5 days per week. Students were taught to listen to teacher presentations and record notes organized by main ideas and details. The expectation to take notes in class improved on-task behavior, and taking notes and having them available during study hall increased scores on assignments. This intervention strategy has been shown to be effective with postsecondary students as well, increasing active engagement, abbreviation use, and overall note-taking organization of students with ADHD and mild LD (Boyle, 2001; Hughes & Suritsky, 1994). Middle school students have been taught to use these same note-taking techniques when reading class texts; however, this application of note-taking techniques has not been formally evaluated.

One advantage of note-taking training procedures is that they require students to be actively engaged in the spoken or written material in order to identify meaningful points that need to be organized and prioritized. This is in stark contrast to the passive and disorganized approach to learning that frequently characterizes these youth. The Evans, Pelham et al. (1995) study is demonstrative of how the provision of a facilitative structure can increase the academic engagement of students with ADHD. As a pilot study, it is a valuable addition to the scant research literature on academic interventions for students with ADHD.

INTERVENTIONS IN POSTSECONDARY SETTINGS

Very little research has been conducted examining psychosocial and educational interventions for college students with ADHD and/or LD. In fact, a recent review of the literature regarding functioning, assessment, and treatment of college students with ADHD (DuPaul, Weyandt, O'Dell, & Varejao, 2009) identified only three empirical studies examining academic interventions for students with ADHD alone or with comorbid LD. These studies examined the effects of strategy instruction to increase course-specific skills (Allsopp, Minskoff, & Bolt, 2005), assistive software to enhance reading performance (Hecker, Burns, Elkind, Elkind, & Katz, 2002), and extended time on the Scholastic AptitudeTest (Lindstrom & Gregg, 2007). Allsopp et al. found that the grade point averages of 18 students with ADHD (some of whom also had LD) increased by 0.55 on average as a function of receiving course-specific strategy instruction that was individualized to meet student needs. For example, students who needed assistance with reading comprehension were taught to use the RAP paraphrasing strategy, which involves R—read a paragraph; A—ask what the main ideas are; and P—put the ideas in your own words (Schumaker, Denton, & Deshler, 1984). Unfortunately, there was no control condition, and these results may be open to various threats to internal validity (e.g., history and maturation). Similar positive findings were obtained for assistive software; however, again, no control condition was included (Hecker et al., 2002). Thus, the effects of specific academic interventions for the postsecondary ADHD and LD population are relatively unknown and require extensive empirical study.

CONCLUSIONS

The provision of services to ameliorate the functional impairment of students with ADHD and/or LD in the secondary school setting is particularly challenging due to the developmental characteristics of adolescent students and the limited amount of time students spend with individual adults. The psychosocial treatment approaches reviewed in this chapter have initial empirical support in addressing school functioning in this population. Nevertheless, the literature examining school-based interventions for adolescents with ADHD is particularly sparse. Few studies examine treatment effects in general education settings—the classrooms in which most adolescents with ADHD are placed. Unfortunately, the strategies reviewed here stand in stark contrast to much of what currently is being done to help many of these youth. Individualized education plans and other well-intentioned efforts all too often reduce expectations for students with ADHD and/or LD without delineating an intervention plan to help them individually manage the academic and social demands required in secondary schools. Accommodations including extended time on tests, providing teacher-prepared copies of class notes to students, maintaining a list of assignments for students without requiring the student to gather or record the information, and placing students in alternative classrooms with reduced demands for independent functioning and academic productivity do little to prepare students for the transition to adulthood. At this time, there is no evidence that these techniques improve the functioning of adolescents with ADHD, yet their use appears to be widespread or, at the very least, more common than many of the interventions described here.

In this chapter we have provided information concerning interventions that require little teacher time, target key areas of functional impairment, and are designed to develop student self regulation. Although the need for additional research concerning school-based interventions for students with ADHD is palpable, initial results are encouraging, and the literature concerning younger children with the disorder offers many tools that may prove adaptable for older students. Moreover, particularly in the realm of academic skills, interventions that have demonstrated efficacy for students that do not necessarily have ADHD offer an additional pool of tools that might be considered for evaluation in samples of adolescents.

REFERENCES

Achenbach, T. M., Howell, C. T., & McConaughy, S. H. (1995). Six-year predictors of problems in a national sample of children and youth: II. Signs of disturbance. *Journal of the American Academy of Child and Adolescent Psychiatry, 34,* 488–498.

Allsopp, D. H., Minskoff, E. H., & Bolt, L. (2005). Individualized course-specific strategy instruction for college students with learning disabilities and ADHD: Lessons learned from a model demonstration project. *Learning Disabilities Research & Practice, 20,* 103–118.

American Psychiatric Association. (2000). *Diagnostic and statistical manual of mental disorders* (4th ed., Text Revision). Washington, DC: Author.

Ausubel, D. P. (2002). The adolescent peer culture. In D. P. Ausubel (Ed.), *Theory and problems of adolescent development* (3rd ed.; pp. 371–416). Lincoln, NE: Writers Club Press.

Barkley, R. A. (2005). Major life activity and health outcomes associated with Attention-Deficit/Hyperactivity Disorder. *Journal of Clinical Psychiatry, 63,* 10–15.

Barkley, R. A. (2006). *Attention-Deficit Hyperactivity Disorder: A handbook for diagnosis and treatment* (3rd edition). New York, NY: Guilford Press.

Barkley, R. A., Anastopoulos, A. D., Guevremont, D. C., & Fletcher, K. E. (1991). Adolescents with ADHD: Patterns of behavioral adjustment, academic functioning, and treatment utilization. *Journal of the American Academy of Child and Adolescent Psychiatry, 30,* 752–761.

Barkley, R. A., Fischer, M., Edelbrock, C. S., & Smallish, L. (1990). The adolescent outcome of hyperactive children diagnosed by research criteria, I: An 8-year prospective follow-up study. *Journal of the American Academy of Child and Adolescent Psychiatry, 29,* 546–557.

Barkley, R. A., Fischer, M., Smallish, L., & Fletcher, K. R. (2002). The persistence of attention deficit hyperactivity disorder into young adulthood as a function of reporting source and definition of disorder. *Journal of Abnormal Psychology, 111,* 279–289.

Barkley, R. A., Murphy, K. R., & Fischer, M. (2008). *ADHD in adults: What the science says.* New York, NY: Guilford.

Bender, W. N. (2008). *Learning disabilities: Characteristics, identification, and teaching strategies*. New York, NY: Pearson.

Biederman, J., Faraone, S. V., Taylor, A., Sienna, M., Williamson, S., & Fine, C. (1998). Diagnostic continuity between child and adolescent ADHD: Findings from a longitudinal clinical sample. *Journal of the American Academy of Child and Adolescent Psychiatry, 37*, 305–313.

Boyle, J. D. (2001). Enhancing the note-taking skills of students with mild disabilities. *Intervention in School and Clinic, 36*, 221–224.

Campbell, A., & Anderson, C. M. (2008). Enhancing effects of check-in/check-out with function-based support. *Behavior Disorders, 33*, 233–245.

Chafouleas, S. M., Riley-Tillman, T. C., & McDougal, J. L. (2002). Good, bad, or in-between: How does the daily report card rate? *Psychology in the Schools, 39*, 157–169.

Cole, C. L. (1992). Self-management interventions in the schools. *School Psychology Review, 21*, 188–192.

Creel, C., Fore, C., & Boon, R. T. (2006). Effects of self-monitoring on classroom preparedness skills of middle school students with attention deficit hyperactivity disorder. *Learning Disabilities: A Multidisciplinary Journal, 14*, 105–113.

Crone, D. A., Horner, R. H., & Hawken, L. (2004). *Responding to problem behavior in schools: The behavior education program*. New York, NY: Guilford Press.

Dey, A. N., Schiller, J. S., & Tai, D.A. (2004). Summary health statistics for U.S. children: National health interview survey, 2002. *National Center for Health Statistics. Vital Health Statistics, 10*(221), 1–78.

DuPaul, G. J. (2007). School-based interventions for students with attention deficit hyperactivity disorder: Current status and future directions. *School Psychology Review, 36*, 183–194.

DuPaul, G. J., & Eckert, T. L. (1998). Academic interventions for students with attention-deficit/hyperactivity disorder: A review of the literature. *Reading and Writing Quarterly: Overcoming Learning Difficulties, 14*, 59–82.

DuPaul, G. J., & Evans, S. W. (2008). School-based interventions for adolescents with ADHD. *Adolescent Medicine: State of the Art Reviews, 19*, 300–312.

DuPaul, G. J., Ervin, R. A., Hook, C. L., & McGoey, K. E. (1998). Peer tutoring for children with attention deficit hyperactivity disorder: Effects on classroom behavior and academic performance. *Journal of Applied Behavior Analysis, 31*, 579–592.

DuPaul, G. J., & Stoner, G. (2003). *ADHD in the schools: Assessment and intervention strategies* (2nd ed.). New York, NY: Guilford Press.

DuPaul, G. J., Weyandt, L. L., O'Dell, S. M., & Varejao, M. (2009). College students with ADHD: Current status and future directions. *Journal of Attention Disorders, 13*, 234–250.

Evans, S. W., Allen, J., Moore, S., & Strauss, V. (2005). Measuring symptoms and functioning of youth with ADHD in middle schools. *Journal of Abnormal Child Psychology, 33*, 695–706.

Evans, S. W., Langberg, J., Raggi, V., Allen, J., & Buvinger, E. C. (2005). Development of a school-based treatment program for middle school youth with ADHD. *Journal of Attention Disorders, 9,* 343–353.

Evans, S. W., & Pelham, W. E. (1991). Psychostimulant effects on academic and behavioral measures for ADHD junior high school students in a lecture format classroom. *Journal of Abnormal Child Psychology, 19,* 537–552.

Evans, S. W., Pelham, W. E., & Grudberg, M., V. (1995). The efficacy of notetaking to improve behavior and comprehension with ADHD adolescents. *Exceptionality, 5,* 1–7.

Evans, S. W., Pelham, W. E., Smith, B. H., Bukstein, O., Gnagy, E. M., Greiner, A. R., ... Baron-Myak, C. (2001). Dose-response effects of methylphenidate on ecologically-valid measures of academic performance and classroom behavior in adolescents with ADHD. *Experimental and Clinical Psychopharmacology, 9,* 163–175.

Evans, S. W., Serpell, Z. N., Schultz, B., & Pastor, D. (2007). Cumulative benefits of secondary school-based treatment of students with ADHD. *School Psychology Review, 36,* 256–273.

Evans, S. W., Vallano, G., & Pelham, W. E. (1995). Attention-Deficit Hyperactivity Disorder. In V. B. Van Hasselt & M. Hersen (Eds.), *Handbook of adolescent psychopathology. A guide to diagnosis and treatment* (pp. 589–617). New York, NY: Lexington Books.

Fabiano, G. A., Vujnovic, R. K., Pelham, W. E., Waschbusch, D. A., Massetti, G. M., Yu. J. et al. (2010). Enhancing the effectiveness of special education programming for children with attention deficit hyperactivity disorder using a daily report card. *School Psychology Review, 39,* 219–239.

Fischer, M., & Barkley, R. A. (2006). Young adult outcomes of children with hyperactivity: Leisure, financial, and social activities. *International Journal of Disability, Development and Education, 53,* 229–245.

Fischer, M., Barkley, R. A., Edelbrock, C. S., & Smallish, L. (1990). The adolescent outcome of hyperactive children diagnosed by research criteria: II. Academic, attentional, and neuropsychological outcomes. *Journal of Consulting and Clinical Psychology, 58,* 580–588.

Fischer, M., Barkley, R. A., Smallish, L., & Fletcher, K. (2002). Young adult follow-up of hyperactive children: Self-reported psychiatric disorders, comorbidity, and the role of childhood conduct problems. *Journal of Abnormal Child Psychology, 30,* 463–475.

Filter, K., McKenna, M., Benedict, E., Horner, R. H., Todd, A., & Watson, J. (2007). Check in/check out: a post-hoc evaluation of an efficient, secondary-level targeted intervention for reducing problem behaviors in schools. *Education and Treatment of Children, 30,* 69–84.

Francis, D. J., Shaywitz, S. E., Stuebing, K. K., Shaywitz, B. A., & Fletcher, J. M. (1996). Developmental lag versus deficit models of reading disability: A longitudinal, individual growth curves analysis. *Journal of Educational Psychology, 88,* 3–17.

Frazier, T. W., Youngstrom, E. A., Glutting, J. J., & Watkins, M. W. (2007). ADHD and achievement: Meta-analysis of the child, adolescent, and adult literatures and a concomitant study with college students. *Journal of Learning Disabilities, 40,* 49–65.

Greenwood, C. R, Delquadri, J., & Carta, J. J. (1988). *Classwide peer tutoring.* Seattle, WA: Educational Achievement Systems.

Gresham, F. M., MacMillan, D. L., & Bocian, K. M. (1997). Teachers as "tests": Differential validity of teacher judgments in identifying students at-risk for learning difficulties. *School Psychology Review, 26,* 47–60.

Gureasko-Moore, S., DuPaul, G. J., & White, G. P. (2006). The effects of self-management in general education classrooms on the organizational skills of adolescents with ADHD. *Behavior Modification, 30,* 159–183.

Hawken, L. S., & Horner, R. H. (2003). Evaluation of a targeted intervention within a schoolwide system of behavior support. *Journal of Behavioral Education, 12,* 225–240.

Hecker, L., Burns, L., Elkind, J., Elkind, K., & Katz, L. (2002). Benefits of assistive reading software for students with attention disorders. *Annals of Dyslexia, 52,* 243–272.

Hook, C. L., & DuPaul, G. J. (1999). Parent tutoring for students with Attention-Deficit/Hyperactivity Disorder: Effects on reading performance at home and school. *School Psychology Review, 28,* 60–75.

Hughes, C. A., & Suritsky, S. K. (1994). Note-taking skills of university students with and without learning disabilities. *Journal of Learning Disabilities, 27*(1), 20–24.

Kelley, M. L. (1990). *School-home Notes: Promoting children's classroom success.* New York, NY: Guilford Press.

Kuhne, M., & Wiener, J. (2000). Stability of social status of children with and without learning disabilities. *Learning Disability Quarterly, 17,* 140–153.

Lewis, K., & Taymans, J. A. (1992). An examination of autonomous functioning skills of adolescents with learning disabilities. *Career Development for Exceptional Individuals, 15*(1), 37–46.

Lindstrom, J. H., & Gregg, N. (2007). The role of extended time on the SAT® for students with learning disabilities and/or attention-deficit/hyperactivity disorder. *Learning Disabilities Research & Practice, 22,* 85–95.

Mace, F. C., Belfiore, P. J., & Hutchinson, J. M. (2001). Operant theory and research on self-regulation. In B. Zimmerman & D. Schunk (Eds.), *Learning and academic achievement: Theoretical perspectives* (pp. 39–65). Mahwah, NJ: Erlbaum.

Mannuzza, S., Gittelman-Klein, R., Bessler, A., Malloy, P., & LaPadula, M. (1993). Adult outcome of hyperactive boys: Educational achievement, occupational rank, and psychiatric status. *Archives of General Psychiatry, 50,* 565–576.

Margalit, M. (1998). Resilience models among individuals with learning disabilities: Proximal and distal influences. *Journal of Learning Disabilities, 31,* 173–181.

Martinez, R. S., & Semrud-Clikeman, M. (2004). Emotional adjustment and school functioning of young adolescents with multiple versus single learning disabilities. *Journal of Learning Disabilities, 37*(5), 411–420.

Molina, B., Pelham, W. E., Blumenthal, J., & Galiszewski, E. (1998). Agreement among teachers' behavior ratings of adolescents with a childhood history of Attention Deficit Hyperactivity Disorder. *Journal of Clinical Child Psychology, 27*, 330–339.

National Longitudinal Transition Study II. (2003). *National Center for Special Education Research at the Institute of Education Sciences*. Washington, DC: U.S. Department of Education.

Pelham, W. E., Burrows-MacLean, L., Gnagy, E. M., Fabiano, G. A., Coles, E. K., Tresco, K. E., . . . Hoffman, M. T. (2005). Transdermal methylphenidate, behavioral, and combined treatment for children with ADHD. *Experimental and Clinical Psychopharmacology, 13*, 111–126.

Pelham, W. E., & Fabiano, G. A. (2008). Evidence-based psychosocial treatment for ADHD: An update. *Journal of Clinical Child and Adolescent Psychology, 37*, 184–214.

Pelham, W. E., Fabiano, G. A., & Massetti, G. M. (2005). Evidence-based assessment of attention deficit hyperactivity disorder in children and adolescents. *Journal of Clinical Child and Adolescent Psychology, 3*, 449–476.

Pelham, W. E., & Hoza, B. (1996). Intensive treatment: a summer treatment program for children with ADHD. In E. D. Hibbs & P. S. Jensen (Eds.), *Psychosocial treatments for child and adolescent disorders: Empirically based strategies for clinical practice* (pp. 311–340). Washington, DC: American Psychological Association.

Pelham, W. E., Wheeler, T., & Chronis, A. (1998). Empirically supported psychosocial treatments for attention deficit hyperactivity disorder. *Journal of Clinical Child Psychology, 27*, 190–205.

Pfiffner, L. J., Barkley, R. A. & DuPaul, G. J. (2006). Treatment of ADHD in school settings. In R. A. Barkley (Ed.), *Attention-Deficit/Hyperactivity Disorder: A handbook for diagnosis and treatment* (3rd ed., pp. 547–589). New York, NY: Guilford Press.

Power, T. J., Karustis, J. L., & Habboushe, D. F. (2001). *Homework success for children with ADHD: A family-school intervention program*. New York, NY: Guilford Press.

Raggi, V. L., & Chronis, A. M. (2006). Interventions to address the academic impairment of children and adolescents with ADHD. *Clinical Child and Family Psychology Review, 9*, 85–111.

Reid, R., Trout, A. L., & Schartz, M. (2005). Self-regulation interventions for children with Attention Deficit/Hyperactivity Disorder. *Exceptional Children, 71*, 361–377.

Riley-Tillman, T. C., Chafouleas, S. M., & Briesch, A. M. (2007). A school practitioner's guide to using Daily Behavior Report Cards to monitor interventions. *Psychology in the Schools, 44*, 77–89.

Rogevich, M. E., & Perin, D. (2008). Effects on science summarization of a reading comprehension intervention for adolescents with behavior and attention disorders. *Exceptional Children, 74*, 135–154.

Schultz, B. K., Evans, S. W., & Serpell, Z. N. (2009). Preventing failure among middle school students with Attention Deficit Hyperactivity Disorder: A survival analysis. *School Psychology Review, 38*, 14–27.

Schumaker, J. B., Denton, P. H., & Deshler, D. D. (1984). *The paraphrasing strategy*. Lawrence, KS: University of Kansas Press.

Semrud-Clikeman, M., Biederman, J., Sprich-Buckminster, S., et al. (1992). Comorbidity between ADDH and learning disability: A review and report in a clinically referred sample. *Journal of the American Academy of Child & Adolescent Psychiatry, 31*(3), 439–448.

Shimabukuro, S. M., Prater, M. A., & Jenkins, A. (1999). The effects of self-monitoring of academic performance on students with learning disabilities and ADD/ADHD. *Education and Treatment of Children, 22*, 397–414.

Smith B. H., Waschbusch, D. A., Willoughby, M. T., & Evans S. (2003). The efficacy, safety, and practicality of treatments for adolescents with Attention-Deficit/ Hyperactivity Disorder (ADHD). *Clinical Child and Family Psychology Review, 3*, 243–267.

Spires, H. A., & Stone, D. P. (1989). The directed notetaking activity: A self-questioning approach. *Journal of Reading, 33*, 36–39.

Stanovich, K. E. (1986). Matthew effects in reading: Some consequences of individual differences in the acquisition of literacy. *Reading Research Quarterly, 21*, 360–406.

Stecker, P. M., Whinnery, K. W., & Fuchs, L. S. (1996). Self-recording during unsupervised academic activity: Effects on time spent out of class. *Exceptionality, 6*(3), 133–147.

Stimmel, G. L. (2009). Addressing the chronicity of ADHD across the life span: Implications for long-term adherence. *Psychiatric Times, 26*, 1–8.

Torgesen, J. K., & Burgess, S. R. (1998). Consistency of reading-related phonological processes throughout early childhood: Evidence from longitudinal-correlational and instructional studies. In J. Metsala & L. Ehri (Eds.), *Word recognition in beginning reading* (pp. 161–188). Hillsdale, NJ: Erlbaum.

Trammel, D. L., Schloss, P. J., & Alper, S. (1994). Using self-recording, evaluation, and graphing to increase completion of homework assignments. *Journal of Learning Disabilities, 27*(2), 75–81.

U.S. Department of Education, Institute of Education Science, National Center for Education Statistics. (2007). *Dropout rates in the U.S.: 1995*. Retrieved from: http:// nces.ed.gov/pubs2009/2009064.pdf

Weyandt, L., Iwaszuk, W., Fulton, K., Ollerton, M., Beatty, N., Fouts, H., . . . Greenlaw, C. (2003). The Internal Restlessness Scale: Performance of college students with and without ADHD. *Journal of Learning Disabilities, 36*, 382–389.

Willcutt, E. G., & Pennington, B. F. (2000). Comorbidity of reading disability and attention deficit/hyperactivity disorder: Differences by gender and subtype. *Journal of Learning Disabilities, 33*, 179–191.

Wilson, J. M., & Marcotte, A. C. (1996). Psychological adjustment and educational outcome in adolescents with a childhood diagnosis of attention deficit disorder. *Journal of the American Academy of Child and Adolescent Psychiatry, 35*, 579–587.

CHAPTER

18

Medications Affecting Behavior and Learning

ANTHONY L. ROSTAIN

INTRODUCTION

Pharmacologic management of older adolescents and adults with Attention-Deficit/ Hyperactivity Disorder (ADHD) and Learning Disabilities (LD) has become an integral part of the multimodal treatment approach that is now considered standard care. Perhaps because of the relatively short time in which ADHD has been studied in this age group, many questions remain about optimal medical approaches, especially for patients with comorbid medical or psychiatric conditions. Unlike studies in children, which are much more numerous and extend back over four decades, empirical trials of medications for adolescents and adults with ADHD are fewer in number and more limited in time and scope. There are also distinct challenges in conducting research in older patients with ADHD, including variable symptom presentation and duration of the disorder, diagnostic and functional heterogeneity (often due to the presence of comorbid conditions), greater reliance on self-report measures (as opposed to teacher and parent ratings) to assess treatment response, short-term study design, and the presence of a large set of variables (e.g., treatment adherence, physical health concerns, developmental differences, contextual influences) that make it difficult to generalize the findings of clinical trials to clinical practice.

This chapter provides a summary of clinical research findings and current trends in medication management of adolescents and adults with ADHD, a review of the mechanisms of action of the major pharmacologic agents currently in use, and a guide to introducing medication into the treatment setting. It emphasizes practical ways to integrate existing research studies with clinical judgment and patient preferences and advances some basic principles for working collaboratively with physicians and patients to promote successful outcomes. It begins with a brief review of evolving paradigms for understanding the neurobiology of ADHD, including new directions in thinking about executive functioning deficits and in psychopharmacologic research (i.e., pharmacogenomics, neuroimaging of medication action) that will undoubtedly influence the way medications are used to treat the disorder. The extant literature regarding medications for learning disorders in older adolescents and adults is very sparse, and it is reviewed and commented on. Given the limitations of what is known about LD medication treatment, the bulk of this chapter focuses on medications for ADHD in this age group.

PATHOPHYSIOLOGY OF ADHD

Over the past 25 years, research into the pathophysiology of ADHD has seen a convergence of findings from various scientific disciplines (e.g., neuropsychology, neuroimaging, neuropharmacology, genetics) supporting a cognitive neuroscience model of the disorder. Although there still is no single unifying theory of ADHD, numerous authors have proposed that ADHD is a developmental disorder of executive functioning, involving underperformance of key neural circuits that subserve alertness, orientation, attention, motor learning and control, inhibition, and working memory (see Arnsten, 2005; Arnsten & Li, 2009; Barkley, 2006; Brown, 2005; Castellanos, Sonuga-Barke, Milham, & Tannock, 2006; Makris, Biederman, Monuteaux, & Seidman, 2009; Nigg & Casey, 2005; Pliszka, McCracken, & Maas, 1996). It is beyond the scope of this chapter to review all the existing scientific evidence in support of the cognitive neuroscience paradigm of ADHD; however, it is worthwhile to examine those that are most salient to pharmacologic treatment.

Catecholamine dysregulation, particular dopamine and norepinephrine functioning, has long been postulated to be causative of ADHD. Zametkin and Rapoport (1987), in a prescient review of the pathophysiology of ADHD, advanced this model:

> Given the current interest in frontal lobe function in this disorder and the intricate relationship between cortex and striatum, a comprehensive model of the pathophysiology of this disorder and drug action should postulate the inhibitory influences of frontal cortical activity, predominantly noradrenergic acting on lower (striatal) structures that are driven by both direct dopamine agonists and controlled or modulated by higher inhibitory structures sensitive to adrenergic agonists. Such a model might account for the wide array of agents effective in treating symptoms of ADHD. Different sites of dysfunction in this "circuit" would account for the array of presenting symptomatology from the pure attentional to the more impulsive. (p. 684)

Since then, dozens of studies have confirmed essential elements of this model while at the same time elucidating details of the underlying circuitry of ADHD.

It appears that neural circuits governing attention, executive functions, motor regulation, reward, and emotional regulation are to varying degrees less efficient at performing their functions in individuals with ADHD. The clinical heterogeneity of the disorder makes it very difficult to delineate the nature and extent of these "circuit malfunctions" and their precise correlations with symptomatology, disease course, and treatment response. Despite these limitations, however, great progress is being made in mapping central nervous system (CNS) anatomic and functional pathology in ADHD.

Pliszka, McCracken, and Maas (1996) advanced an interesting model of ADHD focusing on imbalances of catecholamine functioning in two primary attentional systems: a posterior one (that mediates alerting and orienting) and an anterior one (that subserves executive functioning). Insufficient responsiveness of the posterior attention system to novel stimuli is proposed to be due to a hypoactive central norepinephrine system (via the locus coeruleus). The dopaminergically mediated anterior attention system may also be underactive, leading to poor planning, faulty working memory, lack of attention to details, and inefficient problem solving. The peripheral epinephrine system is hypothesized to play a role in mediating individual responses to psychostimulant medication. This model integrates neurochemistry, neuroanatomy, and neurophysiology and also explains why neurotransmitter studies have failed to show a specific deficiency pattern in patients with ADHD.

A recent paper by Makris et al. (2009) advances a neuroanatomical substrates model of ADHD that maps clinical symptoms onto neural networks. For instance, problems pertaining to hyperactivity are hypothesized to localize to a network involving the dorsolateral prefrontal cortex, dorsal anterior cingulate cortex, supplementary motor area, caudate, and cerebellum (see Figure 18.1)—the so-called fronto-striatal-cerebellar circuit. Impulsivity is proposed to arise from damage to or dysfunction in the circuit involving the orbital frontal cortex, the perigenual anterior cingulated cortex, the nucleus accumbens, and the cerebellar vermis. Inattention is postulated to involve the dorsolateral prefrontal cortex, dorsal anterior cingulate, inferior parietal lobule/temporo-occipito-parietal junction, thalamus, and cerebellar hemisphere. Emotionality (i.e., emotional dysregulation) is proposed to result from disruptions of the circuit involving the perigenual anterior cingulated cortex, orbital frontal cortex, amygdalae, and cerebellar vermis. These authors go on to suggest that the clinical heterogeneity seen in ADHD arises from different patterns of circuit functioning and that better characterization of these systems will enable researchers to identify valid structural endophenotypes that will assist the work of identifying links between genes and behavior.

Even more pertinent to a consideration of pharmacologic treatment of ADHD, Arnsten (2009) proposes a model that emphasizes prefrontal cortex (PFC) dysfunction

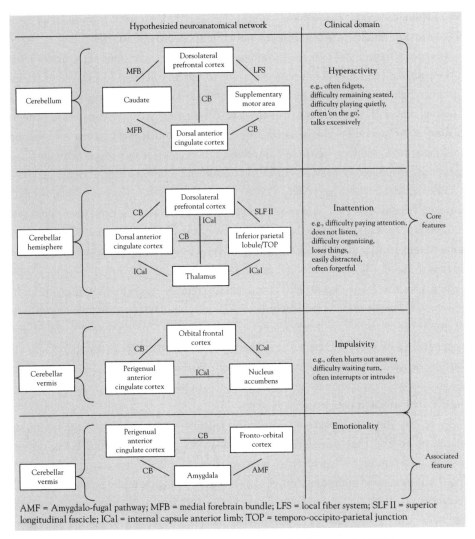

Figure 18.1   Conceptual Model of the Neuroanatomical Substrates of ADHD
Source: Makris, N., Biederman, J., Monuteaux, C., & Seidman, L. J. (2009). Toward Conceptualizing a Neural Systems-Based Anatomy of Attention-Deficit/Hyperactivity Disorder. *Developmental Neuroscience,* 31, 38. doi: 10.1159/000207492. Used with permission.

in ADHD. The neuropsychological deficits seen in ADHD strongly suggest the involvement of the PFC (especially in the right hemisphere), where classical studies of patients with damage to this area show patterns of loss of working memory, forgetfulness, increased susceptibility to interference, distractibility, poor concentration, impulsivity, and poor organization. The PFC has been shown to regulate attention based on relevance (salience), suppress processing of irrelevant stimuli, enhance processing of relevant stimuli, sustain attention on relevant sources, and shift attention to relevant dimensions. The PFC functions to screen distractions, maintain purposeful attention, regulate emotions and behavior, and support the brain's executive functions (i.e., planning, forethought, and the organization of complex behavior). The cellular matrix of the PFC is largely composed of pyramidal neurons that are organized into higher-order networks that utilize glutamate as a primary neurotransmitter. These cells are also rich in dopamine (DA) and norephinephrine (NE) receptors that are highly innervated by inputs from other brain regions (e.g., brainstem arousal systems). The PFC is extremely sensitive to alterations in DA and NE levels, as numerous pharmacologic studies have demonstrated. It appears that NE enhances PFC functioning by strengthening functional connections among cells in critical neural networks and by enabling them to maintain firing for longer periods of time (i.e., "signal strengthening"). By contrast, DA stimulates D1 receptors in the PFC, which, in turn, weaken inappropriate connections (i.e., "noise reduction"). Depletion of DA or NE leads to profound reductions in PFC functioning; enhancement of DA and NE levels (to a moderate degree) improves functioning. These differences are described by an inverted-U plot (see Figure 18.2) such that extremes of these two catecholamines are marked by worsening PFC performance. It is important to keep this in mind when considering medication choice and dosage strategies in treating ADHD.

Another set of insights into the pathophysiology of ADHD comes from the work of Volkow et al. (2009a), who have studied motivation/reward pathways, particularly the nucleus accumbens and related brain regions, of patients with cocaine and other addictive

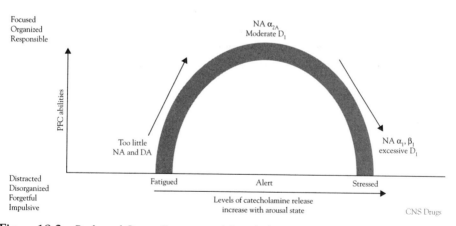

Figure 18.2   Prefrontal Cortex Function and Catecholamine Receptor Stimulation

The prefrontal cortex (PFC) is very sensitive to its neurochemical environment. The catecholamines are released in the PFC according to an arousal state, based on the relevance of the stimuli occurring in the environment. Either too little or too much catecholamine release impairs PFC function. Moderate levels of noradrenaline (NA) engage postsynaptic α2A-receptors to improve PFC function, while high levels engage α1 and β, which impair PFC function. Animal studies suggest that therapeutic doses of stimulants improve PFC function by increasing endogenous NA and dopamine (DA) stimulation of α2A and D1 receptors, respectively.

Source: Arnsten, A. F. (2009). Toward a New Understanding of Attention-Deficit Hyperactivity Disorder Pathophysiology. *CNS Drugs, 23*(1), 37. Used with permission.

disorders. They found abnormalities in the mesoaccumbens dopamine pathway (composed of DA cells in the midbrain and their projections to the nucleus accumbens) in actively addicted patients. Recently this group investigated reward pathways in adults with ADHD by measuring D2/D3 receptor and dopamine transporter (DAT) availability in these same anatomical areas. A marked reduction in these dopamine markers was seen and linked to inattention symptoms in ADHD subjects.

Pharmacogenomics is a rapidly evolving field of inquiry into the interaction of multiple gene functions and drug effects. The contribution of several candidate genes to the onset and course of ADHD has been the focus of genetic research over the past two decades. Specifically, polymorphisms in two dopamine receptors (DRD4 and DRD5), the dopamine transporter (SLC6A3), the enzyme dopa-β-hydroxylase (DBH), the serotonin receptor (HTR1B), the serotonin transporter (SLC6A4), and the synaptosomal-associated protein 25kDa (SNAP25) have been implicated in the etiology of the disorder (Faraone et al., 2005; Swanson et al., 2007). New susceptibility studies have identified catechol-O-methyltransferase (COMT), adrenergic α_{2A}-receptor (ADRA2A), and noradrenaline transporter protein (SLC6A2) polymorphisms as playing a role as well.

Using these findings, investigators have attempted to link these genetic polymorphisms to medication outcomes in an effort to predict which patients will respond best to which pharmacologic agents (see Froehlich, McGough, & Stein, 2010, for an excellent review). Recent research findings are contradictory at best, making it difficult to use these particular candidate genes to predict treatment outcome. Future studies will need to integrate the role of drug-metabolizing enzymes (especially the cytochrome P450 system) along with candidate genes for ADHD into a more nuanced predictive scheme. It is likely that in the near future, clinicians will be able to utilize pharmacogenomic data to prescribe ADHD medication in a more rational, systematic fashion than the current trial-and-error approach.

REVIEW OF THE CLINICAL TRIALS LITERATURE

Medication treatment of ADHD has been comprehensively studied in children for more than 35 years (Barkley, 2006; Biederman & Spencer, 2008; Brown, 2005; Findling, 2008; Wigal, 2009). Fewer studies have been conducted in adolescent and adult ADHD populations, although the past decade has seen a marked increase in the number of published clinical trials. This section reviews randomized, placebo-controlled studies, using either a parallel or a crossover design, of stimulants and nonstimulants. It is important to situate our current knowledge of these agents in a historical context in order to give the reader a better appreciation for the complexities of this body of research. In so doing, it is possible to examine how clinical thinking about patient care has evolved over the past several decades.

Methylphenidate

The first published study of immediate release (IR) methylphenidate (MPH) in adult ADHD was conducted by Wood et al. in 1976. A total of 15 subjects were given a mean dose of 0.4 mg/kg daily over a 4-week period with a response rate of 73% reported. Limitations of this study include the small sample size, the lack of clear diagnostic criteria used, and the absence of standardized outcome measures. Mild side effects were seen in this study.

Mattes, Boswell, and Oliver (1984) conducted a 6-week crossover trial of IR MPH with 26 subjects using a higher mean dose (0.7 mg/kg) than the prior study. The response rate to medication was 25% with mild adverse effects reported. The discrepancy in response rate seen was attributed to the moderate rate of comorbidity of this sample. Interestingly, response rates seen in subsequent studies have varied between roughly 25% and 75%.

Wender, Reimherr, Wood, and Ward (1985) used a crossover design with 37 subjects over 5 weeks using a mean dose of 0.6 mg/kg/day. There was a 57% response rate in the treatment arm compared to 11% in the placebo arm of the study on symptoms of inattention, overactivity, impulsivity, and emotional lability. Interestingly, this sample had a high rate of dysthymia (68%) and cyclothymia (22%).

Gualtieri, Ondrusek, and Finley (1985) studied 8 adult ADHD subjects in a crossover design trial who received an average of 0.6 mg/kg/day and whose plasma level of MPH was measured. The authors reported "mild-to-moderate" response and no association between clinical response and plasma drug levels. The small sample of this study implies that reporting response rates would not be scientifically valid. However, the fact that clinical response was *not* linked to plasma levels of MPH is of both clinical and scientific interest.

Spencer et al. (1995) conducted a 7-week crossover trial of 3 doses of IR MPH (0.5, 0.75, and 1.0 mg/kg/d) with 23 subjects. An overall response rate of 78% was reported (compared to 4% placebo response) with a dose relationship demonstrated (i.e., higher dose was associated with better response). As in the prior study, plasma level of medication was not correlated with clinical response. In addition, neither gender nor comorbidity was associated with outcome of treatment.

Kuperman et al. (2001) used a parallel group design to study 30 subjects over 7 weeks. The mean daily dose was 0.9 mg/kg/d. The response rate was 50% for MPH versus 27% for placebo (higher than usually seen in ADHD treatment studies).

Bouffard, Hechtman, Minde, and Iaboni-Kassab (2003) studied 30 subjects in a 9-week placebo-controlled crossover trial of IR MPH administered on a 3-times-a day (t.i.d.) schedule at 2 different doses (10 mg and 15 mg). For the first 2 weeks, subjects received a total of 30 mg/d (or placebo), and rating scales were obtained on the 14th day of the trial. For the second 2 weeks, the dose was increased to 45 mg/d, and ratings were obtained at the end of this time period. The researchers found a 63% response rate with both doses of MPH, although the placebo response rate was not reported. Performance on the continuous performance test was improved on MPH compared to baseline and to placebo.

Koolj et al. (2004) studied 45 subjects using a crossover design in a trial lasting 3 weeks that compared 2 dosage levels of IR MPH: 0.5 and 1.0 mg/kg/d. The response rate varied between 38–51% for MPH versus 7–18% for placebo. This was the first European study of adult ADHD, and it confirmed findings from the U.S. studies.

Carpentier et al. (2005) used a multiple crossover design to study 25 subjects with comorbid Substance Use Disorder (SUD) who received an average of 0.6 mg/kg/d. No significant differences were seen between MPH response (35%) and placebo (20%) as measured by the Attention-Deficit/Hyperactivity Disorder Rating Scale (ADHD-RS). This study suggests that ADHD with comorbid SUD is more difficult to treat with MPH than ADHD without SUD.

Spencer et al. (2005) studied 146 subjects using a fixed-dose parallel design over a 6-week period, with doses varying from 0.5 mg/kg/d during week 1 up to a maximum of 1.3 mg/kg/d by weeks 5 and 6 (mean daily dose at endpoint was 1.1 mg/kg/d). They found a 76% response rate to MPH versus 19% placebo (effect size [ES] = 1.41) and attributed the robust findings to the higher doses utilized. The study showed that MPH was safe and well tolerated even at higher daily doses. The most commonly reported side effects were appetite suppression (27%), dry mouth (35%), and mild moodiness (30%).

Biederman et al. (2006b) studied OROS (the patented drug delivery system from Concerta referred to as osmotic controlled-release delivery system, see Modi, 2000) MPH in 149 subjects using a parallel group optimal-dosing design over a 6-week period. Doses were titrated up to a maximum of 1.3 mg/kg/d with a 66% response rate seen in the MPH group compared to 39% with placebo. Response was defined as a 30% reduction in ADHD symptoms and a score of 1 or 2 on the Clinical Global Impression - Improvement Scale (CGI-I) Side effects were comparable to those seen with IR MPH. The effect size of OROS MPH (d ≈ 0.5) was reduced because of the high placebo response.

Reimherr et al. (2007) conducted a 4-week crossover study of 41 subjects using OROS MPH titrated up to 0.75 mg/kg/d. They found a response rate of 42% with OROS MPH compared to 13% when subjects were on placebo. This is a lower overall response rate than in the previous OROS MPH study (possibly due to the lower total daily dose). However, the much smaller placebo response seen in this study resulted in a slightly larger effect size (d ≈ 0.57).

Jain et al. (2007) studied biphasic multilayer release (MLR) MPH in 50 subjects over a 3- to 5-week period using a crossover design. The average daily dose of medication was 57.8 mg (≈ 0.68 mg/kg/d). Response rate was 49% in the MLR MPH arm compared to 23% in the placebo arm, resulting in a moderate effect size (d ≈ 0.39).

Side effects were comparable in both arms of the study, indicating that the medication was well tolerated. It is likely that the moderate effect size and the low side effects profile seen in this study were attributable to the moderate dosing levels used.

Spencer et al. (2007) studied the safety and efficacy of extended release dextromethylphenidate (dMPH ER) in 184 subjects using a parallel group design over a 5-week period. Subjects were equally divided into four groups: placebo, 20 mg/d, 30 mg/d, and 40 mg/kg/d. Reduction in ADHD-RS scores were 7.9, 13.7, 13.4, and 16.9 respectively. They concluded that all three doses of dMPH were equally effective in improving ADHD symptoms in this sample.

Medori et al. (2008) conducted a 5-week multicenter study of OROS MPH in 401 subjects using a parallel group design of three different doses: 18 mg (0.24 mg/kg/d), 36 mg (0.50 mg/kg/d), or 72 mg (0.96 mg/kg/d) and placebo. Response rates (defined as at least a 30% decrease in scores on the Conners Adult ADHD Rating Scales (CAARS) were 50.5%, 48.5%, 59.6%, and 27.4% respectively ($p < 0.001$). The safety profile seen in this study was comparable to studies of OROS MPH in pediatric populations. The two major side effects noted were dry mouth and jitteriness.

Amphetamine

Taylor and Russo (2000, 2001) studied the effects of dextroamphetamine (dAMP) on 39 subjects over a 7-week time period using a crossover design. The average dose was 22 mg (0.3 mg/kg/d), and the overall response rate was 48%.

Spencer et al. (2001) conducted a 7-week crossover study of 27 subjects who received three different doses of immediate release mixed amphetamine salts (IR MAS): 10, 20, and 30 mg administered twice daily (0.3–0.9 mg/kg/d). There was a 70% response rate to medication, with a dose relationship observed. However, there were no effects of gender or comorbidity on response rate.

Weisler et al. (2006) carried out a forced-titration parallel group design study of 255 subjects who were given either placebo or three different doses (20, 40, or 60 mg) of mixed amphetamine salts extended release (MAS XR) (equal to roughly 0.3–0.9 mg/kg/d) over a 6-week period. The authors reported an overall response rate of 42% for MAS XR as compared to 20% for placebo (d = 0.38, 0.40 and 0.44 for each of the dose levels). Although there was a trend toward better response at higher doses, the forced titration design made it difficult to draw conclusions about optimal dosing schedules.

Weiss et al. (2006) studied dAMP treatment of 98 subjects over 20 weeks using a parallel group design of four arms: placebo, dAMP only, paroxetine only, and dAMP plus paroxetine. Doses of dAMP were titrated to optimal levels between 5 and 20 mg, with over half (52.6%) receiving the highest dose. Response rates were: dextroamphetamine (85.7%), combined treatment (66.7%), paroxetine (20.0%), and placebo (21.1%), indicating a strong effect of dAMP on ADHD symptoms. Although the presence of a lifetime mood or anxiety disorder increased the efficacy of dAMP, the combination of paroxetine and dAMP seemed to attenuate the stimulant's effects.

Adler et al. (2008) employed a forced-titration parallel group design to study the pro-drug lisdexamfetamine dimesylate (LDX). The sample consisted of 420 adults who were randomized to receive placebo or 30, 50, or 70 mg of LDX daily over a 4-week period. At endpoint, subjects' ADHD-RS scores were reduced by 8.2, 16.2, 17.4, and 18.6, respectively. Response rates (defined as the percentage of subjects receiving a CGI-I score of 1 or 2) for groups were 29% versus 57% versus 62% versus 61% respectively, indicating a significant effect of LDX as compared to placebo on ADHD symptoms. Adverse events were relatively mild and included dry mouth, decreased appetite, and insomnia.

Weisler et al. (2009) conducted an open-label extension study of 349 subjects from the prior LDX trial over a 12-month period to assess the safety and efficacy of this compound. A total of 191 subjects (54.7%) completed the study, and at endpoint, the mean reduction in ADHD-RS was 24.9 ($p < 0.0001$). Treatment-emergent adverse events were relatively mild and included insomnia (19.5%), headache (17.2%), dry mouth (16.6%), decreased appetite (14.3%), and irritability (11.2%). In addition, there were small but statistically significant increases in heart rate and blood pressure seen in the LDX treatment group.

Atomoxetine

The first published study of atomoxetine (ATX), a norepinephrine reuptake inhibitor, in ADHD adults was conducted by Spencer et al. (1998). Using a crossover design of 7 weeks' duration (two 3-week periods separated by a 1-week washout period), 24 subjects were given an average of 76 mg/d of ATX. The response rate was 52.3% for ATX as compared to 9.5% for placebo. The medication also produced improvements in performance on neuropsychological tests of inhibitory control. Adverse events were mild and well tolerated, although one patient became very anxious and had to be withdrawn from the trial.

Michelson et al. (2003) conducted two multicenter studies of a total of 536 subjects who were given either placebo or dose-titrated ATX (60, 90, or 120 mg/d). The most common dose at the end of the study was 90 mg, followed by 60 mg and 120 mg. Subjects on medication reported significantly improved inattentive and hyperactive symptoms of ADHD as compared with controls ($p < 0.01$); however, effect sizes were only moderate ($d = 0.36, 0.38$ respectively). Discontinuation due to side effects was less than 10% across both studies. Open-label extensions of these studies were carried out by Adler et al. (2005) over 97 weeks and by Adler et al. (2008) for up to 4 years (221 weeks) from initial enrollment in the registry trial. There was significant subject dropout over the duration of the studies (i.e., only 33% were still enrolled at 2 years and only 18% at 4 years). For those who remained on medication, the effect of ATX was still significant, with decreases on the CAARS of 33% and 30% respectively. This finding suggests that the clinical effects of ATX can be sustained over long periods of time.

Adler et al. (2006a) conducted a study of the safety and tolerability of once-daily ATX and enrolled 218 subjects who were randomized to either 80 mg once daily or 40 mg twice daily dosing over a period of 6 weeks. Although the once-daily dosing was safe and effective, the twice-daily dosing schedule had a greater clinical effect ($p < 0.001$) and fewer side effects.

Bupropion

Wilens et al. (2001) studied 40 patients using a parallel design over 6 weeks to evaluate the effects of bupropion 200 mg twice daily (mean daily dose = 362 mg). ADHD symptoms were reduced by 42% in the medication group as compared to 24% in the placebo group, with a response rate (= 30% improvement) of 76% and 37%, respectively. Using the CGI-I score of 1 or 2, 52% of the medication-treated subjects improved as compared to 11% of those receiving placebo (d = 0.66). Side effects were reported to be tolerable.

Kuperman et al. (2001) used a parallel group 7-week design to study 30 patients randomized to placebo, MPH (0.9 mg/kg/d in 3 doses), or bupropion (up to 200 mg in the morning and 100 mg in the evening). Response rates based on the CGI-I (1 or 2) were 27%, 50%, and 64%, respectively, which was not statistically significant ($p = 0.14$). The effect size for bupropion was 0.15 and for MPH was –0.24, both of which stand in marked contrast to other studies. This may be due to several factors including small sample size, high placebo response, and a suboptimal dose of bupropion.

Wilens et al. (2005) conducted an 8-week parallel-group design study of bupropion extended release (BP XL) (up to 450 mg daily) in 162 patients with a mean daily dose of 393 mg for those in the treated group. Response rate ($\geq$ 30% improvement in ADHD symptoms) was 53% for BP XL versus 31% for placebo. Treatment effect size for the ADHD-RS total score was calculated to equal 0.60. Effects were seen throughout the day, and side effects were minimal, with a 5% rate of drug-related study discontinuation reported.

Meta-Analytic Studies of Medication Treatment for Adult ADHD

Faraone et al. (2004) published the first meta-analysis of treatment for adult ADHD, focusing exclusively on double-blind placebo-controlled studies of methylphenidate. Six studies were included in this study with a total of 140 MPH-treated and 113 placebo-treated subjects. The pooled effect size of MPH was estimated to be 0.9, with a higher effect size obtained (d = 1.3) when medication dosage was optimized. These authors concluded that "the degree of efficacy of MPH in treating ADHD adults is similar to what has been reported from meta-analysis of the child and adolescent literature" (p. 24).

Koesters, Becker, and Kilian (2009) challenged the findings of Faraone et al. by conducting a meta-analysis of 16 studies of MPH treatment of adult ADHD covering the period 1984 to 2007. These authors found an overall effect size of 0.42 across all studies, with no effect of MPH dose or of type of rating (self versus observer) on effect size. The lower effect size is most likely due to the inclusion of more studies, a higher number of subjects (551 MPH-treated and 494 placebo-treated), and 4 studies of ADHD with comorbid substance abuse.

Peterson, McDonagh, and Fu (2008) performed a meta-analysis on 22 published placebo-controlled studies of medications for adult ADHD ($n = 2,203$) and reported their results using a "relative risk for clinical response" (RR) measure for medication versus placebo. The RR for studies of short-acting stimulants ($n = 8$) was 4.32; for long-acting stimulants ($n = 6$), it was 1.35; and for long-acting bupropion ($n = 3$), it was 1.87. The trials of atomoxetine and of short-acting bupropion were excluded from this particular analysis. Of note, the long-acting stimulant studies included two trials by Levin et al. (2006, 2007) of patients with comorbid Substance Use Disorders for whom the RR was < 1.0. If these studies were excluded, the pooled RR for long-acting stimulants would be 2.0.

Meszaros et al. (2009) conducted a meta-analysis of 12 double-blind, parallel-group randomized design medication trials for adult ADHD involving a total of 1,991 subjects (694 receiving placebo and 1,297 treated with medication). The overall effect size was 0.65, with $d = 0.67$ for stimulant medications and $d = 0.59$ for nonstimulants. Higher effects were seen in the stimulant studies with higher doses ($d = 0.69$). Among nonstimulants, 2 studies of atomoxetine had effect sizes of 0.36 and 0.38; 3 bupropion trials had effect sizes of 0.66, 0.15, and 0.66; and the 1 desipramine study had an effect size of 1.73 (Wilens et al., 1996).

Faraone and Glatt (2010) conducted a meta-analysis of clinical trials of medications for adult ADHD. They included studies using randomized, double-blind methodology with placebo controls that defined ADHD using *Diagnostic and Statistical Manual* (DSM) criteria, lasted for more than 2 weeks, had more than 20 subjects, and reported baseline and endpoint change or rating scale scores. A total of 19 trials studying 13 drugs were analyzed: 7 studied of short-acting stimulants, 5 looked at long-acting stimulants, and 9 examined nonstimulants. (Note: Two trials tested more than one medication.) The overall effect size for short-acting stimulants (adjusting for publication bias) was 0.86; for long-acting stimulants, 0.73; and for nonstimulants, 0.39. These results are somewhat different from those found in the study by Meszaros et al. (2009). The authors were careful to point out that there is a great deal of variability in the methods used by these studies and in the results. Although it is clear that stimulants are more effective than nonstimulants, it is difficult to draw definitive conclusions about the advantages of short- versus long-acting stimulants in actual practice settings.

To summarize the existing literature, stimulants are the most effective medication treatment for adult ADHD, and nonstimulants are an acceptable but less effective option. In terms of response rates, it appears that 75% of patients respond well to stimulants, roughly an equal percentage respond to bupropion, and approximately 60% respond to atomoxetine. Although meta-analytic studies suggest a higher effect size for short-acting stimulants, it is not clear how this translates into the realities of clinical practice, since adherence factors were not considered in the research trials, and since there is some evidence that adherence to long-acting preparations is better than with short-acting preparations. Moreover, the abuse potential of short-acting stimulants is a concern for many practitioners.

At present, it is not possible to predict on the basis of patient characteristics (gender, age, comorbidity) which medication works best for any given patient, nor have sufficient numbers of long-range studies been carried out to determine how long treatment effects persist with any given regimen. Furthermore, there are few controlled studies of combined medication regimens, either for treatment-resistant ADHD or for comorbid ADHD in adults. Finally, it should be kept in mind that subjects in clinical trials are not representative of patients seen in clinical settings and that medication response rates are likely to be higher in published studies for any number of reasons. This makes the clinical decision-making process even more challenging for practitioners working with this patient population.

Studies of Medication Treatment for Learning Disorders in Older Adolescents and Adults

Piracetam and related compounds have been studied for over 30 years as one group of nootropics, or agents that purported to improve cognition, memory, learning, intelligence, or attention/concentration. These compounds are thought to mimic γ-Aminobutyric acid (GABA), although their precise mechanism of action is unclear. Although much remains to be discovered about how they work, a recent review (Malykh & Sadaie, 2010) summarizes their pharmacology in this way:

> These compounds interact with target receptors in the brain and modulate the excitatory and/or inhibitory processes of neurotransmitters, neurohormones and/or post-synaptic signals. The effect(s) on signal trafficking can have an impact on cognition and neurological behaviours. Several groups have suggested the roles of piracetam in energy metabolism, including (i) increased oxygen utilization in the brain, and permeability of cell and mitochondrial membranes to intermediaries of the Krebs cycle; and (ii) synthesis of cytochrome b5.

Piracetam was first investigated for the treatment of dyslexia in 1979 by Wilsher et al. Sixteen male dyslexic adults and 14 matched student volunteers were given a

21-day trial of piracetam. Improvements in verbal learning on medication versus placebo were seen in both groups. A 15% improvement was found for the subjects with dyslexia as compared to an 8.6% improvement for controls. Subsequent studies have had mixed results at best. Rudel and Helfgott (1984) found improved verbal learning in students given piracetam versus placebo. Di Ianni et al. (1985) found improvements in reading speed but no other benefits. Helfgott, Rudel, and Kairam (1986) found no significant improvements with piracetam treatment. Wilsher et al. (1987), in a large study of 225 children with dyslexia, found significant gains in reading ability including comprehension that were sustained up to 36 weeks later. Ackerman et al. (1991) found no benefits of piracetam on children with reading disability. Given that these studies were conducted exclusively in children (except for the 1979 Wilsher study), it is impossible to ascertain what benefits piracetam-group compounds have for older adolescents and adults with LD. It is also significant that recent comprehensive reviews of these agents (see Gouliaev, 1994; Winblad, 2005; Malykh & Sadaie, 2010) make no mention of their benefits for LD other than the papers cited earlier. The paucity of evidence suggests that the piracetam compounds are of limited efficacy, at least with LD. However, they seem to be quite helpful in protecting memory and cognition in patients with acquired brain disorders such as traumatic brain injury, Dementia of the Alzheimer's Type (AD), epilepsy, and mild cognitive impairment.

Methylphenidate and amphetamine have been tested in ADHD children with comorbid LD with mixed results. It appears that stimulants have a clear impact on working memory and attention/concentration in ways that lead to improved academic performance in several domains. What remains controversial is whether these medications actually meliorate the underlying LD or not. A recent review by Tannock and Brown (in Brown, 2009) on the effects of stimulants on LD concludes that these agents improve skills such as phonological processing, word identification, arithmetic procedures, handwriting, and quality of expressive speech. As with the nootropics, these studies have been conducted on children, and there is virtually no evidence regarding the impact of stimulants on underlying mechanisms of LD in older adolescents and adults.

Recent interest in the effects of atomoxetine on conditions comorbid with ADHD has prompted investigations into its effects on dyslexia. Sumner et al. (2009), in an open-label study, treated 20 children with ADHD and 36 children with ADHD and dyslexia (ADHD+D) for 16 weeks. Atomoxetine improved ADHD symptoms and reading scores in both groups, although the subjects with ADHD+D showed greater gains in reading decoding and in phonological scores, suggesting a specific action on reading circuits by ATX.

PHARMACOLOGY OF ADHD MEDICATIONS

This section briefly reviews the mechanism of action, clinical effects, and adverse reactions associated with the medications most commonly used to treat ADHD. Stimulant medications (methylphenidate and amphetamine derived), atomoxetine, and guanfacine are approved by the Food and Drug Administration (FDA). Second-line medications that have been shown to be beneficial but are not FDA approved include bupropion, clonidine, desipramine, and modafanil. Caffeine and nicotine, while not prescribed as medications, are readily available compounds with powerful attention-promoting effects. Newer agents that have not yet been fully tested but seem to show some promise include nicotinic agonists (e.g., varenicline), acetyl-cholinesterase inhibitors (e.g., donezepil) and N-methyl-D-aspartic acid (NMDA) receptor antagonists (i.e., ampakines).

Stimulants

Psychostimulant medications work directly on monoaminergic neurons (especially dopamine and norepinephrine) and enhance neurotransmission in a reversible fashion. There are two major classes of stimulants: methylphenidate compounds and amphetamine compounds (see Table 18.1). Although these agents have been around for decades, the past decade has seen the introduction of novel delivery systems to modify the way they are introduced into the body and released into the circulation, to prolong the duration of their effects, and to modify the rate at which they are metabolized. These newer preparations differ most noticeably in their total duration of action and in the profile of medication release (bolus versus continuous).

Table 18.1 Approved Pharmacologic Treatments for ADHD

Methylphenidate-based formulations	Duration of effect
Concerta®	~12 hours
Ritalin®	3–4 hours
Metadate® CD	8–10 hours
Ritalin® LA	~8 hours
Focalin® (XR)	3–4 (8–10) hours
Daytrana®	~12 hours (worn for 9)
Amphetamine-based treatments	
Adderall XR®	~12 hours
Adderall®	4–6 hours
Dexedrine® Spansule	6–8 hours
Vyvanse®	~12 hours
Nonstimulant treatments	
Strattera®	Up to 24 hours
Intuniv®	Up to 24 hours
Clonicel® (R)	Up to 24 hours

Amphetamine

Amphetamine was first synthesized in 1887 in Berlin. It is derived from the Ma-Huang plant and is chemically related to ephedrine. The medication was initially sold by Smith, Kline and French in a volatile base form as the decongestant inhaler, Benzedrine. It was used by Allied soldiers in World War II to diminish fatigue and increase alertness. It is still being utilized by the U.S. Air Force to reduce pilot fatigue during long-range missions. Amphetamine is currently available as a d-isomer (dextro-amphetamine) that comes in tablets and spansules; as a mixed salt (75% d-isomer, 25% l-isomer) that comes in tablets and capsules; and as a prodrug (lysdexamfetamine) available in capsule form.

Amphetamine moves quickly into catecholamine-containing neurons (most notably DA) and reverses the direction of neurotransmitter transport. In the case of dopamine neurons, the molecule binds to the DAT protein on the outside of the cell membrane and blocks reuptake of DA back into the presynaptic terminal. It also moves into the nerve cell and releases stored DA from the storage vesicles and prevents the reuptake of DA into these vesicles, thereby inducing greater release of DA into the synapse. Amphetamine has similar effects on NE neurons and also interacts with serotonin neurons, particularly in the meso-cortico-limbic pathway. This may explain why it has some transient antidepressant effects. Amphetamine triggers DA transmission in all CNS pathways implicated in the pathophysiology of ADHD. It also works on the ventromedial reward circuits (e.g., nucleus accumbens)—hence its abuse potential—and on striatal structures (e.g., putamen, caudate, globus pallidus)—hence its tendency to induce tics in prone individuals.

Side effects of amphetamine include cardiovascular alterations (e.g., palpitations, tachycardia, hypertension, syncope, and dizziness), CNS arousal (e.g., overstimulation, agitation, restlessness, euphoria, headache, and insomnia), movement difficulties (e.g., tremor, dyskinesia, exacerbation of tics), gastrointestinal (GI) symptoms (e.g., nausea, stomachache, anorexia, weight loss), and psychiatric difficulties (e.g., dysphoria, hostility, paranoia, mania).

Methamphetamine

Methamphetamine, a methylated form of amphetamine, was synthesized in Japan from ephedrine and used in World War II to help Axis soldiers stay awake and fight fatigue. It is currently available in tablet form (manufactured only in Denmark) and is less prescribed than dextro-amphetamine or mixed amphetamine salts because of negative associations with the illegal and commonly abused street drug. Its d-isomer is the active molecule, and although it is very similar to amphetamine (i.e., reverse transport of catecholamine molecules), it is more lipid soluble and has a more rapid onset of action. It is also a far more effective agonist of serotonin, which may account for its being associated with less dysphoria, agitation, and hostility than amphetamine.

Methylphenidate

Methylphenidate (MPH) was first synthesized in 1944, was first recognized as a stimulant in 1954, was introduced in the 1960s as the treatment of choice for "minimal brain dysfunction," and is currently the most widely prescribed stimulant for the treatment of ADHD. It belongs to the piperidine class of compounds: a chain-substituted amphetamine derivative, with a chemical structure similar to cocaine. It has a simpler mechanism of action than amphetamine insofar as it reversibly binds to the DA transporter protein and blocks DA reuptake presynaptically. Its relatively slow uptake and clearance make it less "likable" as a substance of abuse, and its oral administration has less euphoric effects than amphetamine. It is available as a tablet, in several extended-release preparations (beads, osmotic-release systems), and as a transdermal patch. There is also a d-isomer molecule (dexmethylphenidate) available in both tablet and capsule form. MPH has a slightly more favorable side effects profile than amphetamine, although cardiac toxicity is of great concern, as are GI symptoms (e.g., appetite suppression, nausea, vomiting, abdominal pain, and weight loss), insomnia, and psychiatric symptoms.

Nonstimulants

Atomoxetine

Atomoxetine (ATX), a norepinephrine reuptake inhibitor, is the first nonstimulant medication to be FDA approved for ADHD. Its mechanism of action includes selectively blocking the NE reuptake transporter located on the presynaptic neuron, increasing the concentration of NE in the synaptic cleft, and thereby enhancing the transmission along NE-innervated pathways. Although the precise mechanism of its clinical effects in ADHD patients is not known, several lines of evidence suggest that it (a) improves alerting and orienting and reduces overreactivity (i.e., exaggerated startle response) in the posterior attention systems mediated by NE, and (b) increases NE and DA neurotransmission in the prefrontal cortex, thereby improving focusing and executive functioning. The increased DA levels seen in the PFC are not observed in either the striatum (which explains the lack of an increase in tics) or in the nucleus accumbens (thereby reducing the abuse potential of ATX) (Bymaster et al., 2002; Swanson et al., 2006). Recent studies suggest that ATX is very helpful in patients with comorbid anxiety (Geller, 2007), social anxiety (Adler, 2009), and/or tic disorders (Spencer, 2008). Studies in children and adolescent samples suggest improved reading task performance with ATX (Sumner et al., 2009).

The most common side effects of ATX are high blood pressure, dizziness, headache, irritability, nervousness, abdominal pain, nausea, vomiting, loss of appetite and weight loss, dry mouth, constipation, urinary hesitation, and decreased sexual desire.

Bupropion

Bupropion is a medication with proven efficacy for treatment of depression, smoking cessation, and adult ADHD. It is an aminoketone, similar in structure to phenylethyl-amine, whose hydroxylated metabolite is the active agent. The regular-release prepa-ration has a half-life of approximately 14 hours while the extended-release form has a half-life of 24 hours. It is a potent DA reuptake inhibitor with less potent inhibi-tion of NE reuptake. Although bupropion is activating (or even stimulating) and can occasionally worsen anxiety symptoms, it produces less sexual dysfunction than other antidepressants.

The most significant side effect of bupropion is an increased incidence of seizures because it lowers of seizure threshold. Seizures are reported to occur in 0.4% of patients taking the immediate-release preparation; the rate probably is lower in patients on the extended-release preparation. Seizures remit with discontinuation of the medication. Other adverse effects include dry mouth, constipation, nausea, vomiting, anorexia, weight loss, headache, dizziness, fainting spells, insomnia, tremor, restlessness, excit-ability, mood swings, and irritability.

Alpha$_2$ Adrenergic Agonists

Alpha$_2$ adrenergic agonists were first introduced as antihypertensive agents over 40 years ago but were supplanted by other medications (e.g., calcium channel blockers) with fewer side effects. Their effects on the CNS include modulation of the tonic and phasic activity of the locus coeruleus (major source of NE in the brain) and enhanced adrenergic activity in the PFC. Their effects on NE neurotransmission are achieved via up-regulation of intracellular cyclic adenosine monophosphate (cAMP) which, in turn, improves signal conduction along the axon (Arnsten, 2009; Arnsten, Scahill, & Findling, 2007). Clonidine works on alpha$_{2A}$, $_{2B}$, and $_{2C}$ receptors (which are located throughout the CNS, including the brain stem), leading to its producing more hypotensive and sedative effects than guanfacine, which is selective for the alpha$_{2A}$ receptors. There is some evidence that the alpha$_2$ agonists can improve symptoms in adults with ADHD. A double-blind placebo-controlled study comparing guanfacine to dextroamphetamine in adults with ADHD found that each were comparable in their clinical effects as well as their impact on neuropsychological measures (Taylor & Russo, 2001). Clinical trials of extended-release guanfacine (GXR) have shown it to be effec-tive as monotherapy for ADHD in children and adolescents (Sallee et al., 2009a,b).

The fact that these agents reduce hyperactivity, impulsivity, and oppositional behavior and increase attention span and concentration in youth suggests that they can be helpful in adult patients as well. Clinical experience with these agents suggests that they are particularly useful in reducing irritability, overarousal, emotional lability, and explosiveness in adults with ADHD. They are also useful in controlling tics and managing high blood pressure. The most common side effects seen with alpha$_2$ adrenergic agonists are sedation, fatigue, dizziness, syncope, cardiac rhythm disturbances, dry mouth, indigestion, nausea, nightmares, insomnia, anxiety, dysphoria, and depression. In addition, hypertensive crises can be induced by sudden discontinuation of these medications.

Modafanil

Modafanil is a novel wake-promoting medication approved for the treatment of daytime sleepiness secondary to narcolepsy, obstructive apnea, and work-related shift disorder. Its mechanism of action is quite distinct from that of amphetamine and methylphenidate insofar as it promotes the action of multiple neurotransmitters including the catecholamines, serotonin, glutamate, GABA, orexin, and histamine (Kumar, 2008; Minzenberg & Carter, 2008). Although it is reported to have little abuse potential and is less "activating" than the psychostimulants, concerns have been raised recently about the risks of modafanil addiction and dependence (Volkow et al., 2009b). Research into its clinical efficacy with patients with ADHD has focused primarily on children and adolescents, where it was found to have beneficial effects in several randomized controlled trials (RCTs). However, FDA approval for this indication was withheld due to the appearance of suspicious rashes in some subjects. A double-blind, placebo-controlled, triple-arm crossover study of 22 adult patients treated with placebo, modafanil, or amphetamine found clinical improvements in ADHD-RS scores in the two active arms (Taylor & Russo, 2000). The average dose of modafanil used in this study was 207 mg day, lower than the dose used to treat daytime sleepiness.

The half-life of modafanil is 10 to 12 hours, and its onset of action is approximately 2 to 3 hours. Typically, 100 to 400 mg twice daily is prescribed for treatment of sleepiness. Dosage ranges for ADHD have not been established since it is still not FDA approved. Nevertheless, in clinical usage, similar doses are used to improve focusing and concentration and to reduce hyperactivity/impulsivity. Adverse events associated with modafinil (>5%) include nausea, insomnia, headache, and feeling jittery.

Desipramine

Desipramine (DMI), a desmethylated derivative of imipramine, is similar to other tricyclic antidepressants (TCAs) in its structure and neurochemistry (Schatzberg & Nemeroff, 2009). It has prominent effects on NE reuptake inhibition, with little effects on dopamine (DA) or serotonin (5-hydroxytryptamine, 5-HT), which means it is very similar to atomoxetine. DMI demonstrates high affinity for alpha$_1$ and muscarinic receptors, with virtually no effect on alpha$_2$ or histaminic receptors, thereby making it relatively less sedating as compared to imipramine, amitriptyline, and other TCAs. It is well absorbed and achieves peak concentrations in the plasma in 2 to 6 hours, with a mean half-life of 18 hours (range 10–31 hr). It is metabolized in the liver by the cytochrome

P450 CYP2D6 isozyme and takes about 2 to 4 weeks to exert its antidepressant effects. Clinical trials of DMI for adult ADHD indicate that its attention-promoting effects can be seen in the first 2 weeks.

The usual initial dose of DMI is 25 to 50 mg daily, which can be titrated over 2 to 3 weeks to 150 to 200 mg daily, depending on the patient's tolerance of side effects. In some cases, the dosage can be raised to 300 mg daily. Monitoring of cardiovascular status should include following vital signs and electrocardiograms, looking for prolongation of heart conduction (which carries with it high risk for arrhythmia). Only rarely are blood levels indicated. Major side effects include blurred vision, dry mouth, sinus tachycardia, constipation, urinary retention, dizziness, drowsiness, sedation, weight gain, and extrapyramidal movement disorders. There is a black box warning about the risk for suicidal ideation following treatment with DMI (similar to other antidepressants), which is particularly germane given the potential for an overdose of this medication to be fatal.

Novel Agents

Many novel agents for ADHD fall under the rubric of cognitive enhancers, "a general term that denotes a pharmacological or nutraceutical intervention that improves cognitive functioning in an impaired or normal brain by reversing or delaying underlying neuropathological changes within the brain or by modulating the existing neurochemistry to facilitate a desired performance differential" (Bostrum, 2009, p. 312). This section explores new areas of research into cognitive enhancers that show promise for the treatment of ADHD, including nicotinic agonists, acetylcholinesterase inhibitors, and N-methyl-D-aspartic acid (NMDA) receptor antagonists.

Nicotinic Agonists

Nicotine

Nicotine has wide ranging cognitive-enhancing, rewarding, and addicting effects that are well characterized and documented (Levin, McClernon, & Rezvani, 2006; Swan & Lessov-Schlaggar, 2007). It enhances DA release in the CNS by acting as a direct agonist at nicotinic acetylcholine receptors (nAChRs), especially the $\alpha 4\beta 2$ subtypes, in the mesocorticolimbic and nigrostriatal systems. Nicotine has indirect effects on glutamate and GABAergic signaling via the nAChRs. In particular, the $\alpha 4\beta 2$ nAChRs play a significant role in cognition. Over time, nicotine induces higher DAT function via indirect mechanisms that are poorly understood but are thought to be related to increases in DAT cell surface expression. There is evidence that nicotine also enhances amphetamine-stimulated DA release (see Zhu & Reith, 2008).

It has long been noted that individuals with ADHD have higher rates of smoking and lower quit rates than the general population (Fuemmeler, Kollins, & McClernon,

2007; Kollins, McClernon, & Fuemeler, 2005; Wilens et al., 2008b). Adolescents with ADHD have an increased chance of becoming cigarette smokers and do so at a younger age than their peers without ADHD. Lambert and Hartsough (1998) found 46% of youth with ADHD were smoking cigarettes daily compared to 24% of age-mate controls. Studies of cognitive performance have found beneficial effects of nicotine administration in nonsmoking adolescents as well as young adults with ADHD (Potter & Newhouse, 2004, 2008), leading some to suggest that cigarette smoking may function as "self-medication" for individuals with ADHD.

ABT-089

ABT-089 is an investigational nicotinic receptor partial agonist that has been studied in adults with ADHD (Wilens et al., 2006b). Eleven adults with ADHD were given varying doses of ABT-089 (2 mg, 4 mg, or 20 mg twice a day [bid]) versus placebo for 2 weeks in a double-blind, crossover design study. CAARS total symptom scores were used as the outcome measure, with significant improvements seen at the lower doses (ES = 0.92 and 0.76, respectively) and approaching significance at the highest dose. Of note, impulsive/hyperactive symptoms on the CAARS improved more than the inattentive ones. No significant side effects were reported, although the study was small and of short duration.

Varenicline

Varenicline is a α4β2 nAChR partial agonist that is FDA approved for smoking cessation. Typically, dosage is titrated up to 1 mg bid for up to 12 weeks. Long-term usage in smokers has not been studied systematically. Studies of its effects on brain activity and working memory in abstinent smokers report improved cognitive performance on working memory tasks that are associated with increased brain activity in the dorsal anterior cingulate/medial frontal cortex and the dorsolateral PFC (Loughead et al., 2010; Xu et al., 2005). Although there are no RCTs of its use for ADHD, a recent case report suggests that it may prove to be effective (Cocores & Gold, 2008). The major side effects associated with varenicline are nausea, insomnia, and abnormal dreams.

Mecamylamine

Mecamylamine is a noncompetitive nicotinic antagonist that has a paradoxical cognitive-enhancing effect at low doses. It has been used clinically for patients with tic disorders to reduce reactivity and irritability. Potter, Ryan, and Newhouse (2009) studied 15 nonsmoking adult subjects with ADHD and found that ultra-low-dose mecamylamine (0.5 mg) administered in a single daily dose significantly improved recognition memory. Doses of 0.2 mg and 1.0 mg also resulted in some improvements, but the best results were obtained with 0.5 mg. Unfortunately, mecamylamine increased both delay aversion and subject-reported irritability, which may limit its use in this population. Investigations are under way to determine its efficacy in Autism, Schizophrenia, and other neuropsychiatric disorders.

Acetylcholinesterase Inhibitors

Acetylcholinesterase is the main enzyme involved in the degradation of acetylcholine. A class of agents known as acetylcholinesterase inhibitors (AChEIs) has been introduced as cognitive enhancers for the treatment of Dementia of the Alzheimer's Type (AD) and other forms of dementia. Recent work has investigated the role these agents might play in the treatment of ADHD, tics, and Tourette's Disorder, Autism, LD, and related neuropsychiatric disorders. Current evidence does not support the use of these compounds as first-line agents, but there is some suggestion they *may* be helpful in certain cases. The major side effects of these agents include dizziness, nausea, vomiting, fatigue, insomnia, muscle cramps, loss of appetite, and weight loss.

Donepezil

Donepezil, a reversible AChEI, was approved for the treatment of AD in 1996. It is prescribed in daily doses of either 5 mg or 10 mg and has a long plasma half-life (70 hours). Cubo, Jaén, and Moreno (2008) conducted a prospective, open-label trial of donepezil in 20 patients ages 7 to 17 years with ADHD and comorbid tic disorders in escalating doses up to 10 mg daily over 18 weeks. By the end of the study, clear improvements were seen in tic scores but not in ADHD scores.

Galantamine Hydrobromide

Galantamine hydrobromide is another reversible AChEI with a short half-life (6–8 hours) approved in 2001 for the treatment of AD. It is distinct from other AChEIs in that it modulates nicotinic receptors. The optimal dose range is 16 to 24 mg in divided doses. A 12-week double-blind RCT of 36 adults (18–55 years old) with ADHD administered up to 24 mg/day of galantamine failed to show much improvement in ADHD scores. Only 22% of subjects given the medication were classified as responders, leading the authors to conclude that there is limited clinical utility of galantamine for the treatment of ADHD (Biederman et al., 2006b). It is not clear what future role, if any, AChIEs will play as adjunctive agents in the treatment of ADHD.

NMDA Receptor Antagonists

NMDA receptors are a specific type of glutamate receptors that are involved in synaptic plasticity and memory function. Overactivity of NMDA receptors is thought to play a role in the neurodegenerative process of AD.

Memantine

Memantine is a noncompetitive NMDA receptor antagonist that has been shown to improve the symptoms of AD. An open-label 8-week study of memantine in children ages 6 to 12 with ADHD by Findling et al. (2007) demonstrated that 20 mg/day was safe, well tolerated, and moderately effective in reducing symptoms. A recent animal study (Sukhanov et al., 2004) demonstrated that memantine blocked NMDA-induced membrane currents, linking faulty glutamatergic transmission to ADHD and its reversal to clinical improvement. Future studies are likely to expand on these observations as well as clarify the role these agents will play in treating ADHD.

Piracetam-Related Compounds

As noted earlier, there is some evidence that piracetam-related compounds can facilitate reading skills in patients with dyslexia, although there are no clinical trials as yet in adults with LD. The two positive studies in boys with dyslexia (Di Ianni et al., 1985; Wilsher et al., 1987) used 3.3 g daily in 2 divided doses. For adults, the recommended dosage is 50 to 300 mg/kg/d, which amounts to a maximum of approximately 37 g/d. A related compound, leveriacetam (Keppra), is commonly used for the treatment of seizure disorders at doses of up to 3 g/d (roughly 20–60 mg/kg/d), but it is not clear what the recommended dose for treating LD might be since there have been no clinical trials with this agent. A recent report of its use in adult patients with seizures with and without LD found equivalent seizure effects, more behavioral side effects and fewer somatic CNS side effects in the group with LD (Brodtkorb et al., 2004).

CLINICAL APPROACHES

Practice guidelines for the treatment of ADHD have been developed by a number of working groups, including the American Academy of Child and Adolescent Psychiatry (1997, 2002), the British Association for Psychopharmacology (Nutt et al., 2007), the Canadian ADHD Resource Alliance (Jain et al., 2006), the European Network for Hyperkinetic Disorders (Taylor et al., 2004), the National Institute for Health and Clinical Excellence (Kendall et al., 2008), and the National Institutes of Health (NIH Consensus Statement, 1998). Although the majority of these guidelines focus on the treatment of children, there are sections devoted to older adolescents and adults for whom the evidence base of treatment is considerably more limited. In view of this fact, some would argue that it is still too early in the evolution of this field to publish practice guidelines for the treatment of ADHD in adults. This is particularly true when considering issues such as long-term effects of medications on health status and outcomes, consistency of medication effects over time, use of combination regimens to treat comorbid conditions and/or difficult-to-treat cases, integrating medical and psychosocial approaches, and targeting functional outcomes (e.g., work performance, interpersonal success, marital satisfaction) as opposed to symptom amelioration. Despite these limitations, it is important to review what is emerging as a growing consensus regarding the "standards of care" for medication management of ADHD in adults.

The next section begins with a summary of the recommendations for which there appears to be agreement among the published practice guidelines. It is followed by discussions of: (1) practical aspects of introducing medication into the treatment plan; (2) advantages and disadvantages of different medication options; (3) techniques for monitoring treatment outcome, adherence, and side effects; (4) making adjustments for comorbid conditions and side effects; (5) handling inadequate response to treatment; and (6) improving adherence.

Practical Aspects of Introducing Medication

It is clear from the published guidelines that appropriate medication management of adult ADHD necessitates four things:

1. Thorough medical and psychiatric evaluation of the patient with consideration of differential diagnoses and comorbid conditions
2. Comprehensive, user-friendly psychoeducation to enable the patient to make informed choices about recommended treatment options
3. Prioritization of treatment objectives
4. Utilization of a targeted multimodal treatment approach that integrates medical, psychosocial/behavioral, and other interventions (e.g., environmental restructuring, accommodations, coaching)

Diagnostic procedures should include thorough medical and developmental history, careful delineation of school performance and adjustment, employment and military history (if relevant), and social history. Family medical and psychiatric history is critical, particularly regarding experiences of first-degree relatives with school and occupational achievement. A thorough evaluation of current functioning and mental status should include screening for learning disabilities, ethanol and substance abuse or dependency, problems with current role performance (i.e., school or work), status of important relationships, and co-occurring psychiatric conditions. Medical status should also be evaluated including screening for sleep apnea, metabolic and endocrine disorders, and neurological disorders that are associated with mild cognitive impairment. The use of collateral informants is widely considered to be a standard of care, both to provide important data regarding current and past difficulties and to verify the patient's descriptions of his or her symptoms and impairments from ADHD. The use of collateral informants also helps to reduce false positive (i.e., factitious) and false negative (i.e., poor memory or insight) diagnoses of ADHD.

Several reliable rating scales are widely available for confirming a diagnosis of ADHD, including the Barkley Current and Childhood Symptom Checklists (Barkley, 2006), Brown Attention-Deficit Disorder Scale for Adults (BADDS-A) (Brown, 2005), Conners Adult ADHD Rating Scales (CAARS) (Conners et al., 1999), Wender

Utah Rating Scale (WURS) (Ward, Wender, & Reimherr, 1993), and World Health Organization-Adult ADHD Self-Report Scale (WHO-ASRS) (Adler, Kessler, & Spencer, 2003). (See Rosler et al., 2006 for an excellent comparative review.) All of these measures enable the clinician to quantify the patient's symptom profile against a normative sample, to determine the severity of the symptoms, and to ascertain whether these meet criteria for a *DSM-IV* ADHD diagnosis (and subtype). Some of these tools (e.g., WURS, CAARS, BADDS) explore common comorbid symptoms (e.g., mood, memory) that may be affecting the patient's condition. Some (Barkley, 2006; BADDS) have versions for significant others to complete and return for scoring. Newer scales have been developed to measure patient functioning, quality of life, and degree of impairment (e.g., Weiss Functional Impairment Rating Scale [WFIRS], Adult ADHD Quality of Life Scale [AAQoL]). In addition, it is sometimes helpful to use other self-report scales (e.g., Beck Depression Inventory, Beck Anxiety Inventory) to quantify the degree of distress from these conditions. Taken together, these scales provide a broad view of the patient's presenting complaints and place these in context.

Once the assessment is completed, the clinician should sit down with the patient (along with significant others, if appropriate) to review major findings and to provide understandable explanations of what is known about ADHD and related executive function disorders to assist the patient with informed choices about treatment. Psychoeducational materials about adult ADHD are now in great abundance via the Internet, where patient-oriented manuals and treatment guides are readily obtainable. This initial step of providing clear and up-to-date information gives patient and family an opportunity to ask questions and clarify misconceptions. It also enables the clinician to get a better sense of the "mindset" that is guiding the patient's requests for help as well as his or her biases and preconceptions about potential interventions.

The next step is to help the patient prioritize the goals of treatment with an eye toward specifying target symptoms that he or she would most like to address. ADHD symptoms and certain comorbid symptoms (e.g., anxiety, dysthymia, depression) are the most amenable to medication treatment. Other problems (e.g., executive dysfunction, academic or occupational difficulties, relationship issues) are likely to require psychosocial interventions to effect meaningful improvements.

It is helpful to assign the patient a brief homework assignment of reviewing the treatment options that are most appealing and readily accessible for him or her. For instance, if patients are particularly interested in stimulant medications for ADHD, a brief handout of the most common pharmacologic agents should be provided. This serves three functions:

1. It enables patients to gather sufficient knowledge to make an informed choice.
2. It saves time in the office and enables the clinician to address questions and concerns patients have in a straightforward fashion.

3. It helps to clarify the patient's stance ("stage of change") toward treatment. If a patient does not carry out a minimal assignment like reading up on medication options, it is likely that he or she will have trouble adhering to treatment recommendations.

When referring a patient for medication treatment, it is important to talk with the prescribing physician to share information and to discuss medication options before the patient's visit to the physician. Communication about the patient's attitudes, expectations, hopes, and fears facilitates the multimodal treatment approach and enhances the efficacy of each component of the intervention plan. Practical aspects of collaborative care will be discussed in a subsequent section

Advantages and Disadvantages of Different Medication Options

In patients with relatively straightforward symptoms of ADHD, stimulant medication is usually the first line of treatment. The advantages of stimulants include rapidity of onset, immediate efficacy, tolerability, ability to titrate dose to different demands, and the scientific evidence that has led to FDA approval of these agents. At the present time, four of the five medications approved for adults with ADHD are stimulants— Adderall XR, Concerta, Focalin XR, and Vyvanse—which lends further weight to the selection process.

Disadvantages of stimulant treatment include time limitation of medication effects (i.e., early morning and late evening); variability of effects throughout the day; subjective reports of altered mentation that might not be desirable (e.g., "personality blunting," "rote thinking"); and the emergence of side effects, most notably anorexia, sleep disturbance, jitteriness, and cardiovascular toxicity. The misuse and abuse potential of stimulants also needs to be considered carefully. In patients with a history of substance abuse (especially cocaine, methamphetamine, or prescribed stimulants), physicians will likely avoid prescribing stimulants unless the patient is clearly abstinent. Other risk populations, such as college students, might be tempted to misuse stimulants (i.e., to lose weight, stay up late, or combine with alcohol) and should be prescribed these agents with caution (Rostain, 2006).

There is no clear evidence-based rationale for choosing which type of stimulant (MPH versus AMP) to start with, hence these decisions are often made on the basis of patient clinical profile and practitioner predilection. Prior experience with medications is certainly an important guide to choice of the initial agent. If a patient has had a positive experience with one or another compound, or, inversely has had a negative reaction, it is important to factor this into the decision tree. If all things are equal, and there is no past history of stimulant treatment, the tendency is to recommend methylphenidate first, because its mechanism of action is simpler and its side effects tend to be less pronounced. With patients who have a tendency to be "overaroused" or who are particularly sensitive to side effects, amphetamine might be too "stimulating." With individuals who are sluggish, anergic, or dysphoric, however, use of an amphetamine compound might be the preferable option since it also has an impact on the serotonin system.

The general framework for dosing stimulants includes starting with a reasonably low initial dose (e.g., 10 mg) of immediate-release medication given 3 times daily, with incremental titration upward (in 10 mg increments) up to approximately 30 mg per dose. Once the effective dose is established, it is relatively easy to switch patients from immediate-release to extended-release agents. Although it is certainly acceptable to start with extended-release medications, and many physicians prefer this approach, it makes sense to make sure that the stimulant choice (MPH versus AMP) is correct before switching to longer-acting agents. Higher doses may be required to see optimal effects in patients who are "fast metabolizers," but given concerns about exceeding FDA recommended doses, it might be prudent to seek consultation from an experienced adult ADHD clinician. Two recent papers have documented the safe use of "supertherapeutic" doses of stimulant medications without adverse effects (Parasampuria, et al., 2007; Stevens, et al., 2010).

When stimulant medications are not the preferred option, for whatever reasons, atomoxetine is the only nonstimulant medication for the treatment of ADHD in adults that is FDA approved (Adler et al., 2005, 2006a, 2008; Michelson et al., 2003; Spencer et al., 1998). The primary advantages of ATX are its duration of action (24 hours), its ease of administration (once or twice daily), and its relatively benign side effects profile. It can be combined safely with stimulant medications and selective serotonin reuptake inhibitors (SSRIs). It also appears to be particularly helpful for patients with ADHD and comorbid conditions such as anxiety and tic disorders, as described later.

The initial dose of ATX is 40 mg daily for a few days, followed by an increase to 80 mg daily (either in a single or a divided dose). This initial target dose should be maintained for 2 to 4 weeks before making any further adjustments. For patients who develop prominent side effects (approximately 17% are "slow metabolizers"), it is best to drop the dose back down to 40 mg daily, observe how the patient tolerates this, and then increase in 10 mg increments to 50 or 60 mg daily. For patients who do not appear to benefit from 80 mg daily, it is appropriate to increase to 100 mg or 120 mg and observe for an additional 3 to 4 weeks. Absence of any clinically significant improvement after 4 weeks on this maximum dose suggests that the patient is ATX nonresponsive.

Alpha-adrenergic agonists are another option to stimulants. In addition to their ADHD treatment effects, their primary advantages are a positive impact on "overarousal" and "emotional reactivity," on promoting sleep, and on reducing aggression and anxiety. Although they are not FDA approved for treatment of ADHD in adults, extended-release guanfacine and clonidine are approved for children and adolescents.

There is good reason to believe that guanfacine and clonidine are beneficial, either alone or in conjunction with stimulants, for ADHD adults, although their side effects (especially sedation and heart rate slowing) may limit their usefulness (see Taylor, 2001; Muir, 2010).

Immediate-release clonidine (0.1 mg tablets) and guanfacine (1 mg tablets) can be introduced by starting with ½ tablet at bedtime for a week, increasing to ½ tablet twice daily for an additional week, and continuing to titrate the dose by ½ tablet increments on a weekly basis until a target of 4 tablets daily (0.4 or 4 mg) is reached. The speed of dose titration is usually dependent on patient tolerance of side effects.

Bupropion is a unique antidepressant with DA and NE reuptake inhibitor effects that is quite effective for patients with ADHD, and has found a niche in the clinical world as a reasonable treatment for comorbid ADHD and Depressive Disorders. The sustained-release and extended-release preparations have the advantage of extended efficacy (12 or 24 hours), ease of administration (once daily), and lower risk of medication-induced seizure. The major disadvantage of bupropion is that it is an "activating" agent that can interfere with sleep onset and sleep maintenance—hence, some patients may find it overstimulating. Anecdotally, it has been reported to exacerbate nervousness and related symptoms in patients with Anxiety Disorders. As noted earlier, other adverse effects include dry mouth, constipation, nausea, vomiting, anorexia, weight loss, headache, dizziness, fainting spells, tremor, restlessness, excitability, mood swings, and irritability.

Patients should be started on sustained-release bupropion 100 mg twice daily in order to facilitate adherence and minimize side effects. After 2 weeks, if there is no clear clinical benefit, it is advisable to increase the dose to 400 mg daily. After an observation period of 4 weeks, its clinical effects should be assessed. If it appears to be of some benefit, and if the side effects are tolerable, it is acceptable to combine it cautiously with other ADHD agents.

Techniques for Monitoring Treatment Outcome, Adherence, and Side Effects

Once the decision to initiate medication treatment has been made, the target symptoms have been identified, and the initial agent has been selected, it is important to monitor carefully treatment outcomes, adherence, and side effects. It is common practice to utilize one of the standardized rating scales to monitor interim changes in ADHD symptoms, and it is advisable for clinicians to record these changes frequently throughout the initial phase of treatment. An individualized medication log is also useful for getting daily observations of treatment response (see Table 18.2). It is also important to obtain data from multiple sources (e.g., spouse, partner, close friend) to improve the reliability of clinical information. Most physicians will begin a medication at a low dose and titrate incrementally until the target response is achieved and/or side effects are causing concern. It is often helpful to have side effect questionnaires

Table 18.2 Monitoring Treatment Response

MEDICATION RESPONSE FORM

Patient Name _____

Medication _____   Dose, Schedule _____

Instructions: Please rate the following factors on a scale of 1–10 where 1 = poor, 5 = average, and 10 = excellent. Please write comments in the appropriate column

Day	Time	Dose	Concentration	Task Completion	Mood	Comments

available to monitor these issues. Additional strategies for improving outcomes include increasing dosage, switching to other medications, and combining medications, all of which will be considered in greater detail next.

Treatment adherence should be investigated at each visit, including the timing of each dose, the onset and duration of action, and the patient's experiences with forgetting to take pills. Rather than ask "Do you ever forget to take a medication?" a preferred inquiry might be "On average, how many doses would you estimate you miss every week?" This approach normalizes (destigmatizes) the occurrence of nonadherence and promotes more open clinician-patient communication. It also facilitates inquiry into the factors that promote or deter medication adherence. Common causes of failure to adhere to the treatment regimen include inattentiveness, prospective memory difficulties (i.e., forgetting to remember), preoccupation with other tasks, inconvenience, haste, disorganization (misplacing or losing the pill bottle), time mismanagement, and ambivalence about taking medication. Numerous cognitive behavioral strategies can be employed to address these obstacles in the course of a routine follow-up visit with the prescribing physician and can serve as the focus for the work of therapy. Other barriers to nonadherence are discussed in a later section.

Making Adjustments for Comorbid Conditions

Comorbid medical and psychiatric disorders frequently necessitate adjustments in medication management strategies. The presence of hypertension or other cardiovascular problems (e.g., palpitations or arrhythmias, syncope, dizziness, shortness of breath upon exertion, exercise intolerance, recent myocardial infarction) necessitates a comprehensive cardiac workup prior to starting most ADHD medications. The presence of cardiac risk factors such as smoking, high body mass index (obesity), diabetes, and metabolic syndrome also warrants careful evaluation. It is now the standard of care to treat all existing signs or symptoms of heart disease with cardiac medications and lifestyle adjustments to minimize any ongoing risks of ADHD medications. Once cardiovascular symptoms are well controlled, it is appropriate to introduce stimulants or other medications at low doses and to titrate upward slowly while monitoring blood pressure, heart and respiratory rate, and electrocardiogram regularly (Gutgesell et al., 1999; Warren et al., 2009). Recent studies indicate that stimulants and nonstimulants for ADHD have clinically insignificant effects on blood pressure in treated hypertensive patients who are normotensive (Jain et al., 2006; Nutt et al., 2007; Wilens et al., 2006a).

It is unclear what effects ADHD medications have on glucose control and diabetes. Although there is no evidence of primary glucose dysregulation with these agents, it is clear that their anorexogenic effects may alter eating habits. When appetite suppression leads to decreased food intake, and/or when there is rebound binge eating after the medication effects wear off, it is possible that glucose metabolism is adversely affected. In cases where patients suffer from diabetes, it is vital to get tight control of glucose before introducing stimulants and to monitor for signs and symptoms of dysregulation at regular intervals (Satterfield, Schell, & Barb, 1980).

The medication management of ADHD and comorbid psychiatric disorders is an area of active investigation and clinical controversy. The absence of large-scale randomized controlled trials for these patients makes it difficult to delineate precise guidelines for combining pharmacologic agents. Despite these limitations, a clinical consensus is emerging that rational polypharmacy strategies are acceptable for comorbid patients. For instance, with comorbid dysthymia and/or depressive disorders, it is reasonable to treat first with bupropion, which will improve mood and ADHD symptoms. Another approach would be to add an SSRI to stimulant medication. Less commonly, psychiatrists may choose to prescribe a tricyclic antidepressant or a serotonin-norepinephrine reuptake inhibitor (SNRI), either alone or in combination with low-dose stimulant medication (see Rostain, 2008; Spencer, 2008).

ADHD is common in patients with Bipolar Disorder (approximately 10–20%) (Kessler et al., 2006; Nierenberg et al., 2005) yet there are no RCTs in adults to support a treatment algorithm (Goodman & Thase, 2009; McIntyre, 2009). Clinical consensus favors tight control of manic and hypomanic symptoms with appropriate agents (e.g., lithium, anticonvulsants, novel antipsychotics) prior to introducing ADHD medications. Although stimulants and bupropion are safe and effective in combination with mood stabilizers, atomoxetine poses a potential danger because it is similar to TCAs in its pharmacologic profile, and these are generally avoided in patients with Bipolar Disorder. Consultation with an expert in the medical treatment of patients with ADHD is recommended in these cases.

In cases of comorbid Anxiety Disorders (including Generalized Anxiety Disorder, Separation Anxiety Disorder, Obsessive-Compulsive Disorder, or Panic Disorder), it is common to combine SSRIs with stimulant medication, although care must be taken to ensure that these latter agents do not exacerbate the anxiety. As noted previously, recent studies have documented that atomoxetine can be helpful in patients with comorbid anxiety (Geller et al., 2007), social anxiety (Adler et al., 2009; Durell et al., 2010) and/or tic disorders (Spencer et al., 2008). Hence, it might make sense for clinicians to begin with ATX in these patients. If these approaches are not successful, it is reasonable to consider guanfacine, clonidine, or a TCA for these comorbid conditions.

Patients with comorbid substance use disorders present a tremendous challenge since these conditions are already difficult to treat, and the presence of ADHD renders them even more resistant to intervention. Moreover, there is a paucity of clinical trials to inform patient care decisions. Two studies of cocaine abusers with ADHD (Levin, Evans, Brooks, & Garawi, 2007; Schubiner et al., 2002) found that MPH (immediate release and sustained release) had no overall improvement in cocaine use but some improvement in ADHD symptoms. A study of ATX in alcohol-abusing patients with ADHD showed some decreases in heavy drinking but no differences in relapse rates (Wilens et al., 2008a). An open trial of sustained-release bupropion in 32 adults with ADHD and Substance Use Disorder (SUD) found improved ADHD without much change in substance use (Wilens et al., 2010). These studies suggest that while pharmacotherapy alone is not sufficient to reduce substance use in these patients with ADHD, the addition of MPH, ATX, or bupropion was somewhat successful and did *not* worsen SUD symptoms. These results suggest that these medications can be introduced safely into a comprehensive treatment protocol. In order to minimize the risk of diversion, it is important to keep track of pills and refills, use extended-release formulations of stimulants, obtain urine toxicology frequently, discuss safe storage methods, and emphasize the importance of not sharing medications. "Red flags" requiring careful consideration include: (a) demands for immediate-release stimulants, (b) repeatedly discordant pill counts, (c) frequently lost prescriptions, and (d) repeated requests to increase dosage.

Managing Common Side Effects of Stimulants, Atomoxetine, and Alpha Agonists

The most common adverse effects seen with stimulants are gastrointestinal symptoms (e.g., abdominal pain, nausea, and constipation), cardiovascular symptoms (mild increases in heart rate and blood pressure), appetite suppression and consequent weight loss, insomnia (difficulty falling asleep and interrupted sleep), motor tics, mood disturbance (e.g., dysphoria, moodiness, irritability, hypomania), jitteriness, jumpiness, and personality suppression. Rarely, mania, paranoia, and psychosis can result from the use of these agents. Most of these side effects can be managed with dose adjustments and switching from short-acting to long-acting agents, and some of them abate with time (e.g., GI symptoms, jitteriness).

Sleep disturbances may need the addition of other agents, such as melatonin, clonidine, trazadone, mirtazapine, TCAs, or antihistamines (Tjon Pian Gi et al., 2003; Kratochvil, Lake, Pliszka, & Walkup, 2005; Pliszka et al., 2007; Prince et al., 1996; Weiss et al., 2006b).

The onset of stimulant-induced tics may be bothersome or upsetting to the patient, depending on their severity. If they are mild, it may be possible to continue at a lower dose. If they are causing interference with daily activities or subjective distress, it is advisable to switch to a nonstimulant medication (i.e., atomoxetine or alpha-adrenergic agonists). Rarely, it might be necessary to add an atypical antipsychotic to the stimulant.

Mood disturbances from stimulants are especially important to manage carefully. Mild symptoms can be minimized by dose adjustments and the addition of alpha-adrenergic agonists, but more prominent symptoms should prompt a thorough investigation for the emergence of depression, Bipolar Disorder, or stimulant abuse. Similarly, the appearance of thought disturbance, paranoia, or psychosis should be addressed by immediate cessation of the stimulant and a full psychiatric workup.

Atomoxetine-induced side effects are similar to stimulants: GI upset (abdominal pain, nausea, vomiting), cardiovascular alterations (hypertension, mild increased heart rate), decreased appetite and weight loss, and mood disturbance (irritability, nervousness, hypomania, suicidality). Additionally, due to its chemical resemblance to TCAs, anticholinergic side effects, such as dizziness, drowsiness, sedation, headache, dry mouth, constipation, urinary hesitation, and decreased sexual desire, can emerge. GI symptoms can be minimized by dividing the daily dose and by taking the medication immediately after meals (breakfast and dinner). Sedation, cardiovascular changes, and appetite suppression might require dose reductions. Mood disturbances (especially irritability and temper outbursts) should be monitored very closely because of concerns that ATX, like TCAs, can prompt the emergence of manic symptoms in patients at risk for mood disorders. Some clinicians advise the co-administration of mood stabilizers (e.g., carbamazepine or risperidone) for these situations (Niederhofer, 2009), but it is advisable to seek consultation before proceeding with combination treatment. Symptoms of urinary hesitancy and retention can be treated with alpha1A-adrenoceptor antagonists (e.g., tamsulosin, doxazosin) commonly used to treat benign prostatic hypertrophy (Kasper & Wolf, 2002; Szabaldi, 1998). Suicidality and inhibited sexual desire are best managed by discontinuing the medication.

Alpha-adrenergic agonists can cause sedation, fatigue, dizziness, syncope, arrhythmias, dry mouth, indigestion, nausea, nightmares, insomnia, anxiety, dysphoria, and depression. Modifying the dose and administering most of the medication at bedtime can minimize the sedation and fatigue and reduce many other adverse effects. It is important to monitor the patient's blood pressure and heart rate at each visit and to obtain electrocardiograms regularly so as to detect rhythm disturbances before they cause clinical symptoms. The emergence of insomnia, anxiety, dysphoria, and depression are indications to discontinue these medications, although it is important to taper them slowly in order to reduce the chances of rebound hypertension.

Handling Inadequate Response to Treatment

Reviews of clinical trials of medication treatment for ADHD indicate that patients respond well, partially, or poorly in roughly equal numbers (Wilens, 2003). It is unclear why this is occurs, and there are, as yet, no patient predictors of medication treatment response. It is important to keep in mind that treatment response in clinical trials tends to be higher than that seen in clinical practice (Elia, Borcherding, Rapoport, & Keysor, 1991), most likely due to factors such as patient selection (i.e., generally lower comorbidity), patient motivation (i.e., higher in clinical trials), and treatment protocols (e.g., aggressive titration, close follow-up).

When patients are not responding as expected to medication treatment, it is important to establish that they are taking the medication as prescribed and that the diagnosis is accurate. If comorbid disorders are more prominent than ADHD, it might be important to switch the focus of treatment to these concerns. Sometimes an inadequate response may be due to insufficient dosing of medication, which is often seen in the case of stimulants, where the current FDA dosage limits may lead to undermedication. A significant percentage of patients will not respond unless stimulant dosage is raised above these levels. In other cases, patients may need additional medication doses at specific times when increased focus and concentration is required (e.g., studying for examinations, working late into the evening). It is acceptable to combine short- and long-acting stimulant preparations or to combine ATX and stimulants for these patients (Adler, Reingold, Morrill, & Wilens, 2006b; Adler et al., 2008, 2009).

At present, there are no officially sanctioned algorithms for modifying medications to treat ADHD in adults. Pliszka et al. (2006) proposed an algorithm for ADHD treatment for children and adolescents (see Figure 18.3) that includes starting with one class of stimulant (MPH or AMP) at appropriate doses, then switching to the other class of stimulant before adding or switching to ATX. Alternatively, bupropion, alpha-adrenergic agonists, or TCAs can be used before seeking consultation with an ADHD expert. Clinical trials have been conducted on combinations of ATX and MPH, desipramine and MPH, and clonidine and MPH (Cohen et al., 1999; Hazell & Stuart, 2003; Palumbo et al., 2008; Rapport, Carlson, Kelly, & Pataki, 1993; Tourette's Syndrome

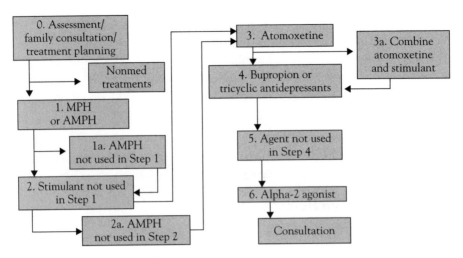

Figure 18.3   ADHD Treatment Algorithm

Source: Adapted from Pliszka, S. R., Crismon, M. L., Hughes, C. W., Texas Consensus Conference Panel on Pharmacotherapy of Childhood Attention Deficit Hyperactivity Disorder (2006). The Texas Children's Medication Algorithm Project: Revision of the algorithm for pharmacotherapy of Attention-Deficit/Hyperactivity Disorder. *Journal of the American Academy of Child and Adolescent Psychiatry, 45*(6), 642–657.

Study Group, 2002) with no serious adverse effects reported. Anecdotally, it is possible to combine bupropion with stimulants or alpha-adrenergic agonists as well as TCAs with stimulants or bupropion, although caution must be exercised here because of potentially additive effects. Whenever polypharmaceutical regimens are introduced, it is important to consult with experts in clinical psychopharmacology.

Improving Adherence

The key to improving patient adherence is a strong therapeutic alliance. Partnership in real-life problem solving, especially with respect to medication management, is essential. Clinicians should inquire in an open-ended fashion about the patient's attitudes and feelings about the medication he or she is taking and should answer all questions regarding perceived or actual barriers to adherence (e.g., side effects, costs, inconvenience, efficacy, and schedule of administration). If nonadherence appears to be a central theme in the patient's course of treatment, it is vital to make this a focus of intervention.

Distorted beliefs about medications may contribute to nonadherence (see Ramsay & Rostain, 2008). For instance, the views that taking a medication is similar to being a "drug addict," is a sign of weakness, or is a form of "cheating" will certainly impede compliance. Similarly, a mindset that "doing better" (i.e., completing tasks, accomplishing goals) on the medication is not the result of the patient's hard work but solely due to an external agent's effects tends to undermine the patient's self-esteem and sense of self-efficacy. It is useful to explore these attitudes and beliefs, to trace their origins, to see their impact on the patient's behavior, and to challenge their validity in a Socratic fashion. Over time, the clinician can assist the patient to come up with a more balanced view of the role that medication plays in his or her treatment plan and to effectively tackle any other barriers to adherence.

There is no doubt that treatment adherence improves with strong social support (Kripalani, Yao, & Haynes, 2007). The involvement of significant others can be helpful, either by suggesting strategies to increase the patient's compliance or by assisting directly (e.g. prompting the patient to take medication at appropriate times). When social supports are not directly available, it is helpful to focus on organizational and time management strategies to build medication administration into daily routines. (Note: See Ramsay & Rostain, 2008; Safren et al., 2005; Solanto et al., 2008, 2010; and Chapter 14 in this text for cognitive behavioral therapy approaches to these issues.)

Adherence improves with repeated educational sessions and continuous assessment and feedback, as these serve to maintain a motivational attitude. It is also the case that adherence improves with dose simplification, including switching to long-acting (i.e., once-daily) medications (Sanchez et al., 2005). Regular contact between therapist and prescribing physician is another strategy to help effectuate adherence. New technologies (like personal digital assistants and cell phones) are playing an increasingly vital role in this regard (Adler & Nierenberg, 2010).

REFERENCES

Ackerman, P. T., Dykman, R. A., Holloway, C., et al. (1991). A trial of piracetam in two subgroups of students with dyslexia enrolled in a summer tutoring. *Journal of Learning Disorders, 24*(9), 542–549.

Adler, L. A. (2009). Pharmacotherapy for adult ADHD. *Journal of Clinical Psychiatry, 70*(5), e12.

Adler, L. A., Dietrich, A., Reimherr, F. W., et al. (2006a). Safety and tolerability of once versus twice daily atomoxetine in adults with ADHD. *Annals of Clinical Psychiatry, 18*(2), 107–113.

Adler, L. A., Goodman, D. W., Kollins, S. H., et al. (2008). Double-blind, placebo-controlled sudy of the efficacy and safety of lysdexamifetamine dimesylate in adults with attention-deficit/hyperactivity disorder. *Journal of Clinical Psychiatry, 69*(9), 1364–1373.

Adler, L. A., Liebowitz, M., Kronenberger, W., et al. (2009). Atomoxetine treatment in adults with Attention-Deficit/Hyperactivity Disorder and comorbid Social Anxiety Disorder. *Depression and Anxiety, 26*(3), 212–221.

Adler , L. D., & Nierenberg, A. A. (2010). Review of medication adherence in children and adults with ADHD. *Postgraduate Medicine, 122*(1), 184–191.

Adler, L. A., Reingold, L. S., Morrill, M. S., & Wilens, T. E. (2006b). Combination pharmacotherapy for adult ADHD. *Current Psychiatric Reports, 8*(5), 409–415.

Adler L. A., Spencer, T. J., Milton, D. R., et al. (2005). Long-term, open-label study of the safety and efficacy of atomoxetine in adults with Attention-Deficit/Hyperactivity Disorder: An interim analysis. *Journal of Clinical Psychology, 66,* 294–99.

Armstrong, C. L., Hayes, K. M., & Martin, R. (2001). Neurocognitive problems in Attention Deficit Disorder, alternative concepts and evidence for impairment in inhibition of selective attention. In J. Wasserstein, L. E. Wolf, & F. F. LeFevre (Eds.), Adult Attention Deficit Disorder, brain mechanisms and life outcomes. *Annals of the New York Academy of Sciences, 931,* 196–215.

Arnsten, A. F. T. (2009). Toward a new understanding of Attention-Deficit Hyperactivity Disorder pathophysiology: An important role for prefrontal cortex dysfunction. *CNS Drugs, 23,* Supp. 1, 33–41.

Arnsten, A. F. T., & Li, B. M (2005). Neurobiology of executive functions, catecholamine influences on prefrontal cortical functions. *Biological Psychiatry, 57,* 1377–1384.

Arnsten, A. F. [T.], Scahill, L., & Findling, R. L. (2007). Alpha(2)-adrenergic receptor agonists for the treatment of Attention-Deficit/Hyperactivity Disorder: Emerging concepts from new data. *Journal of Child and Adolescent Psychopharmacology, 17* (4), 393–406.

Barkley, R. A. (2006). *Attention Deficit Hyperactivity Disorder: A handbook for diagnosis and treatment* (3rd ed.). New York, NY: Guilford Press.

Biederman, J., Mick, E., Faraone, S., et al. (2006a). A double-blind comparison of galantamine hydrogen bromide and placebo in adults with attention-deficit/hyperactivity disorder: A pilot study. *Journal of Clinical Psychopharmacology, 26*(2), 163–166.

Biederman, J., Mick, E., Surman, C., et al. (2006b). A randomized, placebo-controlled trial of OROS methylphenidate in adults with Attention-Deficit/Hyperactivity Disorder. *Biological Psychiatry, 59*(9), 829–835.

Biederman, J., & Spencer, T. J. (2008). Psychopharmacological interventions. *Child and Adolescent Psychiatric Clinics of North America, 17*(2), 439–458.

Bloch, M. H., Panza, K. E., Landeros-Weisenberger, A., & Leckman, J. F. (2009). Meta-analysis, treatment of Attention-Deficit/Hyperactivity Disorder in children with comorbid tic disorders. *Journal of the American Academy of Child and Adolescent Psychiatry, 48*(9), 884–893.

Bostrom, N., Sandberg, A. (2009). Cognitive enhancement: Methods, ethics, regulatory challenges. *Science and Engineering Ethics, 15,* 311–341.

Bouffard, R., Hechtman, L., Minde, K., & Iaboni-Kassab, F. (2003). The efficacy of 2 different dosages of methylphenidate in treating adults with Attention-Deficit Hyperactivity Disorder. *Canadian Journal of Psychiatry, 48*(8), 546–554.

Brodtkorb, E., Klees, T. M., Nakken, K. O., et al. (2004). Levetiracetam in adult patients with and without learning disability: Focus on behavioral adverse effects. *Epilepsy & Behavior, 5*(2), 231–235.

Brown, R. T., Amler, R. W., Freeman, W. S., et al. (2005). Treatment of Attention Deficit/Hyperactivity Disorder: Overview of the evidence. *Pediatrics, 115,* e749–e757.

Brown, T. E. (2005). *Attention deficit disorder: The unfocused mind in children and adults.* New Haven, CT: Yale University Press.

Brown, T. E. (Ed.). (2009). *ADHD comorbidities: Handbook for complications in children and adults.* Washington, DC: American Psychiatric Publishing.

Bymaster, F. P., Katner, J. S., Nelson, D. L., et al. (2002). Atomoxetine increases extracellular levels of norepinephrine and dopamine in prefrontal cortex of rats: A potential mechanism for efficacy in Attention Deficit/Hyperactivity Disorder. *Neuropsychopharmacology, 5,* 699–711.

Carpentier P. J., de Jong C. A., Dijkstra B. A., Verbrugge C. A., Krabbe P. F. (2005). A controlled trial of methylphenidate in adults with Attention Deficit/Hyperactivity Disorder and substance use disorders. *Addiction, 100,* 1868–74.

Castellanos, X., Sonuga-Barke, E., Milham, M., & Tannock, R. (2006). Characterizing cognition in ADHD: Beyond executive dysfunction. *Trends in Cognitive Sciences, 10,* 117–123.

Cocores, J. A., & Gold, M. S (2008). Varenicline and adult ADHD. *Journal of Neuropsychiatry and Clinical Neurosciences, 20*(4), 494–495.

Cohen, L. G., Prince, J., Biederman, J., et al. (1999). Absence of effect of stimulants on the phamacokinetics of desipramine in children. *Pharmacotherapy, 19,* 746–752.

Conners, C. K., Erhardt, D., & Sparrow, E. (1999). Conners Adult ADHD Rating Scales (CAARS). New York, NY: Psychological Corporation / Harcourt Brace.

Cubo, E., Jaén, A. F., & Moreno, C. (2008). Donepezil use in children and adolescents with tics and Attention-Deficit/Hyperactivity Disorder: An 18-week, single-center, dose-escalating, prospective, open-label study. *Clinical Therapeutics, 30,* 182–189.

Di Ianni, M., Wilsher, C. R., Blank, M. S., et al. (1985). The effects of piracetam in children with dyslexia. *Journal of Clinical Psychopharmacology, 5,* 272–278.

Dulcan, M., and the Work Group on Quality Issues, American Academy of Child and Adolescent Psychiatry. (1997). Practice parameters for the assessment and treatment of attention-deficit/hyperactivity disorder. *Journal of the American Academy of Child and Adolescent Psychiatry, 36,* 85S–121S.

Durell, T., Adler, L. A., Liebowitz, M., et al. (2010). An 8-week, open-label extension period study of atomoxetine in adults with Attention-Deficit/Hyperactivity Disorder and comorbid Social Anxiety Disorder. *Journal of ADHD and Related Disorders, 1*(3), 36–52.

Elia, J., Borcherding, B. G., Rapoport, J. L., & Keysor, C. S. (1991). Methylphenidate and dextroamphetamine treatments of hyperactivity: Are there true nonresponders? *Psychiatry Research, 36,* 141–155.

Faraone, S. V., & Glatt, S. J. (2010). A comparison of the efficacy of medications for adult Attention-Deficit Hyperactivity Disorder using meta-analysis of effect sizes. *Journal of Clinical Psychiatry, 71,* 754–763.

Faraone, S. V., Perlis, R. H., Doyle, A. E., et al. (2005). Molecular genetics of Attention-Deficit/ Hyperactivity Disorder. *Biological Psychiatry, 57,* 1313–1323.

Faraone, S. V., Spencer, T., Aleardi, M., et al. (2004). Meta-analysis of the efficacy of methylphenidate for treating Adult Attention-Deficit/Hyperactivity Disorder. *Journal of Clinical Psychopharmacology*, 24(1), 24–29.

Findling, R. L. (2008). Evolution of the treatment of Attention-Deficit/Hyperactivity Disorder in children: A review. *Clinical Therapeutics*, 30(5), 942–957.

Findling, R. L., McNamara, N. K., Stansbrey, R. J., et al. (2007). A pilot evaluation of the safety, tolerability, pharmacokinetics, and effectiveness of memantine in pediatric patients with Attention-Deficit/Hyperactivity Disorder combined type. *Journal of Child and Adolescent Psychopharmacology*, 17(1), 19–33.

Froehlich, T. E., McGough, J. J., & Stein, M. A. (2010). Progress and promise of Attention-Deficit Hyperactivity Disorder pharmacogenetics. *CNS Drugs*, 24(2), 99–117.

Fuemmeler, B. F., Kollins, S. H., & McClernon, F. J. (2007). Attention Deficit Hyperactivity Disorder symptoms predict nicotine dependence and progression to regular smoking from adolescence to young adulthood. *Journal of Pediatric Psychology*, 32, 1203–1213.

Geller, D., Donnelly, C., Lopez, F., et al. (2007). Atomoxetine treatment for pediatric patients with Attention-Deficit/Hyperactivity Disorder with comorbid Anxiety Disorder. *Journal of the American Academy of Child and Adolescent Psychiatry*, 46(9), 1119–1127.

Goodman, D. W., & Thase, M. E. (2009). Recognizing ADHD in adults with comorbid mood disorders, implications for identification and management. *Postgraduate Medicine*, 121(5), 20–30.

Gouliaev, A. H., & Senning, A. (1994). Piracetam and other structurally related nootropics. *Brain Research Reviews*, 19(2), 180–222.

Greenhill L. L., Pliszka S., Dulcan M. K., et al., (2002). Practice parameter for the use of stimulant medications in the treatment of children, adolescents and adults. *Journal of the American Academy of Child and Adolescent Psychiatry*, 41(2 Supplement), 26S–49S.

Greydanus, D. E., Pratt, H. D., & Patel, D. R. (2007). Attention Deficit Hyperactivity Disorder across the lifespan: The child, adolescent and adult. *Disease-a-Month 53*, 70–131.

Gualtieri, C. T., Ondrusek, M. G., & Finley, C. (1985). Attention deficit disorder in adults. *Clinical Neuropharmacology*, 8(4), 343–356.

Gutgesell, H., Atkins, D., Barst, R., et al. (1999). Cardiovascular monitoring of children and adolescents receiving psychotropic drugs: A statement for healthcare professionals from the Committee on Congenital Cardiac Defects, Council on Cardiovascular Disease in the Young, American Heart Association. *Circulation*, 99(7), 979–982.

Hazell, P. L., & Stuart, J. E. (2003). A randomized controlled trial of clonidine added to psychostimulant medication for hyperactive and aggressive children. *Journal of the American Academy of Child and Adolescent Psychiatry*, 42(8), 886–894.

Helfgott, E., Rudel, R. G., & Kairam, R. (1986). The effect of piracetam on short- and long-term verbal retrieval in dyslexic boys. *International Journal of Psychophysiology, 4*(1), 53–61.

Canadian Attention Deficit Hyperactivity Disorder Resource Alliance (CADDRA). (2006). *Canadian ADHD Practice Guidelines, First Edition*. Toronto, ON: CADDRA.

Jain, U., Hechtman, L., Weiss, M., et al. (2007). Efficacy of a novel biphasic controlled-release methylphenidate formula in adults with Attention-Deficit/Hyperactivity Disorder, results of a double-blind, placebo-controlled crossover study. *Journal of Clinical Psychiatry, 68*(2), 268–277.

Kasper, S., & Wolf, R. (2002). Successful treatment of reboxetine-induced urinary hesitancy with tamsulosin. *European Neuropsychopharmacology, 12*(2), 119–122.

Kendall, T., Taylor, E., Perez, A., et al. (2008). Diagnosis and management of Attention-Deficit/Hyperactivity Disorder in children, young people, and adults: Summary of NICE guidance. *British Medical Journal, 337*, 751–754.

Kessler, R. C., Adler, L., Barkley, R., et al. (2006). The prevalence and correlates of adult ADHD in the United States: Results from the National Comorbidity Survey Replication. *American Journal of Psychiatry, 163*(4), 716–723.

Koesters, M., Becker, T., & Kilian, R. (2009). Limits of meta-analysis, methylphenidate in the treatment of adult Attention-Deficit/Hyperactivity Disorder. *Journal of Psychopharmacology, 23*(7), 733–744.

Kollins, S. H., McClernon, F. J., & Fuemmeler, B. F. (2005). Association between smoking and Attention-Deficit/Hyperactivity Disorder symptoms in a population-based sample of young adults. *Archives of General Psychiatry, 62*, 1142–1147.

Kooij, J. J., Burger, H., Boonstra, A. M., et al. (2004). Efficacy and safety of methylphenidate in 45 adults with Attention-Deficit/Hyperactivity Disorder: A randomized placebo-controlled, double-blind cross-over trial. *Psychological Medicine, 34*(6), 973–982.

Kratochvil, C. J., Lake, M., Pliszka, S. R., & Walkup, J. T. (2005). Pharmacological management of treatment-induced insomnia in ADHD. *Journal of the American Academy of Child and Adolescent Psychiatry, 44*(5), 499–501.

Kripalani, S., Yao, X., & Haynes, R. B. (2007). Interventions to enhance medication adherence in chronic medical conditions: A systematic review. *Archives of Internal Medicine, 167*(6), 540–550.

Kumar, R. (2008). Approved and investigational uses of modafinil: An evidence-based review. *Drugs, 68*(13), 1803–1839.

Kuperman, S., Perry, P. J., Gaffney, G. R., et al. (2001). Bupropion SR vs. methylphenidate vs. placebo for Attention Deficit Hyperactivity Disorder: A pilot study. *Annals of Clinical Psychiatry, 13*(3), 129–134.

Lambert, N. M., & Kartsough, C. S. (1998). Prospective study of tobacco smoking and substance dependencies among samples of ADHD and non-ADHD participants. *Journal of Learning Disabilities, 31*, 533–544.

Levin, E. D., McClernon, F. J., & Rezvani, A. H. (2006). Nicotinic effects on cognitive function, behavioral characterization, pharmacological specification, and anatomic localization. *Psychopharmacology, 184*, 523–539.

Levin, F. R., Evans, S. M., Brooks, D. J., & Garawi, F. (2007). Treatment of cocaine dependent treatment seekers with adult ADHD: Double-blind comparison of methylphenidate and placebo. *Drug and Alcohol Dependency, 87*, 20–29.

Loughead, J., Ray, R., Wileyto, E. P., et al. (2010). Effects of the alpha4 beta2 partial agonist varenicline on brain activity and working memory in abstinent smokers. *Biological Psychiatry, 67*(8), 715–721.

Makris, N., Biederman, J., Monuteaux, M. C., & Seidman, L. J. (2009). Towards conceptualizing a neural systems-based anatomy of Attention-Deficit/Hyperactivity Disorder. *Developmental Neuroscience, 31*(1–2), 36–49.

Malykh, A. G., & Sadaie, M. R. (2010). Piracetam and piracetam-like drugs, from basic science to novel clinical applications to CNS disorders. *Drugs, 70*(3), 287–312.

Mattes, J. A., Boswell, L., & Oliver, H. (1984). Methylphenidate effects on symptoms of attention deficit disorder in adults. *Archives of General Psychiatry, 41*(11), 1059–1063.

McIntyre, R. (2009). Bipolar disorder and ADHD: Clinical concerns. *CNS Spectrums, 14*(7), (Suppl. 6), 8–9.

Medori, R., Ramos-Quiroga, J. A., Casas, M., et al. (2008). A randomized, placebo-controlled trial of three fixed dosages of prolonged-release OROS methylphenidate in adults with Attention-Deficit/Hyperactivity Disorder. *Biological Psychiatry, 63*(10), 981–989.

Meszaros, A., Czobor, P., Balint, S., et al. (2009). Pharmacotherapy of adult Attention Deficit Hyperactivity Disorder (ADHD): A meta-analysis. *International Journal of Neuropsychopharmacology, 12*, 1137–1147.

Michelson, D., Adler, L., Spencer, T., Reimherr, F. W., West, S. A., Allen, A. J., . . . Milton, D. (2003). Adults with ADHD: Two randomized, placebo-controlled trials. *Biological Psychiatry, 53*(2), 112–120.

Minzenberg, M. J., & Carter, C. S. (2008). Modafinil: A review of neurochemical actions and effects on cognition. *Neuropsychopharmacology, 33*(7), 1477–1502.

Modi N. B., Lindemulder B., & Gupta S. K. (2000). Single- and multiple-dose pharmacokinetics of an oral once a day osmotic controlled-release OROS (methylphenidate HCL) formulation. *Journal of Clinical Pharmacology, 40*, 379–388.

Muir V. J., & Perry C. M. (2010). Guanfacine Extended-Release in Attention Deficit Hyperactivity Disorder. *Drugs, 70*, 1693–1702.

Niederhofer, H. (2009). Combining atomoxetine with carbamazepine or neuroleptics reduces adverse side effects. *Journal of Paediatric and Child Health, 46*, 66.

Nierenberg, A. A., Miyahara, S., Spencer, T., et al. (2005). Clinical and diagnostic implications of lifetime Attention-Deficit/Hyperactivity Disorder comorbidity in adults with Bipolar Disorder: Data from the first 1000 STEP-BD participants. *Biological Psychiatry, 57*(11), 1467–1473.

Nigg, J. (2006). *What causes ADHD?* New York, NY: Guilford Press.

Nigg, J. T., & Casey, B. J. (2005). An integrative theory of Attention-Deficit/ Hyperactivity Disorder based on the cognitive and affective neurosciences. *Developmental Psychopatholgy, 17*, 785–806.

NIH Consensus Statement. (1998). Diagnosis and treatment of Attention Deficit Hyperactivity Disorder (ADHD). *National Library of Medicine, 16*(2), 1–37.

Nutt, D. J., Fone, K., Asherson, P., et al., British Association for Psychopharmacology. (2007). Evidence-based guidelines for management of Attention-Deficit/Hyperactivity Disorder in adolescents in transition to adult services and in adults: Recommendations from the British Association for Psychopharmacology. *Journal of Psychopharmacology, 21*(1), 10–41.

Palumbo, D. R., Sallee, F. R., Pelham, W. E., Jr., et al. (2008). Clonidine for Attention-Deficit/Hyperactivity Disorder: Efficacy and tolerability outcomes. *Journal of the American Academy of Child and Adolescent Psychiatry, 47*(2), 180–188.

Parasrampuria D. A., Schoedel K. A., Schuller R., et al. (2007). Assessment of pharmacokinetics and pharmacodynamic effects related to abuse potential of a unique oral osmotic-controlled extended-release methylphenidate formulation in humans. *Journal of Clinical Pharmacology, 47*, 1476–1488.

Peterson, K., McDonagh, M. S., & Fu, R. (2008). Comparative benefits and harms of competing medications for adults with Attention-Deficit Hyperactivity Disorder: A systematic review and indirect comparison meta-analysis. *Psychopharmacology, 197*, 1–11.

Pliszka, S., & AACAP Work Group on Quality Issues. (2007). Practice parameter for the assessment and treatment of Attention-Deficit/Hyperactivity Disorder in children and adolescents. *Journal of the American Academy of Child and Adolescent Psychiatry, 46*(7), 894–921.

Pliszka, S. R., Crismon, M. L., Hughes, C. W., et al. Texas Consensus Conference Panel on Pharmacotherapy of Childhood Attention Deficit Hyperactivity Disorder (2006). The Texas Children's Medication Algorithm Project: Revision of the algorithm for pharmacotherapy of Attention-Deficit/Hyperactivity Disorder. *Journal of the American Academy of Child and Adolescent Psychiatry, 45*(6), 642–657.

Pliszka, S. R., McCracken, J. T., & Maas, J. W. (1996). Catecholamines in Attention-Deficit Hyperactivity Disorder: Current perspectives. *Journal of the American Academy of Child and Adolescent Psychiatry, 35*(3), 264–272.

Potter, A. S., & Newhouse, P. A. (2004). Effects of acute nicotine administration on behavioral inhibition in adolescents with Attention-Deficit/Hyperactivity Disorder. *Psychopharmacology* (Berlin),*176*(2), 182–194.

Potter, A. S., & Newhouse, P. A. (2008). Acute nicotine improves cognitive deficits in young adults with Attention-Deficit/Hyperactivity Disorder. *Pharmacology, Biochemistry and Behavior, 88*(4), 407–417.

Potter, A. S., Ryan, K. K., & Newhouse, P. A.(2009) Effects of acute ultra-low dose mecamyl-amine on cognition in adult attention-Deficit/Hyperactivity Disorder (ADHD). *Human Psychopharmacology*, 24(4), 309–317.

Prince, J. B., Wilens, T. E., Biederman, J. B., et al. (1996). Clonidine for sleep disturbances associated with Attention-Deficit Hyperactivity Disorder: A systematic chart review of 62 cases. *Journal of the American Academy of Child and Adolescent Psychiatry*, 35(5), 599–605.

Ramsay, J. R., & Rostain, A. L. (2008). *Cognitive behavioral therapy for adult ADHD: An integrative psychosocial and medical approach.* New York, NY: Routledge, Taylor & Francis Group.

Rappley, M. D. (2005). Attention Deficit-Hyperactivity Disorder. *New England Journal of Medicine*, 352, 165–173.

Rapport, M. D., Carlson, G. A., Kelly, K. L., & Pataki, C. (1993). Methylphenidate and desipramine in hospitalized children: I. Separate and combined effects on cognitive function. *Journal of the American Academy of Child and Adolescent Psychiatry*, 32(2), 333–342.

Reimherr, F. W., Williams, E. D., Strong, R. E., et al. (2007). A double-blind, placebo-controlled, crossover study of osmotic release oral system methylphenidate in adults with ADHD with assessment of oppositional and emotional dimensions of the disorder. *Journal of Clinical Psychiatry*, 68(1), 93–101.

Rösler, M., Retz, W., Thome, J., et al. (2006). Psychopathological rating scales for diagnostic use in adults with Attention-Deficit/Hyperactivity Disorder (ADHD). *European Archives of Psychiatry and Clinical Neuroscience*, 256 (Suppl. 1), i3–i11.

Rostain, A. L. (2006). Addressing the misuse and abuse of stimulant medications on college campuses. *Current Psychiatry Reports*, 8, 335–336.

Rostain, A. L. (2008). Adult ADHD and depressive disorders, prevalence, significance, and clinical presentation. *CNS Spectrums,13*(5, Suppl. 8), 8–10.

Rudel, R., & Helfgott, E. (1984). Effect of piracetam on verbal memory of dyslexic boys. *Journal of the American Academy of Child and Adolescent Psychiatry*, 23(6), 695–699.

Safren, S. A., Otto, M. W., Sprich, S., et al. (2005). Cognitive-behavioral therapy for ADHD in medication-treated adults with continued symptoms. *Behaviour Research and Therapy*, 43, 831–842.

Sagvolden, T., Johansen, E. B., Aase, H., & Russell, V. A. (2005). A dynamic developmental theory of Attention-Deficit/Hyperactivity Disorder (ADHD) predominantly hyperactive-impulsive and combined subtypes. *Behavioral and Brain Sciences*, 28, 397–408.

Sallee, F. R., Lyne, A., Wigal, T., & McGough, J. J. (2009b). Long-term safety and efficacy of guanfacine extended release in children and adolescents with Attention-Deficit/Hyperactivity Disorder. *Journal of the American Academy of Child and Adolescent Psychiatry*, 9(3), 215–226.

Sallee, F. R., McGough, J., Wigal, T., et al. (2009a). Guanfacine extended release in children and adolescents with Attention-Deficit/Hyperactivity Disorder: A placebo-controlled trial. *Journal of the American Academy of Child and Adolescent Psychiatry*, 48(2), 155–165.

Sanchez, R. J., Crismon, M. L., Barner, J. C., et al. (2005). Assessment of adherence measures with different stimulants among children and adolescents. *Pharmacotherapy*, 25(7), 909–917.

Satterfield, J. H., Schell, A. M., & Barb, S. D. (1980). Potential risk of prolonged administration of stimulant medication for hyperactive children. *Journal of Developmental & Behavioral Pediatrics*, 1(3), 102–107.

Scahill, L., Chappell, P. B., Kim, Y. S., Schultz, R. T., Katsovich, L., Shepherd, E., et al. (2001). A placebo-controlled study of guanfacine in the treatment of children with tic disorders and Attention Deficit Hyperactivity Disorder. *American Journal of Psychiatry*, 158, 1067–1074.

Schatzberg, A. F., & Nemeroff, C. B. (Eds.). (2009). *The American Psychiatric Publishing textbook of psychopharmacology* (4th ed.). Washington, DC: American Psychiatric Publishing.

Schubiner, H., Saules, J. J., Arfken, C. L., et al. (2002). Double-blind placebo-controlled trial of methylphenidate in the treatment of adult ADHD patients with comorbid cocaine dependence. *Experimental and Clinical Psychopharmacology, 10,* 286–294.

Singer, H., Brown, J., Quaskey, S., et al. (1995). The treatment of Attention-Deficit Hyperactivity Disorder In Tourette's syndrome: A double-blind placebo controlled study with clonidine and desipramine. *Pediatrics*, 95, 74–81.

Solanto, M. V., Marks, D. J., Mitchell, K. J., et al. (2008). Development of a new psychosocial treatment for adult ADHD. *Journal of Attention Disorders, 11*(6), 728–736.

Solanto, M. V., Marks, D. J., Wasserstein, J., et al. (2010). Efficacy of meta-cognitive therapy for adult ADHD. *American Journal of Psychiatry,167.*

Spencer, T. J. (2008). Treatment of adult ADHD and comorbid depression. *CNS Spectrums, 13*(5 Suppl. 8), 14–16.

Spencer, T. J., Adler, L. A., McGough, J. J., et al. (2007). Efficacy and safety of dexmethylphenidate extended-release capsules in adults with Attention-Deficit/ Hyperactivity Disorder. *Biological Psychiatry*, 61(12), 1380–1387.

Spencer, T., Biederman, J., Wilens, T., et al. (1998). Effectiveness and tolerability of atomoxetine in adults with Attention Deficit Hyperactivity Disorder. *American Journal of Psychiatry*, 155(5), 693–695.

Spencer, T., Biederman, J., Wilens, T., et al. (2001). Efficacy of a mixed amphetamine salts compound in adults with Attention-Deficit/ Hyperactivity Disorder. *Archives of General Psychiatry*, 58(8), 775–782.

Spencer, T., Biederman, J., Wilens, T., et al. (2005). A large, double-blind, randomized clinical trial of methylphenidate in the treatment of adults with Attention-Deficit/Hyperactivity Disorder. *Biological Psychiatry*, 57(5), 456–463.

Spencer, T., Wilens, T., Biederman, J., et al. (1995). A double-blind, crossover comparison of methylphenidate and placebo in adults with childhood-onset Attention-Deficit Hyperactivity Disorder. *Archives of General Psychiatry*, 52(6), 434–443.

Spencer, T. J., Sallee, F. R., Gilbert, D. L., et al. (2008). Atomoxetine treatment of ADHD in children with comorbid Tourette syndrome. *Journal of Attention Disorders*, 11(4), 470–481.

Stevens, J. R., George, R. A., Fusillo, S., et al. (2010). Plasma methylphenidate concentrations in youths treated with high-dose osmotic release oral system formulation. *Journal of Child and Adolescent Psychopharmacology*, 20, 49–54.

Sukhanov, I. M., Zakharova, E. S., Danysz, W., Bespalov, A. Y. (2004). Effects of NMDA receptor channel blockers, MK-801 and memantine, on locomotor activity and tolerance to delay of reward in Wistar-Kyoto and spontaneously hypertensive rats. *Behavioral Pharmacology*, 15, 263–271.

Sumner, C. R., Gathercole, S., Greenbaum, M., et al. (2009). Atomoxetine for the treatment of Attention-Deficit/Hyperactivity Disorder (ADHD) in children with ADHD and dyslexia. *Child and Adolescent Psychiatry and Mental Health*, 3(40), 1–9.

Swan, G. E., & Lessov-Schlaggar, C. N. (2007). The effects of tobacco smoke and nicotine on cognition and the brain. *Neuropsychology Review*, 17, 259–273.

Swanson, C. J., Perry, K. W., Koch-Krueger, S., et al. (2006). Effect of the Attention Deficit/Hyperactivity Disorder drug atomoxetine on extracellular concentrations of norepinephrine and dopamine in several brain regions of the rat. *Neuropharmacology*, 6, 755–760.

Swanson, J. M., Kinsbourne, M., Nigg, J., et al. (2007). Etiologic subtypes of Attention-Deficit/Hyperactivity Disorder, brain imaging, molecular genetic and environmental factors and the dopamine hypothesis. *Neuropsychology Review*, 17(1), 39–59.

Szabadi, E. (1998). Doxazosin for reboxetine-induced urinary hesitancy. *British Journal of Psychiatry*, 173, 441–442.

Tannock, R., & Brown, T. E. (2009). ADHD with language and/or learning disorders in children and adolescents. In T. E. Brown (Ed.), *ADHD comorbidities: Handbook for complications in children and adults* (pp. 189–231). Washington, DC: American Psychiatric Publishing.

Taylor, E., Dopfner, M., Sergeant, J., et al. (2004). European clinical guidelines for hyperkinetic disorder—first upgrade. *European Child & Adolescent Psychiatry*, 13, Suppl. 1, 17–30.

Taylor, F. B., & Russo, J. (2000). Efficacy of modafinil compared to dextroamphetamine for the treatment of Attention Deficit Hyperactivity Disorder in adults. *Journal of Child and Adolescent Psychopharmacology*, 10(4), 311–320.

Taylor, F. B., & Russo, J. (2001). Comparing guanfacine and dextroamphetamine for the treatment of adult Attention-Deficit Hyperactivity Disorder. *Journal of Clinical Psychopharmacology, 21*, 223–228.

Tjon Pian Gi, C. V., Broeren, J. P., Starreveld, J. S., & Versteegh, F. G. (2003). Melatonin for treatment of sleeping disorders in children with Attention Deficit/Hyperactivity Disorder: A preliminary open label study. *European Journal of Pediatrics, 162*(7–8), 554–555.

Tourette's Syndrome Study Group. (2002). Treatment of ADHD in children with tics: A randomized controlled trial. *Neurology, 58*, 527–536.

Turner, D. C., Clark, L., Dowson, J., Robbins, T. W., & Sahakian, B. (2004). Modafinil improves cognition and response inhibition in adult Attention-Deficit/Hyperactivity Disorder. *Biological Psychiatry, 55*, 1031–1040.

Volkow, N. D., Wang, G. J., Kollins, S. H., et al. (2009a). Evaluating dopamine reward pathway in ADHD: Clinical implications. *Journal of the American Medical Association, 302*(10), 1084–1091.

Volkow, N. D., Fowler, J. S., Logan, J., et al. (2009b). Effects of modafinil on dopamine and dopamine transporters in the male human brain: Clinical implications. *Journal of the American Medical Association, 301*(11), 1148–1154.

Ward, M. G., Wender, P. H., & Reimherr, F. W. (1993). The Wender Utah Rating Scale: An aid in the retrospective diagnosis of childhood Attention Deficit Hyperactivity Disorder. *American Journal of Psychiatry, 150*, 885–890.

Warren, A. E., Hamilton, R. M., Bélanger, S. A., et al. (2009). Cardiac risk assessment before the use of stimulant medications in children and youth: A joint position statement by the Canadian Paediatric Society, the Canadian Cardiovascular Society, and the Canadian Academy of Child and Adolescent Psychiatry. *Canadian Journal of Cardiology, 25*(11), 625–630.

Weisler, R. H., Biederman, J., Spencer, T. J., et al. (2006). Mixed amphetamine salts extended-release in the treatment of adult ADHD: A randomized, controlled trial. *CNS Spectrums, 11*(8), 625–639.

Weisler, R. [H.], Young, J., Mattingly, G., et al. (2009). Long-term safety and effectiveness of lisdexamfetamine dimesylate in adults with Attention-Deficit/Hyperactivity Disorder. *CNS Spectrums, 14*(10), 573–585.

Weiss, M., Hechtman, L., & the Adult ADHD Research Group. (2006a). A randomized double-blind trial of paroxetine and/or dextroamphetamine and problem-focused therapy for Attention-Deficit/Hyperactivity Disorder in adults. *Journal of Clinical Psychiatry, 67*(4), 611–619.

Weiss, M. D., Wasdell, M. B., Bomben, M. M., et al. (2006b). Sleep hygiene and melatonin treatment for children and adolescents with ADHD and initial insomnia. *Journal of the American Academy of Child and Adolescent Psychiatry, 45*(5), 512–519.

Wender, P. H., Reimherr, F. W., Wood, D., & Ward, M. (1985). A controlled study of methylphenidate in the treatment of attention deficit disorder, residual type, in adults. *American Journal of Psychiatry, 142*(5), 547–552.

Wigal, S. B. (2009). Efficacy and safety limitations of Attention-Deficit Hyperactivity Disorder pharmacotherapy in children and adults. *CNS Drugs*, *23* Suppl. 1, 21–31.

Wilens, T. E. (2003). Drug therapy for adults with Attention-Deficit/Hyperactivity Disorder. *Drugs*, *63*(22), 2395–2411.

Wilens T., Biederman J., Prince J., et al. (1996). Six-week, double blind, placebo-controlled study of desipramine for adult attention deficit hyperactivity disorder. *American Journal of Psychiatry* 153, 1147–1153.

Wilens, T. E., Adler, L. A., Weiss, M. D., et al. (2008a). Atomoxetine treatment of adults with ADHD and comorbid alcohol use disorders. *Drug and Alcohol Dependence*, *96*(1–2), 145–154.

Wilens, T. E., Biederman, J., & Spencer, T. J. (2002). Attention Deficit/Hyperactivity Disorder across the lifespan. *Annual Review of Medicine*, *53*, 113–131.

Wilens, T. E., Haight, B. R., Horrigan, J. P., et al. (2005). Bupropion XL in adults with Attention-Deficit/Hyperactivity Disorder: A randomized, placebo-controlled study. *Biological Psychiatry*, *57*(7), 793–801.

Wilens, T. E., Prince, J. B., Waxmonsky, J., et al. (2010). An open trial of sustained-release bupropion for Attention-Deficit/Hyperactivity Disorder(ADHD) in adults with ADHD plus substance use disorders. *Journal of ADHD and Related Disorders*, *1*(3), 25–35.

Wilens, T. E., Spencer, T. J., Biederman, J., et al. (2001). A controlled clinical trial of bupropion for Attention Deficit Hyperactivity Disorder in adults. *American Journal of Psychiatry*, *158*(2), 282–288.

Wilens, T. E., Verlinden, M. H., Adler, L. A., et al. (2006b). ABT-089, a neuronal nicotinic receptor partial agonist, for the treatment of Attention-Deficit/Hyperactivity Disorder in adults: Results of a pilot study. *Biological Psychiatry*, *59*(11), 1065–1070.

Wilens, T. E., Vitulano, M., Upadhyaya, H., et al. (2008b). Cigarette smoking associated with Attention Deficit Hyperactivity Disorder. *Journal of Pediatrics*, *153*, 414–419.

Wilens, T. E., Zusman, R. M., Hammerness, P. G., et al. (2006a). An open-label study of the tolerability of mixed amphetamine salts in adults with Attention-Deficit/Hyperactivity Disorder and treated primary essential hypertension. *Journal of Clinical Psychiatry*, *67*, 696–702.

Wilsher, C., Atkins, G., & Manfield, P. (1979). Piracetam as an aid to learning in dyslexia. Preliminary report. *Psychopharmacology (Berlin)*, *65*(1), 107–109.

Wilsher, C. R., Bennett, D., Chase, C. H., et al. (1987). Piracetam and dyslexia: Effects on reading tests. *Journal of Clinical Psychopharmacology*, *7*, 230–237.

Winblad, B. (2005). Piracetam: A review of pharmacological properties and clinical uses. *CNS Drug Reviews*, *11*(2), 169–182.

Wood, D. R., Reimherr, F. W., Wender, P. H., & Johnson, G. E. (1976). Diagnosis and treatment of minimal brain dysfunction in adults: A preliminary report. *Archives of General Psychiatry*, *33*(12), 1453–1460.

Xu J., Mendrek A., Cohen M. S., Monterosso J., Rodriguez P., Simon S. L., et al. (2005). Brain activity in cigarette smokers performing a working memory task: Effect of smoking abstinence. *Biological Psychiatry* 58, 143–150.

Zametkin, A., & Rapoport, J. L (1987). Neurobiology of Attention Deficit Disorder with hyperactivity: Where have we come in 50 years? *Journal of the American Academy of Child and Adolescent Psychiatry, 26,* 676–686.

Zhu, J., & Reith, M. E. A. (2008). Role of the dopamine transporter in the action of psycho-stimulants, nicotine, and other drugs of abuse. *CNS & Neurological Disorders—Drug Targets, 7,* 393–409.

19

Vocational Programs and Practices

ROB CRAWFORD

This chapter provides an overview of vocational assessment and guidance issues for older adolescents and young adults with various "hidden" or nonapparent disabilities who lack a vocational identity or possess limited insight about making informed decisions to create a career path. An overview of the Life Development Institute model of prevocational and life preparation for people with Attention-Deficit/Hyperactivity Disorder (ADHD) or Learning Disabilities (LD) is presented. Vocational strategies for college graduates and possible accommodations in the workplace are also discussed.

VOCATIONAL ASSESSMENT AND GUIDANCE

Current governmental and private-sector employment and higher education reform initiatives continue to neglect or ignore adults with ADHD or LD. Yet adults with these disorders represent the largest single identified population of special needs learners seeking employment. Many of these individuals are nontraditional learners. They often do not present their best capabilities in assessment approaches that rely on traditional, norm-referenced measurements. In order to produce a vocational assessment that accurately reflects the individual's true interests, abilities, and aptitudes, the clinician and client should thoroughly investigate these five areas:

1. Level of client involvement
2. Methods used in securing previous employment
3. Background information from previous employers and coworkers
4. Level of functional skills required for targeted employment
5. Availability of support services

Level of Client Involvement

The most important user of the vocational assessment is the client, and, therefore, the client must be the focus of the assessment process. This is a commonsense statement, but all too often, the typical assessment reports reveal—at best—that only superficial information was collected that can demonstrate the presenting level of self-advocacy, presence of age-appropriate peer relationships, understanding of previous testing experience, perception of what constitutes the individual's view of quality of life, or stress and personal conflict issues present at the time of assessment in making career decisions. Making assessments client centered can become a useful and meaningful method of facilitating self-advocacy. The person being assessed then becomes primarily responsible for the direction and quality of choices rather than relying on the clinician, a teacher, or a parent to make decisions. Assessments that lack meaningful consumer input run the risk of creating an entitlement mentality as opposed to an empowerment mentality.

Previous studies examining vocational guidance and career education approaches for working-age persons with LD and ADHD suggest that career development needs to be an experiential learning process that gives clients opportunities to make logical connections between wants and needs and to understand the demands of the work setting (Rosenthal, 1989; Schaller, 1994). When an assessment is conducted *for* the client rather than *by* the client, the client does not learn how to use community information sources.

A client can learn important basic career advocacy skills by, for example:

- Interviewing local employers to gain an understanding of the basic skills needed for entry-level positions.
- Determining the level of literacy required to benefit from a vocational-technical training program.
- Recognizing the time management requirements for scheduling, confirming, and conducting informational interviews at local community-based resources.

Competency in advocating for oneself should also involve social competency, especially as it relates to interpersonal relationships. Young adults with ADHD or LD who are becoming independent for the first time often equate advocacy with pushiness. Frequently, they are reluctant to speak up strongly on their own behalf for fear of seeming too aggressive or to avoid retaliation from coworkers, parents, and professionals—for example, being asked, "What do you know? You're just a dishwasher," or being told "What you say you want doesn't make any sense. Those meds don't seem to be working."

During assessments, clients can behave in a way that indicates their unawareness of social graces, making off-the-wall comments unrelated to the conversation, avoiding eye contact in conversations, or exhibiting poor taste in personal hygiene or grooming habits (e.g., picking nose or playing with hair). Many times clients are unaware of how this behavior affects the positive development of peer relationships because they lack experience interacting with older adults.

When asked specific questions about activities of adult living—such as: What is your medication for? What is your social security number? Why did you leave your last job? How long were you employed at your last job?—clients may defer to parents for the answers. In these situations, clients lose valuable practice in responding to an "authority figure" and continue to depend on others to handle things instead of assuming that responsibility.

Adults living outside of their parents' residence interact with many types of personalities and communication situations each day. Collecting information about how clients handle day-to-day interactions with adults in a variety of situations (recreation, work, and home) can make it possible to discover what seems to upset or center them. This method is helpful in ascertaining how capable they are of filtering information, organizing possible responses, and choosing the best way to handle a conflict. It is not unusual for young adults with ADHD or LD to operate on both extremes of the relationship spectrums. At one end, a client may have had limited dating experience, casual opposite-sex conversations (outside of family members), and not know how to initiate these interactions. On the opposite extreme, charismatic and charming clients may happily relate that they have "dated," been a "friend with benefits," or had intimate relationships with any-/everyone!

Obtaining this type of information in the assessment allows the practitioner to understand how clients can or will handle social interaction in the workplace. Social situations are potentially more difficult to deal with than any learning or attention barrier as they are unscripted spontaneous experiences that have a lot of gray areas that complicate what constitutes effective client action/reaction.

Moya and O'Malley (1994) noted the shortcomings of limited client involvement in assessments controlled by the clinician. Some of the limitations that result from single-measured approaches are:

- Low scores yield little information about strengths to build on.
- Attention is focused on lower-level skills.
- The process fails to take into account thought processes and reasons for the answers given.
- Quantitative outcomes are emphasized more than instructionally useful feedback.

Attention should also be paid to what constitutes "quality of life" in the eyes of the client, and from more than just the employment perspective. Additional values related to what Halpern (1992a) and others identified as a holistic conceptual quality-of-life model are found in Figure 19.1. This model emphasizes personal choices and needs

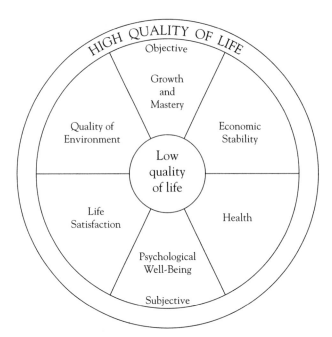

Figure 19.1   Objective and Subjective Dimensions of Quality of Life
Source: From R. Brown, M. Bayer, and C. MacFarlane, "Quality of life amongst handicapped adults," in
Quality of Life for Handicapped People: A Series in Rehabilitation Education, ed. by R. Brown (London: Croom
Helm, 1988). Used with permission.

(the subjective perspective) versus social norms and expectations (the objective perspective) in identifying quality-of-life outcomes.

Putting this model into practice allows the clinician to understand the subjective
dimensions of the client's idea of quality of life. A full array of psychological issues,
including but not limited to employment options, is considered. Halpern (1992a) identifies 15 types of outcomes from the three basic quality-of-life domains. Most of these
outcomes can be measured objectively (e.g., is the person living independently?) and
subjectively (is the person satisfied with where she lives?).

Physical and material well-being
- Physical and mental health
- Food, clothing, and lodging
- Financial security
- Safety from harm

Personal fulfillment
- Happiness
- Satisfaction
- Sense of general well-being

Performance of adult roles
- Mobility and community access
- Vocation, career, and employment
- Leisure and recreation
- Personal relationship and social networks
- Educational attainment
- Spiritual fulfillment
- Citizenship (e.g., voting)
- Social responsibility (e.g., doesn't break laws)

From *Duality of Life as a Conceptual Framework for Evaluating Transition Outcomes* by A. Halpern.

Examining these areas allows the practitioner to help clients achieve the highest quality of life possible from an individual frame of reference as well as the perspective of what is considered socially appropriate. This collaborative approach reduces situations in which the assessment team does a great deal of developmental work to place clients in a training or employment setting and clients sabotage the placement because they are not "happy" with being "controlled" by expectations of performance.

Impulsive behavior leading to job or program termination can be minimized by taking the time to understand what constitutes job satisfaction from the clients' point of view and by explaining that employers expect *all employees* to perform certain job functions in specific ways. Stress is inevitable when an individual unaccustomed to being involved in or responsible for critical decisions about life tries to make correct decisions that are both personally satisfying and acceptable to other adults involved in the process. Each decision that clients must make about a vocational future requires them to take a chance and risk failure.

The amount of vocational stress adults with ADHD or LD experience is directly related to personal uncertainty about employment goals and the perceived needs associated with those goals. If client expectations are not met and the alternatives proposed do not seem viable to either client or practitioner, avoidance behavior on the part of clients usually results. Clients may miss scheduled appointments, be hypersensitive to the "messenger" bringing the bad news, and fail to follow through with school and work requirements.

Janis and Mann (1977) contend that in their conflict model of career decision making, the process of choosing the best vocational path threatens the decision maker. By working to identify the trade-offs and consequences of the risks of "failing" as possible, the practitioner can help clients to objectively consider the positive and negative outcomes of various alternatives.

Frequently, the helping professional will be working with clients who are struggling to make wise career choices and fall victim to the "eight career myths":

1. *I want to be sure I choose exactly the right career.* While it is understandable for a client to want to make a sound career choice, the simple truth is that there is no such thing as the "right" choice. Not only is this approach stifling and self-limiting, it allows for procrastination and indecision because the client's expectations are too high. The best way to refocus an individual who insists on finding a career using this approach is to point out that there are no more perfect jobs than there are perfect people. Each workplace offers both good and bad conditions that must be compared to the client's current wants and needs. Clients must look at the overall picture of the career path in question. If they can identify more positive aspects than negative ones in relationship to areas of personal job satisfaction, the choice can be a sound one.

2. *When I choose my career, I'm deciding for a lifetime.* Given the likelihood that clients lack extensive exposure to the world of work or a strong vocational identity, the clinician would explain that what looks good now may not be satisfying 10, 20, or 30 years from now. People change their priorities and interests over time. A substantial body of statistics shows that people change jobs many times over the course of a lifetime. This would also be a good time to suggest that clients interview parents, employers, or administrators of training programs who have frequently changed jobs themselves.

3. *Most people have made a definite decision about what they want to do when they have reached my age.* There is no research to support the notion that a person has an "internal alarm clock." A time when clients will be ready to make a career decision is unique to their circumstances. Often clients do not know what they *really* want to do in life and, because of this apparent indecision, feel something is wrong with them because everyone in their family or peer group seems to know exactly where they fit in the job market.

   It is very common to encounter and process the numerous invalid comparisons by clients who try to measure their life progress against that of their parents, siblings, or peers at the same age. This comparison is usually heard most often from clients coming from very successful, affluent families and communities. Most of their family members have graduated from prestigious colleges or are attending college, have excellent-paying jobs, and are solidly independent. The pressure to catch up with people who seem better than they are many times drives clients to make vocational choices that reflect someone else's life rather than their own deeper values, interests, abilities, and aptitudes.

4. *I would like to take a test that will tell me what I should do.* No such test exists! Vocational testing and assessment can take clients only *part* of the way in making

a good career decision. In the interests of enhancing personal responsibility, clients must understand that the ultimate answer to what is workable lies within themselves.

5. *I think that if I like to do something, I should be good at it.* Many times adults with ADHD or LD working with Life Development Institute (LDI) staff who have been conducting job placement activities were ready to take a job with a company that has placed a classified ad or posted a sign on a telephone promising to pay "up to $200 an hour to start, no experience necessary." Obviously, the money is attractive to someone who does not understand that if a job looks too good to be true, it probably is. If good pay and the lack of a work experience requirement are the primary motivators for clients, however, most professionals and practitioners would acknowledge these two factors to be a good starting point for job exploration. Practitioners would also ask clients to compare their personal functional abilities and aptitudes with the daily requirements of the job. Also, if the job does not work out, what do they propose for plan B or plan C? It never hurts to prequalify the prospective employer by conducting an informational telephone interview to find out what specifically the company does, basic skills needed for entry-level employment, and opportunities for growth in the future.

It would help to suggest that if the company has what a client seeks and is qualified to do, the client can schedule a trip to the place of business where they can discuss individual qualifications in person. In this way, the client can make an informed decision about the suitability of the company and at the same time find out from the employer what level of effort would be needed to succeed in that employment setting.

6. *I must develop all of the stages in my career plan as soon as possible.* Impulsive, do-it-now planning with "kamikaze" follow-through is typical of clients who subscribe to this myth. Clients may place undue or unnecessary pressure on themselves to have a plan, without having a clear idea of the steps needed to develop a thorough plan. The local community usually has many types of vocational and educational resources. In order to find the best one to commit to, clients must undertake a certain amount of deliberate investigation first.

7. *If I don't succeed in reaching my career goals, then I have failed.* Many clients approach vocational choices with an "all-or-nothing" attitude. The practitioner should ask, "What would your life be like if you hadn't tried at all?" Clients may then acknowledge that most people do not even try to define specific career goals, let alone pursue them. Making an effort requires clients to expose themselves to risk by taking a chance on a particular future path. Although they may not have achieved all of the specific career objectives, they are better people for the attempt. Recognizing incremental personal successes toward

achieving a career objective and developing an increased awareness of the targeted career leaves the door open to discovering other occupational possibilities that would accomplish the purpose originally intended.

8. *Since I am confused about my career plans, I'll take time out so I'll know when it's the right time to come back.* Practitioners should ask these clients two questions: "When/how will you know the right time to come back to your career plan?" and "What productive use will you make of your extra time?" Lengthy experience working in assessment situations with adults who are unaccustomed to filtering and synthesizing vocational information compels practitioners to push for a specific action plan that justifies a course of temporary nonaction on the clients' part. If clients are able to outline solid reasons for taking time off, such as *analyzing* the potential risks involved in making a job change, then it is probably appropriate to allow that time for reflection.

Often clients may face time limitations due to lack of funding or unemployment. In these cases, procrastination often results in job plans and vocational assessments that are practitioner-driven because clients are unwilling or unable to commit to a specific course of action. When a practitioner has a client engaged in avoidance behaviors, an approach that Janis and Mann (1977) call "bolstering" can assist the process of decision making.

In reviewing all information collected by clients, the practitioner can suggest that clients objectively consider all the positive and negative consequences of different choices. During this review, clients will begin to recognize they have truly covered all the aspects of the decision and done their best in arriving at a decision that makes sense in terms of the career choice. For example, a client who has lost a successful position will likely approach getting a new position from a decidedly defensive posture. If there are also pressing financial concerns, a client may take the first job that is offered or find reasons to reject opportunities because they are not exactly like the position held previously. Although no decision is perfect, getting clients to review objectively all of their perceived risks and gains makes it more likely that they will reach a satisfactory decision.

Whether clients obtaining the vocational assessment are just entering the adult world or are older, more vocationally mature people looking toward a career change, it is imperative that they be the center of the learning process. By minimizing the risks of change and eliminating their need to have others tell them what to do, adults with ADHD or LD come to see themselves as capable, self-directed learners.

Methods Used in Securing Previous Employment

Noticeably absent from most vocational reports is information about how adults with ADHD or LD conducted job search activities in the past. Such information allows the practitioner to identify any approaches that were successful in securing the client employment and the client's level of involvement in the search process.

The National Longitudinal Transition Study II of Special Education Students published findings on job search activities that detailed the methods used by young adults with LD and ADHD to identify and secure employment opportunities (NLTS II, 2009). The good news is that 50% of these youth conducted their job searches themselves. The bad news is that this statistic represents a drop from 60% in 1997. The primary sources of information were reading the classified section of the newspaper, Internet searches, and walking in off the street and filling out an application for employment. Relying primarily on these resources overlooks the larger "hidden job market" of unadvertised employment openings. Youth using this approach were in direct competition with all job applicants for these advertised positions and were likely hard-pressed to find a suitable job because they lacked specific information about employers' requirements.

The most readily available resource for job seekers with ADHD or LD remains the local yellow pages. The yellow pages list every company doing business in the local area and should be used in conjunction with other employment-related Internet sites, such as Craig's list, Jobing.com, Monster.com, and the like to survey and speak to a group of local employers. The job seeker will then ask each of these employers for background information on what the company does, position requirements for entry-level positions, and potential opportunities for growth in the future. In this way, a job seeker can obtain a tremendous amount of useful information about vocational possibilities and employer expectations for each position, and accomplish this from a relatively controlled, safe environment. In addition, the job seeker also learns how to make direct contact with the company's key decision makers. This is an advantage that allows the job seeker to prequalify the company and ask "Do I want to work for them?" rather than "Will they want me to work for them?" Job-seeking adults with ADHD or LD are in a much better negotiating position using this kind of direct approach than randomly applying for the first position that comes their way.

A large percentage of job seekers depend on job leads and contacts from family, friends, or outside agencies. It is important to document the level of involvement of these other individuals in the job development process. In particular, the practitioner should ascertain to what extent they assisted in identifying acceptable employment, provided transportation to the interview, made sure that all necessary identification was present, corrected spelling on the application, filled in all the blanks on the application, and participated on behalf of the client in the interview phase of the application process. Many well-meaning individuals actually detract from the abilities of the job seeker by "fixing" the interview and application until the adult with ADHD or LD is virtually guaranteed a job. In this case, unfortunately, the ownership of the job lies with the individuals working with the job seeker rather than with the client him- or herself.

It is important to determine whether the client went through a true interview, was given the job as a result of outside involvement, or simply showed up at the right time when the employer was desperate for a "warm body" and would hire anybody with a pulse. If others performed all job search activities for the client, he or she will lack functional expertise in conducting an independent job search.

Developing independent job search capabilities in the client is critical to the successful implementation of the vocational assessment. Time and attention will need to be devoted to facilitating experiential learning activities, such as how to use public transportation, "elevator speech" techniques to summarize personal qualifications, and how to answer behavior-based interview questions that are position/company specific.

BACKGROUND INFORMATION FROM PREVIOUS EMPLOYERS AND CO-WORKERS

Many adults with ADHD or LD are capable of initiating and conducting successful job searches independently but are unable for any number of reasons to maintain job stability. In contrast, many adults with this profile experience excellent job stability and retention but feel they are underemployed and need better vocational opportunities. In order to measure individual competency and identify probable stumbling blocks, professionals and practitioners will find it useful to survey the opinions of current or former employers and coworkers familiar with the work habits and functional social skills displayed by the client in the work setting.

For both un- and underemployed adults with ADHD or LD, the practitioner should identify how the client was trained (hands on, verbal explanation, etc.), how long the training took, what shifts the client worked, how many hours the client worked per shift and per week, and how much support coverage the client received from coworkers and employers. This information may uncover strategies and techniques that the client used successfully at the work site that resulted in enhanced work performance. If the interventions used by coworkers and employers required a high level of supportive maintenance, that particular work experience would be difficult to replicate without a similarly broad-minded employer willing to invest the extra time and attention. Also, for adults hoping to upgrade their current work situation, job accommodations requiring extensive coworker assistance may negate their ability to perform the essential functions of a more responsible position.

Other important background information the practitioner should obtain includes coworkers' and employers' opinions about the types of training methods that seem to be most or least effective for clients. Depending on the particular kind of job, training and instructions usually are provided through demonstration, orally, or from a written manual. A comparison of baseline psychometric information with feedback from the work site often shows discrepancies between what the testing indicates to be the functional levels of clients and how they perform in an actual work setting.

Some individuals work very well in quiet, controlled test situations but fall apart when asked to make decisions based on multiple priorities in the face of a lot of extraneous auditory and visual stimuli.

Others thrive in a work environment characterized by high levels of stress but may not be able to demonstrate these skills in the assessment process. Talking to people who know the client outside of an assessment setting can provide an extra dimension of knowledge that may encourage investigation of other vocational possibilities that would not have been suggested by traditional testing procedures.

Although they cannot be expected to have specialized knowledge about ADHD and LD, previous employers and coworkers can fill in some of the missing background information on a client's work performance by providing objective recollections. One area of particular interest would be their opinions of the client's work-related social skills. Did clients work better alone or as part of a team? If the organizational culture places a premium on being a team player and clients tended to keep to themselves, they may not have fared very well with that company. In another case, the organization may prefer self-directed workers, whereas clients were social butterflies who frequently visited coworkers or texted on social media sites rather than tending to business.

Former coworkers and employers can also give practitioners before-and-after snapshots of the relative improvement of client social skills at the workplace. Many young adults with ADHD or LD present themselves to their peers as being somewhat immature or different because they lack direct experience in workplace social situations. As the client adjusted to the new work setting, did coworkers and employers observe a leveling out of behavior? This adjustment is common with younger individuals or those new to the workforce.

The practitioner also needs to find out whether clients started out on good footing but developed increasingly disruptive behaviors that interfered with job performance or that of other coworkers. Frequently, young adults with ADHD or LD get themselves into trouble with their coworkers and employers by being too relaxed or becoming overly familiar. Client recollections of how people felt about them usually differs sharply from information gathered from the perspective of coworkers at the receiving end of these behaviors. Especially damaging to clients are reports of disruptive social habits that went unremediated, such as interrupting others, correcting others by pointing out their mistakes, or being unable to accept responsibility for doing a job a certain way without complaining about it. Clients and practitioners have their work cut out for them if these situations consistently recur throughout a client's work history.

Minimizing the likelihood of future occurrences of this sort will require prior knowledge of the specific expectations of the targeted work site. In addition, clients must learn what constitutes fair and reasonable treatment of coworkers, perhaps by scripting or role-playing situations similar to those that occurred at previous work sites. A major benefit of this exercise is to provide practice time for clients to identify the conditions and circumstances in which it is appropriate for them to assert personal opinions. This practice time also allows clients to learn how to accept work-related criticism of their performance gracefully and use it to improve personal work quality without personalizing it.

Adults with ADHD or LD often derive their primary social relationships from employment. When they sense or experience failure, rejection, or exclusion at work, the effect is similar to the feelings of social failure they may have experienced in school. A significant number of adults who have suffered humbling social experiences at work would rather interact with people like themselves than be "mistreated" by people who do not understand. It makes little difference to this subgroup that they may have brought their social isolation on themselves; all they know is that they are not comfortable with their coworkers and it is easier for them to take fewer risks by remaining alone or being with a similar peer group.

Finally, the practitioner should obtain a thorough description of all tools and equipment that clients used to perform essential or assigned work tasks. Sometimes, for example, clients believe that because they once started a forklift, they have mastered all operational aspects of its use. Previous employers can give a much clearer picture of all work technologies and standard operating procedures that were introduced to and mastered by clients. If possible, it is also useful to know specific examples of a client's best/worst performance areas and the conditions or situations in which work rate or quality was affected.

Every employee on the job today has a wide range of functional work performances impacted by events in daily life and on the job. When debriefing the employer about the client's performance in different work situations, the clinician should interpret this information in the context of what was happening in that client's life at the time. In some cases, clients may have been experiencing emotional upheaval that affected them on the job. These types of existential stresses affect *all* employees, not just those who have ADHD or LD. The goal for clients and clinician is not so much to review the past as to reframe the experiences and develop effective coping strategies that enable clients to achieve greater emotional control while maintaining satisfactory job performance.

Level of Functional Skills Required for Targeted Employment

The demands of today's workplace, with its emphasis on high technology, strong interpersonal skills, and maintaining market share against global competition, are driving forces behind reform themes in adult and workplace education programs. The higher expectations of the workplace have changed the way that assessment and placement of young adult students with high-incidence or nonapparent "hidden" conditions, such as LD and ADHD, possessing literacy problems into education, instruction, and employment programs are conducted.

Increasingly, entry-level employees will find themselves in work settings committed to excellence, product quality, and customer satisfaction with far different metrics than traditional academic settings. In order to translate functional, performance-based ideas of quality into usable vocational data, the clinician must go beyond traditional job descriptions as a primary basis of summary recommendations and use information from other sources to identify the specific skills needed for employment in these high-performance workplaces.

Two such sources are the report of the Secretaries' Commission on Achieving Necessary Skills (SCANS, 1991b) and the New Commission Report on the Skills of the American Workforce: Tough Choices or Tough Times (2007). These reports provide broad conceptual frameworks for the generic skills required in the workplace as well as a description of how the skills are used in a variety of tasks clients are likely to encounter. In recommending that performance be assessed in ways that recognize incremental progress toward a level of mastery, the SCANS report suggested six criteria for an effective assessment system:

1. It defines and communicates what is to be learned—the expected outcomes of the knowledge and skills of the students. In effect, these outcomes become standards for all. A useful assessment does not merely indicate success or failure in meeting the standards but identifies the degree of progress made in meeting them.
2. It assures [that] students are taught what the system calls for and that teachers are significantly involved in determining educational standards, outcomes, and goals.
3. It permits comparison of local performance to national benchmarks.
4. It protects students against sorting and labeling by moving away from distinguishing between "good" and "bad" to measuring performance against standards of what students should know and be able to do.
5. It is dynamic, meaning [that] it can be improved on the basis of experience and of advances in knowledge.
6. It motivates students who believe that the assessment will count in the world beyond school because they see that employers make decisions based on the assessment. (Secretaries' Commission on Achieving Necessary Skills, 1991a, pp. 60–62)

The clear and consistent assessment standards for all individuals recommended by the commission would be an excellent first step toward identifying specific marketable skills and would remove the stigma of being a low achiever from adults with ADHD or LD. The design of a vocational assessment system that provides more than one way to evaluate performance and measure success for adults with special learning needs, English-language fluency, and culturally sensitive was identified by both commissions as areas unaddressed.

The need to develop alternative assessment packages acceptable to employers that do not solely rely on traditional academic measurements of skills is critical to overcoming barriers inherent in presenting oneself as a qualified applicant capable of performing essential job functions despite not being able to demonstrate this proficiency in test-taking situations.

A major international electronics firm in Arizona is a good example of an otherwise outstanding corporation that needs to overhaul its screening methods. Candidates applying for a job first must fill out a six-page application. Most applicants do not successfully complete this initial task, according to the corporation's human resource department. The human resource officer reports that the department has a bank of filing cabinets filled with thousands of applications missing such basic items as work history information (e.g., duties and dates of employment), containing misspelled words, or missing entire sections of the application. Presuming that interested applicants can successfully pass the application hurdle, the next step of the process involves taking a timed battery of academic tests encompassing reading comprehension, mathematical computation, tracking the path of an electrical circuit, inventory process control, and a videotape of what-if situations. The videotape section asks applicants to determine the proper action to take from three different perspectives:

1. What your supervisor would want you to do
2. What your coworkers would do
3. What you should do

Typical accommodations, such as having a test reader or getting more time to respond to some or all of the test battery, can be granted if they are formally requested at the beginning of the application process.

Applicants are not required to provide proof of a disability, and the corporate psychologist decides whether a requested accommodation is workable within the context of the test situation. The functional level of literacy required to comprehend test questions is at approximately the ninth-grade level. Applicants must pass all components of this battery to demonstrate the ability to learn and perform effectively in a high-technology manufacturing environment.

This firm offers no alternative assessments for prospective employees (with or without disabilities) seeking to demonstrate that they can perform the essential functions of the job. This deficiency stands in sharp contrast to the amount of individualized training that occurs at the work site. Most of the systems infrastructure that this company uses to design 3G wireless technology applications has been developed in-house.

Each process requires custom production engineered for specific applications of that product and customer requirements. This means that for most entry-level technical positions at this company, there exist no career colleges or occupational-specific programs to train future employees in the specific skills needed to meet the business demands and workplace realities. Since formal training must be conducted by members of the work team and training divisions, it is unclear how a traditional battery of academic tests can truly reflect the workplace capabilities of prospective employees with ADHD or LD.

The issue of developing effective national linkages among education, employment, and relevant assessments of competency-based outcomes has been a stated national priority since the 1980s. The report "Tough Choices or Tough Times" (New Commission Report on the Skills of the American Workforce, 2007) sounds a clear alarm and call for action. The Commission identified the core problem as being education, training, and assessment systems built for another era, an era in which most workers needed only a rudimentary education. The Report points out that there is not enough money available at any level of our intergovernmental system to fix this problem by spending more on the system we have currently in place. According to the conclusions in the report, an inclusive, relevant, and truly world-class educated workforce can occur only by changing the system itself.

Nearly two thirds of states have exit tests that all students, including those with disabilities, must pass to graduate from high school. But few of these high-stakes exams require more than an 8th-grade level of literacy in international terms. The data from the commission's report indicates that many states have increased the proportion of the test that enables students to construct their own answers to questions rather than select an answer from a preselected list. However, these tests still have a way to go to provide the kinds of information that the world's best high school exit examinations could provide, graduating students with LD and ADHD need, and the corporate/business community expects.

On balance—and relative to the high-tech skills barrier described previously—state exit exams are designed to measure the acquisition of discipline-based knowledge in the core subjects in the curriculum. More often than not, however, little or nothing is done to measure many of the other qualities that both SCANS and "Tough Choices" have suggested may spell the difference between success and failure for the students with LD and ADHD who will grow up to be the workers of 21st century America: creativity and innovation, facility with the use of ideas and abstractions, the self-discipline and organization needed to manage one's work and drive it through to a successful conclusion, the ability to function well as a member of a team, and so on.

Neither the SCANS nor the New Commission's reports, at present, provide recommendations or research on alternative assessments for potential employees who are nontraditional learners, come from culturally diverse backgrounds, or have limited proficiency in English. Predicting job success for this rapidly growing subpopulation will require the development of assessments that address learning differences, are respectful of linguistic semantics, and take into consideration cultural differences.

The 2007 U.S. census shows that the largest percentage of new immigrants to the United States comes from countries where Spanish, Asian, or Pacific Island languages are spoken. This trend is expected to continue well into the 21st century, resulting in a workforce that will have significant literacy development and training needs. This changing workforce will require considerable retooling of the assessment and hiring methods currently in use in corporate America. As employers are compelled to modify their hiring practices, alternative assessment packages will be developed that will benefit individuals who are unintentionally penalized by employment decisions based on traditional assessments.

Employer interviewing, hiring, and evaluation practices for nontraditional learners have changed as a result of the Americans with Disabilities Act (ADA; 1990) and the recently passed American with Disabilities Amendment Act (2008), which require the focus of these HR processes to be on what the job involves and not on the disability of the applicant or employee. The Alexander Hamilton Institute (1993) published a useful booklet outlining practices that are both effective and legal that human resource professionals can use in determining the capabilities of the members of their workforce who have a disability. For example, the institute points out that in order to avoid discrimination charges of disability bias, three interview practices are essential:

1. *All questions should be job related.* Do not ask questions such as How would you get to work? or Are you taking any medications that could make you drowsy?
2. *Do not jump to conclusions about whether a disabled person can perform the job or not.* Some disabled persons are able to come up with ideas that might make accommodation easy and inexpensive. Others may remove themselves from contention after they realize the physical or mental demands of the job.
3. *Let applicants visit the job site.* This will allow them to judge the accessibility and comfort level of the workplace. It will also let them decide whether

reasonable accommodation will allow them to do the job. This process is particularly effective when combined with a detailed job description that identifies and assesses the employer's functional job requirements for that specific work site. From the job seeker's point of view, for each targeted employer there will need to be an investigation of what constitutes a complete job description. Such a description should contain the following components:

- *Essential duties.* Obtain a description of what is to be accomplished, in terms of both guidelines and methods of performing duties. For example, "communicating information" could mean writing information on a notepad. It also could mean that an opportunity exists to perform this task in an another way, such as typing or tape-recording the information, if the applicant with ADHD or LD has problems with writing. It may not have occurred to the employer that tasks accomplished through written communication can be dispatched as effectively through alternative strategies. Part of the process of determining whether the client is suitable for a specific job is to find out whether certain job tasks can be modified to accommodate the applicant's learning needs without raising objections from others about perceived special treatment.
- *Mental functions.* Obtain a list of all required job elements, such as coordinating, analyzing, and synthesizing, so the client can determine what abilities are required. For instance, if the job requires providing emergency medical treatment to accident victims, the ability to handle stress is required.
- *Physical functions.* Each task should be broken down into elements such as standing, squatting, reaching, lifting, and grasping. The duration and frequency of these tasks should be part of this analysis.
- *Methods, techniques, and procedures.* Obtain a list of the procedures for accomplishing the essential duties of the job, for example, the amount of time spent working as a member of a team, the type of in-house communications used for memoranda, and the procedure for seeking help with specific job tasks.
- *Working conditions.* Obtain information about such factors as work site locations (indoors or outdoors), potential work hazards, safety considerations, and level of auditory and visual stimuli.
- *Technology, equipment, and work materials.* Establish what types of tools or knowledge of work-specific technologies are needed for the applicant to perform the job effectively. Ascertain the possibility of modifying, replacing, or adjusting products and materials used to perform the job without affecting the quality of work performed. (Alexander Hamilton Institute, 1993, pp. 8–10)

Availability of Support Services

Both client and clinician must familiarize themselves with available community resources that could provide direct services in the areas of job development and job placement, vocational-technical training, work-related literacy, and independent living skill development. These adult agencies and service providers have different eligibility criteria and funding priorities. Those who seek these services should familiarize themselves with the jargon, application procedure, and referral processes that are unique to each agency.

For example, a vocational rehabilitation (VR) counselor working in a rural location quite often is responsible for job development, job placement, and job maintenance efforts. The lack of local service providers means that rural VR counselors must accept a higher level of personal involvement than do their counterparts situated in urban and suburban settings where there are ample vocational opportunities, public transportation, and private contractors to provide support services.

Appropriate services for adults with ADHD or LD in most communities are either nonexistent or fragmented. Individuals seeking to tap into public or private resources can expect to go to one agency for vocational assessment, another for job training, and still another for job placement and job crisis intervention. Most service providers have limited resources—as measured in both time and money. Vocational guidance efforts must focus on providing a clear picture of the specific nature and manifestations of a client's disability in terms of its potential vocational impact while demonstrating how the client meets the demands of a targeted job or training opportunity for a specific employer.

In addition, the knowledgeable consumer takes the time to become familiar with regional and national resources and programs that address the specific needs of the adult with ADHD or LD. Resources such as the National Association for Adults with Special Learning Needs (NAASLN) Literacy and Learning Disability Center, U.S. Business Leadership Network, Disability.gov, and the Job Accommodation Network (JAN) are examples of programs that specifically address the employment, literacy, and training needs of adults with ADHD or LD. They provide a wealth of user-friendly information on how to access local and national programs, identify best practices in assessment and employment, and conduct numerous training sessions disseminating information to both the public and private sector about the unique nature of the adult with ADHD or LD.

Advocacy groups such as the Learning Disabilities Association of America (LDA), Children and Adults with Attention Deficit Disorder (CHADD), and the American Association of People with Disabilities (AAPD) offer other excellent resources for individuals seeking support groups, knowledgeable consumers who understand the rights and responsibilities assigned to the public by various federal mandates, and state and national conferences spanning the full continuum of issues facing adults with ADHD or LD.

Local resources specializing in direct service provision include state departments of VR, Career One Stop Center programs, Adult Basic Education/GED (ABE/GED) programs, and private vendors providing specialty services (supported employment, psychological testing, etc.). The ABE/GED programs offer literacy instruction free of charge to individuals 16 years of age and older. Relying primarily on traditional paper-and-pencil approaches to education, most ABE/GED programs provide some adult contextually related instruction that updates rusty literacy skills and can be beneficial when it is time to draft a cover letter, fill out a job application, or write a resume.

Career One Stop Center programs are comprehensive centers that provide a full range of job seeker, youth, and employer services. Services for job seekers include resume writing, training in new job skills, preparing for job interviews, job referrals, counseling, preparing for GED exam, accessing financial aid for higher education, and other supportive services. They also offer services for employers that include help writing job descriptions, access to resumes, and strategies for recruiting and interviewing workers. Each site in the Arizona area is staffed with a "Disability Navigator," who is the in-house resource that individuals with LD and ADHD would seek.

VR services are available to anyone covered under the Americans with Disabilities Act who has a documented or suspected disabling condition. Assessment, diagnostics, counseling, training, job placement, and educational opportunities are some of the funded services available through this agency. Recently, the Rehabilitation Services Administration (2009) initiated an order of selection process giving priority to those clients considered severely disabled. Many VR counselors tend to view adults with ADHD or LD as being only mildly disabled by their condition. Dowdy (1995) points out that this misconception about the severity of these conditions is difficult to dispel in the presence of diagnostics that lack in scope and sensitivity and fail to pinpoint specific functional limitations and their vocational effects on the adult with ADHD or LD.

A specific LD task force established through the Rehabilitation Services Administration (2005) sought a way to measure the serious vocational barriers faced by adults with ADHD or LD. The task force identified specific vocational limitations that could be encountered by these individuals and tied them to seven major life functions identified in the ADA as a way of documenting the severity of these limitations and of establishing a rationale for service provision. In order to be considered severely disabled, two or more of the major life functions must be significantly affected by the condition to warrant consideration for VR services.

The client and clinician should carefully review the list in preparation for making a case for service provision through VR:

1. *Mobility.* Problems reading and interpreting bus or train schedules, road maps, and signs; problems budgeting and paying for public transportation; impaired sense of direction resulting in getting lost; deficient sense of time resulting in

chronic tardiness; inability to arrange transportation (e.g., taking the wrong bus, getting off at the wrong stop, taking wrong turns while driving, and forgetting landmarks and directions); gross motor coordination problems causing difficulties in using elevators and escalators

2. *Communication.* Difficulties in following oral and written instructions; difficulty interpreting written materials, particularly job manuals, work orders, diagrams, and signs; difficulty understanding complex sentences or language subtleties, including work-related items such as job applications; difficulty learning new tasks or procedures from written materials or verbal instructions; difficulty remembering multistep directions; difficulty differentiating important from unimportant information; tendency to transpose words and delete parts of language such as prepositions, articles, and connectors; illegible handwriting; difficulties in using the telephone; inability to repeat instructions to coworkers and others

3. *Self-care.* Problems with reasoning, processing, and cognition that may cause the individual to repeatedly make poor decisions about basic life activities (health, safety, grooming, dressing, and managing finances); difficulty with shopping and banking; impulsive and explosive behaviors; distractibility

4. *Self-direction.* Lack of insight; inability to monitor performance; tendency to shift from one activity to another without purpose; lack of follow-through; inability to set up and implement a study schedule or job search

5. *Interpersonal skills.* Inability to interact in a mature, socially acceptable manner with peers and supervisors; inability to accept supervisory monitoring and criticism; inappropriate behaviors and language; lack of inhibitions; explosiveness; withdrawal; low frustration; task avoidance; unpredictability

6. *Work tolerance.* Inability to carry out required physical and cognitive work tasks in an effective manner over a sustained period of time; feelings of restlessness or tendency to flee the job site; distractibility on the job; inability to adjust to increased production demands or unexpected changes in job duties

7. *Work skills.* Inability to benefit from training and to perform job tasks that rely on written instructions or materials; inability to take messages or develop written reports; difficulty recalling instructions or following task sequence language; high-level conceptual deficits; deceptive language deficits; expressive language deficits; inability to understand multistep instructions; tendency to transpose words and delete less concrete parts of language; inability to repeat or relay instructions

Documenting or specifying how the ADHD or LD interferes with the adult's daily activities and will impose severe functional limitations throughout the individual's life creates a compelling case for services through VR.

LIFE DEVELOPMENT INSTITUTE PROGRAM

Since 1982, the Life Development Institute (LDI), a private, community-based organization, located in Glendale, Arizona, has been helping older adolescents and young adults struggling with LD, ADHD, Asperger's syndrome, or related conditions overcome the often demoralizing effects of years of school failure by providing them the instruction and real-world experience and tools they need to lead meaningful, productive, and independent lives.

LDI provides a supportive campus and residential community that gives individuals the education, skills, and training they need to live independently. By offering programs in a community-based environment, they give students a chance to feel and know independence and instill in them a desire to succeed. The unique residential setting gives program participants the opportunity to live in an apartment community with a minimum of staff supervision and a moderate amount of structure. LDI is part of the community, not an island. The usual limitation of most residential or boarding school situations is that they are "sheltered" or "institutional" in their orientation. At LDI, the setting is an actual apartment complex, not a dormitory, institutional setting, or group home.

LDI can help students who are 16 years of age and older through several levels in their transition to independent and self-supported living: from earning their high school diplomas, starting college, to achieving careers through employment that is compatible with their unique capabilities. LDI focuses its classroom instruction on career planning, secondary/postsecondary instruction, social/emotional maturity, and job development/placement.

The Institute is fully accredited through the North Central Association Commission on Accreditation and School Improvement, approved as a noncollege program through the Veteran's Administration Vocational Rehabilitation Program, and authorized under federal law to issue M-1 visas to enroll nonimmigrant foreign students through the Department of Homeland Security. LDI also has contracts with the State of Arizona Rehabilitation Services Administration, is an Arizona Department of Education Exceptional Student Services approved private special education program, and an approved vendor for numerous other states that refer students for out-of-district placement into the LDI school program.

LDI utilizes extensive linkages with area employers, vocational/technical education providers, the community college system, and other related state agencies to provide holistic services to program participants. LDI is recognized nationally for its exemplary literacy program for adults with LD and literacy disorders. In 1992, it was a recipient of the coveted Presidential Points of Light award (one of the 21 selected from among 4,500 nominees) presented by President and Mrs. Bush.

Profile of Program Participants

For most students entering LDI, educational and employment success have been elusive. Their educational and employment difficulties have adversely affected how many view themselves and their opportunities for the future.

As stated earlier, LDI's student population is 16 years old and older. Participants come primarily from three referral sources. The first group are referrals from local school districts in the northwest metropolitan area of Phoenix. These individuals are students who are severely credit deficient and for whom the least restrictive setting is no longer the home school campus. Most of these young people have made little or no progress toward graduation and possess limited marketable skills. Without an alternative educational environment, they will not graduate, will drop out, or will be asked to leave due to performance or behavioral problems.

The second group of participants are referrals from out-of-state school districts. The school system and parents have determined through mediation or due process that a more intensive educational setting is needed to meet the needs of the student, and LDI is selected after proper admission interviews and consideration of all available alternatives. The majority of these individuals lack the educational, employment, and residential options needed to facilitate successful transition into adult life as well as complete diploma requirements to graduate from high school.

The third group of program participants has been referred through educational consultants, advocacy organizations, or other parents who have their adult children in the program. This group of individuals is privately funded for services offered through LDI. These young people have been unable to succeed in traditional learning environments. Their needs include remediation, improvement in learning abilities and processing, postsecondary training and education, and competitive employment commensurate with their individual capabilities.

A "typical" program participant would have many or all of these characteristics:

- Diagnosed "hidden disabilities" such as LD, ADHD, Autism Spectrum Disorders, or related neurological conditions.
- 16 to 30 years old
- Little or no work history
- Little or no clearly defined vocational objectives
- Academic skills ranging from 5th-grade mathematical/6th-grade English levels of literacy to postcollegiate academic capacities
- Social, emotional, and behavioral functioning lower than chronological age
- Has not successfully lived away from home
- Has not competently or consistently managed money before

- Lack of or inappropriate experience dating or establishing age-appropriate peer relationships
- Unable to define specific disability, learning style, or coping and compensatory strategies
- Tested IQ averaging from low 70s to 130s
- Does not know how or is reluctant to advocate for self
- Home situation and/or family relationships unstable or dysfunctional
- Lack of, or limited, appropriate local community resources and economic opportunities available

Referral sources with prospective LDI student participants recognize that graduation or completion of the institute's program requires fulfilling 120 days of continuous competitive employment; completion of all class projects, assignments, and related work; and a presentation of a career plan. The career plan combines vocational assessments and exploration targeting individual education, training, and employment needs pursued through the completion of a vocational research project. This project establishes personal values of the central meaning of what matters most in a career to the individual, prospective career ladder, justifies future vocational/technical training, addresses individual vocational deficits and barriers, and matches the individual's transferable skills with appropriate employment and training opportunities. All students present their findings through a multimedia PowerPoint presentation.

Assessment Process

In consideration of the unique needs of LDI students and the thrust of the program, an assessment focus on Adult Life Domains (based on Halpern's Quality of Life method) attempts to organize the various day-to-day demands of living into a useful format. Adult domains are those areas of adult functioning that require certain minimal degrees of competence and independence.

LDI uses a combination of standardized and in-house–developed assessment tools to measure student performance, capacity, and growth. The basis for selecting these tools is found through an understanding of authentic assessment. Students attending LDI programs do not typically fit the mold of the traditional student; hence the use of alternative ways to collect and identify outcomes relevant to the type of student who attends LDI rather than sterile statistics that have little meaning or value to these at-risk learners.

The authentic assessment word system used by LDI has been developed to provide an abilities-based evaluation of such processes. Authentic assessments are realistically structured, taking into account real-world constraints typically encountered outside the learning environment (e.g., time, production-level requirements). Academic design factors for authentic assessment require that testing occur in the context of actual learning situations that are relevant to students. Focus on the mastery and measurement of true essential skills and competencies—which are the basis of assessment and LDI program courses—facilities the ability to uncover students' working knowledge, skillful utilization of course competencies, and transferability of applied learning into real-life situations.

The Vocational Research Institute's CareerScope Version 10 (CareerScope, 2010) is a self-administered system that measures both aptitude and interest through valid and reliable assessment tasks. The results are instrumental in helping an individual with LD and ADHD begin the career or educational planning process. Some of the features of this assessment include:

> It eliminates paper-and-pencil tests.
> It is a self-administered assessment.
> Results are available immediately.
> It matches high aptitudes with high interest areas.
> Assessment is automatically timed and scored.
> It provides concrete results for the career exploration process.
> It is appropriate for high school and adult clients.

The person's cognitive, perceptual, and physical skills for jobs are established using the Occupational Aptitude Pattern (OAP) structure. OAPs are closely related to the work groups of the *Guide for Occupational Exploration* (GOE, 2006).

The Educational Skills Development Battery screens for levels of General Educational Development as defined by the U.S. Department of Labor's *Dictionary of Occupational Titles* (DOT). Every job in the *DOT* and O*Net has been rated in terms of required levels of mathematical development and language development. Scores derived from the Educational Skills Development Battery allow for a general estimate of an individual's ability to handle the workplace literacy requirements of a given job.

Both aptitude and educational skills batteries are important indicators of where an individual is performing relative to all other job seekers. Very few employers are willing to allow a worker unlimited time to perform the essential functions of a job. A qualified worker, with or without disabilities, must expect to do the same job with the same quality and rate of output as everyone else in order to earn the same wage.

The CareerScope Occupational Interest Inventory measures individuals' interests according to the GOE, which classifies all Department of Labor titles recognized in the *DOT*. The goal of this measurement is to assist an individual's vocational exploration by identifying occupational possibilities that are compatible with expressed personal preferences. Since many applicants are unsure of their vocational direction, information derived from this inventory gives many opportunities for exploration of their vocational future. A person with a future is much more inclined to investigate, consider alternatives, and take responsibility for a vocational plan than one who is unwilling to express personal preferences.

The results from these test batteries and interest inventories are subsequently entered into the Occupational Awareness System (OASYS) program (Vertek, 2009). OASYS is a computer-aided counselor support system that matches a person's skills and abilities to employer job demands. The database in OASYS contains the entire *DOT* and *O*Net* Resource Center databases, including all job descriptions, job performance criteria, and operational definitions of job performance variables. The version used at LDI complies with ADA criteria, which establish essential job functions, physical demands, environmental conditions, and the frequency with which tasks or functions are performed.

A case record is opened by the LDI program participant (LDI staff members act as facilitators) by entering information into sections profiling work history, personal skill, and work ability. The student then asks the computer to conduct a search for job matches. The type of job matches found in this search depends on the individual's highest demonstrated skill profile from his or her work history, levels of demonstrated performance from the aptitude and educational batteries, and identified areas of occupational interest from the inventory.

Each job match contains a complete description of all tasks required to perform the job and of related jobs listed under alternative titles. This information allows the development of a career ladder made up of an occupational cluster of jobs directly related to the targeted position. Each job match states the Specific Vocational Preparation (SVP) required learning the techniques, acquiring the information, and developing the facility needed for average performance in a specific work situation. The nine SVP levels range from unskilled jobs requiring a short demonstration only to skilled positions requiring over 10 years to master.

OASYS can compare an individual's skills and abilities to *DOT* and *O*Net* performance variables. In situations where the person has a career goal or knows about a possible job opening, Occupational Goal Analysis (OGA) allows comparisons of the person's skills and aptitudes to each job performance variable required for the job. This comparison makes it possible to identify potential barriers to employment that may exist for a particular job. The barrier may be significant, such as the client's having a much lower level of literacy than the job requires, or may be minor, such as having no demonstrated work history for the particular job.

Vocational Programs and Practices

Combining career ladder and OGA information allows clients and LDI staff to explore hunches about different kinds of jobs clients could perform. Frequently, individuals at LDI need a career goal reality check in order to be candid with themselves about whether their abilities meet the job requirements. Their initial career goal may involve more training or experience than they currently possess, and it is important to identify any vocational barriers involving academic enrichment, job modification, or skill development that must be overcome in order to achieve their career goal. This realization must come primarily from the individuals' investigating the occupation, allowing them to recognize current limitations with respect to this choice and encouraging them to develop alternative vocational strategies.

Following the hypothetical case of a job seeker with previous experience working as a diet clerk in a nursing home can clarify this process. This person is interested in staying in the same occupational cluster but is not sure what career path to take. When OASYS is asked to construct a career ladder for health-related occupations that take no more than one to two years of training and experience to master, it produces the ladder shown in Table 19.1. This career ladder contains occupations identified by DOT code number, occupational title, SVP level, strength required (STR), and *companion O*Net crosswalk code number* needed to fulfill the literacy requirements of this position.

This hypothetical career seeker decides that being a paramedic looks interesting. They begin to explore what the National Employment Outlook is for this occupational category. Table 19.2 represents an employment growth projection based on the

Table 19.1 OCCUPATION LIST (Career Ladder) Occupations with DIC Code: 573 Medical Services

DOT Code	DOT Title	SVP	Str	GED
079.362-014	Medical Record Technician	6	L	434
079.364-026	Paramedic	6	V	434
079.374-014	Nurse, Licensed Practical	6	M	434
079.374-026	Psychiatric Technician	6	M	434
079.374-010	Emergency Medical Technician	5	M	434
245.362-010	Medical-Record Clerk	4	L	433
355.354-010	Physical Therapy Aide	4	M	323
355.377-014	Psychiatric Aide	4	M	323
355.674-014	Nurse Assistant	4	M	322
074.382-010	Pharmacy Technician	3	L	333
079.364-022	Phlebotomist	3	L	323
245.587-010	Diet Clerk	3	S	333
323.687-010	Cleaner, Hospital	2	M	212
355.677-014	Transporter, Patients	2	M	212

Source: OASYS (Occupational Access SYStem), 2010, SkillTRAN, LLC, Spokane WA. Used with permission.

Table 19.2 National Employment Outlook 2008 to 2018

Title: Paramedic

DOT Code: 079.364-026

Industry: Medical Services

SOC Category: Emergency Medical Technicians and Paramedics

SOC Code: 29-2041

2008 Total Employment – Number	210,670
2008 Total Employment – Percent of Industry	0.13%
2018 Total Employment – Number	229,710
2018 Total Employment – Percent of Industry	0.13%
Employment Change 2008–2018 (Percent Change)	9.04%
Employment Change 2008–2018 (Numeric Change)	19,050

This SOC Occupation group includes 2 DOT Occupations
OES Nationwide Employment by Industry

NAICS	Industry	Actual	% Actual	Cum. %	Growth	% Change
621400,500,900	Outpatient, laboratory, and other ambulatory care services	97,570	46.31%	46.3%	8,930	9.14%
621910	Ambulance services	94,720	44.96%	91.3%	7,820	8.25%
934300	Local government, excluding education and hospitals	60,040	28.49%	119.8%	4,860	8.09%
622000	Hospitals, private and private	41,090	19.50%	139.3%	3,020	7.35%
621100	Offices of physicians	1,980	0.93%	140.2%	720	36.24%
561900	Other support services	1,260	0.59%	140.8%	90	7.42%
485900	Other transit and ground passenger transportation	1,250	0.59%	141.4%	210	16.38%
933300	State government, excluding education and hospitals	1,240	0.58%	142.0%	130	10.20%
SE1300	Self-employed workers; all jobs	880	0.41%	142.4%	60	7.28%

Source: OASYS (Occupational Access SYStem), 2010, SkillTRAN, LLC, Spokane WA. Used with permission.

U.S. Department of Labor, Employment Training Administration data. Annual growth or decline in the number of jobs is projected from 2006 to 2016, and nationwide employment in this category by industry is broken out by the number of individuals actually employed in 2006, percentage of the total workforce in this category employed in that industry, and the estimated change by 2016 in terms of additional jobs gained or lost.

Local listings of educational and training organizations and employers who can be sources of information about the targeted occupation will be identified after the client has conducted an OGA. The OGA will correlate national employment demographics found in the *DOT* and *O*Net* with local requirements for the desired position.

The next step is to compare the job performance requirements to the person's current abilities (see Table 19.3). In the table, occupational variables analyzed are in the first column, the person's work traits are in the second column (Person), job performance variables are in the third column (Occupation), and the fourth column comments on the comparison of the Person and Occupation variables.

All searches conducted in the OGA are based on federal definitions of skills transferability. Hypothetical career seekers are considered to have transferable skills when the work activities they performed in past jobs can be used to meet the requirements of skilled or semiskilled work activities in other jobs or kinds of work. The extent to which transferable skills are identified in the OGA depends on the similarity between occupationally significant work activities in an individual's work history and those in the targeted occupation.

Table 19.3 Placement Goal Comparison

Name: sample case **SSN:**
DOT Title: Paramedic
DOT Code: 079.364-026

Variables Analyzed		Seeker	Occupation	Comment
Work Field	**MPSMS**			
Same	Same			No Match
Same	Similar	SVP Level 4	SVP Level 6	Under Qualified
Similar	Same			No Match
Similar	Similar	SVP Level 4	SVP Level 6	Under Qualified
Same	Different	SVP Level 4	SVP Level 6	Under Qualified
Similar	Different	SVP Level 4	SVP Level 6	Under Qualified
Different	Same			No Match
Different	Similar	SVP Level 4	SVP Level 6	Under Qualified

This table shows at which level(s) Transferability of Skills occurs between the seeker's SVP, Work Fields & MPSMS and the occupational requirements. Each Level of Transferability contains different inferences concerning:

— a. The amount of training required to perform the Job Goal.
— b. The suitablity of the Job Goal for the person.
Levels 1-4 are Skills Transfer levels per the definition.
Levels 5-8 do not reflect the operational definition of Transferability.

Transferability is further qualified by the analysis of each worker trait as follows:

Specific Vocational Preparation

Seeker Minimum	Level 1	Level 6	

General Education

Reasoning	Level 5	Level 4	Exceeds Demand
Mathematics	Level 3	Level 3	
Language	Level 5	Level 4	Exceeds Demand

Strength

Lift, Carry, Push, Pull	Very Heavy Work	Very Heavy Work	

Physical Demands

Climbing	Constantly	Occasionally	Exceeds Demand
Balancing	Constantly	Occasionally	Exceeds Demand
Stooping	Constantly	Frequently	Exceeds Demand
Kneeling	Constantly	Frequently	Exceeds Demand
Crouching	Constantly	Occasionally	Exceeds Demand
Crawling	Constantly	Occasionally	Exceeds Demand
Reaching	Constantly	Frequently	Exceeds Demand
Handling	Constantly	Frequently	Exceeds Demand
Fingering	Occasionally	Frequently	Under Qualified
Feeling	Constantly	Occasionally	Exceeds Demand
Talking	Constantly	Frequently	Exceeds Demand
Hearing	Constantly	Frequently	Exceeds Demand
Tasting/Smelling	Constantly	Occasionally	Exceeds Demand
Near Acuity	Constantly	Frequently	Exceeds Demand
Far Acuity	Constantly	Frequently	Exceeds Demand
Depth Perception	Constantly	Frequently	Exceeds Demand
Accommodation	Constantly	Frequently	Exceeds Demand
Color Vision	Constantly	Frequently	Exceeds Demand
Field of Vision	Constantly	Frequently	Exceeds Demand

Environmental Conditions

Exposure to Weather	Constantly	Frequently	Exceeds Demand
Nonweather Extreme Cold	Constantly	Never	Exceeds Demand
Nonweather Extreme Heat	Constantly	Never	Exceeds Demand
Wet-Humid	Constantly	Never	Exceeds Demand

(Continued)

Table 19.3 (*continued*)

Vibration	Frequently	Never	Exceeds Demand
Atmospheric Conditions	Frequently	Never	Exceeds Demand
Moving Mechanical Parts	Constantly	Never	Exceeds Demand
Electrical Shock	Occasionally	Never	Exceeds Demand
High, Exposed Places	Occasionally	Never	Exceeds Demand
Radiant Energy	Occasionally	Never	Exceeds Demand
Explosives	Occasionally	Never	Exceeds Demand
Toxic/Caustic Chemicals	Frequently	Never	Exceeds Demand
Other Hazards	Constantly	Constantly	
Noise	Moderate	Loud	Under Qualified

DOT Aptitudes

General Learning Ability	3 (34–67 Percentile)	2 (68–90 Percentile)	Under Qualified
Verbal Aptitude	3 (34–67 Percentile)	3 (34–67 Percentile)	
Numerical Aptitude	3 (34–67 Percentile)	3 (34–67 Percentile)	
Spatial Aptitude	3 (34–67 Percentile)	3 (34–67 Percentile)	
Form Perception	4 (11–33 Percentile)	2 (68–90 Percentile)	Under Qualified
Clerical Aptitude	3 (34–67 Percentile)	2 (68–90 Percentile)	Under Qualified
Motor Coordination	3 (34–67 Percentile)	2 (68–90 Percentile)	Under Qualified
Finger Dexterity	3 (34–67 Percentile)	2 (68–90 Percentile)	Under Qualified
Manual Dexterity	3 (34–67 Percentile)	2 (68–90 Percentile)	Under Qualified
Eye-Hand-Foot Coordination	3 (34–67 Percentile)	3 (34–67 Percentile)	
Color Discrimination	4 (11–33 Percentile)	3 (34–67 Percentile)	Under Qualified

Job Components

WORK FIELDS
294   Health Caring-Medical
MPSMS
929   Medical and Other Health Services, NEC
SVP: 6

Seeker Components

WORK FIELDS	**SVP(s)**	
294 Health Caring-Medical	4	Same as Job
COMPONENTS OF COMBINATION WORK FIELDS	**SVP(s)**	
None		
MPSMS	**SVP(s)**	
926 Medical Assistant, Aide, Attendant Services	4	Similar to Job

Source: OASYS (Occupational Access SYStem), 2010, SkillTRAN, LLC, Spokane WA. Used with permission.

Machines, Tools, Equipment, and Work Aids (MTEWA) describes the instruments and devices that are commonly used to carry out the specific functions of a job. MTEWA should be thought of as "what you do on a job."

Material, Products, Subject Matter, and Services (MPSMS) describes the end results on which the work activities are performed. MPSMS characteristics can be viewed as "what you do it to" on a job and the type of business.

The transferability of a person's skills is most probable and meaningful among jobs in which

- The same or a lesser degree of skills (SVP) is required.
- The same or similar tools and machines (MTEWA) are used.
- The same or similar raw materials, products, processes, or services (MPSMS) are involved.

A person reviewing the OGA would see that while an exact match between abilities and the demands of the occupation is not present, there is indication that she should consider further career exploration in this area based on matches at Level 6 and Level 8. Job matches identified at Level 6 include the same work activities as in previous jobs but with a different type of employer. Occupation-specific training in this area and strategies on how to use past skills will most likely be necessary. Job matches at Level 8 include similar work activities as in previous jobs but again with a different type of employer. Extensive training in both job-specific work activities and a thorough orientation to the business type will be necessary for success.

Further exploration of this OGA (which lists over 130 traits, each with a one-to two-paragraph description) reveals that the individual's General Educational Development exceeds the reasoning and language requirements for this position and current mathematical competence is at an appropriate level of literacy. Therefore, the client has the academic competence to learn the job requirements. Because she is young and lacks work experience, this client has not had the opportunity to pursue this type of employment. The potential to benefit from a learning environment offering a job-specific course of instruction seems evident.

Reviewing the physical demands required by this position raises only one red flag. The client's states a capacity of using her fingers only occasionally to perform essential physical functions, whereas the position would require using them frequently. Work situations requiring fine motor finger skills pertinent to this occupation, such as finding a vein to give an injection or ascertaining a pulse or heart rate, would be explanations of the importance of this particular demand.

The client's capacity to perform effectively in various environmental conditions shows high transferability to the requirements of being a paramedic, except that a personal response limiting the level of performance under the condition of *noise* is found to be considered underqualified. Noise levels and situations typical of crime and accident scenes would require the individual to be able to handle pandemonium and extreme auditory stimuli. It turns out, however, that our career seeker is a semiprofessional rock musician accustomed to high noise levels. This additional information would be used to change the previous response to one that better indicates her current level of ability. If a person with ADHD or LD (or anyone) is unable to handle the noise level involved in working as a paramedic, a severe vocational limitation would be identified because of the possibility that a person with this deficit could make a life-threatening mistake.

DOT aptitudes indicate that some significant review will be required to determine whether the dexterity, perception, and coordination qualifications can be met at the level needed to perform essential functions of this job. On closer questioning, our career seeker acknowledges that she just "worked to get the sub-tasks of the CareerScope over with" and wants to have another chance to produce a personal best performance. This is a fairly common occurrence among people who have been extensively tested throughout their lives and who have come to see little connection between these measures and their wants and needs.

At all stages of this analysis, the emphasis is on the prospective candidate's capabilities. Employers hire, train, and employ workers based on their abilities to make them money, fit in, and be functioning members of the company. The focus, then, should first be on the bigger picture of what the applicant *can and will* do for the employer and should then circle back to any areas in the OGA found lacking or in need of further development.

The assessment information is part of the overall LDI curricular approach, which is designed to address the specific developmental, academic, and career needs of underprepared or inexperienced young adults. Activities and assignments include:

- Building self-esteem and self-confidence.
- Improving basic study skills.
- Acquiring knowledge and skills related to self-advocacy and leadership.
- Identifying academic and career goals.

The key ingredient in achieving successful outcomes using these approaches is the linkage of learning to know with learning to do. Providing multiple opportunities to practice and become proficient in the areas described in this section of the proposal requires instructors and staff knowledgeable in the ever-changing demands of Corporate America. In addition, both students and LDI staff must develop an appreciation of the barriers adults with hidden disabilities and related literacy difficulties will face in gaining access to appropriate programs that use criterion-referenced assessments and traditional instructional techniques. The LDI program has not shied away from these challenges but rather approaches them with the expectancy of finding the right niche for each student through development of educational, instructional, and employment curricula that match the essential functions of targeted careers with the individual's expressed desires, abilities, and impairments as well as available local resources.

Students engage in both academic and experiential learning to demonstrate knowledge and skills especially pertinent to self-advocacy and leadership. General education outcomes as well as specific course competencies are then assessed using a variety of performance-based rubrics, learning matrices, and other assessment tools.

Classroom instruction seeks to enhance practical education skills in reading, language, mathematics, and oral/written expression in subject matter of high importance to adult skill building and personal competence. These skills are needed and used in problem solving, critical decision making, and living itself.

Many adults with ADHD, LD, or other disorders seeking vocational assessment lack or cannot demonstrate competency in the skills they need to show employers. These individuals must learn to recognize the abilities that will enable them to perform the essential functions of a desired job and the aptitudes that will help them acquire the new job skills needed to be part of a self-directed work team.

The core curriculum offers the time for students to gain exposure to the vast array of Phoenix area colleges, training, and employment options prior to making a commitment to a specific career direction. Simultaneously, each student is also developing proficiency in managing the responsibilities of independent adult living and learning to make healthy choices for her or his social and emotional well-being.

The foundation for occupational exploration and career development begins with an emphasis on developing employability skills that lead to work experience in the community. Through engaging experiential activities, demonstrations, and simulations, students learn by developing and applying competencies that incorporate employment-related and job development concepts into daily classroom and community activities. These type of assignments help students become informed decision makers in their own career development.

As one of several related written and oral projects, clients review a checklist (Dowdy, 1995) that screens for ADHD or LD characteristics, determines what effect these characteristics might have in their desired occupation, and identifies specific strategies or techniques that could be implemented to work around the barriers presented by her condition. Students then draft a cover letter to a potential employer, outlining the position desired, mentioning the potential impact of the condition, suggesting training interventions they will implement to minimize this impact, and stressing a strong personal desire to be evaluated by the same standards as coworkers. When the letter is completed, clients present it orally to program peers, who review the presentation using the LDI oral and written rubrics. This exercise is very important because many individuals who come to LDI are unable or reluctant to identify their specific ADHD or LD. This exercise helps them to recognize that the interference caused by ADHD and LD is selective, not global, in nature. It also provides utilization of clear, performance-related assessment tools, practice in giving direct feedback to peers, and ability to apply best/avoid worst practices of peers from these assignment reflection sessions.

At this point, the program emphasizes that being comfortable with what makes one a unique human being allows others to feel comfortable with one's uniqueness. An empowered person is strong enough to recognize both personal strengths and personal weaknesses and still be able to respect him- or herself as a whole human being capable of performing as well as anyone on the job. This abilities-based approach is at the center of this communication, and it permeates all interaction between LDI staff and program participants. The consistent and persistent message presented to program members is that they are responsible for determining their quality of life.

In 2009, the Phoenix metropolitan area had over 300 vocational-technical schools; 28 universities; the nation's largest community college and workforce development system serving over 300,000 people for continuing education, training, employment, or business activities; and nearly 100,000 businesses. Field investigations into which of these settings is the most appropriate for LDI participants are now initiated by staff and LDI participants and are limited only by an individual's intellectual capabilities, personal desire to succeed, and the thoroughness of the career plan. Site visits of various programs and schools that offer vocational training are scheduled and conducted by the program participant—for example, eight schools and vocational-technical programs in Phoenix offer training leading to emergency medical technician or paramedic certification.

Information gathered from these visits would include but should not be limited to:

- Levels of literacy required for admissions test.
- Levels of literacy in classroom instruction.
- Methods of instruction used in classroom or lab.
- Accommodations for ADHD and LD.
- Tutorial support available.
- Qualifications of staff providing tutorial assistance.
- Length of training, cost, and financial aid availability.
- Personal observations about condition of campus and facilities.
- Any and all promotional literature regarding program of instruction.
- A list of current students and graduates willing to provide testimonials.
- A list of employers who have hired graduates.

Once these tours have been completed, clients follow up by interviewing consumers of the program's educational or training services. It is at this stage that clients would compare local labor market information with that gathered from the OASYS program. Interviews are conducted with persons who have finished training and with local employers who have hired graduates from these programs. These interviews allow LDI program participants to gauge the market value potential of training, the qualifications employers are looking for, training satisfaction among current students, factors constituting job satisfaction among current employees, average wage information, and other pertinent information affecting the career choice.

Participants then develop a multimedia presentation using Microsoft's PowerPoint program to evaluate and synthesize the relative trade-offs and consequences of each education or training program option in relationship to accomplishing career/life values they identified as mattering most to them in such a major decision. The presentation incorporates the information identified by program participants as being essential to making an informed, intelligent decision. Participants present this information on slides that use words, designs, pictures, photographs, video, audio, and many other options to present the results of the vocational investigation.

The end result of this investigation is that the person looking for the right training program—leading to paramedic certification, for example—becomes the expert on all available and appropriate opportunities. Now in possession of a high-quality vocational plan, the program participant can act on it with a high degree of personal confidence.

Vocational Strategies for College Graduates

Adults with ADHD or LD should feel great satisfaction in completing the degree requirements of a specific program of study. The difficulty of completing a college program for many individuals in this population makes the success of those who do finish very inspiring.

The next challenge is applying theoretical concepts to workplace situations and problems. In the workplace, standards of acceptable performance are measured quite differently from in the college environment. Employer expectations about the ability of college graduates to handle multiple tasks and priorities smoothly and effectively require advance preparation on the part of the job-seeking college graduate.

Suggested guidelines, strategies, and accommodations that clinicians can use to help the college graduate with ADHD or LD make a successful transition from education to employment are presented next (Lieb, 1995; Payne, 1993, pp. 2–6):

1. *Seek employment that uses identified abilities and college education.* Decide on a job or career after carefully looking at what is required both during training and on the job. Avoid job searches that are too narrowly or broadly focused. Resist the impulse to go after employment opportunities because of primarily financial

motivations; instead, concentrate on the opportunities inherent in the position itself.

2. *Assess the targeted employer's awareness of and efforts to work with employees who have ADHD or LD.* Ascertain whether personal work habits (e.g., messy desk, need to walk around, need for quiet work area, receptivity to practical jokes) are compatible with company culture.

3. *Develop a long-term career ladder that includes the estimated amount of time needed to move up to successive levels of responsibility, the number of potential openings in the targeted area, and anticipated future learning needs.* It is in the best interests of career-minded job applicants to focus on companies that offer in-house continuing education programs. Once competency and capabilities have been established, employers can deal with any academic difficulties much more flexibly because the individual has proved himself.

4. *Find out how companies that offer continuing education programs deliver these services.* Is service delivery by traditional paper-and-pencil techniques, or is it industry specific and taught in the context of the job? Be aware of the accommodations individuals used successfully in school and do not assume that they will automatically be allowed on the job.

5. *Ask for specific timelines for performance evaluations, and understand when and how performance will be evaluated.* If accommodations will be needed, propose an evaluation process through which the employee and supervisor can review the effectiveness of the accommodations and the possibility of adjustments.

SUGGESTED ACCOMMODATION STRATEGIES FOR SUCCESS IN THE WORKPLACE

College graduates with ADHD or LD need to have compensatory strategies ready to offer employers once they succeed in securing employment. A list of accommodations for specific deficits that are easily operationalized in just about any work setting at little or no cost to the employer is presented next.

- *Needs oral directions.* Provide written copy or picture, model, flow chart, or diagram; shorten directions; use simple sentences and explain one step at a time; have employee repeat directions in own words; have trainer physically demonstrate the task.
- *Learns erratically.* Have model of finished product available for review; record or videotape instructions; repeat activity until learning is accomplished.
- *Is distracted by irrelevant details.* If unable to focus, clarify directions and provide clear, reasonable expectations; underline or number key points using color; break activities or tasks into small, sequenced steps.

- *Struggles with expression of ideas.* Keep responses simple (yes-or-no choices); keep questions short and direct, clearly expressed; focus on the order of events; use clues to help person get through steps or explanation (e.g., first, second, third).

- *Perseverates—has trouble moving to new tasks.* Identify time frames or limits for tasks; help create lists, checking off as it is completed; design a task chart with time frames; keep a calendar with start and end dates; give regular feedback.

- *Is unorganized—has difficulty planning.* Provide concise directions; spell out all steps of tasks; specify time limitations for activities; organize work spatially so sequence and structure are more visible.

- *Is easily frustrated—lacks self-confidence.* Make task assignment short to promote quick success; teach to self-rate quality; give or repeat work tasks person enjoys; praise.

- *Is impulsive—rushes tasks.* Emphasize intent or purpose of task; concentrate on accuracy rather than deadlines.

- *Lacks time orientation.* If person has difficulty tracking time or staying on time, check to see whether he or she has difficulty telling time; identify which time-telling device is best—digital or analog clock; encourage use of a watch with an alarm or use of a stopwatch; have person time activities to experience completion time; give task assignments time frames; monitor time, eventually have person monitor own time; team up with coworker with similar schedule.

- *Struggles with attention—is easily distracted.* Place person in stimulus-free environment; use time chart; identify expected and actual finish times; minimize distractions (visual or auditory); have person focus on supervisor's or trainer's eyes when giving or receiving instructions.

- *Lacks direction orientation.* Encourage person to ask questions when confused; suggest he or she carry small notepad; use landmarks or color when giving directions; use maps and models with landmarks and street names.

- *Has spatial judgment difficulties that interfere with reading.* Suggest use of a ruler as a guide; cut a window in a piece of cardboard; use magnifiers, colored markers, and overlays.

- *Struggles with writing and copying tasks.* Have person copy from notes or outline, not the board, flip chart, or overhead; carbon copy or photocopy another's notes; photocopy or duplicate worksheets; encourage use of outlines.

- *Struggles with written directions.* Tape-record or read the printed information; demonstrate directions in an oral and hands-on fashion if possible; print directions on 3-by-5 cards with step-by-step instructions (one instruction per card).

- *Struggles with integration of work tasks.* Have example of finished product; demonstrate how parts fit into a meaningful whole.

- *Struggles when coping with changing environments.* Try to keep tasks and activities highly structured; minimize changes and distractions whenever possible.

- *Has poor social judgment.* Create buddy system with senior employee in the same section who will advise and explain hidden rules, nonverbal communication, and culture of the organization; role-play or discuss group situations; reinforce positive behaviors; help person identify and respond to nonverbal cues and information.
- *Is vulnerable to auditory distractions.* Try to eliminate open, noisy spaces; place person in small quiet office or room; utilize headsets or earphones; supplement information with written instructions and outlines.
- *Struggles with handwriting and forms.* Make sure person can read supervisor's handwriting; provide person with samples or examples of forms, worksheets, and time sheets; color-code similar tasks for processing (colored baskets, folders, or labels). (Payne, 1994, pp. 52–54).

SUMMARY

Many adults with ADHD or LD seeking vocational assessment lack or cannot demonstrate competency in the skills they need to show employers. These adults must learn to recognize the abilities that will enable them to perform the essential functions of a desired job and the aptitudes that will help them acquire the new job skills needed to be part of a self-directed work team.

This task is made more difficult by a shortage of appropriate training programs providing services to this population, limited understanding of how to make reasonable accommodations in the workplace, and lack of insight of many adults with ADHD or LD into how they can cope with and compensate for their deficits.

This writer's experience as both service provider and adult with comorbid ADHD and LD has taught that when reasonable expectations of personal performance are combined with appropriate treatment, individuals with ADHD or LD can and do succeed at levels of accomplishment commensurate with their nondisabled peers.

Society has expected too little from those with special learning needs, and, sadly, it has not been disappointed. These individuals are chronically un- and underemployed and at risk of becoming involved in the welfare, criminal justice, and mental health systems as consumers of public resources instead of providers to the community. The Bureau of Labor Statistics has kept track of employment for working-age adults with disabilities, and close to 75% are unemployed and 40% did not finish high school. Where in the future of the high-performance workplace do they fit in?

Clinicians must approach vocational planning by dealing with the characteristics and demands of global workplace and workforce realities within an aggressively developed consumer-directed vocational assessment. Targeted occupational clusters can be examined in order to identify a career ladder, tasks essential to a desired job, and general literacy requirements.

Client-directed vocational assessments provide depth and meaning to background information on the individual's interests, abilities, and aptitudes. But more critically, they facilitate personal buy-in. Because the occupational goals identified in this process are set by the individual with clinician support, they can take ownership of and thus responsibility for the action plan.

Discovering a personally satisfying occupational niche and learning how one can achieve it produces dramatic positive changes in life. The goal for those of us who work with this population must be to provide the tools, techniques, and vision necessary to help our clients start, sustain, and complete this vocational journey successfully.

REFERENCES

Americans with Disabilities Act of 1990, Pub. L. No. 101-336, § 2, 104 Stat. 328 (1991).

ADA Amendments Act of 2008, Pub. L. No. 110-325, § 2, 122 Stat. 3553, 3554.

Alexander Hamilton Institute. (1993). *What every manager should know about the Americans with Disabilities Act*. Maywood, NJ: Author.

CareerScope (2009) Vocational Research Institute. Philadelphia, PA

Dowdy, C. A. (1995). Attention deficit rating scale. In C. A. Dowdy, J. R. Patton, T. E. C. Smith, & E. A. Polloway (Eds.), *Attention-Deficit Hyperactivity Disorder in the classroom: A practical guide for teachers*. Austin, TX: Pro Ed.

Guide for Occupational Explorations. (2006). Washington, DC: U.S. Government Printing Office.

Halpern, A. (1992b). Quality of life as a conceptual framework for evaluating transition outcomes. *Exceptional Children, 59*, 202–213.

Janis, I. L., & Mann, L. (1977). *Decision making: A psychological analysis of conflict, choice, and commitment*. New York: Free Press.

Lieb V. (1995). *Choosing careers*. St Louis, MO: People Achieving Results Together.

Life Development Institute. (2009). Glendale, AZ.

Moya, S. S., & O'Malley, J. M. (1994). A portfolio assessment model for English as a second language. *Journal of Education Issues of Language Minority Students, 13*, 13–36.

National Center on Education and the Economy. (2007) New Commission Report on the Skills of the American Workforce: Tough Choices or Tough Times. Washington, DC.

National Longitudinal Transition Study 2. (2009) SRI International, Menlo Park, CA.

Occupational Awareness System. (2009) Vertek, Inc. Bellevue, WA.

Payne, N. (1993). *What employers want in an employee*. Olympia, WA: Payne and Associates.

Rehabilitation Services Administration. (2009, October 1). RSA: Monitoring Reports on the Vocational Rehabilitation and Independent Living Programs Required under Section 107. Washington, DC.

Rehabilitation Services Administration. (2005, January 10). TECHNICAL ASSIS-TANCE CIRCULAR RSA-TAC-05-01. Washington, DC.

U.S. Census Bureau. (2007). Washington, DC: U.S. Government Printing Office.

U.S. Department of Labor. (1991). Dictionary of Occupational Titles. Washington, DC: U.S. Government Printing Office.

U.S. Department of Labor. (2009). Bureau of Labor Statistics. Washington, DC: U.S. Government Printing Offiice.

CHAPTER

20

Lifestyle and Family Issues

ARTHUR L. ROBIN

Attention-Deficit/Hyperactivity Disorder (ADHD) has classically been thought to be a neurobiological disorder of attention, impulse control, and hyperactivity having its onset in childhood and often continuing across the life span into adulthood (Barkley, 2006). Specific Learning Disabilities (LD) have classically been defined as disorders in one or more of the basic psychological processes involved in understanding or using spoken or written language, which manifest themselves as problems with speaking, listening, writing, spelling, or doing mathematical calculations (Katz, Goldstein, & Beers, 2001); more generically, LD refer to a heterogeneous group of disorders characterized by significant difficulties in acquiring and using listening, speaking, reading, writing, reasoning, or mathematical skills (Gregg, 2009). There is overlap between LD and ADHD, with anywhere from 4% to 40% of adults with ADHD also displaying LD, depending on the type of LD and the method used to define it (Barkley, Murphy, & Fischer, 2008). Contemporary researchers have recast ADHD and LD within the framework of executive functions and neuropsychological processes (Barkley, 1997a; Gregg, 2009; Mapou, 2009). Executive functions are higher-order controlling functions of the brain that direct the individual's actions in a goal-oriented fashion. Brown (2005) has likened executive functions to the conductor of an orchestra. The conductor selects the musicians and the music; directs rehearsals; directs the musicians during the concert; and tells various musicians when to start, stop, play louder, softer, and how to interpret the music. The brain's executive functions guide the individual to get focused on a task, get organized to complete the task, sustain attention and effort to the task, resist distraction, remember verbal and nonverbal information as the task is completed, control emotional interference, creatively

The author would like to acknowledge the helpful feedback and suggestions of Dr. Philip Parker, Dr. Sally Palaian, Dr. J. Russell Ramsey, and Mrs. Mary Jo Schuster, who reviewed earlier versions of this manuscript.

recombine elements of a problem to solve it, and the like. When the conductor directs the orchestra effectively, the music sounds harmonious; when the conductor does not direct the orchestra effectively, the music sound cacophonous. When the brain's executive functions work efficiently, the individual completes the tasks of daily life effectively. When the brain's executive functions do not work reliably or efficiently, the individual displays impairments in daily functioning. The executive functions are not operating reliably or efficiently for individuals with ADHD or LD, leading to significant impairments in many of the major activities of daily life.

In order to survive and thrive as an adult in contemporary society, the individual with ADHD or LD, like others without the disorders, must take care of his or her health, complete his or her higher education, maintain a job or career to earn a living, manage the money that is earned effectively, take care of a household, drive safely or take public transportation appropriately, interact appropriately with other people and/or sustain long-term relationships or marriages effectively, and if he or she has children, parent them effectively. The impaired executive functions intrinsic to ADHD or LD can interfere with functioning in all of these areas (Barkley & Benton, 2010). Higher education and vocational/career issues have been discussed in earlier chapters of this book. Driving has been discussed in detail elsewhere (Barkley et al., 2008). The current chapter focuses on money management, health, marriage and committed relationships, and parenting. In each case, we describe the types of impairments that occur, the research data documenting these impairments, and the types of interventions that might help individuals cope with these impairments.

UMASS AND MILWAUKEE STUDIES

The data describing the impairments suffered by adults with ADHD come primarily from two large studies conducted by Dr. Russell Barkley and his colleagues (Barkley et al., 2008). These two studies are briefly summarized next.

The University of Massachusetts (UMASS) study was a comparison of the functioning of 146 clinic-referred adults with ADHD, 97 clinic-referred adults without ADHD (Clinical Control group), and 109 non-referred community adults (Community Control group). The first two groups were obtained from consecutive referrals to an adult ADHD clinic at the University of Massachusetts Medical School. To be placed in the ADHD group, participants had to meet the *Diagnostic and Statistical Manual of Mental Disorders* (4th ed.; *DSM-IV*) ADHD criteria, except for the age-of-onset criterion, as judged by an experienced clinician. All clinic-referred adults not meeting the ADHD criteria were placed in the Clinical Control Group. This group included 43% with Anxiety Disorders, 15% with Substance Related Disorders, 12% with Mood Disorders, 4% with LD, 4% with partner relationship disorders, 1% with Personality Disorders, 4% with Adjustment Disorders, 1% with Oppositional Defiant Disorder, and 1% with no diagnosis. The Community Control Group did not have ADHD and were not taking medication for any psychiatric or medical disorders that might interfere with the assessment. All participants in the UMASS study were assessed at intake into the clinic at a single point in time.

The Milwaukee Study was a prospective, longitudinal follow-up study comparing the adult functioning of children with or without hyperactivity initially recruited in 1979 to 1980, when they were age 4 to 12, at the Milwaukee Children's Hospital in Milwaukee, Wisconsin. Follow-up data was collected three times: age 12 to 20, age 19 to 25, and age 27. To be in the Hyperactive Group ($n = 158$) at initial recruitment, the children had to:

1. Score 2 or more standard deviations above the normal mean for same-age and sex children on parent rating scales.
2. Exhibit parent- and/or teacher-reported short attention span, impulsive behavior, and high activity level.
3. Have developed these problems prior to age 6 and had them for at least 12 months.
4. Not have Autism, psychosis, other psychiatric disorders, mental retardation, epilepsy, or a thought disorder.

To be in the Community Control group ($n = 81$), the children had to have no history of referral for mental health services, no current parent or teacher reports of significant behavior problems, no psychiatric disorders, and score within 1.5 standard deviations of the normal mean on parent rating scales.

At age 27, the follow-up assessments included comprehensive *DSM-IV* ADHD symptom interviews independently conducted with the participants and their parents. After careful consideration, Barkley et al. (2008) decided to base their adult ADHD diagnoses on the interview with the participants, not the interviews with the parents, as was done with the childhood diagnoses. They adjusted the number of symptoms required for a positive diagnosis developmentally to be at least 2 standard deviations above the mean of ADHD symptoms exhibited by the Community Control Group; for example, 4 out of 9 inattention and/or 4 out of 9 hyperactivity/impulsivity symptoms. They also required evidence of impairment to a major life activity, such as education, work, or home life. Using these criteria, 44% of the original hyperactive children had ADHD (H + ADHD Group) and 56% did not have ADHD (H-ADHD Group) at age 27. These two groups were compared to each other and the Community Control group on all of the measures.

Although these follow-up studies do not address outcomes for adults who have LD alone, they are relevant to those individuals who have both ADHD and LD. Follow-up research with adults who have LD has generally focused on educational and occupational outcomes, not the lifestyle challenges discussed in this chapter (Gregg, 2009; Katz et al., 2001).

BARKLEY'S THEORY OF ADHD

Also pertinent to understanding the impairments and treatments for these impairments discussed in this chapter is Dr. Russell Barkley's executive function theory of ADHD (Barkley, 1997a, 2006). Barkley considers behavioral inhibition to be a central executive function from which follows four other important executive functions: nonverbal working memory, verbal working memory, self-control over affect/motivation/arousal, and reconstitution. Behavioral inhibition involves the individual's ability to stop before immediately acting when faced with a life situation, to continue to inhibit impulsive action long enough for thinking to have a chance to occur, and to tune out any interfering stimuli that would distract the individual from thinking through a reasoned response to the situation. For example, when an adult with ADHD goes to balance the checkbook using computer software, he may experience the temptation to go on eBay and search for interesting things to purchase. With strong behavioral inhibition, the individual would tell himself that he needs to refrain from going on eBay, stick to balancing the checkbook, and continue to tune out tempting thoughts to go on eBay, recognizing as he balances the checkbook that such purchases would be frivolous and break the budget. Many adults with ADHD go on eBay and mindlessly buy attractive items without considering whether they have the money to pay for them, getting distracted to many different eBay sites, overspending rather than balancing the checkbook. The term "nonverbal working memory" refers to the retention and reactivation of prior visual and auditory sensory representations, prolonging these stimuli long enough for them to help guide action; this involves our sense of time, hindsight and forethought, and the organization of behavior in time. Adults with ADHD have a very poor sense of time, living in the moment rather than considering the past and the future, procrastinating and failing to learn from past mistakes. The term "verbal working memory" refers to self-directed, covert speech, the internalization of language, and the ability to behave in accordance with rules and guidelines. Adults with ADHD have very poor internalization of language and self-directed speech, resulting in poor adherence to rules, poor memory of information, poor acquisition of social conventions and social skills, and lack of consideration of the future. The term "self-control over affect, motivation, and arousal" refers to the ability to generate and release emotions in a self-controlled manner rather than in huge, impulsive bursts, the maintenance of motivation to complete mundane and uninteresting but necessary life tasks, and arousal and alertness. Adults with ADHD have grave difficulties with controlling extreme emotional outbursts, especially anger, generating motivation to carry out many of the tasks of daily life, and maintaining alertness and arousal. The term "reconstitution" refers to analysis of a problem situation, breaking it down into its elements, and synthesizing a novel or creative way to solve the problem. Adults with ADHD often exhibit cognitive inflexibility when they fixate on a single way of approaching a problem and are unable to look at it differently and come up with creative solutions. Adults with LD often also have difficulties with verbal and nonverbal working memory, self-control over affect/motivation/arousal, and reconstitution, but they may always not have the poor behavioral inhibition common with ADHD.

TREATMENT IMPLICATIONS

If adults with ADHD or LD have executive function deficits, and the impairments to money management, health care, relationships, and parenting are in part a result of impaired behavioral inhibition, then interventions for these lifestyle problems must take this into account. As Barkley has said, the problem of impaired behavioral inhibition is not knowing what to do but rather doing what one knows; intervention needs to be aimed at helping the individual do what he or she knows at the point of performance in the natural environment where the behavior needs to occur, not primarily provision of knowledge or skill training in an office setting (Barkley & Benton, 2010; Barkley et al., 2008). Treatments will be helpful when they assist the individual with performing the target behavior in the natural environment at the time and place where it is supposed to be performed. The farther away in space and time that treatment is from this point of performance, the less effective it is likely to be in assisting with coping with executive function deficits.

For example, to help adults with ADHD or LD save for retirement, clinicians might have them, while in the therapist's presence, arrange for an automatic monthly electronic transfer of funds to their retirement account, or alternatively (a) specify the time and place during the month for a manual transfer of funds to their retirement account, (b) set electronic alarms to go off and remind them to carry out the manual transfer, and (c) agree to send an e-mail to or leave a phone message for the therapist confirming the transfer and bring the receipt to the next therapy session. The therapist then might help the patient to anticipate and plan to overcome any obstacles, such as spending the money earmarked for the retirement account impulsively. More traditional therapists unaccustomed to dealing with such performance problems might regard this intervention as "codependency," "babying the patient," or doing the patient's work, and the patient "must be ready psychologically to save for retirement." However, the nature of these conditions demands creative solutions to performance problems along with methods of helping patients call forth these solutions and implement them at those moments in the environment when they are needed (Barkley & Benton, 2010).

MONEY MANAGEMENT

Barkley et al. (2008) studied the money management habits of the adults with ADHD in both the UMASS clinic study and the Milwaukee Follow-Up Study. In the UMASS study, the ADHD, psychiatric control group, and Community Control groups were compared on 12 areas of money management. Relative to the Community Control group, a higher proportion of the group with ADHD reported eight types of money problems: (1) overall money management, (2) difficulty saving, (3) buying on impulse, (4) nonpayment of utilities resulting in their termination, (5) missing loan payments, (6) exceeding credit card limits, (7) having a poor credit rating, and (8) not saving for retirement. Relative to the psychiatric control group, a higher proportion of the group with ADHD reported four problems: (1) trouble saving money, (2) buying on impulse, (3) not paying utilities resulting in their termination, and (4) not saving for retirement; thus, these four areas were specific risks associated with ADHD. Similar results were found in the Milwaukee Follow-Up study in that more of the H + ADHD group than the community controls had difficulties with overall money management, difficulty saving, impulsive buying, missed rent payments, utility shut-offs, missed credit card payments, exceeding credit limits, repossessed vehicles, declarations of bankruptcy, and poor credit ratings. The severity of ADHD symptoms during childhood predicted financial problems at age 27. Some of these problems were partially replicated in an online survey of 111 partners of adults diagnosed with ADHD described in detail later in the chapter (Pera, 2008). Pera asked the partners several questions about money and their relationships with their spouses with ADHD. The percentage of partners endorsing each problem were:

My partner won't or just can't save money—60%

ADHD has been an expensive disorder, from the money spent on traffic tickets, late fees, doctors' bills, therapy for our kids, and more—59%

A large percentage of our income goes to my partner's fines, late fees, and finance charges—26%

Although researchers have not extended such studies to adults with LD, clinicians find that many of the same challenges occur for such adults.

A comprehensive approach is needed to address the money management problems of adults with ADHD or LD. As far as this author knows, there are no evidence-based interventions for helping older adolescents and adults with ADHD or LD improve money management behaviors. Instead, the next suggestions are based on promising approaches that have proven useful in clinical practice.

Dr. Sally Palaian (2009) has applied her comprehensive intervention for money management problems to adults with ADHD or LD. She outlines a continuum of money behaviors, ranging from a healthy relationship with money through a problematic relationship with money to a money addiction. In a *healthy relationship with money*, the individual spends money consciously, with planning and self-discipline, and lives within the limits of his or her own income, only charging what there is money in the bank to cover. A *problematic relationship with money* involves buying things primarily to obtain happiness and starting to lose control over spending habits—charging items without knowing how they will be paid for, having difficulty paying off credit cards, and having difficulty adhering to self-imposed spending limits. The *money addict* is an out-of-control spender who buys things on impulse, does not respect any spending limits, maxes out credit cards and tries to get more of them, and borrows money from friends or relatives with no plan to repay it, and has no internal spending controls and ignores external attempts to control spending. Adults with ADHD or LD range widely in their money behaviors, but many have problematic or addictive relationships with money.

Integrating cognitive behavioral therapy (CBT) with a 12-step model, Palaian (2009) outlines six phases of recovery from money problems:

1. Hitting bottom
2. Accepting and following guidance
3. Creating a life vision
4. Living within a spending plan
5. Changing thoughts, feelings, and impulsive actions
6. Living the abundant life

This intervention can take the form of individual therapy sessions, group therapy sessions, or psychoeducational workshops. *Hitting bottom* involves becoming aware of the seriousness of one's problematic money behaviors, poor spending habits, and inability to meet financial obligations, and moving beyond denial to own responsibility for these problems. Using a series of structured, pointed questions, the therapist helps individuals "break through denial," stop making excuses, acknowledge that they are powerless to control their urges to spend, and acknowledge that they have a serious money problem or in some cases a money addiction. The contributions of these factors to problematic money behavior are explored: neurobiological disorders such as ADHD, LD, family-of-origin money problems (a financially stressed childhood, begrudging parents, parents with money addictions and conflict), the attitudes towards money of the generation into which the patient was born, cultural factors, and unexpected changes in life circumstances. Palaian strongly recommends that her patients also join a 12-step program, such as Debtors Anonymous.

Accepting and following guidance involves patients overcoming the shame of having money problems, gathering all relevant financial records, reviewing them with a trusted friend or the therapist, writing a list of debts, stopping credit card use, and regularly recording all spending. Palaian encourages adults with ADHD or LD to get a portable file, put all financial records in this file, bring it to therapy sessions, and take it to the library or other quiet places where they can work on it. Many patients need therapist coaching to open bills, list debts, prioritize which bills to pay, write checks, or pay bills online. Sometimes the adult is unable to write a list of debts but can dictate it to the therapist. Palaian provides a detailed analysis of the reasons why it is essential to stop credit card use, so that the therapist can effectively use cognitive restructuring to help the patient buy in to this step. She also asks patients to record all spending and practices this with them; they tell her what they spend, and at first she writes it down for them, then later they keep their own records.

Next, patients are asked to create a life vision, a fantasy of the ideal life where money is no object. The life vision is designed to motivate patients to take the difficult steps necessary to improve money management and may go beyond money to include anything that they want to accomplish. Palaian encourages her patients to collect images associated with the life visions and create collages or other pictorial representations of their ideals, to keep handy when making difficult financial decisions. From the life vision follows a list of long- and short-term personal and financial goals. The financial goals are listed in a table with estimated costs and a projected time frame to attain them. Such lists can be generated during the therapy session or at home.

With the help of templates provided in her book or available free on the Internet at www.hazelden.org/bookstore ("Spent" page, under "reproducible journal with worksheets"), the patients translate the previously collected spending record into a detailed spending plan. The spending plan includes the annual amount of all expenses organized in meaningful categories, the monthly amounts for these items, a reconciliation of income with expenses, and a plan to reduce or adjust expenses so that they can live within their income. This task is often overwhelming. It helps for the therapist to review the spending records with patients and coach them, step by step, to develop the spending plan; patients read out the item, and the therapist lists it under the appropriate category on the plan. The therapist keeps asking "What else?" until the entire spending plan has been written out. Then the therapist coaches patients to use a variety of time management and organizational tools to implement the spending plan effectively. The therapist should break the plan into small units, assign implementation of one unit at a time, arrange for significant others in a patient's environment to prompt and reinforce the patient for carrying out each stop, and monitor implementation closely between sessions through e-mail and phone messages.

As the adult with ADHD or LD implements the spending plan, he or she must recognize, challenge, and replace distorted thinking with more reasonable thinking about finances and money. Palaian exhaustively catalogs common extreme cognitions that interfere with effective financial management. A few examples follow, with more reasonable beliefs in parentheses:

- I can't make it without credit cards. (Remember, credit cards are what got me into trouble in the first place; I can survive without them.)
- Only money matters. (There are many interesting dimensions of life for me to participate in.)

- If I don't buy it now, there will never be another one as nice. (Nice things are always available; every day offers new opportunities to get nice things.)
- I am worthless because of my debt. (I am not my debt.)
- The world owes me—I deserve to have the best. (It is my responsibility to take care of myself, not others.)

Such extreme thoughts trigger negative emotions, which dramatically increase the chances of poor financial choices and impulsive spending. The therapist helps patients logically challenge such distorted thinking and replace it with more reasonable thinking, decreasing the triggers for impulsive spending.

In the final phase of the intervention, *Living the abundant life*, Palaian helps patients recognize the signs of a now-healthy relationship with money, transcend materialism, and recognize how abundance also involves living life with balance, flexibility, meaningful relationships, and in accordance with authentic values.

This intervention may need to be tailored further for patients who have an LD in mathematics. The therapist may need to simplify the arithmetic steps, carry them out with patients during the sessions, create spreadsheets that automatically calculate the numbers for the spending plan, and alleviate mathematics anxiety through the use of relaxation and in vivo desensitization.

Although this intervention does not yet have any research to test out its effectiveness, it is conceptually consistent with the point of performance philosophy articulated throughout this chapter. The therapist guides the patient to carry out a series of cognitive and behavioral tasks to improve money management both in the session and in the natural environment, programming prompts and consequences for performing these steps into the environment. Barkley (2010) provides similar, practical advice in a recent book for adults with ADHD.

HEALTH

Alice, age 35, is an adult with ADHD and an LD in mathematics who has a full-time office job, a husband, two children ages 9 and 6, and a home to manage. Her 9-year-old also has ADHD. Alice is overweight, was recently diagnosed with type II diabetes but does not reliably remember to check her blood sugar, does not accurately compute the amount of insulin to give herself, often eats junk food on the run, gets 4 to 5 hours of sleep her night, belongs to a gym but does not have time to exercise, and has 2 glasses of wine with her husband most evenings after her children go to sleep to help her "unwind." She cannot remember when she last had an annual physical or a gynecological checkup and mainly goes to urgent care centers when she is sick or her diabetes gets out of control. It takes all of her energy, focus, and time to take care of her children, her husband, and her job, with little time left for herself or her health.

Alice is typical of many adults with ADHD and LD when it comes to taking care of their health. Lifestyle is a significant contributor to health and longevity (McGinnis & Foege, 1993), and Alice's lifestyle is likely to shorten her life span. These factors contribute to longevity: proper exercise; good nutrition; appropriate body weight; adequate sleep; safe sexual practices; moderation in the use of caffeine, tobacco, and alcohol; safe driving; adequate medical and dental care; and adherence to medical regimens for chronic conditions. Optimizing these factors involves effective planning, organization, follow-through, time management, impulse control, self-regulation, and regard for the future consequences of one's behavior. The impaired executive functioning and poor behavioral inhibition that are central problems for older adolescents and adults with ADHD or LD lead to reduced concern about the future consequences of one's behavior and inconsistent follow-through with all of these health-conscious behaviors. Thus, such individuals would be predicted to display problems in all of these health-related areas and as a result would be predicted to be at risk for a shorter life span.

The UMASS and Milwaukee studies shed some light on these hypotheses. The Skinner Computerized Lifestyle Assessment was administered in both studies. This software program computes scores for strengths, concerns, and risks in these areas: nutrition, eating habits, caffeine use, physical activity, body weight, sleep, social relationships, family interactions, tobacco use, alcohol use, nonmedical drug use, medical/dental care, motor vehicle safety, sexual activities, work and leisure, and emotional health. In the UMASS study, a significantly higher percentage of the group with ADHD than the Community Control group had concerns or risks regarding sleep, social relationships, family interactions, tobacco use, nonmedical drug use, medical/dental care, motor vehicle safety, work and leisure, and emotional health. More participants in the group with ADHD than the Clinical Control group had concerns or risks for nonmedical drug use, motor vehicle safety, and emotional health. In the Milwaukee study, significantly higher percentages of the group with H + ADHD than the Community Control group had concerns or risks regarding eating, sleep, social relationships, tobacco use, nonmedical drug use, and emotional health.

In addition, in the Milwaukee study detailed medical histories, current medical concerns, physical exams, and lab studies were collected. Results revealed that the group with H + ADHD had more problems in their medical histories, more current medical concerns, poorer exercise habits, higher body mass indices, and greater risks for future medical problems than the Community Control group. Although space limitations preclude a detailed presentation of these results, two poignant findings will be highlighted. Using a risk factor consisting of smoking, blood pressure, serum cholesterol, body mass, diabetes, and exercise, Barkley et al. (2008) found that the group with H + ADHD had a greater risk for future coronary heart disease at 5 or 10 years than the Community Control group. Using another set of risk factors, they also found that the group with H + ADHD had a greater risk for current and future atherosclerosis of the coronary vessels than the Community Control group.

Taken together, the results of the UMASS and Milwaukee studies paint a picture of a less healthy lifestyle in adults with ADHD compared to adults without ADHD, with increased risks for life-threatening medical problems that might shorten their life expectancy.

Although no research has examined patterns of health care in adults with LD, clinicians might expect that LD will interfere with adherence to medical regimens—for example, the individual with Reading Disabilities (RD) may not correctly follow written instructions for taking medication.

The task for the clinician working with adults with ADHD or LD is to help them embrace and act on a healthy lifestyle, compensating for the executive dysfunction that might prevent them from naturally doing so. In addition, the clinician should communicate to the patient's primary care physician the special challenges that the patient will face because of ADHD and LD and enlist the cooperation of that physician in helping to address these challenges. To the author's knowledge, there are no controlled studies evaluating interventions for increasing health care behaviors in older adolescents and adults with ADHD or LD, although there is a case study using behavioral interventions to increase diabetes care in younger adolescents who have ADHD (Sanchez, Chronis, & Hunter, 2006). However, there is research on the use of implementation intention approaches to increase adherence to health behaviors in adults without ADHD (Gollwitzer & Oettingen, 2007), and such approaches have been found to be beneficial in improving self-control of children with ADHD (Gawrilow & Gollwitzer, 2008).

For now the clinician should use an approach based on sound behavioral programming. The first step is for the therapist and the patient to take an inventory of the patient's current acute and chronic medical conditions; weight; nutrition and eating; exercise; sleep; intake of nicotine, caffeine, and alcohol; and health prevention behaviors (e.g. annual physical, regular dental checkups, gynecological checkups for women, etc.). What is the person actually doing to take care of each of these areas of health, and how does current functioning compare to the regimens recommended by the individual's physicians, dentists, and allied health professionals in order to produce positive health outcomes? The therapist might prompt the individual to write a list in two columns, "Current Health Behaviors" and "Recommended Health Behaviors." If the patient is unsure of what health behaviors are recommended, the therapist should prompt him or her to make appointments with the primary care physician, dentist, and any other relevant allied health professionals (e.g., dietician) and take the list to these appointments, asking the professional to write in the recommended behaviors. With those patients who are skeptical about the need to follow such recommendations, the therapist might take a motivational interviewing approach (Miller & Rollnick, 2002) by asking them to discuss how long they want to live and what they want to accomplish during the remainder of their lives; then the therapist might highlight the discrepancy between patients' life goals and specific examples of poor adherence to a healthy lifestyle plan, asking how they expect to achieve those goals when an unhealthy life style may shorten their lives.

Table 20.1 lists Alice's current and recommended health behaviors. The recommended health behaviors become goals for change in therapy. Keeping in mind ADHD and LD as point of performance problems, the therapist and patient select one goal at a time, translate the goal into a list of specific daily behaviors to perform, set times to engage in each behavior, arrange for time-based memory prompts to perform each response (electronic alarms on cell phone, alarm clocks, kitchen timers, or people reminding her), and arrange the environment to provide positive reinforcement for engaging in each behavior. The patient's significant other, family, friends, and physicians might be enlisted to praise the patient for engaging in the targeted health care behaviors. The therapist also anticipates any cognitive distortions or extreme beliefs that might interfere with this intervention and uses cognitive restructuring to address these cognitions. When the individual is reliably performing the first target behavior, a second one is added, and over time the remaining target behaviors are added. Slowly, over many months, the individual begins to make significant changes in health-related target behaviors and associated cognitions. It is important to help instill the belief that engaging in recommended health behaviors is a lifestyle change, not a "cure for a symptom." Inevitably, there will be setbacks, and the therapist needs to help the individual plan to cope with such setbacks without giving up.

Alice selected checking her blood sugar 4 times per day as an initial health target behavior. Although her endocrinologist indicated that it was essential to know her blood sugar before each meal so she could supplement her oral medication with insulin if her blood sugar was very high, Alice was convinced that "I can never remember to do it." Before intervention, she checked her blood sugar in the morning and sometimes before bedtime. The therapist asked how she remembered to feed her children and put

Table 20.1 Alice's Current and Recommended Health Behaviors

Current Health Behavior	Recommended Health Behavior
Checks blood sugar irregularly	Check blood sugar 4 times per day
Eats junk food at irregular intervals	Follow food plan from dietician
Does not exercise	Walk for 30 minutes 4 times per week. Go to gym once per week; husband watches kids.
Sleeps 4–5 hours per night	Aim for 6–7 hours per night of sleep
Drinks a glass of wine daily	Drink a glass of wine every other evening

them to bed. She responded that they told her they were hungry and that looking at the clock cued her that it was bedtime. The therapist used her response to point out that since reminders help her complete other tasks, perhaps they would help her remember to check her blood sugar four times per day. Although hesitant, she agreed to try. She set an alarm on her cell phone to go off at noon and at 6 P.M.; her husband agreed to call her at work at noon and also remind her. He also agreed to give her a back rub every evening on days when she checked her blood sugar 4 times and showed him the stored meter readings. Slowly, over the next month, she increased the number of days that she checked her blood sugar 4 times. To her great surprise, about half the time she discovered that she needed insulin, and when she took it, she felt much better.

Her second target for change was calculating the correct amount of insulin and self-administering it. Counting carbohydrates and looking up the correct amount of insulin in a table supplied by her physician made her very anxious because of her LD in mathematics. The therapist taught her relaxation skills and coping self-statements to use in this situation. Then the therapist and Alice practiced counting carbohydrates and calculating insulin doses until she became comfortable with these tasks. Eventually, Alice became accustomed to this procedure and experienced less anxiety. Three months later, she was ready to tackle another goal on her list, but this time she was much more optimistic about achieving it.

Alice's case illustrates that change in health care behaviors may be a tedious, long process. Research is needed applying these approaches to individuals with ADHD and LD. Until then, the individual clinician must rely on tried-and-true cognitive behavioral interventions to promote positive health outcomes. Barkley (2010) also has some very useful pointers for adults with ADHD to maintain a healthy lifestyle.

MARRIAGE AND COMMITTED RELATIONSHIPS

In this section the term "marriage" will be used to include both actual marriages and other committed relationships. Consider Paul and Brenda to understand the impact of ADHD and LD on marriage and committed relationships. Paul came home from work 2 hours late for the fifth time this month. He did not pick up the dry cleaning, bread, or milk, and missed dinner and his son's soccer game. He had no recollection of Brenda asking him to do these chores. Earlier that day, he had invited Brenda to have lunch with him, but he got busy with work and never showed up for lunch. Brenda has been nagging him to complete a variety of home chores, but he does not get around to them. In the case of buying and hanging new doors, he bought the doors and figured he would put them up next weekend, but it took 18 months before he finally hung them, and then only after a huge argument the previous day about his failure to keep his promises. During this argument he lost his cool, blew up at Brenda, and called her all kinds of nasty names. She threatened divorce, and he hung the doors soon thereafter.

The marriage had started on a positive note after Paul had swept Brenda off her feet with a whirlwind courtship characterized by excitement, fun, and a great deal of passion. However, things deteriorated after the honeymoon. At first Brenda gave Paul the benefit of the doubt when he forget things, failed to keep his commitments or follow through on things, and slipped into irritability and blaming communication. When her attempts to get him to change failed and he made the same mistakes over and over, she came to think that he was self-centered, inconsiderate and irresponsible, and did not really care about her. A seemingly endless cycle of nagging, excuses, yelling, and negative communication set in, and intimacy suffered. She wondered how this could this be the same man she married.

Careful examination of this vignette illustrates how the couple experiences most of the top 10 relationship challenges found in a survey of 80 heterosexual married couples where one spouse had ADHD (Robin & Payson, 2002): does not remember being told things, says things without thinking, zones out in conversations, has trouble dealing with frustration, has trouble getting started on a task, underestimates the time needed to complete a task, leaves a mess, does not finish household projects, does not respond when spoken to, and does not plan ahead. For couples like Paul and Brenda, the neurobiology and executive function deficits of ADHD and LD interact with the dynamics of marriage, the backgrounds and personalities of the partners, and their negative communication/problem-solving skills and negative beliefs to produce a highly conflictual relationship often doomed to failure. Researchers are beginning to document these patterns of negativity that clinicians, advocates, journalists, and support group leaders have known about for a long time (Halverstadt, 1998; Pera, 2008). In both the UMASS and Milwaukee studies, Barkley et al. (2008) found that clinic-referred adults with ADHD and their partners reported significantly less marital satisfaction than the Community Control groups, although in the UMASS study the group with ADHD did not differ from the clinical control group. The group with H + ADHD in the Milwaukee study also reported more extramarital affairs than both the Community Control group and the group with H-ADHD. Findings regarding divorce rates are mixed, with some studies reporting higher divorce rates in adults with ADHD compared to control groups and others reporting comparable divorce rates in both groups (Barkley et al., 2008).

Eakin et al. (2004) compared the marital adjustment and family functioning of 33 married adults with ADHD and their spouses to 26 control couples. Adults with ADHD reported poorer marital adjustment and more family dysfunction than the control group, although there were no significant differences reported by the spouses without ADHD. Pera (2008) completed an extensive, online survey of 148 spouses of adults with ADHD and reported the results for 111 whose partners had officially been diagnosed as having ADHD (86% male partners with ADHD, age 22 to 75, upper-middle socioeconomic class). She was careful to point out that this was a convenience sample derived from participants in her online support groups and may not be representative of couples with ADHD in general. This survey replicated the results of the Robin and Payson study (2002) with regard to the issues that the spouse without ADHD considered a major problem, and a few selected results will be summarized. The following percentages of the partners of the spouses with ADHD rated each item as a significant problem: 72%—organization; 70%—starting and finishing tasks; 67%—remembering things; 61%—listening; 54%—mood/temper; and 52%—sleep habits (Pera, 2008). Before learning that their spouse had AD/HD, the partners made a variety of negative attributions about their behaviors. The most common attributions were (numbers are percentages of partners making each attribution): 61%—being scatterbrained or absentminded; 56%—being immature; 55%—came from a dysfunctional family background; 47%—being selfish; 39%—passive, lazy, or introverted; 35%—free-spirited or eccentric; and 35%—passive aggressive (Pera, 2008).

No research addresses the impact of LD without ADHD on marriage and committed relationships. LD may impact marriage less than ADHD. Although individuals with either disorder may be poorly organized, have low self-esteem, and show inconsistent follow-through, those with ADHD are more likely to lash out impulsively at the spouses than those with LD.

A number of authors have described the clinical process of conducting marital therapy for couples with ADHD (Kilcarr, 2002; Pera, 2008; Ramsay, 2010; Robin, 2006), but there have not yet been any controlled outcome studies. There is no literature on the treatment of couples with LD, but the clinical approaches taken with ADHD are also likely to be applicable to couples with LD. Marital therapy for couples with ADHD usually integrates cognitive behavioral, imago, structural, and contextual therapies with medication management and is based on research findings suggesting that these factors characterize successful marriages (Gottman, 1998; Kilcarr, 2002; Ramsay, 2010): high self-esteem and self-worth; toleration of each other's idiosyncrasies and foibles; the ability to communicate about difficult issues; good humor; expression of affection; minimal displays of negative affect; and acceptance and normalization of the ebbs and flows of life. The therapist might sequence such intervention in five steps:

1. Optimize ADHD education and adjust attitudes.
2. Maximize medication.
3. Improve communication and problem solving.
4. Learn effective time management and organizational skills.
5. Deal with family-of-origin problems.

Optimizing ADHD education involves getting an ADHD evaluation if this has not yet been completed, overcoming denial about the presence of ADHD and its impact on the relationship, and learning how the neurobiology of ADHD promotes poor coping skills and escalating negative interaction in a marriage. After Paul has been diagnosed with ADHD, the therapist provided ADHD education to Paul and Brenda, for example, by explaining how Paul's forgetfulness followed from his poor working memory and his failure to follow through on hanging the doors followed from his poor planning, organizing, and managing time. Brenda interrupted to express concern that Paul would be "off the hook," his irresponsible behavior seemingly sanctioned. The therapist indicated that ADHD is a challenge, not an excuse, and Paul must take responsibility for his actions, although he might need Brenda's assistance to learn new habits. The therapist suggested that the couple remove blame and label such situations "ADHD moments," so they could work as a team to employ effective problem-solving and time management tools rather than argue. The therapist then provided Internet sites, support group information, and reference lists for the couple to educate themselves about ADHD.

Denial about ADHD often impedes getting an evaluation and utilizing strategies for coping effectively with ADHD in a marriage. The individual with ADHD may deny the possibility that the disorder applies or may minimize its impact on the marriage. Pera (2008) distinguishes between two types of denial: (1) "psychological denial"—misinformation and/or extreme cognitions promote fear about undergoing an ADHD evaluation or examining how ADHD impacts a marriage; and (2) "biological denial"—when poor working memory, poor self-observation, difficulty linking cause and effect, and other executive dysfunctions intrinsic to the neurobiology of ADHD cause the adult with ADHD to fail to perceive his or her own symptoms and their impact on the marriage. The marital therapist can use cognitive therapy (Ramsay & Rostain, 2008), the LEAP (Listen, Empathize, Agree, Partnership) method (Amador, 2007), or motivational interviewing techniques (Miller & Rollnick, 2002) to circumvent denial.

The therapist should assist the couple to *maximize medication* by guiding them to:

1. Select specific and reasonable target behaviors sensitive to medication effects.
2. Develop a simple monitoring system to record the daily occurrence of the target behaviors.
3. Review the records at subsequent therapy sessions.
4. Coach them to provide accurate feedback to their physicians so that medication can be optimally titrated.

Paul's medication regimen consisted of 54 mg Concerta. Paul and Brenda picked three medication targets for Paul: (1) listen to Brenda attentively and calmly on weekday evenings and weekends; (2) help the children with homework without getting frustrated and angry; and (3) touch base with Brenda daily by phone at noon and carry out all of the items she requested him to do within 24 hours. The therapist affirmed the first two goals but told the couple that the third goal took place over too long a time span and involved a variety of executive functions to be a realistic medication target; they modified it to be "touch base with Brenda by noon and put her requests on his electronic to-do list in his cell phone." The therapist prompted the couple to rate attainment of each goal daily on a 5-point Likert scale (5 being most positive) and bring the ratings to the next session. For the first week the ratings were in the 2 to 3 range on weekdays and 4 to 5 on weekends; the medication was wearing off too soon on weekdays. Paul took the ratings to his physician, who added 10 mg of short-acting methylphenidate at the end of the Concerta dose; the weekday ratings increased to 4s over the next 2 weeks.

Behavioral interventions help couples *improve communication and problem solving*. Couples with ADHD spouses often slip into free-for-all shouting matches, during which many hurtful comments are impulsively uttered. Structuring communication through the use of the imago marital therapy technique known as the dialogue corrects such negative interactions. In the dialogue, one partner starts as the speaker, calling for a dialogue about a specific topic. The other partner starts as the listener, paraphrasing whatever the speaker says. After several exchanges, the partners switch roles, so each has a turn as speaker and as listener. The therapist keeps the discussion on track. After the couple can successfully engage in a dialogue during a therapy session, they are assigned the task of practicing and using it at home. Initially, the primary purpose of the dialogue is to facilitate an exchange of ideas without negative communication. Later, the therapist uses this forum to introduce five steps of problem solving as a structure for resolving disputes (Robin & Foster, 1989):

1. Define the problem.
2. Generate a list of solutions.
3. Evaluate the solutions.
4. Reach a compromise.
5. Plan to implement this solution.

After sufficient coaching to problem-solve during the therapy session, the couple is assigned the task of practicing at home. This crucial step of marital therapy is often very difficult to implement fully and may take weeks or months because negative communication patterns are deeply ingrained.

Next, marital therapy shifts to *learning and implementing effective time management and organizational strategies*. This portion of the intervention may be relevant both to patients with ADHD and to those with LD. The therapist coaches the adult to put all time-locked responsibilities in a paper or electronic calendar while the therapist observes. In the case of an electronic calendar (personal digital assistant [PDA], cell phone, computer), the adult also sets alarms to go off sufficiently in advance of the time to prompt him or her to engage in the task at the required time. Afterward, the therapist prompts the patient to make prioritized daily and weekly to-do list and to set alarms in cell phones, computers, or PDAs to go off and remind him or her to look at the list and carry out the items on the list in order of their priorities. A variety of materials have been published to help therapists guide adults with ADHD or LD to carry out such steps (Kolberg & Nadeau, 2002; Safren, Perlman, Sprich, & Otto, 2005; Tuckman, 2007). Although it is ultimately the responsibility of the person with ADHD to get organized, track responsibilities, and carry them out on time, the therapist enlists those partners who are willing to provide prompts, reminders, and positive affectionate incentives to the adult with ADHD for effective habit change and task completion. Paul, for example, was asked to put a prioritized daily to-do list in his cell phone and set alarms to go off to remind him to carry out the daily items on the list. Brenda wanted to establish a daily check-in time when Paul would report his progress on the day's list and they could plan for tasks to be done during the next day. The couple agreed that he would call her daily at 1:00 P.M., and they would review the lists together. He set an alarm to go off at 12:50 P.M. to remind him to call Brenda. She praised him when he called, and the couple planned tasks to be done later that day.

The *family of origin* in which each spouse grew up often strongly influences their marital interactions. Individuals may unwittingly re-create in their own marriage conflicts and patterns that they observed in their parents' marriage, or they react against their observations of their parents' marriage and act in a very different way toward their spouses. Unresolved difficulties between an adult and a parent may play themselves out in the adult's marriage. ADHD exponentially complicates this process. The astute therapist assesses the impact of the family of origin on the marriage and helps the couple deal with problems that are found, using cognitive restructuring and behavioral interventions. Paul, for example, grew up with a highly critical parent who endlessly berated him for even minor problem behaviors. Having undiagnosed ADHD, Paul did many things "wrong" in his father's eyes. Such a childhood predisposed him to be hypersensitive to any criticism by Brenda; he reacted with angry outbursts. By contrast, Brenda's family was "perfect." Everyone did whatever was expected in a highly organized manner, but they were emotionally unexpressive. After the honeymoon ended, she found it very difficult to tolerate Paul's foibles and his emotional outbursts. The therapist brought these patterns to the couple's attention and helped them identify "family of origin" moments, step back, take a deep breath, laugh a bit, and try to move forward.

In clinical practice, after initially cycling through the steps of marital therapy outlined here, the therapist will focus more intensely on the steps necessary to help each couple improve their relationship. Rosenfield, Ramsay, and Rostain (2008) illustrate how the therapist integrates these various stages of marital therapy with individual cognitive behavioral therapy and medication in the treatment of complex adult ADHD.

PARENTING

Life at the Johnsons' house is like a "three-ring circus." Sally and Bill both have ADHD, as does their 8-year-old son, Matthew. Sally also has a LD in written expression. Only 6-year-old Alice "escaped" ADHD. School mornings are a disaster. The children do not have any clean clothes. Lunches are half-packed. Shoes, coats, hats, and gloves are nowhere to be found amid the endless piles of clothing strewn around the house. Homework is rarely in the right section of the folders, and Matthew's backpack looks like a tornado recently passed through, also grazing his room. Matthew is playing video games instead of getting dressed, ignoring Sally's ear-piercing screeches. Alice is huddled in a corner, ready for school. Sally is madly rushing around, trying to get Matthew ready, getting dressed herself, scrambling to make breakfast, find their stuff, and get them out the door to the cacophonous sound of the school bus horn as the bus is preparing to leave without the children. Instead of helping Sally, Bill loses his cool and puts her down for being an incompetent parent, all the time unable to find his own keys, wallet, and cell phone. As the children race to the bus, Sally and Bill argue vehemently until Bill storms out of the house, forgetting his lunch, to go to work. Overwhelmed and exhausted, Sally gets to work 25 minutes late.

Adult ADHD clearly impairs parenting, and when one of the children also has ADHD, the problems grow exponentially (Weiss, Hechtman, & Weiss, 2000). LD may further interfere with parenting when the parent with the LD needs to complete tasks that tax the area of the disability: for example, Sally helping her children with written homework or writing lists for herself. Sally's executive function deficits with attention, planning, organizing, time management, multitasking, attending to detail, and following through make it difficult to complete the daily tasks of parenting. Bill's poor self-control of emotion and impatience lead him to lash out at Sally rather than helping her while he is displaying the same executive function deficits. The couple fails to work as a team, the marriage suffers, and parenting is rendered ineffective. The sibling without ADHD, Alice, suffers silently as this daily drama unfolds.

Researchers have begun to document this clinical picture of parenting difficulties when adults with ADHD parent children, especially children with ADHD. There is no research on the impact of adult LD on parenting. In the UMASS study Barkley et al. (2008) studied the association between child inattention, hyperactivity, Oppositional-Defiant Disorder (ODD) symptoms, parental depression, and parenting stress. A mixture of both parental depression and child ODD contributed the most to overall parenting stress, accounting for 55% to 62% of the variance. Chronis-Tuscano et al. (2008) found that mothers with higher levels of ADHD symptoms displayed lower levels of positive parenting and involvement with their children and higher levels of inconsistent discipline; these findings were evident both with direct observations of mother-child interactions and through maternal self-reports. Harvey, Danforth, McKee,

Ulaszek, and Friedman (2003) found that fathers' self-reported inattention and impulsivity symptoms were strongly associated with lax discipline, and their impulsivity symptoms were associated with a tendency to argue with their children; similar but weaker effects were found for mothers.

The question arises as to whether having ADHD helps a parent better understand and be sympathetic to their child with ADHD and thereby ameliorates negative interactions. Based on temperament theory, this "goodness of fit hypothesis" has been tested in two studies. Using both self-report measures and direct observations of mother-child dyads, Psychogiou, Daley, Thompson, and Sonuga-Barke (2008) examined whether similarity between mothers and children with regard to high ADHD symptoms would improve or worsen parenting. High parental ADHD symptoms ameliorated the effects of child ADHD symptoms on negative parenting; parental response to children with high ADHD symptoms was more positive and affectionate when the mother also had high ADHD symptoms. In a study that included mothers and fathers (Psychogiou, Daley, Thompson, & Sonuga-Barke, 2007), the results for mothers were replicated, but opposite results were found for fathers; high paternal ADHD symptoms exacerbated the effect of high child ADHD symptoms on negative parenting. These two studies suggest that the goodness-of-fit hypothesis applies more to mothers than fathers. However, it is important to note that in these two studies, the mother-child interactions that served as the basis for the analyses consisted of the mother playing with the child, not attempting to do a structured task such as homework, chores, or getting ready for school in the morning. As suggested by the case example earlier with Sally, Bill, and Matthew, the results of a goodness-of-fit study using actual task-oriented interactions may be vastly different and more negative than in a study where mothers play with their children. Clearly, more research is needed to understand the goodness-of-fit hypothesis and its relationship to interventions designed to improve parenting for adults who have ADHD.

The same team of investigators who conducted the goodness-of-fit studies also evaluated whether high parental ADHD symptoms reduce the effectiveness of behavioral parent training. Sonuga-Barke, Daley, and Thompson (2002) studied 83 3-year-old children with ADHD and their mothers who completed an 8-week behavioral parent training program. A parental ADHD checklist divided the mothers into three groups: (1) high (>16), (2) medium (8–15), and (3) low (0–7) ADHD symptoms. Using a composite score from three parent-completed behavior checklist, Sonuga-Barke et al. (2002) found that children of mothers in the high-ADHD symptom group displayed no improvement after parent training, but children of mothers in the low- and medium-ADHD symptom groups showed considerable improvement. These results persisted even after controlling for maternal demographic and mental health histories. Thus, even though mothers with high ADHD symptoms may be positively predisposed toward their children with ADHD, they still fail to benefit from parent training and may not be consistent in their disciplinary practices. Although the results of this study need to be replicated, they are certainly consistent with the picture painted by clinicians, who find that parental ADHD reduces the effectiveness of family interventions (Phelan, 2002; Ramsay, 2010).

What is the best way to help families such as the Johnsons? Medication is effective for modifying the core symptoms of ADHD in children and adults (Barkley, 2006). Behavioral interventions are effective for modifying problem behavior in children and adolescents with ADHD (Barkley, 1997b; Barkley, Edwards, & Robin, 1999). Learning compensatory and/or bypass strategies may help the adult who also has an LD. CBT helps adults with ADHD change extreme thinking and improve life management skills (Ramsay & Rostain, 2008). Therefore, combining these three interventions and keeping in mind the point-of-performance problem should prove effective for helping adults with ADHD parent children with ADHD more effectively.

First, medication must be maximized and coordinated for all members of the family who have ADHD. Either the children's physician and the parents' physician need to coordinate their efforts, or the family needs to see a physician who treats both children and adults, as do family physicians and many child psychiatrists. Each family member needs to be on effective doses of a stimulant or nonstimulant medication that provides coverage during important family interaction times, including mornings, evenings, and weekends. This may mean taking medicine as soon as one awakens or parents awakening a child 30 minutes early, giving the medication, and letting him or her sleep for another 30 minutes. It also may mean supplementing long-acting stimulants with short-acting stimulants in the late afternoon or early evening. For example, Dr. Jones, a family physician working with the Johnson family, prescribed Concerta for both Sally and Bill, taken at 6:00 A.M. as soon as they awoke. Then, at 5:00 P.M., they supplemented it with short-acting methylphenidate , which lasted into the evening. Fortunately, this regimen did not interfere with getting to sleep. Matthew needed a stimulant to start acting quickly in the morning, so Dr. Jones prescribed short-acting methylphenidate given 30 minutes before he needed to stay awake, followed by Concerta after breakfast. The short-acting methylphenidate helped him get up and ready for school while the Concerta helped throughout the school day and early evening. The family attended medication follow-up visits together, so that Dr. Jones could get input from each family member and adjust the doses of medicine accurately.

Second, behavioral parent training needs to be augmented with CBT for parents with ADHD. At the University of Pennsylvania and the Children's Hospital of Philadelphia such a collaborative intervention has been developed and piloted (Ramsay et al., 2009; Ramsay, 2010). The adult ADHD and child ADHD programs have combined their efforts to develop and pilot a 13-session intervention that includes 6 multifamily group sessions without the children, 4 individual family sessions with each family and the child, 1 session devoted solely to meeting with the parents alone, and 2 school consultation meetings with the family and the teacher (Ramsay et al., 2009). The intervention is designed to emphasize relationships, communication strategies, anticipation and management of adult ADHD-related barriers to implementation, and correction of distorted cognitions, along with providing modeling of desired behavior and check-ins between sessions. The sequence of 13 sessions includes (Ramsay et al., 2009):

1. *Multifamily group.* Introduction to Guiding principles and positive attending
2. *Individual family session.* Preparing for school meeting
3. *Family school meeting.*
4. *Individual couple session.* Adult relationships in context of parental ADHD
5. *Multifamily group.* Adult ADHD issues and introduction to behavior management
6. *Multifamily group.* Applications of behavior management and barriers for parents with ADHD
7. *Multifamily group.* Making behavior management work and household organization
8. *Individual family session.* Homework intervention and goal setting
9. *Individual family session.* Goal-setting practice and management of barriers
10. *Family school meeting.*
11. *Multifamily group.* Effective use of punishment
12. *Individual family meeting.* Refinement of punishment and monitoring of intervention application
13. *Multifamily group.* Integrating skills and planning for the future

The sessions are sequenced to introduce new material and then consider potential barriers to implementing the new material caused by adult ADHD, for example, point-of-performance problems. Initial piloting of this intervention proved promising, so the authors are planning controlled clinical trials to evaluate its effectiveness.

Meanwhile, what might a behavioral intervention look like for the Johnson family, when one clinician is available to treat one family without a group? The therapist first would meet with the couple, make sure that all relevant family members have received ADHD evaluations, and then remove blame by reframing negative parent-child and negative spouse interactions as "ADHD moments" that follow from the genetics and neurobiology of AD/HD. The therapist would use cognitive restructuring to help them replace these types of unrealistic thoughts with more realistic alternatives (Phelan, 2002):

- My child should behave like any other child.
- My child has ADHD because I somehow messed him up by my bad parenting.
- If ADHD is not caused by my faulty parenting, I'm off the hook.

- I hope the kids don't fight today.
- If my child makes a fool out of me in public and people think I'm a lousy parent, I'll never live it down.
- It's awful and I'm a bad parent because I don't even like my child.

Third, the therapist would refer the family to a knowledgeable physician to start the kind of medication regimen discussed earlier in this chapter. The therapist then would meet all family members together and assess their direct interactions. During this session, positive attending (also known as special time) would be introduced as a fun activity designed to break the seemingly endless cycle of negative parent-child interactions (Barkley, 1997b; Barkley et al., 1999). The family would be assigned positive attending as homework, and Sally and Bill would return to the next session. In assigning the homework, the therapist would prompt the parents to pick times for the homework and set electronic reminders on their cell phones to go off at the selected time so they would remember to carry out the assignment. Any other barriers to carrying out the assignment would be considered. In this way, management of adult ADHD is integrated into assignment of behavioral tasks for parenting. Fourth, the parents would return to the next session to report the results of implementing positive attending. If they carried it out as planned, the therapist would congratulate them and invite to start working on the problems that occur in the morning. If they did not carry it out as planned, the therapist would consider what adult ADHD and/or other factors interfered, develop strategies to circumvent these obstacles, and re-assign the task. The therapy would continue in this way: Pick a target behavior, develop a parenting intervention, consider how adult ADHD might get in the way of the parenting intervention, develop adult-focused interventions for such obstacles, and carry them out.

CONCLUSION

The research reviewed in this chapter clearly documents that adults with ADHD have lifestyle and family problems in the areas of money management, health, marriage/committed relationships, and parenting. Very little research exists regarding the impact of LD on these lifestyle problems, but clinicians find that the executive function difficulties of LD do create interference. With the exception of Ramsay et al.'s (2009) pilot of a family intervention for adults with ADHD parenting children with ADHD, very little research has been conducted evaluating the effectiveness of interventions designed to ameliorate these lifestyle and family problems. In the absence of evidence-based interventions, this chapter provided illustrations of how clinicians have applied sound cognitive, behavioral, and family intervention principles to craft interventions for these problem areas. Clearly, researchers need to evaluate these and other interventions.

The chapter also demonstrates how the executive function deficits inherent in ADHD and LD require interventions that target the *point of performance* where the patient must actually perform the appropriate behaviors and inhibit the impulse to respond reactively rather than reflectively. Case examples illustrate how clinicians intervene at the point of performance for adults with ADHD and LD.

REFERENCES

Amador, X. (2007). *I am not sick, I don't need help*. Peconic, NY: Vida Press.

Barkley, R. A. (1997a). *ADHD and the nature of self-control*. New York, NY: Guilford Press.

Barkley, R. A. (1997b). *Defiant children: A clinician's manual for assessment and parent training*. (2nd ed.). New York, NY: Guilford Press.

Barkley, R. A. (2006). *Attention Deficit Hyperactivity Disorder: A handbook for diagnosis and treatment* (3rd ed.). New York, NY: Guilford Press.

Barkley, R. A., & Benton, C. M. (2010). *Taking charge of adult ADHD*. New York, NY: Guilford Press.

Barkley, R. A., Edwards, G., & Robin, A. L. (1999). *Defiant teens: A clinician's manual for assessment and family intervention*. New York, NY: Guilford Press.

Barkley, R. A., Murphy, K. R., & Fischer, M. (2008). *ADHD in adults: What the science says*. New York, NY: Guilford Press.

Brown, T. (2005). *Attention Deficit Disorder: The unfocused mind in children and adults*. New Haven, CT: Yale University Press.

Chronis-Tuscano, A., Ragg, V. L., Clarke, T. L., Rooney, M. E., Diaz, Y., & Pian, J. (2008). Association between maternal Attention-Deficit/Hyperactivity Disorder symptoms and parenting. *Journal of Abnormal Child Psychology, 36,* 1230–1250.

Eakin, L., Minde, K., Hechtman, L., Ochs, E., Krane, E., Bouffard, R., . . . & Looper, K. (2004). The marital and family functioning of adults with ADHD and their spouses. *Journal of Attention Disorders, 8,* 1–10.

Gawrilow, C., & Gollwitzer, P. M. (2008). Implementation intentions facilitated response inhibition in children with ADHD. *Cognitive Therapy and Research, 32,* 261–280.

Gollwitzer, P. M., & Oettingen, G. (2007). The role of goal setting and goal striving in medical adherence. In D. C. Park & L., L. Liu (Eds.), *Medical adherence and aging: Social and cognitive perspectives* (pp. 23–47). Washington, DC: American Psychological Association.

Gottman, J. M. (1998). Psychology and the study of marital processes. *Annual Review of Psychology, 49,* 169–197.

Gregg, N. (2009). *Adolescents and adults with learning disabilities and ADHD: Assessment and accommodation*. New York, NY: Guilford Press.

Harvey, E., Danforth, J. S., McKee, T. E., Ulaszek, W. R., & Friedman, J. L. (2003). Parenting of children with Attention-Deficit/ Hyperactivity Disorder (ADHD): The role of parental ADHD symptomatology. *Journal of Attention Disorders, 7,* 31–42.

Halverstadt, J. S. (1998). *A.D.D. and romance: Finding fulfillment in love, sex, and relationships*. Dallas, TX: Taylor.

Katz, L. J., Goldstein, G., & Beers, S. R. (2001). *Learning disabilities in older adolescents and adults: Clinical utility of the neuropsychological perspective*. New York, NY: Kluwer Academic/Plenum Press.

Kilcarr, P. (2002). Making marriages work for individuals with ADHD. In S. Goldstein & A. T. Ellison (Eds.), *Clinician's guide to adult ADHD: Assessment and intervention* (pp. 220– 240). San Diego, CA: Academic Press.

Kolberg, J., & Nadeau, K. (2002). *ADD-friendly ways to organize your life*. New York, NY: Brunner-Routledge.

Mapou, R. L. (2009). *Adult learning disabilities and ADHD: Research informed assessment*. New York, NY: Oxford University Press.

McGinnis, J. M., & Foege, W. H. (1993). Actual causes of death in the United States. *Journal of the American Medical Association, 270,* 2207–2212.

Miller, W. R., & Rollnick, S. (2002). *Motivational interviewing: Preparing people for change* (2nd ed.). New York, NY: Guilford Press.

Palaian, S. (2009). *Spent: Break the buying obsession and discover your true worth*. Center City, MN: Hazelden.

Pera, G. (2008). *Is it you, me, or adult A.D.D.?* San Francisco, CA: 1201 Alarm Press.

Phelan, T. W. (2002). Families and ADHD. In S. Goldstein & A. T. Ellison (Eds.), *Clinician's guide to adult ADHD: Assessment and intervention* (pp. 241–260). San Diego, CA: Academic Press.

Psychogiou, L., Daley, D., Thompson, M., & Sonuga- Barke, E. (2007). Testing the interactive effect of parent and child ADHD on parenting in mothers and fathers: A further test of the similarity-fit-hypothesis. *British Journal of Developmental Psychology, 25,* 419–433.

Psychogiou, L., Daley, D., Thompson, M., & Sonuga- Barke, E. (2008). Do maternal Attention-Deficit/Hyperactivity Disorder symptoms exacerbate or ameliorate the negative effect of child Attention-Deficit/Hyperactivity Disorder symptoms on parenting? *Development and Psychopathology, 20,* 121–137.

Ramsay, J. R. (2010). *Nonmedication treatments for adult ADHD: Evaluating impact on daily functioning and well-being*. Washington, DC: American Psychological Association.

Ramsay, J. R., & Rostain, A. L. (2008). *Cognitive-behavioral therapy for adult ADHD: An integrative psychosocial and medical approach*. New York, NY: Routledge.

Ramsay, J. R., Rostain, A. L., Power, T. P., Soffer, S., Wiley, P., & Mantone, J. (2009, October). *PENN- CHOP family ADHD treatment collaboration*. Program presented at the CHADD National Conference, Cleveland, OH.

Robin, A. L. (2006). How to succeed in marriage with ADHD. *Attention, 13,* 5–8.

Robin, A. L., & Foster, S. L., (1989). *Negotiating parent-adolescent conflict: A behavioral family systems approach*. New York, NY: Guilford Press.

Robin, A. L., & Payson, E., (2002). The impact of ADHD on marriage. *ADHD Reports, 10,* 9–14.

Rosenfeld, B. M., Ramsay, J. R., & Rostain, A. L. (2008). Extreme makeover: The case of a young adult male with severe ADHD. *Clinical Case Studies, 7*, 471–490.

Safren, S. A., Perlman, C. A., Sprich, S., & Otto, M. W. (2005). *Mastering your adult ADHD: A cognitive-behavioral treatment program–Therapist guide.* New York, NY: Oxford University Press.

Sanchez, L. M., Chronis, A. M., & Hunter, S. J. (2006). Improving compliance with diabetes management in young adolescents with Attention Deficit/Hyperactivity Disorder using behavior therapy. *Cognitive and Behavioral Practice, 13*, 134–145.

Sonuga-Barke, E., Daley, D., & Thompson, M. (2002). Does maternal ADHD reduce the effectiveness of parent training for preschool children's ADHD? *Journal of the American Academy of Child and Adolescent Psychiatry, 41*, 696–702.

Tuckman, A. (2007). *Integrative treatment for adult ADHD.* Oakland, CA: New Harbinger Publications.

Weiss, M., Hechtman, L., & Weiss, G. (2000). ADHD in parents. *Journal of the American Academy of Child and Adolescent Psychiatry, 39*, 1059–1061.

Author Index

Subject Index